US Agricultural and Food P

Policy analysis is a dynamic process of discovery rather than a passive exercise of memorizing facts and conclusions. This text provides opportunities to "practice the craft" of policy analysis by engaging the reader in realistic case studies and problem-solving scenarios that require the selection and use of applicable investigative techniques.

US Agricultural and Food Policies will assist undergraduate students to learn how policy choices impact the overall performance of agricultural and food markets. It encourages students to systematically investigate scenarios with appropriate positive and normative tools. The book emphasizes the importance of employing critical thinking skills to address the complexities associated with the design and implementation of twenty-first-century agricultural and food policies. Students are asked to suspend their personal opinions and emotions, and instead apply research methods that require the careful consideration of both facts and values. The opportunities to build these investigative skills are abundant when we consider the diversity of modern agricultural and food policy concerns.

Featuring case studies and critical thinking exercises throughout and supported by a Companion Website with slides, a test bank, glossary, and web/video links, this is the ideal textbook for any agricultural policy class.

Gerald D. Toland, Jr. is a Professor of Economics at Southwest Minnesota State University, USA.

William E. Nganje is a Professor in the Department of Agribusiness and Applied Economics, North Dakota State University, USA.

Raphael Onyeaghala is a Dean of the College of Business, Education, Graduate, and Professional Studies at Southwest Minnesota State University, USA.

ROUTLEDGE TEXTBOOKS IN ENVIRONMENTAL AND AGRICULTURAL ECONOMICS

US Agricultural and Food Policies

Economic Choices and Consequences

Gerald D. Toland, Jr., William E. Nganje, and Raphael Onyeaghala

Routledge
Taylor & Francis Group

LONDON AND NEW YORK

First published 2018
by Routledge
2 Park Square, Milton Park, Abingdon, Oxon, OX14 4RN

and by Routledge
711 Third Avenue, New York, NY 10017

Routledge is an imprint of the Taylor & Francis Group, an informa business

© 2018 Gerald D. Toland, Jr., William E. Nganje, and Raphael Onyeaghala

British Library Cataloguing-in-Publication Data
A catalogue record for this book is available from the British Library

Library of Congress Cataloging-in-Publication Data
Names: Toland, Gerald, author. | Nganje, William Evange, 1966- author. |
    Onyeaghala, Raphael, author.
Title: US agricultural and food policies : economic choices and
    consequences / Gerald D. Toland, Jr., William Nganje, and Raphael
    Onyeaghala.
Other titles: United States agricultural and food policies
Description: Abingdon, Oxon ; New York, NY : Routledge, 2017. |
Identifiers: LCCN 2017017914| ISBN 9781138208285 (hardback) |
    ISBN 9781138208292 (pbk.) | ISBN 9781315459530 (ebook)
Subjects: LCSH: Agriculture and state—United States. | Agriculture—
    Economic aspects—United States. | Food supply—Government
    policy—United States.
Classification: LCC HD1761 .T598 2017 | DDC 338.1/873—dc23
LC record available at https://lccn.loc.gov/2017017914

ISBN: 978-1-138-20828-5 (hbk)
ISBN: 978-1-138-20829-2 (pbk)
ISBN: 978-1-315-45953-0 (ebk)

Typeset in Goudy
by Swales & Willis Ltd, Exeter, Devon, UK

Contents

Figures

Tables

Check boxes

Preface

In Shakespeare's *Hamlet*, Polonius offers fatherly guidance to his son Laertes: "To thine own self be true." Four centuries later, that piece of advice still rings true. In 2015, we viewed the prospect of writing a textbook to address twenty-first-century US agricultural and food policy as both an exciting opportunity and a serious challenge. Should we embark on this task? This field of study is complex and dynamic. Previous publications on farm and food policy set high standards for organization, readability, and comprehensive coverage. Any new entry into this textbook arena should make a distinct contribution to the discipline while also meeting expectations for superior educational quality.

As in all economic activity, we balance risks against benefits, and make a choice. In our case, we followed Shakespeare's counsel. To be true to ourselves, we knew this project was worthwhile and that we had the capacity to undertake it. While there are risks in producing a textbook that can pass market scrutiny in this demanding field, we can bear these risks if we adopt the proper attitude, make extensive preparations, and engage in a lot of hard work. Some authors indicate that their publications are a labor of love. We can agree with that sentiment. We also observe that copious amounts of both labor and love are needed to begin and fully complete such a project.

Why write this book? We believe we are filling a real need. Important changes are taking place in the "farm-to-fork" supply chain. Some policies are well coordinated with the market changes; they contribute to increased economic efficiency and equity. Other policies are a source of consternation because they are out of date or contradictory.

Increasingly diverse and decidedly vocal constituent groups are influencing the political and economic arenas of farm and food policy. The result is a very dynamic policy environment. Policymakers must respond to the growing demand for action in the areas such as food safety, food security, sustainability, climate change, and international trade conditions. If we are to develop policies properly suited to address the current and future challenges, we need rational and effective tools to properly analyze them. We must also increase our capacity to design and implement new policy designs that successfully tackle the problems and help create a desired outcome. Our textbook is an effort to supply our readers with economic analysis tools that they can use to improve the layout of farm and food policies, and ultimately facilitate real progress in achieving more efficient and equitable results.

We offer some suggestions on how to read this book and realize the best net return for the effort:

- Set aside time to carefully read this text. Much learning will be lost if a decision is made to simply read the summaries at the end of each chapter. Farm and food policy, if it is to be understood properly, requires a dedicated and deliberate study.
- Read interactively. We encourage you to take real ownership of the book. Make notes in the margins and use a highlighter.
- Chapter 3 of this textbook offers a set of economic analytical tools that have applicability to the problems and policy challenges that arise throughout our farm and food system. Refer back to this chapter whenever the need for a refresher arises.
- Research topics raised in each chapter often need additional facts or background information to be properly analyzed and understood. Take advantage of the references and citations provided in the endnotes at the back of each chapter.

Writing and publishing a textbook does not happen without the support of family, friends, co-workers, and many others. It is risky to begin naming names, but we feel it is essential to recognize those who have been instrumental in the project's completion. First, we are grateful to our families who made the time allowances necessary for this textbook to go from idea to publication. Next, Dr. Toland appreciates his year-long sabbatical granted by Southwest Minnesota State University to create the work time necessary to research, draft, and edit the book. Routledge Publishing has been very supportive throughout this entire project, and it has been very heartening to work alongside such a highly professional organization.

Mentors who go above and beyond the call of duty have a special place in our lives and careers. During his professional career, Dr. Brian Schmiesing reached out to many friends and colleagues, helping them to become better versions of themselves. Before his untimely death in 1997, Dr. Schmiesing used his considerable mentorship skills and caring nature to instruct his friend Gerry Toland on what it takes to be an academic professional and careful writer. As a coauthor of this textbook, Dr. Toland dedicates his portion of the work to his friend Brian. The publication of this book would not have been possible without Brian's intervention. Dr. Toland strives each day to do his best as a father, husband, friend, and colleague to pass on that mentorship to others. Thank you, Brian.

Chapter 1

An introduction to policy analysis

"If we could first know where we are, and whither we are tending, we could then better judge what to do, and how to do it."

Abraham Lincoln. Excerpt from his "House Divided" speech in Springfield, Illinois. June 16, 1858.[1]

An initial perspective on policymaking

Whether we realize it or not, agricultural and food policies influence the quality of our daily lives. We expect our agri-food system to produce a safe, nutritious, reliable, and abundant food supply. But perhaps we do not fully appreciate how remarkable our system is. What is more, we continue to enhance our expectations. For example, we now seek food production and distribution methods that are environmentally friendly and sustainable.

Are today's farm and food policies adequate to meet the challenges? How will we determine and implement programs that can effectively and equitably balance economic incentives, resource constraints, and distributional outcomes, now and in the future?

This textbook is designed to help the reader address these and other important questions. If we follow Abe Lincoln's advice (quoted above), then we will carefully examine the status of our agricultural and food system performance today, and begin formulating a way forward for the future.

The dynamic changes taking place in our agri-food system point towards a future of both challenge and opportunity. We are frustrated by the problems of food insecurity and child-hood obesity, while we marvel at the speed and power of our technological advances.

We gain a sense of optimism when we view the amazing impact of precision agriculture, agricultural genomics, supply-chain management, and nanotechnology. Our current agricultural and food system strongly benefits from noteworthy improvements in knowledge, efficiency, and overall productivity in our modern economy.

In the midst of our optimism, there are real concerns. We need to fully address how our farm-and-food system will endure the effects of climate change, food safety issues, and related factors that threaten food system resiliency.

Considerable effort is required, if we are to design and implement agricultural and food policies[2] that can capitalize on the promising opportunities while offering real solutions to the vexing problems.

When we examine what is at stake – such as, determining how best to sustainably feed a hungry world – then the search for effective agricultural and food policies is readily understood as an enterprise worthy of our full attention.

This book aims to assist undergraduate students (and other interested readers) to learn how alternative policy choices impact the overall performance of agricultural and food markets. This text also provides opportunities to apply economic principles to improve the efficiency and equity of policy design and implementation.

Readers of this text can sharpen their ability to analyze scenarios and review case studies to determine how policy choices create desired results. We also identify when well-intentioned policies are sometimes responsible for unintended economic impacts.

"Choices have consequences" is a nearly universal piece of advice. This motto is particularly relevant for our investigation of agricultural and food policies. Using appropriate methods of analysis, we can predict how policy changes create a wide range of important economic consequences for real-world decision-makers.

Role of this chapter and the educational aims of this textbook

The objectives for this first chapter are to:

- Introduce the field of study known as "Agricultural and Food Policy." Why is it a productive area of research and discussion?

- Identify the goals and purpose of this textbook. This book offers analytical frameworks and learning strategies to help students understand and evaluate US agricultural and food policy choices and evaluate economic consequences.
- Provide readers with an overview of key policy forces currently influencing the economic performance of the agricultural and food sectors in the United States.
- Explain the textbook's organizational logic and sequence of chapter topics.

Why study agricultural and food policy?

We all have an interest in learning more about a food and agricultural system that supplies our society with the sustenance for life. Beyond this obvious concern for feeding a hungry world, we can readily cite additional reasons to learn more about farm and food policy.

Agri-food markets are unique. They are regularly affected by highly volatile prices, perishable products, societal safety concerns, and uncontrollable natural production conditions. The impact of these unique conditions, in combination with the influence of private sector economics and government policies, means that policy analysis is always interesting, never boring (at least for true policy analysts), and intellectually challenging.

In this text, we assume readers are motivated to improve the performance of our agri-food systems. If you are a member of this club, then it is necessary to study the socio-economic relationship between public-sector policy options and private-sector decision making.

There are plenty of twenty-first-century instances where we know that policy analysis and effective policy intervention are needed. For example:

- We are encountering health issues associated with child obesity and food waste, and at the same time we are trying to overcome household nutritional deficits connected with food insecurity.
- We need a coordinated policy approach to manage a range of issues that include: increasing our sustainable food production potentials; keeping pace with dynamic domestic and international food markets; and creating efficient systems for renewable energy output and utilization.
- We must address the questions surrounding food system integrity. This agenda includes the pursuit of food safety policies that incorporate HACCP and related performance-based practices. Today's consumers expect their food purchases to be healthy, nutritious, good-tasting, and free from all pathogens and related threats.
- We need policies that can transform challenges into economic opportunities. For example, can we structure government-subsidized federal crop insurance to efficiently and equitably use taxpayer dollars?

We must pay attention to the details if we are to design successful agricultural and food policies. We need good analysts who recognize the complexity of these problems, and then formulate methods that correctly assess choices and evaluate results.

The stakes are high. We need a properly functioning farm-and-food system. Effective policy analysis can help us "get there." If we are to increase our resource efficiency and economic welfare, then we must strive to understand the goals of private-sector participants, the motives for government intervention, and the relevance of market outcomes.

General purposes of this text

Given the rapid pace of change in our agricultural and food economies, it is essential that students be properly equipped to assess new policy situations, apply appropriate analytical techniques, and arrive at conclusions based on sound research.

In light of the pressing need to design effective policies, this textbook serves two major purposes:

- It is a tool for students to learn and apply research-based skills for policy analysis.
- It offers students the opportunity to explore how alternative agricultural and food policies influence the economic outcomes for farmers, agribusinesses, domestic consumers, international markets, and other important constituencies.

Policy analysis is a dynamic process of discovery rather than a passive exercise of memorizing facts and conclusions. This text provides opportunities to "think critically" by asking the reader to consider alternatives and identify solutions for real-world policy problems.

Systematic policy analysis requires considerable effort. As we embark upon our extensive study of policy choices and their economics consequences, it is reasonable to address a very basic and utilitarian question: what difference will it make?

Challenges and efficacy of policy analysis

In the sixteenth edition of his world-renowned textbook, *Economics*, the late Nobel Laureate Paul Samuelson noted that there is a "world of difference between informed economics and just plain bad economics."[3] He observes that policies based on imprudent analysis can be very costly; and conversely, he effectively argues that thoughtful inquiry is a worthy enterprise.

Samuelson also reminds us that while we have made notable advances in research methodology, we are far from conducting policy analysis as an exact science. Objectivity requires that we understand and respect the limitations of our investigative approaches, while taking advantage of the important insights that careful study can yield.

We also must recognize that the economic analysis of policy making goes beyond the efficiency criteria of calculating benefits and costs. There are distributional consequences. Which individuals, groups or organizations stand to benefit from a policy decision? What economic participants will shoulder the costs associated with a new policy?

In many policy situations, some participants gain, and others lose. As a result, questions about fairness and equity are unavoidable. Balancing the efficiency and equity impacts of a new approach is not a task that can be completely addressed by science-based methods. The effort also requires normative evaluation.

Policies are typically introduced to solve a problem or achieve a desired end. Both economics and philosophy are intertwined in such instances. Recognition of this complexity is intellectually demanding. It is also essential, if we are to make good policy choices.[4]

Effective policy making is both art and science. In addition, agricultural and food policies are generally initiated and implemented by governments. As soon as we enter the realm where government activity and private decision making are mixed, it is inevitable that the efficacy of a policy will also be judged based on political and ethical considerations.[5]

Ideally, we hope properly designed policies produce measurable net ⸗ equitably shared by all economic participants. The reality of a policy sit⸗ that we simply seek to avoid costly pitfalls.

The approach taken in this textbook is that we can learn and apply teᴄ⸗ enhance our ability to choose policy options that are appropriately adapted to chaɴɢ⸗ economic circumstances. Well-informed policymaking can make a difference.

Transition from general philosophy to pragmatic matters

In the discussion above, we identify some broad philosophical foundations for the work ahead. Such wide-ranging considerations are important prerequisites to properly engage in the pragmatic aspects of policy analysis.

We are about to embark upon an exciting and challenging enterprise. We will investigate real-world policy choices, and predict their economic consequence for farm and food systems in the USA and globally. Let's now apply our general philosophy to create practical methods that will guide our approach.

Tools for policy analysis and evaluation

Policy analysis is a multidimensional field of study. The work of policy analysts includes both quantitative and qualitative studies. There are a variety of methods available to gain important insights when we investigate the efficacy of agricultural and food policies.

Mayer, van Daalen, and Bots (2004) introduced an innovative model to integrate a broad spectrum of diverse techniques that are applicable to policy analysis.[6] In our textbook, we require only a subset of the available policy analysis tools. The methods of primary interest here are categorized as "Applied Research and Problem Solving."

Using the Mayer, et al. framework for policy analysis, the activities of applied research and problem solving are subdivided into two primary areas of study:[7]

- The science-based methodologies of positive economics (research and analysis).
- The evaluative approach of normative economics to judge policy options and make recommendations (design and recommend).

Disciplines in the social sciences, such as economics and political economy, have particular relevance in positive and normative analysis.

When positive economics is employed, policy analysis methods must be scrutinized for their scientific validity, reliability, and consistency. The goal is to gain accurate and objective observations of cause and effect.

When normative economics is applied, the goal is to design, recommend, and implement better policies. Evaluation of the "goodness" of a policy is judged with criteria such as fairness, equality, and transparency. After a systematic review of policy options, the recommendation to move forward with a particular policy derives from its instrumental value as a relevant, usable, accessible, and action-oriented choice.[8]

In the next section, we review a recent change in agricultural policy. Our aim is to illustrate the importance of using both positive and normative economics to properly organize the investigation of policy choices and consequences.

Discontinuation of the Direct Payment Program (DPP): a case study

When the 2014 Farm Bill was signed into law, the new legislation discontinued a farm subsidy known as the Direct Payment Program (DPP). Prior to its elimination, the DPP had been a steady source of revenue for participating US crop producers between the years 1996 and 2013.

Whenever a policy is established or eliminated, we can gain immediate insight by examining the event from the perspectives of both *positive economics* and *normative economics*.

As indicated above, positive economics is science-based, emphasizing the importance of impartial and reliable facts and investigative methods. On the other hand, normative economics is focused on philosophical issues and value judgments. For example, we can use normative methods to gauge whether implementing a new policy will leave participants economically better off, worse off, or unaffected.

Positive economics includes the identification of objective facts. For example, we engage in positivism by accurately describing the history of the DPP as a farm policy. We objectively establish that before the 2014 Farm Bill became law, qualified participants in selected USDA commodity programs received steady DPP payments based on validated production history and a fixed per-bushel payment rate established in previous farm bills.[9]

Positive economics also encompasses objective predictions of policy impacts. Positivism requires that such estimates be generated using modern and valid modeling techniques, and that the results be reported without any comment on the "goodness" or "badness" of the outcome. For example, we can make an unbiased forecast of the federal government deficit reduction that are associated with the discontinuation of DPP expenditures.

One estimate, based on a 10-year forecast, predicts that the demise of DPP will produce about $50 billion in deficit reduction.[10] However, when the House and Senate were struggling to pass the 2014 Farm Bill, compromises led Congress to reallocate some of the savings from the DPP removal to enact new farm subsidies for crop insurance and other farm safety-net programs. This compromise increased spending, adding $15 to $30 billion to the estimated cost of the 2014 Farm Bill commodity and crop insurance titles.

Using basic arithmetic to offer a more accurate estimate, we project that the 10-year deficit reduction achieved by eliminating DPP would only be $20 to $35 billion (not $50 billion). And, to be completely transparent, positive economics would demand that we place more conditions on these predicted cost savings.

The forecast of deficit reduction (by eliminating DPP) is *entirely dependent* on what happens with the programs that "replaced" the DPP. These are subsidized variable payment programs. Federal spending could increase dramatically if there are downturns in markets or weather conditions that trigger additional government payouts. Depending on what circumstances prevail, new farm subsidy spending could actually increase dramatically over the 10-year period rather than decline.[11] When we strive to inform policy makers about the full range of possible outcomes using appropriate estimation techniques, we are utilizing the power of positive economics.

Every policy decision also has a *normative component*. For example, with normative economics we can examine why various interest groups believed that Congress *should* eliminate the DPP in 2014. Or, if we look back at the DPP's origins, we observe that a majority in Congress voted to create the DPP as a *worthwhile policy* in 1996. Of course, a majority vote means there was also a minority who did not think the DPP was needed. This case study is an opportunity to understand why reasonable people can normatively disagree about policy choices.

Let's examine the normative elements of establishing the DPP as part of the 1996 Farm Bill. Normativism means that basic philosophy and values spark the search for compatible policies. In 1996, the US Congress expressed a change in its fundamental philosophy towards US farm subsidy policy. Congress sought policy reform to emphasize market-driven motives to guide farm-producer decisions. As Congress moved in this direction, it simultaneously introduced the DPP as a "bridge" or transition to financially help producers adjust. When fully implemented, in 1996 the overall new market-driven policy meant that farm operators would have greater exposure to price volatility in commodity markets.

The 1996 Congress made a normative choice. These legislators signaled that supply and demand *should* guide resource allocation in agriculture, rather than artificial prices associated with farm-program participation. At the same moment, the DPP was created as "a means to an end," because Congress also sought to foster farm financial stability while converting the system of farm support away from public funds and towards private-market forces. Normatively, the 1996 Congress placed a value on creating a "stable transition," and funded that priority by establishing the DPP.

The 1996 Congress was also seeking to reduce federal government spending and taxpayer burdens by taking farm policy in a new direction. Normatively, the values associated with promoting increased resource efficiency and reduced taxpayer responsibility were viewed as real ways to change farm policy "for the better." Whenever we are trying to determine whether a new state of affairs leaves participants better off, worse off, or indifferent, then normative activity is in play, and normative analysis is completely appropriate.

In the above discussion, we use the DPP case study as an opportunity to explore both positive and normative consequences of a policy decision. We now introduce a basic sequential and analytical approach that can be applied to a broad range of policy scenarios.

A systematic method for applied policy research

In policy analysis, we often seek to determine the evidence for a cause-and-effect relationship between a policy decision and its results. For example, will the elimination of the DPP produce a federal budget savings of $15 billion over a 10-year time horizon?

Unlike natural science research, where we can design and execute controlled experiments, policy analysis often requires that we utilize social science research methods such as modelling and statistical estimation.

While there are real differences in natural science and social science methodologies, the ultimate goal is the same: to prudently establish a body of evidence that either supports or contradicts the existence of cause-and-effect relations between variables of interest.

Careful analysis of observed phenomena can improve our chances of uncovering true cause-and-effect relationships. We need valid research to plan effective policy. In this textbook, we define careful analysis as a systematic approach that we summarize into the following steps:[12]

1   Identify a clear and definite purpose for the policy analysis.
2   Use both positive and normative economics to define the policy question (or questions) to be investigated.
3   Gather and organize preliminary information – e.g. perform a literature search, assemble secondary data, engage focus groups, and conduct informal and formal interviews.

4   Create or adopt an appropriate theoretical framework (or model) to identify policy options and formulate testable hypotheses.

5   Engage in scientific data collection, and use appropriate data analysis techniques (such as statistical tests, simulations, etc.) to test hypotheses and evaluate the predicted impact of alternative policies.

6   Interpret results, reach conclusions, and make recommendations (when appropriate) about alternative policies and their consequences.

Both positive and normative aspects are included in the above step-by-step approach to applied policy research. The logical progression of this sequential methodology is necessarily reliant on the principles of positive analysis. In this case, the prominence of positivism is entirely appropriate. Our goal with this organized approach is to consistently produce good policy analyses that are valid, reliable, and transparent. Ultimately, if our policy analysis is sufficiently rigorous, then we are more likely to help identify pragmatic policy choices that are equitable, workable, and efficient.

Elected officials often rely upon policy analysts to provide objective and reliable information. After the policy analyst has produced impartial and science-based research on the available policy options, then the authorized policy makers can use the analytical results as input to normatively select a preferred policy option.

Some policy situations do require the policy analyst to act normatively and recommend policy options. For example, if the desirability of alternative policies is evaluated using the applicable techniques of cost-benefit analysis, then a policy analyst would rank policy options according to their respective economic efficiency impacts.

The choice to recommend and implement a policy option, while others are rejected, is not entirely a scientific conclusion. The selection of the most preferred policy alternative is highly dependent on the appraisal criteria. For example, if we evaluate the desirability of a range of policy alternatives based on ethical standards or political attractiveness, then the relative ranking of the policy options could easily differ from their relative status based on economic efficiency.

In normative analysis, we cannot use "the scientific method" to determine which value system is the "best" for ranking alternatives. In this situation, the most transparent method is to simply announce that a particular criterion for comparing values is selected, and that the resulting priorities are a reflection of that value choice.

The science and art of policy design

The above considerations imply that policy analysis is often strongly influenced by the methods of positive economics. Equally important, the role of normative evaluation is essential in policy making. We need a policy design that can properly integrate these crucial elements of the policy process.

The challenge of determining the proper balance between policy analysis and policy making means that the policy design process is both an art and a science. The purpose of building better connections between analysis and implementation is to strengthen the overall effectiveness of policy design.

Mayer, van Daalen, and Bots argue that policy design is more effective when analysts are "knowledge generators." In applied research, knowledge creation happens when research efforts produce new policy options with real problem-solving potential. In such cases, the policy analyst creates fresh opportunities for policy makers to consider. Policy design is strengthened.

One quick way to summarize how knowledge generation can improve policy design is this logical sequence: "actions–means–ends." The innovative policy analyst "opens the door" for policy makers to have a start-to-finish knowledge of how a policy option is expected to work.[13]

When new knowledge is transferred from the policy analyst, policy makers can:

- Identify a policy option as a definite *action*,
- Access the *means* for implementing it, and
- Accurately predict the *end results* of making that decision.

A comprehensive policy design will produce an entire set of these policy option sequences. Each option is an alternative strategy, with its associated implementation tactics, and its specific aims or goals to be accomplished.[14]

The above review reveals that effective policy design is no accident. Careful planning, clear communication, and productive research results can all make a difference in translating the results of policy analysis into usable knowledge for policy making.

Summary of applied policy research

A systematic approach to policy analysis is a primary focus in this text. The methods of both normative and positive economics help guide the investigation of policy scenarios. Policy analysis is directed by a step-wise methodology. Policy recommendations and the process of policy making require normative choices that involve value judgments and the pursuit of desired outcomes. An effective policy design will transform the knowledge obtained from policy analysis into policy options/strategies that can be evaluated and implemented by policy makers.

Policy analysis: a worthy undertaking

Earlier in this chapter, we learned that the cessation of the DPP is projected to have a multi-billion dollar impact on the US federal budget deficit. Such case studies offer concrete evidence that agricultural and food policy choices are consequential.

The outcome of policy decisions have real and measureable influences on the welfare of farmers, consumers, and taxpayers (to name just a few of the stakeholders). Therefore, if we can identify and implement good policy, then the potential beneficial results are substantial. On the other hand, policy mistakes are expensive.

The large economic scale of farm and food policy impacts reminds us that careful analysis is a worthwhile activity. Normatively, we can make the judgment that the cost of developing a better policy design has the potential of yielding a sizable payoff.

Part of the process of effective policy design requires that we become acquainted with current policies and economic conditions in the farm and food sectors of the US economy. In the next section, we briefly examine how a selected set of today's policies are influencing economic conduct and performance.

We will also review the textbook's sequence of chapters and case studies. We have some exciting work ahead, as we continue our campaign to understand the opportunities and challenges associated with agricultural and food policies in the United States.

Influential US Policies in the 21st Century: the 2010 FSMA, the 2014 Farm Bill, and the 2015 Trade Act

On any given day, there are variety of policies creating real consequences for US agricultural and food systems. Within the boundaries of a single textbook, it is not possible to evaluate all of the influences. But we can still learn a great deal about the impact of policy choices on economic outcomes by focusing on key elements that we know will be important.

In this textbook, we will explore case studies and scenarios for policy analysis that arise primarily from three recent large-scale legislative initiatives of the US Congress, namely:

- The FDA Food Safety Modernization Act (FSMA) (Passed by the US Congress in December 2010, and signed into law by the US President on January 4, 2011.)
- The Agricultural Act of 2014 (i.e. the 2014 Farm Bill)
- The 2015 Trade Act (H.R.1314 – 114th Congress) (Creating the Trade Promotion Authority (TPA) for the US President to negotiate trade agreements such as the Trans-Pacific Partnership (TPP), and for Congress to reject or approve the negotiated trade agreements with an "up-or-down" vote.)

As we strive to discern important twenty-first-century trends for agriculture and food, we expect that the trio of legislated policies listed above will be very influential in determining economic performance over both the short term and the long term.

Because these laws are so significant, it is essential that we become acquainted with their content and purpose. In addition, we will be referring to these three laws to generate policy discussions throughout the rest of this textbook. What follows next are introductions to fundamental aspects of these major policy initiatives.

The FDA Food Safety Modernization Act (FSMA)

When the twenty-first-century American consumer enters a retail supermarket or a favorite restaurant to buy groceries and/or enjoy a meal, he/she expects food products to be high in quality and fully screened against any threats or contaminants. However, documented episodes of food poisoning in recent years have eroded the perception that the US food supply is consistently and reliably safe.

Some examples illustrate that the threats are real. The DailyMeal.Com website highlights the 1993 E. coli outbreak where 732 consumers were sickened and four children died from under-cooked hamburgers consumed at Jack-in-the-Box fast-food outlets. In 2003, tainted green onions at Chi-Chi restaurants in Pennsylvania were responsible for the spread of Hepatitis A among 640 consumers – where four died. In 2008, contaminated peanuts infected more than 700 people, and nine died.[15] There are plenty of other recent episodes; we do not have the space to identify all of them here.

The US Centers for Disease Control and Prevention ("the CDC") estimates that 48 million people (one in six Americans) are poisoned and about 3,000 die each year from food-borne contaminants. In the past, the primary government response to outbreaks of food-related illnesses has been to create new regulations and guidelines *after* the contamination event has taken place. In an effort to lessen the frequency and severity of these preventable public health threats, the US Congress passed the FDA Food Safety Modernization Act

(FSMA) in 2010. When the FSMA was signed into law on January 4, 2011, Congress set new goals to shift the paradigm from reaction to *prevention*.[16]

The FSMA dramatically increased the US Food and Drug Administration's (FDA's) authorities to create and enforce new food safety standards. For example, the FSMA almost immediately granted the FDA new powers to force food companies and agribusinesses to issue food recalls when circumstances warrant them. The FDA's international reach also was extended to imported foods – the FDA can now compel foreign food suppliers to adhere to the same safety standards as domestic foods. The FDA is further empowered to enter into alliances and partnerships with the US Department of Agriculture (USDA) and other federal agencies, as well as state and local authorities. The process of establishing a new prevention-oriented food system is time-consuming work. In 2015, nearly four years after the FSMA became law, the FDA was only beginning to implement strategies dictated by the FSMA's legislative language.

The FSMA promises to create sweeping changes throughout the US farm and food system. As the FDA moves forward with the mandates in the FSMA, there will be numerous policy scenarios to examine and analyze. The economic benefits and costs of adhering to the new regulations and guidelines should be estimated and assessed. We can explore questions of how to structure new food safety policies in ways that are effective in achieving the desired goals while also being economically cost efficient.

Distributional consequences are also a very important consideration. We can determine which groups are likely to shoulder the major costs of meeting the new FSMA standards, and also what constituencies stand to most benefit from the enforcement of FSMA authorities. And ultimately, there is the overarching question of how much safer will the US farm and food system really be as a result of establishing the new paradigm of prevention that is the FSMA centerpiece.

The FSMA is likely to be a major transformational influence on the overall safety and economic conditions in our farm and food systems. But FSMA is not the only law with enormous consequences. The massive multi-year impacts of policies known collectively as "the Farm Bill" are another key influence. We now turn our attention to this next major policy initiative.

The Agricultural Act of 2014 (i.e. the 2014 Farm Bill)

After three years of debate, the US Congress passed the 2014 Farm Bill, and on February 7, 2014 President Obama signed it into law. The Farm Bill is an omnibus[17] piece of legislation. The 2014 Farm Bill is certainly expected to impact US farming in the coming years; but its effects go far beyond the farm gate.[18]

The Agricultural Act of 2014 has twelve different titles (Commodities, Conservation, Trade, Nutrition, Credit, Rural Development, Research and Extension, Forestry, Energy, Horticulture, Crop Insurance, and Miscellaneous) that guide federal government expenditures. The Congressional Budget Office (CBO) predicts a total cost of $489 billion over five fiscal years (FY2014-FY2018) for this latest farm bill.[19]

Compared to previous farm bills, the 2014 Farm Act transformed commodity programs, expanded multi-peril crop insurance, restructured conservation programs, adjusted the Supplemental Nutrition Assistance Program (SNAP), and reorganized programs for beginning farmers and ranchers, bioenergy, organic farmers, and specialty crops. Because of its large and multi-dimensional nature, it is difficult to briefly summarize this wide-ranging law.[20]

Some observers examine the breakdown of expenditures in this omnibus act, and wonder how this law continues to be called the "Farm Bill." CBO projections demonstrate that 80 percent of the outlays in the 2014 Farm Bill will actually fund nutrition programs. We can argue that the remaining 20 percent of government expenses in this law are farm-focused, but the fact remains that the term "Farm Bill" oversimplifies the purpose of a multifaceted piece of government policy.

We can investigate the economic effect of the 2014 Farm Bill in relation to the stated goals of the policy makers who legislated it. The full heading of the 2014 Farm Bill is:

> "An Act – To provide for the reform and continuation of agricultural and other programs of the Department of Agriculture through fiscal year 2018, and for other purposes."[21]

Our analysis of this important law can begin with its identified purpose for the "reform and continuation" of programs. We can scour the twelve titles of the 2014 Farm Bill to determine whether there are distinguishable patterns or relationships. In some cases, we may uncover a real effort to reform a set of related policies, while in other areas there may be a clear trend towards maintaining support for goals established in earlier farm bills.

The 2014 Farm Bill is a complex piece of legislation. It may initially seem to be unmanageable as a focus for policy analysis. But we can use the "principle of parsimony," sometimes known as Occam's razor, to search for distinct patterns and critical variables that will help us to achieve important insights. With sufficient intellectual effort, we can distinguish systematic tendencies from apparent chaos and complexity.[22]

We can apply economic principles and theories of political economy to postulate general relationships, construct manageable models, and make testable inferences.

The wide scope of the 2014 Farm Bill means that even if we focus our efforts, there is still considerable work to do. We also need to recognize that other pieces of legislation are worthy of our attention. The next policy initiative that we will introduce is in the area of international trade. Let's take an initial look at the proposed trade agreement known as the "Trans Pacific Partnership (TPP)" in relation to its potential effect on the food and agriculture sectors of the US economy.

The 2015 Trade Act ("TPA for the TPP")

If we decipher the acronyms associated with international trade agreements, then we discover a very fertile area for farm and food policy analysis.

In June of 2015, Congress passed H.R.1314 (The Trade Act) and opened the door for the President to temporarily exercise negotiating powers known as "Trade Promotion Authority (TPA)." TPA is also known as "Fast-Track." In essence, when the US Congress legislates a temporary TPA, then the constitutional authority for international commerce (that resides with Congress) is briefly "on loan" to the executive branch to facilitate negotiations and produce an international trade agreement proposal in a timely way. When a trade agreement proposal is ready for final consideration, then the TPA law guides Congress to consider the proposed trade agreement as a legislative bill that is *not* subject to amendments. The proposed agreement (in its entirety) is brought to Congress for an "up-or-down" vote. In 1994, the TPA process brought the North American Free Trade Agreement (NAFTA) before Congress for a vote, and it passed.

In October 2015, with the help of TPA negotiating powers, the US International Trade Representative was able to negotiate a new trade agreement proposal known as the Trans-Pacific Partnership (TPP). The US Congress will ultimately decide whether the United States will formally join with eleven other Pacific Rim countries to be a member in this proposed trade partnership.

In terms of an opportunity for policy analysis, the US decision to either accept or reject membership in the TPP will have important implications for US agriculture. If the TPP is adopted, the agreement will reduce barriers to free trade among the TPP members. In particular, the TPP is expected to reduce or eliminate tariffs and tariff-rate-quotas (TRQ's). In a study performed by the USDA's Economic Research Service (ERS), Burfisher et al. predicted significant US agricultural trade impacts if the US agreed to join the TPP.[23]

Using the Global Trade Analysis Project's (GTAP) static computable general equilibrium model, Burfisher et al. forecasted US agricultural trade flows through the year 2025. US agricultural trade within the TPP was compared to a baseline without the TPP. Burfisher et al. estimated that total US agricultural trade (as a TPP member) would increase by 6 percent above the baseline projection. When this noticeable increase in US agricultural trade is broken out into its components, US agricultural exports would increase by about $3 billion over the baseline, while US agricultural imports would rise by $1 billion. Such increases would be a significant boost in economic activity for US agriculture. In addition, the American food consumer would most likely benefit from access to tariff-free and TRQ-free imported products.[24]

This textbook aims to encourage students to engage in policy analysis exercises that are both stimulating and relevant. If modeling projections are correct, then the policy questions associated with whether the USA should participate in the TPP is a decision where billons of trade dollars are at stake for US agriculture.

From this perspective, the textbook authors think that analyzing a trade policy scenario (such as the US TPP membership issue) is a meaningful and exciting area of study. We hope that our student-readers share our enthusiasm for this opportunity to think critically about policy questions that really matter.

Summary

The FSMA, the 2014 Farm Bill, and the 2015 Trade Act are real pieces of legislation that will shape the policy environment for US food and agriculture in the twenty-first century. This textbook is an opportunity to learn analytical skills and apply them to better understand the policy impact emanating from these legislative initiatives. The breadth and depth of the policy changes associated with these three laws means that we will have no shortage of policy scenarios to consider. In addition, we can also begin to explore the question of whether the range of policies encompassed by these three laws are in harmony or in conflict.

To what extent will the pursuit of food safety in the FSMA have an influence on the subsidized nutrition programs in the 2014 Farm Bill? What will be the interactions between FSMA rules and trading relationships if the USA was to join the TPP agreement? These are interesting questions that should be addressed with the systematic approaches that arise from proper application policy analysis methods.

The next section of this introductory chapter offers guidelines intended to help the reader "reap the harvest" of educational potential associated with utilizing this textbook on agricultural and food policy analysis.

Suggested guidelines for using this textbook

"An investment in knowledge pays the best interest." This piece of advice is attributed to American scientist and activist Benjamin Franklin.[25] In relation to this textbook, we use the quote as an invitation. Seize the learning opportunity offered here, and your effort will earn you a valuable return.

Use this text to sharpen your analytical skills. Learn about the exciting changes taking place in our agricultural and food economies. The knowledge will benefit you, and you can educate others too. We all eat to survive; and consequently, we all have a stake in creating a more successful farm and food system.

The application of policy analysis techniques in problem-solving scenarios and case studies is an active learning process. Each chapter in this textbook is accompanied by opportunities to address issues, apply theoretical frameworks, formulate hypotheses, gather evidence, draw conclusions, and make recommendations. Students are strongly encouraged to seek out these opportunities to practice policy analysis.

Policy choices have economic consequences. The design of this textbook can help students learn to appropriately assess policy options and reasonably predict changes in economic performance. For example, students can use the principles of both positive and normative economics to review the circumstances, decision making, and anticipated economic outcomes associated with the FSMA, the 2014 Farm Bill, and/or the 2015 Trade Act.

Organization of the textbook chapters

There are a variety of ways to organize a wide-ranging analysis of US agricultural and food policies. Our approach is to: (1) first acquaint students with key economic trends that are impacting food and farm; then (2) introduce methods for scenario analysis; and finally (3) apply the investigative methods to explore policy choices and their consequences.

Below is an overview of the sequence and content of the textbook chapters:

- **Chapter 1 – An introduction to policy analysis**. The purpose of Chapter 1 is to: (1) identify why agricultural and food policy is an area worthy of careful study; (2) highlight key policies (e.g. 2014 Farm Bill, FSMA, and TPP) that will be addressed; (3) introduce the principles of policy analysis and evaluation; and (4) outline the overall chapter organization and content of the textbook.
- **Chapter 2 – Twenty-first-century trends, opportunities, and challenges for US agriculture and food systems**. In this chapter, we initially use the agricultural economics literature to review changes in US twentieth-century food and agriculture that continue to influence twenty-first-century economic performance. Next, we examine how the Food Safety Modernization Act (FSMA), the 2014 Farm Bill, and the Trans-Pacific Partnership (TPP) Congressional-decision are expected to influence efficiency and distributional outcomes in the US farm and food sectors. Finally, we review how general macroeconomic, energy, and environmental and climatic factors affect US farm-and-food sector policies and performance.
- **Chapter 3 – A policy analysis toolbox: methods to investigate agricultural and food market scenarios**. This chapter is pivotal. We review the analytical methods of economics that are applicable to case studies and problem solving. We begin with the principles of rational decision making and marginal analysis. Next, we utilize the supply-and-demand

model, and elasticity analysis, to predict to how alternative policies affect market equilibria. We then apply consumer and producer surplus concepts to determine welfare effects when conditions change. Finally, we explore the relevance of the following investigative tools: the law of comparative advantage; market externalities; public goods; and public choice economics.

- **Chapter 4 – Analyzing economic consequences of farm safety net programs in the 2014 Farm Bill.** Chapter 4 takes a look at the Farm Bill Programs known as the "farm financial safety net." We begin with a review of Title I: Commodities. We investigate the Price Loss Coverage (PLC) and Agriculture Risk Coverage (ARC) programs. We also examine the Marketing Assistance Loan Program (MALP), Sugar and Dairy Policies, and the Supplemental Agricultural Disaster Assistance Program. Next, we turn our attention to Title XI: Crop Insurance. Included topics are: Revenue and Yield Insurance, Premium Subsidy Levels, Supplemental Coverage Option (SCO), and the Stacked-Income protection plan (STAX). At the conclusion of Chapter 4, we apply the methods of Chapter 3 to study three case scenarios of selected Farm Bill programs.

- **Chapter 5 – The Food Safety Modernization Act (FSMA): evaluating costs and benefits.** The FSMA promised to improve food safety by creating regulatory policies emphasizing preventative action instead of post-crisis response. Is the FSMA properly designed to reach its stated goals? To answer this question, we apply cost-benefit analysis (CBA) methods in Chapter 5 to investigate the FSMA's economic value. Students will learn techniques to properly measure FSMA's costs and benefits, avoid common pitfalls in CBA analysis, and apply the equi-marginal principle to optimize net gains in policy design.

- **Chapter 6 – US agricultural and food sector connections to the global economy.** In Chapter 6, we investigate the effects of globalization, macroeconomic policy, and currency exchange rates on US food and agricultural markets. We also study US trade policy, where both protectionism and trade liberalization are influential philosophies. Finally, we investigate the influence of changing trade policies on economic efficiency, income redistribution, and consumer-driven global food markets.

- **Chapter 7 – Analyzing effects of USDA nutrition programs on hunger and food security in the US.** Food is one of life's necessities. In this chapter, students investigate nutrition assistance policies in the 2014 Farm Bill and their effects on economic efficiency and equity. Nearly 80 percent of the estimated $489 billion five-year 2014 Farm Bill expense is targeted towards offering financial support for family members who cannot independently afford a complete and healthy diet. Included in Chapter 7 is a review of USDA's *Thrifty Food Plan* and its importance in nutrition policy today. We also examine the purpose of USDA's *MyPlate* and *MyWins* Nutrition Communication Plans.

- **Chapter 8 – Economic choices and outcomes for agriculture, natural resources, and the environment.** Agricultural and food policies are frequently interconnected with trends in natural resource management, energy use, and environmental quality. We begin Chapter 8 by introducing a microeconomic model of intertemporal choice to guide our study. In relation to our economic model, we review key concepts of sustainability. We then focus our attention on empirical indicators of the "stocks and flows" of agricultural, environmental, and natural resources. We pay particular attention to measurements of land use, soil conservation, and water use economics. Finally, we take a look at policies influencing agriculture's role in energy markets and climate change.

- **Chapter 9 – Research, technology, and the growth of sustainable agricultural production**. After World War II, research and technology investments were largely responsible for a strong record of US agricultural productivity growth. In Chapter 9, students examine how trends in public and private research funding are related to changes in productivity. In light of the natural resource constraints just studied in Chapter 8, students are encouraged to examine how future policies are expected to influence the sustainable growth of food-production potentials.

- **Chapter 10 – Exploring the multi-dimensional aspects of food security**. Poverty and food insecurity are among the most troubling challenges facing agri-food system policy. The approach that we take in Chapter 10 is to first define the meaning of "food-secure" and "food-insecure" households. Next, we review US domestic food security policy. Then we widen our perspective to include the multi-national and global efforts to improve nutritional conditions for households worldwide. We also investigate the food security problems of areas that are "food deserts," and the role of "food hubs" in achieving efficient and equitable food distributional outcomes.

- **Chapter 11 – Twenty-first-century perspectives on rural development**. In the US, rural development has been a long-term focus of multiple farm bills. Modern agricultural production and marketing trends are changing the meaning of rural development. Agriculture can be an important driver to advance regional success, but not by itself. In Chapter 11, we examine the need for a comprehensive approach. We review proposals to modernize rural development policies. We study US and global rural development patterns. Finally, we anticipate future challenges and opportunities in rural development policy.

- **Chapter 12 – Current developments and new dynamics influencing agricultural and food policy**. Traditional social images of farm producers and food systems are being transformed by increasingly diverse demographics and new patterns of consumer-driven markets. Interactions between these new social dynamics and related government policies (2010 FSMA and the 2014 Farm Bill) provide a rich area for analysis and evaluation. In this chapter, students have the opportunity to explore how policy choices can influence the growth of women and socially disadvantaged groups in agriculture. In addition, this chapter examines the significant impacts on policy design that new consumer expectations are having on food supply chains, locally grown foods, expanding organic markets, urban farms, food cooperatives, and related innovations in food production, delivery, and consumption.

- **Chapter 13 – When policies work at cross-purposes: addressing challenges and pursuing opportunities**. This chapter highlights the challenges that often arise in the design and implementation of agricultural and food policies. Using research-based policy analysis techniques, we examine instances when well-intentioned policies create outcomes that are contradictory to other policy goals. For example, when government subsidies are capitalized into farm assets, the goal of achieving competiveness in global food markets is compromised. In this chapter, we contrast ideal policy scenarios to real situations where political pressures and special-interest agendas influence policy outcomes.

- **Chapter 14 – Anticipating future trends in agricultural and food policy**. This final chapter offers summaries and conclusions about the predictive powers and the real limitations of research-based policy analysis. We make educated guesses about the future trends in policy design for the agricultural and food sectors of the US economy, and beyond.

The chapter topics and organization indicated above are intended as a reasonable cross-section of key aspects of agricultural and food policy. The coverage is not fully comprehensive because our goal is to create a textbook that combines active learning opportunities with important policy content. Normative judgments were necessary in creating a text of manageable length that balances the practice of policy analysis with the very interesting knowledge about our agricultural and food systems.

Summary

In this first chapter, we established the overall educational goals for this textbook. We introduced a science-based framework for policy analysis, and briefly introduced some critical aspects of agricultural and food policy that are currently influencing economic performance.

The remainder of this textbook is designed to help students become better policy analysts, and hopefully be more informed about key aspects of our agricultural and food economy. In the next chapter we will examine the current conditions and driving forces that shape the economic choices faced by participants in our agricultural and food systems. Returning back to Lincoln's suggestion presented at the beginning of this chapter, we aim to "know where we are and whither we are tending, so that we can better know what to do, and how to do it."

Notes

1 Abraham Lincoln Online. "House Divided Speech: Springfield, Illinois, June 16, 1858." Retrieved from: www.abrahamlincolnonline.org/lincoln/speeches/house.htm
2 What is a policy? Merriam-Webster offers this definition – a definite course or method of action selected from among alternatives and in light of given conditions to guide and determine present and future decisions. Retrieved from: www.merriam-webster.com/dictionary/policy
3 Samuelson, Paul A. and William D. Nordhaus. *Economics*. Sixteenth Edition. New York: Irwin/McGraw-Hill, 1998, p. xxiv.
4 Johnson, Glenn L., and Lewis K. Zerby. *What Economists Do About Values*. East Lansing, MI: Michigan State University, 1973, p. 1.
5 Rosen, Harvey and Ted Gayer. *Public Finance*. Ninth Edition. New York: Irwin/McGraw Hill, 2010, p. 5.
6 Mayer, Igor, Els Van Daalen, and Pieter Bots. "Perspectives on Policy Analysis: A Framework for Understanding and Design." International Journal of Technology Policy and Management. 01/2004; 4(2). DO, p. 1. Retrieved from: www.researchgate.net/publication/249921167_Perspectives_on_Policy_Analysis_A_Framework_for_Understanding_and_Design
7 Ibid, p. 7.
8 Ibid, p. 17.
9 Shields, Dennis. Farm Commodity Provisions in the 2014 Farm Bill (P.L. 113-79). Washington: US Congressional Research Service. CRS Report 7-5700, R43448. March 28, 2014, p. ii. Retrieved from: http://nationalaglawcenter.org/wp-content/uploads/assets/crs/R43448.pdf
10 Keeney, Roman. "The End of the Direct Payment Era in US Farm Policy." Purdue Extension: APEX – Ag Policy Explained. EC-477-W, Dec. 2013, p. 2. Retrieved from: www.extension.purdue.edu/extmedia/ec/ec-774-w.pdf
11 Ibid, p. 2.
12 This science-based approach is a modification of the hypothetico-deductive method that is described in Uma Sekaran's research methods textbook. Sekaran, Uma. *Research Methods for Business*, Fourth Edition. New York: John Wiley and Sons, 2003, p. 29.
13 Mayer, Igor, Els Van Daalen, and Pieter Bots. "Perspectives on Policy Analysis: A Framework for Understanding and Design." International Journal of Technology Policy and Management. 01/2004; 4(2). DO, p. 7. Retrieved from: www.researchgate.net/publication/249921167_Perspectives_on_Policy_Analysis_A_Framework_for_Understanding_and_Design

14 Ibid, p. 7.
15 Myers, Dan, (ed). "The World's Biggest Food Poisoning Scares." *The Daily Meal*. May 26, 2016. Retrieved from: www.thedailymeal.com/historys-worst-food-poisoning-outbreaks
16 Department of Health and Human Services, Food and Drug Administration. FSMA Facts: Background on the FDA Food Safety Modernization Act (FSMA). Washington: FDA. July 2011. Retrieved from: www.fda.gov/downloads/Food/GuidanceRegulation/UCM263773.pdf
17 An "omnibus bill" jointly addresses several areas of law that previously were treated separately. See Jim Monke, Randy A. Aussenberg, and Megan Stubbs. "Expiration and Extension of the 2008 Farm Bill." Congressional Research Service, 7-5700, R42442, Sept. 16, 2013, p. 2, and Renée Johnson and Jim Monke. "What Is the Farm Bill?" Nov. 8, 2016. CRS Report RS22131, Retrieved from: https://fas.org/sgp/crs/misc/R42442.pdf and https://fas.org/sgp/crs/misc/RS22131.pdf
18 Zulauf, Carl and David Orden. "U.S. Agricultural Act of 2014: Reaffirming Countercyclical Support." July 16, 2014, p. 1. Retrieved from: file:///C:/Users/User/Downloads/zulauf_and_orden_narrative_final_synopsis_to_accompany_policy_seminar_powerpoint_-_july_21_2014.pdf
19 Monke, Jim. "Budget Issues That Shaped the 2014 Farm Bill." Congressional Research Service, 7-5700, R42484, April 10, 2014, p. 1. Retrieved from: http://nationalaglawcenter.org/wp-content/uploads/assets/crs/R42484.pdf
20 USDA, ERS. "Agricultural Act of 2014: Highlights and Implications." Retrieved from: www.ers.usda.gov/agricultural-act-of-2014-highlights-and-implications.aspx
21 113th US Congress, H. R. 2642: Agricultural Act of 2014. Retrieved from: www.gpo.gov/fdsys/pkg/BILLS-113hr2642enr/pdf/BILLS-113hr2642enr.pdf
22 The principle of parsimony undergirds all scientific analysis and modelling. If we are faced with a group of equivalent models that can explain events occurring within a scenario, then choose the approach that is the most streamlined or simplest model. Occam's razor lets us "shear away" concepts or variables that are redundant or unnecessary. Parsimonious investigation will reduce the likelihood of introducing contradictions or irregularities that can prevent the discovery of key relationships. Retrieved from: http://pespmc1.vub.ac.be/occamraz.html
23 Burfisher, Mary E., John Dyck, Birgit Meade, Lorraine Mitchell, John Wainio, Steven Zahniser, Shawn Arita, and Jayson Beckman. "Agriculture in the Trans-Pacific Partnership." Washington: ERR-176 Economic Research Service/USDA, October 2014, p. 1. Retrieved from: www.ers.usda.gov/media/1692509/err176.pdf
24 Ibid, pp. 23–24.
25 Google Search Result. Benjamin Franklin. Retrieved from: www.google.com/webhp?sourceid=chrome-instant&ion=1&espv=2&ie=UTF-8#q=benjamin%20franklin

Chapter 2

Twenty-first-century trends, opportunities, and challenges for US agriculture and food systems

Earth's population is was estimated to be 7.3 billion in 2015, and will reach approximately 9.6 billion by the year 2050.[1,2] A dramatic expansion in agriculture's production capacity will be required over the next 35 years, if we are to satisfy the food demands of an additional 2.3 billion persons.

US food and agricultural systems are just beginning to respond to this global challenge. The question of how to manage this worldwide growth in food requirements is very important. But there are additional concerns. For example, twenty-first-century farm-and-food markets must seek effective ways to create a safer and sustainable food supply while simultaneously responding to an increasingly sophisticated set of consumer preferences.

The need for informed policy making has never been greater. Individual farm producers, agribusinesses, government agencies, and other interest groups are seeking strategies to accurately identify the trends and successfully adapt to them.

Purpose and organization of chapter

Global population trends virtually guarantee that agricultural and food sector performance will be a highly visible agenda item for US policy-makers throughout the twenty-first century.

Food is a necessity for life, and is consequently always on the minds of people everywhere. Rural or urban, local or global, food and agricultural markets are vital. The proper design of agricultural and food policies must take into account how decisions influence market performance at all levels of the agri-food system.

Successful policies and insightful analyses rely on having accurate knowledge of the market environment. Consequently, Chapter 2 aims to provide readers with baseline information on current and expected future conditions in the food and agricultural sectors of the US economy.

The value of this chapter stems from its instrumentality. Just as a surveyor carefully examines the arrangement of key landscape features before mapping an area, we develop a wide-ranging perspective on the state of the agricultural economy prior to conducting a policy analysis. The process of evaluating and recommending policy choices is more effective when we integrate relevant facts and background information into our research.

We organize Chapter 2 to highlight major economic factors and trends, as follows:

- We utilize the Dmitri et al. (2005) framework, and additional intellectual contributions to the professional Agricultural Economics literature, to review how changes in US twentieth-century food and agriculture continue to influence twenty-first-century economic performance.[3]
- We examine how the FSMA, the 2014 Farm Bill, and the TPP Congressional-decision are likely to influence future efficiency and distributional outcomes in the US farm and food sectors.
- We review how general macroeconomic, energy, and environmental and climatic factors affect US farm-and-food sector policies and performance.

After we review the diverse forces at work within the farm and food sectors of the economy, we summarize and draw conclusions. Chapter 2 serves as an empirical foundation to help readers comprehend and apply the policy analysis tools that we introduce in Chapter 3.

Twentieth-century influences on current US agriculture and food systems

From farm to table: a dynamic era

Today we live in a world where precision agriculture and laser-guided drones are commonly used farming technologies. While we accept these advanced techniques as part of a normal and competitive farm operation, we also know that these practices are relatively recent innovations. The pace of technical change in agriculture and food systems is remarkable. Making predictions can be a speculative business, but we can confidently forecast that even more dramatic changes are on the horizon.

If we are to make reasonable estimates of twenty-first-century developments, we need to understand our current status. And, since our present state is influenced by ongoing trends, we begin by examining the past forces of change that continue to shape our market conditions today.

US agriculture and food systems experienced dramatic and complex changes during the twentieth century. These transformations jointly affected the farm and food sectors. Nevertheless, we can gain valuable insights by studying each sector independently.

We begin by examining how the "farm sector" evolved over the period of 1901–2000. We subsequently focus our attention on the twentieth century innovations that transformed the "food sector" of the US agri-food system.

US agriculture responds to powerful twentieth-century influences

While a variety of phenomena influenced the progress of twentieth-century American agriculture, the role of changing technology, growing global markets, and evolving consumer expectations are among the most important long-run driving forces.[4]

Technology and US agricultural productivity

Technological innovation in US agriculture during the twentieth century can be characterized as broad in its scope and dramatic in its impact. From the very beginning of the era, a wide range of technical improvements dramatically changed US agriculture.

Advances in plant and animal breeding were accompanied by the rapid adoption of new petroleum- and electrical-powered machinery (a process simply called "mechanization"). In plain terms, farmers substituted mechanical for animal power because of efficiency gains, and they also adopted many labor-saving technologies.

Farming is a competitive business. Market economics meant that rational profit-oriented farm owners increased their use of technology and capital investment while they reduced their demand for human labor and animal inputs.[5]

New agricultural technologies necessitated on-farm resource reallocations. The restructuring of farm inputs radically altered the connection between agriculture and the broad rural economy. The Gross Domestic Product (GDP) of rural areas became less reliant on agricultural activity. Rural areas experienced a *long-term labor exodus* to urban centers. Simultaneously, farm households became increasingly dependent on *non-farm income* to supplement their farm business earnings.[6]

After World War II (post-1945), chemical industry innovations meant that yield-enhancing inorganic fertilizers and pesticides could be applied at low cost, and farm producers quickly incorporated these cheap but productive inputs into their operations. In the final twenty years of the twentieth century, US agriculture began to benefit from research and development (R&D) in areas such as genetics, information technology, no-till, and related new knowledge. The improved agricultural productivity associated with the widespread adoption of these new technologies is still considered to be quite extraordinary.

To gain additional insight into the important economic effects of technology adoption, we can statistically estimate technological impacts on agricultural productivity growth. To this end, the Economic Research Service (ERS) of the US Department of Agriculture (USDA) developed a measurement tool known as Total Factor Productivity (TFP). Using TFP, the ERS can determine the separate effect of technological change on productivity, unconnected from the influences of hired inputs on agricultural output growth.[7]

TFP can be measured as an index value. ERS set the TFP index equal to 100 in 1948. Using a consistent estimation approach across all years, the ERS determined that the TFP index gradually trended higher, and reached 266 by the year 2004. Assuming that our measures are reliable, we can say that US agricultural productivity improved 2.66 times over the period 1948 to 2004.[8]

If we annualize the growth rate during this 56-year span, we estimate that TFP grew at an average rate of 1.8 percent per year. Over the same time frame, ERS estimated that *aggregate input use in US agriculture actually decreased slightly*. When we logically connect these observations, we conclude that *technological change was largely responsible* for US agriculture productivity improving 2.66 times in just over half a century.

This result is impressive, when agriculture's productivity record is compared to the rest of the US economy. ERS cited another related study, conducted during 1960–2004, where agriculture was determined to be the source of 12.1 percent of all TFP growth in private industry, while agriculture accounted for only 1.8 percent of industrial GDP.[9]

Throughout the twentieth century, the intensely competitive nature of farm commodity markets meant that producers were highly motivated to adopt a variety of new cost-saving technologies.

As farmers incorporated these technical innovations into their business operations, they soon discovered that ongoing improvements in their profitability were linked to a long-run production phenomenon known as "increasing returns to scale" (or "economies of scale").

When economies of scale influence the performance of an expanding operation, farm managers notice that their percent gain in productive output value *exceeds* the proportional increase in their input hiring costs. Simply put, larger-scale farm operations gained a competitive advantage by producing at a lower average total cost per unit output than smaller-sized farms.

The influence of economies of scale, in combination with a variety of other factors, led to a strong and relentless trend of *US farms becoming larger in size and fewer in number*. This pattern has continued into the twenty-first century.

The total amount of US land in farm production has varied little. However, the structure of agriculture, as gauged by who owns and controls the majority of agriculture's productive resources, shifted significantly in the last century. The forces prompting farm consolidation are still at work. As a result, it is very likely that the *structure of US agriculture* will continue to change.

The growth of global agricultural markets

Ongoing adjustments in the organization of US agriculture are also connected to the expanding influence of the global economy. Today's US farm and food sectors are strongly linked to world markets.

From an historical standpoint, a growing international role for the US agricultural economy is a trade pattern that was often interrupted during the twentieth century. Policies towards agricultural trade between 1901 and 2000 were inconsistent. They were buffeted by major political and economic events.

From 1910–1914, just prior to World War I (WWI), powerful foreign demand for US food and fiber created a "golden age for US Agriculture." It was a period of exceptionally high exports, strong commodity prices and above-normal profits (adjusted for price inflation) for US farmers. The belief that there should be "parity prices for US commodities" in farm markets is rooted in the unique conditions of that time period. However, the advent of WWI and US post-WWI isolationism reversed the tide, and led to depressed US export demand and reduced commodity prices. The slowdown in trade contributed to harsh US farm financial conditions throughout the 1920s.

The next set of events did *not* help US agriculture. The US Congress passed the protectionist Smoot-Hawley Tariff Act in 1930. Smoot-Hawley increased US Tariff rates on imported goods to an average of 53 percent.[10] Trading partners retaliated against the US with their own high tariffs on US exports. The resulting "trade war" coincided with, and contributed to, the Great Depression. US Real GDP growth was negative for four consecutive years (1930 to 1933).[11] *These combined economic circumstances were responsible for a dramatic decline in overall US international trade*. US agricultural exports in the 1930s were particularly hard hit – *a 20 percent reduction* as compared to the average trade level in the 1920s.[12] The extraordinary Smoot-Hawley import tariffs were the "high watermark" of US trade protectionism.[13] It is difficult to imagine worse economic conditions for US Agriculture than what transpired during the 1930s.

With the passage of the Reciprocal Trade Agreements Act (RTAA) of 1934, the US began a *departure away from trade protectionism*. By the late 1940s, the US had utilized the RTAA to repair trade relationships, and US import tariff rates dropped to an average of 13 percent, compared to the 53 percent average import tariff levels of Smoot-Hawley.

For the remainder of the twentieth century, US *trade policy trended towards trade liberalization* (intentionally reducing and/or eliminating tariffs and other trade barriers).

The US role in World War II (WWII) (1940–1945) began an expansion of US Agricultural Exports.[14] In the post-WWII period, the US continued on the path towards trade liberalization as one of twenty-three nations that established the General Agreement on Tariffs and Trade (GATT) in October 1947. For 48 years, the GATT sponsored eight rounds of negotiations that substantially reduced tariffs among its members. The GATT was succeeded by the World Trade Organization (WTO) in 1995.

The WTO oversees ongoing implementation of the GATT accords, and has a larger span of authority than the GATT to help resolve trade disputes. Although member nations (including the US) exempted many agricultural products from the GATT disciplines, US participation in the GATT established a US trade philosophy that would gradually aim to *liberalize (move towards tariff-free)* trade for all goods and services, including an increasing number of farm and food products.

The change in the general US trade stance away from protectionism and towards trade liberalization is one major reason for the growing influence of global commerce on US agriculture. To learn more about additional factors that increase trading potentials, please see the inserted Check Box 2.1

☐ Put your check in the box, if you have read and mastered its content.

Check Box 2.1   Factors facilitating free trade

Advances in technology for *communication, information transfer,* and *transportation* in the twentieth century greatly reduced the transaction costs of international trade. As a result, the separation of space and time between foreign suppliers and their consumers is a much less burdensome trade barrier. These technological efficiencies that encourage international connections have spurred real growth in US trade for all products. Consequently, while agriculture is not alone in experiencing the trade impact of improved transportation and communication technologies, the effect on US agriculture are nonetheless substantial.

As new technologies reduce logistical costs, and as trade negotiations diminish tariffs and related barriers, *market-driven incentives can motivate new trade activity. The Law of Comparative Advantage [LCA]* is a powerful argument demonstrating the potential for growth in global markets. Simply put, the LCA tells us that international trade is an opportunity to stimulate mutually beneficial transactions. With respect to US Agriculture, there are a variety of food and fiber products where the US has a *comparative advantage* because the US can export the output to its trade partners at a lower opportunity cost. And, since *trade is a two-way street,* there are segments of agricultural markets where it is rational for the US to be a net importer.

If the proper economic conditions for the LCA can be met, then two trading nations determine the terms of trade with reciprocal net benefits. The trading partners achieve real efficiencies in utilizing scarce resources while simultaneously fulfilling potentials for real GDP growth. In pure economic terms, as the government engages in true trade liberalization, then there will be significant capacity to expand US Agricultural Trade.

Trade liberalization (*also known as a "free trade policy"*) an essential element if the LCA is to spur the growth of global markets for US agriculture. In addition to its membership in the WTO, the US has been actively seeking and establishing free trade agreements with selected trading partners. In 1994, the US began a new relationship with Canada and Mexico as part of the North American Free Trade Agreement (NAFTA).

By 2004, the US had expanded NAFTA with a another new agreement, known as DR-CAFTA (Dominican Republic-Central American Free Trade Agreement) with the countries of Guatemala, El Salvador, Honduras, Costa Rica, Nicaragua, and the Dominican Republic. A quick review of the website for the US Trade Representative in 2015 indicates that the US now has free trade agreements with 20 different countries.[15]

While the details of these various free trade agreements may differ in certain details, there is the *common thread of reducing trade tariffs and barriers*. At the time that this text was being written, the US (through its International Trade Representative) had reached a final free trade agreement via a proposal for the *Trans-Pacific Partnership (TPP)*. Ultimately, the US Congress must decide if the TPP will become a reality for trade in the US economy.

Independent of the efforts to develop the TPP in 2015, the US International Trade Representative was also engaged in creating a comparable proposal known as the Trans-Atlantic Trade and Investment Partnership (TTIP). From the "Atlantic to the Pacific," the US was participating in negotiations aiming to liberalize trade in 2015.

Recent developments in the politics of international trade

During the 2016 US presidential campaign, international trade policies and proposals became topics for intense debate. Strong media coverage of the TTP and TTIP placed substantial emphasis on how trade policies influence the economic viability of domestic industries, as well as the competitiveness of domestic labor markets. Trade agreements can also affect the decision of private domestic firms to contract out their production to foreign sources.

Political debates about trade policy put a spotlight on the fact that all international trade agreements, even when they help the overall economy, create "winners" and "losers" in domestic markets. A high-pressure political arena, such as a presidential race, is a prime opportunity for economically threatened domestic interests to campaign against trade proposals such as the TPP and TTIP. When the US electoral period concluded in November 2016, both major political parties were vowing to reject US involvement in the TPP and TTIP multinational trade negotiations.

A review of US history shows that reluctance to participate in free-trade agreements is *not* a new idea. As noted earlier in this chapter, the US instituted the 1930 Smoot-Hawley tariff law to establish very high trade barriers of imported goods. Such actions are pleasing to domestic interests who stand to gain from trade protection.

Unfortunately, US trading-partner nations have the option to retaliate in kind with tariffs and restrictions on US-made products. Export-dependent US industries can suffer considerably when they are caught in the middle of a "trade war" between nations who escalate trade barriers to protect their selected domestic producers from foreign competition.

In the future, if the US was to *reverse* its trade liberalization policies, and choose protectionism instead, then we will have plenty of new economic scenarios to investigate in this textbook. For example, we can study what sectors of the US ag-and-food system stand to benefit from trade protectionist policies, and which ones do better when the US is promoting trade liberalization.

One fact is relatively easy to establish. The overall trade policy of the US, whether it emphasizes liberalization or protectionism, will affect the economic performance of the US agricultural and food system. As we look ahead to the upcoming changes in globalization and US international trade, we will have a rich source of material to investigate with our tools of policy analysis.

The rising influence of consumer expectations on the organization of US agriculture

Globalization is more than just an expansion of international commerce. It is a key factor contributing to the *evolution of consumer expectations*. Global influences have combined with important post-industrial societal phenomena to prompt the emergence of new consumer behaviors in modern agricultural markets.[16]

Thanks to rising living standards, US middle-income consumers experienced fundamental changes in their economic opportunity set of available choices during the twentieth century. Advancing technology, developing socio-economic conditions, and upwardly mobile aspirations all helped to create a new reality for the typical US household. Recent reports highlight the agricultural implications of these distinct changes in consumer perceptions, expectations, and behaviors that evolved between 1901 and 2000.[17, 18, 19]

Senauer (2001) observed that US consumers in the first half of the twentieth century exhibited relatively homogeneous food consumption patterns. Simple economic models could predict food demand patterns using basic demographic factors such as region, age, and household size. By the end of the century in the information age, consumers had progressively increased their range of knowledgeable choices via digital access. Their demand behaviors increased in complexity, and traditional demand analysis was unable to provide adequate forecasts of food consumption patterns.[20]

Senauer (2001) postulates that Maslow's Hierarchy of Needs is an appropriate construct for understanding the evolution of consumer attitudes towards food. Maslow's theory suggests that humans will seek to satisfy new higher-level needs as economic progress produces a higher living standard for the typical consumer household.

In this sense, as prosperity improves the economic status of consumers, Maslow's pyramid predicts that food choices will be more closely associated with meeting the human need for esteem and self-actualization, rather than just satisfying the more basic drives associated with hunger and safety. Using this psychological approach, it is not surprising to discover that consumer households integrate their food choices with their personal goals for sustainability, optimal nutrition, and convenience.[21]

Saxowsky and Duncan (1998) characterize the adjustment in modern consumer behavior with this statement: "Consumers expect what they want, rather than accept what is available." In the information age, consumers have faith that *the satisfying food that they seek is accessible*; if the product does not seem to be locally available, then it can be obtained elsewhere. The role of globalization is definitely contributing to this consumer attitude.[22]

The conviction "that what I want is just a click away" reflects consumers' self-assurance that current technologies can deliver. Simply put, if a food item does not satisfy consumer requirements, then they can access alternatives with relative ease.

Consumers are confident that their suppliers will be responsive to new requests for service and convenience. And, if consumers are dissatisfied with the service that they are receiving, then they can exercise other options, including imports from abroad. As a result of these new consumer expectations, which are definitely related to the influence of globalization, the competitiveness of the agricultural business environment has moved beyond the perfectly competitive model of uniform commodity markets. In the twenty-first century, as contrasted with the simpler twentieth-century markets, agriculture must make adjustments to compete in a world where product differentiation must be taken into account.

What do these new consumer behaviors mean for farm producers and agribusinesses? Agriculture's gains in productivity may be remarkable, but they are not sufficient to meet the full set of consumer expectations in the modern age.

The farm-to-fork system must have the capacity to adjust to new patterns of consumer non-price preferences, such as the demand for food products that are compatible with environmental sustainability.

Ray and Shaffer (2014) observe that Walmart and McDonald's are being pressured by customer concerns and preferences to market foods that are convenient, healthy, and more environmentally friendly, while also meeting expectations for good taste and affordability. Many affluent consumers have demands that go much further than maximizing food quantity for the lowest price. They expect full transparency on how the food was produced and where it originated. Taken as a whole, these new consumer attitudes set a standard that can be tougher for agribusinesses to meet than compliance with any new federal government regulations.[23]

The need to respond to these sophisticated consumer preferences is a real force for change in agriculture's approach to production and marketing. Agribusiness is increasingly characterized by new organizational adaptations. The establishment of coordinated food systems is one of the more important institutional changes that has occurred, and is continuing to evolve. A careful review of the increasing importance of contracting as a vertical coordination response to consumer food demands appears in Check Box 2.2.

☐ Put your check in the box, if you have read and mastered its content.

Check Box 2.2   Vertical coordination in the value chain

In the early- to mid-twentieth century, it was typical for farm producers to perceive the local grain elevator or auction barn as their customer. But as the expectations of the late twentieth and early twenty-first-century consumer evolve into a much wider range of concerns, there is a growing need to effectively respond to the transmission of these new demands up and down the entire "value chain" (consumer–retailer–wholesaler–producer). The multi-dimensional nature of modern consumer expectations requires an intentional and systematic effort to vertically coordinate or integrate the process.[1]

Vertical coordination via production and/or marketing contracts (as contrasted with the use of traditional spot markets) is one method of assuring customers that their product purchases have met the full range of their demands and expectations. Contractual arrangements provide a vehicle for participants to specify their desired food product characteristics. Contract language can offer the final consumer transparency, by stipulating the product's traceability, production methods (e.g. organic, free-range, etc.), content (GMO, or not), and other consumer-relevant characteristics.

(continued)

(continued)

MacDonald et al. (2004) observe that 36 percent of US agricultural production is currently guided by production and marketing contracts. In 1969, contracts guided just 12 percent of farm output. In livestock commodity markets, including milk, hogs, and broilers, contracting is the dominant production and marketing mechanism. Contracts are also the prevailing coordination device for major crops such as sugar beets, fruit, and processed tomatoes.[2]

The frequency of using agricultural contracts has increased for a variety of reasons, including the ability to certify that a final product meets consumer requirements. Contracts can also be used as a means of managing or transferring price risks or production risks. There are costs to contracts too. Contracts limit the freedom of farm producers to control their own operations, and legal requirements often mean that contracts are costly to write, monitor, and enforce.[3]

1   "In the Future, Farmers' Fiercest Taskmaster May Be Consumer Expectations." Daryll E. Ray and Harwood D. Schaffer. Knoxville, TN: Agricultural Policy Analysis Center, University of Tennessee, Policy Pennings. Oct. 17, 2014. www.agpolicy.org/weekcol/742.html#
2   "Contracts, Markets, and Prices: Organizing the Production and Use of Agricultural Commodities." James MacDonald, Janet Perry, Mary Ahearn, David Banker, William Chambers, Carolyn Dimitri, Nigel Key, Kenneth Nelson, and Leland Southard. Washington: AER-837 Economic Research Service/USDA. November 2004, pp. 1, 29.
3   Ibid, p. 29.

There are other ways to organize production and delivery, including the traditional spot markets and vertical integration. The issue at hand here is that consumer expectations for food products have changed dramatically since the past century, and these consumer preferences have required the agricultural economy to make large adjustments to satisfy the "multi-dimensional consumer" of the twenty-first century.

The response of the US food system to twentieth-century influences

Changing consumer expectations, expanding global markets, and productivity enhancing technologies are among the driving forces that have transformed American agriculture. These same factors have also influenced the "food side" of the US agri-food system.

Many of the economic effects associated with the driving forces in agriculture are similarly interpreted for their influence on the food processing and distribution network. New technologies have vastly improved productivity and efficiency in food markets; growth in international trade has diversified the range of imported and exported food products; and the final consumer's increased sophistication has required food marketers to adjust product offerings to properly serve new and important customer niches.

In addition to the forces of change that have influenced both food and agriculture, the role of science-based research has been a primary influence on US *food*-system performance.

Floros et al. attributes major accomplishments in the efficiency and safety of our food system to the combined contributions of new scientific knowledge, originating from diverse (but related) disciplines, including microbiology, biochemistry, physics, engineering, computer science, toxicology, materials science, and other key fields of study.

The food system components that have most benefitted from this twentieth-century science-based progress include food storage, manufacturing, transportation, distribution, retailing, and consumption.

Floros et al. notes that the speed of innovation in the development of food and beverage processing technologies during the twentieth century is unparalleled in human history. Between 1901 and 2000, food system research quickly produced new knowledge about how to dry, can, chemically preserve, and refrigerate foods for longer and safer shelf lives and more efficient transport. Advances in nutritional knowledge led to the discovery of how appropriate levels of vitamins and micronutrients could overcome deficiencies and dramatically improve human health.

From this perspective, *scientific breakthroughs* can be collectively viewed as the single most important influence on the success of the US food system in the twentieth century. The ability to produce safe, nutritious, and satisfying foods in our US economy today is largely the result of integrating the new knowledge obtained from both basic and applied research to continually improve the performance of our food system.

Ongoing research and development (R&D) in the food-related scientific disciplines (e.g. genomics, biotechnology, etc.) will most likely continue to play a prominent role in advancing food system performance in the twenty-first century.

Summary

The twentieth-century economic performance of the US food and agriculture sectors was strongly influenced by productivity enhancing technologies, market globalization, changing consumer behaviors, and science-based research. These driving forces are ongoing trends. They continue to be powerful sources of change in the twenty-first century. They constitute key aspects of the market environment that must be taken into account when current policies are being reviewed and when new policies are being contemplated.

In the next section of this chapter, we examine how recently modified US policies are likely to interact with the driving economic forces to achieve targeted outcomes in some cases and create undesirable results in other circumstances. One of the ongoing goals of policy analysis and design is to figure out policies that can efficiently produce desired outcomes while avoiding unwelcome consequences.

Twenty-first-century policy choices and consequences for US farm and food systems

There are a variety of recent policy initiatives expected to have noticeable impacts on US food and agriculture in the twenty-first century. While it is not feasible to examine all possible influences, we can select and study those policies that are most likely to create important effects. As mentioned in Chapter 1 of this textbook, three key initiatives are the FSMA, the 2014 Farm Bill, and the TPP Proposal.

To better understand the nature and direction of expected future trends in the US agrifood system, we can explore how these three policies and their associated incentives might influence future economic performance in the US agricultural and food sectors. We can also examine how these policies are expected to interact with the driving forces in the agri-food system: advancing science and technology, increasing global markets, and evolving consumer expectations.

Expected economic effects of the FSMA

The FDA Food Safety Modernization Act (FSMA) became law on January 4, 2011. The main purpose of FSMA is to change the US Food and Drug Administration's (FDA's) paradigm for controlling foodborne contaminations from reaction to prevention. Accomplishing this laudable goal creates both challenges and opportunities, not just for the FDA but for all participants in the food value chain.

The FSMA is a wide-ranging and ambitious policy change that has the potential to make real and measurable improvements in the safety of our food system. It also could run into difficulty, if the FSMA becomes a very costly policy to implement. We should evaluate the economics of the FSMA as one way of assessing whether or not it has the capacity to be a successful policy that achieves its aims.

An economic perspective on the FSMA can be organized as follows:

* Articulate what the FSMA is, how it will be implemented, and who will be affected by it.
* Estimate the FSMA's costs and benefits.
* Analyze the FSMA's cost-incidence impacts on market participants.
* Predict the FSMA's performance outcomes – both desirable and undesirable.

FSMA: goals, implementation, and anticipated effects

The intent of the FSMA is to reform the US food system by actively preventing the entry of foodborne contaminants, rather than simply reacting to the hazards. When examined in detail, it is clear that the FSMA is focused on the FDA as the primary agency that will carry out this new safety agenda. The FSMA expands the FDA's span of authority and increases its range of responsibility. The FDA can now conduct mandatory recalls and shut down food facilities by cancelling their registrations to operate.

As the FDA strives to meet the FSMA's legislative mandates, the regulatory footprint of this federal agency noticeably increases. The FSMA specifically sets deadlines for the FDA to issue rules that implement the law's intent. As the FDA follows through, the FMSA will create real impacts in the food industry. The FMSA will obligate human-food providers (processors, manufacturers, some farmers, transporters, and retailers) and also animal feed suppliers to:[24]

* Determine potential threats that can cause contamination at their respective facilities.
* Design and implement written preventive plans, monitor safety at the critical control points, record monitoring practices and results for a minimum of two years, and assess the success of the preventive plan every three years.
* Keep written procurement records of suppliers and their delivered ingredients, as well as sales records of products to customers (e.g. industrial, wholesale, retail).

- Introduce initiatives that can decrease the likelihood of intentional contamination of high-risk foods.
- Ensure that equivalent preventive safety standards are applied to foreign ingredient suppliers as they export food and feed products to the US.
- Permit the FDA to inspect records in any instance where a valid food safety issue arises, let the FDA inspect relevant facilities every five years, and allow inspections of high-risk facilities every three years.

The above FSMA-initiated activities are definitely consistent with a focus on prevention. But these programs and actions will require both the FDA and the participating food- and agri-businesses to dedicate scarce resources to perform these new tasks. In short, implementing the FSMA will be costly.

FSMA: costs and benefits

Developing reasonable estimates of FSMA's costs and benefits requires careful attention to basic economic principles. We can focus on an incremental approach, and analyze how implementation of FSMA will change the allocation of scarce resources in comparison to a baseline scenario where FSMA is absent.

We can organize a cost-benefit examination of the FSMA as follows:

- **Cost of FSMA:**
  - *Private sector cost of FSMA compliance:*
    - Extra cost of new testing and monitoring procedures.
    - Additional cost of new governmental reporting requirements.
    - New user fees to food suppliers for preventive government inspections.
  - *Public sector cost of FSMA implementation:*
    - Extra FDA staffing requirements for FSMA rulemaking and enforcement.
    - Extra FDA cost of changing priorities from a reaction-based approach to a preventive-control food safety system – need additional research, standard setting, inspections, and technical assistance.
- **Benefit of FSMA:**
  - *Private sector saving – attributable to preventive controls that:*
    - Reduce the frequency and severity of costly foodborne illnesses.
    - Decrease the frequency and size of expensive product recalls.
    - Result in fewer litigation costs associated with contamination occurrences.
  - *Public sector saving – attributable to preventive controls that:*
    - Increased efficiency of maintaining a safe food system
    - Improved coordination of federal agencies to eliminate both contradictory policies and duplication of effort.
    - Decreased frequency and size of government agency costs associated with "reactive" emergency government responses to contamination incidents (such as less frequent need for product recalls).

Based on the above outline, it is apparent that a full assessment of the overall FSMA benefit/ cost impact requires a serious research effort. Later in this textbook, we will examine this estimation challenge in more detail. Some already completed studies can offer a glimpse of the effort needed to evaluate the FSMA's effect on our economy.

The Congressional Budget Office (CBO) produced a cost estimate of the FSMA in 2010. The CBO's primary role is to serve the US Congress with its substantial analytical resources. The CBO provides objective estimates of legislative budgetary impacts. As a result, the CBO report is heavily weighted towards estimating the public sector cost of the FSMA.[25]

For example, taking into account all anticipated activities necessary to carry out the FSMA over a five-year period, the CBO estimated that the law would increase cumulative federal budgetary spending by $1.4 billion between fiscal years 2011 and 2015. Without offering any numerical estimate, the CBO refers to the benefit of FSMA as the improved federal government capacity to "ensure the safety of commercially distributed food."

Ribera and Knutson engaged in a broader examination of the FSMA's economic implications.[26] They analyze its distributional effects, and also investigate the FSMA's likely effects on the efficiency and competitive market structure of the entire US agri-food system. Ribera and Knutson rely on the CBO study for numerical FSMA cost estimates, and their study did not extend to calculating a dollar estimate of the FSMA's economic benefit.

FSMA's cost incidence effects

Current economic studies of the FSMA do not directly measure its monetary benefit. But the CBO and related reports clearly indicate that there will be extra costs of implementing this food safety law. In the private sector, food suppliers and related agribusinesses are allocating additional resources to comply with FSMA's new testing protocols, additional monitoring, inspection fees, and related expenses for engaging in the new paradigm of hazard prevention.

There are also cost consequences for food-related firms who are not directly subject to the new FSMA regulations. Why? The answer lies in the economic connections that naturally exist in the food-industry value chain. If the FSMA is impacting the business customers of a supply-chain firm, then those customers may require their suppliers to meet the same standards.[27]

The ripple effect of absorbing the costs of FSMA regulatory requirements throughout the supply chain also introduces the question of cost incidence. Who will pay the extra cost? Will the cost be entirely passed on to the consumer, or will the additional expense be shared by both supplier and customer? Traditional supply-and-demand analysis provides some insight for addressing this question.

We evaluate the added cost of meeting new FSMA regulations as a supply-side effect. In a graphical analysis (see Figure 2.1 below), the impact of increased production cost creates a "decrease in supply," and therefore shifts the supply curve of the regulated food product up and to the left. The market adjusts to a more restricted supply by increasing the food price (and reducing the transacted quantity) to re-establish a market equilibrium.

In Figure 2.1, we can observe the cost incidence of compliance with the new FSMA regulation. When the market equilibrium price is established at (New P_{eq}), the market price has not increased by the full cost of regulatory compliance. Part of the cost (Distance BC) is shouldered by food suppliers, while the remainder of the extra expense (Distance AB) is passed on to the consumer.

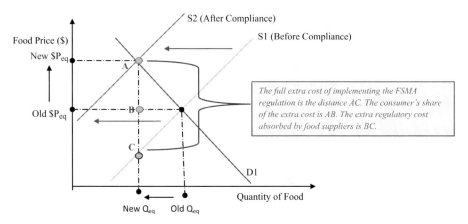

Figure 2.1 Impact of food industry compliance with a higher-cost FSMA regulation.

The relative elasticities of supply and demand determine the cost incidence results. *Ceteris paribus*, as the *demand* for a food product becomes more *price inelastic*, then the consumer pays an *increased* proportion of the extra regulatory cost. Conversely, if demand is more price elastic, then the consumer's cost share is less.

In comparison, as the *supply* function becomes more *price inelastic*, then the consumer pays a *decreased* percent of the extra regulatory cost. Equally, if supply is price elastic, then food consumers bear a larger proportion of the regulatory cost burden.

Food is a consumer necessity, and other things being equal, we expect necessities to exhibit price-inelastic demand. On the supply side, we also expect a price-inelastic function because both food and agricultural production is characterized by a high proportion of fixed inputs. A price-inelastic response is also predicted because agriculture's supply function is biologically influenced and weather-dependent.

The combination of price-inelastic supply and demand in a typical food market means that we expect the average food consumer to pay for a portion of the extra cost of FSMA regulation in the form of a higher food price. We also anticipate that a price-inelastic supply response will cause food industry firms to share the burden of the additional regulatory cost.

Some food businesses will exit because FSMA compliance causes a higher production cost and a reduced market equilibrium quantity. Firms leave the market because they can no longer consistently earn a normal profit in a more highly regulated environment.

FSMA's performance outcomes

The FSMA is ultimately aimed at establishing a safer US food system. Measures of success such as reduced rates of contamination and less frequent food-product recalls are likely candidates for assessing the benefits of FSMA. Hopefully the FSMA is properly designed to produce such desirable outcomes.

The cost of implementing FSMA is another outcome that should be monitored. If real and perceived regulatory costs become excessive, then a re-assessment of how best to achieve the goal of a safe food supply may be necessary. Basic supply-and-demand analysis reveals that FSMA compliance will increase food prices for consumers and also increase the average cost of production for food industry firms.

Ribera and Knutson's economic analysis of FSMA offers valid arguments and evidence that FSMA is likely to cause unintended and undesired consequences, in addition to contributing to a more secure food system.[28] Ribera and Knutson raise concerns that the cost of FSMA compliance (such as implementing complete HACCP plans) will require high fixed-cost investments by food industry firms. In this scenario, smaller firms suffer increases in the average total cost (ATC) of production that are avoided by larger firms with scale economies. We can expect a disproportionately higher rate of market exit by smaller firms (with increased ATC) who cannot regularly earn a normal profit. An unintended FSMA "performance outcome" is to create more highly concentrated and less competitive markets in the agri-food system.

Summary

The US Congress created the FSMA to establish a preventive approach to food safety in the US agri-food system in the twenty-first century. We have introduced an economic perspective to examine the FSMA. Our overview of the FSMA in this chapter provides a framework to evaluate how well the FSMA will perform in comparison to what the US Congress intends.

Our initial review reveals that this law generates both costs and benefits. To gain a balanced view of what the FSMA can accomplish, it is important to evaluate overall gains and losses associated with the details of its actual policies. For example, we can investigate the cost-incidence effects of FSMA compliance. Then we can interpret what those effects mean in terms of the FSMA's capacity to improve the effectiveness of our agri-food system.

There are many interesting and researchable questions about the FSMA that remain. We know that the future of the US agri-food system is being shaped by the forces of advancing technology, increased global influences, and a growing sophistication in consumer preferences. How will the FSMA interact with these driving factors? After learning additional analytical tools in Chapter 3, we can explore these important questions in more detail later on in this textbook.

Effective policy analysis relies on the ability to generate unbiased and reasonable assessments of policy choices. When we examine the FSMA and its performance outcomes in Chapter 5, we will continue to employ the powerful organizing principles of economics to help us systematically analyze the most critical aspects of this complex legislative initiative.

Expected economic effects of the 2014 Farm Bill

The Agricultural Act of 2014 became part of US federal law in early February 2014. Better known as the 2014 Farm Bill, it is a large, multifaceted piece of legislation that is expected to influence US farm and food policy through the year 2018, and likely beyond.

The 2014 Farm Bill is important to food, agriculture, and the rest of the US economy for many reasons, not the least of which is its budgetary size. The Congressional Budget Office (CBO) estimates that the 2014 Farm Bill will result in $956 billion in federal government spending over ten fiscal years (FY2014–FY2023). In round numbers, this amounts to nearly $100 billion per year of the federally budgeted expenditure of taxpayer dollars.

Our interest here is to carefully consider how the US agri-food system's twenty-first-century economic performance is linked to the numerous programs, subsidies, and related incentives that collectively define the 2014 Farm Bill.

An organized strategy can help us make sense of the 2014 Farm Bill's intricacies. Following the pattern of our earlier FSMA review, we address the economics of the 2014 Farm Bill as follows:

- Articulate the goals of the 2014 Farm Bill, how it will be implemented, and who will be affected by it.
- Identify costs and benefits associated with 2014 Farm Bill.
- Anticipate the 2014 Farm Bill's efficiency and distributional impacts.
- Predict the 2014 Farm Bill's performance outcomes – desired and undesired.

2014 Farm Bill: goals, implementation, and anticipated effects

As noted in Chapter 1, the US Congress stated the purpose of the 2014 Farm Bill as "the *reform and continuation* of agricultural and other programs of the Department of Agriculture".

This brief statement of the lawmakers' intentions indicate that the future of US farm and food policy will be a combination of past trends and new approaches. A review of the 2014 Farm Bill's twelve different titles confirms that the new law does continue some programs relatively unchanged from previous farm bills, while other areas are altered or restructured.

The 2014 Farm Bill also clearly identifies the US Department of Agriculture (USDA) as the primary federal agency that will implement the law. This is similar to the role of the FDA in relation to the FSMA.

After the 2014 Farm Bill passed, the USDA quickly engaged in the task of rulemaking to execute the law. For example, following the law's directives in Title I: Commodities, the USDA *dismantled* the Direct Payment Program (DPP), the Counter-Cyclical Payment (CCP) program, and the Average Crop Revenue Election (ACRE) program. While these previous commodity programs were being eliminated, the USDA also developed the mechanisms necessary to create the Price Loss Coverage (PLC) and the Agriculture Risk Coverage (ARC) programs that are authorized in the 2014 Farm Bill.

The Agricultural Act of 2014 also instructs the USDA to consolidate conservation programs, increase the size and scope of multiple peril crop insurance, create a Foundation for Food and Agricultural Research, renew a partially revised Supplemental Nutrition Assistance Program (SNAP), and engage in many other required actions specified in the multi-page document that encompasses the entire law.

In one way or another, the USDA's implementation of the 2014 Farm Bill will affect the lives of most Americans. Food consumers, taxpayers, agribusinesses, school lunch program managers, scientific researchers, conservationists, environmentalists, farmers, export/import firms, and many other interest groups have a stake in how the benefits and cost of this wide-ranging law will affect them.

2014 Farm Bill: costs and benefits

A fundamental economic principle is that we live in a world of scarce resources. As the saying goes, "there is no such thing as a free lunch." Anyone involved in the farm and food economy knows the truth of this statement. The food on our tables does not magically appear.

Hard-working farmers and food providers dedicate their valuable time and resources to make it all possible.

Our resources have opportunity costs. Time or money allocated to one purpose means those resources are not available for other beneficial pursuits.

When we learn that the 2014 Farm Bill will account for $956 billion of federal spending over the next ten years, we can also emphasize that these funds originate primarily from tax-payers' wallets and purses. It is perfectly rational for the average US citizen to ask how the 2014 Farm Bill resources are being used. If those dollars were not supporting agricultural and food programs, then they would be freed up to create value elsewhere.

What are citizens gaining in relation to the cost? One answer to this question is that the farm bill primarily helps to create a national economy where the food supply is reliable and households are food secure. The farm bill establishes and maintains large-scale safety-net systems to accomplish this end result.

While the goals of stability and security are commendable, the economic perspective encourages us to ask whether we should be pursuing other objectives. Another concern is whether funds are being wisely spent. Also, are there better and more efficient ways to achieve our objectives?

There are some aspects of the current farm bill, such as renewed support for research and development, which are truly worthwhile and can yield measurable benefits. But careful analyses of the 2014 Farm Bill reveal that it has many inefficiencies and imperfections. It is useful and appropriate to examine the pitfalls associated with the farm bill, and begin to figure out how future policies might be improved.

2014 Farm Bill: efficiency and distributional effects

After the 2014 Farm Bill became law, Goodwin and Smith (2014) coordinated with other scholars to produce a series of professional articles that explored the law's anticipated efficiency and distributional consequences. Collectively, this research team raises a variety of sobering questions and serious concerns about the economic effect of the farm bill.[29]

Using traditional supply-and-demand analysis, Goodwin and Smith demonstrate that the taxation systems supporting the farm program, as well as the subsidies for crop insurance and the commodity programs, create deadweight market losses by artificially altering equilibrium market prices. The market inefficiencies of farm bill programs create extra costs for the economy. Additional aspects of the farm bill also require a critical review.

In this textbook, we have noted that technological advance, globalizing trade, rising consumer sophistication, and ongoing scientific discovery are twentieth-century driving forces that continue to shape our twenty-first-century agri-food system. How does the farm bill interact with these dynamics? Unfortunately, it appears that very little of the farm bill is a purposeful effort to connect with the ongoing forces of change. Goodwin, Smith and their companion researchers provide evidence that the farm bill is *not* well-equipped to help produce a more economically efficient and equitable agricultural economy.[30]

Ideally, the design and implementation of any policy should be a process where choices are intentionally made to harmonize with overall goals and objectives. In a few instances, such as resource conservation and support for scientific research, the 2014 Farm Bill is deliberately structured to synchronize with stated goals.

However, much of this omnibus law produces discordant impacts. For example, Glauber and Westhoff (2015), Smith (2014), and Carter (2014) use both empirical observations and objective simulation models to demonstrate scenarios where farm subsidies included in the 2014 Farm Bill's Commodities (I) and Crop Insurance (XI) Titles will cause the US to exceed its WTO trade limits on total allowed subsidy levels.[31] It is disconcerting for the US to engage in trade negotiations as a proponent of liberalization, when the US is simultaneously approving expensive and protectionist agricultural policies.

Goodwin and Smith (2014) also describe how the design of the Commodities and Crop Insurance programs in the 2014 Farm Bill will offer substantial subsidy assistance for the farms and households who least require it. These support programs have also served to accelerate the technologically driven trend towards larger and fewer farms.

Nearly eighty years ago, in the midst of the US Great Depression, the first farm bill was legislated to pursue the goal of "saving the family farm". In that era, the financial threat to agriculture was real, and the reason for creating a farm safety net was self-evident. Eight decades later, we can truthfully say that "times have changed".

Using USDA financial data, Goodwin and Smith indicate that in 2012, median farm household income was $68,298, 34 percent higher than the median total income of $51,017 received by all US households. Not only that, USDA data lets us establish that approximately 98 percent of US farms have "high wealth". This affluent status for farms is defined as household wealth greater than the US economy's median wealth level.

More research is needed to gather all the distributional details, but current financial data indicates that not much of the farm economy actually needs saving. Farm operations have largely saved themselves. Producers in today's market have survived competitive market pressures and adopted many productive improvements in the eighty-some years since the Great Depression.

In today's media, commentators often say that facts are "stubborn". The facts about the connection between farm wealth and farm subsidies are stubbornly breaking down the argument that government programs are still needed to save the family farm. Given the state of affairs today, it is not surprising that many observers of agricultural policy question why we have a government farm safety net that subsidizes some of our nation's wealthiest citizens.

2014 Farm Bill's performance outcomes

Our economic examination of the 2014 Farm Bill's expected performance identifies genuine shortcomings. Is this an unexpected result? The deficiencies are not so surprising, if we take into account the realities associated with the passage of a complex, multi-year, and multi-billion-dollar legislative act.

The actual process of enacting the 2014 Farm Bill is clearly characterized by the political lobbying efforts of powerful and very divergent economic interests. Various groups (businesses, non-profit institutes, trade associations, volunteer organizations, etc.) vie with one another to ensure that the legislative content is consistent with, and supportive of, their own personal preferences and financial interests.

Let's take a brief look at the challenge of creating a farm bill that can actually be acceptable to a majority of both houses of Congress. Congressional representatives must seek compromises when powerful stakeholders are on opposite sides of the issues. In addition, coalitions of very diverse organizations often unite to jointly produce enough votes for a proposal to pass with a majority. An original legislative bill that had a clear focus on economic efficiency (or some other desired goal) may end up as a very different program because of the compromises inherent in crafting a plan acceptable to the various members of the coalition.

It is also common for phenomena such as logrolling (issue trading) and agenda manipulation (strategic voting patterns) to develop as legislators balance the powers of the various interests and arrive at a legislative proposal that gathers sufficient votes to be viable.

Pragmatism, and not idealism, is the ruling philosophy as a complicated and expensive piece of legislation makes its way through the many committees and voting rules. Even if members of Congress understand and value the ideas of economic efficiency and distributional equity, the actual lawmaking process often relegates these idealistic concerns to a lower priority as the pressures to find votes take precedence.

Finally, the US House and Senate generally work on their own versions of the farm bill, and differences between the two legislative bodies are ironed out in joint conference committees where additional "horse trading" of proposals and legal language can take place.

Summary

The 2014 Farm Bill, and other similar legislative initiatives, can be found wanting in terms of their economic performance. But when we consider the political economy of how a bill becomes law, these outcomes are not entirely unexpected.

In Chapter 4 of this textbook, we take a more in-depth look at the structure and performance of the farm subsidy programs included in the 2014 Farm Bill. We can examine the decision-making process and associated outcomes in more detail, and also suggest policy changes that can increase the benefits and limit the costs of this important legislative initiative.

Expected economic effects of the TPP

The US Congress passed H.R.1314 (The Trade Act) in June 2015, and momentarily delegated its constitutional power to negotiate trade agreements to the executive branch of the federal government. This legislative act is known as "Trade Promotion Authority" or TPA. TPA authority does not last for long; under H.R. 1314, TPA will expire by July 1, 2018, or it could be extended to July 1, 2021 with Congressional approval.

The US Trade Representative (USTR) exercised H.R. 1314's TPA "Fast Track" authority, and after months of intense negotiations, the US agreed with its trade partners to a negotiated proposal known as the Trans-Pacific Partnership (TPP) on October 5, 2015. The proposal requires final Congressional approval. H.R. 1314 instructs the US Congress to schedule an "up-or-down" vote (with no opportunities for additional amendments) on whether to approve or reject the TPP Proposal as a trade agreement to guide US export and import policies.

The recent 2016 US presidential election season may have convinced some observers that the sitting US president decides whether the US enters or rejects a trade agreement. This perception is not correct. The language in the US Constitution determines that the power to establish US international trade policy ultimately lies with the US Congress.

Using the TPA legal timetable, a final US Congressional decision on TPP participation could have occurred as early as February 2016. When this textbook went to press, the US Congress had not yet acted on the TPP. If the Congress chooses not to act, or simply rejects the agreement, the TPP proposal will no longer directly influence US trade patterns. The remaining eleven TPP nations can choose to go ahead with their own parts of the TPP agreement.

Although US participation in the TPP now appears doubtful, we can make an educated guess on the economic effects if the Congress had approved US participation. If the US was to become a TPP member, then the agreement would reduce trade barriers between the US and eleven other nations that share the "Pacific Rim": Australia, Brunei Darussalam, Canada, Chile, Japan, Malaysia, Mexico, New Zealand, Peru, Singapore, and Vietnam.[32]

The TPP is a wide-ranging agreement. It is best understood in an organized format. Following the pattern of our earlier FSMA and 2014 Farm Bill policy reviews, we address the economics of the TPP as follows:

- Articulate the TPP's goals, how the agreement could be implemented, and who would be affected by it.
- Identify costs, benefits, and distributional impacts associated with the TPP.
- Predict the TPP's performance outcome – desired and undesired.

Trans-Pacific Partnership (TPP): goals, implementation, and anticipated effects

The twelve-nation TPP proposal in 2015 was the result of an evolutionary process. In 2003, Chile, New Zealand, and Singapore began negotiations that produced the TPP's forerunner, known as the Trans-Pacific Strategic Economic Partnership Agreement. Brunei Darussalam joined this trio in 2005, and a four-nation trade pact was established by 2006. The accord included a pledge to invite other countries, with a goal of ultimately expanding the global reach of the agreement.[33]

President George W. Bush informed the US Congress in 2008 of the US intention to join trade discussions with the original four TPP nations. The US entry was also accompanied by three additional partners: Australia, Peru, and Vietnam. President Obama continued US involvement in 2009. The eight-member group agreed to invite Malaysia in 2010. Mexico and Canada joined the trade cluster in 2012, and Japan officially agreed to become a negotiating partner in 2013.

Most of the TPP participants visualize this trade pact as a "comprehensive and high-standard" Free Trade Agreement. When negotiations began in earnest, the ideal goal was to liberalize trade in nearly all goods and services. The agreement would aim to establish rules-based commitments that matched or exceeded the trade-treaty standards adopted by the World Trade Organization (WTO).[34]

From the US vantage point, the TPP would reinforce and expand the US capacity for increased trade and investment among a group of nations whose collective GDPs represent close to 40 percent of the world's economy. In addition, the TPP might have generated some far-reaching and strategic impacts.

As indicated earlier, it appears that the US will not enter into the TPP Agreement. There will be US industries who benefit from this refusal. However, as in all choices, opportunity costs occur.

The terms of the TPP settlement might have been a blueprint for future US trade policy. For example, the guidelines developed in the TPP could have profited the US, as it begins to pursue other trade agreements. At this juncture, it is unclear whether the US gained economically from its participation in the TPP negotiations. There may have been benefits of the US learning "negotiation tactics" associated with the long process of developing the TPP proposal. Those types of gains, though real, are not easily measured.

One final consideration is the US strategy relative to the growing economic power of the People's Republic of China. The US might have used the TPP to leverage its position within the TPP to compete with China. The TPP represented an opportunity for the US to directly determine how trade rules are applied in the Asian-Pacific area of the globe.

Trans-Pacific Partnership (TPP): costs, benefits, and distributional effects

The TPP's economic impacts on the US economy are dependent on many factors. The primary consideration for the US is whether or not the Congress approves or rejects the trade proposal. Two alternative realities are possible, but only one can emerge. Either the US joins the TPP, or it does not.

Both scenarios deserve analysis. Admittedly, it now appears that the US will refuse to participate in the TPP. US President Trump has vowed to keep the US out of the TPP in 2017. His stated goal is to pursue bilateral trade agreements instead. All US Presidents have the "bully pulpit" to influence national policy.

While the president's voice is an important political power, we again observe that US participation in TPP is a Congressional decision. In 2016, most of the powerful members of Congress indicated that they will work to prevent US participation in the TPP.[35] [36] On the other hand, the US Trade Representative has urged approval of the TPP.

Let's consider the scenario where the US rejects the TPP. In some respects, US withdrawal from the TPP will not dramatically influence the US trading relationship with countries such as Australia, Canada, Chile, Mexico, Peru, and Singapore – the US has already signed bilateral free trade agreements (FTAs) with each of these six nations.

But the US will forego any trade negotiation progress it achieved with the other five TPP nations where the US lacks such an agreement. The economic opportunity cost of not gaining a greater access to the markets in Japan, New Zealand, Brunei, Vietnam, and Malaysia will be considerable, assuming the US rejects the TPP.

The TPP proposal not only produced settlements for greater US market access at lower (or zero) tariff rates with the eleven other participants, it also was a negotiation about the rules that govern trade relations. All of the efforts to negotiate trading rules that would be acceptable to both the US and its trading partners will be abandoned in the scenario where the US cancels its participation in the agreement.

It may be difficult to estimate a monetary figure that properly measures this lost opportunity, but the forgone economic value might be sizable. Similarly, any Asian-Pacific strategic advantage for US leadership associated with TPP participation will be set aside.

Of course, US rejection of the TPP will be viewed as a huge benefit by sectors of the US economy where TPP adoption would be connected with declines in jobs, wage rates, and/or profit levels. It is undeniable that policy transitions from protectionism to liberalized trade reduce or terminate the economic viability of a domestic economy's less globally competitive sectors.

If the TPP was approved, a policy switch from high barriers to tariff-free and quota-free markets will increase the strength and vitality of those US economic sectors that are poised to increase their exports, because of their comparative advantage in producing/marketing a product or service.

The transition from protectionist policy to free trade always generates winners and losers in a domestic economy. If the law of comparative advantage is truly at work, then free-trade policies will create a net overall economic gain in a nation's real GDP.

Many governments who seek to adopt a trade liberalization policy must be prepared to re-allocate some of the net GDP gains from free trade to compensate or re-train those individuals and/or organizations that are negatively affected by free-trade initiatives.

For the purpose of comparison, we make projections for the results if the US agreed to join the TPP. In 2015, the CBO prepared a report for the US Congress to highlight specific negotiated items and offer background information on trade issues that are likely to be controversial in the US.[37] The CBO cited a 2011 economic analysis performed by Petri, Plummer, and Zhai on the expected GDP and distributional effects of TPP implementation.[38]

This quantitative modeling effort predicted a small net percent gain in US Real GDP, if the US became a TPP member. The US service sector would gain considerably, while the joint impact on agriculture and mining would be net-neutral, and US manufacturing would be expected to incur a welfare loss.

The results of Petri, Plummer, and Zhai's economic analysis illustrate why Congressional approval of a trade agreement is politically divisive and difficult to approve. The domestic sectors and industries who stand to lose economic ground lobby the voting process to prevent the agreement from taking hold. Or, economically threatened groups can pressure politicians to radically modify these trade deals to soften the economic pain associated with the transition to a free-trade economy.

In this textbook, we have a special interest in the expected impact of US participation in TPP on the agricultural and food economies. Petri, Plummer, and Zhai reported a joint net-neutral economic outcome caused by TPP participation, when the US agriculture and mining sectors are considered as a single unit.

It is possible to separate out the predicted TPP effects of the two different industries. Burfisher et al. (2014) performed a more narrowly focused economic simulation of US participation in the TPP to identify expected impacts on US agriculture. The results of the Burfisher et al. (2014) in-depth USDA modeling of TPP interactions with the US agricultural economy is displayed in Check Box 2.3.

☐ Put your check in the box, if you have read and mastered its content.

Check Box 2.3   Economic modeling of the TPP's influence on US agriculture

Burfisher et al. forecasted a scenario where agricultural and nonagricultural tariffs and tariff-rate quotas (TRQs) are abolished, along with the assumption of the US as a TPP member, through the year 2025. These USDA researchers compared the expected results with a baseline model where the US has rejected the TPP.

With US TPP participation, the model estimates a net gain in real GDP of 6 percent, or about $8.5 billion for US intraregional agricultural trade by the year in 2025 under a tariff-free and quota-free scenario. The model predicts US agricultural exports to expand by about five percent, or an increase of $3 billion. US agricultural imports from TPP members would rise by two percent in 2025, or a $1 billion increase compared to baseline values.

(continued)

(continued)

Burfisher et al.'s model predictions for US agricultural economic performance mean that US agricultural interests, as a whole, have financial reasons to support US TPP participation. Following the October 2015 announcement that a TPP settlement proposal had been negotiated, many agricultural organizations indicated that they were pleased that a TPP pact had been drafted, and that they were anxious to review the specifics in the deal.[1]

1 Mary E. Burfisher, John Dyck, Birgit Meade, Lorraine Mitchell, John Wainio, Steven Zahniser, Shawn Arita, and Jayson Beckman. Agriculture in the Trans-Pacific Partnership. USDA, ERS, Report 176, October 2014. www.ers.usda.gov/media/1692509/err176.pdf

The results of the Burfisher, et al. modeling forecast demonstrate noticeable gains for the US agricultural economy associated with US participation in the TPP (if the US joins TPP). However, even within the agriculture sector, not all specific US products and markets end up reaping net economic benefits from free trade. Similar to any other industry, there will be opposition to this agreement from those agricultural interests likely to lose ground if the TPP removes their trade protections.

News reports about the October 2015 TPP accord indicate that the US sugar and dairy industries were largely (but not entirely) exempt from the "disciplines" of the agreement.[39] In plain terms, the ongoing exemptions mean that the sugar and dairy sectors of US agriculture will be able to retain many protectionist import tariffs, quotas, and trade rules, and shield themselves from the competitive pressures of free trade in the agreement.

Powerful lobbying efforts by US interest groups (American Sugar Alliance, National Milk Producers Federation, and US Dairy Export Council) representing the sugar and dairy markets were able to penetrate the TPP negotiating process. Their political clout was sufficiently strong to maintain preferential status in US trade, much to the chagrin of lower-cost TPP exporters such as Australia and New Zealand.[40][41]

The TPP's expected performance outcomes

The US agri-system economic performance will be affected by either the absence or the presence of the US as a TPP member. If the US chooses to reject TPP affiliation, the results will *not* be catastrophic for the US economy. The consequences will be the costs associated with lost trade opportunities. Also, in the short run, by refusing to join the TPP, the US will avoid the domestic economic and political upheaval that normally accompanies the implementation of a large free trade agreement.

As an alternative to the TPP, the US will likely decide to separately pursue bilateral free trade agreements with individual TPP member nations. However, if the TPP economic models are correct, many segments of US agriculture will expand more slowly without TPP membership. US agricultural interests will be seeking new export markets without the advantage of reduced trade barriers helping to open up opportunities in the TPP economies.

If the US chooses to accept TPP membership, then a different set of events is predicted to be set in motion. The United States Trade Representative Michael Froman states that the TPP agreement will remove 18,000 tariffs that other TPP countries have imposed on US exports. The US will eradicate 6,000 of its own import tariffs. The Peterson Institute for International Economics forecasts that TPP membership will expand all American exports by 4.4 percent, as compared to the scenario without US TPP membership. If the US accepts TPP, the forecast is also an increase in both US imports and real GDP by 3.7 percent and 0.2 percent, respectively.[42]

Another valid economic question is whether a regional trade agreement creates costs for an economy because of "trade diversion". Trade diversion occurs when a regional free trade agreement (FTA) creates incentives for FTA member nations to redirect their imports away from global low-cost suppliers who are not members of the pact. When it occurs, trade diversion stimulates the purchase of goods and services from higher-cost FTA members.

The USDA analysis of US TPP participation includes an economic simulation that determines whether the trade agreement encourages trade diversion, as compared to "trade creation" – where the conditions spur extra real welfare gains that generate additional value for the global economy. The USDA economic model predicts that additional trade stimulated by the TPP will spur more trade creation than it does trade diversion.

USDA analysts make one more prediction that can happen if the TPP is fully supported by all twelve members. If the absence of trade barriers in a fully participative TPP has sufficient time to allow new rules and incentives to work properly, then the remnants of costly trade diversion tendencies associated with the pre-existing FTAs between TPP members will dissipate. Without the drag of trade diversion, then the full potential of the TPP to create additional real GDP will be realized in the long run.

Aside from trade diversion, imperfections in the TPP will serve to make the agreement less economically beneficial to the economy as a whole. In particular, when exemptions for US sugar and dairy products are built into the trade pact, then the capacity of free trade to deliver its full economic value in the TPP is weakened.

Undoubtedly, the ability of these particular industries to insulate themselves from the normal terms of the agreement will be seen as a trade victory for their lobbyists. These outcomes, where special interests are awarded exemptions, will almost certainly strengthen the capacity of these interests to permanently influence the terms of all future free-trade agreements that might be proposed or envisioned. A question for policy makers, and for all citizens, is whether the public good is served by the perpetual power of these groups to prevail.

Summary

The Trans-Pacific Partnership (TPP) was a proposed free trade agreement among twelve nations (including the US). In October 2015, negotiators for the each of the prospective TPP national participants concluded their work. They transferred the proposed trade pact to their respective governments. The government authorities in each country will review the contents of the settlement, and then decide to reject or approve the TPP agreement as a real guide for future trade.

Our interest here is the likely impact of the TPP decision on America's farm and food economies. There are economic consequences for either cancelation or confirmation of the proposed trade agreement.

Rejection of the TPP will offer economic relief to all US industries (including some agricultural and food industries) that would likely suffer losses if US protective tariffs and non-tariff barriers were to decrease or disappear under the terms of the agreement. US dismissal of the TPP also means that some highly competitive American industries (including those in US agriculture) will lose opportunities to further expand their export markets. New markets can become accessible to US exporters, if burdensome tariffs and related barriers of the other TPP member nations could be eliminated by the terms of the trade agreement.

It is an established fact that national transitions from protectionism to free trade will create turmoil in economic sectors that are unable to withstand the onslaught of tough global competition. When nations decide to walk away from free trade agreements, there are generally real and strong political reasons why that outcome is the final result.

We have also examined evidence of the anticipated economic effects if the US was to agree to TPP membership. On the whole, US agriculture would experience noticeable incentives to expand its market influence, and the economic models consistently predict a net gain in US agriculture's real GDP as a result of US participation in the TPP.

Some US agricultural sectors, such as sugar or dairy, would experience real downward economic trends under the normal terms of a free trade agreement. Powerful US lobbies for sugar and agriculture have thus far been awarded exemptions from most of the TPP's free trade disciplines. While these exempted industries have successfully protected themselves, the overall impact of these special arrangements on the entire economy is not calculated as a net gain, when the standard economic models for determining overall welfare are objectively applied.

When free trade regimes (such as the TPP) do replace long-standing protectionist policies, many economists recommend that governments seriously consider redirecting the net GDP gains of trade liberalization to help compensate and re-train domestic economic participants who are financially damaged by the transition in trade policy.

Macroeconomic influences on twenty-first-century US farm and food sector performance

If a national government makes a major trade policy decision, such as the approval or denial of TPP participation, then the economic considerations for making that choice will necessarily extend beyond the costs and benefits of any one sector. While agriculture and food are certainly important, the interests of other stakeholders will also be reflected in making that choice. Policy makers normally take into account the effect of a trade policy on the *entire economy* before taking a position and casting a vote.

We study macroeconomics to better understand the performance of the economy as a whole. The national and global implications of trade and related policies are matters for macroeconomic analysis. We enter into the realm of macroeconomic policy when we incorporate large-scale aggregate economic factors (such as inflation, unemployment, and real economic growth) in our decision making.

A straightforward question to ask is, "How do US macroeconomic policies influence the agricultural and food sectors?" The answer to this query requires an organized response, because the effects of macroeconomic policies are varied. The question may be simple to ask, but an honest answer requires careful thought, if the response is to be both accurate and transparent.

Fiscal and monetary policies and their impacts

When we investigate choices and consequences in macroeconomics, a good place to start is to examine changes in monetary and fiscal policy. *US monetary policy* affects aggregate demand through the actions of the US Federal Reserve Bank ("the Fed"). The Fed's "tools" for managing monetary policy are: (1) changing the money supply; (2) determining the base interest rate level; and (3) occasionally managing the US exchange rate with other nations' currencies. On the other hand, US *fiscal policy* alters national aggregate demand when intentional (and sometimes unintentional) changes in government spending and taxes occur.

Macroeconomic policies aim to solve national problems. Production agriculture accounts for about two percent of the US Real GDP. The phases of the national economy and the agricultural economy lack synchronicity. In the past fifty years, there are numerous instances where agriculture is prosperous while the rest of the economy is struggling, and vice versa.

There are consequences for this disconnect between agriculture's financial condition and the circumstances faced by the other 98 percent of the economy. Macroeconomic policies are targeted at solving "mainstream" problems. Negative side effects of national policies on agriculture can easily happen. For example, in the early 1980s the US Federal Reserve chose a strategy of vastly increased interest rates to extinguish a national crisis of price inflation. While the aims of this Fed policy were rational from an aggregate economic viewpoint, the interest rate policy financially devastated US agriculture. The frequency of farm foreclosures, rural bank failures, and overall farm business stress in the 1980s created agricultural hardships not seen since the 1930s Great Depression.

To drive home the main point, macroeconomic changes can have dramatic and sometimes destructive effects on the agriculture's economic viability. But aggregate national policies may move forward anyway, because the actions are aimed at solving problems unrelated to agriculture's economic situation.

What are the problems that most macroeconomic policies seek to overcome? Since the Great Depression in the 1930s, the Fed and the US government have actively used monetary and fiscal policies to partially mitigate the undesirable effects of the national "business cycle." In macroeconomics, the national business cycle is the tendency of modern-day economies to periodically exhibit unstable real GDP growth. National economies experience recurring phases of economic "booms" (strong positive real GDP growth), followed by slowdowns towards recession (negative real GDP growth). The recession eventually "hits bottom," and a resurgence takes place. The economy revives into a recovery (positive real GDP growth returns), reaches a peak, and then the cycle repeats itself.

When a government engages in "counter-cyclical macroeconomic policy," the instruments of monetary and fiscal policy are used to moderate the most severe effects of the cycle. The Fed and/or the government's fiscal budget create a change in aggregate demand that is "counter" to the phase of the cycle. If the economy is booming too quickly, counter-cyclical policy would attempt to slow growth. If the economy is in deep recession, then fiscal and monetary instruments are manipulated to stimulate demand.

What does national counter-cyclical policy mean for the financial conditions faced by food and agriculture? While there is not a single answer to this question, we can nonetheless examine some key scenarios.

Counter-cyclical macroeconomic policy: scenario of the "Great Recession"

For example, a typical case study is to examine the effects of a counter-cyclical policy that aims to mitigate a national recession. Between 2008 and 2010, the US experienced the "Great Recession" subsequent to a severe disruption in US financial markets. Real GDP growth was negative (−5.1 percent) during 2008–2010, and the unemployment rate rose from 4.7 percent in 2007 to 10 percent in October 2009.[43]

The countercyclical response to the Great Recession was both monetary and fiscal. The Fed reduced the Federal-Funds interest rate to 0.25 percent (nearly zero percent), and also engaged in "quantitative easing" (which increased the money supply). On the fiscal side, Congress passed the American Recovery and Reinvestment Act of 2009, which was a package of tax cuts and spending increases. There are ongoing debates as to whether these monetary and fiscal actions had their intended impacts of moderating the recession, but the fact remains that these government actions did happen. Our goal here is to examine macroeconomic consequences of policy actions for the agriculture and food sectors.

Let's look at the Fed's decision to reduce interest rates. A decrease in interest rates tend to reduce the cost of borrowing. *Ceteris paribus*, agribusinesses and food businesses will be able to invest in a wider range of capital-enhancing projects because net rates of return are positive when lower interest rates create an additional incentive for increased investment spending.

There is a connection between interest rates and the *US currency exchange rate*. When interest rates are relatively lower in the US, compared to those in other nations, then international investors will take their funds elsewhere to locations where they can enjoy more lucrative interest-rate returns. A reduced flow of foreign investment funds will decrease the "demand for US dollars" in currency markets. Other things being equal, the less scarce US dollar depreciates in foreign exchange.

How does a depreciation of the US dollar affect the trade position of US agriculture? A cheaper US dollar spurs US agriculture exports, and inhibits US agriculture imports. When the US dollar is inexpensive in currency markets, foreign consumers discover that US food and agricultural products are more affordable.

Well, if the Fed's low-interest-rate policy stimulates additional export trade for agriculture, what about the fiscal stimulus? The results of this intentional macroeconomic policy are mixed. Fiscal stimuli, such as tax cuts and spending increases, will increase the federal budget deficit. Budget deficits, *ceteris paribus*, tend to tighten the borrowed-funds markets, and increase interest rates, and subsequently place upward pressure on the US currency value. Appreciation and depreciation of the US dollar have opposite effects on US agricultural exports and imports.

In addition, if a fiscal stimulus is successful in inducing an increase in household consumer spending, then US food and agricultural firms may benefit from a modest increase in domestic demand for food products. But when US households are in a position to spend more, they also have the freedom to purchase from any source that they desire, and some of the increased household expenditures will be directed to acquire foreign-made products (increasing agri-food imports).

Macroeconomic policy, currency exchange rates, and US agricultural trade

The discussion above clearly indicates that it is important to study both the domestic and international effects of macroeconomic influences on US agriculture. In this chapter, we have argued that international trade is a primary force driving change in US agriculture. The key interactions between macroeconomics and trade are often reflected in currency exchange rate markets. Twenty-first-century US agricultural producers and agribusinesses know that foreign demanders will take advantage of globally competitive markets, and transfer their business to the nation that can offer the best value. As a result, US farm and food producers are highly attuned to the effect of currency markets on their exports and imports.[44]

The central role of exchange rates in shaping the ongoing relationship between US agriculture and the global economy was highlighted in G. Edward Schuh's 1974 seminal article on the topic.[45] Post-WWII US macroeconomic policy during 1945–1970 had emphasized stability in trade and exchange. Over time, a policy of fixed exchange rates had allowed the US dollar to become overvalued against a "basket" of foreign currencies.

International markets began to experience a dramatic change when the US adopted a floating currency rate in 1971. Schuh contends that the previous high-dollar value had overly discouraged US agricultural exports. Further, Schuh maintains that US agriculture's post-WWII financial struggles were at least partly attributable to US macroeconomic policies that had stressed post-war stability instead of allowing open market forces to determine trade patterns. Orden (2002) and other scholars have expanded and further developed the founding ideas in Schuh's research.[46]

Twenty-first-century environmental, energy, and climatic effects on US farm and food sector policies and performance

The recently completed overview of macroeconomic connections to the US agri-food system is another reminder that farm-and-food sector decision making occurs within a larger context. Our studies have established a genuine linkage between the microeconomics of individual choice and the macroeconomics of aggregate markets.

This last section of Chapter 2 continues the connectivity theme. We know that singular actions have broader effects. For example, as a farm manager adopts a technology or hires a scarce resource, the choice generates an array of consequences that stretch beyond the individual producer.

In the twenty-first century, there is a heightened awareness that our planet's environmental quality, energy availability, and climatic change are phenomena related to human economic activity, including the decisions we make in our agricultural and food sectors.

Controversies often arise when the topics about the environment, energy, and climate are discussed, especially in relation to production agriculture and food marketing. It is a challenge to study these sensitive areas in an unbiased and objective manner. The authors of this textbook are aware of the highly charged nature of the subject matter. But we cannot take the "ostrich approach", and simply bury our heads. These are real issues that require our best effort to be objective and fair-minded. There are risks associated with addressing these issues. We think the payoffs are worth the risks.

Environmental connections to food and agriculture

Earlier in this chapter, we examined the remarkable growth of US agricultural productivity associated with technology adoption. While the benefits of those gains are undeniable, costs accompanied the advances. Agriculture is not alone in this instance; the majority of US markets and industries generate costs as they make valuable economic contributions to our economy.

The costs that are of particular interest here are unintended environmental and detrimental side effects of economic activity in our food and agricultural sectors. In economic theory, extra impacts that are outside of private market valuation are identified as "spillover effects" or "externalities."

Spillover effects can either be beneficial or create costs. Food and agriculture generate both types of side effects. On the positive side, agriculture can help sequester carbon and therefore contribute to climate change management. At the rural-urban interface, farmland can provide valued green space in areas dominated by concrete sprawl. An emphasis on healthy diets can reduce the demand for food products associated with increased global carbon emissions.

The spillover cost of food and agricultural activities often impair or damage resources for economic participants who are downwind or downstream from the agricultural source. Among the side effects are:

- Impaired soil quality, damaged watersheds, and extra dust pollution – When farming practices are responsible for excess water and/or wind erosion.
- Reduced water quality of aquifers, lakes, rivers, and oceans – When chemicals, pesticides, and surplus nutrients run off into watersheds, or drain down through the soil.
- Diminished air quality – As pesticides drift into neighboring areas, or odors from confined livestock facilities affect the welfare of residential areas.
- Reduced biodiversity – As monoculture dominates the landscape, wildlife, and wetland habitats are converted to crop production.
- Landfill waste challenges – Extra packaging and health-related container requirements associated with food marketing and sanitation add to solid waste burdens in public landfills.

In the US, the establishment and enforcement of new regulations has been a commonly used policy technique for reducing the occurrence of costly externalities.

Authoritative regulatory systems aimed at decreasing the environmental spillover effects of food and agriculture have often been unsuccessful in efficiently achieving the desired results. Why? Standardized regulatory enforcement mechanisms often ignore important economic differences in farm operations and food markets, and consequently the cost of compliance with the new rules becomes prohibitive, particularly for smaller farms and food retailers who lack economies of scale to absorb the costs.

As a result, instead of helping to alleviate externalities, regulatory enforcement can drive smaller operations out of the market. Even if externalities are reduced, the regulatory effort simply saddles the economy with a different set of new costs. When market structures become more concentrated, as a result of regulatory enforcement, then market power can be exercised by the larger firms remaining in the industry.

Also, from a socio-cultural perspective, there is natural resistance among all decision makers to compliance with unfunded mandates. Farm owners and food-business managers highly value their independence, and often respond better to voluntary requests for assistance rather than edicts requiring compliance.

To the extent that regulatory approaches have been inefficient and/or ineffective, the search for innovative means to reduce harmful externalities is ongoing. Roberston et al. (2004) are an interdisciplinary team of researchers who have been active in creating a new paradigm for productive relationships that benefit both the agri-food system and environment.

The policy approach that Robertson et al. recommends is similar to the driving principle of prevention in the FSMA. Namely, this research team argues for a "new vision" that anticipates possible environmental problems associated with agricultural technology prior to its adoption. They especially note that *environmental research has overlooked the capacity of food and agriculture to generate real natural benefits*, as compared to the viewpoint that farm and food management practices are an ecological challenge. A fresh approach is to examine how food and agriculture become part of the solution instead of being perceived as part of the problem.

In the past, the question of how to respond to food and agricultural externalities was often a case of reacting to them one at a time. Solutions to individual situations were proposed and implemented, but common patterns among similar problems remained undetected, and there was an absence of follow up after the 'treatment' to determine if it made a difference in improved environmental quality.

Robertson et al. are strongly supportive of a more systematic approach that puts greater emphasis on pre-planning and emphasizes the positive contributions that agricultural practices can make. They advocate for broader consideration of how rural landscapes and watersheds can interact with agriculture to improve environmental performance. If the "preventative model" can be applied in the realms of environmental and food safety, then perhaps we have arrived at a twenty-first-century policy approach that is a step ahead of reactive regulatory paradigm of the past. A very good example of innovative approaches that can jointly improve farm economics and environmental quality is the adoption of sustainable agricultural systems, as described in Check Box 2.4.

☐ Put your check in the box, if you have read and mastered its content.

Check Box 2.4   Sustainable agriculture: profitable integration of economic and environmental systems

A holistic approach that joins farm economics with environmental well-being is the establishment of sustainable food and agricultural systems. Similar to the work by Robertson et al., an interdisciplinary effort by researchers at Kansas State University examines scenarios that can meet the following standards (established in 1990) for long-term viability of an integrated system of plant and animal production practices:[1]

- Satisfy human food and fiber needs.
- Enhance environmental quality and the natural resource base upon which the agricultural economy depends.
- Make the most efficient use of nonrenewable resources and on-farm resources and integrate, where appropriate, natural biological cycles and controls.
- Sustain the economic viability of farm operations.
- Enhance the quality of life for farmers and society as a whole.

Further evidence supporting the beneficial potentials for systems that are agriculturally productive, economically profitable, and ecologically sound were conducted by teams of scientists at the Universities of Nebraska and Minnesota.[2,3] While it will be necessary for

(continued)

(continued)

additional sustainability "experiments" to be designed and implemented, the research thus far is promising.

1 https://www.nal.usda.gov/afsic/sustainable-agriculture-information-access-tools
2 http://digitalcommons.unl.edu/cgi/viewcontent.cgi?article=1317&context=agronomyfacpub
3 www.misa.umn.edu/prod/groups/cfans/@pub/@cfans/@misa/documents/asset/cfans_asset_287080.pdf

Still another innovative approach that seeks to identify mutually beneficial interactions between agriculture and the environment is a USDA initiative. USDA has created a research effort to *establish markets for environmental services*.[47] Researchers are examining the possibilities to measure the supply of environmental services from agriculture, the demand for environmental services from the public, and the use of market instruments such as trading and auctions to enable the forces of supply and demand to allocate environmental services efficiently.

Later in Chapter 8 of this textbook, we will examine the challenges and opportunities associated with the linkages between the agri-food system and the environment. The recent multi-disciplinary research in this area of study offers some important and exciting policy options that are worthy of further investigation.

Energy connections to food and agriculture

An engaging discussion about the relationship between agriculture and the environment is often a logical prelude to an inquiry into the production and use of energy in the agri-food system. As in other policy areas, it is instructive to understand the twenty-first-century agriculture-to-energy relationship in light of actions and trends that began prior to 2001.

In the early to mid-twentieth century, the US agricultural and food sectors were primarily *demanders of energy products* (such as petroleum-based fuels and electricity). New technology, infrastructure investment, and efficiency advances spurred strong growth in energy use by the US agri-food system. As discussed earlier in this chapter, technological innovations in agriculture motivated rational producers to mechanize and modernize their operations. Farm-labor and animal-power were displaced by productivity-enhancing capital investments in petroleum- and electrical-powered farm equipment. Increased use of energy intensive inorganic fertilizers and chemical pesticides further boosted agri-system energy demand.

The 1930s Great Depression generated severe consequences for US agriculture, but one policy response to that era's stark conditions had a lasting impact on farm-energy use patterns: rural electrification. Development of the electrical grid in rural America provided agricultural producers the access they needed to adopt electric-powered technologies that increased output and profit-earning potentials.

As the agri-food sector adopted energy intensive technology and equipment, the search for increased energy efficiency was another important phenomenon. Over time, the demand for energy became more sophisticated and selective, because agricultural and food producers sought out practices and devices that were more energy efficient. Numerous innovations that increased the amount of output per unit of energy emerged, particularly after fuel costs increased dramatically as a result of the 1970s "energy crises". US farm energy productivity increased an average of approximately 29 percent between the five-year periods of 1948–52 and 2007–2011.[48]

In the late 1970s, research on large-scale fermentation facilities began to make it possible to produce corn-based ethanol as an energy source. New federal energy policies, starting in 1979, were primarily aimed at reducing the US dependence on imported fuels. One of the energy alternatives to "foreign oil" involved new Congressional incentives to produce corn-based ethanol.

Initially, corn-to-ethanol conversion rates were not economically competitive. Government subsidies were introduced to encourage both ethanol production and consumption. Publicly funded grants stimulated research to improve ethanol production technologies. Subsidies also enticed consumers to purchase corn-based ethanol as a partial replacement for petroleum-based liquid fuels. Even though the initial ethanol production methods were primitive by twenty-first-century standards, the introduction of corn-based ethanol into fuel markets marked an important transition for US agriculture. *The farm sector became a supplier, and not just a user, of energy.*

US ethanol production rates originally increased at a moderate pace, rising from 175 million gallons in 1980 to 1.8 billion gallons in 2001. More dramatic jumps in US ethanol production occurred subsequent to two legislative initiatives:

1) The Energy Policy Act of 2005 – This law established the first Renewable Fuel Standard RFS) for biofuels, and it mandated that ethanol gradually replace MTBE (a petroleum derivative) as an oxygenate additive. Increased subsidies and research for soybean-based biodiesel as a transportation fuel was also included in this 2005 statute.
2) The 2007 Energy Independence and Security Act (EISA) – EISA dramatically increased the 2005 mandate for renewable fuels. EISA set a goal for the US to produce 36.5 billion gallons of alternative fuels annually by the year 2022. In 2015, this steep RFS has come into question. Powerful lobbies are seeking to pare back the 2007 RFS. Even if there is an RFS reduction, the built-up US ethanol production capability will remain strong for some time.

The mandate to reach the new RFS by 2022 sparked large investments in ethanol plant production capacity and advanced research on enzymes increased corn-to-fuel conversion rates. As a result, ethanol output briskly increased. In 2014, the annual ethanol production rate was nearly 14.3 billion gallons.[49] As ethanol production rose, so did the usage rate for its primary input: corn. Large increases in corn demand occurred subsequent to the 2007 EISA. In the 2014/2015 Marketing Year, total US corn plantings were nearing 90 million acres, and ethanol production was absorbing about 38 percent of all corn bushels produced.[50]

The enormous increase in corn demand and production associated with the growth of the ethanol market has created side effects. Concerns have been voiced about adverse effects on food prices and the global food supply, as more than one third of US corn production is now servicing energy markets instead of feed-and-food markets. Environmental and resource conservation issues have also arisen as farmers engage in resource re-allocation to enable additional growth of corn acreage.

Instead of engaging in a corn-soybean biannual crop rotation, many producers have adjusted input usage to accommodate continuous year-on-year corn production. Additional resource adjustments have involved converting pasture and fallow lands into additional corn acres. Finally, a noticeable number of producers have allowed contracts for the Conservation Reserve Program (CRP) to expire, and then farm operators have brought those lands back into production. Much of that acreage is now devoted to corn output. Groups such as Pheasants Forever have noticed the impacts associated with the loss of wildlife habitat as CRP acres diminish.

Questions about how to balance the competing interests for renewable fuels, affordable food, and sufficient wildlife habitat create real challenges for proper policy design. In Chapter 8, when we examine conservation and environmental considerations with increased focus, we can explore how innovative policy approaches (such as sustainable agriculture or preventative systems solutions) can address multiple concerns more efficiently and effectively.

One mechanism that consistently balances the forces of economic scarcity is a market. In the case of energy allocation for agriculture, the dynamics of supply and demand are always at work. Farm managers actively respond to market incentives as both users and producers of energy. Agriculture in the twentieth century figured out numerous ways to be more efficient demanders of energy. An exciting trend for twenty-first-century farmers is the opportunity to supply energy – and not just in the form of ethanol.

Farm producers are increasingly generating their own electricity. Farms often have the open space and related landscape qualities to provide good sites for wind turbines, solar panels, and anaerobic energy units. The USDA reports that 17,358 US farms in 2008 produced energy from wind or solar technology, methane digesters, and related technologies. By 2011, twice that number of farms were generating additional power on-site.[51]

Climate connections to food and agriculture

Wind turbines, solar panels, and anaerobic digestion are prime examples of how agriculture continues to seek out and adopt more affordable technologies. Geothermal and biomass are related energy options gaining attention as alternative energy platforms. Discussions about renewable energy sources are typically spawned when the overarching question of global climate is considered.

What can we, or should we, say about the relationship between the US agri-food system and climate change? Is there an approach to this question that will largely be perceived as unbiased and objective?

Earlier in this chapter, we acknowledged that controversies often arise when relationships between the agri-food system and environmental quality are examined. Contentiousness of the issues did not prevent us from investigating them. Instead, we moved forward with a review, seeking to be as transparent as possible. Honesty and straightforwardness continue to be our guideposts as we now address how the agri-food system interacts with global climate conditions.

Scientists have carefully examined the evidence and concluded that a changing climate is already underway and that human activity is a major contributing factor.[52]

Recent observations are worth noting. According to the United Kingdom's (UK's) Meteorology Office, the January–September 2015 average worldwide temperature was 1.02°C above the overall global temperature average that existed between 1850 and 1900[53]. This 1850–1900 fifty-year period is used as a reference for when the world's industrial revolution began to burn fossil fuels for energy generation. A temperature difference of 1-degree Centigrade is the equivalent of a temperature difference of 1.8°F.[54]

The United Nation's (UN's) World Meteorological Organization reported that world-wide carbon dioxide and methane levels reached record highs in 2014. The overwhelming majority of scientists have concluded that it is not merely a coincidence that we have simultaneously increased global average temperatures and ever-increasing greenhouse gas volumes in the atmosphere. The two phenomena are connected.

Former US Secretary of Agriculture Dan Glickman contends that our changing climate is not a media discussion. He argues that it is not an operative plan to believe that climate change will go away if we pay no attention to it. Disruptive weather patterns are already a reality.

US agricultural producers can respond to more frequent extreme weather events (such as extended drought or torrential rainfall) by taking a pragmatic approach. Farmers are already producing their own renewable energy and using precision agriculture to achieve maximum energy-use efficiency. With the appropriate technologies and decision tools, the farm and food system can prudently address the challenges that lie ahead.[55]

What are functional methods to adjust to a changing climate? A variety of studies have suggested a three-pronged approach: (1) Agricultural Production and Food Security, (2) Adaptation, and (3) Mitigation.

Agricultural production and food security

Article Two of the United Nations treaty known as the UN Framework Convention on Climate Change (the UNFCCC or "the Convention") directly addressed the key importance of the agri-food system to both the global climate and the world economy.

In particular, the Convention states that actions to stabilize greenhouse gas emissions (GHGs) should be designed to ensure that agricultural production is not threatened, and that food security is not compromised. In addition, the Convention sets a goal for climatic adjustments of human-based activities to occur within a timeframe sufficient to allow ecosystems to adapt naturally, and also enable economic development to proceed in a sustainable manner.

At the beginning of this chapter, it was noted that the global human population will be over 9 billion people by the year 2050. Substantial increases in agricultural productivity will be needed to meet the food needs associated with the anticipated world population growth. To ensure global food security for vastly larger numbers of humankind, now and in the future, it is unlikely that a "carbon-neutral" agri-food system will be possible.

However, there is a considerable contribution that the farm and food economy can offer to alleviating problems associated with a changing climate. New technologies and improved management practices can concurrently increase productive efficiency and consequently decrease the GHG emissions per unit of farm (or food) output. Farm practices can sequester GHGs in soils and biomass.

Adaptation

Increased investments in research and development (R&D) can accelerate the discovery of crop varieties and animal breeds with increased stress resistance, and consequently enhance production capacity without any additional GHG emissions.

Modifications of the timing and locality of crop production, and updated water and/or fertilizer management regimes can increase yields and limit harmful climate side effects. Soil and water conservation technologies can help producers to engage in climate-friendly practices that increase output while simultaneously managing soil moisture, prevent water-logging, control erosion, and reduce nutrient leaching. Innovations in integrated pest management can be combined with new crop or livestock varieties to isolate and control destructive biological vectors. Increased accuracy and availability of forecasted weather events and seasonal climate trends can assist producers to adapt their plans and therefore reduce production risks.

Many economically rational farm managers will voluntarily utilize these climate-safe adaptations because they enhance the profit potentials of their operations. One role for pub-lic policy is to ensure that sufficient funding is directed towards the R&D needed to create and disseminate new knowledge and practices.

Mitigation

As indicated above, the priorities for feeding a growing and hungry world may mean that the agriculture and food sector cannot both increase production and reduce overall emissions. Nevertheless, there is plenty that the agri-food system can accomplish in mitigating the effects of climate change.

A simple but powerful contribution for limiting GHG emissions is to stimulate gains in productive efficiency. It should be a policy priority to figure out ways to reduce the amount of wasted feed and food connected with logistical challenges or inadequate sanitary practices.

There are additional climate-responsive management changes. For example, there are crop- and grazing-land management strategies that specifically improve both farm output and soil health. Livestock management approaches, including cutting-edge dietary addi-tives, advanced breeding and manure management, have strong potentials to limit or reduce climate threats.

Summary

We can think of mitigation, adaptation and production as "three legs of the stool" for the agri-food systems policy response to the challenges of a changing climate. The content of this three-way approach puts emphasis on using the general tools of agricultural, food, and rural development to foster the capacity and resilience of farm and food producers to be prepared for climate change impacts.

Many of the most promising policies are founded on how farmers, and their input and ser-vice providers, apply current practices and upcoming technologies. In many ways, the farm and food sectors have always been managing climatic risks for centuries. While the climate changes of the twenty-first century certainly introduce new uncertainties, there are reasons to be hopeful. The greatest challenge may be the realization that climate change is a real phenomenon that requires serious attention. Take a look in Check Box 2.5 to see why an inclination to have doubts about long-term complex problems is a typical human response.

☐ Put your check in the box, if you have read and mastered content of Check Box 2.5.

Check Box 2.5   The psychology of doubt in relation to climate change

Recent scientific research by professional psychologists demonstrates that the tendency to harbor doubts about the reality of phenomena such as climate change is not a new human behavior. It is quite common. A recent formal study makes this observation:

> ...psychological barriers...impede behavioral choices that would facilitate mitigation, adaptation, and environmental sustainability. Although many individuals are engaged in some ameliorative action, most could do more, but they are hindered by seven categories of psychological barriers, or "dragons of inaction." [1]

To ensure that we examine all points of view, then we also have to recognize that the psychologists themselves are targets for "doubt": they are placed under suspicion as they get involved in the discussion. It does not matter that their intentions are purely scientific:

> Upon hearing about APA's climate change task force report (American Psychological Association Task Force on the Interface Between Psychology and Global Climate Change, 2009), the host of a popular show on a leading US television network held up a copy of Aldous Huxley's *Brave New World* and said, "The shrinks are trying to brainwash us again."[2]

A volunteer association of 250 global companies, known as Business for Social Responsibility (BSR), emphasizes that it is important for citizens to face facts about our changing climate. There is simply too much objective evidence that a new era has already begun. The BSR group, and other professional organizations, emphasize that there are no enemies in these circumstances; it is useless and counterproductive to assign blame.[3, 4]

1 www.researchgate.net/profile/Robert_Gifford3/publication/254734365_The_Dragons_of_
   Inaction_Psychological_Barriers_That_Limit_Climate_Change_Mitigation_and_Adaptation/
   links/0c96052047aaad383e000000.pdf
2 Ibid, p. 296
3 www.bsr.org/en/our-insights/report-view/climate-change-implications-for-agriculture
4 www.agri-pulse.com/Climate-change-and-agriculture-challenges-and-opportunities-09222015.asp

As suggested in Check Box 2.5, there is no real value in placing the blame for climate change on any one group or nation. Rather, the twenty-first-century approach encourages the private sector, governments, scientists, and individuals to work together on solutions. The agriculture and food sectors of the economy have much to offer in this team approach, particularly with an emphasis on increasing production, economical adaptations, and research-supported mitigation strategies.

Review of challenges and opportunities influencing the US agri-food system's future

The objective of this chapter is to "survey the twenty-first century landscape" of the US agri-food system. The effort helps us to develop an economic roadmap for efficiently navigating a complex policy environment.

As we plot a path to the future, there are *three twentieth-century agricultural signposts* that will continue to guide the *twenty-first century* journey: productivity enhancing technological change; ongoing growth in global trade; and the rising power of the savvy food consumer. We also know that scientific research and discovery will pave the route to continued systematic improvements in food safety and quality.

Our destination is an agricultural and food economy that can grow sustainably, safely, and securely. Our goal in this textbook is to determine how to design and implement policies that will assist decision makers to find and travel the right road. We also may be able to warn against policies that are blind alleys or unnecessary detours.

The *FSMA*, the *2014 Farm Bill* and the *Trans-Pacific Partnership* constitute important landmarks that belong on the map of the US agricultural and food economy in the twenty-first century. The guidance offered by these policies will affect the direction that the US agri-food system takes.

Our chart for the future of the farm and food system would not be complete unless we carefully consider how *macroeconomic forces* will create twists and turns along the way. Finally, the course taken by the US agri-food system will encounter both smooth passageways and challenging obstacles as we travel a landscape that requires our attention to *environmental quality*, *energy management* and *climatic adaptation*.

In the next chapter, we journey into the field of policy analysis. The goal will be to learn how to properly use the investigative tools of economics to gain insights for improved policy design and implementation. There is much at stake in guiding the farm and food system along the pathways to sustainable growth and a food-secure global economy. Creating and implementing the right policies can make a difference in the pursuit of a more effective and efficient agri-food system.

Notes

1   United Nations, Department of Economic and Social Affairs, Population Division (2015). "World Population Prospects: The 2015 Revision, Key Findings and Advance Tables." Working Paper No. ESA/P/WP.241, p. 1. Retrieved from: http://esa.un.org/unpd/wpp/Publications/Files/Key_Findings_WPP_2015.pdf
2   UN News. "World Population Projected to Reach 9.6 Billion by 2050." New York: United Nations ESA, June 13, 2013. P. 1. Retrieved from: www.un.org/development/desa/en/news/population/un-report-world-population-projected-to-reach-9-6-billion-by-2050.html
3   Dimitri, Carolyn, Anne Effland, and Neilson Conklin. "The 20th Century Transformation of U.S. Agriculture and Farm Policy." USDA, Economic Research Service. EIB-3, 2005. Retrieved from: www.ers.usda.gov/webdocs/publications/eib3/13566_eib3_1_.pdf
4   Ibid, p. 6.
5   Ibid.
6   Ibid, p. 2.
7   Fuglie, Keith O., James M. MacDonald, and Eldon Ball. "Productivity Growth in U.S. Agriculture." Washington: USDA, ERS. Economic Brief Number 9, September 2007, p. 2. Retrieved from: https://pdfs.semanticscholar.org/ecee/972700b4c4dc83f4e57833b8a11649513bc9.pdf
8   Ibid, p. 2.

9 Jorgenson, Dale W., Mun S. Ho, John Samuels, and Kevin J. Stiroh. October 2006. "The Industry Origins of the American Productivity Resurgence." Working Paper, Department of Economics, Harvard University, Cambridge, MA. Retrieved from: http://people.hmdc.harvard.edu/~mho/jhss_industry_100606.pdf

10 Carbaugh, Robert J. *International Economics*. Mason, OH: Southwestern Cengage Learning, 2011, p. 188.

11 Creative Commons. "The Components of GDP during the Great Depression." Retrieved from: http://2012books.lardbucket.org/books/theory-and-applications-of-economics/s26-03-the-components-of-gdp-during-t.html

12 Dimitri, Carolyn, Anne Effland, and Neilson Conklin. "The 20th Century Transformation of U.S. Agriculture and Farm Policy." USDA, Economic Research Service. EIB-3, 2005, p. 7. Retrieved from: www.ers.usda.gov/webdocs/publications/eib3/13566_eib3_1_.pdf

13 Carbaugh, Robert J. *International Economics*. Mason, OH: Southwestern Cengage Learning, 2011, pp. 188–189.

14 Wessel's Living History Farm, York, Nebraska. "Farming in the 1940s." Retrieved from: www.livinghistoryfarm.org/farminginthe40s/money_09.html

15 Office of the US Trade Representative. "Trade Agreements." Retrieved from: https://ustr.gov/trade-agreements/free-trade-agreements

16 Senauer, Ben. Department of Applied Economics, University of Minnesota. "The Food Consumer in the 21st Century: New Research Perspectives." The Retail Food Industry Center. Working Paper 01-03. April 2001, p. 1. Retrieved from: http://ageconsearch.umn.edu/handle/14346

17 Saxowsky, David M., and Marvin R. Duncan. "Understanding Agriculture's Transition into the 21st Century Challenges, Opportunities, Consequences and Alternatives." Fargo: NDSU, Agricultural Economics Miscellaneous Report No. 181, March 1998. Retrieved from: https://ideas.repec.org/p/ags/nddmrs/23112.html

18 Boehlje, Michael, Craig Dobbins, and Allan Gray. "The Competitive Environment: New Realities." West Lafayette: Department of Agricultural Economics, Purdue University. EC-717, May 2004. Retrieved from: www.extension.purdue.edu/extmedia/EC/EC-717.pdf

19 Becker, Tilman C. "Consumer Behavior Research in the Advent of the 21st Century." Stuttgart, Germany: Hohenheim University. Institute of Agricultural Policy and Markets. Cahiers Options Méditerranéennes. 01/2005; 64: 5–16. Retrieved from: https://marktlehre.uni-hohenheim.de/fileadmin/einrichtungen/marktlehre/Forschung/Verbraucherverhalten/consumer_behavior21.pdf

20 Senauer, Ben. Department of Applied Economics, University of Minnesota. "The Food Consumer in the 21st Century: New Research Perspectives." The Retail Food Industry Center. Working Paper 01-03. April 2001, p. 1. Retrieved from: http://ageconsearch.umn.edu/handle/14346

21 Ibid, pp. 2, 25.

22 Saxowsky, David M., and Marvin R. Duncan. "Understanding Agriculture's Transition into the 21st Century Challenges, Opportunities, Consequences and Alternatives." Fargo: NDSU, Agricultural Economics Miscellaneous Report No. 181, March 1998. Retrieved from: https://ideas.repec.org/p/ags/nddmrs/23112.html

23 Ray, Daryll E. and Harwood D. Schaffer. "In the Future, Farmers' Fiercest Taskmaster May Be Consumer Expectations." Knoxville, TN: Agricultural Policy Analysis Center, University of Tennessee, Policy Pennings. Oct. 17, 2014. Retrieved from: www.agpolicy.org/weekcol/742.html#

24 Agralytica Consulting. "Food Safety Modernization Act: Economic Analysis." Prepared for the United Soybean Board. Alexandria, VA: October 17, 2012. Retrieved from: http://unitedsoybean.org/wp-content/uploads/2013/07/FSMA-Economic-Analysis-Final-Oct-16.pdf

25 Harvey, Holly. Deputy Assistant Director for Budget Analysis. "Congressional Budget Office Cost Estimate: S. 510 Food Safety Modernization Act." August 12, 2010. Retrieved from: www.cbo.gov/sites/default/files/s510.pdf

26 Ribera, Luis A. and Ronald D. Knutson. "The FDA's Food Safety Modernization Act and Its Economic Implications." *Choices Magazine* 26(4). October 2011. Retrieved from: www.choicesmagazine.org/choices-magazine/submitted-articles/the-fdas-food-safety-modernization-act-and-its-economic-implications

27 Agralytica Consulting. "Food Safety Modernization Act: Economic Analysis." Prepared for the United Soybean Board. Alexandria, VA. October 17, 2012. Retrieved from: http://unitedsoybean.org/wp-content/uploads/2013/07/FSMA-Economic-Analysis-Final-Oct-16.pdf

28 Ribera, Luis A. and Ronald D. Knutson. "The FDA's Food Safety Modernization Act and Its Economic Implications." *Choices: The Magazine of Farm, Food and Resources*. Vol. 26, Number 4. October 2011. Retrieved from: www.choicesmagazine.org/choices-magazine/submitted-articles/the-fdas-food-safety-modernization-act-and-its-economic-implications

29 Goodwin, Barry K. and Vincent H. Smith. "Theme Overview: The 2014 Farm Bill – An Economic Welfare Disaster or Triumph?" *Choices: The Magazine of Farm, Food and Resources*. 3rd Quarter 2014. Retrieved from: www.choicesmagazine.org/choices-magazine/theme-articles/3rd-quarter-2014/theme-overview-the-2014-farm-billan-economic-welfare-disaster-or-triumph

30 Ibid, p. 1.

31 Glauber, J. and P. Westhoff (2015). "50 Shades of Amber: The 2014 Farm Bill the WTO." Invited Paper presented at the session The 2014 Farm Bill: An Economic Post Mortem. Allied Social Science Associations (ASSA) Meetings. Boston, Massachusetts, 4 January.

32 Office of the US Trade Representative. "Overview of the Trans Pacific Partnership." Retrieved from: https://ustr.gov/tpp/overview-of-the-TPP

33 Canadian Federation of Agriculture. "Trans-Pacific Partnership." Retrieved from: www.cfa-fca.ca/hot-topics/trans-pacific-partnership

34 Fergusson, Ian F., Mark A. McMinimy, and Brock R. Williams. "The Trans-Pacific Partnership (TPP) Negotiations and Issues for Congress." Congressional Research Service. R42694, March 20, 2015. Retrieved from: www.fas.org/sgp/crs/row/R42694.pdf

35 Katz, Richard. "Free Trade and the TPP: Will Republicans Defeat the Trans-Pacific Partnership?" Foreign Affairs: Snapshot: October 7, 2015. Retrieved from: www.foreignaffairs.com/articles/united-states/2015-10-07/free-trade-and-tpp

36 Mauldin, William. "U.S. Reaches Trans-Pacific Partnership Trade Deal With 11 Pacific Nations." *Wall Street Journal*. October 5, 2015. Retrieved from: www.wsj.com/articles/u-s-reaches-trade-deal-with-11-pacific-nations-1444046867

37 Fergusson, Ian F., Mark A. McMinimy, and Brock R. Williams. "The Trans-Pacific Partnership (TPP) Negotiations and Issues for Congress." Congressional Research Service. R42694, March 20, 2015. www.fas.org/sgp/crs/row/R42694.pdf

38 Petri, Peter, Michael Plummer, and Fan Zhai. "The Trans-Pacific Partnership and Asia-Pacific Integration: A Quantitative Assessment." Peterson Institute for International Economics, October 2011: www.usitc.gov/ research_and_analysis/documents/petri-plummer-zhai%20EWC%20TPP%20WP%20oct11.pdf

39 Wardell, Jane and Krista Hughes. "Faint Corporate Praise for TPP as Winners, Losers Sought." Reuters: World News, Oct. 6, 2015. Retrieved from: www.reuters.com/article/2015/10/06/us-trade-tpp-business-idUSKCN0S00I820151006#hjboKoJ7VsGAg0rj.97

40 Vidot, Anna. "TPP to Cut Agricultural Tariffs across the Board, but US Sugar Protections Remain." ABC News Australia. Oct. 6, 2015. Retrieved from: www.abc.net.au/news/2015-10-06/agriculture-tariffs-to-fall-under-tpp/6830138

41 Mauldin, William. "U.S. Reaches Trans-Pacific Partnership Trade Deal With 11 Pacific Nations." *Wall Street Journal*. October 5, 2015. Retrieved from: www.wsj.com/articles/u-s-reaches-trade-deal-with-11-pacific-nations-1444046867

42 Katz, Richard. "Free Trade and the TPP: Will Republicans Defeat the Trans-Pacific Partnership?" Foreign Affairs: Snapshot: October 7, 2015. Retrieved from: www.foreignaffairs.com/articles/united-states/2015-10-07/free-trade-and-tpp

43 National Bureau of Economic Research. "Business Cycle Dating Committee, National Bureau of Economic Research." Retrieved from: www.nber.org/cycles/sept2010.html

44 Orden, David. "Exchange Rate Effects on Agricultural Trade and Trade Relations." 2000. Policy Harmonization and Adjustment in the North American Agricultural and Food Industry; Proceedings of the 5th Agricultural and Food Policy – 1999. Farm Foundation, Agricultural and Food Policy Systems Information Workshops. Retrieved from: www.farmfoundation.org/news/articlefiles/887-orden.pdf

45 Schuh, G. Edward. 1974. "The Exchange Rate and U.S. Agriculture." *American Journal of Agricultural Economics*. 56(1) (February): pp. 1–13.

46 Orden, David. "Exchange Rate Effects on Agricultural Trade and Trade Relations." 2000. Policy Harmonization and Adjustment in the North American Agricultural and Food Industry; Proceedings of the 5th Agricultural and Food Policy – 1999. Farm Foundation, Agricultural and Food Policy Systems Information Workshops. Retrieved from: www.farmfoundation.org/news/articlefiles/887-orden.pdf

47 Ribaudo, Marc, Leroy Hansen, Daniel Hellerstein, and Catherine Greene. "The Use of Markets to Increase Private Investment in Environmental Stewardship." USDA, ERS. Report # 64. Sept. 2008. Retrieved from: www.ers.usda.gov/webdocs/publications/err64/11931_err64fm_1_.pdf

48 Mercier, Stephanie. "The U.S. Agriculture and Energy Sectors – A Complex Love Affair." Farm Journal Foundation. Straight from D.C.: Agricultural Perspectives. May 27, 2015. Retrieved from: www.agweb.com/blog/straight-from-dc-agricultural-perspectives/the-us-agriculture-and-energy-sectors-a-complex-love-affair/

49 Voegele, Erin. "EIA Predicts Increased Ethanol Production in 2015 and 2016." *Ethanol Producer Magazine*. Jan. 13, 2015. Retrieved from: http://ethanolproducer.com/articles/11825/eia-predicts-increased-ethanol-production-in-2015-and-2016

50 USDA, ERS. "Corn Supply, Disappearance, and Share of Total Corn Used for Ethanol." Oct. 2016. Retrieved from: www.ers.usda.gov/data-products/us-bioenergy-statistics/us-bioenergy-statistics/#Supply and Disappearance

51 Beckman, Jason, Allison Borchers, and Carol A. Jones. "Agriculture's Supply and Demand for Energy and Energy Products." USDA, ERS. May 2013. Retrieved from: http://ageconsearch.umn.edu/bitstream/149033/2/eib-112.pdf

52 Nelson, Gerald, et al. "Climate Change Effects on Agriculture: Economic Responses to Biophysical Shocks." *Proceedings of the National Academies of Sciences*. Vol. 111, No. 9, 3274–3279, doi: 10.1073/pnas.1222465110. Retrieved from: www.pnas.org/content/111/9/3274.full

53 McGrath, Matt. "Warming Set to Breach 1C Threshold." BBC News, Science and Environment. November 9, 2015. Retrieved from: www.bbc.com/news/science-environment-34763036

54 Metric Conversions. "Celsius to Fahrenheit." Retrieved from: www.metric-conversions.org/temperature/fahrenheit-to-celsius.htm

55 Glickman, Dan. "Climate Change and Agriculture: Challenges and Opportunities." Sept. 22, 2105. Agri-Pulse Communications, Inc. Retrieved from: www.agri-pulse.com/Climate-change-and-agriculture-challenges-and-opportunities-09222015.asp

Chapter 3

A policy analysis toolbox

Methods to investigate agricultural and food market scenarios

US agricultural and food policy is a meaningful field of study. Anyone who cares about how we feed a hungry world can appreciate its significance. It is also intellectually challenging. Complete mastery of the topic requires wide-ranging skills.

This chapter aims to help the reader acquire some of the important skills needed for policy analysis. We know that we can investigate agri-food policy matters from a variety of perspectives – political, psychological, sociological, and economic. Each of these viewpoints can advance our knowledge of farm and food issues. But within the confines of a single textbook chapter, we must narrow our focus.

The approach taken here is to use *economic analysis* as a means to investigate farm and food policies. Our decision to emphasize the economic approach does *not* mean that we overlook other scientific disciplines. Wherever possible, we supplement our analysis with relevant ideas and alternative perspectives.

In this chapter, we assemble a set of investigative methods that we collectively describe as a "policy analysis toolbox". This intellectual toolbox includes applicable economic models that readers can use to explore policy scenarios throughout the remainder of the textbook.

The reader can also go beyond the confines of this textbook to investigate *new* agricultural and food policy options and outcomes. We intend the toolbox to be portable and versatile.

In addition to developing a repertoire of analytical methods for policy appraisal, a related goal is to match the tool to the task. To improve our understanding of how policy choices influence food and agricultural market performance, we must learn to recognize how specific analytical techniques are best suited to address distinct problems or unique situations.

Organization of chapter

The first three chapters of this textbook are preparatory. They establish a solid foundation for the reader to efficiently engage in a wide range of farm and food policy analyses. Chapter 1 provides a broad overview of the policy environment, and a roadmap for the entire textbook. Chapter 2 describes key features of the twentieth and twenty-first century policies that are relevant, if we are to more fully understand the economic landscape of the US agri-food system.

To complete the process of laying the groundwork for effective policy assessment, this third chapter offers an array of economic models for logical analysis and problem solving.

This textbook (and especially this chapter) aims to serve upper-division undergraduate students engaged in food- or agriculturally-related curricula. We expect our readers' academic performance level to be the equivalent of juniors or seniors in a baccalaureate degree program.

For those who have successfully completed courses in microeconomics and macroeconomics principles, Chapter 3 is an opportunity to refresh memories and renew skills. If there are readers examining economic models for the first time, they may wish to refer themselves to one of the standard texts in introductory economics.

We organize the techniques for policy analysis as follows:

- We review the principles of rational decision making, opportunity cost, optimized resource allocation, and marginal analysis in an economy where scarcity is ubiquitous.
- We brush up on the model of supply and demand, and elasticity analysis. The supply-and-demand model is important because it is the primary tool for all fundamental market analysis. Elasticities reveal the sensitivity of markets to changing conditions. We can predict market equilibrium price and quantity responses to a wide range of policy scenarios using the model of supply and demand in combination with elasticity analysis.
- We develop and use the concepts of consumer surplus and producer surplus to determine who gains and loses potential market revenues when new policies alter market outcomes.

- We examine the law of comparative advantage and its consequences for international trade policy.
- We explore the concepts of externalities and public goods in relation to the public policies that influence economic performance in the farm and food sectors.
- We review the analytical techniques of public choice economics to better understand the intersection between the realities of agri-food policy making and the ideal goals of economic efficiency and equity.

Tools for positive economic analysis

As we established in Chapter 1, positive economics is focused on using logical and unbiased methodologies to make valid predictions and determine objective results. *"Tell it like it is"* is a slogan that capsulizes the positivist approach.

Much of economic analysis emphasizes positivism. Decision makers who utilize economic models expect these tools to provide reliable insights into how markets work. In this section of the chapter we primarily review important positivist concepts and models.

Scarcity, opportunity cost, and rationality

Scarcity is the fundamental concept that underlies all economics. Relatively unlimited human wants continually interact with limited resources to generate pervasive scarcity in all economies.

Scarcity necessitates *choice*, and choice creates *opportunity cost*. In a farm operation, when a manager places acreage into the Conservation Reserve Program (CRP), then that resource cannot be simultaneously allocated towards crop production. If crop output is the next best alternative to CRP for the land resource, then the value of the sacrificed crop production is the opportunity cost of choosing to keep the land in CRP.

The economic perspective presumes that decision makers are *goal-oriented, self-interested* and *rational*. In a world where resources are limited, rationality predicts that people normally weigh the extra benefit against the extra cost before making an intentional choice. For example, when buyers and sellers participate in an open-air farmer's market on an early Saturday morning, smiles on the faces of the providers and consumers of the fresh produce are evidence of a very *rational* and enjoyable activity that *creates value for all participants*.

Self-interest in economics is a predicted human behavior; we hypothesize that people typically make choices based on how decisions affect their own welfare. Simply put, self-interest suggests that people choose options that increase their well-being, and shy away from alternatives that leave them worse off. Self-interest does *not* mean selfishness. Self-interested and rational decision makers often give funds to charity and volunteer their time because those actions increase people's feelings of self-worth – they choose activities that leave them better-off.

Economic rationality also implies *optimizing behavior*. Rather than settling for second-best outcomes, the rational decision maker seeks the best result possible. A rational head of household has a goal of seeking the *maximum total satisfaction* within the constraints of limited time and income. As product prices or household income changes, the rational household manager responds by rearranging purchases (more of one item, less of another) to seek a new maximum level of attainable satisfaction.

Similarly, the rational entrepreneur reallocates resources and production to achieve a *maximum attainable profit level*, taking advantage of new revenues and costs created by changing market conditions.

The *rational economic model* predicts that farm managers maximize total net returns by skillfully handling both the costs and revenues of their operations. On the cost side, producers hire natural resources (land, fertility, water, etc.); choose productive technologies (GPS, machinery, fertilizers, and advanced seed varieties); employ appropriate labor time/skills, and endure the weather (both good and bad). On the revenue side, farm managers must choose enterprises (crops, animals, CRP, etc.) and marketing strategies (spot markets, contracting, futures) to generate sales levels that can produce the best possible net returns.

Marginal analysis and optimization

When we apply rationality theory, we declare that economic participants make purposeful and optimal choices. The rational model is also designed to be fully logically consistent. All decisions, large and small, are governed by the same motives.

In economic analysis, we often examine decision making "at the margin." If the decisions guiding an overall operation are rational, then the same standard of rationality should logically apply when managing each associated incremental (i.e. marginal) transaction.

When we break down a larger system into its smaller components, we reveal the power of marginal analysis in economics. The usefulness of economics as a policy analysis tool often stems from applying the marginal principle to address challenging problems.

Marginal analysis is a step-by-step process. We incrementally weigh extra benefits against extra costs to guide our choices. To achieve a maximum total net return from an activity, we rationally expand the activity while the extra benefit of another unit exceeds its additional cost. We achieve an optimum activity level, and cease its expansion, when the *marginal cost of the last unit just equals its marginal benefit*.

The *equi-marginal principle* is very important. It tells us how an economy achieves the best overall gain in efficiency. Economically efficient resource allocation occurs at the point where marginal benefit and marginal cost are equal. Why is this true? Will policy makers pay attention to the recommendation?

Marginal analysis of the Minnesota farmland-waterway buffer-strip scenario

To address the potential role of the equi-marginal principle, let's use an example. Suppose the State of Minnesota (MN) considers a policy proposal requiring MN farm producers to increase the width of buffer-strips on their farmland adjacent to waterways.

Buffer strips are a natural protection against extra farm-sourced pollutants entering into watersheds. Buffer strips, when they perform as designed, act as a natural "sponge" that absorb excess soil and nutrient runoff from acreages in crop production. The basic idea behind establishing *wider* buffer-strips is to further reduce runoff and achieve additional improvement in water quality.

In the MN buffer-strip scenario, if we apply the principle of marginal analysis, then the *most economically efficient* amount of new buffer-strip acreage would occur in the instance where the *extra benefit* of new water quality improvement *just equals* the *extra cost* of establishing another acre of buffer-strip-coverage along waterways. This is the equi-marginal principle in action.

The question of buffer-strip widths on MN farms was a real policy consideration in the 2015 session of the MN Legislature.[1] When the initial policy proposal was reviewed by legislative committees (before a final version came to a full-floor vote), the suggested plan was to *increase the minimum buffer-strip width* from 16-and-a-half feet on either side of waterways to a 50-foot width on each side. Promoters of the proposal argued that a significant increase in buffer-strip area was needed to make a noticeable improvement in the quality of MN waterways. Detractors argued that the *33-and-a-half foot increase* in buffer-strip width was a "one-size-fits-all" prescription that would divert thousands of acres of land from valuable crop production.

In this scenario, *both sides* of the MN buffer-strip debate discussed benefits and costs, but *neither side* focused on the efficient equi-marginal principle as a possible solution. If the debate had considered the economic perspective of marginal analysis, then different types of questions could have been addressed.

For example, what is the extra value gain in water quality associated with widening a buffer-strip by 1-foot? What is the extra opportunity cost of lost crop output value associated with diverting a 1-foot wide swath of land into buffer-strip plantings? Economists would argue that we need to gather such marginal cost and benefit measurements if we care about achieving an outcome that is economically efficient for the overall economy.

How would we recognize the "economically efficient solution" in a graphical analysis? Please examine Figure 3.1 below.

When we consider *marginal benefit*, we can reasonably hypothesize that the *"law of diminishing returns"* is applicable to extra 1-foot swaths of buffer strips. The first few feet of buffer-strip widening would likely have significant impacts on improved water quality. But, at some point, as additional feet of buffer-strip width occur, the marginal gains in improved water quality would decrease. Consequently, the slope of the marginal benefit curve would be negative – as the area of buffer-strips increases, the marginal benefit of another acre of buffer-strip land would decrease.

When we consider *marginal cost*, we can reasonably assume that there would be rising extra costs to increase buffer-strip widths. As producers hire the resources to convert cropland into cover-crops for buffer-strips, the scarcity of the equipment, labor, and supplies for buffer-strip establishment would increase, based on the *"law of increasing opportunity cost."* Consequently, the slope of the marginal cost curve would be positive – as the area of buffer-strips increases, the marginal cost of establishing another acre of buffer-strip land would increase.

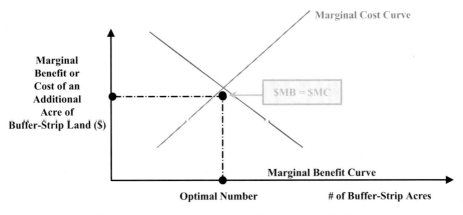

Figure 3.1 Marginal benefit and marginal cost of an additional acre of buffer-strip land.

Ideally, MN should add new acres of buffer-strip land right up to the point where the marginal cost of another buffer-strip acre just equals the marginal benefit of the gain in water quality associated with that extra acre of buffer-strip land. From the standpoint of marginal analysis, the "*optimal total number*" of buffer-strip acres occurs at the intersection of the marginal benefit and marginal cost curves.

The logic of the equi-marginal principle has the potential of contributing rational economic reasoning to a highly contested policy debate. Economic principles offer a solution that balances the extra cost and extra benefit of widening MN's farmland-waterway buffer-strips.

Supply and demand: fundamentals of market analysis

A competitive market is also a mechanism that balances out benefits and costs. Without direction from any central authority, buyers and sellers voluntarily participate in markets and establish equilibrium prices for scarce goods and resources.

Are agri-food markets alive and well in the twenty-first century? Evidence of market activity is everywhere. For example, in 2014 the Chicago Mercantile Exchange, Inc. (CME) (where farm commodity futures market contracts are actively traded) reported a *daily average* of over 3.2 million contracts exchanged. The average CME trading volume grows larger each year.[2]

Markets are a key allocator for food, agriculture, and the entire US economy. How do we analyze them? In 1890, Alfred Marshall developed and graphically illustrated the model of supply and demand.[3] He also introduced and demonstrated how elasticity measurements provide key insights into market-price responsiveness.

Marshall's contributions are remarkable, measured by any standard. One hundred and twenty-five years later, supply-and-demand analysis continues to be the backbone of all microeconomics. Elasticity studies are vital tools in economic research. If markets are the major driving force in the US economy, then the model of supply and demand is the primary means for understanding how and why those individual markets guide the economy's performance.

This section of Chapter 3 aims to renew the reader's familiarity and skills in applying the supply-and-demand model. The usefulness of elasticities in predicting market responsiveness and volatility is also reviewed. This presentation is intended for an audience with previous exposure to these techniques in an economics principles course.

Foundations and organization of the supply-and-demand model (S&D Model)

Buyers and sellers in the S&D Model are rational decision makers seeking to conduct transactions in a competitive market. They pursue their respective self-interests as they modify quantities demanded and supplied in response to price changes (and to variations in other market determinants). The S&D Model predicts that the opposing but rational behaviors of buyers and sellers ultimately produce an equilibrium price and quantity that clear the market of any surpluses or shortages.

To review the S&D Model, we first explore the supply side, then the demand side, and finally examine the price determination process produced by interactions of supply and demand.

The supply function

Ceteris paribus, the *Law of Supply* predicts that sellers increase their quantity supplied in response to an increase in market price; and conversely, sellers react to a decreased market price by reducing their quantity supplied. In a two-dimensional graph, market price is an independent variable measured on the vertical axis, and quantity supplied is a dependent variable gauged on the horizontal. The Law of Supply is a direct relationship, and is commonly displayed as a positively sloped straight line. See Figure 3.2 below.

The marginal cost function is the supply offered by a single competitive firm. The horizontal summation of firms' individual curves is the market supply function.

Firms' quantity-supplied responses to price changes occur *along the slope* of the supply function. In Figure 3.2, the quantity reaction to price would be a "sliding movement" up and down the slope of the supply function.

Variability of the non-price supply determinants *shifts the supply function*. An "increase in supply" is a rightward shift, and a "decrease in supply" is a leftward shift. See Figure 3.3 below. Non-price supply determinants include:

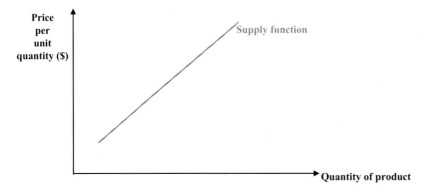

Figure 3.2 Supply function: positive slope illustrates the law of supply.

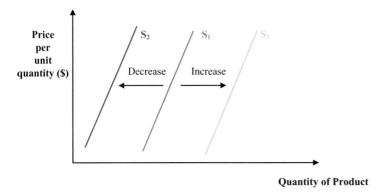

Figure 3.3 Increases and decreases in the supply function.

- Changes in prices of resources (land, labor, capital, entrepreneurship).
- Changes in government subsidies and business taxes.
- Changes in technology; changes in natural production conditions.
- Changes in the prices (profitability) of other products.
- Changes in expected future prices by sellers.
- Changes in the market supply caused by changes in the number of individual suppliers.

Changes in demand are *not* a supply determinant. As demand shifts, the market equilibrium price adjusts, and the supply slope determines the seller's response to new prices. The converse is also true; supply changes are not demand determinants.

The demand function

Ceteris paribus, the *Law of Demand* predicts that buyers increase their quantity demanded in response to a decrease in market price; and conversely, buyers react to a decreased market price by increasing their quantity demanded. Similar to the supply side, the market price is the independent variable and quantity demanded is dependent. The Law of Demand is an inverse relationship, and is commonly displayed as a negatively sloped straight line. See Figure 3.4 below.

The demand function represents the price response of a utility optimizing consumer. Horizontal summation of individual consumer demand curves produces the market demand function.

Consumer reaction to variations in the price determinant occur along the demand function slope. In Figure 3.4, the quantity reaction to price would be a "sliding movement" up and down the slope of the demand function.

Changes in non-price demand determinants shift the demand function. Rightward shifts indicate increasing demand, and leftward shifts signal decreased demand. See Figure 3.5 below. Non-price demand determinants include:

- Changes in consumer income (changing demand for normal and inferior goods).
- Changes in prices of consumer substitutes and/or consumer complements.
- Changes in consumer tastes and preferences.
- Changes in expected future prices by consumers.
- Changes in the market demand caused by changes in the number of individual buyers.

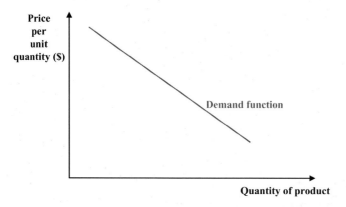

Figure 3.4 Demand function: negative slope illustrates the Law of Demand.

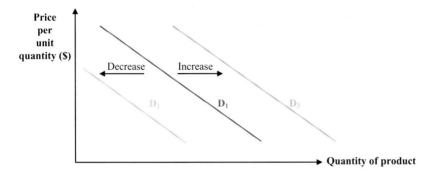

Figure 3.5 Increases and decreases in the demand function.

Shifts of the demand curve illustrate that consumers are willing and able to alter their quantities purchased at different price levels, as they respond to changes in relevant non-price determinants.

When demand movements are considered in concert with the supply function, then we are prepared to predict how equilibrium prices are initially established, and then change, as market forces are exerted.

Supply and demand together: market price determination

In the S&D Model, all participants are price takers; buyers and sellers react to price changes, they do not control them. Similar to real-world bidding practices, such as the CME's open outcry method (or its present-day electronic equivalent), the S&D Model is a process of price discovery.[4]

The S&D Model includes mechanisms to ensure that market-price determination occurs. Bidding processes in the model can begin at any price level. Ultimately, the rational decisions of many buyers and sellers create a stable equilibrium price that clears the market of surpluses or shortages.

Scenarios of how markets free themselves of temporary surpluses or shortages demonstrate how stable equilibria are established. In Figure 3.6 below, a buyer-driven auction

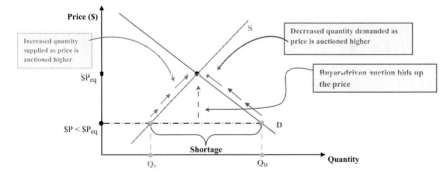

Figure 3.6 Temporary market shortage cleared by buyer-driven auction process.

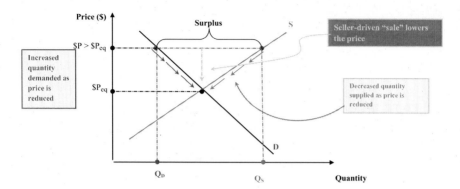

Figure 3.7 Temporary market surplus cleared by seller-driven "sale" process.

process eliminates a shortage. Or, if suppliers offer reduced prices ("have a sale"), then surpluses are dissipated. See Figure 3.7.

Market shortage analysis

Shortages are temporary in the S&D Model. A market shortage occurs when:

Current Market Price ($P) < Equilibrium Price ($P$_{eq}$), and consequently,

Quantity Demanded (Q$_D$) > Quantity Supplied (Q$_S$)

Because buyers cannot obtain the entire quantity demanded at the current price, the shortage triggers an auction. As displayed in Figure 3.6 above, the buyer-driven auction bids up the price until the shortage = 0 at the equilibrium price, and then the auction ceases. Because auctions instantly form when shortages occur, the S&D Model predicts that shortages are temporary. The market moves toward the equilibrium price. When a news agency reports that a "price spike" has occurred in a commodity market, or in food retailing, we can often link that rapid price change to a market shortage adjustment

Market surplus analysis

Surpluses are temporary in the S&D Model. A market surplus occurs when:

Current Market Price ($P) > Equilibrium Price ($P$_{eq}$), and consequently,

Quantity Demanded (Q$_D$) < Quantity Supplied (Q$_S$)

Because suppliers cannot sell the entire quantity supplied at the current price, the surplus triggers a "sale." As displayed in Figure 3.7 above, the seller-driven sale decreases the price until the surplus = 0 at the equilibrium price, and then the sale ceases. Because sales instantly arise when surpluses occur, the S&D Model predicts that surpluses are temporary. The market again moves toward the equilibrium price.

In 2015, news reports of a "glut" in fuel markets have been associated with dropping energy prices. Such events are logically consistent with S&D Model's prediction of how markets manage surpluses.

Market equilibrium analysis

After market mechanisms have reduced both surpluses and shortages to zero, the current market price becomes the equilibrium market price. In a modern world where technology allows market participants to make market adjustments in microseconds, surpluses and shortages disappear rapidly. Market equilibria are established in an instant of time. What are the characteristics of these equilibria?

Examine Figure 3.8 below. When a market reaches an equilibrium point, then buyers and sellers are agreed on the same quantity to transact. The absence of surpluses and shortages means that *no* market participants are motivated to create auctions or sales. Because buyers or sellers are not exerting any pressure, the market price stabilizes. As a result, we can think of an equilibrium price as relatively steady. We can use that equilibrium as a reference point for future analysis.

As in all of economics, there are provisos that must be stated, even in the case of a market equilibrium. A very important proviso, or stipulation, about the stability of an equilibrium price is its dependence on *relative calm* amid non-price market determinants. If neither the supply nor the demand function has any reason to shift, then we can think about an equilibrium as an enduring market price level. Such a tranquil scenario, which may only briefly exist in the real world of a fast-paced society, is illustrated in Figure 3.8

Equilibria are stable in the S&D Model, when market non-price determinants are constant. A market equilibrium occurs when:

Current Market Price ($P) = Equilibrium Price ($P$_{eq}$), and consequently,

Quantity Demanded (Q$_D$) = Quantity Supplied (Q$_S$)

Because suppliers and consumers agree to transact the exact same quantity at the current price, there are no surpluses or shortages to trigger price movements. As displayed in Figure 3.8 above, both buyers and sellers are satisfied at the equilibrium price. The price remains steady because no market participant has a motive to change it, and no curve is currently shifting. The market converges to the equilibrium price, and remains there (until the market is "stirred up" by a change in a market non-price determinant).

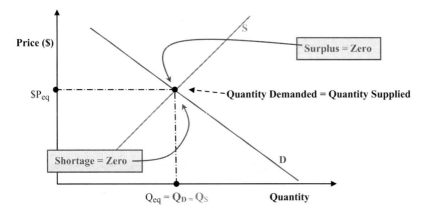

Figure 3.8 Current market operating at an equilibrium price and quantity.

Analysis of changing market equilibria

Using the S&D Model, we predict that shifts of either/both supply and/or demand alter the market's equilibrium position.

On any given day in the real-world economy, market equilibrium prices are typically very fluid. There are good reasons for this fluidity. Non-price market determinants vary daily, or even more rapidly.

Farm producers and food procurement managers who frequently check their smartphones to see "how the markets are doing" are fully aware that market prices can change quickly. When we think about this in the context of S&D analysis, we can conclude that the compulsion to "check markets" is a good indication that non-price determinants are rarely static; in fact, they are very dynamic at all times.

The S&D Model is a well-tested apparatus for making logical connections between price movements and market events. When we properly employ our knowledge of how non-price determinants influence markets, then we have a good chance of developing an accurate picture of what markets are doing, and why. Intellectual mastery of the S&D Model's analytical powers will serve us well as we begin to make predictions of how new government policies might affect market performance.

Changes in market equilibria: some examples

In the above discussion, we established that a pair of supply-and-demand functions create a market system that converges on an equilibrium price and quantity. We can put this knowledge to work, and examine some typical scenarios that arise in agriculture and food markets. Let's take a look at three scenarios:

- Scenario One – The US Food and Drug Administration (FDA) requires farms and agribusiness firms to meet new science-based standards for the growing, harvesting, packing, and holding of fresh produce for human consumption. What is the immediate expected impact on the equilibrium price and quantity in produce markets?
- Scenario Two – The US Dollar strengthens significantly in global currency markets, causing foreign consumers to encounter a noticeable change in the price of US beef exports, and foreign beef producers to view the US consumer as a more lucrative market opportunity. What is the immediate expected impact on the equilibrium price and quantity in US beef markets?
- Scenario Three – Breakthroughs in breeding technology produce a new strain of sweet sorghum that is higher-yielding, more disease-resistant, and has increased adaptability for cultivation across a much wider range of climate zones. What is the immediate expected impact on the equilibrium price and quantity in the sweet sorghum market?

Detailed S&D Modeling of the three identified scenarios follows below. Our goal is to examine each situation, determine if the primary impact is on the supply side or the demand side, predict if the change will cause an increase or decrease in supply or demand, and finally track the net changes in equilibrium price and quantity associated with the scenario event.

Scenario One: supply-and-demand analysis of the fresh produce market

Industry compliance with new FDA science standards:

- Assume there is a market for fresh produce; then we can analyze the interaction of produce supply and demand.
- Assume that compliance with new science standards requires extra resources – therefore implementing the new standards *increases produce's marginal cost* of production.
- Because the new FDA regulation is directly affecting firms (not consumers), we analyze this situation as a change in a supply-side non-price determinant.
- A *decrease in supply* is associated with an increase in marginal cost – as a result, the produce supply function shifts to the left.
- Market Response – The immediate impact of industry compliance with the new FDA science-based standards is an *increase in the equilibrium produce price* and *a decrease in equilibrium produce quantity*. See Figure 3.9 below.

Scenario Two: supply-and-demand analysis of the US beef market

The US dollar strengthens in global currency exchange markets:

- Assume there is a US Beef Market. We analyze the interaction of the supply and demand for beef in the US. Both domestic beef demand and domestic beef supply can be supplemented by foreign sources.
- A currency value appreciation of the US Dollar increases the cost of US beef exports for foreign consumers. *Export demand for US beef decreases.*

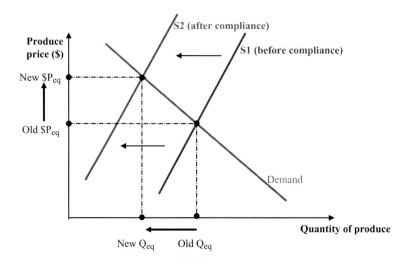

Figure 3.9 Immediate impact in Scenario One: decrease in produce supply caused by increased marginal cost of new FDA science-standard compliance.

- A strong US Dollar also encourages foreign beef producers to increase their sales to US consumers. US imports of overseas beef increase, supplementing the supply of US beef. The supply of beef (*domestic- plus foreign-produced*) increases. *Beef supply in the US shifts to the right.*
- Because the stronger dollar affects overall demand and supply, we analyze this situation as both a *change in demand* and a *change in supply* associated with a non-price determinant (the US Currency value).
- We predict a *decrease in US beef demand* because of the increased US Dollar value – therefore the beef demand (domestic plus foreign) function shifts to the left. We also predict an *increase in the supply of beef in the US*, as foreign producers export larger amounts their beef to the US. The supply of beef in the US shifts to the right.
- Market Response – The immediate impact of a stronger US Dollar in currency markets is a decrease in the equilibrium US Beef price and an indeterminate change in equilibrium beef quantity (without more data on the size of the opposing shifts of supply and demand, we do not know which change in Qeq will dominate). See Figure 3.10 below.

Scenario Three: supply-and-demand analysis of the sorghum market

New technology increases yield, disease resistance, and geographic climate range

- Assume there is a sorghum market. We analyze the interaction of sorghum's supply and demand.
- New technology increases sorghum production output and efficiency.
- Farm operations who grow sorghum directly benefit from the higher yields, better resistance, and wider planting range. We analyze this situation as a change in a supply-side non-price determinant.
- An *increase in supply* is associated with an increase in productivity-enhancing technology. Consequently, the sorghum supply function shifts to the right.
- Market Response – The immediate impact of improved sorghum production technology is a *decrease in the equilibrium sorghum price and an increase in equilibrium sorghum quantity.* See Figure 3.11 below.

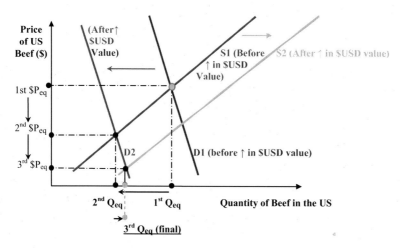

Figure 3.10 Immediate impact in Scenario Two: a decrease in US beef demand, and an increase in US beef supply, caused by increased us dollar value in global currency markets.

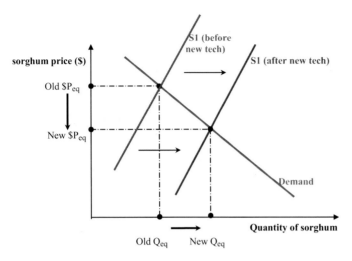

Figure 3.11 Immediate impact in Scenario Three: increase in sorghum supply caused by improved production technology.

What are the "lessons learned" as we use the S&D Model to examine various market scenarios, such as the three examples above? We can summarize some of the major analytical contributions as follows:

- In every scenario, it is important to identify whether the studied events are primarily *supply-side* or *demand-side* phenomena, or sometimes both. In the real world, there are often more complex scenarios (such as Scenario Two) where combinations of supply-side and demand-side influences are simultaneously at work. The contributing factors must be properly sorted out. We are seeking well-reasoned and accurate analyses. This step in S&D modeling is often difficult, but it is critical. We need to know what types of forces are driving market changes.
- Once we have figured out if an event is a supply determinant or a demand determinant or both, then the next step is to *observe the direction of the change(s)*. Is the event causing an increase or a decrease in the market function? Will the function shift left or right? It may seem simple to make this determination, but appearances can be deceiving. Again, the analyst may want to proceed as a carpenter does: "Measure twice, cut once." Make sure you know the direction that the market is headed.
- As a market's equilibria vary, there are always two fluctuations worth reporting: *the net changes in both Equilibrium Price and Equilibrium Quantity*. Supply-and-demand analysis is often referred to as a "model of price determination." While this observation is true, in many cases it is also important to know about how the product volumes are changing.

Analyzing proportionate market responses: demand-and-supply elasticities

As noted above, S&D analysis allows us to predict the direction of change for a market's equilibrium price and/or quantity. While knowledge of these S&D results is useful, we can learn more. We can unearth additional market information if we measure the price-to-quantity relationship proportionately. In the lexicon of an economist, we use the concept of "elasticity" to examine proportional change. There are solid reasons to study and apply elasticities.

For example, it might be important to know whether wheat demand is more sensitive to price changes than is beef demand. Wheat volume is usually determined in bushels (bu), and commercial beef quantities are often measured in hundred-weights (cwt). Is the bushel comparable to the hundred-weight, when we want to know which product is more price responsive? If our measurements are not equivalent, then we need a more universal approach. If we convert our data into proportions (percentages), then we have a convenient way to compare the market sensitivities of commodities with dissimilar units of measure.

General principles guiding elasticity measurements

An elasticity is a ratio. An elasticity determines a coefficient that expresses the proportional responsiveness of a dependent variable in relation to an independent variable. For example, the Price Elasticity of Demand (ε_D) gauges the proportional response of quantity demanded in relation to a proportional price change.

In mathematical notation, we can display ε_D as:

$$\varepsilon_D = (\Delta Q_D/Q_D) \div (\Delta P/P)$$

Where:　ε_D = Price Elasticity of Demand

ΔQ_D = Change in Quantity Demanded

Q_D = Base Quantity Demanded Level

ΔP = Change in Price

P = Base Price Level

To consistently determine an elasticity ratio coefficient, the dependent variable is placed in the numerator, and the independent variable is in the denominator.

Using mathematical definitions, the "slope" of an economic relationship is a ratio of variables measured in natural units, whereas *elasticities are ratios of proportions*. Consequently, an elasticity is not a slope. However, when we study a particular relationship, we observe that both slope and elasticity ratios share the same sign. For example, in the case of a demand function, if the slope is negative, then the corresponding elasticity will also be negative.

We have a nomenclature to help interpret the meaning of elasticity coefficient values. We can identify relationships as elastic, unitary elastic, inelastic, or unrelated, based on the measurement outcome. For example, if the absolute value of an elasticity coefficient (ε) is greater than +1.0, we classify that relationship as "elastic" – which means that the quantity response to the change in the independent variable is considered "strong" or "sensitive." We can develop a small table (Table 3.1) to conveniently connect the coefficient values to their classifications and interpretations, as follows:

Table 3.1 General guidelines for interpreting elasticity (ε) coefficients

Elasticity Coefficient (ε) Value	Classification of the ε coefficient	Interpretation of the ε Coefficient Value
$|ε| > +1.0$	Elastic	Relatively sensitive response of dependent variable to changes in independent variable.
$|ε| = +1.0$	Unitary Elastic	Proportional value of dependent variable equals proportional value of independent variable.
$0.0 < |ε| < +1.0$	Inelastic	Relatively insensitive response of dependent variable to changes in independent variable.
$|ε| \approx 0.0$	Perfectly Inelastic	Changes in Dependent Variable not consistently related to Changes in Independent Variable. The slope is perfectly vertical.
$|ε| \approx +\infty$	Perfectly Elastic	An infinitely large change in the dependent variable related to an infinitely small change in the independent variable. the slope is perfectly horizontal.

Demand-side elasticities

Elasticity measurements can help relevant economic participants more accurately gauge market responsiveness to changing conditions. A better understanding of *consumer sensitivity* to variations in price and consumer income is useful information for a variety of decision makers.

Agribusinesses, food retailers, and government agencies (e.g. FDA, USDA) can utilize demand-side elasticities to better anticipate consumer purchasing patterns, and consequently improve their ability to satisfy demand with more effective prhoduction schedules, delivery patterns and incentive programs.

While a variety of elasticity coefficients can be determined, three of the more important demand-side elasticity ratios are:

- Price Elasticity of Demand ($ε_D$).
- Cross-Price Elasticity of Demand ($ε_X$).
- Consumer Income Elasticity of Demand ($ε_I$).

Immediately below, we review key aspects of these three demand-side elasticities, and their particular relevance to the US farm and food system.

Price elasticity of demand ($ε_D$)

Whenever a discussion of market economics arises in relation to food and agriculture in the US, the topic of Price Elasticity of Demand ($ε_D$) almost inevitably is included. This ($ε_D$) measurement is often identified as the "own-price" demand elasticity. Certain distinguishing market characteristics heavily influence the nature of the $ε_D$ coefficient that predominates throughout the agri-food system. Those characteristics are:

- Food is a necessity of life.
- Consumers do not have realistic substitute products that can reasonably replace the nutritional value of food.

- Many foods are perishable; they have short shelf lives that limit storage capacity.
- There are important segments of the food consumer markets that must adhere to strict dietary requirements (e.g. lactose intolerance, gluten-free diets, food allergies, etc.).

How does this set of special conditions influence the prevailing ε_D in the agri-food system? Considered together, the above-mentioned food attributes mean that food consumers are very likely to exhibit an insensitive quantity-demanded response to price changes. In other words, we can reasonably expect that *the market-level ε_D for many food and agricultural products is* **inelastic**:

$$0 < \left| \varepsilon_D \right| < +1.0$$

What are some consequences associated with the predominance of price-inelastic market demand for food and agriculture? One outcome is the pattern of total revenue for food producers. Total Revenue (TR) is equal to price times quantity ($TR = P \times Q$). Inelastic market demand implies that an increase in food prices generates an increase in total revenue, while a price decrease is associated with decreased total revenue.

Price elasticity of demand and revenue volatility

As the $\left| \varepsilon_D \right|$ coefficient decreases in value, the demand relationship becomes *more price-inelastic*. In the case of highly price-inelastic demand, then the *net change in total revenue* associated with price variation becomes *more volatile* (changes by a greater proportion).

In some instances, the demand for specific food items can be *very inelastic*. Most experienced farm producers know that total revenue for their operations can swing rapidly from hefty net increases to large net decreases. *Price-inelastic market demand is a major contributing factor that creates high volatility in the total revenue of farm operations.* When farm producers say that they need effective strategies to cope with market financial risks, they are "telling it like it is."

Knowledge is power. Decision makers who understand the price elasticity of demand in their markets are in a better position to more effectively manage risks, costs, and revenues in their operations.

For example, we know that the perfectly competitive market model is a close approximation of a farm operator's economic situation. We observe that each farm firm is a price-taker for its marketed product. The single farm owner-operator has no control over the product's market price, and therefore the individual price-elasticity of demand is "perfectly elastic." The farm operator encounters the very challenging situation of enduring volatility in total revenue caused by an *industry-level price-inelastic demand*, while simultaneously managing the farm as a "price-taker" that faces *perfectly price-elastic demand at the firm level*.

Price elasticity of demand and the cost-price squeeze

The price elasticity of demand is also a tool for understanding the "*cost-price squeeze*" that continually challenges participants in food and agricultural markets. When a farm producer enters input markets to hire productive resources (such as fertilizers, pesticides, specialized farm equipment, etc.), then the price-elasticity of the factor demand function must be considered.

The modern farm business often requires specialized technological inputs that have few substitutes. Consequently, price-inelastic factor demand functions are common in food and agricultural production. When we combine a perfectly-elastic demand curve on the product revenue side with price-inelastic factor demand function on the resource cost-side, the scenario of the cost-price squeeze comes into focus.

When farm input prices rise, *price-inelastic factor demand* means the producers cannot easily reduce their quantity demanded for these resources, and their total cost expenditures increase. At the same moment, *price-elastic demand for their product-output* means that farm producers have no individual power to pass along cost increases to their consumers. Costs rise, and revenues do not; therefore, we have a classic case of the cost-price squeeze that challenges individual farm and food producers.

Elasticity tools help us to comprehend why certain types of financial challenges will likely always be a part of participating in the farm and food economy. Successful management outcomes for farm and food firms will involve accurate assessments of how price-elasticity conditions influence net returns. This knowledge also highlights the importance of developing strategies that help farm and food businesses anticipate and endure the financial stress. Apparently, elasticity conditions will persistently test the business acumen and adaptability of agri-food system participants.

Cross-price elasticity of demand (ε_x)

Why is the measurement of ε_x important? The short answer to this question is that we engineer better-designed policies if we take into account secondary or tertiary policy effects. We can attain increased understanding of how industries are economically interconnected if we have an idea of how changes in one industry influence the performance of other industries. Reliable estimates of ε_x can provide insights in these cross-industry linkages.

Policy makers and related interests often view new policy initiatives in terms of their primary goals or major impacts. Earlier in Chapter 2, we learned that policies can also have unintended and/or unanticipated consequences. A more thorough review of what to expect from a policy initiative involves recognition of additional effects. In some cases, side effects are key economic considerations for entire industries.

For example, the implementation of new government-mandated food safety practices may disproportionately increase the cost burden on smaller-sized firms. The cost imbalance may be the impetus for creating markets that have more highly concentrated competitive structures where larger firms wield increased market power.

In the case of ε_x, we use the economic theory of household consumer expenditure patterns and relevant data to determine estimates of whether pairs of goods are substitutes, complements, or unrelated. We can examine Table 3.2 to associate the ε_x coefficient values to their appropriate categories:

Substitutes and the cross-price elasticity of demand (ε_x)

Based on the ε_x classifications in Table 3.2 above, we can identify some agri-food examples of how product pairs are economically related. When we consider the impact of an increase in the price of beef on the quantity demanded for pork, we can cite a USDA study that identifies beef and pork as consumer substitutes. The USDA beef price-to-pork quantity unconditional estimate is +0.48. This positive ε_x coefficient is evidence of consumer substitutes.

Table 3.2 Interpreting cross-price elasticity (ε_x) coefficient values

Elasticity Coefficient (ε_x) Value	Interpretation of the ε_x Coefficient for Products A & B	Classification of the ε_x Coefficient Value
$\varepsilon_x > 0$	Direct relationship between price of Product A and Quantity of Product B	Evidence that Products A&B are **Substitutes**
$\varepsilon_x < 0$	Inverse relationship between price of Product A and Quantity of Product B	Evidence that Products A&B are **Complements**
$\varepsilon_x \approx 0$	No regular relationship between Price of Product A and Quantity of Product B	Evidence that Products A&B are **Unrelated Products**

It is perhaps no surprise that US households consume increased pork quantities in response to increased beef prices.[5]

Complements and the cross-price elasticity of demand (ε_x)

Consumer complements are products that households commonly consume jointly. For example, when a household orders a pizza or serves pasta, it is typical for a tomato-based marinara sauce to be part of that cuisine. It is also true that annual US tomato consumption is very large. Next to potatoes, tomatoes are the second-most US-consumed vegetable.[6] Tomatoes have many more uses beyond combinations with pizza and spaghetti. While the nature of tomatoes as a complement for popular consumer menu items (e.g. pizza) is easily identifiable, the tremendous volume of overall tomato consumption can overwhelm the influence of particular cross-price consumer behaviors.

When the USDA consumer expenditure study examined the cross-price elasticity for tomato quantities and the price of the "rice and pasta" category, the estimated ε_x was negative, but only by a slight margin (−0.07). Similarly, the ε_x between tomato quantities and "other bakery products" was (−0.08).[7] These estimates, statistically speaking, are not significantly different from zero. In these instances, our statistical estimation methods may be detecting some product complementarity, but the relationship is overshadowed by the sheer volume of tomato usage. The ε_x estimate might also be more accurate if the paired variable of "rice and pasta" could be disaggregated into its component products.

Unrelated products and the cross-price elasticity of demand (ε_x)

There are pairs of products where typical household purchasing decisions are not logically connected. For example, the USDA category of "coffee and tea quantity" was estimated to have an ε_x equal to 0.00 in relation to the price of tomatoes.[8] In this case, the typical household has little reason to engage in a predictable purchasing pattern with respect to tomato price and purchases of tea and coffee. We can normally expect that these two product categories should have a $\varepsilon_x = 0.0$, indicating that they are unrelated.

On the other hand, when the price of tomatoes is compared to the category of "processed fruits and vegetables," the USDA reports an ε_x equal to −0.77.[9] There are salsas, sauces and juices where tomatoes are combined with other vegetables to please consumer palates.

Here we have evidence of product complements. As the prices of other vegetables decrease, it is rational to combine additional quantities of tomatoes to complement the other vegetables and produce more affordable and appealing combinations that increase household consumer satisfaction.

Consumer-income elasticity of demand (ε_I)

If consumer households become more affluent, then their definition of what is considered "affordable" can change. It is reasonable to expect that consumer expenditure patterns evolve as average household income rises.

In Chapter 2, we explored how US consumer household spending on food-related items became increasingly sophisticated as the socio-economic status of the typical US household continually evolved during the twentieth century. That evolution continues in the twenty-first century. The gradual but unrelenting changes in the typical US household are affecting the Consumer-Income Elasticity of Demand (ε_I) for a variety of food items and categories. We can examine Table 3.3 to identify particular classes of goods as household consumer income changes:

The ε_I Coefficient values in Table 3.3 have applications in the food and agricultural economy. One dynamic household food consumption habit affected by ε_I is the location where the consumption occurs. Wealthier consumers can afford to enjoy Food Away From Home (FAFH). Lower-income households, or households who experience loss of employment and income during recessions, are associated with an increased frequency of consuming Food At Home (FAH). In the 2012 USDA consumer expenditure study, a combination of empirical evidence and advanced economic modeling provided important insights into linkages between changing household budgets and the consumption patterns for FAFH and FAH.

In 2009, FAFH accounted for about 41 percent of the average US household food budget. In 1984, the FAFH proportion of household food expenditures was only 29 percent. Household food consumption patterns are definitely changing.[10]

Collected data provide evidence that the nutritional nature of FAFH is noticeably different than FAH. Household demand elasticities for FAH and FAFH are also unalike. For example, if we allow household total expenditure to serve as a proxy for household income, then the USDA can approximate the household ε_I response to changing income levels.

Table 3.3 Interpreting household consumer-income demand elasticity (ε_I) coefficient values

Elasticity Coefficient (ε_I) Value	Classification of the ε_I Coefficient	Interpretation of the ε_I Coefficient Value
$\varepsilon_I < 0$	Inferior Good	Good's quantity demanded inversely related to consumer income
$\varepsilon_I \approx 0$	Income-Neutral Good	Good's quantity demanded not related to consumer income
$0.0 < \varepsilon_I < +1.0$	Normal Good	Good's quantity demanded directly related to consumer income
$\varepsilon_I > +1.0$	Superior Good	Good's quantity demanded is elastic and directly related to consumer income

The 2012 USDA consumer study determined that FAFH demand is more sensitive to changing income than is FAH. During the 2009–2011 US "great recession," the FAFH household budget share markedly decreased, while FAH share of the household food budget increased.[11]

To sketch an image of US household expenditures and the associated elasticities, we should first examine the budget shares for food and non-food categories. The 2012 USDA expenditure study determined that the average US household spends 19 percent on food, and 81 percent of total expenditures on non-food items. US households are very fortunate that food is generally affordable and a relatively smaller budget expenditure.[12]

Of course, within this 19 percent of the total US household budget, FAFH has grown in importance. FAFH occupies more than 40 percent of the food budget for the typical US household. When we examine income demand elasticities, we discover that the household ε_I equals +1.21 for non-foods, +0.21 for Food Away From Home (FAFH), and +0.11 for dairy products consumed at home.[13] Using the ε_I classification system in Table 3.3, non-foods are a superior good – the non-food expenditures change proportionately more than does household income.

On the other hand, FAFH and at-home dairy products are normal goods – and, we can observe that FAFH is nearly twice as income-responsive as compared to at-home consumption of dairy products. In another expenditure study (Bergtold, Akobundu and Peterson 2004), the at-home production of "biscuits, rolls and muffins" exhibited an $\varepsilon_I = -0.55$.[14] This negatively signed ε_I estimate suggests that food items produced at home are inferior goods – households purchase and consume lesser quantities of these items as household income rises.

The 2012 USDA expenditure study also referenced other studies indicating that consumers are purchasing greater amounts of "less healthy" foods. Household food choices are contributing to a serious US obesity problem. The increased prevalence of "less healthy" food consumption is connected to the increase in the FAFH share of the food budget. Another recent policy concern is whether the food and agriculture sector can reduce its carbon footprint as part of an overall effort to reduce the adverse effects of climate change.[15]

One of the important conclusions in the USDA 2012 expenditure study is closely connected to proposals that aim to encourage healthier food choices. The USDA expenditure study determined that US household choices between FAFH and FAH exhibit significant and complex differences in demand elasticities.

Any single policy initiative (such as advocacy for healthy food consumption) is likely to face difficulties because household own-price, cross-price, and income-demand elasticities produce diverse and unexpected responses to new policy incentives. The USDA expenditure study demonstrated considerable *dissimilarity* between household consumer behavior in the FAH and FAFH markets.[16]

The continued growth of FAFH markets means that the policy challenges will also expand. Additional expenditure studies and very carefully crafted policies will be needed, if there are to be policy initiatives that successfully redirect household consumer incentives in the pursuit of broad societal goals (e.g. healthier food consumption, low-carbon-footprint foods, etc.).

Price-elasticity of supply (ε_s)

An appreciation for the importance of the Price Elasticity of Supply (ε_s) in agri-food markets requires that we give the question of price volatility a second look.

We just finished a discussion of the US Food Away From Home (FAFH) market. We placed extra focus on the rising economic status of the average US consumer household. If we solely concentrate on US average household trends, we can blind ourselves to the economic realities for participants who are below or above the average. Below-average income households are often challenged by food insecurity. A major concern of most food-insecure households is market uncertainty associated with volatile food prices.

A deeper inspection of agri-food markets reveals a tendency toward heightened price volatility. As "the food-price standard deviation" increases, additional market uncertainty will adversely affect food-insecure households. Earlier in this chapter, we observed that food markets generally exhibit *inelastic own-price demand elasticity* (ε_D). It is now time to learn "the rest of the story". We have good reasons to expect that the agri-food *Price Elasticity of Supply* (ε_S) *is also inelastic* in the short term.

Why is (ε_S) for food and agriculture price-inelastic, particularly in the short run? A combination of factors create this inelastic response:[17]

(1) Food production is often season-dependent. For example, once spring-planting has concluded and the "crop is in the ground", then the producer's management skills and cooperating weather can increase yield per acre. But any sizable expansion of crop output and acreage response to increased crop prices cannot take place until the next growing season.
(2) In animal agriculture, the time needed to either expand or reduce production (increase or decrease herd size) often extends beyond one season. It is necessary to understand the "cattle cycle" or the "hog cycle", if the overall supply of animal products is to be properly measured.
(3) Modern agriculture makes a large investment in fixed inputs and unique technologies. In any given growing season, it is difficult to increase or decrease these hired resources. As the name "fixed" implies, these are resources that do not vary much in the short term.
(4) Alternative uses for many farm-related resources are very limited. This phenomena is sometimes identified as "*agricultural asset fixity*." The salvage value of a crop harvester in some non-farm use is worth much less than its acquisition price. As a result, resources do not easily enter and leave agriculture as market product prices fluctuate.

Price-elasticity of supply and market price volatility

If the (ε_D) and the (ε_S) in a market are both price-inelastic, then highly volatile equilibrium price movements are the result whenever a market "shock" occurs. Random and non-random shocks frequently affect agricultural markets. Sizable shifts of crop supply functions can occur when there are large-scale changes in weather or climate (such as droughts, excess moisture, late-spring or early-fall frosts, widespread disease or pests, etc.). Other shocks can be the result of intentional choices. For example, governments can interfere with markets by imposing high tariffs or food embargoes.

Whenever "across-the-board" events are powerful enough to shift either/both supply and/or demand, the combined price-inelastic nature of both (ε_D) and (ε_S) creates very sizable changes in equilibrium market prices. This phenomenon is known as *high market price volatility*. Extreme price volatility is the enemy of household food security. In periods of low prices, households may be able to "stock up" some food stores to weather periods when prices rapidly swing to high levels. But not all foods have a long shelf life, and consequently food-insecure households often find themselves in a precarious situation because price-inelasticity means the food markets have a built-in potential for serious price volatility. For a visual illustration of how market shocks are associated with large swings in equilibrium prices, please review Figure 3.12 below:

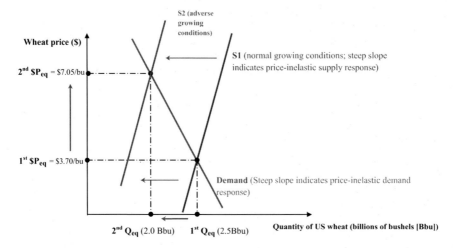

Figure 3.12   Increased US wheat market-price volatility occurs with a combination of price-inelastic supply and price-inelastic demand.

Scenario analysis for Figure 3.12: US wheat market-price volatility associated with a supply-shock, inelastic supply, and inelastic demand

- Assume there is a US Wheat Market. Wheat supply is price-inelastic $(0 < \varepsilon_s < +1)$ and wheat demand is also price-inelastic $(0 < |\varepsilon_D| < +1)$.
- A large-scale adverse weather event (e.g. a massive Midwest US drought) or a widespread disease (e.g. wheat rust) causes a "Decrease in Market Wheat Supply." The Wheat Supply Function shifts to the left. This is an unplanned "shock" in the wheat market. The equilibrium market wheat quantity decreases from 2.5 billion bushels to 2.0 billion bushels. This is a 20 percent reduction in the equilibrium quantity of marketed wheat.
- The severity of the supply shock produces a sizable equilibrium price increase in the wheat market. Compared to $3.70/bushel under normal growing conditions, the shock to the wheat market produces a new price: $7.05/bushel. The new equilibrium wheat price is 90.5 percent higher, compared to the price under normal market supply conditions. Food-insecure households struggle to survive when food prices nearly double.

- Price-Inelastic Market Response – The 90.5 percent jump in the market wheat price is evidence that wheat prices are *highly volatile* (they exhibit a large standard deviation) when shocks affect the wheat market. The increased price volatility reflects the price-inelastic nature of both the wheat supply and demand functions. In summary, a large-scale "decrease in wheat supply" *nearly doubles the Equilibrium Wheat Price* and *decreases the Equilibrium Wheat Quantity by 20 percent.* When a proportionately smaller quantity response is paired with a proportionately larger price change, then we have a price-inelastic and price-volatile market.

Undoubtedly, food-insecure households are adversely affected by the severe price volatility associated with price-inelastic markets. It is also important to highlight the fact that farm producers must figure out management strategies to financially survive the ups and downs of markets that naturally lend themselves to volatile swings in product prices. If we examine the stated motivations of the policy makers who authored the 2014 Farm Bill, they argue that government commodity programs offer a financial safety net against downside price and revenue risks for farm producers. The market price volatility associated with price-inelastic (ε_D) and (ε_S) is an important factor that provides one rationale for initiating these government-sponsored financial safety-net programs.

Summary of market-elasticity analyses

Analysts can utilize Supply and Demand Elasticities to increase their accuracy in predicting outcomes for new policy initiatives. When we employ elasticity measurements to examine the proportionate consequences of new policy choices, the data requirements and research efforts are significant. Rigorous elasticity analysis generally requires considerable intellectual discipline and meticulous attention to appropriate estimation procedures.

The attention to minute details in elasticity analysis has its payoffs. As indicated earlier in Chapter 2, government activity within agricultural and food markets has financial implications that are measured in the billions of dollars, or more. Resources are scarce, and consequently we have good reason to utilize elasticity studies and related techniques to carefully design beneficial and cost-efficient policies when billion-dollar policy decisions are being made and implemented.

How will we know when a new policy is creating cost-efficient or cost-inefficient outcomes? While this is not a simple question to answer, we have tools to address it. Elasticity analysis and applications of the Supply-and-Demand Model offer us baseline estimates of how markets determine economically efficient results.

A new government policy, such as the establishment of an import tariff, often creates new market outcomes. Elasticities of supply and demand can offer us estimates of how new policies proportionately change market outcomes. Fundamental supply-and-demand analysis guides us towards logical predictions of the nature and direction of market responses to new policy influences.

The next logical step in our analysis is to use measurement tools known as "consumer and producer surplus" to estimate benefits and costs when policies alter market economic efficiency. In these cases, we can compare the outcomes of policy-altered markets to the market results produced in the absence of these government policies.

Using consumer and producer surplus to estimate changes in economic welfare and efficiency

As the US Congress decides to reject or approve US participation in the proposed Trans-Pacific Partnership (TPP) (see Chapter 2), future levels of US agricultural import and export tariffs are in the balance. Potential changes in US international trade relationships provide us with an important opportunity to explore the economic welfare and efficiency outcomes associated with alternative policy choices.

We have just reviewed the use of market-equilibrium models and elasticity analyses to predict changes in the US food and agricultural economy. Our next challenge is to examine how the related analytical tools known as "consumer surplus and producer surplus" offer additional insights into predicting economic consequences. After we have developed these additional tools, then we apply them to better understand the outcomes of changes in international trade policy.

What is consumer surplus (CS)?

Consumer surplus (CS) is a measure of the economic value enjoyed by consumers when they purchase a product in a competitive market at a single equilibrium product price (P_{eq}) and quantity (Q_{eq}).

The CS value is partially determined by integrating knowledge from two important concepts: (1) the *theory of consumer choice*, and (2) the *law of demand*. Consumer choice theory emphasizes the *law of diminishing marginal utility* (LDMU). The LDMU predicts that consumers derive a *heightened marginal utility* from the first few units of a product, and a *reduced marginal utility* from additional units of the same product. Similarly, the Law of Demand predicts that consumers are willing and able to pay increased prices to obtain initial quantities of a product. Decreased product prices are necessary to stimulate purchases of additional product quantities.[18]

When we combine the law of demand and consumer-choice theory with the equilibrium results of a competitive market, then the CS value can be fully derived. In a free and open market, buyers and sellers negotiate a single equilibrium product price. The entire equilibrium quantity is bought and sold at the agreed-upon price. Consumers do *not* pay higher prices for the initial quantities, even though they value the first few units more. The "consumer surplus" is the *positive difference* between the *higher prices* that consumer are willing to pay for the initial quantities, and the actual quantities purchased at the *lower agreed-upon equilibrium price*.

From a geometrical viewpoint, CS is a triangular area that is underneath the consumer demand curve but above the equilibrium price (P_{eq}). See Figure 3.13 below:

In Figure 3.13, CS is a dollar value equal to the triangular area underneath the demand function. The P_{eq} in a competitive market creates mutual net benefits for buyers and sellers. The CS is a measure of the consumer benefit on the *demand side*.

While it is likely an obvious statement, we observe the following: *A consumer is better-off if the size of the CS increases, and the consumer is worse off if the size of the CS decreases.* If a new government policy has the effect of increasing or decreasing the CS value, then consumer welfare (satisfaction) changes accordingly in the economy.

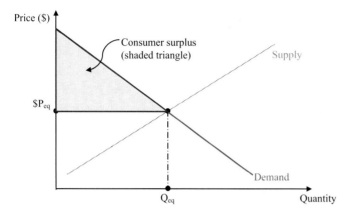

Figure 3.13   Consumer surplus generated in a competitive market.

What is producer surplus (PS)?

Producer surplus (PS) is a measure of the economic value realized by sellers when they supply a product in a competitive market at a single equilibrium product price (P_{eq}) and quantity (Q_{eq}).

The PS value is partially determined by integrating knowledge from two important concepts: (1) the *law of increasing marginal cost*, and (2) the *law of supply*. Increasing marginal cost of production is the logical result of the *Law of Diminishing Returns* and the *Law of Increasing Opportunity Cost*. The initial quantities of a product can be rationally produced at a *lower cost per unit output*. Reduced marginal productivity and increased opportunity costs cause increased marginal cost for additional output units. Similarly, the Law of Supply predicts that suppliers are willing and able to sell initial product quantities at decreased prices. Increased product prices are necessary to stimulate sellers to offer additional units of product output.[19]

When we combine the law of supply and increasing marginal cost with the equilibrium results of a competitive market, then the PS value can be fully derived. In open markets, sellers and buyers transact the entire equilibrium quantity (Q_{eq}) at the agreed-upon equilibrium price (P_{eq}). Producers receive higher prices for the initial quantities, even though their marginal cost for the first few units is less. The "producer surplus" is the *positive difference* between the *higher equilibrium price* that producers receive for the initial quantities, and the actual *lower marginal cost for supplying these initial product-output units*.

From a geometrical viewpoint, PS is a triangular area that is above producer supply curve but below the equilibrium price (P_{eq}). See Figure 3.14 below:

In Figure 3.14 above, PS is a dollar value equal to the triangular area above the supply function. At the P_{eq} in a competitive market, the PS is a measure of the seller's benefit on the *supply side*.

A seller is better off if the PS area (value) increases, or worse off if the PS value decreases. A new government policy that expands or contracts the PS area is definitely altering the net welfare position of sellers in the economy.

Equipped with PS and CS to evaluate changes in producer and consumer welfare, we can now apply these tools to evaluate the economic impacts of a new international trade policy.

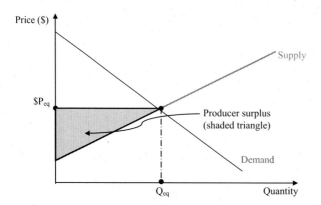

Figure 3.14 Producer surplus generated in a competitive market.

Changes in consumer and producer surplus: an international trade scenario

Let's begin this scenario with simplifying assumptions. We are interested in the welfare and efficiency effects of a hypothetical US Congressional decision to accept entry into the Trans-Pacific Partnership (or TPP).

Prior to becoming a TPP member, let's assume that the US government had been applying a $0.50/gallon import tariff on ethanol supplied to the US by TPP members. Also assume that the TPP negotiations completely eliminate the ethanol import tariff. As a member of the TPP, the US effectively reduces its ethanol import tariff to $0.00 per gallon of imported ethanol. What are the predicted welfare impacts, as the US ethanol market adjusts to the total removal of the ethanol import tariff?

We will use changes in Consumer Surplus and Producer Surplus, as we track the adjustment to a tariff-free ethanol market. Carefully examine Figure 3.15 below. This scenario has complexities, but they can be overcome if we take a step-wise approach to understanding the US ethanol market status before and after the tariff is abolished.

Let's initially examine the welfare gains and losses that exist in the case where the $0.50/gallon tariff on ethanol imports remains in place. This situation would be relevant if the US chose to reject TPP membership. The US would maintain the status quo of using the tariff to protect domestic US ethanol producers from the full brunt of TPP competition in supplying ethanol to US consumers.[20]

What are the welfare impacts on US consumers when the $0.50/gallon tariff increases the cost of importing ethanol from other TPP countries? Let's use the "consumer surplus" tool to figure this out. Remember that consumer surplus is the triangular area underneath the demand curve at all prices that exceed the relevant market price.

The most straightforward method to predict the welfare impact of maintaining the tariff is to determine the amount of the consumer surplus (CS) with and without the tariff. An inspection of Figure 3.15 reveals that the net consumer welfare with a $Zero import tariff is Triangle AMH. On the other hand, if the $0.50/gallon tariff is applied, then the surplus for US consumers shrinks to Triangle ABF.

If we were supplied with all prices and quantities, we could calculate the net loss of consumer welfare caused by the full tariff as equal to the dollar value of Trapezoidal

Area FBMH. This *loss of consumer welfare* means that US consumers have reduced buying power for other goods in the economy as a result of bearing the $0.50/gallon import tariff as they purchase ethanol.

What happens to the dollars in Trapezoid FBMH that are no longer controlled by US consumers? The breakdown of what happens is worth investigating. First of all, some of that buying power is transferred to domestic ethanol producers who can afford to supply more ethanol at the tariff-elevated $price (located at Point B). In fact, US consumers transfer the value in Trapezoid FHKE to US Ethanol producers.

US consumers also contribute Rectangle EBCD to the US Treasury in the form of the government's tariff revenue on the imported ethanol gallons.

Finally, there are two instances where the US consumer loses consumer surplus, and so does the rest of the economy. An inspection reveals consumer surplus losses in Triangle EDK and Triangle BCM. The sum of these two triangular areas is known as the "deadweight loss" of the tariff. A deadweight loss means that the entire economy is less efficient in resource use as a result of imposing a tariff on the market.

In addition, because the US economy is huge relative to those of other nations, the US decision to place a tariff on imported ethanol changes the world price of ethanol. A careful inspection of Figure 3.15 reveals that when the $0.50/gallon tariff is applied, the world price of ethanol does not increase by the full amount of the tariff. In effect, other nations who supply ethanol to the US absorb part of the cost of the tariff. In this instance, US consumers "pick up part of the tab" associated with the tariff, and the countries exporting their ethanol to the US pay for the rest of the tariff. See Rectangle DCGJ in Figure 3.15 for the foreign income transferred to the US when the US tariff is applied on imported ethanol.

The US import tariff partially changes the international "terms of trade" by redistributing income from a foreign nation into the US economy. Because US trading partners are not receiving anything in return for this loss of income, it can become a "sore point" in trade. This negative impact on the incomes of US trading partners is known in international trade as a "beggar thy neighbor policy." Ultimately, the impacts of US import tariffs on the terms of trade can be a reason for US trading partners to retaliate by creating their own import tariffs on US-produced exports.

The astute reader who has been following the logical arguments presented above will discern that import tariffs redistribute the consumer surplus to domestic producers and to the government treasury. The tariff also actually reduces overall resource efficiency in the economy. Finally, a US import tariff might motivate US trading partners to establish import tariffs that reduce the commercial viability of US exports. Advocates of free trade agreements are quick to point out these drawbacks to protectionist trade policies that discourage imports.

A final question is what happens if a tariff is eliminated? We began this sophisticated scenario with the situation where the US Congress passes legislation to let the US join the free trade agreement encompassed by the TPp. If we use the analysis in Figure 3.15, we can reverse the discussion. The transition from the $0.50/gallon import tariff to a $Zero tariff will *help consumer welfare* with a net gain of Trapezoid FBMH. The economy as a whole recaptures net efficiency, because the *deadweight losses are reversed*.

Who loses when the import tariff goes away? The domestic ethanol industry does. The at-home producers of ethanol will compete unprotected in an open global market. The price of ethanol drops to its free-trade level. See Point M in Figure 3.15. Domestic consumers will enjoy the gain in consumer surplus, but domestic producers lose part of their producer surplus as the market price falls to the globally competitive level. After adjusting for the

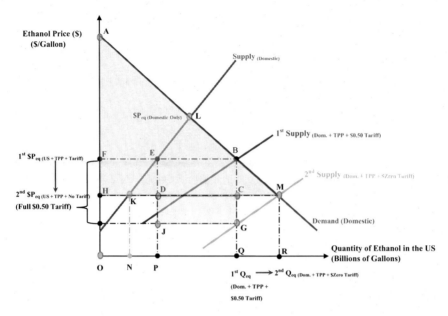

Figure 3.15 Scenario: US participation in the TPP reduces an import tariff on ethanol.

financial loss of the domestic ethanol industry, calculations demonstrate the overall economy's GDP is actually better off and more efficient in the absence of the tariff.

When the tariff is lifted, there is no denying that dislocations will occur in the domestic
US ethanol industry. A complete understanding of this scenario provides plenty of reasons
why domestic industries often vigorously lobby legislators to either put new import tariffs in
place, or maintain those tariffs if they already exist.

Many journalists and other pundits have noted that lobbyists for the US sugar and dairy
industries fully understand all of the results of the above analysis. Representatives of US
sugar and dairy interests have been very successful in their efforts to maintain import tariffs
and related protections for their industries, even as the US considers entry into the TPP and
similar free-trade proposals.

Scenario analysis for Figure 3.15: US participation in the TPP reduces an import tariff on ethanol

- Assume there is a US Ethanol Market. It is comprised of a US Domestic Ethanol Supply,
  and a Global Ethanol Supply from TPP nations, and a Domestic Ethanol Demand.
- There are three possible positions for US ethanol equilibrium price (P_{eq}) and quantity
  (Q_{eq}):

  ○ At Point L: Completely isolated US ethanol market (no international trade). The etha-
    nol market equilibrium P_{eq} and Q_{eq} would be entirely determined by only US domes-
    tic supply and demand. In this situation, the US Ethanol P_{eq} > World Ethanol P_{eq}.

- o At Point B: Domestic plus foreign (TPP) ethanol supply affects US ethanol market. A $0.50 per gallon import US ethanol tariff increases the US Ethanol P_{eq} above the free-trade P_{eq} level.
- o At Point M: Domestic plus foreign (TPP) ethanol supply affects US ethanol market. A $Zero US import tariff causes the US Ethanol P_{eq} to be equal to the free-trade P_{eq} level at Point M.

- Assume the US market equilibrium is initially at Point B: US allows international trade in ethanol, but establishes a $0.50/gallon ethanol import tariff. Domestic ethanol production is Distance OP, and imported ethanol is Distance PQ on the Quantity axis. US Ethanol P_{eq} > Free-Trade Ethanol P_{eq}.
- Change in Policy: US joins the TPP and adopts $0/gallon import tariff. New US Ethanol equilibrium is at Point M. Domestic output = Distance ON. Foreign Imports = Distance NR. US Ethanol P_{eq} = Free-Trade Ethanol P_{eq}.

Summary and conclusions associated with producer and consumer welfare analyses

As illustrated in the international trade scenario (Figure 3.15) above, we can learn how policy changes influence the economic welfare of market participants, and also affect the overall resource efficiency of our economy.

Our example involved market outcomes with and without the influence of an import tariff. What are some additional lessons that we can learn from this exercise?

One generalization is that any new government initiative is likely to change efficiency and economic welfare outcomes in a competitive market. Our analysis of import tariff impacts is not an isolated case. There are broader implications.

A tariff, whether it be placed on imports or exports, is a type of sales tax. Whenever governments introduce either taxes or subsidies into the economy, the action creates a "wedge" between the equilibrium of a competitive market and the new market equilibrium outcome associated with the tax or subsidy.

We can arrive at a far-reaching conclusion about the market "wedge" created by any new tax or subsidy (with few exceptions). We observe that the policy intervention produces economic losses for some participants, economic gains for others, and deadweight efficiency losses for the entire economic system. In other words, whenever we "tamper" with the results normally achieved in a competitive market, there should be an accounting of all the consequences.

If situations arise where a new policy is under consideration, then we should understand that ideal economic outcomes will be difficult to achieve. For example, in the field of welfare economics, nineteenth-century economist Vilfredo Pareto introduced the idea of seeking out transactions that can improve the economic welfare of some participants without making any other participants worse off.

For a moment, let's follow the line of logic that Pareto pursued. Trades that benefit some without hurting others are identified as "Pareto-Better"; and, from an economic efficiency standpoint, it is rational to create market conditions where Pareto-Better transactions can easily occur.

Pareto also concluded that, in a world of scarce resources, only a limited number of Pareto-Better transactions are possible in any set of circumstances. When all Pareto-Better trades have been exhausted, then a Pareto-Optimum is reached where it is no longer possible to make someone better off without making someone else worse off. From an efficiency standpoint, it does not make sense to encourage additional trades, once a Pareto-Optimum is attained.[21]

How does Pareto's study of welfare economics apply in our discussion of alternative farm and food policies? Let's directly answer this question now. Nearly all new policies, such as proposals to subsidize one activity or tax another, will produce mixed welfare results. Pareto-Better proposals will be rare or impossible – few new policies can produce outcomes that improve the welfare of some groups without adversely affecting others. And, we have discovered that when policy proposals cause competitive markets to diverge from their "free-trade" equilibria, then we generate deadweight losses that reduce the system's overall economic efficiency.

The above discussion *is not intended* to promote an agenda where we will never again subsidize or tax an economic activity. Rather, we simply need to realize that the standard types of government interventions (such as tariffs on imports) are naturally imperfect. We need to think twice when a policy is helping some, hurting others and perhaps creating a drag on the efficiency of our economic system. In other words, as a new policy comes under consideration, we need to examine it with our eyes "wide open."

Update on our policy analysis toolbox

We have just applied the concepts of Consumer Surplus (CS) and Producer Surplus (PS) to study changes in economic welfare associated with alternative policies. The content of our intellectual toolbox is growing. Thus far, we have utilized marginal analysis, supply-and-demand modeling, elasticity estimations, and CS and PS evaluation as we expand our capacity to investigate the economics of US agricultural and food policy choices and consequences. Because international trade is a large and growing area of economic activity for the US agri-food system, we next review the principle of comparative advantage as a rationale for efforts to negotiate and implement the TPP and related free trade agreements.

The economic influence of the law of comparative advantage on US food and agriculture

In the economic welfare analysis above, removal of an import tariff on ethanol *improved* consumer surplus and *increased* overall economic efficiency by eliminating deadweight market losses.

Because of redistributive effects, not all participants are likely happy with the tariff-free outcome. The US government's tariff revenues fall to zero, and the producer surplus decreases for domestic ethanol firms. However, when the arithmetic is performed, the decrease in the market ethanol price *increases domestic consumer surplus* by an amount that is *larger than* the combined reductions in producer surplus and government revenue. Net economic value increases.

If political opposition from domestic producers can be overcome, nations can move forward with proposals to eliminate tariffs and other barriers. In such cases, governments often declare that they are strengthening their economies by replacing trade-protection policies with a "free-trade" approach. Other than eliminating deadweight losses in international markets, what are the additional "gains from free trade"? To answer this question, we utilize the "*law of comparative advantage*" as an analytical tool to guide patterns of production and trade.

Comparative advantage and its relationship to the opportunity cost principle

Debates about the benefits and costs of protectionism versus a free trade policy are not new. In the early 1800s, economist David Ricardo was a critic of trade barriers, and put forward his argument for open trade based on comparative advantage. Ricardo's model refined Adam Smith's earlier "absolute advantage" proposal that focused on the lowest cost of production as the guidepost to determine international trade patterns. Ricardo credited Smith's contribution, and then employed the principle of opportunity cost to broaden and strengthen Smith's reasoning.[22]

Ricardo demonstrated benefits that jointly accrue to two trading partners when they produce and export products at *lower opportunity cost*. For example, if Canadian farms give up less soybeans than the US when Canadians produce flax, then *Canada has a comparative advantage in flax production*, compared to the US. Similarly, when the US produces soybeans, if US farms forego less flax production than does Canada, then the *US has a comparative advantage in soybeans*, relative to Canada. In this scenario, Ricardo would recommend that the US and Canada determine terms of trade where the US exports soybeans to Canada in exchange for importing flax from Canada.

Both Ricardo and Smith believed that protectionist policies prevent the occurrence of mutually beneficial trades, and therefore tariffs and other restrictions are impediments to overall global economic growth.

What exactly is the link between open trade, comparative advantage, and economic growth? We can create a twenty-first century example that largely follows Ricardo's nineteenth-century numerical illustration. He argued that England's and Portugal's economies would be better off if they mutually lifted trade restrictions on Portugal's wine and England's cloth production.

In our example, we examine different production potentials for corn and tomatoes in the US and Mexico. Then we use Ricardo's "comparative advantage tool" to develop a reciprocal agreement that benefits production and resource efficiency in both nations.

A comparative advantage scenario

Let's assume that we can create two "representative" 600-acre crop-farm operations. One is in Mexico, and the other is in the US. For simplicity, allow that the respective US and Mexican farm managers allocate available acreage between corn and tomatoes. Assume no double cropping. The opportunity cost of growing an acre of tomatoes is the corn that is not produced.

Suppose the initial trading relationship between the US and Mexico is non-existent. The US and Mexico are each separately self-sufficient in corn and tomatoes.

Based on the initial conditions outlined above, we can develop Tables 3.4 and 3.5 to illustrate per acre production potentials, opportunity costs and initial crop acreage allocations.

Table 3.4 Mexican and US production on a per acre basis. Opportunity Costs of producing one
crop *instead of* another are displayed.

Nation	Bushels of Corn per Acre	or	Tons of Tomatoes per Acre
Mexico	50	or	30
United States	160	or	40

In Table 3.4, we can use the production potentials to illustrate basic trade concepts. For example, the US has an *absolute advantage* in corn and tomatoes. The US yield per acre is simply larger for each crop.

Comparative advantage is a different story. Each time Mexico grows one (1.0) ton of tomatoes, Mexico has an opportunity cost of (1.67) bushels of corn not produced. When the US grows one (1.0) ton of tomatoes, the US gives up the chance to produce (4.0) bushels of corn.

A comparison of the opportunity cost ratios in this scenario allows us to conclude that *Mexico has a comparative advantage in tomato production* relative to the US. It costs Mexico less corn foregone to produce tomatoes relative to the US.

To complete this picture, let's examine the opportunity costs of corn production. Each time Mexico grows (1.0) bushel of corn, Mexico gives up (0.60) tons of tomatoes. When the US grows (1.0) bushel of corn, the US has an opportunity cost of (0.25) tons of tomatoes. The US can grow corn at a lower opportunity cost than can Mexico, so the *US has the comparative advantage in corn production*.

If the US and Mexico shut off their common border to trade, then we can examine how their farm managers have independently allocated acreages between the two crops. Take a look at Table 3.5. Notice that the US and the Mexican farms have each used their entire 600-acre allotment.

Table 3.5 indicates that, prior to any trade, Mexico has concentrated two-thirds of its acreage in corn, leaving one-third for tomatoes. In contrast, the US has equally divided its acreage between corn and tomatoes.

Next we allow the scenario to change in the direction suggested by David Ricardo over 200 years ago. We follow comparative advantage, and reallocate acreages accordingly. Earlier (see above), we have learned the following:

- Mexico gives up 1.67 bushels of corn per 1.0 ton of Mexican tomatoes grown.
- US gives up 4.0 bushels of corn per 1.0 ton of US tomatoes grown.

In this modified scenario, we need appropriate terms of trade that will allow both Mexico and the US to capitalize on their respective comparative advantages. David Ricardo used

Table 3.5 Total production, before trade and specialization, on 1,200 total acres.

Nation	Total # Bushels of Corn Produced	and	Total # Tons of Tomatoes Produced	
Mexico	20,000 bu. (400 acres)		6,000 tons (200 acres)	(Sum = 600 acres)
US	48,000 bu. (300 acres)		12,000 tons (300 acres)	(Sum = 600 acres)
Sum Total For Both Nations Combined	50,000 bu. (700 acres)		18,000 tons (500 acres)	(Sum = 1,200 acres)

basic mathematics to determine the terms of trade. He discovered that a mutually acceptable ratio of tomatoes-to-corn should be within the production trade-off ratios of the two trading partners. In this case, a mutually beneficial trading rate occurs in-between the 1.0 : 1.67 Mexican ratio and the 1.0 : 4.0 US Ratio.

While any trading rate *within the production boundaries* will suffice, let's say that the terms of trade are negotiated as 1.0 ton of tomatoes per 2.67 bushels of corn. Further, the actual trade proposal based on these terms of trade determines that *Mexico exports 6,000 tons of tomatoes to the US in exchange for importing 16,000 bushels of US-produced corn*. Both nations must reallocate acreages to ensure that each nation is "made whole" after the trade, as compared to their pre-trade quantities of the commodities. A careful inspection of Table 3.6 below reveals that, after the acreage-reallocations and the agreed-upon terms-of-trade are executed, both nations can reach their trade goals while using *50 less acres each* (a total savings of 100 acres). Mexico also receives a bonus of total corn bushels that are larger than pre-trade levels. Examine Table 3.6 below.

In Table 3.6 above, Mexico trades 6,000 tons of its tomatoes for 16,000 bushels of US-produced corn. Compared to the collective national production totals in Table 3.5, total corn production is up by 3,500 bushels, total tomato production is constant, and each nation has "freed up" 50 acres for other uses.

After the trade, the US is made whole in commodities and has extra acreage to devote to other purposes. In particular, the US pre- and post-trade amounts of corn (48,000 bushels) and tomatoes (6,000 tons) are identical. And, the post-trade US farm has *50 extra acres* to dedicate to additional productive uses. The US is better off after the trade.

Mexico ends up with 3,500 additional bushels of corn, the same amount of tomatoes, and 50 extra acres to dedicate to other uses. Like the US, Mexico is better off after the trade.

Following the Law of Comparative Advantage, acreage allocations have changed in each country. *Post-trade Mexico allocates 27.3 percent of its planted acreage into corn and 72.7 percent of Mexican farm acreage into tomatoes*. This acreage result is nearly the opposite of Mexico's pre-trade position; the new allocation allows Mexico to specialize its land resource in tomato production, where it has the comparative advantage. Similarly, *post-trade US acreage allocation is 72.7 percent in corn* and 27.3 percent in tomatoes, reflecting the US comparative advantage in corn relative to Mexico.

The post-acreage allocations for Mexico and the US pertain to 1,100 total acres. The US and Mexico can each use their freed-up 50 acres as they see fit.

Table 3.6 Total production and allocation, after trade and specialization, on 1100 total acres.

Nation	Total # Bushels of Corn Produced	and	Total # Tons of Tomatoes Produced	
Mexico	23,500 bu. (= 7,500+16,000) (150 Mex. acres)		6,000 tons (= 12,000−16,000) (400 Mex. acres)	= (Sum = 550 acres)
US	48,000 bu. (= 64,000−16,000) (400 US acres)		12,000 tons (=6,000+6,000) (150 US acres)	= (Sum = 550 acres)
Sum Total For Both Nations Combined	71,500 bu. (550 total acres)		18,000 tons (550 total acres)	= (Sum = 1,100 acres)

By following the Law of Comparative Advantage, each nation uses its land resource more efficiently. Post-trade additional output of both crops occurs at reduced opportunity costs. The net gain in post-trade collective corn production is interpreted as net positive economic growth. If and when Mexico and the US each employ their freed-up farm acreages for productive uses, then additional economic growth can take place.

Comparative advantage and economic realities

The Mexico-US trade scenario above indicates that nations who use the Law of Comparative Advantage (LCA) to guide trading relationships can profit from more efficient resource use and increased collective total output.

When the World Trade Organization (WTO) and similar agencies actively promote free-trade policies, the LCA and its economic benefits are considerations that lie at the heart of their advocacy. Support for approval of US participation in the Trans-Pacific Partnership (TPP) is also closely connected with the LCA and its potential contributions to efficiency and growth.

Of course, political support for free trade and the LCA is far from universal. Debates over trade policies are often vigorous and protracted. What are the drawbacks to the removal of trade barriers and allowing relative opportunity costs to determine trade patterns?

Earlier in this chapter, we used the tools of consumer and producer surplus to demonstrate that domestic producers often experience reduced revenues when import tariff restrictions are lifted. The lesson to learn is very important. Specifically, when free trade improves efficiency and total output, the market cannot evenly spread those benefits to all participants. To be blunt, a decision to drop trade-protection polices creates winners and losers.

Governments should realistically consider creating "trade adjustment assistance" programs to help economically injured participants transition to the new market conditions that prevail when free-trade policies replace protectionist regimes. Contrary to the ideal conditions included in the LCA economic model, there are real transaction costs to reallocating resources from one end-use to another.

In the Mexico-US trade example above, the illustration implicitly assumes that changing production between corn and tomatoes is a simple and costless transition. The reality is far removed from this assumption. Considerable costs, in terms of additional time and new investments, are generally necessary to reallocate resources among alternative uses.

Hesitation to follow the LCA and adopt free-trade policies also stems from concerns about the real-world trade risks and competing national priorities. One risk associated with free-trade policy is whether both trading partners will consistently follow through on their trade agreements. Trade partners become *mutually dependent* on each other for the transacted products that flow back and forth across borders. If one nation's government unilaterally decides to change the terms of trade (such as initiating an embargo or renewing protectionist practices), then the projected gains from trade are not realized.

Finally, national governments can decide that some policy priorities supersede the LCA goals of economic growth and efficiency. Policy makers may impose trade restrictions because they view national security, environmental quality, human rights, etc. or other goals as objectives that should take precedence over the economic benefits of free-trade policies.

For example, debates over whether the US should join the TPP include the issue that some TPP trading partners gain a comparative advantage through cost-saving production methods that compromise environmental quality. The concern is whether there will be a "level playing field" where all TPP nations create cost-neutral policy environments that adjust to the external economic effects of markets and public goods in similar ways.

In the next section, we explore how we can apply the economics of market externalities and public goods to identify how economic outcomes in the farm and food sectors are influenced by alternative policy options.

Probing US agri-food sector economic performance using the concepts of market externalities and public goods

As we have seen, advocates for free-trade policies and the Law of Comparative Advantage (LCA) typically emphasize the LCA's economic efficiencies and positive growth effects. At the core of the LCA is an accurate assessment of relative opportunity cost to determine the pattern of specialization and trade that should take place. As we use the LCA to make trade-policy recommendations, we depend on the idea that our market mechanisms determine equilibrium prices that fully reflect the true scarcity of resources and outputs in our economy, and in other nations' economies.

When market prices consistently provide the proper signals to guide consumer and producer responses to economic scarcity, then economies are socially efficient. What does this mean? In effect, social efficiency means that all decision makers regulate their choices according to opportunity cost indicators. Efficient prices signify the genuine value of scarce resources in alternative uses. *Ceteris paribus*, social efficiency is a desirable economic outcome.

What is market failure?

We are likely all familiar with the expression that "Nobody's perfect." This adage also applies to markets. There are conditions where social efficiency does not occur, and it makes sense to discuss market failure. Fortunately, we have access to the economic models known as "market externalities" and "public goods" to effectively investigate these failures and their consequences. We can also explore what remedies are available when markets fall short of delivering what they promise.

By the way, if we are being completely even-handed and transparent, we also should mention that we have economic models to explore the causes and consequences of government failure. Yes, nobody's perfect.

Market externalities: origins, challenges, and alternatives

Situations where economic activities have positive and negative side effects are more common than we expect. A homeowner makes landscape improvements, and the real estate values in the entire neighborhood benefit. A tobacco user's second-hand smoke creates adverse health effects for others. A beekeeper's hives produce not only honey, but help the fruit-grower reap a harvest. A child receives a polio vaccine, gains personal immunity, and helps prevent the disease from spreading to others.

When the market fails to measure the economic value of an activity's side effect, then a market externality is in progress. For example, suppose a farmer's intensive crop tillage practices have a side effect of triggering extra soil erosion. The lost soil travels downstream and affects a regional watershed. Additional silt in streams and rivers spoils fish habitat and reduces river navigability. The downstream fishermen and boat owners are economically worse off while erosion-prone crop-production upstream is artificially cheaper. The farm is "hiring" a scarce resource: the watershed's limited natural capacity to absorb eroded soil. What price is the market charging for this valuable resource?

Private markets require clearly defined property rights to assign prices and efficiently allocate resources. In the case of a watershed, it is very difficult to define who owns its natural potential to sustainably serve as a receptacle for product residuals. If the watershed's ecological, recreational, and navigable values have no identifiable owner, then the legal authority to charge a user fee is absent, and the private market often assigns a zero-price to this open-access resource.

Of course, the zero-price is erroneous. The watershed is a scarce and valuable resource. But without additional effort to determine clear property rights, the market mechanism's normal role as a socially efficient system to determine resource prices is incapacitated. We identify this failure as a "market externality" because resource-using transactions are occurring *outside* the typical process for establishing market prices.

The inefficient outcomes associated with market-external effects create real challenges for economic participants and policy makers. For example, downstream communities may be burdened with river-dredging costs because of soil erosion upstream. We can apply the economics of market externalities to identify policies to restore market system efficiency. This process of reestablishing market efficiency is known as "internalizing" the externalities.

In the next section, we examine a scenario where various internalization options are considered as means to counteract a market externality that has various effects on US agriculture.

A market externality scenario

As discussed above, externalities are a category of market failure. Externalities are economic activities that generate beneficial or costly side effects that are not properly accounted for by the market. If an externality persists, then private marginal resource costs are not equal to full social marginal costs, and inefficient market performance is the end result.

Real-world externalities can be fascinating case studies. Unexpected side effects occur that make for interesting analyses. For example, let's consider outcomes associated with fossil-fuel powered electric-generating plants that have the residual effect of airborne emissions.

We build power plants and burn fossil fuels for the primary purpose of producing electrical energy. Electricity is a very important resource in modern society. Unfortunately, burning fuels to obtain electrical power also means that we emit smoke, ash, and other by-products into the air.

Simply put, fuel combustion and airborne emissions go hand-in-hand. When combustion residuals reduce air quality, then we have air pollution. Air pollution is a typical case example of an externality. Power-plant emissions create impacts for downwind third parties. When the power plant has no market pressure to adjust production and account for the economic effects of the emissions, then we end up with inefficient results.

Power plants that combust coal and oil emit a variety of chemicals and particulates. Two of these residuals are sulfur dioxide and various nitrogen oxides. These chemical emissions combine with water vapor and other atmospheric elements to create a mixture known as "acid rain." Clouds capture the acidic droplets and carry them hundreds of miles before they fall to earth. Acid rain affects plant and animal life in both soils and waterways.[23]

Acid rain impedes the growth and productivity of forests and a variety of vegetables (such as tomatoes and spinach). This is a case where power-plant emissions create a "negative externality" for agricultural production enterprises. Foresters and vegetable farmers do not have any effective means of receiving compensation from the power-plant producers for the damage done to their operations. Because the market mechanism is absent, the acid rain's external diseconomy means that we produce too much electric power, and not enough trees and vegetables. The misallocation is clear evidence of economic inefficiency.

How can externalities be resolved? Farmers and foresters might petition all power plants in the nation to voluntarily reduce their emissions. But rational power-plant owners are not likely to incur extra pollution control expenses and reduce their profit margins. If appeals for voluntary emission controls are ignored, then the externality continues. When voluntary measures fail, a role for government intervention can arise. In the latter half of the twentieth century, especially after the mid-1970s, US federal and state governments legislated mandatory regulations and/or tax programs requiring power plants to control their emissions.

Analyzing an externality's economic efficiency impacts

What economic tools can we use to clearly demonstrate the adverse results of externalities, as well as the effects of policies that reduce or eliminate externalities? Fortunately, we can utilize the concepts of marginal analysis, opportunity cost, and the market's supply-demand equilibrium to display the inefficient effects of externalities. These same tools also illustrate how policies can stimulate market participants to internalize the externalities and generate more economically efficient outcomes.

In Figure 3.16 below, we use the Supply and Demand for Electrical Power to illustrate how externalities cause the Marginal Social Cost (MSC) of electric-energy generation to diverge from Marginal Private Cost (MPC) of electric power. The "wedge" between private and social cost is created because the external costs of electricity generation (e.g. acid rain's damages to forest and vegetable production) are not internalized in the private electric energy market.

When the externality is exerting its influence, the private market for electric power reaches an equilibrium price and quantity (See P[1], Q[1] in Figure 3.16). This market price is not an optimal equilibrium. The private market solution produces too much electric power at a price that is too low.

In contrast, because of reduced productivity and higher cost, forest and vegetable product outputs are reduced and their product prices are artificially high. The acid rain externality creates an inefficient market signal, indicating that forest and vegetable products are scarcer relative to other resources. Resources are not efficiently allocated when too much of one product, and not enough of another, are produced.

Figure 3.16 demonstrates the market inefficiencies associated with power plant emissions that create a negative externality. What realistic remedies can reverse this scenario, and transfer the emission costs back to the power-plant owners? Transactions costs are likely too high for forest- and vegetable-producers to voluntarily negotiate with power-plant owners to receive compensation for the damages, or obtain relief in the form of reduced emissions.

In the absence of any private-sector solution, a public policy to adjust the externality may be justified. In economic theory, we can consider a government introducing a marginal tax or subsidy to change the incentives of the industry that is the source of the externality. Ideally, the extra tax or subsidy should be just equal to the externality's marginal damage.

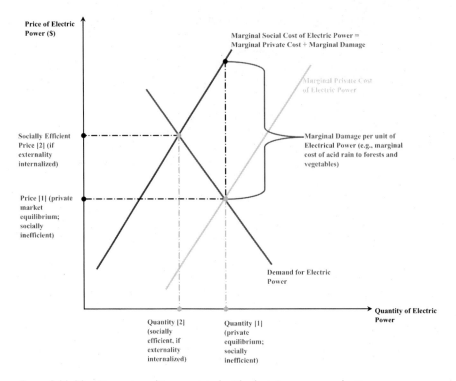

Figure 3.16 Negative externality associated with electric power production.

In Figure 3.16, the offsetting tax or subsidy would have the effect of shifting the Private Marginal Cost Curve to the left by an amount that would cause the supply of electric power to coincide with the Social Marginal Cost Curve. From an economic standpoint, the externality would have been internalized.

There are many real-world limitations to the tax-or-subsidy solution for an externality. Transactions costs (e.g. measurement, supervision, monitoring, etc.) inside government hinder the establishment of a tax-or-subsidy rate that properly matches the "marginal damage value." Even if the extra damage value can be approximated, there are administrative costs (e.g. collection, enforcement, updating, etc.) of a tax-or-subsidy policy. It is also important to realize that if an "externality tax" is applied, the revenue goes to the government and not to those injured by the emissions. Similarly, if the government subsidizes the power industry to help control the emissions, then income is being redistributed to the industry emitter and not to the victims downwind.

One other solution, which also has adverse efficiency consequences, is for the government to exercise its regulatory and enforcement powers, and mandate a cut-back in power industry emissions. For better or worse, US federal and state governments have often chosen this government "command-and-control" option to legally limit the emission volumes.

Careful reflection on this scenario reveals an interesting conclusion: achieving emission control via policy edict may be less economically efficient than simply allowing the externality to continue without intervention. However, in these situations, economic efficiency concerns may not be the dominant consideration. Instead, politics and questions of fairness may be the deciding factors that determine whether or not a public policy is adopted to regulate power plant emissions. In the US today, power plant emissions have been regulated by federal and state laws and agencies since the mid-1970s.

Unexpected side effects of successful air pollution control programs

From a scientific standpoint, there is one additional scenario to consider when we examine the side effects of regulated power-plant emissions. Namely, have there been any unanticipated externalities associated with *decreased fossil-fuel emissions*, as the power-plant industry has complied with federal and state air pollution control standards?

The Pacific Northwest National Laboratory (PNNL) studied Sulphur Dioxide (SO_2) emissions of power plants in the US. PNNL determined that atmospheric releases of SO_2 peaked in 1980, and measurably decreased afterwards.[24] In 2007, Iowa State University (ISU) agronomists determined that decreased alfalfa production in Northeast Iowa (NE-IA) was associated with soils exhibiting sulfur (S) deficiencies.[25] The ISU alfalfa yield study noted that NE-IA producers now need to include S in their cropland fertilization schedules to compensate for reductions in atmospheric S deposited into NE-IA soils.

It would seem that the effectiveness of post-1980 US power-plant air pollution controls created an unexpected side effect of changing NE-IA's soil chemistry and consequently influencing alfalfa production. We can hypothesize that the extra amounts of pre-regulatory power-plant sulfur (S) emissions actually generated a *positive externality for alfalfa producers*. If our observations are correct, increased power-plant atmospheric emissions benefited Iowa's alfalfa growers while simultaneously damaging forest and vegetable production. Real-world externalities are often more complex scenarios than we typically examine in a college-level economic principles course.

Public goods and the US agri-food system

Externalities and public goods create similar economic challenges for private markets. Both create incentives and outcomes that the market mechanism struggles to properly address.

What exactly is a public good? When the scale of a positive externality becomes very large, we can classify it as a public good. We can define a pure public good as a product that exhibits two consumption-based characteristics: (1) non-rival and (2) non-exclusion.

One person's satisfaction from consuming a *non-rival public good* does not reduce the good's value to other users. For example, we can view "global food security" as a type of non-rival good. When an individual benefits from living in a healthier food-secure world, there is no loss of food security available to other consumers.

Non-exclusion of a public good implies unconditional consumer access to the good's benefits. In contrast, the condition for consumer access to a private good is routinely based on a voluntary transaction followed by a consumer purchase. We can illustrate non-exclusion in the food system. If improvements to the food industry's HACCP procedures increase overall safety levels for food consumers, then access to that protective benefit is non-exclusionary. All consumers have equal access a safer food supply, regardless of their circumstances.

Let's distinguish public from private goods, to add clarity to this discussion. *Pure private goods dominate in market-based economies.* Food in a vending machine is a simple example of a private good that has exclusion and is rival. The machine will only dispense an item after receiving a payment, and a consumed candy bar cannot be used again.

While public goods are less numerous in modern society, they can be high-profile products that require large resource allocations. For example, national defense and homeland security are well-known public goods, and the US government budgets more than half a trillion dollars annually to provide these protective services.

Governments often provide public goods because private markets cannot efficiently allocate them. The non-rival character of public goods often means that the marginal cost of an additional consumer is nearly zero. In addition, while all consumers basically use the same quantity of a public good, the perceived value of the public good varies by the individual.

Some consumers are willing to pay a great deal to maintain a national defense system, while others wish that national defense would simply go away. In theory, if all consumers self-revealed how they value a unit of a public good, then a voluntary payment system could be devised. Unfortunately, there would a rational incentive for consumers to reduce their "public good fee" by understating their true valuation of the service.

Similarly, non-exclusion is a product characteristic limiting the normal market mechanism. Rational consumers figure out that they can "free ride" (i.e. unconditionally receive public good benefits) as long as some "good neighbor" pays for the public good to be produced.

In a private market, a public good would be under-allocated. A public good's non-rival and non-exclusion qualities prevent the good's true valuation (its demand curve) from being voluntarily and fully expressed by market consumers.

Private-market limitations mean that we will seek other options to supply public goods. In many instances, governments are authorized to provide them. Governments can rely on taxes, fees, and subsidies to increase the allocation of scarce resources towards the production of public goods. Because governments can use their administrative and enforcement powers to collect revenues, take on debt, and authorize direct expenditures, greater amounts of resources can be redirected to provide public goods.

How are public goods and the agri-food economic system connected? Agriculture produces public goods. At the broad societal level, a highly developed and successful agricultural supply chain is an essential ingredient for modern civilization as we know it. While we can understand and respect the hunter-gatherer skills of our ancestors, we also know that agriculture made it possible for developed human settlements to replace a more primitive and transient lifestyle. The health, safety, and quality-of-life advantages of an advanced society, made possible by modern agricultural and food systems, is a public good with non-rival and non-exclusion benefits.

Agriculture also exercises a powerful influence on the earth's landscape. We can identify agricultural practices that can either add or subtract from the public goods that originate across vast regional areas. For example, US intensive crop-tillage production practices in the 1920s and early 1930s increased the susceptibility to soil erosion. When drought conditions in the mid-1930s combined with the erosive farm systems, the infamous "Dust Bowl" occurred. Before soil management improvements were subsequently introduced, agricultural practices associated with the "Dirty Thirties" created landscapes that damaged the public goods of clean air and water.

Moving forward in time to the twenty-first century, agricultural technologies and conservation systems have advanced considerably. Agricultural landscapes dominated by "low-till" and "no-till" practices conserve soils to benefit the farm producers themselves, as well as creating a public good of cleaner air and water because soils are safeguarded from excessive erosion.

Agriculture is also a beneficiary of public goods. Let's consider the services of "agricultural research and extension" as public goods. When we can produce and disseminate new knowledge, and share modern updates with all farm operators, then we harness the power of non-rival and non-exclusive goods to create a more productive economic sector.

As we look ahead, it is likely that the rest of society will have an ongoing interest in how our food and agricultural economy influences the production of public goods. For example, how does the US farm and food sector affect public good production associated with environmental quality, food security, or biodiversity? Industry leaders, government officials, agricultural researchers and other interest groups should be prepared to address these questions. The "public nature" of public goods often generates demands for transparency and accountability, and the agri-food system will be expected to respond.

Using public choice economics to interpret and improve US agri-food system policies

In the above discussion, we examined how externalities and public goods influence US agri-food system's economic performance. Inefficient outcomes associated with market failure cannot always be resolved by private sector action, and the search for alternatives opens the door for a public sector (i.e. government) role.

Earlier in this chapter, we also stated that public policies have their limitations. Not only are there circumstances where markets fail, government action can fall short too. Situations can and do arise where both private and public sector solutions to market challenges are imperfect. How do we choose a reasonable path under these conditions?

An immediate thought is to select the option that is the "lesser of two evils." While determining what policy action is best can be difficult, it is important to understand that inaction is a choice in itself. One definite step we can take is to equip ourselves with relevant knowledge and improve our understanding of the forces that influence public and private choices and their associated outcomes.

Our next discussion examines consequences when collective decision making, exercised primarily via the democratic (small "d") process of majority rule, determines how we allocate public goods and manage externalities. One conclusion that we reach is the importance of an electorate that is vigilant, rational, and fully informed when choosing policies and seeking outcomes consistent with real progress and development.

What is public choice economics? How does it contribute to policy analysis?

It is perhaps surprising to discover that the fundamentals of Public Choice Economics are based on analyzing the choices and consequences of *rational individual decision making*. Public choice theory makes predictions about collective decision making only after carefully analyzing individual citizens' incentives and behaviors.

The public choice paradigm assumes that individuals are self-interest optimizers who are active members of a democracy. As these rational citizens vote and use majority rule to make political decisions (*such as whether to provide public goods, and on what scale*), we can evaluate the economic consequences.

Nearly all decision processes have imperfections. We need to understand the strengths and weaknesses of democracies as public choice mechanisms. Public choice models offer logically consistent models to predict results. We can employ tools to forecast the economic performance of collective choices that emerge when individuals seek to improve their own welfare.

Public choice models have predictive power, and we can apply them to improve public policy design. Public choice theory offers insights into a wide range of collective decision-making mechanisms. Selected concepts that are central to public choice analysis follow:

- Models of alternative voter preferences predict both efficient and inefficient majority-rule election outcomes.
- *Arrow's Impossibility Theorem:* Nobel economist Ken Arrow carefully studied the connections between individual preferences and collective decision making, and concluded that *no collective choice mechanism* (including majority rule) can guarantee logical, rational, and efficient outcomes.[26]
- *Buchanan and Tullock's Calculus of Consent:* Building on Ken Arrow's research, economists James Buchanan and Gordon Tullock emphasized the proposition that majority-rule democracy is an ongoing experiment. The results of collective decision making (including voting) are likely to be imperfect. They argue that democracies still have the capacity to encourage efficient and equitable outcomes. However, that capacity must be exercised to be realized. Electorates should be vigilant in reviewing existing policies, cognizant of alternative competing policies, and active in replacing outdated policies.[27]
- Models of political economy can be used to analyze relationships between rent-seeking special interests and policy choices.
- Models of bureaucratic behavior predict a phenomenon known as "empire building."

Consequences of alternative voter preferences

Most modern democracies determine outcomes using majority-rule voting systems. Public choice analysis reveals that collective choices can be logically inconsistent when individual preferences are rational. Scenarios such as voting paradoxes, vote cycling, logrolling, and vote manipulation are possible when majority rule is the mechanism that determines public choice.[28]

From a policy-making standpoint, the potential failures of majority-rule voting is a cautionary note. We discussed market failure earlier in this chapter. Public choice theory tells us that we can encounter flaws in collective decision making too.

What are the lessons to be learned in agricultural and food policy when these imperfections are taken into account? Buchanan and Tullock's observations about participants being knowledgeable and vigilant are appropriate. A reasonable guideline is to set aside any assumptions that majority rule is a dependable mechanism that automatically seeks out the best economic end results. Any complacent notion that the "system always works" is likely a costly mistake. Instead, agri-food system participants should equip themselves with accurate knowledge of how the policy-making process takes place, and actively work to shape that process to achieve effective results.

Impossible outcomes and the rational choice calculus

The potential for imperfect results arising from majority-rule decision-making is to be expected, when Arrow's Impossibility Theorem is applied. Arrow concluded that we cannot guarantee logically transitive outcomes when we use reasonable rules to convert individual preferences into collective choices.

As stated above, Buchanan and Tullock use Arrow's theorem as a springboard to argue that the effectiveness of policies is highly dependent on how the politics of majority rule is managed. In this sense, politics and policy differ. *Politics determines the rules of the game, while policy involves designing and implementing strategies that can be successful within those rules.*

The ideas of Arrow, Buchanan, and Tullock have value for agri-food system policy. Using their recommendations, we discover that farm and food policy effectiveness goes beyond pure market economics. Developing a real political astuteness and paying strict attention to the details of policy making are also important. A successful agri-food system must be able to navigate both the rational demands of the market economy as well as the less predictable effects of the political economy.

The world of rent-seeking interests and empire-building bureaucracies

Up to this point, our focus has been the effect of individual voter incentives on collective choice. While this perspective is important, just as significant (maybe even more so) is the phenomenon of multiple participants banding together around a common interest to influence public outcomes.

When individuals coalesce into a special interest group, they can exert proportionately larger economic power than if the group members were to act separately to achieve the same end-goal. In public choice analysis, when these groups can influence government programs to gain above-normal economic returns, their actions are known as "rent seeking." Rents are a powerful incentive to engage in an activity.[29]

If we borrow Buchanan's terminology, we can explain the "benefit-cost calculus" of special interests and their pursuit of rents. At the heart of an interest group's power is often a differentiating characteristic or quality in comparison to the overall population. The group's membership may have a higher voter participation rate, a greater willingness to make financial sacrifices, or simply a higher income or wealth than the general populous.

When special interests are successful in their lobbying efforts, they benefit from unique program or policy provisions that improve their economic circumstances. Taxpayers, consumers or other economic participants pay the cost. Why does this happen? There a number of reasons.

Interest group members develop natural networks that reduce connection costs as they internally gather and share vital information about policy-making opportunities. The most effective interest groups are highly organized. Consequently, they can more easily wield their influence at the right time and place to obtain economically favorable legislative provisions for their members. The benefits of successful lobbying tend also to be concentrated. Each member of the interest group can have a large economic stake in the effectiveness of their collective lobbying effort.

What is the situation for those who ultimately shoulder the cost of special interest programs? Individual taxpayers or consumers may not even be aware that others' lobbying efforts have increased living costs. As already stated, the advantages of new programs clearly benefit the special interests, and the financial gains are concentrated among relatively few recipients. In contrast, the costs are frequently uncertain and widely dispersed. Even if taxpayers and/or consumers do know that they carry the burden, the costs of organizing opposition to special interest proposals are considerable. The broadly distributed interests discover that the expense of mounting a resistance to the well-organized special interests is simply not worth the effort.

Rent seeking by *special interests* is just one element in the evolution of public policy. The other key participants are legislators and bureaucracies. *Legislators* sanction new policies and *bureaucracies* implement them. Public choice theory studies the incentives that drive the choices and actions of legislators and bureaucrats. In brief, legislators are assumed to be vote maximizers, while bureaucrats seek to increase the size of their budgets as a means to maximize their spheres of power and influence.

Let's examine bureaucratic economic tendencies first. We will shortly return to their connections with the legislators and also with the special interest groups.

William Niskanen pioneered research on bureaucracy behavior. Economic inefficiency is a predicted result of his hypothesis that bureaucrats maximize agency budgets. Bigger budgets generally enlarge an agency's authority and increases its prestige. Unfortunately, when we examine this budget expansion tendency in detail, we find that *agencies tend to operate where total benefits equal total costs.* Economic efficiency demands that operations produce where marginal benefit equals marginal cost. The bureaucratic incentive is to inflate the agency budget beyond where marginality would determine an optimal size. Niskanen used the "empire building" terminology to characterize the expansive nature of bureaucratic agencies and the inefficient consequences.[30]

The Iron Triangle

In the discussion directly above, we examined the phenomena of empire building, vote maximizing, and rent seeking. What happens when these three powerful incentives are joined together by political and policy-making processes? The results are important to understand.

We have already used the tools of public choice economics to establish the significant roles of special interests, bureaucrats, and legislators.

When these three major participants organize themselves to make decisions on major policy initiatives (such as the Farm Bill, the FSMA, and the TPP), we discover that their motivations are mutually reinforced. Their three-way relationship is known as the "Iron Triangle." The term indicates a three-sided association where the connecting bonds are very strong.[31]

The iron triangle is a powerful mechanism for legislators, special interests, and bureaucracies to support each other's economic agendas. Public choice theory emphasizes that individual incentives drive these policy participants to form a triad of mutual cooperation. Unfortunately, rent-seeking, vote-maximizing, and empire-building are not behaviors that we expect to improve national economic performance. Iron triangles have no built-in systems translating individual incentives into efficient or equitable outcomes that benefit the entire economy. If contributions to the "greater good" arise from iron triangle relationships, those results are as likely to be coincidental as compared to any outcome associated with some grand design.

The way forward

Any serious study of public choice economics dispels the notion that government is a simple tax-funded mechanism to produce public goods and improve societal welfare. Thoughtful insights, such as Arrow's Impossibility Theorem or Buchanan's Calculus of Consent, clearly demonstrate the limitations of collective decision making.

As indicated earlier in this chapter, "government failure" and "market failure" are real phenomena that fully test our ability to design and implement effective policies. The iron triangle and market externalities are reminders of the imperfections that characterize real-world political and economic systems. Our decision-making systems do create inefficient and inequitable outcomes. These results seem far removed from the ideal conditions discussed and predicted in our economic models. A reasonable question is whether any action can make societal improvements in actual policy situations.

Are our systems damaged beyond repair? The answer is no, if we follow the recommendations of scholars such as Nobel laureate James Buchanan. Buchanan capsulized his optimistic perspective in 1960 when he observed:[32]

> Majority rule allows a sort of jockeying back and forth among alternatives, upon none of which relative unanimity can be obtained.It serves to insure that competing alternatives may be experimentally and provisionally adopted, tested and replaced by new compromise alternatives approved by a majority group of ever-changing composition.

Buchanan is effectively arguing that knowledgeable and engaged participants retain the opportunity to make progress. Economist Harvey Rosen similarly observes that those who prefer to utilize private markets as resource allocation mechanisms consistently pursue innovations to enhance their performance. Rosen confidently asserts that improvements in public sector outcomes are equally possible.[33]

Conclusions

We just completed a brief outline of the challenges and opportunities for policy design and analysis using the concepts of public choice economics.

In combination with the various analytical tools that we have studied throughout this chapter, we are now better prepared to investigate the diverse policy challenges arising within our dynamic agricultural and food economy.

Looking ahead to the remaining chapters of this text, we are equipped to explore opportunities and address questions central to twenty-first-century US farm and food sector economic performance. The investigations into our agri-food system will require us to engage in important and interesting policy work. Mastery of the analytical tools in this chapter will enable our efforts to be both worthwhile and productive.

Most policy makers support the goal of improving our capacity to feed the world in an economical, equitable, and sustainable manner. You can use this policy textbook as a vehicle to increase your expertise on the very issues that are at the heart of creating a more efficient, food-secure, and environmentally sound world.

If you are ready, let's move onto investigating the policy choices and consequences that lie ahead.

Notes

1 Krohn, Tim. "Buffer Strip Proposal to be Discussed at Minnesota Farm Forum." The Free Press, Mankato, MN, AgWeb, Farm Journal, Dec. 31, 2015. www.agweb.com/article/buffer-strip-proposal-to-be-discussed-at-minnesota-farm-forum—naa-news-wire/

2 Chicago Mercantile Exchange (CME) Inc. "CME Reports Average Daily Volume of More Than 3.2 Million Contracts in November, Up 40 Percent from Prior-Year Period." Chicago, Dec. 1, 2004.   PRNewswire-FirstCall.   http://investor.cmegroup.com/investor-relations/releasedetail.cfm?ReleaseID=159301

3 The Concise Encyclopedia of Economics. "Alfred Marshall (1842–1924)." 2008 Liberty Fund. Library of Economics and Liberty. www.econlib.org/library/Enc/bios/Marshall.html

4 Kleinman, George. "The Exchange, 'Open Outcry' and the Clearinghouse." *Trading Commodities and Financial Future: A Step by Step Guide to Mastering the Markets*, 3rd Edition. Upper Saddle River, NJ : FT Press. 2004. www.Ftpress.Com/Articles/Article.Aspx?P=360436&Seqnum=8

5 Okrent, Abigail M., and Julian M. Alston. "The Demand for Disaggregated Food-Away-From-Home and Food-at-Home Products in the United States." ERR-139, U.S. Department of Agriculture, Economic Research Service, August 2012. www.ers.usda.gov/media/875267/err139.pdf

6 Bentley, Jenine. "Food Availability and Consumption." USDA, Economic Research Service. Ag and Food Statistics: Charting the Essentials. Sept. 18, 2015. www.ers.usda.gov/data-products/ag-and-food-statistics-charting-the-essentials/food-availability-and-consumption.aspx

7 Okrent, Abigail M., and Julian M. Alston. "The Demand for Disaggregated Food-Away-From-Home and Food-at-Home Products in the United States." ERR-139, U.S. Department of Agriculture, Economic Research Service, August 2012. www.ers.usda.gov/media/875267/err139.pdf

8 Ibid, pp. 43–60.

9 Ibid.

10 Ibid.

11 Ibid.

12 Ibid, pp. 6, 18.

13 Okrent, Abigail M. and Julian M. Alston. "The Demand for Disaggregated Food-Away-From-Home and Food-at-Home Products in the United States." ERR-139, U.S. Department of Agriculture, Economic Research Service, p. ii, August 2012.

14 Bergtold, Jason, Ebere Akobundu, and Everett B. Peterson. "The FAST Method: Estimating Unconditional Demand Elasticities for Processed Foods in the Presence of Fixed Effects." *Journal of Agricultural and Resource Economics* 29(2): 276–295, p. 28, 2004.

15 Okrent, Abigail M., and Julian M. Alston. "The Demand for Disaggregated Food-Away-From-Home and Food-at-Home Products in the United States." ERR-139, U.S. Department of Agriculture, Economic Research Service, p. 28, August 2012.

16 Ibid.

17 Dahl, Dale C. and Jerome W. Hammond. *Market and Price Analysis: The Agricultural Industries.* New York: McGraw-Hill, 1977, pp. 100–109.

18 Rosen, Harvey and Ted Gayer. *Public Finance.* Ninth Edition. New York: McGraw Hill Education, 2010, pp. 556–557.

19 Ibid, pp. 557–558.

20 This scenario borrows the analysis of the Large Nation Model for Tariff Welfare Effects, developed by Robert Carbaugh on pp. 131–134 in his textbook on international economics. Citation: Carbaugh, Robert J. *International Economics.* Thirteenth Edition. Mason, OH: Southwestern Cengage Learning, 2008, pp. 131–134.

21 Rosen, Harvey. *Public Finance.* Sixth Edition. New York: McGraw Hill Education, 2002, pp. 34–37.

22 Carbaugh, Robert J. *International Economics.* Thirteenth Edition. Mason, OH: Southwestern Cengage Learning, 2008, pp. 32–36.

23 Cohen, C.J., L.C. Grothaus, and S.C. Perrigan. "Effects of Simulated Sulfuric Acid Rain on Crop Plants." Agricultural Experiment Station, Oregon State University, Corvallis. Special Report 619, May 1981.

24 Smith, S.J., E. Conception, R. Andres, and J. Lurz. "Historical Sulfur Dioxide Emissions 1850-2000: Methods and Results." Battelle Pacific Northwest National Laboratory. PNNL-14537. January 2004. www.pnl.gov/main/publications/external/technical_reports/PNNL-14537.pdf

25 Lang, Brian J., Sawyer, John E., and Barnhart, Stephen K. (2007) "Dealing with Sulfur Deficiency in Northeast Iowa Alfalfa Production." Animal Industry Report: AS 653, ASL R2202. Available at: http://lib.dr.iastate.edu/ans_air/vol653/iss1/28
26 Arrow, Kenneth J. *Social Choice and Individual Values*. New York: Wiley Publishers, 1951.
27 Buchanan, James and Gordon Tullock. *The Calculus of Consent: Logical Foundations of a Constitutional Democracy*. Ann Arbor, MI: University of Michigan Press, 1965.
28 Rosen, Harvey and Ted Gayer. *Public Finance*. Ninth Edition. New York: McGraw Hill Education, 2010, pp. 110–114.
29 Ibid, pp. 124–126.
30 Niskanen, William A. *Bureaucracy and Representative Government*. Chicago, IL: Aldine Publishers, 1971.
31 Rosen, Harvey. *Public Finance*. Sixth Edition. New York: McGraw Hill Education, 2002, pp. 124–125.
32 Ibid, p. 116.
33 Ibid, p. 133.

Chapter 4

Analyzing economic consequences of farm safety net programs in the 2014 Farm Bill

When we visit the USDA website to review the Agricultural Act of 2014, a pie chart reveals that household nutrition programs constitute 80 percent of the Act's total budget.[1] Additional research tells us that the purposes of the Agricultural Act extend considerably beyond the farm sector. The 2014 Agricultural Act funds initiatives such as the Supplemental Nutrition Assistance Program (SNAP) and the Commodity Supplemental Food Program (CSFP). Nevertheless, Congressional representatives, journalists, and many other interests simply refer to this Act as the "Farm Bill". Why?

The "Farm Bill" has a long history. The familiar label for this Act is easy to remember. Funding included in the Act continues to support core agricultural programs traceable to eight decades of legislative tradition. For these reasons, and additional rationales not enumerated here, we have confidence that the "Farm Bill" moniker will persist.

The educated observer knows that the "Farm Bill" is an unpretentious name for an omnibus piece of legislation that provides funding for a complex set of multi-year farm-and-food programs.[2]

What are the origins of the farm safety net?

"Permanent" farm bill legislation influences the agricultural side of the 2014 Act. When the US Congress passed the 1938 Agricultural Adjustment Act, and later the 1949 Agriculture Act, it designated a subset of farm commodity price-support programs as perpetual.

Why does this matter? The law's durability is political leverage to take action. Unless the US Congress suspends the law's permanent sections when the Farm Bill is renewed, then these selected commodity programs revert back to their original 1938 and 1949 formats.

As explained in Chapter 2, the 1930s Great Depression financially devastated the US farm economy. Congress enacted the 1930 Smoot-Hawley tariffs, foreign trade dropped precipitously, and the negative impacts on American agriculture were particularly harsh.

Repeal of Smoot-Hawley and the creation of reciprocal trade agreements in the mid-1930s did reopen US agricultural trade. The recovery rate was regrettably sluggish.

A toxic combination of farm foreclosures, bank failures, depressed commodity prices, and the "Dust Bowl" challenged the conventional logic that the private market would rebound on its own.

Severe economic circumstances created sufficient political pressure to institute a farm financial safety net. Congress responded with the first Farm Bill in 1933. The US Supreme Court struck down parts of the 1933 farm bill as unconstitutional. Revisions were made, and the 1938 Agricultural Adjustment Act emerged. Not including 1933, there have been 16 farm bills up through 2014.[3]

Our particular interest in this chapter is an analysis of the 2014 Farm Bill programs that serve as the core components of the farm safety net. History demonstrates that congressional efforts to lessen downside farm financial risks are consistent with the original farm bill's stated purposes.

Organization of chapter

Economic and technological advances have vastly transformed US Agriculture since the first constitutionally valid 1938 Farm Bill. One constant in this dynamic environment is the predictable tendency of the US Congress to offer producers financial safeguards in successive farm bills. The ongoing purpose of "farm commodity programs" is to secure farm income against market and production risk.

The 2014 Farm Bill is a large and multifaceted legislative initiative. We constrain our investigation to the most prominent safety net programs. We consequently organize this chapter to review the following sequence of topics, based on selected titles in the 2014 Farm Bill:

- Title I   Commodities

  o   Commodity Policy: Price Loss Coverage (PLC) and Agriculture Risk Coverage (ARC)
  o   Marketing Assistance Loan Program
  o   Sugar and Dairy Policies
  o   Supplemental Agricultural Disaster Assistance

- Title XI – Crop Insurance

  o   Revenue and/or Yield Insurance
  o   Premium Subsidy Levels
  o   Supplemental Coverage Option (SCO)
  o   Stacked-Income protection plan for producers of upland cotton (STAX).

- Economic Effects of the 2014 Farm Bill's Farm Safety Net

  o   Influences on Production, Trade, and Economic Efficiency
  o   Income Distribution Effects
  o   Political Economy of Current and Future Farm Bills

A continuing goal for this textbook is to promote thoughtful reflections on policy choices and their consequences. The content of this chapter is well suited to our main objective. Title I commodity programs, along with Title XI subsidized federal crop insurance, are the 2014 Farm Bill's main mechanisms fostering the financial survival of farm producers. These farm bill programs are counter-cyclical – they aim to restore farm incomes damaged by market downturns and/or natural catastrophes.

There are many important perspectives to consider when exploring these traditional agricultural programs. Farm managers and US Congressional representatives often emphasize different aspects. The farm producer-operator typically stresses an overall risk management viewpoint. Participation in a government-sponsored commodity or insurance program is just one of several tools that producers can use to manage risk in their farm operations.

On the other hand, as stated by Chairman of the House Agriculture Committee Representative. Frank Lucas, the public policy outlook on these programs is to create a "safety net" that helps the overall farm economy survive the financial extremes caused by natural disasters and/or difficult market conditions.[4]

Commodity and crop insurance programs offer a rich source of scenarios suitable for policy analysis. The work we will be doing is both interesting and meaningful. Let's begin.

A review of the 2014 Farm Bill's Title I – Subtitle A: commodity policy

Public Law (P.L.) 113-79, better known as the 2014 Farm Bill, is a 357-page legislative document subdivided into twelve titles (major provisions). Title I establishes the federal commodity policy that will remain in force through the end of Fiscal Year 2018.

Title I's policy impact combines continuity and reform. A carry-over from previous farm bills is the Congressional effort to maintain an effective farm safety net within Title I. The reform involves the discontinuation of prior commodity programs and the creation of new ones.

Repeal of the previous Direct Payment Program (DPP), Counter-Cyclical Payment Program (CCP), and the Average Crop Revenue Election (ACRE) Program was the first order of business in Title I. Elimination of these three programs, particularly the annual DPP producer payments, created projected federal budget savings of $47 billion over the next 10 years. The savings were determined relative to what government spending would have been if the baseline 2008 farm bill budget had continued unchanged.[5]

The US Congressional Research Service (CRS) estimates that nearly 75 percent of the expected 10-year budget savings (about $35.3 billion) *was redirected* within the 2014 Farm Bill to expand current programs and/or create new ones.[6] Consequently, the projected *net* federal budget savings associated with repealing the previous Title I programs was only about $11.7 billion (not $47 billion).

How were the original savings from the program repeals reallocated? Some funds were designated to permanently create disaster assistance programs for qualified producers of livestock, honeybees, and farm-raised fish. The remainder of the reallocated budget dollars expanded support for Title XI federal crop insurance programs, as well as helping to establish two new commodity programs under Title I.

Creation of the PLC and ARC programs within Title I

Congress filled the void of the eliminated 2008 commodity programs by instituting the Price-Loss Coverage (PLC) and the Agriculture Risk Coverage (ARC) Programs in 2014.

PLC and ARC are financial safety-net alternatives available to eligible producers of selected crops covered within Title I. In brief, PLC is a traditional counter-cyclical program where farmers receive government pay-outs when market prices fall below legislated reference prices. If a producer believed that depressed commodity prices would continuously prevail through 2018, he/she would likely be considering a PLC enrollment. On the other hand, ARC is a program that provides revenue protection (price multiplied by yield). ARC is attractive to producers seeking a safeguard against revenue falloffs associated with either price or yield reductions.

Farm producers eligible for Title I program-benefits were encouraged to educate themselves on the possible impacts of PLC or ARC participation on their operations. Then, prior to the publicized April 8, 2015 deadline, make an irrevocable choice to protect themselves against downside market- and/or yield-risk *under* **one** *of these two programs*. Funding was included in the 2014 Farm Bill for the USDA and land-grant universities to offer seminars, create scenario-simulation software programs, and disseminate information to help producers with the decision-making process.

Why create the PLC v. ARC choice?

Both politics and economics were important considerations when Congress decided to structure Title I participation as a producer choice between PLC and ARC. Politically, the design of the ARC program is popular with farm producers in the US Midwest and upper Great Plains, whereas the PLC program is a better fit for farm operators in the South.[7] Coalitions are necessary to obtain a majority vote in favor of any farm bill. Title I program choices helped create broader geographic support for the 2014 Farm Bill.

There are various economic rationales favoring a producer choice between competing alternatives to manage downside risk (such as PLC v. ARC). One aspect is the diversity of farm operators. Not all producers have the same risk attitudes. Some have substantial risk aversion, while others favor risk-neutral or risk-loving behaviors. Differing degrees of financial risk tolerance means that the PLC v. ARC decision is significantly influenced by the preferences of farm operators (and their financial advisors).

In addition, the optimal risk management strategy for one farm enterprise might not be the same as for another. Small, medium, and large-scale operations often have different production economies. Farm managers can and should perform scenario simulations to make rational determinations of the optimal program choice. The USDA and university software packages funded by the 2014 Farm Bill proved to be highly valued analytical tools. Numerous producers were able to simulate alternative program impacts and make informed decisions about their Title I options.[8]

Detailed aspects of the PLC v. ARC enrollment decision

It is very important to outline additional enrollment options and requirements that influence the producer's rational choice to be a PLC or ARC participant. Let's examine these considerations:[9]

Option to update Title I commodity payment yields

This option is primarily relevant for PLC participants. On a crop-by-crop basis, producers have the opportunity to reset their crop yield values for determining PLC payouts.

Subsequent to the elimination of previous Title I programs (DPP, CCP, and ACRE), US Congressional leaders sought to offer producers a one-time opportunity to update their

"farm profiles" as a means of maximizing benefits associated participation in th
Commodity programs.

Title I disbursements to producers are determined using *historical* "progr
yields" when unfavorable market conditions trigger PLC pay-outs to producers.

Prior to the 2014 Farm Bill, many payment yields were 93.5 percent of 1998–2001 crop
yield averages. If a producer updates, then the payment basis changes to 90 percent of
2008–2012 average yields. If the 2008–2012 average yields are 3.9 percent higher than the
1998–2001 averages, then a participating PLC producer is better off with the increased
payment yield.[10]

What is the policy aspect of this update? The PLC payment calculation is based on *historical
yields*, not on current or expected yields. This is a key feature. No matter what the farm
operator does in the current growing season, the historical payment yield is unaffected. As a
result, the producer has no incentive to alter current production methods in relation to program participation. The *decoupling of the government program yield* from the farmer's production decision is a good outcome. The likelihood of a program creating a "distorted market"
is reduced.

Market distortions reduce economic efficiency, and they adversely affect the economy's
potential to fully benefit from free trade agreements. When programs have a decoupled design,
distortions are largely avoided. One lesson to draw from this discussion is the improved
economic performance that can be achieved if we pay attention to policy design details.

Option to reallocate within program base acres

This provision permitted each producer to *reallocate* Title I program crop acres within a
constant overall base. The goal is to let producers change their program structure to better
match their current ratio of alternative crops. This reallocation option is relevant for either
PLC or ARC enrollment.[11] No increase in total base acres occurs.

After a producer reallocates the crop mix within the base program acres, the change
becomes permanent over the life of the 2014 Farm Bill (at least through FY 2018). What is
the policy impact? Similar to the effect of the historical yields, payments to producers are
determined by program acres, not planted or harvested acres. Producers *cannot increase* their
PLC or ARC payments by placing more acres of a crop into current production. The impact
of the Title I program-acres is *decoupled* from the current production decision. A program
where the production-acreage decision is decoupled from market distortions is a more efficient and trade-friendly outcome.[12]

It is important to point out that the PLC and ARC programs are only partially decoupled
from market distortions. Because program payments are triggered when market prices fall
below the legislated reference prices, both PLC and ARC are "coupled" to the market via
the price mechanism. A degree of market distortion is associated with program coupling to
market prices.

Counter-cyclical or shallow-loss coverage

PLC and ARC offer producers fundamentally different methods of risk management. Making
an informed choice on whether PLC or ARC is the best fit for downside risk protection
requires detailed analysis. We can outline some prominent factors that should play a role in
the decision:

- The choice between PLC and ARC should be evaluated for *interactions with other risk management tools*. For example, the producer's decision on crop insurance coverage levels, in combination with PLC or ARC protection, has a significant bearing on the producer's overall capacity to reduce income variability.
- The PLC v. ARC decision also depends on whether it is better for a producer to seek a *counter-cyclical safeguard* against downside price risk (lean towards the PLC option), or if it is just as important to have coverage against decreases in either crop yield and/or crop price (lean towards ARC's revenue protection).
- If producer chooses to enroll in PLC, then a related decision arises: should the producer pay an extra premium to purchase the Supplemental Coverage Option (SCO)?

    SCO is a risk protection tool newly introduced by the 2014 Farm Bill. SCO is a type of *"shallow loss coverage."* SCO Shallow loss protection allows a producer to purchase a crop insurance "rider" to shelter the producer from most of the specific risk exposure associated with the insurance deductible.
- If a producer chooses an ARC enrollment, then SCO is not available. However, the producer still faces an additional decision: choose to participate in ARC-County (ARC-CO) or ARC-Individual Coverage (ARC-IC).

    If a producer enrolls in ARC-County, then the decision to be a PLC or ARC participant can be made crop-by-crop.

    Farmers who elect the ARC-IC option cannot enroll in PLC; instead, they qualify for payments based on their farm's own yields. ARC-IC, by definition, is a self-contained whole-farm coverage program that protects the sum of all farm-level program revenues from downside risk. ARC-IC's unique aspects are expected to limit its popularity as a Title I commodity program choice.

    ARC-County is another shallow loss coverage program. Revenue payments to producers are triggered when actual county revenue falls below 86 percent of a county revenue benchmark. Producers receive payment revenues only within a narrow window equal to 10 percent of the county revenue benchmark. Consequently, shallow loss coverage in ARC-CO happens between 86 percent and 76 percent of the revenue benchmark.

Revenue caps and conservation requirements

Two additional aspects of Title I programs apply equally to PLC and ARC participants. Maximum program payment level per producer is one consideration. Compliance with USDA resource conservation rules is the other.

Why impose payment-ceilings on Title I revenues? As discussed in Chapter 2, *average annual US farm household income* in the twenty-first century dramatically increased in comparison to its low levels in the twentieth century. In fact, the typical income of a US farm household today *is well above the average income of all US households.* At one time, it made sense to use farm programs to redistribute income towards undervalued farm households. That era has passed.

There are political consequences associated with the improved financial status of US farm households. Lobbyists working on behalf of taxpayers and related interests have pressured Congress to place limits on the maximum payment dollar amounts that producers can receive from government programs. In the case of Title I benefits in the 2014 Farm Bill, the cap is set at $125,000 for a single producer, or $250,000 for married couples.[13] The 2014 Farm Bill also created a new Title I program eligibility criterion based on the tax code's

Adjusted Gross Income (AGI) measure. If a producer's AGI is above $900,000, then the producer no longer qualifies for Title I payments.[14]

Why is program eligibility tied to conservation practices? Both politics and economics influence this requirement. Politically, the voting majority needed to pass a Farm Bill depends on garnering a broad coalition of interest groups. Vocal segments of the conservation coalition include volunteer organizations and commercial interests whose preferences and livelihoods are dependent on access to a "clean" natural environment. These groups lobby Congress to introduce conservation incentives into the farm bill.

Economically, as discussed in Chapter 3, the proper management of externalities creates efficient market outcomes. When the beneficiaries of Title I safety-net programs engage in production practices that *prevent* excessive soil erosion and preserve key wetlands, then downwind and downstream externalities are avoided.

US Congressional policies specifically require that Title I beneficiaries *refrain from* production practices that employ highly erodible lands, or "dry up" essential wetlands. These linked policies are known respectively as the "Sodbuster" and "Swampbuster" provisions of Title I eligibility. When participation in one program (Title I) is contingent on following the rules of other programs (such as Resource Conservation), the connection is known as "cross-compliance policy."

Lessons learned from analysis of the PLC and ARC Title I programs in the 2014 Farm Bill

Congress restructured the Title I Crop Commodity Program to become the PLC v. ARC producer-decision within the 2014 Farm Bill. The creation of these new programs is an indication of the federal government's ongoing interest in supporting the US agricultural economy. We can summarize that support as follows:

- Looking forward, Congress's goal is to be a force for farm financial stability. Title I programs safeguard producers against unstable market and production conditions.
- The status of household farm incomes in relation to the non-farm economy has changed. Average household farm income is no longer undervalued. As a result, Congress will face political pressure to limit the total benefits that a producer can receive from government farm-program participation.
- Congress reserves the right to place conditions on the production decisions of farmers who participate in government programs and receive public payments. For example, producers are expected to abide by resource conservation rules as a condition for receiving Title I payments.
- Congress intends to offer producers the resources and options they need to maximize their available benefits from farm programs. Research, education, and extension are the "three legs of the stool" that help make this a successful effort. Congress also has an interest in policies that encourage free trade and prevent market distortions.

Title I – Subtitle B: Marketing Assistance Loan Program

The 2014 Farm Bill renewed the long-standing Marketing Assistance Loan Program (MALP) in Title I with few changes. What is MALP?

MALP is a voluntary program where a producer can inexpensively borrow funds that are secured by the value of harvested Title I commodities.

An eligible MALP producer offers all or part of his/her harvested commodity's production as collateral, and then borrows funds for nine months from the federally subsidized Commodity Credit Corporation (CCC) at a crop-specific per-unit "county loan rate" (or price). MALP county loan rates are noticeably lower than their counterpart PLC reference prices.

Farm managers often use MALP as a low-cost cash-flow management tool to help administer their marketing expenses after harvest. MALP interest rates are inexpensive. In December 2015, the USDA Farm Service Agency indicated a 1.375 percent annual interest rate on 9-month CCC loans.[15]

There are three options for producers to settle their MALP loans with the CCC:[16]

- Producers repay the CCC at the statutory county loan rate, plus interest.
- If county market prices decrease below the county loan rate (plus interest), then producers are allowed to repay the CCC at a reduced alternative county loan repayment rate.
- If market prices decrease below the county loan rate, the producer can choose to forfeit the crop to the CCC at loan maturity. Legislatively, the CCC is required to accept the forfeit as a sufficient loan settlement. The CCC cannot take any recourse action against the producer. As a result, this type of borrowing agreement is known as a *non-recourse loan.*

MALP also serves as an additional farm safety-net program. When commodity market prices have fallen dramatically, MALP can be a source of funds (called "deficiency payments") for qualified producers.

For example, in cases where market commodity prices have "crashed" to very low levels, then MALP's safety-net role will likely apply. In these instances, market prices fall below the loan rates, and a producer can repay the CCC loan at a reduced alternative rate. In effect, part of the CCC loan has been forgiven, and this arrangement is a *measurable program benefit.*

When market prices are this low, producers who have not taken out loans through MALP qualify to receive the loan program benefit. Eligible producers apply for a source of funds known as a "*loan deficiency payment*" or LDP. An LDP is the net difference between the normal loan rate and the lower alternative rate. Basically, the safety-net function of MALP is available to all eligible producers, current borrowers or not.

There are "circuit-breaker" regulations that prevent the potential abuse of MALP payments. Any producer-borrower who has already received the MALP program benefit is not eligible for further loans. Similarly, if a producer has received an LDP, those funds cannot be used as collateral for obtaining a new marketing loan or another LDP.[17]

Marketing assistance: distortions, payment limitations, and cross-compliance

In our earlier discussion of the Title I PLC program, we noted that eligible producers receive payments when the national average annual commodity price decreases below the legislated reference price. We also observed that PLC payments are determined using historical program acres.

The conditions that trigger Loan Deficiency Payments (LDPs) from the MALP program are noticeably different. Statutory loan rate prices are significantly below comparable PLC reference prices. MALP uses county-level loan rates, while PLC reference prices are national averages. County-level market prices are compared to statutory county loan rates to determine if loan program benefits or loan deficiency payments are activated. PLC and ARC payments are calculated with historically determined base acres, whereas MALP payments vary by current production volume.

The MALP program design clearly distorts markets. MALP program payments increase as the market price diverges further below the loan rate. An increase in total harvested production also leads to larger MALP payments to producers. Producers have incentives to "farm the program" both on the basis of price and production. In situations where market prices are extremely low, the market is sending out a signal to curtail production because of an over-abundance of the commodity. When producers are receiving MALP program benefits and LDP's, the program is encouraging them to supply more. This market-distorting result is problematic, especially when the US is promoting participation in free trade agreements that depend on adhering to market-friendly policies.

Fortunately, in recent years, commodity market prices have not been hovering at the low levels that cause MALP payments to be distributed. Critics point out, however, that even in years where LDPs and program benefits do not happen, producers still can use MALP as a subsidized loan mechanism. They question why producers are allowed to pay below-market interest rates for marketing loans in seasons when commodity market prices are profitable for producers.

MALP payments, as a highly visible Title I program, also place participating producers under increased scrutiny for the total amount of government support that they receive. The same caps or limits that apply to PLC or ARC payments also include any funds received through MALP. As a result, producers who qualify for Title I safety-net coverage must "keep track" of their overall benefits from all Title I programs summed together. Producers with an AGI of $900,000 or more cannot receive any Title I funds. More generally, an individual producer cannot receive any additional Title I funds beyond a $125,000 cap written into the 2014 Farm Bill.

Cross-compliance with "Sodbuster and Swampbuster" conservation provisions of the farm bill is another policy area where MALP, PLC, and ARC are all connected. MALP participants are required to adhere to production practices consistent with soil and wetland conservation requirements.

It makes sense to design programs with integrated goals and purposes. Connecting eligibility for the farm safety-net to conservation-friendly production practices is an idea can be defended as a logical and equitable policy. One drawback to conservation cross-compliance is its mandatory nature. It does restrict the producer's freedom to choose production methods. On the other hand, it is also societally and economically efficient to encourage practices that limit or prevent the occurrence of externalities such as erosion or chemical runoff into waterways. The policy-making process often involves balancing pluses and minuses.

Title I – Subtitle C: The US Sugar Program

Our above compliance-policy discussion seemingly indicates that Congress designs farm programs to function cohesively together. Appearances can be deceiving. A unified farm policy is theoretically a desirable outcome. In reality, logically consistent farm policy is very difficult to achieve.

When we examine the elements of the US Sugar Program, we discover that logical connections to decoupling policies and the pursuit of economically efficient markets is just not a relevant consideration. The design of the Sugar Program has few parallels elsewhere in farm policy today.

Let's begin our review by noting that the current Sugar Program structure *was approved unchanged as part of the 2014 Farm Bill*. The continuation of this program "intact" without any reforms is an amazing result. Prior to its passage, there were vigorous Congressional debates about sugar program provisions, and a number of bills were introduced by prominent senators and representatives to alter the policy. All attempts to amend the program failed, and its current structure will likely remain in place at least until FY 2018.[18]

The US Sugar Program's uniqueness reveals itself throughout the entire supply chain. Beginning with farm production, the program explicitly identifies sugarcane and sugar beets as the sugar sources processed into a humanly consumed final product. As raw commodities, sugarcane and sugar beets are cumbersome and perishable. They are not easily standardized to become a basis for establishing a government payment program. As a result, the Sugar Program's primary point of contact occurs at the supply chain's processing stage.

Other Title I programs, such as PLC and MALP, directly provide payments to *farm producers*. In contrast, the Sugar Program offers low-interest, 9-month CCC non-recourse loans to *sugar processors*. Sugar processors, as part of the loan qualifying process, must promise to distribute payments to producers in proportion to the value of the CCC loans that processors receive. Congress empowers the USDA to set minimum producer payment amounts.

The 2014 Farm Bill authorizes the USDA (via its CCC division, between Fiscal Years 2011 to 2018) to extend these short-term loans to sugar processors at the following loan rates (price support levels):[19]

- 18.75 cents per pound for raw cane sugar, and
- 24.09 cents per pound for refined beet sugar.

Processors can also obtain loans for in-process sugar and syrups at 80 percent of the applicable loan rate. Reflecting value-added processing, the refined beet sugar loan rate (24.09¢/lb.) is greater than the raw sugar cane loan rate (18.75¢/lb.)

Qualified sugar processors use their sugar as collateral, and receive non-recourse CCC loans. Under certain prescribed market conditions (when market prices are low enough), processors are permitted to forfeit their collateral to settle the loan, and the USDA's CCC division becomes the party that must dispose the asset.

Under normal market conditions, if the CCC were to simply sell forfeited sugar onto the open market, the equilibrium sugar price would decrease further and the CCC would experience a loss. The market loss would normally be a cost shouldered by the government. But the sugar program does not follow typical market processes.

By law, the US Sugar Program cannot create a cost to the government. How does the Sugar Program avoid normal market processes? The answer is an ingenious set of rules that require careful study to be fully understood. Some observers who prefer to see regular market forces at work also find the Sugar Program requirements to be troubling.

So, how does the CCC handle a sugar-processor loan forfeiture, and avoid a government cost? The 2014 Farm Bill empowers the USDA to use a payment-in-kind (PIK) authority. Basically, the USDA returns control of the CCC sugar to the processors in exchange for decreased production. Planted-sugar acres are required to decrease, restoring the supply and demand balance. If the sugar acres are already planted, then the processor is not permitted to sell the crop other than as a feedstock to produce biofuel.[20]

There is no doubt that the details of the entire sugar program are difficult to understand. One way to simplify the program is to identify it as a *substantial supply management program that has one very specific objective: control the overall supply-demand balance such that the Sugar Program operates at no cost to the Federal Government.*

To achieve this objective, the USDA must estimate national demand patterns, and then work hard to manage the national supply of sugar from all sources, both foreign and domestic. The USDA's goal is to create a managed market price that is above the loan forfeiture rate. To accomplish this delicate task, the Congress empowers the USDA to use a combination of domestic marketing allotments and tariff-rate-quotas on imports to generate a supply-demand balance-price that is above the forfeiture loan rate (support price).[21]

The US forfeiture loan rate is a *sugar price level* that is considerably above the typical world price for sugar on open international markets. The US sugar market is basically insulated from the normal influences of global free trade.

There is not enough space in this chapter to examine all of the US Sugar Program's intricate details. Those interested in the full pursuit are encouraged to access the cited sources in the chapter's endnotes.

Before leaving this topic, a key question deserves attention. Exactly how does the Sugar Program maintain its power? The short answer lies in the political economy of the program's supporters. Known as the American Sugar Alliance (ASA), they are a knowledgeable and tightly knit group of farm producers, sugar processors, and national farm organizations (Farm Bureau and Farmer's Union). They also include a league of seventeen developing nations that have lucrative allocations within the overall US sugar-import Tariff-Rate-Quota (TRQ). The US Sugar TRQ is a WTO-approved minimum total of 1.139 million metric tons of imported sugar.[22]

The ASA promotes a Sugar Program agenda of US job creation, high product quality, and a system that costs the American taxpayer $0 to operate. While ASA members understand the importance of the Sugar Program to their industry, the mix of marketing allotments, sugar-processing loan rates, and sugar-import TRQ's are very difficult for the average citizen to fully comprehend. ASA has been very successful at "driving home" the simpler agenda items (such as the $0 government cost) to gain the votes they need to keep the program in place.[23]

Title I – Subtitle D: The US Dairy Program

In contrast to the stable Sugar Program, considerable changes affected the US Dairy Program in the 2014 Farm Bill. Three programs were discontinued: the Dairy Product Price Support (DPPS) program; the Milk Income Loss Contract (MILC) program; and the Dairy Export Incentive Program. Congress established a new insurance-based program, known as the Dairy Margin Protection Program (DMPP) to replace DPPS and MILC. Congress also used the 2014 Farm Bill to create a safety-net program known as the Dairy Product Donation Program (DPDP).[24]

Dairy farm operations occasionally confront catastrophic circumstances not caused by adverse market conditions. Biological, chemical or environmental threats are the source. Since its original 1968 authorization, the Dairy Indemnity Payment Program (DIPP) offers financial assistance to dairy producers when pesticides or other residues contaminate the farm's production, and a government agency compels the producer to remove his/her milk from the commercial market. DIPP continues under the 2014 Farm Bill.[25,26]

Dairy program changes in the 2014 Farm Bill and trade impacts

The US decision to remove the DPPS, MILC and Export Incentive programs improves the US trade position. How is this trade impact measured?

The World Trade Organization's (WTO's) classification system outlined within the Agreement on Agriculture (AoA) measures this type of progress. AoA determines the amount of market distortion caused by national farm programs. AoA distinguishes greater or less distortion using a colored-box traffic-light analogy. For example, a "green box" program is non-distorting, while a blue box category is minimally distorting.

Government programs that create the worst distortions are known as "amber box." The sum of all amber box producer-payments are subject to WTO spending limits. Each WTO member nation has a calculated limit. US spending on amber-box programs cannot exceed $19.1 billion. WTO transparency obligations require that member nations (such as the US) publish notifications of how much amber-box spending occurs in each of their programs.[27]

The 2014 Farm Bill's elimination of the DPPS and MILC programs is estimated to release the US from $4.2 billion and $287 million of amber-box notifications, respectively. Added together, the *reduction in US amber-box spending* by dropping these dairy programs is substantial. To the extent that new 2014 Farm Bill programs generate additional amber-box spending, there is now "leeway" within the AoA limit to include new programs.[28]

More detail on the new DMPP and DPDP dairy programs

Let's sort through the "alphabet soup," and learn more about amended US Dairy Policy in the 2014 Farm Bill.

The Dairy Margin Protection Program (DMPP) is a new type of financial safety net for dairy producers. The deleted DPPS and MILC programs offered downside protection via price supports. The recently introduced DMPP is a counter-cyclical program that safeguards against decreases in net income.

With DMPP, Congress transformed the dairy safety net from a price-support system to an insurance-style deficiency payment program. Qualified participants in DMPP can choose to pay increased premiums for increased net income coverage. In an effort to spur strong participation in this new program, the DMPP insurance premiums are subsidized. Reducing producer premiums as an incentive to encourage DMPP membership is also a strategy that has successfully sparked increased federal crop insurance enrollment.[29]

Producers seeking DMPP participation pay a $100 administrative fee to register their entry into the DMPP system. Dairy producers elect to insure a minimum milk margin (the margin is determined as the average farm milk price minus the cost of a formula-based average feed ration). The insurable margin lies between $4.00 and $8.00 per hundredweight (cwt). The premium for the minimum $4.00/cwt margin coverage is $0. Margins greater than $4.00/cwt (via 50 cent/cwt increments) require increasingly higher premiums, up to the maximum insurable $8.00/cwt margin.[30]

The Dairy Product Donation Program (DPDP) is an additional safeguard system initiated when extreme market conditions reduce the milk margin below the $4.00/cwt threshold for two consecutive months. Under DPDP, the USDA is obliged to purchase consumer-ready dairy products to tighten the dairy supply-demand balance. This USDA action authorized by DPDP actually serves two purposes: (1) the USDA dairy product purchases aim to stimulate upward price pressure in the dairy market and restore the national milk margin above the

$4.00/cwt level, and (2) the DPDP is designed to provide real assistance to food banks and related low-income nutrition programs in the form of food donations.[31]

Future potential trade impacts of the DMPP dairy program

As noted above, elimination of previous US Dairy Programs (DPPS and MILC) improved the US trade position by reducing WTO amber-box spending. As we look ahead, we can make educated guesses about potential impacts of the new DMPP on US amber-box spending.

An initial review of the DMPP might indicate that its market-distorting effects are less severe than its predecessor price support programs. However, if we are to make a fair assessment of its effects on the US trade stance, we may simply have to observe how the DMPP affects dairy market performance over the life of 2014 Farm Bill (FY 2014–2018).

The DMPP's design is coupled to the dairy market in measurable ways. While DMPP insures producers against decreases in milk margins, the primary reason for margin shrinkage is likely to be decreased dairy market prices. Consequently, changes in market prices and DMPP benefits are coupled.

DMPP payments are calculated using recent historical production (highest output/year during 2011–2013). Some degree of market *decoupling* is associated with the use of a *historical production value*. On the other hand, the DMPP payment is based off a maximum historical number, rather than a historical average. *Coupling to the market* can happen as producers seek to set new output maximums for increased program payouts. We can reasonably speculate that rational producers will be encouraged to continually *increase production to improve future DMPP benefits*. If producers change their output in response to DMPP incentives, instead of reacting to market motives, then *distortions are occurring*.[32]

When exploring areas of concern with respect to market distortions and the resulting trade effects, it is best to "put all the cards on the table." For example, in contrast to the PLC, ARC, and MALP programs explored earlier in this chapter, recipients of the new DMPP benefits are *not subject to any payment limits* or restrictions. The absence of caps on producer benefits means that federal spending on DMPP could increase rapidly when difficult market conditions reduce milk margins and trigger producer payments.

If we assume that DMPP expenditures are classified as a WTO amber-box notification, then any savings achieved by eliminating the previous dairy programs could be offset by unrestricted payouts of DMPP benefits. We also must mention the government subsidies used to reduce DMPP insurance premiums. These are real expenditures that will happen annually regardless of market conditions. We can reasonably argue that the premium subsidies will be classified as WTO amber-box expenditures in the future.

Special policy considerations influencing US dairy markets

If we are to have a more complete picture of how government involvement in dairy programs impacts both national and international markets, we should examine some of the unique rules governing the pricing and availability of dairy products in the US.

General background

Earlier in this chapter, we explored complexities in US sugar policy. US dairy markets are similarly intricate. For example, US imports of dairy-related products are governed by tariff-rate quotas (TRQs). A TRQ is trade-policy device that predetermines a fixed annual volume of an imported product that can enter the US subject to a low tariff rate. Any imported amount beyond the initial quota level (known as a "tier") is subject to a prohibitively high tariff rate that economically eliminates any further imports.

A visit to the USDA's Foreign Agricultural Service (FAS) website for dairy imports demonstrates that nations who seek to export dairy products to the US at the reduced TRQ tier-rate must annually apply for a license to sell an approved volume of a selected dairy product.[33] Countries hoping to export multiple dairy products to the US must apply for the individual associated licenses. The FAS assembles monthly and annual databases to track the import volumes of the various dairy products, nation by licensed nation. It is an amazing system.

Milk marketing orders

The domestic US milk market is equally fascinating. Just as parts of the 2014 Farm Bill continue to be influenced by permanent legislation passed during the 1930s Great Depression, the fluid milk market and its related value-added products (cheese, yogurt, ice cream, etc.) are affected today by the 1937 Agriculture Marketing Agreement Act (AMAA).[34]

The AMAA is another permanent farm-related legislative measure. AMAA authorizes dairy producers (and/or dairy cooperatives) to conduct a referendum on the establishment of a "milk marketing order". If two-thirds or more of qualified producers approve a federal marketing order, then USDA implements it.

What exactly is a marketing order? A marketing order is a binding set of government-enforced regulations that structure and monitor the market relationship between handlers and producers of a designated commodity.

A *milk marketing order* is similar to a licensing system. Milk handlers are at the heart of a milk marketing order. These milk handlers are certified to operate as part of a marketing order by agreeing to applicable regulations within a specific geographic Marketing Area. Handlers process milk into a variety of consumer products. Milk marketing orders ensure that handlers monitor the milk and its many by-products for quality, weight, and related consumer-oriented concerns for safety and satisfaction.[35]

Federal milk marketing orders are USDA enforced. There are currently eleven federal milk marketing areas. State governments can also oversee milk marketing orders. Many US dairy farmers rely upon milk marketing orders to consistently receive a satisfactory minimum milk price. The regulations also safeguard a dependable and steady milk supply with predictable prices for consumers.[36]

Similar to the design of the sugar program, the operation of milk marketing orders requires no tax funding. Handlers in the dairy industry pay administrative fees to underwrite the operating costs of the federal order. This is a politically astute design.

Why institute a milk marketing order?

Fluid milk is a highly perishable and staple food product. Milk production is a 24/7, capital-intensive and a highly management-dependent operation. Pasteurization and refrigeration are essential technologies that require constant supervision to prevent milk from becoming a disease-carrying agent. The combined impacts of these production conditions cause milk's *own-price elasticity of supply to be highly inelastic.*

Today's consumer tends to view milk as a necessity, and expects the dairy industry to deliver a safe, sanitary, and high-quality product. Own-price elasticity of demand estimates for whole milk, 1 percent and skim milk vary between –0.79 and –0.75, respectively.[37] This is *inelastic demand*.

As demonstrated in Chapter 3, any market comprised of both inelastic supply and inelastic demand is susceptible to sizable market price volatility. This is especially the case with dairy markets. Fluid milk has a very short shelf life. It cannot be stored in times of surplus to alleviate inadequate supplies during market shortages. Seasonal supply and demand patterns create real challenges. Milk cows have natural cycles, and production tends to be higher in spring and summer. Dairy consumers, driven by cultural influences, tend to enjoy more milk products in the fall and winter. The natural imbalance of dairy supply and demand, combined with perishability and inelastic price responses can create markets where prices gyrate, milk spoils, producers fail, and consumers protest.

Marketing orders tend to smooth out dairy market conditions. What are the origins of this increased stability? There are two contributing factors: (1) classified pricing, and (2) cooperative pooling.[38]

Classified pricing

Classified pricing is a marketing-order mechanism that allocates alternative uses for the available fluid milk supply. Fluid milk has value as a directly consumed beverage, but it also can be further processed into additional satisfying consumer products such as cheese, yogurt, ice cream, etc. The federal classified pricing system divides the range of milk-related products into four classes, identified as follows:

Class I – Consumer-Ready Beverage – Fluid Milk

Class II – "Soft" Dairy Products – Yogurt and Frozen Desserts

Class III – "Hard" Dairy Products – Cheeses

Class IV – Nonfat Dry Milk and Butter

As argued earlier, shortages or surpluses in the Class I Milk market can create chaotic market results. The classified pricing system limits the volatile impacts of market disequilibrium. When delivered milk volumes are greater than the Class I Milk demand, then the surplus milk is subsequently designated for further processing in the alternative markets for Classes II, III, or IV.[39]

In terms of reducing price volatility in dairy markets, the federal milk marketing order designates differential minimum prices for each of the four milk classes. Classified pricing assigned by the federal milk marketing order means that any excess supply in the very volatile and perishable Class I Milk Market is a reduced threat of instability. The excess Class I milk becomes a source of supply for the remaining three dairy product classes.

Handler participants within the marketing order control any excess Class I milk volume by paying a "uniform blend price" to their producer-suppliers. The blend price is the weighted average of all four price categories. The allocated milk amount to each class determines the associated weighted price value.

Undoubtedly, classified pricing does *not* eliminate all downside risk in dairy markets. Instability issues can still arise in the subsequent product classes. But additional efforts are made to control the risk. For example, carefully calibrated pricing formulas in the milk marketing order determine minimum monthly prices for all four classes. The goal of the formulas is to approximate supply and demand forces, and strive for efficient market results. In addition, processed milk products (Classes II, III, and IV) have longer shelf lives than Class I milk. Consequently, it is relatively easier to manage the supply-demand balance and prevent chaotic market scenarios.

Cooperative pooling

The Capper-Volstead Act of 1922 empowered US agricultural producers to establish cooperative market organizations that can act collectively on behalf of their members without the threat of antitrust action.[40] In the second half of the twentieth century, agricultural cooperatives became an increasingly effective means for agricultural producers to exercise countervailing market power in industries dominated by large agribusinesses.

The rise of successful dairy cooperatives is notable. Dairy cooperatives demonstrated a real economic capacity to generate profitable sales of Class I fluid milk. They subsequently evolved into effective marketers of Class II, III, and IV processed dairy products on a regional and national scale.

Cooperatives in the twenty-first century account for approximately eighty percent of the milk marketed in the US.[41] Cooperatives originated the practice of pooling in dairy markets. A cooperative combines the milk from many producers; each producer who contributes to the pool earns a milk price associated with their participation in the pool. Membership within a cooperative pool is a means of diversifying and *reducing the price volatility faced by any one producer*.

Marketing orders require handlers to recognize a cooperative as single milk supplier. Each cooperative acts on behalf of its membership. Cooperatives can legally sell milk to processors in multiple regions regulated by different marketing orders. The federal or state order within each Marketing Area determines the uniform blend price received by the cooperative.

Cooperatives who sell milk products across multiple marketing order areas develop their own pool price formulas to determine how much to pay each cooperative member from the total cooperative revenues earned from the multiple area sources.[42] The ability of a cooperative to reach alternative market areas with their dairy products increases the cooperative's capacity to earn additional returns for its members.

Summary: US Dairy Program impacts

A comprehensive study of the US Dairy Program requires a much deeper inquiry than we can offer within a textbook chapter. While there is more to learn, we can make observations based on our limited review.

Dairy products are a very important component in US consumer diets. Societal expectations demand a safe and dependable supply of milk and milk-derived products at predictable and affordable prices. Milk is a highly perishable product requiring the entire supply chain to pay special attention to timeliness and sanitary technologies to create market stability and consumer trust.

History and political economy are very significant factors that continue to drive US Dairy Program design and implementation. Even in the twenty-first century, events 80 years earlier during the Great Depression reverberate in the form of government interventions that aim to establish "stable" market conditions. The definition of this stability has evolved. Today, US Dairy policy strives to create an environment where dairy producers and handlers are less prone to experience dramatic price swings, fluctuating supplies, and consumer dissatisfaction.

There are trade-offs when we choose market stability as the highest policy priority. The economic performance of today's US dairy industry is influenced by international trade protections (TRQ's), farm safety net programs (DMPP), classified pricing within milk marketing orders, and producers' cooperative pooling to manage risk and gain bargaining power.

The origins of our dairy market "infrastructure" can be explained in reasonable terms. However, these characteristics are *not* necessarily in harmony with other important policy goals. Dairy programs are not well-aligned with a US trade policy focused on reducing market distortions, decreasing WTO "amber box" spending, and promoting free entry and free exit market conditions to achieve improved allocative efficiency.

These observations about "trade-offs" are not meant to discredit the outcomes achieved under the current system. There is a lot to be said for a dairy system that daily delivers safe and affordable fluid milk products offering nutritional value to consumers of all ages. But it is also important to understand our opportunity costs. As we make future choices for dairy program policy, an awareness of the "price" of our programs is a useful consideration in informed and rational decision making.

Title I - Subtitle E: Supplemental Agricultural Disaster Assistance Programs

Our review of dairy, sugar, and related federal programs reveals a high degree of government involvement in selected agricultural markets. But the US farm safety net is not equal and universal in coverage. Some commodities qualify for considerable support, while others receive much less attention.

The uneven nature of the farm safety net has its consequences. For example, on past occasions when massive droughts and similar natural disasters damaged agricultural production on a large scale, a frequent federal government response in the twentieth century was to establish "emergency relief disaster programs" that offered assistance to a broad cross-section of producers. These on-the-spot (a.k.a. "ad hoc") disaster programs were often hastily designed and implemented. Ad hoc programs are well-intended, but they are often expensive for taxpayers and uneven in the distribution of their benefits. Problems with "waste and abuse" are also associated with the ad hoc approach.

The political landscape in relation to all federal program spending has changed in the twenty-first century. Budgets are being sequestered and programs are being held accountable for their costs and outcomes. The popularity of ad hoc programs in almost all circumstances, including agriculture, is waning.

The treatment of agricultural disaster programs in the 2014 Farm Bill is reflective of this new era of accountability. After gaining experience with the administration of five disaster programs initiated in the 2008 Farm Bill, Congress took definitive action in the 2014 Farm Bill to discontinue one of them, and establish the remaining four as permanent programs.

The Supplemental Revenue Assistance (SURE) crop disaster program was not reauthorized in 2014. The safety-net design for whole-farm revenue coverage in the new 2014 ARC-IC Commodity Program overlapped with SURE. To prevent program duplication, SURE was terminated.[43] Three programs offering disaster relief to livestock producers and one program for tree-fruit farmers were reauthorized in 2014 with no sunset date.

The 2008 Farm Bill initiated a transition away from ad hoc and towards permanent disaster programs. An additional trend was to extend the farm safety net to a broader cross-section of agricultural producers (including livestock, tree fruit, honeybees, and farm-raised fish).

The focus on permanency was further supported with an identifiable funding source.[44] The 2008 farm bill legislation approved the creation of an Agricultural Disaster Relief Trust Fund with a genuine revenue source: 3.08 percent of annual collected US tariff duties.[45] Establishing a revenue source to support a permanent program is a different philosophy than fashioning ad hoc programs on the spur of the moment and figuring out later how to pay for those programs.

The Supplemental Agricultural Disaster Assistance Programs permanently reauthorized in the 2014 Farm Bill are:[46]

- Livestock Indemnity Program (LIP) – When adverse weather is responsible for disproportionate livestock mortality rates, then eligible livestock owners and contract growers can receive LIP payments at a rate of 75 percent of market value.
- Livestock Forage Disaster Program (LFP) – If eligible livestock producers incur grazing losses on drought-affected pasture or grazing land, or on federally managed rangeland affected by a qualifying fire, then LFP payments can occur.
- Emergency Assistance for Livestock, Honey Bees, and Farm-Raised Fish Program (ELAP) – In cases where disease, adverse weather, and feed or water shortages cause damages, then ELAP offers payments (capped at $20 million per year) to the covered producers.
- Tree Assistance Program (TAP) – If natural disasters damage vines, trees, or bushes, then TAP makes payments to orchardists/nursery tree growers for losses in excess of 15 percent associated with replanting.

LIP, LFP, ELAP, and TAP were reauthorized with the stipulation that pre-2014 losses would retroactively qualify for assistance. By supporting producers who happened to incur disaster losses in the time gap between the end of the 2008 Farm Bill and start of the 2014 Farm Bill, Congress was aiming to treat all producers with recent disaster damages equitably.

This even-handed action also increased the upfront cost of reauthorizing the permanent programs in 2014. Barring an unnatural string of new disasters taking place, the expenditure rate on the permanent disaster programs should subside to lower and more manageable levels, going forward.[47] In relation to the "retroactive payments" that assisted producers with disaster losses since FY2012, the USDA has already distributed $5.3 billion in payments.[48]

In all of these permanent disaster programs, Congress has enforced the individual producer payment limit of $125,000 (as is the case in PLC, ARC, and similar programs). This is another point of differentiation for permanent programs. The totality of government support to any one producer is taken into account. Payment limits per person are not always included in ad hoc disaster programs.

To offer a comparison, the thirty-three ad hoc disaster programs enacted between FY1989 and FY2006 (to date) were responsible for about $55.4 billion in total USDA supplemental disaster funding. Most of the ad hoc supplemental spending on disaster programs over this time period was not offset with specific new tax revenues or equivalent cutbacks in other programs.[49]

A review of the 2014 Farm Bill's Title XI: Crop Insurance

The congressional decision to permanently fund supplemental disaster programs and widen commodity coverage to include fruit trees, honeybees, fish farms, and livestock is consistent with the large-scale policy initiatives being pursued within federal crop insurance.

Federal crop insurance became a permanent program with broadened commodity coverages after Congress passed the Crop Insurance Act of 1980. Today, the powerful and wide-ranging nature of this twenty-first-century insurance program is hardly recognizable in comparison to its more humble beginnings. Federal Crop Insurance originated in 1938 as an experimental government project offering a very limited range of crop coverages.[50]

Federal crop insurance is now entirely serviced and sold nationwide through eighteen approved private companies. Any unusual losses experienced by these private insurers are fully reinsured by USDA. The federal government also reimburses a portion of the private firms' operating and administrative expenses. Over 100 different commodities are insurable.

This crop insurance program offers producers a range of safeguards, including loss protection against decreases in yield, crop revenue, or whole farm revenue. The 2014 Farm Bill increased federal funding for crop insurance by $5.7 billion over 10 years, compared with the original 2008 baseline farm-bill projection.[51]

The twenty-first-century dominance of federal crop insurance as a US farm safety net mechanism is clear. Let's examine additional metrics. USDA's Risk Management Agency (RMA) reported that producers insured 294 million acres in 2014.[52] If we compare the insured area to the National Agricultural Statistics Service (NASS) estimate of 326.8 million total US planted acres in 2014, the insured-to-planted ratio is approximately 89.9 percent.[53]

Based on changes enacted in the 2014 Farm Bill, the Congressional Research Service (CRS) estimates a 10-year projected budget expense of $90 Billion for Federal Crop Insurance. In comparison, CRS predicts a smaller $44 billion budget for Commodity Programs (such as PLC, ARC, etc.) over the same time horizon. Crop Insurance accounts for 9.4 percent of the entire projected 2014 Farm Bill Budget, and is now the second largest Farm Bill expense (after food and nutrition).[54]

From both the budgetary and acres-insured perspectives, federal crop insurance is now the most important US farm safety-net program. The current magnitude and projected growth of crop insurance requires that we examine this program with the depth and attention that it deserves.

2014 Farm Bill impacts on federal crop insurance

Government funding and congressional support for Federal Crop Insurance accelerated with the passage of the 2014 Farm Bill. The rise to prominence of crop insurance as a federal program is stunning. As recently as the 2002 Farm Bill, crop insurance was not assigned a separate farm bill title; it was deemed as miscellaneous and supplementary, relative to other farm support programs. Times have changed.

We can highlight major changes in the dominant and growing crop insurance program under the 2014 Farm Bill. One modification, known as the Stacked Income Protection Plan (STAX), offers a new insurance product for US upland cotton producers.

STAX is designed to safeguard cotton producers from county-level revenue losses exceeding 10 percent of expected revenue, but not more than the individual producer's own crop-insurance deductible level. STAX is a type of "shallow-loss" program that offers producers financial relief when an entire area is exposed to downside financial risk. In many cases, the decline in area revenue is within the deductible range of a typical individual crop insurance policy. STAX offers protection against this loss.[55]

Creation of the STAX policy was triggered when the US discontinued its cotton commodity program to settle a WTO trade dispute with Brazil. STAX is expensive. It is expected to account for $3.3 billion of government expenditures over a 10-year budget horizon.

Similar to STAX, Congress also established another area-based shallow-loss coverage program with the Supplemental Coverage Option (SCO) for other crops. SCO is a safeguard against downturns in county revenue (or yields), and its coverage is limited by the deductible on a producer's individual crop insurance policy.

SCO is also a large expense. The projected 10-year cost is $1.7 billon. Congress set the government subsidies for these new programs as 80 percent for STAX and 65 percent for SCO.[56]

The 2014 Farm Bill additionally introduces cross-compliance policy between crop insurance and conservation requirements. Participants in federal crop insurance must adhere to Sodbuster and Swampbuster conservation provisions to be eligible for the premium subsidies. Plantings on native sod acreage in certain states also decrease or eliminate crop insurance subsidies.[57]

Crop insurance enlarges its sphere of influence under 2014 Farm Bill provisions. The 2014 legislation boosts both opportunities to insure existing crops and to offer new products. Specialty crops and animal agriculture are included in the expansion. RMA is also expected to revise the value of crop insurance for higher-priced organic and similar non-conventional crops.

What key factors are driving the growth of crop insurance?

In the film *Casablanca*, Captain Renault saves his friend Victor Laszlow from arrest by instructing his police corps to "round up the usual suspects."[58] Similarly, as we explore the ascendancy of federal crop insurance as the chief component of federal disaster assistance, we seek to assemble the primary factors that have transformed a pilot program into a fast-growing multi-billion dollar enterprise. The reasons for this program expansion are both political and economic. We can address them as follows:

- Increased premium subsidies, a broadened range of insurable losses (catastrophic risk protection [CAT], revenue insurance, area yield insurance), and an enlarged variety of eligible commodities (fruits, vegetables, hay, etc.).
- Changes in the political economy of crop insurance as a primary component of the farm safety net.
- Mounting strength of the congressional "Iron Triangle" expanding the policy influence of federal crop insurance.

Premium subsidies, product development, and expanded coverage

USDA economist Joseph Glauber's 1990–2011 historical review of federal crop insurance reveals an ongoing congressional interest in establishing crop insurance as the principal federal farm disaster assistance program.[59]

The previously mentioned Crop Insurance Act of 1980 subsidized 30 percent of producer premium costs, empowered private insurers to actively sell policies, and authorized the USDA to act as a reinsurer for the private firms. Producer participation in crop insurance increased to 25 percent by 1990, but this performance fell short of the congressional 50 percent goal.[60]

Crop failures occurred in 1988 and 1989, and insufficient crop insurance coverage led Congress to legislate new ad hoc disaster programs.[61] A 1990 administrative proposal emerged to simply replace crop insurance with permanent disaster programs. Instead, Congress pursued an increase in producer participation with the 1994 Crop Insurance Reform Act (CIRA). CIRA increased premium subsidies further, introduced a catastrophic (CAT) coverage level, and linked eligibility for other farm safety-net programs with crop insurance participation. Insured acres temporarily increased to nearly 80 percent of available production. The 1996 farm bill repealed mandatory insurance sign-up and participation rates predictably fell. Undeterred, Congress authorized additional premium subsidies in 1999, and then passed the 2000 Agricultural Risk Protection Act (ARPA).[62]

ARPA established a pattern of amplified subsidy rates. The changes were very noticeable, and producers easily recognized a marked reduction in the out-of-pocket costs of crop insurance premiums. The ARPA reform of subsidy rates means that the average cost of a producer's crop insurance premium is reduced by 62 percent. Subsidy rates on producer premiums can reach as high as 80 percent higher in some circumstances, and lower in others. Glauber observes that producers have an *own-price inelastic demand for crop insurance.*[63] Under ARPA, subsidies are now sufficiently high to overcome that inelastic demand, and produce crop insurance acreage annual participation rates of nearly 90 percent.

Robust subsidy levels figure strongly in the crop insurance program's rise to dominance. There are additional important factors. One is product innovation. Today, producers have a suite of insurance options to consider. They can purchase low-cost catastrophic (CAT) coverage. Alternatively, they can choose to insure their revenues, their yields only, or buy an area-yield plan. If a producer selects participation in the PLC commodity program, then he/she can purchase a Supplemental Coverage Option (SCO) to provide protection against area-wide shallow losses that are less than the deductible on individual crop insurance policies.

Why does Congress care about product development in crop insurance? The short answer is increased interest and participation. The USDA's Risk Management Agency (RMA) reports that 77 percent of all producer-purchased policies in 2014 are for revenue-based protection. This is a real break with the past. In 1990, revenue protection was not available; all policies were simply protection against decreases in yield. Today, only 23 percent of producers choose plain yield insurance.[64]

The growth of crop insurance as a risk protection mechanism is also the result of research efforts to establish actuarially fair premium rates to cover new alternative crops and enterprises. In 2015 alone, the RMA announced that policies were available for twenty-five additional commodities. In its pre-1980 stages, crop insurance policies were restricted to the large-acreage crops. Today, there is an active effort to make crop insurance widely available to offer safeguards to the majority of all agricultural producers.

Political economy of crop insurance

When the 2014 Farm Bill became law, U.S. Senator Debbie Stabenow, who chairs the Senate Committee on Agriculture, Nutrition and Forestry, commented: "From now on, farmers will protect themselves from disaster with risk management programs like crop insurance. Instead of getting a government check even in good times, farmers will pay an insurance bill every year and will only receive support from that insurance in years when they take a loss."[65]

Senator Stabenow, along with other elected officials, have a vested interest in modifying farm and food policy to meet constituency expectations. In Chapter 3, we reviewed the political economy of policy making, and examined the "vote maximizing hypothesis" as a predictor of legislators' decision making.

Approximately 1.9 percent of the US population is directly involved in production agriculture.[66] If a farm policy is to attract sufficient support for approval, then it is necessary to assemble a coalition of votes that constitute a majority. Building such a coalition requires recognition of societal demands and trends.

We live in an era where the general public increasingly expects legislators to scrutinize public budgets, emphasize personal responsibility, and produce equitable outcomes. The *elimination of Direct Payments in the 2014 Farm Bill* became politically necessary when legislators and news editorials criticized the program as a prime example of misguided federal spending, deficient private accountability and unjustifiable income redistribution.

Direct payments were not the only program to be dismissed. Congress also repealed Counter-Cyclical Payments and the ACRE program. The 2014 Farm Bill also saw the removal of the DPPS and MILC dairy programs, as well as the SURE disaster program. Political and economic considerations required this restructuring to generate sufficient support for the 2014 Farm Bill from reform-minded special interests and politicians.

As discussed earlier in this textbook, the repeal of some farm bill programs was accompanied by the creation and/or expansion of others. PLC, ARC, DMPP, and SCO are all new programs in the 2014 Farm Bill. In addition to these initiatives, Congress markedly increased funding to expand the operations and outreach of federal crop insurance.

A reordering of program priorities appears to be an essential step in making this 2014 omnibus legislation viable. The demise of older programs created openings for the newer initiatives.

Difficult compromises, and some real "give and take" on the issues, were necessary conditions for approval of the 2014 Farm Bill. Some constituencies were heartened by the repeal of programs such as direct payments. Other interests, who sought continued existence of the farm safety net, were satisfied with the program additions and the expansion of crop insurance. Taken together, a coalition of votes large enough to establish a majority approved the 2014 Farm Bill.

Political economy provides a key perspective on how legislative outcomes depend on the interaction of competing interests as they wield their influence and votes.

Iron Triangle theory and the growth of federal crop insurance

We introduced the Iron Triangle theory of policy influence in Chapter 3. Three key participants – legislators, bureaucracies, and special interests – are each predicted to have individual and mutually reinforcing incentives.

No natural rules or mechanisms ensure that an Iron Triangle's interlocking agendas produce beneficial results such as global economic efficiency. While policies emerging from Iron Triangle activity might possibly improve social welfare, the theoretical and empirical evidence suggests that other outcomes are more likely.

We can apply Iron Triangle concepts as a frame of reference to understand the dramatic growth of the federal crop insurance program. Before proceeding with the analysis, let's review some additional aspects of the Iron Triangle model.

The Iron Triangle is a commonly recognized behavioral theory in public choice economics. As indicated in Chapter 3, individual rational motives are the foundation of public choice analysis. As a result, the Iron Triangle predicts that legislators maximize votes, bureaucracies build empires, and special interests seek rents.

Iron is symbolic of strength. Iron Triangle theory suggests that an interconnecting and rational decision-making system is a powerful economic force. Joint cooperation among legislators, special interests, and bureaucratic agencies has a real capacity to command additional resources and expand the sphere of influence.

Let's examine how the Iron Triangle hypothesis offers insights into the forces that are driving change in federal crop insurance. The *vote-maximizing paradigm of legislator decision making* suggests that congressional leaders seek policy stances favorably aligned with their constituencies' priorities. For example, Senator Stabenow argues that a crop-insurance-based safety net policy is appropriate because farm producers pay insurance premiums rather than simply receive government direct payments. She also makes it clear that producers only benefit from the insurance safety net when the need arises.

Clearly, these crop insurance "talking points" aim to satisfy voters' demands for personal accountability and economic equity. By reorganizing the farm safety net to emphasize crop insurance, Senator Stabenow and her fellow legislators hope to secure the support and votes of their constituencies. This is fertile ground for growing the federal crop insurance program.

Rent seeking occurs when individual members of an industry recognize that collective action to influence government policy yields above-normal economic returns. What current market and policy circumstances affect firms' profitability potential in the crop insurance industry?

There are eighteen approved private firms who can offer federal crop insurance. While competition can take place within this design, the industry structure falls short of the entry and exit conditions that would drive down profits to normal levels. The limited number of private crop insurers suggests that profits will be above normal and that rent earning is likely.

Government subsidies that increase insurance demand and reduce production costs are also market conditions favorable to rent-seeking private interests. We noted earlier that government subsidies reduce producers' crop insurance premium rates by 62 percent on average. An "increase in demand" is the typical result when the government subsidizes the crop insurance buyer.

Private insurers incur costs of production. For example, they must reward independent insurance agents with commissions to spur crop insurance sales. But there are additional costs of delivering crop insurance, and private insurers have a real advantage in this instance. Supply-side government subsidies reduce the production costs of private insurers. The USDA reinsures the potential catastrophic losses of private insurers, and USDA also reimburses a portion of their administrative and operating costs. *Ceteris paribus*, reduced private insurer costs will improve their profit levels.

Considering the market structure of the crop insurance industry, as well as the government role in stimulating demand and decreasing production costs, there is a very clear opportunity for rent seeking. The crop insurance industry has substantial incentives to coalesce into a united special interest group to influence policy.

The third "side" of the Iron Triangle hypothesis is a *bureaucracy with empire-building tendencies*. Is this idea applicable for crop insurance? Prior to the 1996 Farm Bill, the USDA's

Farm Service Agency (FSA) was primarily responsible for supervising the delivery of federal crop insurance to producers. FSA is a multi-purpose agency that manages various USDA commodity and loan programs on a day-to-day basis. Crop insurance was simply one of a suite of FSA programs. The 1996 Farm Bill shifted supervisory responsibility for federal crop insurance to a newly established Risk Management Agency (RMA) within USDA.[67] In contrast to the FSA, RMA could focus its efforts on one safety net program: crop insurance.

A USDA-published fact sheet explains the RMA's responsibilities, mission, and vision. Part of the RMA's charge is to offer educational outreach and seminars on overall agricultural risk management.[68] But RMA's main tasks includes management of the Federal Crop Insurance Corporation (FCIC), the development and approval of insurance premium rates on current and new commodities, the administration of crop insurance subsidies on producer premiums and private insurers' expenses, and the reinsurance of private insurers' losses. RMA's mission clearly centers on creating and sustaining a successful crop insurance program.

Whether or not the theory of empire building is applicable, the RMA's financial power and geographical outreach has experienced tremendous growth. RMA's management of crop insurance liability increased from approximately $20 billion in 2001 to about $117 billion in 2012. This is roughly a 16 percent annual growth rate in crop insurance liability coverage. In 2014, RMA was staffed with 68 people at its Washington, DC headquarters, and had an additional 399 employees stationed at field offices across the nation.[69] RMA has evolved into a sizable agency with a considerable range of responsibility and authority.

Federal Crop Insurance appears to exhibit the basic components associated with the Iron Triangle hypothesis: supportive legislators, well-funded industry-based special interests, and a powerful bureaucracy. If the Iron Triangle does exert influence, we should be able to measure its success in terms of policy funding and initiatives. What is the recent "track record" for crop insurance?

Crop insurance protected 294 million acres in 2014. Ratios of total safeguarded acres in 2014 included: cotton, 96 percent; soybeans, 88 percent; corn, 87 percent; and wheat, 84 percent. Policies for "specialty" crops are available in their respective primary growing areas. Overall, crop insurance now covers about 130 crops (including a variety of fruit trees, nursery crops, pasture, rangeland, and forage).[70]

Government subsidy expenditures are also impressive. On the demand side for crop insurance, policy premium subsidies for producers constituted the largest government cost, and they accounted for $6.3 billion in 2014 alone.[71] On the supply side, the RMA developed a Standard Reinsurance Agreement (SRA) determining how the USDA reimburses the administrative and operating (A&O) expenses of the private insurers, as well as setting the terms for the risk-sharing of losses associated with large insurance indemnity payouts.

SRA's terms and conditions translate into a 12 percent A&O reimbursement rate. Each $100 in total premiums generates a federal $12 reimbursement to the private insurers. SRA sets a maximum total A&O reimbursement of $1.3 billion and a minimum of $1.1 billion. The maximum is a RMA budget cost control, and the minimum guarantees private insurers that a predictable portion of their A&O expenses will be subsidized.[72]

If we can attribute even part of federal crop insurance's rapid expansion to the Iron Triangle hypothesis, the impact is remarkable. Very few industries can match the level of policy support and financial growth experienced by federal crop insurance.

Economic effects of the 2014 Farm Bill's farm safety net

One of the goals for this textbook is to encourage students to actively engage in policy analysis. We are now in a position to make that happen. We have genuine policy choices and their consequences to evaluate. The 2014 Farm Bill programs that collectively encompass the US farm safety net through FY 2018 offer wide-ranging opportunities to review policy trends and outcomes.

We have already learned a great deal in this chapter. We identified key farm bill safety-net programs, determined their purposes, and explained their design. There is more to discover. We can employ the tools of positive and normative analysis (see Chapters 1 and 3) to carefully investigate these policies and interpret what they mean for our economy's overall performance.

The full range of possible 2014 Farm Bill safety-net policies to investigate are too numerous for one textbook chapter. But the encyclopedic approach is not necessary. Valuable insights are gained by narrowing the focus, identifying key patterns, and making broadly applicable observations. We can concentrate our efforts, as follows:

- Economic effects of a US farm safety net policy dependent on the continued dominance and ongoing expansion of subsidized federal crop insurance.
- The 2014 Farm Bill farm safety net's impacts on US international trade policy.
- Political-economic analysis of contradictory and consistent program goals within the farm safety net.

A policy analysis framework

As outlined in Chapter 1, systematic policy analysis begins with a clear purpose. A well-articulated purpose translates into researchable questions.

We address these questions through the proper use of sources, methods, and tools of positive and normative analysis. A search of the professional literature yields valuable insights and identifies additional areas for productive inquiry. In this textbook, we can also use the policy toolbox from Chapter 3 to guide the exploration of alternative scenarios.

Policy analysis is a rational process with instrumental value. We summarize and interpret results, draw conclusions, and make recommendations based on the analysis. From a normative perspective, our analytical work can and should yield beneficial contributions.

In the three policy reviews that follow, we engage in focused and manageable scenario analyses.

Analyzing economic effects of a US farm safety net program driven by growth in subsidized federal crop insurance

We organize our analysis of this important policy into a step-wise approach:

- Purpose – A primary reason for investigating changes in the US farm safety net initiated under the 2014 Farm Bill is to predict effects on the economy's welfare and efficiency.
- Researchable Question – What are the predicted market, distributional, and efficiency consequences of using producer subsidies to support crop insurance as the leading farm safety net program included in the 2014 Farm Bill?

- Investigative Model – Predict the outcomes of a subsidized premium for federal crop insurance using (1) market equilibrium analysis and (2) producer and consumer surplus analysis.
  - Scenario – Corn producers have a demand for federal crop insurance to protect their insurable corn yield at the 65 percent level. The insurance policy protects the value of the corn crop from multiple perils (such as drought, flooding, wind, disease, etc.) that reduce the corn-yield by more than 35 percent. The benefit of the policy to the producer is the right to receive indemnity payments for losses greater than the 35 percent "deductible."

    An actuarially fair insurance premium per acre determines the cost per acre for supplying this crop insurance policy.

    The USDA Risk Management Agency (RMA), through private insurers, supplies the federal crop insurance policy with a 60 percent subsidy. The net price offered to producers by the insurers is 40 percent of the true actuarially fair cost of supplying the crop insurance policy.

    A 60 percent reduction in the net crop insurance premium subsidy causes an "increase in supply." In this scenario, the supply curve for federal crop insurance shifts to the right. The proportional subsidy rate creates a non-parallel shift of supply. See the both the graph and the step-wise analysis in Figure 4.1 to predict the consequences of the 60 percent crop insurance premium subsidy:[73]
- Interpreting results of the premium-subsidy scenario – When the RMA introduces a 60 percent subsidy to reduce the producers' premium paid below the actuarially fair level, we can examine market, distributional, and efficiency impacts using changes in producer and consumer surplus.
  - Market Effects – A 60 percent Subsidy that reduces the net price of crop insurance premiums to farm producers has the effect of causing an "increase in supply" of crop insurance, a decrease in the equilibrium premium price, and an increase in the equilibrium number of acres insured. See Figure 4.1.
  - Distributional Effects – We use a "with-and-without" analysis to determine net gains or losses in welfare in Figure 4.1 above. In the crop insurance market, if the policy is sold at the actuarially fair premium price without any subsidy, then the Consumer Surplus equals the sum of areas A + B underneath the Demand Curve for Insured Crop Acres. Similarly, the Producer Surplus without the subsidy is the sum of areas D + G above the supply curve.

    If the policy premium price offered is subsidized, reducing the offered price per acre by 60 percent, then the Consumer Surplus increases in size to areas A + B + D + E. With the subsidy, the area of the Producer Surplus also rises to include: D + G + B + C. In this situation, farm producers who purchase crop insurance gain the Consumer Surplus and Private Insurers who sell the policies enjoy the welfare gain of the Producer Surplus.
  - Taxpayer and Efficiency Effects – What is the cost of the 60 percent subsidy to the taxpayer? If we make the assumption that government spending must ultimately matched with tax revenue, then the taxpayer burden includes all of the

additional Consumer plus Producer Surplus (Area = D + E + B + C), plus a *net decrease in overall market efficiency equal to Area F* in Figure 4.1. Area F is known as the deadweight loss, and this area is a taxpayer burden too. In the end, since all the gains to the consumers and producers are offset by taxpayer cost, plus a loss of economic efficiency, the net effect of the subsidy is a *welfare loss* to the entire economy.

- ○ Interpret the meaning of Area F (deadweight loss) in Figure 4.1 – From the standpoint of economic efficiency, Area F means that the economy *produces too many insured acres, and not enough of other goods in the economy*. The marginal cost of producing the extra insured acres in Area F is greater than the farmers' true market demand value for those insured acres. The subsidy creates a wedge between the market value of the resources used to insure crop acres and their artificially created equilibrium value.

- Conclusions – Our brief analysis predicts that subsidized premiums will:

  - ○ Reduce the net price of crop insurance to producers and increase insured acres.
  - ○ Redistribute income from taxpayers to private insurers and farm producers.
  - ○ Reduce overall economic efficiency, because the economy has too many insured acres and not enough of other goods, based on the true market value of the opportunity cost.

- Recommendations – We examine the rationale for subsidizing federal crop insurance, and suggest alternatives to improve economic performance.

  - ○ Subsidized Crop Insurance: Compare US Congressional Goals to Predicted Market Results – Let's examine the goals of Congress in relation to the simple model of subsidized crop insurance in Figure 4.1.

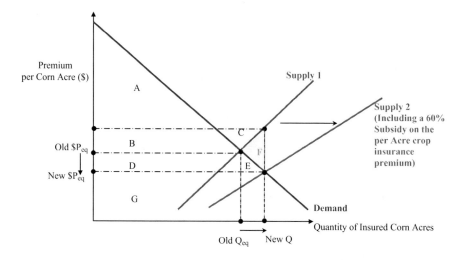

Figure 4.1 Analysis of market, consumer surplus, and producer surplus effects of a 60 percent crop insurance premium subsidy.

Congressional farm safety net goals: Our review of official 2014 Farm Bill language and the professional literature reveals the following goals of the US Congress for the US farm safety during the period between FY 2014 and FY 2018:

- Increase the number of acres and the range of different crops covered by federal crop insurance.
- Reduce the need for ad hoc government-funded disaster assistance programs.
- Create a farm safety net program where producers pay to participate, rather than simply apply to receive government payments.
- Establish a permanent safety net program that has a counter-cyclical purpose – Generating government support only when downside risks reduce farm producer income because of adverse growing and/or market conditions beyond the producer's control.

Relate predicted market results of subsidized crop insurance to congressional goals:

- Our simplified model in Figure 4.1 predicts an increase in equilibrium acres insured and a reduced equilibrium insurance premium per acre.
- Producers pay a premium to qualify for crop insurance indemnity coverage. The premium rate is reduced by the subsidy, and the producer receives the indemnity when the insured event occurs.
- Subsidized crop insurance produces outcomes that are basically consistent with Congressional objectives for programs that increase acres insured and require producer premium payments to participate.
- Normative Observation/Recommendation – Congressional satisfaction with the acreage and participation results of subsidized crop insurance should be tempered by the cost of a program that reduces economic efficiency and transfers income from taxpayers to the suppliers and consumers of the subsidized insurance product.
- Subsidized Federal Crop Insurance – What is the current cost of offering Federal Crop Insurance? What factors contribute to the cost?

  o Budgetary Cost – A 2014 Congressional Budget Office (CBO) study estimated that Federal Crop Insurance Program would account for $41.4 Billion of federal spending over the 5-year span of the 2014 Farm Bill (FY2014–FY 2018). The projected cost is the farm bill's second largest expenditure, next to the Nutrition Title.[74]

  o Production Cost – The "production function" for federal crop insurance includes costly inputs such as administrative oversight, claims adjustment and reinsurance. In addition, the benefit of downside risk protection creates the expensive side-effect problems of adverse selection and moral hazard.[75] Adverse selection means that purchasers of crop insurance may be disproportionately higher-risk producers who collect indemnities more frequently and with larger losses than the typical farmer. Moral hazard is the incentive for insured producers to intentionally change decisions and practices to increase the likelihood of receiving an indemnity payment.

  o Taking into account the challenges that accompany the development, sale, and implementation of multiple peril crop insurance coverage, the cost of offering this protection is an extra 40 cents per dollar of likely indemnity payment.[76]

- ○ Each dollar of premium paid by a producer with federal crop insurance was associated with an average of $1.90 in indemnities. In most insurance markets, the purchase of a policy yields an actuarially fair expected return equal to the premium, minus administrative expense.[77] The high rate of Congressional subsidy provided to both the private crop insurers and their farmer-customers is the reason why the "net return" to crop insurance is 90 cents on the dollar. It is important to remember that the federal government is subsidizing insured farmer premiums at average 62 percent rate, reimbursing administrative expenses for private insurers and reinsuring the private insurers' indemnity losses.[78]
- ○ External Cost – The premium subsidy for federal crop insurance creates a wedge between actual market risk and the artificially reduced equilibrium price of taking on risk. The subsidy encourages producers to assume more than the efficient amount of risk. Goodwin and Smith (2012) cite evidence and effectively argue that subsidized risk is an incentive to take on additional risk at the intensive margin (by changing production decisions within current operations) and at the extensive margin (electing to bring riskier land into to production).[79] Conservation compliance required in the 2014 Farm Bill may limit some, but not all, of these riskier practices that often are also associated with negative environmental externalities.

- • Subsidized Federal Crop Insurance – Opportunity cost as a rationale to recommend future policy alternatives.

  - ○ Applying the Opportunity Cost Principle – The powerful concept of opportunity cost is an important tool in policy analysis. The interpretation of analytical results and the formation of recommendations often benefits when the question of alternative use is raised.
  - ○ In the case of subsidized federal crop insurance, our brief analysis in Figure 4.1 identified "deadweight" efficiency losses (Area F) associated with the market wedge created by the premium subsidy. Deadweight losses are lost market values; no one in the economy captures them. A valid question is to ask about the economic gains that could have been made available to the economy for other productive uses, if the subsidy were reduced or eliminated. This is the type of question is emphasized when the opportunity cost framework is applied.
  - ○ Goodwin and Smith (2012) apply the opportunity cost viewpoint when they indicate that subsidizing crop insurance removes the incentive for producers to be innovative in developing their own market-based risk-management strategies. Without the necessary incentives, decision making may miss opportunities to spur productivity gains and internationally competitive practices. A study by Wang, Hanson and Black (2003) determined that producers tend to forego more efficient risk-management strategies to choose more highly subsidized crop insurance alternatives.[80]
  - ○ Examples of Alternative Premium Subsidy Scenarios – In their review of the 2014 Farm Bill, Orden and Zulauf cite an RMA study indicating that a 35 percent premium subsidy rate would be associated an 80 percent participation rate. They also suggest that subsidies could be determined as a rate that simply covers the catastrophic indemnity costs of systemic risk.[81]

Bruce Babcock (2012) indicates that many producers are attracted to revenue insurance protection. A program that subsidizes premiums sufficiently to encourage producer to insure at an entry level, and then allows producers to increase their higher coverage levels at actuarially fair rates, would achieve high participation rates at much lower government subsidy expense.[82]

Dennis Shields' CBO study (2015) reported on alternative proposals for reducing premium subsidies for crop insurance. Research to determine the elasticity response of farm producers to alternative subsidy levels and limits should be performed to determine the tradeoffs between reduced program subsidy costs and the level of producer participation in crop insurance.[83] Using the opportunity cost principle, these studies should also explore the best alternatives uses of any cost savings produced by a reduced subsidy crop insurance program

o   Recommended Policy Options and Research – The Opportunity Cost perspective opens the door to perform some valuable research. Our policy analysis (above) demonstrates that subsidized crop insurance is expensive, and that improved economic performance is possible if alternative crop insurance designs are tested and adopted. If we can reduce the cost of protection, then it is possible to use the cost savings to return funds to taxpayers or invest in higher-valued economic activities.

Analyzing the effects of agricultural tariff rate quotas (TRQs) on the US commodity markets and the US trade position

Similar to our crop insurance inquiry above, we organize another "policy analysis scenario" by examining the effects of US agricultural-import protection programs with a step-wise approach:

- Purpose – Under the 2014 Farm Bill's Commodities Title, Tariff Rate Quotas (TRQ's) continue to offer protection to US Sugar and Dairy interests against import competition. Our purpose here is to analyze the impact of TRQs on market equilibria, economic efficiency, economic welfare, and the US trade position.
- Researchable Question – Tariff Rate Quotas are a means of limiting imported agricultural products entering the US. What are the costs and benefits of TRQs? Specifically, what are the predicted market, distributional, efficiency, and trade consequences of continued support for TRQs in the 2014 Farm Bill?
- Investigative Model – Predict the outcomes of a dairy Tariff Rate Quota for imported salted butter using (1) market equilibrium analysis, and (2) producer and consumer surplus analysis.

  o   Scenario – A US Tariff Rate Quota (TRQ) license authorizes New Zealand (NZ) to export up to 150,000 kilograms of salted butter at the lower-tier US tariff rate. To simplify the analysis, assume that the US is a relatively "minor player" in terms of the global traded volume of salted butter. In a free-trade global market, if the US did not enforce any quotas, then the US (as a smaller consumer) could pay a constant free-trade world price of $4.64/kilogram (about $2.10/pound) to import alternative quantities of salted butter from NZ.

Assume that NZ has a comparative advantage in salted-butter production and can profitably supply large volumes of salted butter at the $4.64/kg world price.

Suppose that NZ pays a lower-tier $0.20/kg salted-butter tariff to the US within the 150,000 kg NZ quota limit. For NZ salted-butter exports above the US quota limit, the tariff instantly increases to the higher-tier tariff of $3.00/kg. The higher-tier tariff is severe; it eliminates all economic incentive for NZ to export salted butter beyond its licensed quota.

We display the US salted-butter market, and the TRQ impact, in Figure 4.2 below:[84]

- Interpreting results of the US TRQ for imported NZ salted butter – When the US licenses NZ exports of salted butter up to 150,000 kg at the lower-tier $0.20/kg TRQ, and the $3.00/kg upper-tier TRQ, we can examine the market, distributional, and efficiency impacts using changes in producer and consumer surplus.

  o Market Effects – A lower-tier limit of 150,000 kg of imported NZ salted butter for imported NZ butter increases the US salted butter equilibrium price to $5.24/kg, which is $0.60/kg above the free-trade world price of $4.64/kg. The TRQ also has the effect of reducing the equilibrium quantity from 525,000 kg at the free-trade price to 300,000 kg at the TRQ-induced price. See Figure 4.2.

  o Distributional Effects – We again use a "with-and-without" analysis to determine net gains or losses in welfare in Figure 4.2 above. In the salted-butter market, if the US imports NZ salted butter at the *free-trade price* of *$4.64/kg*, the US Consumer Surplus equals the large triangular area identified by Points X, Y, and Z in Figure 4.2.

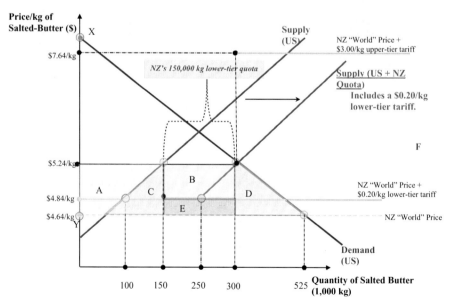

Figure 4.2 Analyze US authorization of a tariff rate quota (TRQ) license to New Zealand to export salted butter to the US. (Within the 150,000 kg quota limit, a lower-tier $0.20/kg tariff applies. Beyond the quota, the higher-tier $3.00/kg tariff is enforced.)

When the TRQ affects the US salted-butter market, the *Consumer Surplus decreases in value* by the sum of the following areas underneath the domestic US Demand Curve: A + B + C + D + E. As we analyze the components of this loss of Consumer Surplus, please refer to Figure 4.2.

We can identify how the reduced Consumer Surplus is either reallocated or lost to the rest of the economy. The trapezoidal *Area A* is known in international economics as the *"redistributive effect"* – this is a transfer of value from US consumers to domestic US producers of salted butter. In this instance, producer surplus grows as consumer surplus declines.

Area B is known as the *"quota rent."* It is a type of above-normal profit created by the TRQ quota restricting the available volume of the product that can be transacted. Quota rents might have accrued to the NZ exporters, except for the licensing process created by the US. NZ must bid for the right to control the license against other nations who could export salted butter to the US. The bidding process typically continues until all of the above-normal quota rent has been absorbed. With competitive bids driving up the prices of quota licenses, the *US Treasury is the most likely beneficiary* of the quota rent. US consumers end up adding to the federal government's account balances as a result of the licensing fee process.

Area E is known as the *"revenue effect,"* and this is clearly a transfer from US domestic consumers to the US Treasury coffers. A TRQ is a tariff; and a tariff is another name for a tax that happens to be applied to international markets. In our example, Area E is the government collecting $0.20/kg of revenue on each kilogram of salted butter imported from New Zealand.

Area C is known as the *"consumption effect"* and *Area D* is the *"protective effect."* When added together (Summed Areas = C + D), the combined impact is known as the *"deadweight loss"* of the TRQ. Deadweight losses occur because valuable market results have been displaced by the artificial effects of the TRQ quota. In the case of Area C, consumers are denied the opportunity enjoy larger volumes of the product at free-market prices. Area D is a loss of efficiency because the quota allows higher-cost US producers *supply* increased product volumes at higher marginal costs than are actually available in the global economy. Basically, it is not efficient to displace lower-cost production with higher-cost production.

- Conclusions – Our brief analysis predicts that US TRQ limits on imported NZ salted butter will:

  o Increase the equilibrium price of salted butter to US consumers, and decrease the market equilibrium quantity, as compared to an unrestricted free-trade market in salted butter.

  o Redistribute income from US salted-butter consumers to domestic US salted-butter producers, and also to the US Treasury in the form of licensing fees and tariff revenue.

  o Reduce overall economic efficiency, because the TRQ artificially restricts the amount of salted butter that could be internationally transacted, if free-trade market at lower global equilibrium prices were allowed to prevail.

- o   TRQ's distort markets. These quotas benefit domestic producers, create costs for domestic producers, and cause deadweight economic losses.

- Recommendations – We examine the rationale for Tariff Rate Quotas to protect domestically produced US agricultural commodities from global competitive pressures, and suggest alternatives to improve economic performance.

  - o   What are the Trade Consequences of TRQ's that limit US Imports? – Let's consider the possible international responses to the effects of TRQs on global trade patterns.

    - o   Our analysis in Figure 4.2 predicts that a TRQ does reduce the trade volume below the amount that would exist at globally competitive free-trade prices.
    - o   US trading partners who have a comparative advantage for exporting selected products encounter these TRQ constraints:

      - ❑   TRQ's prevent US trading partners from exporting efficient volumes of their products to US consumers
      - ❑   US trading partners pay a licensing fee for the right to export the product to the US
      - ❑   Depending on supply and demand elasticities, US trading partners share alternative proportional costs of the lower-tier TRQ tariff; and, the upper-tier tariff is typically so high that economically rational trade cannot occur.

    - o   Potential responses of US trade partners affected by US TRQs:

      - ❑   US trading partners burdened by TRQ volume limits, licensing fees, and tariff costs can retaliate in-kind against US exports. The result can be a global proliferation of TRQs that slow down international trade flows.
      - ❑   Trading partners can enter into trade negotiations with the US in an effort to loosen (increase) the lower-tier TRQ trading volume limit, increase the availability of TRQ licenses, reduce the lower-tier tariff or the lessen the severity of the upper-tier TRQ tariff, or perhaps even eliminate the TRQ altogether.

    - o   Recommended Policy Options and Research

      - ❑   There are considerable deadweight economic costs associated with a status quo policy that maintains TRQs and upholds related barriers to free trade. The USDA's Economic Research Service recommends efforts to *reform US agricultural trade policy*, and estimates that the elimination of all market distortions would increase global economic welfare by $56 billion/year.
      - ❑   Active trade negotiations, such as those sponsored by the World Trade Organization or in proposals such as the Trans-Pacific Partnership, are preferable to scenarios where dissatisfaction among trading partners becomes a scenario of retaliation and trade barrier escalation.
      - ❑   Transitions from protective policies such as TRQs to more liberalized trading conditions does create winners and losers. Any movement towards a free-trade stance should also consider programs known as "Trade Adjustment Assistance" to assist domestic industries that need time and resources to adapt to a new, unprotected, and more competitive trade environment.

Making sense of the consistent and contradictory program impacts in the 2014 Farm Bill's safety net

The effects of the various programs in 2014 Farm Bill vary greatly in relation to the nation's economic goals and policies.

For instance, the US is a prominent World Trade Organization (WTO) member. The US also actively participated in negotiating the proposed the Trans-Pacific Partnership (TPP). US involvement in the WTO and the TPP indicates a national interest in opening up world markets and pursuing free-trade opportunities. When Congress discontinued the DPPS and MILC dairy programs, the US action was entirely consistent with the national goal of reduced distortion and greater economic efficiency in global markets.

In stark contrast, the Congress renewed the market-distorting elements of the MALP and Sugar Programs in the 2014 Farm Bill with little or no reforms.

Congress's differential treatment of these agricultural programs in relation to their effects on US trade policy sends a mixed message to the rest of the global economy. From a simple logical perspective, there is seemingly no distinctive pattern to the economic effects of these programs. Why?

The standard market analysis of price equilibria and consumer surplus cannot fully answer the question. We need an alternative approach. The methods of public choice economics offer us a mode of analytical reasoning to obtain insights and useful explanations. We seek a perspective that lets us effectively address the perplexing questions that often arise in the development and implementation of public policies.

If we apply the step-wise policy analysis method that we used to study the two previous scenarios, we can better understand the major influences on US agricultural and food policy:

- Purpose – The 2014 Farm Bill (PL 113-79) is an Act "to provide for the reform and continuation of agricultural and other programs." PL 113-79 sometimes includes provisions that harmonize with general US economic policy, and at other times the farm programs conflict with stated goals. Our purpose here is to use the analytical methods of *public choice economics* to better understand the forces determining the design of alternative programs within the 2014 Farm Bill, and future farm bills.
- Researchable Question – In the midst of the Great Depression, the US Congress enacted the free-trade-oriented 1934 Reciprocal Trade Agreement Act (RTAA) to effectively repeal the protectionist 1930 Smoot-Hawley Tariff legislation. Since that time, US national economic policy on international trade has mostly emphasized a long-term goal to orient the US economy *towards increased trade liberalization and less protectionism*. Why do some programs in the 2014 Farm Bill correspond to a free-trade agenda, while others are in conflict?
- Investigative Model – Our goal is to apply the models of public choice economics (see Chapter 3) to anticipate the outcomes of political and economic undertakings. As farm participants and legislative representatives respond to the various incentives, their decisions shape the performance of selected agricultural policies and programs.

We begin by borrowing ideas from Nobel Laureate Ken Arrow. He determined that collective choice mechanisms (such as majority rule) have inherent logical flaws. Arrow reminds us that we do not have a sound basis to assume that democracy (or any other process) will naturally convert individual preferences into logically consistent collective choices.

Further analysis is certainly necessary, but the inconsistencies that arise between farm program goals and national economic policy are already less of a surprise, if we fully consider Ken Arrow's insights.

Let's take this further, again using ideas we offered in Chapter 3. Following up on Arrow's admonition, Buchanan (another Nobel Laureate) suggests that participants must be vigilant participants if the democratic (small d) process is to produce rational results. Many voters have busy lives of their own, and do not always have the time and interest to monitor every vote taken in Congress. If the process is not being actively monitored for errors, it can go astray.

Another key perspective is Anthony Downs's (1957) research on coalition building.[85] Downs emphasizes the importance of assembling sufficient support from special interests to achieve a majority vote in favor of a particular policy initiative. Downs's work puts the spotlight on the power of interest groups in the political process.

Almost by definition, a wide spectrum of goals separate diverse interest groups. A humorous but insightful expression is: "Politics makes for strange bedfellows." The process of assembling a coalition capable of creating majority support for a particular policy is complex. A successful policy (garnering sufficient votes) is often a sophisticated arrangement of individual preferences and interest groups with varying degrees of negotiating strength.

At this point, it is also appropriate to again consider the power of the Iron Triangle in policy making. In the general case of garnering sufficient congressional votes to pass the 2014 Farm Bill, the roles of the special interests, the responsible government agencies/departments (e.g. USDA), and the legislators themselves have the highest priority.

How does this line of thought relate to congressional approval of the farm bill? Ultimately, if coalition-building and special-interest theories are substantial, then the goals and benefits of any particular government policy will accrue to the interest groups best able to build effective coalitions with others. These early adopters of selected options have the best potential to lobby congressional representatives and senators to vote for their favored policies.

We began this inquiry by asking why some farm policies are congruent with broad national economic goals, while others seem counterproductive. Public choice economics, to the extent that its insights are accurate, paint a picture clearly indicating that the success of any individual program or policy initiative is dependent on the ability to build a coalition. The collection of interests must be large enough to sustain a vote of the majority. All of this has little to do with aligning alternative national policies into an integrated logical system.

Public Choice Theory has multiple uses. It offers a valid rationale, in addition to other common-sense explanations, to explain why the Direct Payment Program (DPP) was so quickly eliminated as a politically unsustainable program in the 2014 Farm Bill.

Never mind that the WTO classified the DPP as a "green box" trade-friendly US farm support program. Taxpayer outrage over a program (DPP) that delivered cash payments to high-income farmers in the midst of the Great Recession was enough to kill the program. Our public choice economics perspective is entirely consistent with the DPP's demise.

In 1989, prior to the invention of the DPP, Gordon Tullock observed that farm support is frequently provided through subsidy and TRQ programs that create deadweight losses, as opposed to the economically efficient process of simply transferring cash to producers from taxpayers.

The DPP was remarkably similar to a cash transfer program. Publicly available documents were accessed freely to determine which farm producers were DPP recipients. Journalists speedily published this information. Opposition to the DPP easily formed, as most taxpayers had an elementary understanding of the DPP, and could express their dissatisfaction to something that they could comprehend.

Tullock argued that if similar amounts (or greater) of government support to producers were transferred by more complicated and harder-to-track mechanisms, then the programs were likely to gain sufficient interest group support to pass a majority vote.[86] Tullock is perhaps one economist with a forecasting record worth fame. DPP payments were easy to identify. New farm safety net programs in the 2014 Farm Bill are difficult to comprehend.

The 2014 Farm Bill indeed eliminated DPP, diminished the role of other commodity programs, and greatly increased the function of Federal Crop Insurance. The increased crop insurance presence and the decline of commodity policy programs creates a new legal reality. Crop insurance indemnity payments are legally private information.[87] Journalists will have to find farm-program stories elsewhere, because no data on the beneficiaries of crop insurance support are now easily available.

Recommended Policy Options and Research. All three of our policy analyses at the end of this chapter indicate that economic efficiency losses and questionable welfare transfers are associated with re-authorized or new programs included in the 2014 Farm Bill.

Are consumers and taxpayers sufficiently informed and possibly dissatisfied with inefficient or inequitable results in the 2014 Farm Bill to register their opposition to their legislators?

As Buchanan and Tullock remind us, it takes an actively involved and informed electorate to make a difference in the goals and impacts of government policy. Taxpayers who choose "rational ignorance" – calculating that the benefit of their involvement in public decision making is less than the cost – do so at their own peril (if public choice economics is correct).

Nobel Laureate Ken Arrow tells us that democracy is not necessarily a logically driven form of collective decision making. These observations about the imperfections of collective action are equally applicable to farm policy as they are to any other area of public concern. What are the alternative methods to investigate these policy limitations?

Pure market economics is one approach. Markets are based on the premise that mutually beneficial exchanges offer realistic solutions to most problems. When we engage in public policy analysis, we certainly utilize the market principle of reciprocal benefits. But there is more.

Policy making is also a political process. Political exchanges differ from economic markets. Political circumstances are dominated by competitive and conflicting relationships. One party wins, and the other loses.[88]

The win-lose reality of the political environment produces different outcomes than does the win-win result of efficient markets. The competitive political viewpoint is a clear reason to expect that policies within the omnibus farm bill do not naturally synchronize. Actually, the opposite outcome is quite plausible and likely.

What can be recommended? Public choice theory emphasizes that policy change is difficult, but not impossible. Dominant interests will tend to prevail in policy selection unless or until the lobbying power of other groups increases. Any individual or group who is not happy with the results of the current regime must figure out how to exert influence.

The ideas of Buchanan stand out. Active and informed participation is a preferred choice, as compared to passive acceptance. In any decision-making process, there are nuances to be understood and utilized. Policies, in a competitive environment, are channeled by special interests in alternative directions. Taxpayers and other broad interests must consider whether they wish to actively participate in channeling those policies, or will they allow themselves to be channeled by the organized special interests.

The primary lesson from public choice economics is that informed individuals and collective decision making are necessary if new and improved outcomes are to be achieved. No participant, whether he/she be a taxpayer, farm producer or food consumer, should depend on any natural tendencies of the democratic process to seek the best solutions. Such tendencies do not exist. Active and informed participation in the process is the vital ingredient required to produce desired performance.

Summary of chapter and the road ahead

The Title I commodity programs are sometimes referred to as the "heart of the farm bill." They are also important elements of the farm safety net. While the commodity programs still demand considerable attention, other priorities such as crop insurance have increased in relative importance. In the 2014 Farm Bill, the projected budget shows that crop insurance support will be more than twice as large as the funding for Title I commodities.

In this chapter we have explored the workings of these farm safety net programs, and investigated their efficiency and distributional effects. Both economics and politics play key roles in determining whether these programs are the object of reform, or are simply reauthorized from the previous farm bill with little modification.

We also used the broad reach of commodity and crop insurance programs as opportunities to practice policy analysis. We were able to use methods from Chapter 3's toolbox to gain additional insights into farm policy choices and their economic consequences.

As noted at the start of this chapter, the farm bill is not just agricultural legislation. It is also a huge influence on our food system. It is appropriate to follow the supply chain, and move beyond the farm gate to explore the new issues associated with the safety and nutritional quality of food products. We will temporarily change our focus away from the 2014 Farm Bill to look closely at the Food Safety Modernization Act (FSMA). We will return to the farm bill in later chapters. Both of these pieces of legislation are shaping the farm and food system for the rest of the twenty-first century. Let's continue the learning process as we look ahead to Chapter 5.

Notes

1 USDA, ERS. "Agricultural Act of 2014: Highlights and Implications." Retrieved from: http://ers.usda.gov/agricultural-act-of-2014-highlights-and-implications.aspx
2 Johnson, Renée and Jim Monke. "What Is the Farm Bill?" Congressional Research Service 7-5700. Report # RS22131. July 23, 2014, p. ii. Retrieved from: www.fas.org/sgp/crs/misc/RS22131.pdf
3 Ibid, p. 2.
4 Casteel, Chris. "Oklahoma Rep. Frank Lucas says Farm Bill Agreement 'almost a Miracle.'" *The Oklahoman*. Published: January 29, 2014. Retrieved from: http://newsok.com/article/3928268. by Chris Casteel
5 Chite, Ralph M. "The 2014 Farm Bill (P.L. 113-79): Summary and Side-by-Side." Congressional Research Service. 7-5700, R43076. February 12, 2014, p. 6. Retrieved from: http://nationalaglawcenter.org/wp-content/uploads/2014/02/R43076.pdf

6 Ibid.
7 Orden, David and Karl Zulauf. "Political Economy of the 2014 Farm Bill." *Amer. J. Agr. Econ.* 97(5): 1298–1311; doi: 10.1093/ajae/aav028. June 11, 2015, p. 1303. Retrieved from: http://ajae. oxfordjournals.org/content/97/5/1298.full.pdf+html
8 Taylor, Alexis. "Statement before the House Committee on Agriculture." Deputy Under-Secretary for Farm and Foreign Agricultural Services. September 15, 2015. Retrieved from: http://agricul ture.house.gov/uploadedfiles/taylor_testimony_091515_house_ag.pdf
9 AgriBank. "Price Loss Coverage or Agriculture Risk Coverage?" St. Paul, MN: Agribank Insights. July 2014. Retrieved from: www.farmcreditnd.com/documents/Jul14_AgriBankInsights_ PLC-ARC.pdf
10 Ibid, p. 2.
11 Ibid.
12 Babcock, Bruce. "Welfare-effects-of-PLC-ARC-and-SCO." *Choices Magazine*. 3rd Quarter 2014. Retrieved from: www.choicesmagazine.org/choices-magazine/theme-articles/3rd-quarter-2014/wel fare-effects-of-plc-arc-and-sco
13 AgriBank. "Price Loss Coverage or Agriculture Risk Coverage?" St. Paul, MN: Agribank Insights. July 2014. Retrieved from: www.farmcreditnd.com/documents/Jul14_AgriBankInsights_ PLC-ARC.pdf
14 USDA, ERS. "Crop Commodity Program Provisions-Title I – Payment Limitations." Dec. 15, 2015. Retrieved from: www.ers.usda.gov/topics/farm-economy/farm-commodity-policy/crop-commodity- program-provisions-title-i.aspx
15 USDA, Farm Service Agency. "December 2015 CCC lending rates." Current Interest Rates. Retrieved from: www.fsa.usda.gov/about-fsa/structure-and-organization/commodity-credit-corpo ration/current-interest-rates/index
16 USDA, ERS. "Crop Commodity Program Provisions-Title I." Nov. 22, 2016. Retrieved from: www. ers.usda.gov/topics/farm-economy/farm-commodity-policy/crop-commodity-program-provisions- title-i.aspx
17 Ibid, p. 1.
18 Jurenas, Remy. "Sugar Program Proposals for the 2012 Farm Bill." Congressional Research Service, 7-5700. Report# R42551. June 19, 2012. Retrieved from: https://fas.org/sgp/crs/misc/R42551.pdf
19 USDA, ERS. "Sugars and Sweeteners: Policy." Nov. 1, 2016. Retrieved from: www.ers.usda.gov/ topics/crops/sugar-sweeteners/policy.aspx
20 Ibid, p. 1.
21 McMinimy, Mark A. "Sugar Program: The Basics." Congressional Research Service, 7-5700. Report# R42535. April 1, 2014. Retrieved from: http://nationalaglawcenter.org/wp-content/ uploads/assets/crs/R42535.pdf
22 Jurenas, Remy. "Sugar Program Proposals for the 2012 Farm Bill." Congressional Research Service, 7-5700. Report# R42551. June 19, 2012. Retrieved from: https://fas.org/sgp/crs/misc/R42551.pdf
23 Ibid, p. 1.
24 USDA Economic Research Service. "Agricultural Act of 2014: Highlights and Implications – Dairy and Livestock." April 11, 2014. Retrieved from: www.ers.usda.gov/agricultural-act-of- 2014-highlights-and-implications/dairy-livestock.aspx
25 USDA, Farm Service Agency. "What's in the 2014 Farm Bill for Farm Service Agency Customers?" March 2014. Retrieved from: www.fsa.usda.gov/Internet/FSA_File/2014_farm_bill_customers.pdf
26 USDA, Farm Service Agency. "Fact Sheet: Dairy Indemnity Payment Program." September 2010. Retrieved from: www.fsa.usda.gov/Internet/FSA_File/dipp10.pdf
27 Glauber, Joseph W. and Patrick Westhoff. "50 Shades of Amber: The 2014 Farm Bill and the WTO." Allied Social Science Association Annual Meeting, January 3–5, 2015, Boston, MA, p. 8. Retrieved from: file:///C:/Users/User/Downloads/50ShadesOfAmberThe2014FarmBillAn_ preview.pdf
28 Schnepf, Randy. "2014 Farm Bill Provisions and WTO Compliance." Congressional Research Service 7-5700, Report # R43817, April 22, 2015, p. 20. Retrieved from: www.fas.org/sgp/crs/misc/ R43817.pdf
29 Glauber, Joseph W. and Patrick Westhoff. "50 Shades of Amber: The 2014 Farm Bill and the WTO." p. 3.

30 USDA, Economic Research Service. "Agricultural Act of 2014: Highlights and Implications – Dairy and Livestock." April 11, 2014. www.ers.usda.gov/agricultural-act-of-2014-highlights-and-implications/dairy-livestock.aspx
31 Ibid.
32 Schnepf, Randy. "2014 Farm Bill Provisions and WTO Compliance." pp. 20–21.
33 USDA, Foreign Agricultural Service. FAS Import Policies and Export Reporting Division. "Dairy Import Licensing Program." Retrieved from: www.fas.usda.gov/programs/dairy-import-licensing-program
34 USDA Agricultural Marketing Service. "Marketing Orders and Agreements." Retrieved from: www.ams.usda.gov/rules-regulations/moa
35 Cropp, Bob. "History, Function and Future of Federal Milk Marketing Orders." University of Wisconsin-Madison. April 2001, Slide # 5. Retrieved from: future.aae.wisc.edu/publications/federal_orders.ppt
36 Anderson, David, Michael Haigh, Matthew Stockton, and Robert Schwart. "Milk Pricing." Texas Cooperative Extension, Texas A&M University. Report # L-5403, RM2-41.0, 8-01. Retrieved from: www.researchgate.net/publication/26904508_Milk_Pricing
37 Andreyeva, Tatiana, Michael W. Long, and Kelly D. Brownell. "The Impact of Food Prices on Consumption: A Systematic Review of Research on the Price Elasticity of Demand for Food." *American Journal of Public Health*. 2010 February; 100(2): 216–222. Retrieved from: www.ncbi.nlm.nih.gov/pmc/articles/PMC2804646/
38 Anderson, David, Michael Haigh, Matthew Stockton, and Robert Schwart. "Milk Pricing." pp. 1–4.
39 Northwest Dairy Association, Seattle, WA. "From the Farm to the Table: Understanding the Why's and How's of Federal Milk Marketing Orders." Slides # 60–71. Retrieved from: www.fmmaseattle.com/statistics/UnderstandingFMOs.pdf
40 Barnes, Donald and Christopher Ondeck. "The Capper-Volstead Act: Opportunity Today and Tomorrow." University of Wisconsin Center for Cooperatives. August 5, 1997. Retrieved from: www.uwcc.wisc.edu/info/capper.html
41 Anderson, David, Michael Haigh, Matthew Stockton, and Robert Schwart. "Milk Pricing." p. 1.
42 Ibid.
43 Chite, Ralph M. "The 2014 Farm Bill (P.L. 113-79): Summary and Side-by-Side." Congressional Research Service 7-5700, Report # R43076, February 12, 2014, p. 7. Retrieved from: http://nationalaglawcenter.org/wp-content/uploads/2014/02/R43076.pdf
44 Ibid, p. 31.
45 Cornell University Law School. Legal Information Institute. 19 U.S. Code § 2497a - Agricultural Disaster Relief Trust Fund, Section (b): Transfer to Trust Fund. Retrieved from: www.law.cornell.edu/uscode/text/19/2497a
46 Shields, Dennis A. "Agricultural Disaster Assistance." Congressional Research Service, 7-5700, Report # RS21212, August 14, 2015, p. 2. Retrieved from: http://fas.org/sgp/crs/misc/RS21212.pdf
47 Dyer, Graham. "The 2014 Farm Bill and Disaster Assistance for Livestock Producers." Farms.Com Newsletters. Farms.com Ltd., Mar 28, 2014. Retrieved from: www.farms.com/news/the-2014-farm-bill-and-disaster-assistance-for-livestock-producers-74541.aspx
48 Ibid, p. ii.
49 Chite, Ralph M. "Emergency Funding for Agriculture: A Brief History of Supplemental Appropriations, FY1989–FY2006." Congressional Research Service, Order Code RL31095. July 3, 2006. Retrieved from: http://digital.library.unt.edu/ark:/67531/metacrs9308/m1/1/high_res_d/RL31095_2006Jul03.pdf
50 USDA, Risk Management Agency. "History of the Crop Insurance Program." Retrieved from: www.rma.usda.gov/aboutrma/what/history.html
51 Chite, Ralph M. "The 2014 Farm Bill (P.L. 113-79): Summary and Side-by-Side." Congressional Research Service 7-5700, Report # R43076, February 12, 2014, p. 17. Retrieved from: http://nationalaglawcenter.org/wp-content/uploads/2014/02/R43076.pdf
52 Shields, Dennis A. "Federal Crop Insurance: Background." Congressional Research Service, 7-5700, Report # R40532, August 13, 2015, p. 2. Retrieved from: http://ftp.fas.org/sgp/crs/misc/R40532.pdf

53 Scuse, Michael and James Harris. "Crop Production: 2014 Summary." USDA, National Agri-
    cultural Statistics Service (NASS), ISSN: 1057-7823, January 2015, p. 7. Retrieved from: www.
    census.gov/history/pdf/cropan15.pdf
54 Chite, Ralph M. "The 2014 Farm Bill (P.L. 113-79): Summary and Side-by-Side." Congressional
    Research Service 7-5700, Report # R43076, February 12, 2014, p. 4. Retrieved from: http://national
    aglawcenter.org/wp-content/uploads/2014/02/R43076.pdf
55 Shields, Dennis A. "Crop Insurance Provisions in the 2014 Farm Bill (P.L. 113-79)." Congressional
    Research Service, 7-5700, Report # R43494, April 22, 2014, p. 4. Retrieved from: http://national
    aglawcenter.org/wp-content/uploads/assets/crs/R43494.pdf
56 Ibid, p. 12.
57 Ibid, p. 10.
58 IMDb.Com. "Casablanca (1942) Quotes." Retrieved from: www.imdb.com/title/tt0034583/quotes
59 Glauber, Joseph. "The Growth of the Federal Crop Insurance Program, 1990–2011." Amer. J. Agr.
    Econ. 95(2): 482–488, January 2013. doi: 10.1093/ajae/aas091. Retrieved from: https://ajae.oxford
    journals.org/content/95/2.toc
60 Ibid, p. 483.
61 USDA, Risk Management Agency. "History of the Crop Insurance Program." Retrieved from:
    www.rma.usda.gov/aboutrma/what/history.html
62 Glauber, Joseph. "The Growth of the Federal Crop Insurance Program, 1990–2011". p. 483.
63 Glauber, Joseph. "The Growth of the Federal Crop Insurance Program, 1990–2011".
64 Shields, Dennis A. "Federal Crop Insurance: Background." Congressional Research Service, 7-5700,
    Report # R40532, August 13, 2015, p. 7. Retrieved from: http://ftp.fas.org/sgp/crs/misc/R40532.pdf
65 Stabenow, Senator Debbie. "Not your Father's Farm Bill." Huffington Post Politics blog. Feb.
    4, 2014. Retrieved from: www.huffingtonpost.com/sen-debbie-stabenow/not-your-fathers-farm-
    bil_b_4723767.html
66 College of Agriculture and Life Sciences, North Carolina State University. "General Facts about
    Agriculture." Retrieved from: www.cals.ncsu.edu/CollegeRelations/AGRICU.htm
67 Nelson, Frederick J. and Lyle P. Schertz. "Provisions of the Federal Agriculture Improvement and
    Reform Act of 1996." USDA, Economic Research Service. April 22, 2013. Retrieved from: www.
    ers.usda.gov/publications/aib-agricultural-information-bulletin/aib729.aspx
68 USDA, Risk Management Agency (RMA). "RMA Fact Sheet: About the Risk Management
    Agency." Program Aid 1667-02. June 2013, p. 1. Retrieved from: www.rma.usda.gov/pubs/rme/
    aboutrma.pdf
69 Ibid, p. 2.
70 Shields, Dennis A. "Federal Crop Insurance: Background." Congressional Research Service,
    7-5700, Report # R40532, August 13, 2015, p. 2. Retrieved from: http://ftp.fas.org/sgp/crs/misc/
    R40532.pdf
71 Ibid, p. 12.
72 Ibid, p. 18.
73 This graphical analysis follows the farm subsidy example in: Perloff, Jeffrey M. Microeconomics.
    Fourth Edition. Boston, MA: Pearson Addison-Wesley, 2007, p. 287.
74 Johnson, Renée and Jim Monke. "What Is the Farm Bill?" Congressional Research Service 7-5700.
    Report # RS22131. July 23, 2014, p. 5. Retrieved from: www.fas.org/sgp/crs/misc/RS22131.pdf
75 Shields, Dennis A. "Crop Insurance Provisions in the 2014 Farm Bill (P.L. 113-79)." Congressional
    Research Service, 7-5700, Report # R43494, April 22, 2014, p. 2. Retrieved from: http://national
    aglawcenter.org/wp-content/uploads/assets/crs/R43494.pdf
76 Wright, B.D. 2014. "Multiple Peril Crop Insurance." Choices. Quarter 3. Retrieved from: http://choic
    esmagazine.org/choices-magazine/theme-articles/3rd-quarter-2014/multiple-peril-crop-insurance
77 Glauber, Joseph. "The Growth of the Federal Crop Insurance Program, 1990–2011."
78 Shields, Dennis A. "Federal Crop Insurance: Background." Congressional Research Service,
    7-5700, Report # R40532, August 13, 2015, p. 2. Retrieved from: http://ftp.fas.org/sgp/crs/misc/
    R40532.pdf
79 Goodwin, Barry and Vincent Smith. "What Harm is Done by Subsidizing Crop Insurance?" Amer.
    J. Agr. Econ. 95(2): 489–497, January 2013. doi: 10.1093/ajae/aas091. Retrieved from: https://ajae.
    oxfordjournals.org/content/95/2.toc

80 Wang, H. Holly, Steven D. Hanson, and J. Roy Black. "Efficiency Costs of Subsidy Rules for Crop Insurance." *Journal of Agricultural and Resource Economics* 28(1): 116–137. Retrieved from: https://scholars.opb.msu.edu/en/publications/efficiency-costs-of-subsidy-rules-for-crop-insurance-3

81 Orden, David and Karl Zulauf. "Political Economy of the 2014 Farm Bill." *Am. J. Agr. Econ.* 97(5): 1298–1311; doi: 10.1093/ajae/aav028. June 11, 2015, p. 1303. Retrieved from: http://ajae.oxford journals.org/content/97/5/1298.full.pdf+html

82 Babcock, Bruce A. "The Politics and Economics of the U.S. Crop Insurance Program" in *The Intended and Unintended Effects of U.S. Agricultural and Biotechnology Policies*. Joshua S. Graff Zivin and Jeffrey M. Perloff (eds). University of Chicago Press, February 2012. Retrieved from: www.nber.org/chapters/c12109

83 Shields, Dennis A. "Proposals to Reduce Premium Subsidies for Federal Crop Insurance." Congressional Research Service 7-5700. Report # R43951. March 20, 2015, p. ii. Retrieved from: http://nationalaglawcenter.org/wp-content/uploads/assets/crs/R43951.pdf

84 This graphical analysis follows the Import Quota example in: Carbaugh, Robert J. *International Economics*. Thirteenth Edition. Mason, OH: South-Western Cengage Learning, 2011, pp. 157–163.

85 Downs, Anthony. *An Economic Theory of Democracy*. New York: Harper Publishers, 1957.

86 Tullock, Gordon. *The Economics of Special Privilege and Rent Seeking*. Boston, MA: Kluwer Academic, 1989.

87 Freeman, Andrea. "The 2014 Farm Bill: Farm Subsidies and Food Oppression." *Seattle U. L. Rev.* 1271(38), 2015. Retrieved from: http://digitalcommons.law.seattleu.edu/sulr/vol38/iss4/5/

88 International Encyclopedia of the Social Sciences. "Public Choice Theory: Bibliography." Thompson Gale, 2008. Retrieved from: www.encyclopedia.com/doc/1G2-3045302118.html

Chapter 5

The Food Safety Modernization Act (FSMA)

Evaluating costs and benefits

In this chapter, we pursue two goals:

1) Discover why the Food Safety Modernization Act (FSMA) has a key influence on twenty-first-century US farm and food policy, and
2) Learn to apply Cost-Benefit Analysis (CBA) methods to understand the FSMA's economic value.

The material in this chapter is challenging. We have confidence that you are ready to take on this task. As you do, you will acquire some useful and powerful analytical skills.

CBA is a useful investigative device with broad applicability. Mastery of CBA adds to the "toolbox" of techniques that you learned in Chapter 3.

Because the FSMA is a landmark and complicated piece of legislation, we need a systematic methodology to address it. Fortunately, CBA is such an approach. CBA methods offer consistent guidelines to evaluate the economic value of any program.

An even-handed review of the literature demonstrates that FSMA's requirements are not popular with all farm and food systems participants. How will we know if an FSMA rule is effective and rational? We need objective methods to make this determination. CBA can fulfill this role.

CBA analysis is an impartial means for estimating a program's net economic effects. CBA is not an opinion poll, and its methods are not mystical. It is a straightforward and analytical device. If its rules are properly followed, the basis for any CBA recommendation is easily tracked. The validity of its techniques and conclusions can be evaluated by anyone who understands how CBA works.

We also know that CBA is not a universal cure for solving all public policy problems. CBA analysis has its strengths and weaknesses, and we will explore them in this chapter. CBA decision criteria are sometimes a target of criticism, and it is important to understand the limits and the potentials of CBA.

On the other hand, CBA's reasoning and evidence for ranking one program as preferred over another are steady and reliable. A properly performed CBA analysis has the advantage of internal consistency. Generally accepted economic principles guide the use of CBA criteria to arrive at rational outcomes.

As noted earlier in this textbook, the FSMA both authorizes and requires the US Food and Drug Administration (FDA) to change its national food safety policy from one of reaction to that of prevention. Congress specifically wrote FSMA legislative language demanding that the FDA act quickly with its "rule making" for FSMA. Congress clearly sought to speed up the process of implementing the law's preventative intent.

We are in the era of accountability. Congress required that each of the seven proposed FDA Rules to implement the FMSA be accompanied by a Cost-Benefit Analysis (CBA) to estimate its net economic impact. Consequently, our effort to apply CBA principles to interpret the FSMA's effects is entirely consistent with the FDA's congressional mandate.

Fortunately, you can learn to use CBA without having to immediately appear before Congress to explain your analysis. But remember, your career might one day place you in the situation of being on the "hot seat." Therefore, we recommend that you apply yourself to learn CBA principles. Study hard. You never know when you may be called upon to justify your assessments.

Economists are often invited to offer testimony to congressional representatives on why CBA ranks one project higher than another. Elected officials do not always agree with, or prefer, the CBA criteria that favor or disfavor a program. Such disagreement is to be expected. But an analyst who uses CBA properly can stand his/her ground, and clearly state why CBA recommends some projects and not others.

Organization of chapter

Some ideal outcomes of implementing the FSMA include saving lives, reducing outbreaks of foodborne disease, and decreasing the need for costly quarantines and food recalls. Both congressional representatives and everyday citizens understand that it is beneficial to prevent food system contamination. The real challenge is to figure out how to properly quantify these benefits, compare them to the costs of disease prevention, and determine the most efficient ways to keep our food safe and nutritious. CBA Analysis provides a structured format to meet this challenge.

We will follow CBA's logical steps to: (1) sequence this chapter's topics, and (2) analyze the FSMA's economic impact. Our approach is to:[1,2]

- Identify and measure the FSMA's costs and benefits.
- Alert the reader to avoid common pitfalls when enumerating costs and benefits.
- Apply the equi-marginal principle (see Chapter 3) as a guideline to optimize net gains as resources are allocated towards food safety and disease prevention.
- Learn how to properly use the discounting process to convert future values into their present worth, because FSMA's costs and benefits are spread across time.
- Perform sensitivity analysis by employing alternative discount rates to strategically determine the net value of an FSMA rule.
- Demonstrate the superiority of using Net Present Value (NPV) to rank the desirability of FSMA rules, in contrast the more limited applicability of the Internal Rate of Return (IRR) and the Benefit-Cost (B/C) Ratio.
- Interpret the impacts of decision making under uncertainty and income redistribution on CBA outcomes and recommendations.

CBA is a demanding but rewarding methodology. Using CBA, rules and projects are ranked as economically superior or inferior to others based on transparent criteria. We are using CBA to review outcomes of the FSMA. But CBA has versatility. It can be productively applied to gain greater clarity and insight in a variety of policy scenarios.

We now have our roadmap to guide us for the rest of this chapter. Let's follow it.

Recognize and gauge the costs of implementing the FSMA

Cost measurement and/or estimation in a CBA is sometimes considered to be less complex than determining benefits. This viewpoint arises because the completion of a government project, or compliance with a government regulation, involve actions where expenses can be more easily identified. For example, the FDA may require a food business or an agency to perform a water quality test as a means of ensuring consumer safety. Compliance with the rule typically involves measurable testing fees and/or a reported amount of staff time.

Such costs are often obvious or simple to determine. In comparison, gauging the economic benefit of saving a human life through preventative practices is more difficult to quantify.

We will soon turn our attention to benefit estimation. Our current focus is the proper determination of cost, particularly as it applies to implementing the FSMA. This effort has its own set of challenges. Let's explore them.

There will be genuine sacrifices and expenses associated with making the FSMA's "safety by prevention policy" a reality. As noted earlier, the FDA is the primary agency charged with the FSMA's implementation. A court order has set deadlines for the FDA to follow through on seven FSMA "rules." These rules are:[3]

- Standards for the growing, harvesting, packing and holding of produce for human consumption – This rule determines science-based minimum safety standards for fruits and vegetables grown for human consumption.
- Preventive Controls for Human Food – This rule sets requirements for a written food safety plan, hazard analysis, preventive controls, monitoring, corrective actions and corrections, verification, supply-chain program, recall plan, and associated records.
- Preventive Controls for Animal Food – This rule establishes Current Good Manufacturing Practices (CGMPs) for animal food production. Similar to the rule for human food controls, the Animal Food Controls require a written food safety plan, hazard analysis, preventive controls, monitoring, corrective actions and corrections, verification, supply-chain program, recall plan, and associated records.
- Foreign Supplier Verification Programs – This rule requires importers to perform risk-based activities verifying that food imported into the United States is produced in full compliance with applicable U.S. safety standards.
- Accreditation of Third Party Auditors – This rule creates a voluntary program for the accreditation of third-party certification bodies (auditors). These certified accreditors will conduct food safety audits and issue foreign food facilities certifications. Ensuring that the accreditation bodies and third-party certification teams are competent and independent is this rule's purpose.
- Mitigation Strategies to Protect Food from Intentional Adulteration – This rule involves introducing risk-reducing strategies for processes in certain registered food facilities, and it targets the prevention of intentional food adulteration caused by acts of terrorism and/or similar attempts to cause wide-scale harm to the food supply and public health.
- Sanitary Transportation of Human and Animal Food – The FDA's proposed rule requires food transporters to use transportation practices that ensure the safety of the food they carry and deliver. The rule will establish criteria such as identifying the conditions, practices, training, and record keeping needed for safe and hygienic transportation of food.

A brief review of the FDA's seven rules (listed above) for FSMA implementation indicates that farms, food processors, transporters, and retailers will be required to engage in activities such as monitoring, hazard analysis, and auditing. The FDA will also have new supervisory responsibilities to ensure that the rules are implemented as designed. All of these considerations mean that extra resources are expended – generating entries on the cost side of the CBA ledger.

Theoretical and practical cost measurement considerations

Standard economic theory recommends that any cost included in a CBA should accurately measure opportunity cost. We live in a world of scarce resources, and implementing a new food safety law absorbs some of them. The resources could have valuably been employed elsewhere. We need to know how much of a sacrifice the economy makes to move ahead with this food safety initiative.

In a perfectly competitive market, resource prices are efficient measures of opportunity cost. Real-world markets often differ from the competitive ideal; market power or externalities cause equilibrium prices to diverge from efficient levels. In CBA, when we know that current market prices are distorted, we should strive to use *shadow prices* – prices that reflect true social marginal costs.[4]

Estimating shadow prices

Data on shadow prices are difficult to gather. The CBA analyst must make a professional judgment on whether to estimate project costs with market prices (value to the consumer), or with the marginal cost of production (value to the producer). For any new project, if the government's actions causes the good's total market to increase, then producer's marginal cost is a better approximation. If the government activity is expected to displace private users of the product within a constant market, then the market price is appropriate. If the government's impact is only a partial market expansion, then a weighted average of the marginal cost and the market price is needed.

When resources or goods used in a public program are subject to a sales tax, we have a similar cost estimation problem of whether to use the pre- or post-tax price. We follow a comparable process to determine the cost estimate. If the program expands the market, then the producer's pre-tax price is relevant, but when government activity dislodges private purchases, then the consumer's post-tax price should be used. In cases where the market response to the government activity is not complete, then a weighted average of the two prices is recommended.[5]

Unemployment effects on labor's opportunity cost

Another consideration is the opportunity wage cost of hiring labor. The cost is theoretically influenced by whether or not involuntary unemployment influences labor availability. If a government project causes labor to simply migrate from private to public employment, then the private sector wage rate is a reasonable estimate of project opportunity cost.

On the other hand, if the project causes an involuntarily unemployed person to return to the workforce, then technically the government project has not reduced output elsewhere. However, microeconomic analysis informs us that there is a labor-leisure choice; when a person works an additional hour, he/she encounters a real opportunity cost of lost leisure time.

When the results of the labor-leisure model are coupled with national economic stabilization policies, and the uncertain duration of involuntarily unemployment, we can conclude that the opportunity wage cost of labor will generally be some *non-zero* value. Rosen and Gayer (2010) suggest a pragmatic approach and recommend that the going equilibrium wage rate in the labor market is usually a reasonable estimate of the opportunity cost of attracting labor into public employment by a particular project.[6]

Taxation: distributional effects and real costs

In most cases, government projects are funded through taxation. The supporting tax base itself is not an extra cost. Taxes are simply the distribution mechanism that ultimately diverts the resources necessary to support the program or project.

However, there are the administrative costs of collecting the taxes, and the deadweight efficiency losses associated with the market interference caused by sales and income taxes. These additional costs created by the tax revenue-raising process are not always incorporated into a CBA. This is regrettable. Nevertheless, professional economists emphasize that these tax-related costs should be part of the discussion when CBA results are being interpreted.[7]

Summary of CBA cost measurement

In a CBA, we aim to measure the opportunity cost value of the resources that are necessary to implement a project. The primary purpose of this side of CBA is to accurately estimate the cost of complying with and administering a government program. Deadweight efficiency losses associated with financing the project should also be considered. New government initiatives, such as the FSMA, require the economy to allocate scarce resources to meet the program goals. The CBA method demonstrates that we should calculate the economic sacrifices required to implement the project.

Recognize and gauge the benefits of implementing the FSMA

What is the primary benefit of enacting and implementing the FSMA? What is it worth? These are difficult questions to answer, but CBA demands that we respond with accuracy and professionalism. We can think of this effort as a logical two-step process.[8]

A first step in benefit estimation is to determine whether the FSMA has satisfactorily met its comprehensive goals. From a broad perspective, the chief benefit of the FSMA is to create a safer and more advanced US food system. We need metrics to objectively assess how our system has progressed. Basically, we should be able to recognize and measure improvement when we see it. This step is easier said than done.

While the first step in benefit estimation definitely is a challenge, the second step is typically considered to be an even greater obstacle to overcome. In CBA, we need to calculate the value of the identified beneficial effects.

Determining FSMA's beneficial effects on food system safety

The main purpose of the FDA's seven rules for FSMA implementation is to create a safer and more modern food system. When these seven rules are functioning as designed, there should be improved and measurable safety performance.

Let's look at Step One of benefit estimation. We can observe examples of enhanced safety outcomes. Such benefits can be identified as: less frequent product recalls, reduced probability of disease outbreaks in the food system, increased documented instances where system threats are detected and avoided, estimated lives saved, and expected reductions in foodborne illnesses. Step Two would require that we place prices or values on each of these benefits.

We can examine a specific instance where the FDA was required to create a suitable benefit measurement. In particular, FDA is required by law to estimate the benefit (and cost) of enforcing its seven new FSMA rules. One of the seven FDA rules used to implement FSMA is: Standards for the Growing, Harvesting, Packing, and Holding of Produce for Human Consumption (or "the Produce Standards Rule").[9] The process of proposing and issuing the Produce Standards Rule required the FDA to conduct a Regulatory Impact Analysis (RIA).

RIA uses many of the same economic principles and methods as CBA. Two related presidential executive orders (#12866 in 1993, and #13563 in 2011) authorized the FDA to investigate the economic effects of the Produce Standards Rule by carrying out an RIA.[10,11]

The RIA that we will briefly examine is focused specifically on the economic effects of a FSMA rule that intends to increase the safety of fresh produce. This RIA is no trivial exercise. Its final form is a 397-page study. Included in this RIA is an exhaustive analysis of the benefits expected to be generated by implementing the Produce Standards Rule.

To estimate the benefit created by the Produce Standards Rule, the FDA used a detailed technique to determine the FSMA's effectiveness in *preventing and reducing the threat of contamination*. The task of improving prevention performance begins by recognizing that foodborne diseases can damage fresh-produce quality at multiple stages of the supply chain. Contamination can happen during activities such as planting, growth, harvest, and post-harvest.

FDA took the supply-chain system into account, and created a "contamination pathway model" where the threat- probability is calculated at each of eight different pathway points. FDA also estimated the efficacy (success rate) of their new rule in reducing the contamination threat at each point. Overall, FDA estimated that their new FSMA Produce Rule would have an average 64.77 percent efficacy in achieving prevention.[12]

FDA additionally estimated the number of "illnesses prevented" at each of the eight pathway stages. Finally, citing other professional research, FDA assigned an average cost per illness ($592) saved by prevention. *The cost savings is considered the benefit of the FSMA Produce Standards Rule.*

The details of the FDA benefit-estimation methodology are admittedly complex. The main point is that the FDA used a scientifically based research method to estimate the benefit of increased safety.

To summarize, FDA analysts engaged in Step One of benefit estimation when they created the eight-point contamination pathway model. They used the model to demonstrate where the FSMA prevention controls were reducing threats, and consequently increasing system safety.

FDA continued into Step Two when their analysts used research to determine the economic value of preventing illnesses. FDA also offered detailed descriptions of how they arrived at their estimates. Whether it is called RIA or CBA, maintaining transparency is a key aspect of ensuring scientific integrity.

Theoretical and practical benefit measurement considerations

When FSMA implementation increases food system safety, the benefit of illness prevention is not restricted to any one individual. To the extent that the reduced risk of contamination has both non-rival and non-excludable qualities, the FSMA's beneficial effect is a *public good* (see Chapter 3).

In theory, the complete value of a public good is the vertical summation of the individual consumer demand curves for those who benefit from the public good. Because of the practical difficulty of asking individual consumers to reveal their true preference for a public good, we are generally unable to properly measure its true value.

Because it is nearly impossible to determine a perfectly accurate value for a public good, we employ inventive approximations. The FDA's methodology for estimating the benefit of its FSMA Standard Produce Rule illustrates how we can calculate a reasonable public good value for reducing the frequency of foodborne illnesses.

There are also some economic changes originating with public projects that *cannot be included as benefits*. For example, a healthier economy free from illnesses might lead to stronger demand and higher prices for fresh fruits and vegetables. This secondary effect of the project is known as a pecuniary externality. These higher prices further the profits of fresh produce businesses. But these higher prices also represent increased costs for consumers. The market effects are offsetting, and no net benefit is created from pecuniary externalities.

Proper calculation of benefits (and cost) in a BCA requires us to not only what to include, but also what to exclude. The next section addresses possible source of errors, and offers advice on how to avoid them.

Common pitfalls when enumerating costs and benefits

Our discussion above demonstrates that CBA analysis requires considerable skill and resourcefulness to produce unbiased and reasonable estimates. It is important to recognize and respect that effort by preventing common errors that threaten CBA integrity.

Secondary effects and biased estimates

When determining the economic impact of a public project, an analyst *should avoid* calculating the "multiplier or trickle-down effect." Any new program will generate its direct impacts, and CBA aims to measure those outcomes as accurately as possible.

There are also secondary, tertiary, and related effects. These secondary and further impacts on business profits and consumer welfare are a ripple effect of the new program's initial economic results. But it is important to understand that these additional effects are two-sided: generating both benefits and costs. As a result, the majority of secondary effects are transfers of value, not creating new net benefits.

Any attempt to include secondary and later effects is not recommended, because there is no real limit to how far those calculations can go. If taken to the extreme, it would be relatively easy to economically recommend any project, by just including a sufficient number of secondary effects where net benefits are seemingly generated. To prevent bias, it is best to limit the project evaluation to the intended purpose of the program.

Job creation: benefit or cost or both?

Many politicians will proudly proclaim that a government project is responsible for creating a large number of jobs. This viewpoint may aid the reelection prospects of office-holders, but it confuses the theoretical perspective on the role of labor in the economy. Labor is a productive resource; competitive labor wages are part of a firm's cost of production. In a CBA, labor wages are properly a cost side measurement, and not a government project benefit. When we do not clearly identify what is a cost or a benefit, then usefulness of CBA as an evaluation tool quickly fades.

As discussed earlier in this chapter, one impact of a government project that attracts attention is the capacity to bring involuntary-unemployed persons back into the workforce.

The social opportunity cost of hiring these unemployed individuals is less than their actual wage. However, calculating this net benefit to the economy is extremely tricky. Making a determination of how much labor the project draws from the pool of involuntary-unemployed, as compared to transferring labor from private to public sector employment, is often impossible or very difficult to determine.

Avoid double counting

When a project creates direct net benefits that are reflected in annual business profits and an improved consumer surplus, these values are correctly included in CBA calculations.

But suppose the net asset values of these same businesses and consumers also increase. The expanded net worth *should not* be counted as an extra benefit, adding to the original profit and consumer gains. The advance in asset value is simply a reflection of the project's direct gains that are already included in the benefit calculation. It would be inappropriate to count the same benefit twice.

Avoidance of double counting would seem to be relatively easy to accomplish. Surprisingly, analysts make this mistake more often than expected. A recommended practice is to review calculated benefits in a CBA to ensure that double counting has not inadvertently occurred.

Using the equi-marginal principle in CBA to determine optimal resource allocation

In the above discussion, we identified potential sources of error when conducting CBA. We should not only be vigilant to avoid faults in the analysis, but also be knowledgeable about how to apply principles that produce the best results.

Ideally, a Cost-Benefit Analysis can guide a project to an economically efficient outcome. A world of scarce resources is good reason to design and implement programs that optimize net returns from those resources. An underfunded project wastes opportunities for advancement, and an overfunded project robs resources from other areas that could achieve superior outcomes.

The equi-marginal principle (see Chapter 3) is fundamental to all economics, and has particular relevance in CBA. In practice, the equi-marginal principle recommends that a decision maker employ an extra unit of a resource up to the point where the marginal cost *equals* the marginal benefit. When this marginal equality is reached, then the net total benefits from utilizing that resource are maximized.

Applying the equi-marginal principle to FSMA rule implementation

When the FDA's rule-making for implementing the FSMA is fully complete, seven different aspects of the US farm and food system will be affected. While each FSMA has unique elements, the common thread tying them together is the prevention of foodborne threats.

We can apply the equi-marginal principle to identify economic guidelines for FDA rule-making and prevention efforts. For example, when the FDA conducted the Regulatory Impact Analysis (RIA) of the FSMA Produce Standards Rule, they created a probabilistic model of events associated with fresh produce contamination. The FDA used the model to predict the efficacy of preventive controls in reducing the chance of a contamination event at each stage of the supply-chain pathway between the farm and the consumer of fresh produce.

To illustrate how the equi-marginal principle can be applied to FSMA rule-making, we can construct a model that employs fundamental components of the FDA's probabilistic model. We begin with the following concepts and notation:

$P(C_i)$ = Probability of a Produce Contamination Event "C" at Pathway Level (i)

$[1 - P(C_i)]$ = $P(A_i)$ = Probability of Averting (A) a Produce Contamination Event "C" at Pathway Level (i) via FDA Preventive Controls

$TB = \$Total Benefit$ = $f[P(A_i)]$ = Total Benefit is a function f of the Probability of an Averting (A) a Produce Contamination Event at Pathway Level (i)

$TC = \$Total Cost$ = $g[P(A_i)]$ = Total Cost is a function g of the Probability of an Averting (A) a Produce Contamination Event at Pathway Level (i)

$MB = \$Marginal Benefit$ = $f'[P(A_i)] = \Delta(\$TB)/\Delta\{P(A_i)\}$

        = Change in Total Benefit / Change in Prob. Of Averting "C"

$MC = \$Marginal Cost$ = $g'[P(A_i)] = \Delta(\$TC)/\Delta\{P(A_i)\}$

        = Change in Total Cost / Change in Prob. Of Averting "C"

The above notation and model components offer an opportunity to demonstrate the connections between costs, benefits and the FDA's efforts to reduce the probability of a Produce Contamination Event (C) occurring at some point (i) in the supply chain pathway. We make the simplifying assumption that the Probability of Averting a Contamination Event $[P(A_i)]$ is equal to one minus the Probability of a Contamination Event $[1 - P(C_i)]$ occurring.

We also make additional assumptions about the Total Cost ($TC) and Total Benefit ($TB) functions. The Law of Increasing Opportunity Cost is presumed to govern the Total Cost function (g), and the Law of Diminishing Marginal Utility influences the Total Benefit function (f).

Our Marginal Cost ($MC) function measures the change in Total Cost as the probability of Averting a Produce Contamination Event increases.

Our Marginal Benefit ($MB) function measures the change in Total Benefit as the probability of Averting a Produce Contamination Event increases.

We can use a graphical display to demonstrate that if the equi-marginal principle ($MC=$MB) is followed, then the FDA would be informed about the probability of averting a Produce Contamination Event $[P(A_i)]$ that would maximize net benefits to the economy as a whole. See Figure 5.1 below.[13]

What can we learn from the Cost and Benefit model in Figure 5.1? The economic efficiency perspective would argue that it is *not rational* to push the probability of averting a contamination event up to 100 percent. Marginal analysis tells us that any increase of $[P(A_i)]$ beyond the optimal point is a situation where the extra cost to society is greater than the extra benefit.

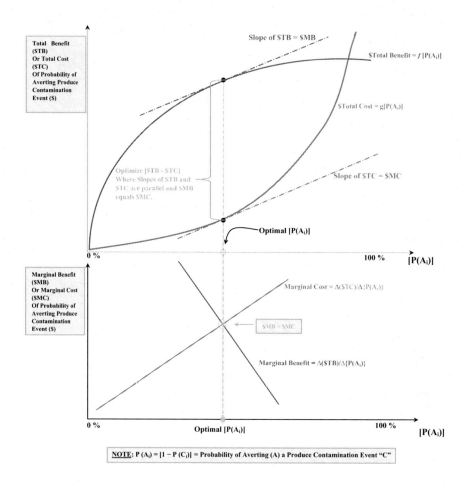

Figure 5.1 Use equi-marginal principle to determine economically efficient probability of averting a produce contamination event.

We can use Figure 5.1 to observe that it is also *not optimal* to increase $[P(A_i)]$ up to the point where $Total Cost = $Total Benefit ($TC = $TB). When ($TC = $TB), the marginal benefit of improving the probability of contamination aversion is far below the marginal cost. Too many resources would be involved in aversion activities, and not enough in the rest of the economy.

Discounting FSMA's future benefits and costs into present values

Benefits and costs of government programs and/or projects are not always concurrently realized. For example, costs may occur "upfront" at the start of a program, while benefits are only gained in future years. A wise student of finance or economics understands that the receipt of $100 in 10 years is not the same value as $100 received today.

Dollars available now can be saved or invested, earning interest into the future. As long as funds are not withdrawn, interest compounds. Consequently, if a project produces $100 in a future year, then the rational step is to discount that amount into a present value using an appropriate interest rate.

The standard formula for determining the present value (PV) of a future benefit or cost can be displayed as follows:

$$PV = FV_i / (1 + r)^i$$

Where: PV = Present Value

FV$_i$ = Future Value in time period i

r = discount or interest rate

If a project is expected to generate a continuous stream of benefits or costs, now and into the future, then the standard formula for determining the present value (PV) of the *sum* of discounted future values can be displayed as follows:

$$PV = \sum_i^T [FV_i / (1 + r)^i]$$

Where: PV = Present Value

FV$_i$ = Future Value in time period i

R = discount or interest rate

i = number of time periods between 0 and year T

Assuming that we have chosen an appropriate discount rate (r), we can separate the PV of a project's overall cost and benefit. We can determine a Net Present Value (NPV) with this formula:

$$NPV = PV (Benefit) - PV (Cost)$$

Conditions:

PV(X) = Present Value of Variable X

NPV = Net Present Value

If NPV > 0, then the project is viable

If NPV ≤ 0, then reject the project

If there are a range of possible projects and a limited budget, then choose the project with the *maximum NPV*. While other ways to rank projects exist, there are key arguments that favor NPV as the best indicator of a project's economic efficiency.

In the case of FSMA Rule Implementation, we are seeking the preventive methods that maximize the NPV of returns. The arrangement of benefits and costs under alternative FSMA rules may or may not yield a viable outcome, depending on what discount rate is applied. A relatively high discount rate will favor projects where benefits are large and early. A lower discount rate will be more favorable to FSMA Rules that yield heavier benefits (relative to costs) in the later years.

Sensitivity analysis of FSMA's value with alternative discount rates

The decision on the appropriate interest rate for discounting future benefits and costs into present value terms is difficult to determine. As a result, rather than settling upon a single discount rate, a project's NPV is reviewed under alternative discount rate scenarios.

Private versus public sector considerations for determining the discount rate. The private sector influences on the selection of an appropriate discount rate for government projects are varied. *The equilibrium private rate of return on capital is a starting point.* There are at least two tax-related considerations. One of them is the tax levied by federal and state entities on investment interest. From a national economic efficiency standpoint, the question of whether private investors or the government receives these net returns is not relevant. The economy is simply better off from good investments, as measured by their market interest rate.[14]

However, to the extent that *income and capital gains taxes create deadweight market inefficiencies*, then the net return to society is less. Taking into account the inefficiencies that the tax code introduces into private capital markets, the US General Accounting Office recommends a *maximum discount rate of no lower than 7 percent* to take into account the market and government forces influencing private capital markets. This 7 percent discount rate is the upper-bound on many sensitivity analyses of government-funded projects.[15]

On the other hand, the question of the social discount rate takes into account *positive (or negative) externalities* that are associated with the implementation of government programs. In an industry-level publication, Robert Rogers noted that the food industry's response to the FSMA rule implementation has been a reassignment of who is ultimately responsible for food safety.[16] The FSMA is compelling upper-level management to respond. Safety controls used to be delegated to on-the-floor production and operations managers. The FSMA-activated transfer of accountability has had a strong positive external effect that we can identify as a public good.

The paradigm shift from production-floor-manager to upper-level executive dramatically changes the safety focus of many companies. The prevention of foodborne system safety threats becomes more than just a cost-minimization scenario. A more sophisticated view of safety as an integral part of production has emerged, as compared to a food safety tool only needed in emergencies.

What does this public good production mean? It means that firms *who proactively adjust to create a safer system* for all consumers do not receive all the net returns for their efforts.

We need a discount rate that reflects the existence of public goods and externalities. The US General Accounting Office recommends that a *minimum discount rate no lower than 3 percent* be used to convert future government project benefits and costs into PV terms.[17]

Sensitivity analysis recognizes the importance of both private capital markets and socially responsible considerations of public goods and externalities. A healthy test of the economic viability of a project or program is to model its NPV between a minimum of a 3 percent discount rate and a 7 percent maximum discount rate. If the project has a positive NPV between the lower and upper bounds for the discount rate, then the project is recommended. The only proviso is a situation where more than one competitive project is evaluated. The project with the highest NPV is economically preferred over others.

Measuring FSMA's worth with NPV methodology, versus the IRR and B/C ratio methods

Professional economists prefer NPV as the primary means to measure the viability of public programs and projects. There are two competing measurements of a project's economic worthiness, and these are the Internal Rate of Return (IRR) and the Benefit-Cost (B/C) Ratio.

Internal Rate of Return (IRR)

The IRR calculation is determined if the project's costs and benefits are inserted into the following PV formula:
   Solve the following to determine the IRR (ρ):

$$0 = \Sigma_i^T [(B_i - C_i) / (1 + \rho)^i]$$

The IRR ρ-value is the discount rate that equates the present value of a project's benefits and costs. The rationale for calculating ρ is to create a rate-of-return measurement that is directly comparable to the market's interest rate (r) cost of capital. In simple terms, the project is judged as viable if [$\rho > (r)$].
   A flaw of using the IRR approach is the inability to detect superior net gains in total profit when projects differ in size. Examine the following scenario of two competing projects:

Project "Small"	Project "Big"
Initial Cost = $100	Initial Cost = $1,000
Year 1 Return = $112	Year 1 Return = $1,100
IRR for "Small" = 12 percent	IRR for "Big" = 10 percent
Market Interest Rate = 7 percent	Market Interest Rate = 7 percent
Net Profit = $12 - $7 = $5	Net Profit = $100 - $70 = $30

In the above scenario, let's assume that both Projects "Small" and "Big" are one-time programs that cannot be duplicated or repeated. If we use the IRR as the criterion for making a choice, then we prefer Project Small over Project Big (12 percent > 10 percent). However, if we examine net profit after paying 7 percent market interest, we know that Project Big should be ranked higher. In comparison, if we had simply used Net Present Value to determine the project choice, the decision would unambiguously be to fund Project Big.[18]

The Benefit-Cost (B/C) Ratio

The rationale for using the Benefit-Cost (B/C) Ratio is convenience. If the net present value of the project benefits are costs are calculated, and those values are respectively placed in the numerator and denominator of the B/C Ratio, then a project will can be judged as admissible if the B/C ratio exceeds one (B/C > 1). Similarly, if competing projects must be ranked, then we would favor projects with higher B/C Ratios.

The potential fault of the B/C criterion occurs when the B/C ratio is modified by our accounting methods. The value of the B/C ratio fluctuates if costs are classified as negative benefits, or if benefits are identified as negative costs. For example:

Project A: "Enforce Critical Controls"	Project B: "Monitor Contaminants"
PV of Direct Cost = $10,000	PV of Direct Cost = $15,000
PV of Direct Benefit = $25,000	PV of Direct Cost = $30,000
B/C Ratio = 2.50	B/C Ratio = 2.00
PV (Negative Externality [NE]) = $4,000	PV of new Negative Externality = $0
[(B – NE) / C] Ratio = 2.10	
[B / (C + NE)] Ratio = 1.79	

In the scenario above, the B/C criterion would initially rank Project A as superior to Project B (2.50 > 2.00). Suppose we later discover that Project A has costly externalities – for example, there are external costs created when "critical controls" are enforced where they are unnecessary. In this case, the question is how to count the externality in determining the B/C ratio for Project A. If the externality is included as a negative benefit, then Project A retains its superior rank. On the other hand, if negative externality value is added to Project A's cost, then Project B is preferred.[19]

The Net Present Value (NPV) criterion

If we do not have clarity on how to include externalities or other project impacts in the calculation, then the guidance from the B/C ratio on project prioritization will also be inconsistent. As was noted already in the IRR discussion, the analyst should use Net Present Value (NPV) to make CBA determinations of project worth and ranking. NPV recommendations will always be accurate and consistent.

Decision making under uncertainty, and its FSMA relevance

On May 30, 2013, the US Centers for Disease Control (CDC) officially announced that a strain of E. Coli had infected the US food system in nineteen states. There were thirty-five reported illness cases, and about one-third required hospitalization. Fortunately, no deaths occurred. A coordinated investigation determined that the outbreak originated with a frozen food plant in Georgia. The company involved issued a food recall for all products sold between July 2011 and March 2013.[20]

This 2013 outbreak is the type of contamination event that the FDA hopes to prevent in the future as the FSMA rules are established and implemented. The FSMA is a costly undertaking. We can debate on how much protection is enough, and how much should be spent to reduce the frequency of foodborne illnesses. As we have been exploring the methods of CBA in this chapter, we have examined trade-offs, and asked questions about how to compare the benefits of protection against the costs.

We can view the FDA's efforts under FSMA as a means of creating greater certainty, and less uncertainty, about the safety of our food system. FDA aims to accomplish this purpose by implementing new methods of treating, monitoring, and testing the foods that move through the supply chain from the farm to the kitchen table.

Increased certainty comes at a cost. But economic theory provides insight into what types of consumer and producer behaviors we can expect under uncertainty. For example, if we consider the following thought experiment about two options available to Tristan, a hypothetical consumer:[21]

Tristan's Option 1	Tristan's Option 2
Receive $1,000	A 50 percent Chance to Receive $2,000,
with 100 percent Certainty.	and a 50 percent Chance to Receive $0.

Which option will Tristan prefer? Both options have the same expected value. The second option includes uncertainty. If Tristan is risk averse, he will prefer Option 1 over Option 2. How prevalent is risk-averse behavior? We can argue that risk aversion is widespread enough to support numerous insurance markets where customers pay premiums in exchange for coverage against infrequent and unpredictable loss events. In financial markets, investors are willing to purchase relatively safe 3-month Treasury bills that yield low interest rates; but they require higher rates of return to attract them to purchase riskier stocks and bonds.

Risk aversion is predominant throughout the market economy. The concept of comparing a risky choice to its "certainty equivalent" is another related analytical tool for understanding risk-based choices. When a decision maker is risk averse, then the certainty equivalent will be some dollar amount that is less than the expected value of a game of chance (the difference is known as the "risk premium"). If a decision maker was completely risk-neutral, then the certainty equivalent and the risky choice's expected value would be equal, and the risk premium would be zero.

The cost of implementing the seven FSMA rules can be thought of as a type of societal risk premium for reducing the probability of a contamination event. When the FDA was developing these rules, the goal was to reduce the likelihood of foodborne illnesses. Using the available technologies and resources, the FDA introduces practices that help prevent disease outbreaks all along the supply chain pathway.

For example, in the case of the FSMA Produce Standards Rule, the FSMA introduces preventive practices at eight different key points along the supply-chain pathway. When the safety measure probabilities are totaled for a collective impact, the FDA estimates that the effectiveness of their efforts will reduce the overall risk of foodborne illnesses by 64.77 percent. FDA assesses the Total Cost of the effort to be $459.56 million and the Total Benefit of $1,036.4 million, for a Net Benefit = +$576.84 Million. The benefit of the FSMA Produce Standards Rule is derived as the cost savings of $592 per illness prevented.[22]

It is worth noting that the FDA's efforts are not aiming to achieve 100 percent prevention. This outcome makes economic sense, as the theory would tell us that attaining full certainty of averting all threats would be cost prohibitive. In addition, our lessons from studying decision making under uncertainty indicate that while risk aversion is an important phenomenon, the aversion is not infinite.

The concept and measurement of certainty equivalents help us to understand that risk-averse consumers are willing to endure a smaller amount of risk in exchange for a risk premium. It is a question of trade-offs again. In the case of FSMA rule implementation, we can examine the risk reduction associated with the preventive measures and weigh that against the costs and cost savings, to make judgments about the economic efficiency impacts of improving food system safety.

CBA, FSMA, and income distribution impacts

Who benefits, and who pays? Cost Benefit Analysis is not designed to answer this distributional question. As the FDA implements the seven FSMA rules, we do not have a scientific way of knowing whether the taxpayers who finance these government activities are the same individuals who benefit from the reduced probability of foodborne illnesses.

Another related issue is whether FSMA benefits are weighted towards higher income households, while lower income households carry a greater part of the tax burden. Traditional CBA is focused on overall economic efficiency, and does not include the analytical tools to take into account differential impacts on the rich, poor, and middle class.

Some proposals have been made to recalculate costs and benefits with a weighting system that would determine that a $1 benefit to a wealthy person be counted as $0.80, and that $1 of benefit to a poor person be treated as $1.20. But such an arrangement is entirely arbitrary, and we do not have a scientific way of determining the exact income levels where a household is considered rich or poor. Finally, such a weighting system would impact the efficiency outcome of the project, and we would likely be able to find a way to deliver more benefits to the poor at a lower cost by simply designing a program with that objective in mind.[23]

Other economists have argued that any methodology to weight CBA outcomes to address distributional inequities is not necessary. Known as the Hicks-Kaldor criterion, this argument suggests that that if a CBA yields a positive NPV, then it would be possible for the "winners" from the project to use some of their gains to compensate the "losers."[24] Hicks-Kaldor simply says that the only requirement that matters is the potential to make a wealth transfer. Not all economists find Hicks-Kaldor to be the final verdict on CBA distributional consequences – they argue that we examine the distributional consequences for what they really are, rather than what they could be.

In truth, Cost Benefit Analysis cannot tell us whether a project will necessarily lead to an overall gain in social welfare. Once we establish this premise, then we can talk about the reasons for performing a CBA.

CBA is an organized method for comparing the gains and drawbacks of introducing a government project into the economy. The difficulties of estimating certain benefits and costs are well known. Because the strengths and weaknesses of CBA methods are transparent, it is always possible to question the methodology when necessary.

The advantage of using a CBA to evaluate a government project is its structured and rational format. The techniques for estimation are not random or arbitrary. In a CBA, it is required to have solid reasoning for using some approximation methods while rejecting others. Finally, to the extent that we live in a world of scarcity, it makes sense to use an evaluation system that intentionally takes into account opportunity cost as the efficiency impact of a government project is evaluated.

Summary

We employed the analytical power of Cost-Benefit Analysis (CBA) to determine the economic effects of implementing the Food Safety Modernization Act (FMSA). We reviewed and used important principles, such as estimating opportunity costs and shadow prices to properly measure the cost side of any FSMA rule or project. We also learned to avoid pitfalls such as double counting and the mistake of including secondary effects. The equi-marginal principle is a key concept to prevent a rule or project from exceeding its optimal size. We also learned that proper calculations of discounted present value are necessary when costs and/or benefits are dispersed over time. Ranking projects Net Present Value is the most preferred method because of its logical consistency.

The focus on "safety" in the FSMA means that risk management is an integral consideration. Risks are typically measured using probabilistic scenarios. When probabilities of events are included, then the notion of risk-averse behavior is analytically relevant when making recommendations in CBA Analysis.

One of the economic areas of the FSMA involves the FDA's new power to regulate the safety of imported foods. Imports and exports, when considered together, are another key economic influence on the agri-food system. We turn our attention to international trade and its relationship to agri-food policy in the next chapter.

Notes

1 Rosen, Harvey and Ted Gayer. *Public Finance*. Ninth Edition. New York: McGraw Hill Education, 2010, pp. 152–174.
2 Browning, Edgar K. and Jacquelene M. Browning. *Public Finance and the Price System*. Second Edition. New York: Macmillan Publishing Company, 1983, pp. 114–125.
3 US Dept. of Health and Human Services, Food and Drug Administration (FDA). "President's FY 2017 Budget Request: Key Investments for Implementing the FDA Food Safety Modernization Act (FSMA)." Feb. 22, 2016. Guidance and Regulation. Retrieved from: www.fda.gov/Food/GuidanceRegulation/FSMA/ucm432576.htm
4 Rosen, Harvey and Ted Gayer. *Public Finance*. Ninth Edition. New York: McGraw Hill Education, 2010, p. 163.
5 Ibid.
6 Ibid, p. 164.
7 Browning, Edgar K. and Jacquelene M. Browning. *Public Finance and the Price System*. Second Edition. New York: Macmillan Publishing Company, 1983, pp. 117–118.
8 Ibid, pp. 114–116.
9 US Food and Drug Administration (FDA). "Analysis of Economic Impacts – Standards for the Growing, Harvesting, Packing and Holding of Produce for Human Consumption." January 4, 2013. Retrieved from: www.fda.gov/AboutFDA/ReportsManualsForms/Reports/EconomicAnalyses/ucm334171.htm
10 Clinton, President William. "Regulatory Planning and Review: Executive Order 12866 of September 30, 1993." Federal Register, Vol. 58, No. 190. Title 3. October 4, 1993.
11 Obama, President Barack. "Improving Regulation and Regulatory Review: Executive Order 13563 of January 18, 2011." *Federal Register*, Vol. 76, No. 14, Title 3. January 18, 2011.
12 Ibid, p. 80.
13 This graphical analysis follows the Cost-Benefit Analysis example in: Perloff, Jeffrey M. *Microeconomics*, Fourth Edition. Boston, MA: Pearson Addison-Wesley, 2007, pp. 612–613.
14 Browning, Edgar K. and Jacquelene M. Browning. *Public Finance and the Price System*. Second Edition. New York: Macmillan Publishing Company, 1983, p. 117.
15 Rosen, Harvey and Ted Gayer. *Public Finance*. Ninth Edition. New York: McGraw Hill Education, 2010, p. 161.

16 Rogers, Robert. "Finding the Unforeseen Benefits of Food Safety Regulation." *Food Manufacturing.* April 2012. Retrieved from: www.manufacturing.net/article/2012/04/finding-unforeseen-benefits-food-safety-regulation

17 Ibid, p. 161.

18 Rosen, Harvey and Ted Gayer. *Public Finance.* Ninth Edition. New York: McGraw Hill Education, 2010, p. 157.

19 Ibid, p. 158.

20 US Centers for Disease Control and Prevention (CDC). "Multistate Outbreak of Shiga toxin-producing Escherichia coli O121 Infections Linked to Farm Rich Brand Frozen Food Products (Final Update)." May 30, 2013. Retrieved from: www.cdc.gov/ecoli/2013/O121-03-13/index.html

21 Rosen, Harvey and Ted Gayer. *Public Finance.* Ninth Edition. New York: McGraw Hill Education, 2010, pp. 170–171.

22 US Food and Drug Administration (FDA). "Analysis of Economic Impacts – Standards for the Growing, Harvesting, Packing and Holding of Produce for Human Consumption." January 4, 2013, p. 301. Retrieved from: www.fda.gov/AboutFDA/ReportsManualsForms/Reports/EconomicAnalyses/ucm334171.htm

23 Browning, Edgar K. and Jacquelene M. Browning. *Public Finance and the Price System.* Second Edition. New York: Macmillan Publishing Company, 1983, pp. 124–125.

24 Rosen, Harvey and Ted Gayer. *Public Finance.* Ninth Edition. New York: McGraw Hill Education, 2010, p. 169.

Chapter 6

US agricultural and food sector connections to the global economy

A student attending a US Midwest College enters an Asian restaurant for lunch. After ordering a meal consisting of Spicy Cumin Lamb, Guatemalan coffee, French cheese, Vietnamese rice, and Brazilian papaya juice, she uses a Finland-made Nokia phone to "Skype" her brother. He is a US exchange student at Queensland University of Technology in Brisbane, Australia.

Our twenty-first-century world is interconnected. Rapidly advancing communication and transportation technologies continue to reduce geographic barriers of time and space. Diverse cultures regularly influence each other via highly interactive networks. The pace of global change is breathtaking.

Organization of chapter

In this chapter, we explore our US agricultural and food system as it progressively integrates itself into the global economy. This topic is deserving of an entire course of study. We cannot cover it all here. We must narrow our focus.

Our chapter plan is to:

1) Evaluate the principal effects of globalization and changing macroeconomic conditions on US food and agricultural markets
2) Examine the political-economic forces fostering a US trade policy that intermixes protectionism with free trade
3) Analyze how global trends and related government policies are affecting the US agrifood system's economic vitality.

International influences on the US food and agricultural economy continue to expand in size and complexity. We need an effective method to organize the core relationships.

We can apply a sequential model to aid our understanding of globalization trends. Our approach is displayed in Figure 6.1:

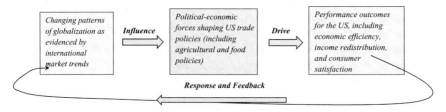

Figure 6.1 Conceptual model of the patterns and forces influencing the international trade performance outcomes for US food and agriculture.

Figure 6.1 offers a straightforward method for analyzing globalization's economic effects. The model helps us to visualize a logical progression. In the model, globalization patterns influence trade policy choices, and then trade policy choices generate new economic outcomes. The feedback loop demonstrates how the three-step process contributes to further developments in the globalization process.

The globalization cycle in Figure 6.1 guides our analytical approach. In Chapter 6, we gather data and perform analyses to discern international market trends. Once we understand

the general direction and volume of international trade, we then connect the empirical observations to developments in trade policy.

Equipped with positivist knowledge of trade trends and associated policies, we examine their
linkages to efficiency and distributional outcomes in the US economy. In this textbook, we are
particularly interested in the effects of globalization patterns on the US agri-food system.

Finally, as we review the model in Figure 6.1, we refer back to the feedback loop. The
performance outcomes of US agricultural and food markets are themselves inputs that alter
the trajectory of future globalization trends.

We have a model to organize our study, and we have an important topic to cover. Let's
move forward.

Globalization patterns and their influence on the economics of US food and agriculture

Since 1990, a variety of economic, technological and cultural factors have opened the door
to increased international trade and global connections. We can quickly review some noteworthy 1990 events:

- Tim Berners-Lee introduced the globe to the first *World Wide Web* browser for a system
  that today we know as "the Internet."[1]
- East and West Germany reunified while the Soviet Union began to dissolve; by the end
  of the 1990s, many former "Eastern Bloc" countries had become European Union (EU)
  members.[2]
- The US and the EU agreed to extend the "Uruguay Round of Talks" to resolve agricultural trade issues as part of the General Agreement on Tariffs and Trade (GATT) negotiations. By 1994, the expanded trade talks established the World Trade Organization
  (WTO) as an effective successor to the GATT.[3]

Further evidence of amplified global linkages is discerned by examining the data. We can
review impacts on the US economy by exploring trends in US Exports and Imports. Let's
take a look at US trade data in Figure 6.2 below.

A visual inspection of Figure 6.2 indicates that both US Exports and US Imports have a
similar upward trajectory over time. Because US Imports have expanded more rapidly than
US Exports, the Net Exports (US Exports – US Imports) measurement has continuously
been in deficit. While large US trade deficits do create economic challenges, there is another
side to this coin.

The Law of Comparative Advantage, when it is applicable in US trade, tells us that the
world's more efficient producers will export goods and services at globally determined prices.
For example, the American consumer can benefit when imports are responsible for creating
more competitive prices in many domestic markets. Global competitive pressures can also
serve as a counter-influence against general price inflation. It is also important to remember
that when US trading partners are successful in marketing their products to US customers,
then their enhanced income provides an economic capacity to purchase US Exports.

Figure 6.2 also reminds us that macroeconomic phenomena influence trade outcomes.
The US experienced national recessions in both 2001 and 2009, and the trade data (see the
graph) reflect those downturns. Similarly, when the US economy resumes positive growth as
it did in 2002 and 2010, there are rebounds in both exports and imports.

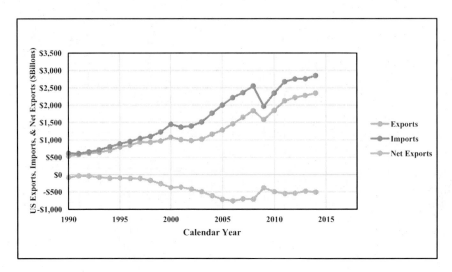

Figure 6.2 US exports, imports, and net exports ($billions), years 1990–2014*.

*Data Source: www.census.gov/foreign-trade/statistics/graphs/gands.html

Another important perspective is the relative contribution of trade to the overall value in the entire economy. In his textbook *International Economics*, Robert Carbaugh uses trade data to create an index of Trade Openness.[4] This trade indicator compares the sum of exports plus imports to the national Gross Domestic Product (GDP). This measurement offers an approximation of trade's national economic significance. See Figure 6.3 below.

If we use the Trade Openness Ratio in Figure 6.3 as a guide, then we can roughly say that the importance of trade has gradually increased (with some macroeconomic fluctuation) from about 20 percent to 30 percent influence in the US economy between 1990 and 2014. It is significant that nearly one-third of all US economic activity is trade-related.

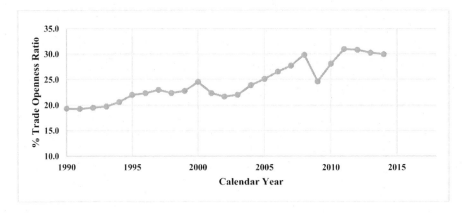

Figure 6.3 US trade openness ratio = (US exports + US imports)/US GDP, years 1990–2014*.

*Data Sources: www.census.gov/foreign-trade/statistics/graphs/gands.html, www.research.stlouisfed.org/fred2/series/GDPCI

Agriculture's contribution to US trade

In Figures 6.2 and 6.3, US national trade trends across all goods and services are displayed. Equipped with this background information, we can return to our focus on US food and agriculture. An initial question is to determine what proportion of US trade originates with agricultural products. We can examine the proportion of US exports attributable to US agricultural products sold overseas, and similarly we can observe the percent of US imports that are agriculturally related. We can explore patterns and trends, and study basic economic relationships that are influencing the outcomes. Let's begin by viewing the graphs in Figures 6.4 and 6.5:

We can make a number of key observations about US agricultural exports and imports during the 1990–2014 period by gleaning information from Figures 6.4 and 6.5. Both graphs indicate an upward trend in the proportion of US agriculturally related trade. The upward trends in both figures indicate that *agricultural markets are expanding more rapidly* than the rising levels of all US exports and imports (ag and non-ag).

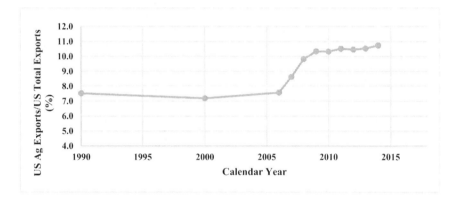

Figure 6.4 US agricultural exports/US total exports (percent), years 1990–2014*.

*Data Source: www.data.worldbank.org/indicator/ne.imp.gnfs.zs/countries?page=5

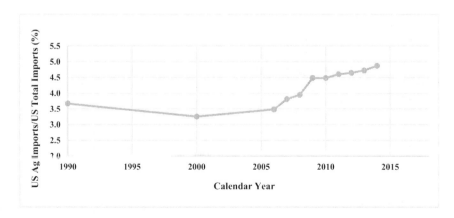

Figure 6.5 US agricultural imports/US total imports (percent), years 1990–2014*.

*Data Source: www.data.worldbank.org/indicator/ne.imp.gnfs.zs/countries?page=5

We can also note that US agricultural exports are a larger proportion of all US exports (ranging between 7 percent and 11 percent), as compared to the similar comparison of US agricultural imports in relation to all US imports (range is about 3 percent to 5 percent).

Finally, both Figures 6.4 and 6.5 indicate that the year 2006 was a turning point for both US agricultural exports and imports. A noticeable uptick in the proportion of US agricultural trade occurs after 2006 in comparison to all US trade. After the agriculture sector makes this jump to a higher level of trade impact, the increases continue at a slower rate through the year 2014. It will be interesting to track the trend of this ratio in future years, and determine if the new level of trade importance for agriculture will be sustained.

From an economic standpoint, we can ask the question of why both US agricultural exports and imports had measurable gains in importance after 2006. The answer to this question offers an opportunity to explore how key market relationships and new government policies can influence trade outcomes.

Research on agricultural trade markets, microeconomic theory and macroeconomic policy can be very helpful in understanding the influence of crucial trade variables.

One reason for the value of agricultural exports and imports to rise in relation to all other exported and imported goods is relative price. Between 2006 and 2012, the Consumer Price Index (CPI) *for all food products* rose by nearly 20 percent, while the CPI *for all items* (food and non-food) increased by only 14 percent. Why did this happen? In the 2006–2012 period, global weather events reduced farm output and annual carry-over levels, while the foreign demand for US-grown corn, wheat, soybeans and other commodities grew in global markets such as South America, Africa, and Southeast Asia. Simultaneously, US federal and state governments' energy policies between 2007 and 2012 triggered increased domestic corn demand for conversion to ethanol as a renewable fuel.[5] Basic supply and demand analysis predicts that a surge in demand will increase a commodity's equilibrium price and quantity.

Macroeconomics: GDP in relation to imports

In macroeconomic theory, we predict a *positively sloped relationship between import purchases and Gross Domestic Product (GDP)*. When "times are good" (meaning GDP is rising at a healthy pace), Americans increase their imports of higher-end food products such as expensive olive oils, fruits, candy, chocolates, nuts, and liquors. Similarly, when a national recession hits, the demand for these luxury-food imports can drop dramatically.[6]

Between 1990 and 2014, US GDP (both real and nominal) displayed an upward trend, even adjusting for the 2001 recession and the 2009 Great Recession. Also, recall from Chapter 3 that inelastic commodity markets generate considerable price volatility when economic forces begin shifting demand and supply. If we statistically map the US Ag Import/ US Total Import Ratio against US GDP, we can view how these two variables are correlated. See Figure 6.6 below.

In Figure 6.6, an Ordinary Least Squares (OLS) straight line of regression is fitted to the actual Ag-Import Ratio (*array of dots*) data. While the estimated Ag-Import Ratio (*line-of triangles*) has an imperfect Correlation Coefficient = 72.1 percent, we have visual evidence that US GDP is positively correlated with the US Ag Import/US Total Import Ratio. This result is consistent with the normally predicted direct relationship between US national income and US imports in macroeconomic models.

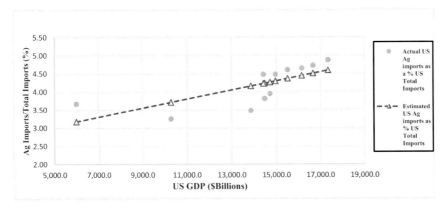

Figure 6.6 US agricultural imports/US total imports (percent) versus US GDP, years 1900–2014*.

*Data Source: www.data.worldbank.org/indicator/ne.imp.gnfs.zs/countries?page=5

Micro- and macroeconomics: currency exchange rate in relation to exports

Another strong influence on import and export trade-flows is the currency exchange rate.

Economic theory predicts that the value of one nation's currency, measured in units of another national currency, is determined by the market forces of supply and demand. For example, if the US trades with Japan, then we can analyze how supply and demand for the US Dollar (USD) determines an equilibrium "price" of *Japanese Yen (¥) per One USD* needed to clear the USD market. See Figure 6.7.

In Figure 6.7, we analyze the *Supply of $USDs* as originating with *US Consumers* who seek to buy (*import*) Japanese-made products. At some point in the supply chain, we visualize that American consumers "supply" USDs to an international exchange bank to obtain Japanese Yen (¥); then those ¥ are used to *import* (purchase) the Japanese-made products.

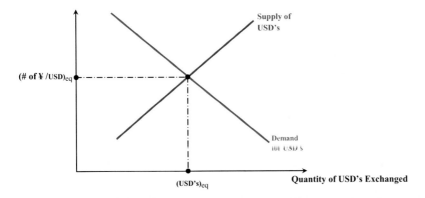

Figure 6.7 US dollar (USD) currency exchange market: determines the equilibrium value of Japanese Yen (¥) per US Dollar (USD), when the US trades with Japan.

The *Demand for $USDs* (see Figure 6.7) originates with *Japanese Consumers* who seek to buy American-made goods (*US Exports*). At some point in the supply chain, the Japanese consumers "purchase" (demand) USDs using the ¥ normally held by Japanese consumers. Once the Japanese consumers have USDs in their possession, then they purchase US-made exports.

An equilibrium exchange rate for the USD is established when the quantity supplied of USDs equals the USD quantity demanded. Shortages of USDs are resolved by auctions, and surpluses of USDs are eliminated by sales (see Chapter 3 to review equilibrating forces within markets).

As a nation's equilibrium currency value fluctuates, the net cost of imports and exports changes for foreign and domestic consumers. For example, when the equilibrium USD value "strengthens" (increases) relative to the Yen (¥), then Japanese consumers experience an increased cost of importing American-made products. Simultaneously, a strong USD causes Japanese imports to be cheaper for American consumers to purchase. *Ceteris paribus*, an appreciating USD (relative to the ¥) encourages US imports and discourages US exports.

Of course, a depreciating USD has the opposite effect of a stronger USD. A weaker USD (relative to the ¥) decreases the cost of US-made goods for Japanese consumers, and increases the cost of Japanese-made imports for American consumers. *Ceteris paribus*, a depreciating USD (relative to the ¥) discourages US imports and encourages US exports.

The above market analysis (Figure 6.7) of currency exchange rate markets is particularly relevant for examining trends in US agricultural export markets. Based on what we have just learned, we can expect a *negatively sloped* (inverse) relationship between the US Ag Export/US Total Export Ratio and the USD indexed-trade-weighted value (in relation to a basket of foreign currencies). In other words, when the dollar (USD) has a high indexed-value, we expect fewer US agricultural exports, and when the indexed-USD-value is cheap compared to other currencies, then we predict increased US agricultural exports.

Finally, two important considerations logically lead us to expect that US agricultural export values will change more rapidly than US non-agricultural exports. These are (1) competitive commodity markets, and (2) volatile price-inelastic agricultural markets.

First, agricultural commodities are largely undifferentiated. A soybean produced in the US is often viewed as mostly equivalent to a soybean produced in Argentina or Brazil. Global consumers will often import commodities from the producers with the "best deal." If the USD is expensive relative to the Brazilian Real or the Argentinian Peso, and if the soybeans from these US competitors are viewed as having equivalent quality, then Brazil and Argentina will "make the sale" and the US soybeans may remain stored in US Midwest bins, or sit on the docks of Seattle or Los Angeles.

Second, as international market pressures ebb and flow, the volatile and price-inelastic commodity-market values *change price more dramatically* than in less competitive markets where differentiated products and market power exist.

Taking into account the nature of currency exchange markets, globally competitive conditions, and volatile prices in commodity markets, we can use the analysis to *anticipate that US agricultural exports will be responsive to changes in the equilibrium USD currency value*. Similar to cases with US agricultural imports that we explored in Figure 6.6 above, we statistically map the US Ag Export/US Total Export Ratio against Trade-Weighted Index of the USD currency value, and we can examine how these variables are correlated. See Figure 6.8 below.

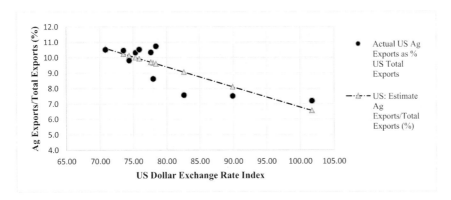

Figure 6.8 US agricultural exports/US total exports (percent) versus US Dollar Exchange Rate Index, years 1900–2014*.

*Data Source: www.research.stlouisfed.org/fred2/series/DTWEXM

In Figure 6.8, an Ordinary Least Squares (OLS) straight line of regression is fitted to the actual Ag-Export Ratio (*array of dots*) data. While the estimated Ag-Export Ratio (*line-of triangles*) has an imperfect Correlation Coefficient = −82.46 percent, we have visual evidence that the Trade-Weighted-Indexed USD Currency Value is negatively correlated with the US Ag Export/US Total Export Ratio. This result is consistent with the normally predicted inverse relationship between USD Currency Values and US Exports in macroeconomic models.

Another lesson to learn from these statistical patterns and predicted relationships is that the "status quo" of an economic era is only temporary. The graphs included in Figures 6.4 and 6.5 above analyze a reality that has already become a memory. After 2014, the year that the Farm Bill was approved, global commodity markets have changed considerably.

After 2014, the USD value has appreciated relative to most other foreign currencies. This situation depresses US agricultural exports, and tends to reduce the prices and profits associated with agricultural production.

Improved weather and natural growing conditions have facilitated increased global production and larger global commodity year-to-year carry-over commodity volumes. As a result, price-inelastic and volatile commodity markets have created situations where agricultural product prices have dropped precipitously, and US farm profit margins have become thin or negative.[7]

Instability in foreign markets and economies have further complicated the situation in 2015, and beyond. Agriculture remains a risky industry; profits and incomes continue to markedly fluctuate.

Summary: globalization patterns and the US food and agricultural economy

Our exploration of US trade data indicate that proper interpretation of international trade markets requires that we pay attention to general import/export trends, national policy decisions (such as the US Renewable Fuels mandate), GDP growth (or its absence), currency value changes, and unique market situations (such as favorable or unfavorable global crop-growing conditions). While this set of variables is complex, if we employ rational models and well-established economic theory, we have tools to examine and make sense of the phenomena.

The next section of this chapter reviews existing national and agricultural policies in relation to the outcomes of international and national markets. A careful examination of US trade policies in 2016 reveals that the US trade position is eclectic. In some cases and markets, the US is actively pursuing free-trade policies. In other situations, the US position changes to the implementation of Tariff Rate Quotas to protect selected US home industries.

The competing roles of multilateralism, regionalism, and protectionism in the establishment of US trade policy

The growing importance of international trade in the US general economy, as well as in the food and agricultural sector, is evident. We have just reviewed some market-related reasons (exchange rates, comparative advantage, etc.) for increased interconnectedness. The changing international market environment provides a backdrop for exploring other key factors and their economic effects.

The conceptual model introduced in Figure 6.1 (see opening of this chapter) indicates that international market trends create incentives for nations to negotiate trade agreements, establish trade associations, and institute government policy reforms. These institutional responses, in turn, have major effects on resulting market outcomes, such as economic growth, market efficiency, and income distribution.

In this section of the chapter, we examine how national governments and multinational organizations seek to shape global trade patterns and policies. Of course, the economic welfare effects of these international "public sector choices" on *US food and agriculture* remains our specific focus.

We can organize our study of global trade strategies by first examining multilateral trade relationships (e.g. the WTO). We subsequently review the recent upswing in regional trade agreements (such as NAFTA). We finally observe how the US government (and other foreign governments) individually influence trade with a mixture of free-trade and protectionist policies.

WTO and the GATT: multilateral efforts to influence international trade patterns and policies

Soon after the end of World War II in 1945, the US and twenty-two other nations resolved to work together towards increasing the "openness" of their economies to worldwide trade. The participants viewed a multilateral trade deal as a means of facilitating war recovery for the world's economy. They also sought to repair the trade damage done by the extremely high "Smoot-Hawley" tariff levels that originated during the 1930s Great Depression.

The General Agreement on Tariffs and Trade (GATT) began in October 1947 as a first round of multilateral trade negotiations in Geneva, Switzerland. Additional nations joined the GATT in subsequent years. Eight GATT rounds occurred between 1947 and 1994. When the last "Uruguay Round" of GATT meetings began in 1986, a total of 123 nations were involved.[8]

At the conclusion of the Uruguay Round in 1994, member nations agreed to replace the GATT with the World Trade Organization (WTO) on January 1, 1995. As compared with the GATT, the WTO is a more powerful and full-time advocate for barrier-reducing multilateral trade agreements. By the end of 2015, WTO membership had expanded to 162 countries. The WTO is committed to establishing and enhancing a truly global approach to free trade.

The *strengths of the WTO's multilateral trade agreement method* include the following globally recognized values:[9]

- Improved trade agreement predictability through *Binding* and *Transparency*:
  - *Binding* – Trade agreement participants promise not to unilaterally increase their tariffs above a negotiated maximum "bound" rate.
  - *Transparency* – Trade agreement participants create and abide by clearly understood and publicly stated trade rules.

- Trade without Discrimination – Any nation who qualifies for "Most Favored Nation" (MFN) status is guaranteed access to tariff rates that are as low as they are for any other nation. So, if a WTO member decreases its tariff rates to one MFN country, then it will lower them to all.
- National Treatment Principle – WTO members agree to apply internal regulations and taxes equally to both domestically- and foreign-produced goods.
- An Even-Handed Trade-Dispute Resolution Process – WTO members agree to resolve disputes with each other while being supervised by a neutral third party; the process includes a formalized complaint procedure and a conciliation panel which conducts a fair and balanced hearing of trade grievances.

The WTO's trade principles are indeed respected and esteemed. When other trade agreements occur outside the WTO's purview, they often borrow the WTO's trade principles because these standards create trust and enforceability within negotiated settlements.

The *drawbacks of the WTO's multilateral approach* stem from the difficulty of reaching agreement among a large number of countries with differing trade-policy agendas. Prior to the establishment of the WTO in 1995, multiple rounds of GATT negotiations over a 47-year period were able to reach agreement on the market areas where compromise was easier to attain. To use a phrase, the GATT meetings were able to harvest most of "the low-hanging fruit."

By the time that the WTO began sponsoring the "Doha Development Round" of trade meetings in 2001, much of the remaining trade policy items to be negotiated were among the most difficult to find a "middle-ground" for agreement. As a result, the WTO Doha Round has not been able to reach a full conclusion.

It is important to understand that while the current WTO Doha Round has been unsettled, much has been accomplished by the WTO and its GATT predecessor. The global tariff levels and general trade conditions that exist today are remarkable, considering the differences and barriers that existed in the mid-twentieth century. Economies are more open, thanks to all the negotiating efforts that have taken place. The WTO is pledged to continue administering the GATT accords that have already been reached. The WTO's negotiating principles are a solid base to build trade relationships.

Agriculture as a "sticking point" in WTO negotiating rounds

Agricultural markets have been, and remain, some of the toughest areas for reaching a multilateral WTO agreement. Many WTO member nations, and not just the US, have substantial domestic and international policies that protect their own farm products from facing the full brunt of global competition. In addition, many governments around the world financially underwrite programs that subsidize farm production. For example, in Chapter 4, we explored how the 2014 Farm Bill includes a US-subsidized farm safety net.

In many nations, the US included, the political reality is that subsidies and protectionist tariffs for farm-related products are very difficult to reduce or remove. When proposals within WTO negotiations ask nations to offer concessions or seek compromise positions in their agricultural policies, the resistance to these suggestions is typically very stiff. In the US and other nations, farm lobbies are very politically effective in garnering the votes and political support they need to retain their subsidies and trade protections. The sugar and dairy lobbies in the US are clear examples of just how influential these political alliances are (see Chapter 4).

The unique position of agricultural markets and trade within WTO trade rules

Multilateral agreements that open up global agricultural trade are difficult to achieve. Consequently, it is a credit to the Uruguay Round GATT negotiators that they were able to establish an agreed-upon and transparent system for trade in farm products. The WTO method accounts for the market-distorting effects of government farm programs. Today, member WTO nations self-report the impacts of their farm policies on normal market processes. The arrangement is known as the Agreement on Agriculture (AoA).

As discussed in Chapter 4, the AoA institutes an official WTO farm-subsidy-program classification system. In the US, the AoA measures the dollars-worth of market distortion caused by US Federal Government farm programs. AoA distinguishes greater or less distortion using a colored-box traffic-light analogy.

For example, a "green box" program is non-distorting, and a blue box category is minimally distorting. Programs generating the most harmful market distortions are classified as "amber box." The sum of all amber box producer-payments within any one nation are subject to WTO spending limits. Each WTO member nation has a calculated limit. US amber-box costs cannot exceed $19.1 billion. WTO transparency obligations require that member nations (including the US) officially notify how much of their amber-box spending occurs in each program.[10]

A historical and political perspective on US trade policy

From the late 1980s to the mid-1990s, US federal government policies were broadly receptive to increased openness in international trade. During this period, the US was engaged in WTO negotiations while it also worked towards approval of the North American Free Trade Agreement (NAFTA) with Mexico and Canada.

The US Constitution specifically assigns trade authority to the US Congress. In the middle of the 1930s Great Depression, President Franklin D. Roosevelt (FDR) asked Congress for its consent to temporarily transfer the right of trade negotiation to the Executive Branch. Congress approved, with the condition that they would review any proposed agreement, and use an up-or-down vote to either approve or disapprove it.

FDR exploited this temporary trade power to quickly negotiate bilateral and reciprocal trade agreements with other nations. His aim was to offset and gradually eliminate the 1930

Smoot-Hawley import tariffs. FDR also sought open trade as a means to help lift up the US economy. This trade legislation created an opportunity for future presidents (after FDR) to make similar trade negotiation requests to Congress.

In 1988, the US Congress temporarily transferred "fast-track" international commerce authority to President H.W. Bush in the Omnibus Trade and Competitiveness Act (OTCA) (P.L. 100–418). After his 1992 election, President Clinton inherited this fast-track authority from President Bush.

Trade negotiations take time, and President Clinton requested a "fast-track" extension to complete trade negotiations, with a new end date of May 31, 1993. Clinton's proposal survived House and Senate resolutions for disapproval.

Under the 1988 OTCA, Congress greatly expanded the President's trade negotiation objectives. With President Clinton's support, his administration proposed the North American Free Trade Agreement (NAFTA) to Congress in 1993 for an up-or-down vote to establish free trade conditions among the US, Canada, and Mexico. It passed.[11]

The 1988 OTCA Act was also amended (P.L. 103–49) to extend fast-track authority to create trade proposals for the WTO's *Uruguay Round of multilateral negotiations*. An agreement was reached before April 16, 1994. The US became a formal member of the WTO soon afterwards. Subsequent to these major trade agreement events, the Congress allowed President Clinton's fast-track trade negotiating authority to expire.

There is a natural constitutional tension between the US Congress and the Executive Branch over the control of international trade policy. That tension continues today.

Why has the US signed numerous regional free trade agreements?

The website for the President's Office of the US Trade Representative indicates that the United States currently participates with twenty different nations in free trade agreements (FTAs). The US decision to join NAFTA in 1993 (see above discussion) was a major turning point for US trade policy. But NAFTA was actually preceded by a US-Canada FTA in 1989 and a US-Israel FTA in 1985.[12]

As discussed earlier in this book, the US recently concluded negotiations for the Trans-Pacific Partnership (TPP) in October 2015. The TPP has the format of a very large free trade agreement among twelve potential Asian-Pacific nations (including the US). It is now up to the US Congress to decide whether the US will or will not join the TPP.

Similarly, the US is still in the midst of negotiating another large-scale "Atlantic" free trade agreement with the European Union (EU). The EU itself is comprised of twenty-eight nations. The proposed agreement is currently identified as the Trans-Atlantic Trade and Investment Partnership (T-TIP). If a final agreement is reached, the T-TIP will also be an FTA to come before Congress for a vote to approve or disapprove.

What about the WTO's role? Why is the US pursuing FTAs? How will additional FTAs (if they are approved) influence US food and agriculture? These are reasonable and important questions that all require thoughtful responses.

First, let's consider the current relationship between the US and the WTO. US membership in WTO continues, but the WTO's recent lack of progress in achieving multilateral solutions to current trade problems has motivated the US to consider other avenues to create a more open economy.

What about the US and its tendency to negotiate FTAs? In many ways, the FTA approach to trading arrangements offers a "good fit" for a nation that values its independence and freedom to choose. Among the various models for organizing a group of countries to cooperate with each other on trade, the FTA allows member nations the most flexibility to pursue their own agendas while simultaneously working out mutually agreeable trading rules within an FTA.

There are other ways to organize cooperative trading arrangements, such as customs unions, common markets or economic unions. The benefit of these other trading models is the increased integration of their economies. Customs unions and common markets allow for high levels of economic coordination. The trade alliance of MERCOSUR in South America (including Brazil, Argentina, Paraguay, Uruguay, and Venezuela) is a common market.[13]

From the US standpoint, the limitation of a common market is that more trade decisions require consultation among the member nations. A common market generally requires all members to set the same levels of tariffs and quotas on imports and exports from any country which is not part of the common market group.

An economic union has trade rules that are even more tightly coordinated than in a common market. For example, we can realistically argue that the fifty states of the US are part of an economic union that shares the same currency.

The common market format for organizing free trade among member nations is not likely to be readily adopted by the US because of its preference to exercise its own authority. The US places a high value on being able to make policy decisions for its own best interest without the need to consult with other nations. Having examined the benefits and drawbacks of other more highly integrated trading arrangements, it is not too surprising that the US prefers the FTA approach to developing trading relationships.

Why are Free Trade Agreements (FTAs) relevant for US food and agriculture?

When the US negotiates and signs a new FTA, the relevance for US food and agriculture is usually economic. One consideration is the potential impact of the FTA on the economic efficiency of farm and food markets. In particular, every regional trade agreement should be examined for its likely effects on "trade creation" and on "trade diversion."

A FTA can enhance economic efficiency if reduced trade barriers create increased access for the FTA participants to be the low-cost producers of farm and food products. This efficiency-enhancing result is called "trade creation." When consumers on both sides of the agreement can now purchase equivalent (or higher) quality goods at lower real market prices, then consumer surplus increases and the protective effect (a deadweight loss) decreases.

On the other hand, if a FTA motivates its participants to discontinue trade with globally efficient suppliers, then we have a case of lost efficiency known as "trade diversion." Every regional FTA has a potential to produce trade-diverting consequences. The question for FTAs is whether, on net, they generate more trade creation than trade diversion.[14]

Thanks to natural endowments, technological advances, and investments in human capital (education, experience, etc.), the US is often a low-cost producer in many agricultural and food markets. The Congressional Research Service (CRS) analyzed the economic potentials of recent US FTA's with South Korea (2012), Colombia (2012), and Panama (2007).[15] The CRS assessment was very optimistic about the US agricultural trade opportunities associated with these agreements.

Additional reviews by the USDA's Economic Research Service (ERS) and Foreign Agricultural Service (FAS) reached similar conclusions.[16] These studies indicate that FTAs can create considerable gains for US agricultural and food markets. The CRS study also noted that US commodity groups, farm organizations, and agribusinesses had made their own assessments, and were very supportive of implementing these FTAs.

If the US Congress was to move forward with large-scale FTAs, such as the TPP and T-TIP, the experience with the more modest-sized bilateral FTAs indicates that the US agriculture and food sectors will view these free-trade proposals as highly relevant.

How does trade protectionism continue to thrive alongside US free-trade policies?

The above discussion of FTAs and US membership in the WTO places a spotlight on how the US has endeavored to reduce trade barriers and increase the international openness of the US economy. All of these trends would seemingly indicate that trade protectionism in the US will gradually wither away. "Appearances can be deceptive" is a particularly applicable catchphrase in this instance.

In many ways, we can confidently make the observation that trade protectionist policies and government farm subsidies are "alive and well," and we do not expect that they will disappear any time soon.

If we perform an in-depth analysis of what actually happens in the formulation and implementation of US farm policy, we become *less surprised* to discover that contradictions do occur between domestic and foreign-trade policy. While it is appropriate for economists to express their concerns about policy outcomes that lack logical consistency and undermine economic efficiency, there are some realities that are simply difficult to change or overcome.

Wanki Moon and Gabriel Saldias (2013) conducted a study of US citizen preferences on the topic of agricultural protectionism. One of the interesting results of this survey is the tendency of higher-income Americans to have a negative preference for government subsidies and related interventions while simultaneously holding a positive preference for American policies that restrict the entry of foreign imports. The survey responses in the Moon and Saldias study indicate that citizens do not perceive a contradiction when they support trade protectionism while they oppose government farm-program interventions. The US sugar lobby demonstrates their understanding of the importance of these citizen beliefs when they ensure that no tax dollars are used to fund the US sugar program while they simultaneously protect the domestic sugar industry with tariff-rate quotas.[17]

In Chapter 4, we explored farm-safety-net aspects of the 2014 Farm Bill, such as PLC, ARC, and SCO. When these new farm programs are reviewed from an international trade policy perspective, we observe that Congress replaced the Direct Payment program (a WTO "green box" subsidy) with *market-distorting policies* that are either "blue box" or "amber box" from an international trade perspective. How did this happen? Is this policy outcome expected, or a considerable shock?

When Congressional representatives and senators craft domestic farm safety-net programs for a farm bill, their focus is on meeting their electorate's expectations. Interest groups who sponsor powerful lobbies also play a role. A key realization is that the final decisions on what Congressional decision makers include or exclude from a farm bill program is governed by both politics and economics.

We briefly explored political-economic theories produced by Ken Arrow, James Buchanan, Gordon Tullock, William Niskanen, and others in Chapter 3 of this text. We learned that government policy development processes are more often responsive to the concentrated efforts of a few rent-seeking economic interest groups than they are to the welfare of large numbers of widely dispersed interests of general consumers and taxpayers.

Ken Arrow's analysis tells us flat out that majority-rule democratic processes cannot always guarantee rational outcomes. James Buchanan admonishes us that we should take Arrow's observations to heart, and participate in the process if we are not satisfied with the results. Dr. Buchanan contends that political processes are experimental by nature. There is no natural tendency for collective decision making to correct itself. If consumers and taxpayers really desire alternative policy outcomes, then they need to make conscious choices to become properly informed and get involved.

Efficiency and distributional outcomes of US agricultural and food trade policies

What is trade liberalization? When nations liberalize trade, they actively negotiate the reduction or removal of trade barriers. Fully liberalized trade is simply identified in the global media as "free trade."

Over a 47-year period in the second half of the twentieth century, eight rounds of GATT negotiations made considerable progress in liberalizing trade on a global scale. The WTO, as the true heir and successor to the GATT, has vigorously pursued the same liberalization agenda in the twenty-first century.

What are the outcomes of trade liberalization? From an economic standpoint, we predict that decreasing trade barriers increases national economic growth, improves economic efficiency and alters the income distribution.

The Law of Comparative Advantage (see Chapter 3) demonstrates how liberalized trade based on relative opportunity cost can mutually *enhance the economic growth* of two trading partners (increasing their Real GDP). A supply-and-demand analysis of import tariff impacts (see Chapter 3) illustrates how tariffs create deadweight economic efficiency losses; tariff reductions (or tariff repeals) *improve economic efficiency* by eliminating deadweight burdens.

The income distribution effects of trade liberalization are also worthy of review. These effects are real and highly visible. Some industries gain from trade liberalization, and others industries falter. *The income redistribution effects of liberalized trade are **at the root** of why "free-trade policies" frequently stir up political and economic controversy.*

It is important to clearly identify *what income redistribution means* when a new free trade policy comes into effect. Let's consider a scenario. Suppose Canada and the US trade with each other by exchanging two commodities: softwood lumber and soybeans.

Just for this example, assume Canada's comparative advantage is in softwood lumber production, while the US has a comparative advantage in soybeans. Finally, let's just say that the 1993 NAFTA agreement was never signed; consequently, the US and Canada both have numerous barriers to protect their home industries from cross-border trade.

In this scenario, the US and Canadian governments are enforcing high import tariffs. Canada has a $1.50/bushel tariff on all imported US-produced soybeans, while the US has an import tariff of $1.00/board-foot of 4"-by-4" Canadian-produced knotty-pine wood.

Under this trade protection plan, the Canadian government shields its soybean producers from US competitors, while the US government protects US foresters who raise knotty-pine trees. Canadian soybean producers and US knotty-pine foresters are satisfied with this arrangement. That is, until a trade policy change occurs that alters the status quo.

Again, for the purposes of this scenario, assume that "times change" and the US and Canadian governments agree to *mutually liberalize all trade between the two nations*. Suddenly, the Canadian soybean import tariff and the US knotty-pine import tariff disappear. What are the income redistribution consequences?

Canadian soybean farmers lose customers to more efficient American producers. If the Canadian soybean growers cannot easily switch operations to another crop, then their incomes will drop, their hired farm labor will be laid off, and their related soy businesses will fail. Similarly, *US knotty-pine producers lose markets to less expensive Canadian foresters.* These US knotty-pine growers experience lost income, lay off US lumbermen, and seek other markets.

In the meantime, *Canadian knotty-pine producers gain additional US customers*, earn additional profits, and begin hiring additional Canadian lumbermen to harvest the trees. Simultaneously, *US soybean producers benefit from increased crop prices, hire additional help, and gain more Canadian customers* for their output.

US soybean producers are supportive of this new US-Canada free trade agreement. US knotty-pine tree producers are very unhappy, write their Congressmen and Senators, and stage protests against the new trade agreement.

In Canada, their national Soybean Production Association is besieging the Canadian Parliament with complaints about the free-trade deal; meanwhile, the Canadian knotty-pine producers are praising the values of liberalized trade and using their extra income to secure winter getaways in the British Bahamas.

The above scenario is fictional but plausible. Clearly, if there are economic stakeholders who stand to lose their livelihoods as a consequence of their government adopting a free trade agreement, then we can reasonably predict that those interests will actively oppose such a policy change. The debate over trade protectionism versus trade liberalization policies is more than an academic exercise; it is based on real differences in economic outcomes. Looking to the future, we can reasonably expect that discussions about trade will continue, and that US trade policy will remain mixed.

The effects of agricultural and food policies on trends to retain or liberalize trade protections

In this textbook, we have emphasized a forward-looking twenty-first-century policy agenda. We focus particular attention on the FSMA, the 2014 Farm Bill, and the Trans-Pacific Partnership as key legislative initiatives. The FSMA and the 2014 Farm Bill have passed into law, and are influencing our economy as this book is being published. The TPP's future is weighing in the balance, but its rejection or approval will guide US agriculture and food trends.

The FSMA's influence on US trade over the long term is expected to be a net positive. We can formally analyze its impacts with Cost-Benefit Analysis (CBA) (see Chapter 5). From the standpoint of international trade policy, the FSMA is expected to be a beneficial influence for economic efficiency in the US, because its design is trade neutral. The FSMA neither favors nor disadvantages a product marketed in the US based on its productive origin (domestic or foreign). The safety provisions are expected to be equally applied. FSMA guidelines are also consistent with WTO rules for transparency and binding.

The 2014 Farm Bill's impact on trade policy is mixed. In the area of dairy policy, three trade market-distorting programs were withdrawn: the Dairy Product Price Support (DPPS) program, the Milk Income Loss Contract (MILC) program, and the Dairy Export

Incentive Program. From the standpoint of the WTO's Agreement on Agriculture (AoA), these dairy program eliminations noticeably reduces US "amber-box" spending, and is considered to be a step forward along the road to trade liberalization.

On the other hand, Congress used the 2014 Farm Bill to create a new insurance-based program, known as the Dairy Margin Protection Program (DMPP) to replace DPPS and MILC. It is unclear how the DMPP will influence US amber box spending. The end results will depend on the extent of dairy farm producers' participation in DMPP and the market price conditions in the dairy industry.

Congress discontinued the Direct Payment Program (DPP), and subsequently created the PLC, ARC, SCO, and STAX programs in the 2014 Farm Bill. Congress also renewed the MALP and Sugar programs with little or no change included, and expanded the role of subsidized crop insurance (see Chapter 4). The collective impact of all these programs is a US decision to continue subsidizing a farm safety net. One consequence of these farm bill decisions is a likely increase in US-government farm support classified by the WTO as market-distorting Amber Box spending.

As discussed in Chapter 2, the Congressional decision to join or reject the Trans-Pacific Partnership proposal is a very considerable economic issue for US food and agriculture. With a very few exceptions, if the US became a TPP participant, then a new range of liberalized markets would open up for US agricultural exporters. US agricultural and food imports would rise as well, because lower tariffs cause reduced net import prices for American consumers. Another consideration is simply that trade is a two-way street. When other nations are successful in breaking through to US agricultural and food import markets, then they earn better incomes, and are soon in an improved position to purchase US-made goods.

A CBO study of US agricultural trade liberalization

In a hypothetical world where all agricultural production and trade conditions are fully liberalized, the US and other nations would discontinue their farm safety nets and eliminate all barriers. What would the efficiency and income distribution consequences be, if such a dramatic movement towards free trade in agriculture were to occur? The US Congressional Budget Office (CBO) examined this question.[18] The CBO reviewed a collection of major professional research studies in 2005 on the question of what outcomes could be expected if agricultural trade liberalization on a global scale took place.

Some conclusions of the CBO study are noteworthy. One liberalization result was the predicted worldwide benefits of improved market efficiency. The anticipated range of gains is somewhere between $50 billion to $185 billion per year (measured in 2001 dollars), which is approximately 0.1 percent to 0.4 percent of the value of all annual world production.

Another observation in the CBO study is the ranking of the protectionist policies that distort markets. Tariffs and Tariff-Rate-Quotas generally create the most distortions, accounting for between 80 percent to 93 percent of the costs of inefficiency. Farm subsidies are next, creating another 5 percent of distortions, and export subsidies generate about 2 percent of inefficiency costs.[19]

Based on the breakdown of lost efficiencies, trade negotiations to improve liberalization are likely to get the most "bang for the buck" by focusing on ways to directly reduce or eliminate agricultural tariffs and quotas.

The distributional consequences of agricultural trade liberalization are complicated, and likely will generate political controversy. For example, the CBO study points out that farm subsidies tend to benefit countries purchasing the subsidized products. Low-income developing nations, especially those who are net importers of subsidized food products, would experience financial stress under a new regime of trade liberalization. As production subsidies disappear, we can expect a "decrease in supply," along with the predicted rise in equilibrium price and fall in equilibrium quantity. Net-food-importing developing countries will struggle in the short run to purchase a smaller supply of food products at higher (non-subsidized) prices.

The other side of the subsidy issue is the impact on nations who are net exporters of farm products. Liberalizing agricultural trade would create a "level playing field" where the countries with the unsubsidized comparative advantage could compete to supply customers in an efficient world market. These exporters would gain considerably in a global setting where they do not have to overcome subsidized farmers to be able to profitably sell their products.

One final note from the CBO study is a realistic assessment that trade proposals, especially those that emerge from current WTO multilateral negotiating sessions, will only likely achieve partial and not full trade liberalization. As a result, the movement towards increased liberalization is an incremental process. At any point in time, it is to be expected that liberalized and protectionist trade policies will exist alongside each other.

Summary

The American agricultural and food economies are dynamic, and the growing influence of international trade is one of the key forces driving the changes that we are experiencing. In this chapter we have explored important economic relationships with a three-stage conceptual model. We began by examining *globalization trends* and interpreting how they affected the growth of US imports, exports, and net exports. We then reviewed how these *political-economic forces* have influenced trade policies such as multilateralism, regionalism, and protectionism. Finally we examined some of the *efficiency and distributional outcomes* associated with the changes in the US agri-food system.

From a purely theoretical and rational standpoint, there would be considerable positive payoffs if the trade policies were consistent and we had a unified approach to trade policy. We have learned that the reality of the policy-making process means that policy inconsistencies are not surprising, especially when we take into account the challenges that arise whenever collective decisions are made. Interest groups who seek different policy outcomes must themselves become better informed and more involved.

In the next chapter, we broaden our perspective further by emphasizing that the decisions and policies of the entire agri-food system ultimately affect the nutritional outcomes of food consumers.

Notes

1   Berners-Lee, Tim. *The WorldWideWeb Browser*. 1994. Retrieved from www.w3.org/People/Berners-Lee/WorldWideWeb.html
2   *The New York Times*. "The End of the Soviet Union; Text of Declaration: 'Mutual Recognition' and 'An Equal Basis'." December 22, 1991. Retrieved from: www.nytimes.com/1991/12/22/world/end-soviet-union-text-declaration-mutual-recognition-equal-basis.html
3   World Trade Organization. *What is the WTO?* WTO, 2016. Retrieved from: www.wto.org/english/thewto_e/whatis_e/whatis_e.htm
4   Carbaugh, Robert J. *International Economics*. Thirteenth Edition. Mason, OH: Southwestern Cengage Learning, 2008, pp. 8–10, 131–134.

5 Volpe, Richard. "Price Inflation for Food Outpacing Many Other Spending Categories." USDA, ERS: Amber Waves, August 2013. Retrieved from: www.ers.usda.gov/amber-waves/2013-august/price-inflation-for-food-outpacing-many-other-spending-categories.aspx#.Vs4cYZwrLIU

6 Hanrahan, Charles E., Carol Canada, and Beverly A. Banks. "U.S. Agricultural Trade: Trends, Composition, Direction, and Policy." July 29, 2011, Congressional Research Service. 7-5700, www.crs.gov, 98-253. Retrieved from: www.fas.org/sgp/crs/misc/98-253.pdf

7 Volpe, Richard. "Price Inflation for Food Outpacing Many Other Spending Categories." USDA, ERS: Amber Waves: August 2013. Retrieved from: www.ers.usda.gov/amber-waves/2013-august/price-inflation-for-food-outpacing-many-other-spending-categories.aspx#.Vs4cYZwrLIUfoodprices between 2006 and 2012 – USDA

8 World Trade Organization (WTO). *Understanding the WTO: Basics. The GATT years: from Havana to Marrakesh.* WTO, 2016. Retrieved from: www.wto.org/english/thewto_e/whatis_e/tif_e/fact4_e.htm

9 Carbaugh, Robert J. *International Economics.* Thirteenth Edition. Mason, OH: Southwestern Cengage Learning, 2008, pp. 190–202.

10 Glauber, Joseph W. and Patrick Westhoff. "50 Shades of Amber: The 2014 Farm Bill and the WTO." Allied Social Science Association Annual Meeting, January 3–5, 2015, Boston, MA, p. 8. Retrieved from: file:///C:/Users/User/Downloads/50ShadesOfAmberThe2014FarmBillAn_preview.pdf

11 Carbaugh, Robert J. *International Economics.* Thirteenth edition. Mason, OH: Southwestern Cengage Learning, 2008, p. 203.

12 Office of the United States Trade Representative. *Free Trade Agreements.* 2016. Retrieved from: www.ustr.gov/trade-agreements/free-trade-agreements

13 Carbaugh, Robert J. *International Economics.* Thirteenth edition. Mason, OH: Southwestern Cengage Learning, 2008, p. 273.

14 Ibid, p. 276.

15 Jurenas, Remy. "Agriculture in Pending U.S. Free Trade Agreements with South Korea, Colombia, and Panama." October 6, 2011 Congressional Research Service 7-5700. www.crs.gov. R40622. Retrieved from: www.fas.org/sgp/crs/misc/R40622.pdf

16 Burfisher, Mary E. and Steven Zahniser. "Multilateralism and Regionalism: Dual Strategies for Trade Reform." Amber Waves. Feature: International Markets and Trade September 01, 2003. Retrieved from: www.ers.usda.gov/amber-waves/2003-september/multilateralism-and-regionalism-dual-strategies-for-trade-reform.aspx#.Vsvug4-cHIV

17 Moon, Wanki and Gabriel Pino Saldias. "Public Preferences about Agricultural Protectionism." Selected Paper prepared for presentation at the Agricultural and Applied Economics Association's 2013 AAEA & CAES Joint Annual Meeting, Washington, DC, August 4–6, 2013. Retrieved from: www.ageconsearch.umn.edu/bitstream/150718/2/Wanki_Moon_June8_Revised_2013_AAEA_manuscript.pdf

18 The Congress of the United States, Congressional Budget Office. "The Effects of Liberalizing World Agricultural Trade: A Survey." December 2005. Retrieved from: www.cbo.gov/sites/default/files/109th-congress-2005-2006/reports/12-01-tradelib.pdf

19 Ibid, pp. 10–15.

Chapter 7

Analyzing effects of USDA nutrition programs on hunger and food security in the US

US Secretary of Agriculture Tom Vilsack visited the Colina Del Sol Recreation Center in San Diego, California near the end of the 2013 school year. Secretary Vilsack's purpose was to highlight the importance of communities cooperating with the USDA's Summer Food Service Program to reduce the incidence of child hunger when school is not in session. Many US low-income families are not "food secure" during the summer months when the USDA's School Breakfast and Lunch Programs discontinue operations. Secretary Vilsack noted that, "USDA's summer meals program helps to fill that gap and is an invaluable investment in the future of America's children."[1]

Organization of chapter

Federal government-sponsored nutrition provisions are worthy of study for several reasons. One justification is their large budgetary size and national reach. For example, about 79 percent of the 2014 Farm Bill's annual budget is needed to fund SNAP and other provisions under Title IV: Nutrition. The USDA reports that an average of 46 million people per month were SNAP recipients in 2012. Millions of children are affected each school day through the School Breakfast and Lunch programs. SNAP and a number of other nutrition provisions are federal entitlement[2] programs with budgets that fluctuate as participation rates ebb and flow.

National nutrition programs have economic impacts that range far and wide. To observe space and time constraints in this chapter, we intentionally narrow our attention to a limited but important set of topics. We organize them as follows:

- A review of federal nutrition provisions
- Evaluating impacts of nutrition programs on food insecurity and hunger

  - Formalizing our definitions: hunger and food insecurity
  - Economic analysis of in-kind transfer programs
  - The challenges of interpreting the evidence for nutrition program effects on food insecurity
  - Nutritional policy paradox: the dual problems of obesity and food insecurity

- The USDA's Thrifty Food Plan

  - What is it, and why is it important?
  - The role of additional USDA food plans

- USDA's Food Pyramid and the MyPlate Nutrition Communication Plans
- Summary and future policy choices

The above outline of this chapter is restricted in comparison to the full range of Nutrition Program impacts. But we can be economical. We can efficiently address the most critical program elements and optimize our efforts to increase our understanding of US nutrition policy.

Food safety nets

Our review of the 2014 Farm Bill's Commodity and Crop Insurance Titles in earlier chapters of this textbook demonstrated a US Congressional intent to create and maintain a *farm* safety net. If we reflect on the USDA Secretary's remarks above, we can say that most of the

USDA-administered Nutrition Programs (such as the Summer Food Service Program) aim to provide a *food* safety net.

The combined impact of all federal nutrition programs is undoubtedly a *large-scale* food safety net. One way to view the substantial impact of these nutrition programs is to determine their effects on the nutritional health status of US households. Research results include:[3]

- Basiotis, Kramer-LeBlanc, and Kennedy (1998) used US food consumption data to determine that each dollar spent in the Supplemental Nutrition Assistance Program (SNAP, formerly known as "food stamps") increases a household's score on the USDA's Healthy Eating Index. The household nutrition benefits were noticeable for vegetable, dairy, meat, and sodium components of the Index.[4]
- Mabli, Castner, Ohls, Fox, Crepinsek, and Condon (2010) conducted research for the USDA, and found that additional SNAP dollars increase household food expenditures, and were also associated with gains in dietary quality, energy density, nutrient density, and fruit and vegetable consumption.[5]

Another way to view the safety net effects of USDA nutrition programs is to examine their macroeconomic impacts. Between December 2007 and June 2009, the Great Recession wreaked economic havoc in the US. Most economic indicators reveal that the 2007–2009 downturn was the most severe since the 1930s Great Depression. The US unemployment rate climbed over 10 percent, and lingered at high levels for many months. What role did the farm bill's Nutrition Programs play during this highly stressful period?

Participation in USDA's Supplemental Nutrition Assistance Program (SNAP) was a bright spot in a very dim time. An article authored by Tim Slack (2014) in the agricultural economics' *Choices Magazine* noted that prior to the Great Recession in 2007, about 26 million people in the US were SNAP participants. By 2011, the number of SNAP beneficiaries had increased to more than 45 million. These new SNAP participants used their EBT cards to buy and consume groceries, and it made a dent in the hunger problem during the Great Recession. This is a good outcome. The program is designed to help people in desperate times, and it did help quite a few.[6]

From a macroeconomic viewpoint, the SNAP program aided the US economic recovery from the recession in a manner that the Temporary Assistance for Needy Families (TANF) program did not. TANF is a cash-transfer program administered by the US Health and Human Services (HHS) Department. Slack (2014) notes that TANF was not much of a factor in offsetting the economic deterioration associated with the Great Recession.[7]

On the other hand, with over 45 million people participating in SNAP, the impact was noticeable and real. SNAP also has a regional macroeconomic multiplier effect: each $1 of SNAP benefit helps produce an extra $1.80 in local spending. SNAP helped reduce hunger and it also acted as an economic stimulus in a distressed economy.[8]

In addition to SNAP serving as a counter-cyclical[9] influence in the US economy, a USDA study (1976–2010) of the relationship between nutrition program participation rates and the national business cycle revealed that the USDA Women, Infant, and Children (WIC) program helped reduce the economy's volatility. USDA also determined that more households participated in the free- and reduced-priced meals offered by USDA's School Lunch, School Breakfast, and the Day Care food programs during the Great Recession. All of these programs offered some financial relief for households facing unemployment, home foreclosures, and other stressors during the 2007–2009 economic downturn.[10]

A review of federal nutrition programs

A 2016 Congressional Research Service (CRS) study by Aussenberg and Collelo[11] reported that as many seventy federal programs had linkages to food and nutrition policy. Their research determined that it is possible to narrow our attention to seventeen federal programs directly related to government-supported food assistance.

The USDA's Food and Nutrition Service (FNS) manages the majority of national food programs. In addition, the Administration on Aging (AOA), which is a US Health and Human Services (HHS) agency, administers a set of food programs for the elderly under the authority of the 1965 Older Americans Act.

When and why did the government become involved in food and nutrition policy? A little history is relevant here. Past events create a momentum for today's programs. A place to start is to understand the origins of SNAP, the largest budgeted federal food program.

A background on SNAP

Prior to the 1930s Great Depression in America, private organizations (churches, volunteer groups, etc.) assumed much of the responsibility for "feeding the hungry." The work of these private associations continues today; community food shelves are as important in the twenty-first century as when the first volunteer extended a meal to a hungry child. Much deserved praise goes to the charitable labors of these privately run US entities who daily provide food and assistance to society's most vulnerable.[12]

As we have learned in previous chapters, the 1930s Great Depression severely challenged the social and economic fabric of the US. Not only can we trace the origins of the farm bill to this cataclysmic period, but we also can identify the beginnings of federal government involvement in food policy. Many events during this decade were linked. Farm and food policy were no exceptions. Connections naturally developed between these programs.

The 1930s farm economy was troubled by large commodity surpluses, low prices, farm foreclosures, and the Dust Bowl. The national economy was also suffering. In 1933, the US unemployment rate reached 24.75 percent; many households were impoverished and hungry. Social unrest became nearly unmanageable when a US government official made a supply-side price-boosting proposal to plow crops under and slaughter baby pigs. Understandably, there was much consternation of living in a time when "food is plentiful and children go hungry."[13]

Initial 1930s federal government food policy did place considerable emphasis on programs that alleviated farm surpluses. But not exclusively. USDA also established alternative consumer food plans, along with associated expenditure budgets, to offer 1930s households with practical and economic guidance on an affordable healthy diet. These 1930s food budgets were the precursors to the USDA food plans that are used today in the SNAP program to establish food-spending levels for participating households.[14]

Corruption and mismanagement in the early 1930s plagued the government's first attempts to create simple food distribution programs. To decrease fraud and improve efficiency, the next trial was the "food stamp plan." Citizens could use $1 in cash to buy a $1 orange food stamp that could purchase nearly any food product; in addition, citizens also received a $0.50 blue food stamp to exclusively purchase low-priced surplus foods. The net gain of 50 cents on the dollar was attractive for consumer households. This mid-to-late

1930s food stamp plan grew in popularity through the end of 1941, but it was discontinued when the outbreak of World War II (WWII) forced the US government to emphasize new priorities.[15]

After WWII, food assistance primarily took the form of commodity distribution programs until the early 1960s when a new food stamp pilot program was re-introduced. Then, in 1964, Congress passed the Food Stamp Act to establish this food assistance and nutrition policy on a permanent basis. Additional pieces of legislation during 1965–1976 followed to further clarify participation requirements and funding levels. The Food Stamp Act of 1977 was a major reform of the program; it eliminated the purchase requirement and focused on simplified organization, increased accuracy, and improved capacity to match program benefits with household need.

Additional legislation during 1978–1989 further improved administrative procedures and encouraged experimentation with an electronic benefit delivery system. Then in 1990, Congress passed the Mickey Leland Memorial Domestic Hunger Relief Act, which included language to establish Electronic Benefit Transfer (EBT) as an alternative to food stamps.

By 2002, USDA required cooperating state agencies to completely implement EBT and phase out the physical stamps. In the 2008 Farm Bill, the program name officially changed over to SNAP as a means for the USDA to emphasize the current goals of the program – increasing the food budgets of needy households, and encouraging recipients to adopt balanced and nutritional diets.[16]

USDA-administered food assistance programs

Today, the USDA's Food and Nutrition Service (FNS) coordinates a considerable range of federal food programs. Some of these programs are re-authorized as part of the farm bill, and others require separate legislative approval. Each program serves particular purposes and intends to meet a targeted set of food and/or nutritional needs for qualified beneficiaries. At this point, we can begin organizing the various programs according to legislative origin and administrative responsibility.

We can inventory the USDA-administered food programs approved under the 2014 Farm Bill. Except for the Community Food Project Program, the USDA Food and Nutrition Service (FNS) is the agency which takes responsibility for the following farm bill programs:

- SNAP – Supplemental Food Assistance Program
- The Emergency Food Assistance Program (TEFAP)
- Community Food Project Grants Program (administered by the USDA's National Institute of Food and Agriculture [NIFA] Agency)
- Commodity Supplemental Food Program (CSFP)
- Fresh Fruit and Vegetable Program
- Senior Farmers' Market Nutrition Program

Additional US Congressional legislation is needed to update and approve these important USDA-administered food programs:

- Special Supplemental Nutrition Program for Women, Infants, and Children (WIC)
- WIC Farmers' Market Nutrition Program

- The following Child Nutrition Programs:
  - School Breakfast Program
  - National School Lunch Program (NSLP)
  - Summer Food Service Program (SFSP)
  - Special Milk Program
  - Child and Adult Care Food Program (CACFP)

Health and Human Services (HHS)-administered food assistance programs

HHS's Administration for Community Living (HHS-ACL) supervises the Administration on Aging (AOA) food assistance programs authorized under the Older Americans Act:

- Congregate Nutrition Program
- Home Delivered Nutrition Program
- Grants to Native Americans: Supportive and Nutrition Services
- Nutrition Services Incentive Program (NSIP)

It is difficult to create a logical format that simplifies the multiple purposes of seventeen different initiatives. In the lists above, we sort them by enacted law and government agency. But to better understand US food policy, we need other ways to organize this catalog of food programs. One method is to identify program similarities and differences.[17]

Certainly, all seventeen programs share a common goal of improving food access, nutritional quality and sufficient consumption levels for vulnerable or needy segments of the US population.

When we examine the programs in more detail, we can discover how they differ. Program demographics, eligibility requirements, and program benefits offer some important program distinctions:

- Targeted demographic segment of the population (intended recipients of alternative food programs vary by people's age and gender)
  - The WIC Program serves pregnant, postpartum, and breastfeeding women, as well as children aged 5 and younger.
  - The School Breakfast and Lunch Program is available to school-age children.
  - The AOA Congregate Nutrition Program targets meals for seniors, age 60 and over, who are members of senior centers and adult day care centers.

- Eligibility requirements (pertaining to qualified household gross- and net-income levels)
  - SNAP eligibility has:
    - A gross income test equal to a monthly cash income below 130 percent of the federal poverty guidelines.
    - A net income test equal to a monthly cash income, subtracting SNAP deductible expenses, at or below 100 percent of the federal poverty guidelines.
    - A liquid assets test – must be under $2,250 (in 2016; if households have seniors or disabled members, then higher thresholds are allowed).

- ○ WIC eligibility has:
    - ○ A household income test equal to or less than 185 percent of the federal poverty guidelines.
    - ○ Applicants must be individually determined to be at "nutritional risk" by a health professional, and must meet state residency requirements.
- • Program Benefits
    - ○ The Commodity Supplemental Food Program and WIC limit recipients to specific foods.
    - ○ SNAP offers a wide variety of food choices at authorized retailers.
    - ○ OAA programs deliver prepared meals for low-income recipients who also cannot prepare meals for themselves.

How food policy works: program connections and agency coordination

It takes considerable synchronization of federal, state, and local offices to properly and efficiently serve the millions of intended recipients of seventeen federal nutrition programs. The Food and Nutrition Service administers many of its programs by utilizing the distributional reach of USDA's ten regional offices, as well as the numerous local USDA offices located throughout the nation.

USDA also works cooperatively with state and local government agencies. For example, USDA coordinates with state departments of education and school districts to manage the School Breakfast and Lunch programs. State and local health departments often work jointly with the USDA to organize and operate the WIC and the Child and Adult Care Food Program (CACFP).[18]

USDA directly purchases and distributes commodities needed to supply The Emergency Food Assistance Program (TEFAP) and the Commodity Supplemental Food Program (CSFP). USDA also coordinates its "farm programs" with its "food programs." For example, USDA buys food identified as producers' surplus goods. The 2014 Farm Bill includes an initiative to facilitate "farm-to-school" endeavors, such as assisting school cafeterias to acquire foods straight from local and regional farms.[19]

As indicated in an earlier footnote, more detailed information on each of the seventeen federal nutrition programs can be studied in Appendix A of this textbook. Our next task, after our very brief introduction to the broad array of food assistance programs, is to more closely analyze the economic choices and consequences associated with offering these programs. A careful review requires us to seek scientifically based terminology and logically structured models to guide our exploration of this very important topic. Let's proceed.

Evaluating impacts of nutrition programs on food insecurity and hunger

In 2006, the National Research Council (NRC) published an in-depth study of how best to measure or define the concepts of hunger, food security, and food insecurity.[20] After consideration, the NRC concluded that while "hunger" is certainly a real phenomenon, it is very difficult to determine an objective measure of hunger for the purposes of policy formation.

The NRC concluded that hunger is a personal physiological state that cannot be properly gauged by a household consumption survey. Hunger can happen because a disadvantaged household has a constricted food budget, but it can also occur because a person decides that she is too busy to take time for a regular meal.

Food assistance programs need to focus on helping the households that are persistently (e.g. daily) anxious about whether they can financially afford to sustain an adequate diet. The NRC invented the term "food insecurity" to identify when a household formally communicates this anxiety. Household consumption surveys can measure this household concern more easily than different states of hunger.

If a household participates in a food assistance program, and if the program achieves its targeted goals, then a food insecurity index should be able to detect improvement in a household's food budget situation. The continuum between a "food secure" and "food insecure" household can be subdivided into various levels. The NRC, in cooperation with USDA's Economic Research Service (ERS), created a four-stage food-security scale:

- Food Security Levels

  o   High Food Security – A household reliably accesses sufficient food.
  o   Marginal Food Security – A household periodically has anxieties about having sufficient food, but consumption is not significantly reduced.

- Food Insecurity Levels

  o   Low Food Security – A household reduces diet quality, but quantity and eating patterns not significantly interrupted.
  o   Very Low Food Security   deficient household income or resources interrupts normal eating patterns and reduces food consumption.

Using the above measurement categories, an ERS study (conducted in conjunction with the NRC) based on US Census Data estimate that 86 percent of the US population had either high or marginal levels of food security. The 14 percent of US "food insecure households" were subdivided into 8.4 percent with low food security and 5.6 percent who experienced "very low food security."

When we can collect household consumption survey data over time, we can assess trends in food security. ERS also uses the data to track food security levels for different types of households. For example, food security can be estimated for households with children or households with seniors.

In August 2013, the USDA's Food and Nutrition Service appointed Mathematica Policy Research to conduct a study of SNAP participation effects on household food security.[21] This commissioned research included interviews of 9,811 households across 30 States. Results indicated that households receiving SNAP benefits for at least 6 months were less likely to be food insecure than new SNAP-participant households. One cross-sectional measurement reveals a 6.7 percent reduction of food insecurity, when comparing newly accepted SNAP applicants to 6-month SNAP-participant households.[22]

Economic analysis of in-kind transfer programs

Empirical research (such as the 2013 USDA food security study) helps us to understand impacts of current nutrition programs on household food security. We also gain useful insights when we apply microeconomic theory to predict program effects. Careful analysis of rational consumer behavior guides researchers and decision makers to focus on those factors most likely to affect program efficiency and effectiveness.

Analysis of household consumer choice

Rational consumer choice theory is central to all economics and well adapted to predicting the effects of federal food assistance programs. We begin with the premise that any household seeks to optimize its satisfaction within scarcity's constraints. We can use a graphical model to demonstrate how consumers express their preferences when they are limited by a finite budget.[23]

To conduct this graphical analysis, we make a few simplifying assumptions. We can divide household consumer purchases into two categories: (1) food and (2) all other goods. For this analysis, let $1.25 =$ per unit food (F) price, and $1.00 =$ per unit "other goods" (O_g) price. A limited household income (I) creates a negatively sloped straight-line budget constraint. See Figure 7.1 below:

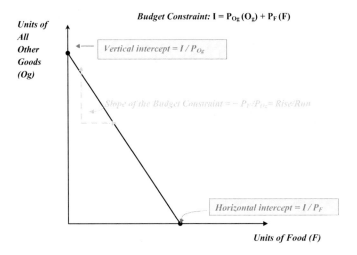

Figure 7.1 Household consumer linear budget constraint.

In Figure 7.1, increases in household income (I) create a parallel shift of the budget line to the right, and vice versa. A change in either the Food Price or the Price of Other Goods causes budget line I to pivot to a different slope.

The consumer household uses the budget constraint displayed in Figure 7.1 to identify its range of possible outcomes. This budget must be combined with a utility function that gauges consumer preferences. In our analysis, we assume that the household utility function includes the normal microeconomic assumptions of: (1) diminishing marginal utility for any one item, and (2) a convex indifference curve indicating a preference for variety in consumption.

The utility function reflects the *Principle of Diversity in Consumption*. This principle suggests that consumers prefer a variety or a "balance" in the amounts of different types of goods that they purchase and use. Let's consider our example of a consumer choosing between food amounts (F) and quantities of other goods (Og). The desire for "balance" changes the rate at which consumers will trade away an amount of Food (F) to receive some of Other Goods (Og) in return, and still remain equally as happy (remain "indifferent").

Here is a scenario: suppose a consumer initially has relatively large amounts of (F) (perhaps 200 units), and very little of Og (10 units). Because the consumer has lots of (F), and only a small amount of (Og), the consumer (*under the Principle of Diversity*), is willing to trade away larger amounts of F to receive relatively smaller portions of Og in return, and remain indifferent. For example, this consumer may willingly give up 10 units of F to receive 2 units of Og in exchange. This consumer is "just as happy" after the trade off, because the consumer is moving towards a "more balanced" distribution of F and Og.

The pace at which the consumer trades off F for Og is called the "marginal rate of substitution (the MRS)." The principle of *Diversity in Consumption* causes the MRS *to diminish* (the trade-off rate decreases), as the consumer's distribution of F and Og becomes more balanced. For example, if past trading of F for Og has caused the consumer to now "own" 150 units of F and 30 units of Og [*instead of 200 Fs and 10 Ogs*], then the trade-off rate could fall off to a 5-to-2 ratio (the consumer will offer only 5 units of F to receive 2 units of Og in return [*instead of a 10F-to-2Og ratio*], and still be indifferent about the exchange.)

Diminishing MRS can be shown as a "convex indifference curve." See the Figure 7.2 below. The function is convex with respect to the origin of the graph. A *diminishing MRS* means the "arc-shaped curve" changes from a steep slope to a flat slope, as the consumer "slides along" the indifference curve from left to right. As the consumer "slides down" the *Indifference Curve*, the consumer gives up units of Og to receive units of F in exchange, and remains equally happy ("indifferent along the curve").

In Figure 7.2 above, we view a single level of consumer satisfaction. How are changes in satisfaction displayed? If the consumer acquires more of all goods (e.g. more of *both* F and Og), then satisfaction rises, because more is preferred to less. In a graph, the entire Indifference Curve shifts up and to the right to demonstrate increased satisfaction. Conversely, if reduced satisfaction occurs, then the Indifference Curve shifts down and to the left. See Figure 7.3 for a visual representation of alternate satisfaction levels:

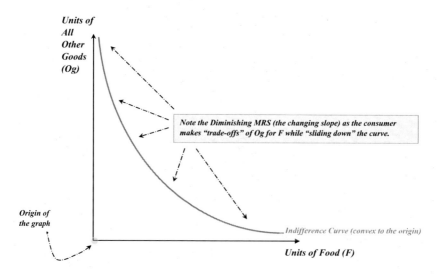

Figure 7.2 Household consumer utility function's convex indifference curve.

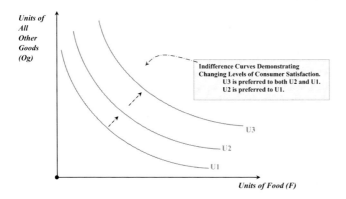

Figure 7.3 Shifting indifference curves to demonstrate alternative consumer utility levels.

Using the budget constraint from Figure 7.1 and the Indifference Curves of Figures 7.2 and 7.3, we predict that the rational consumer household reaches an optimum level of satisfaction by reaching the highest level of indifference while staying within a limited budget. In brief, *Indifference Curves (IC's)* tell us what consumers prefer, and *Budget Constraints (BCs)* tells us what the consumer can afford.

Rational consumers naturally seek their highest satisfaction level. On a graph, let the Budget Constraint (BC) be set or "fixed" by a given level of income (I). Next, along alternative indifference curves, let the consumer experiment with different combinations of Food (F) and Other Goods (Og).

As long as the consumer does not go above the budget, she or he can change the mix of F and Og, until the highest indifference curve is reached. When the *indifference curve is just tangent to the budget constraint*, no further adjustments of F and Og produce any greater utility. *This is the optimum point sought by the rational consumer*. The consumer is still on the BC, so he or she can afford this combination of F and Og. At the tangency, the most preferred combination of F and Og also occurs. See Figure 7.4 below:

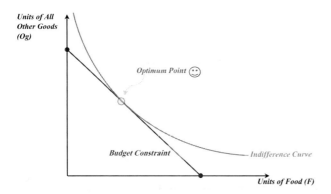

Figure 7.4 Tangency of indifference curve and budget constraint, indicating a consumer optimum.

Consumer analysis of in-kind transfer programs

We can use the consumer optimum displayed in Figure 7.4 as a starting point for determining the effect of an in-kind transfer program such as SNAP.

Suppose the consumer household depicted in Figure 7.4 has just met the qualifications for becoming a SNAP participant. A SNAP food subsidy is transferred to the household. The extra SNAP income can only be spent on food items, and nothing else. For simplicity, we will also assume the household is prohibited from reselling any of the extra food purchased with the SNAP payment. How does this new subsidy affect the household's choices? The initial effect is a shift of the household's budget constraint.

Let's examine how the budget constraint responds to the in-kind transfer in Figure 7.5. Notice that the changed budget is not the typical parallel shift associated with a simple cash transfer. The vertical intercept of the new budget function remains unchanged, because the extra SNAP income *cannot* be used to purchase any "Other goods (Og)."

Using the SNAP budget result displayed in Figure 7.5, we can examine scenarios of how consumer households could respond to the program. We can examine how the outcome changes with a SNAP payment as compared to an equivalent cash transfer. If cash were substituted for a SNAP payment then the new budget line could extend up to a new vertical axis intercept, indicating that cash can be spent on any item (food or other) (see Figure 7.5) Depending on the preferences of the consumer (i.e. the shape of the indifference curve), the consumer outcomes of SNAP or cash subsidies can either coincide or differ.

Let's consider two scenarios below: (1) in Figure 7.6, cash is superior to the SNAP consumer subsidy, and (2) in Figure 7.7, cash and SNAP are equivalent methods of increasing consumer satisfaction.

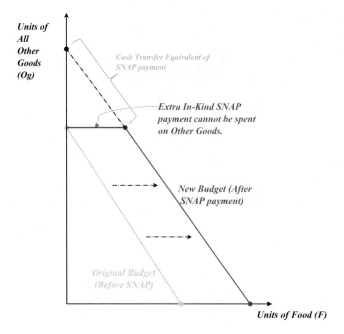

Figure 7.5 Budget impact of in-kind SNAP payment.

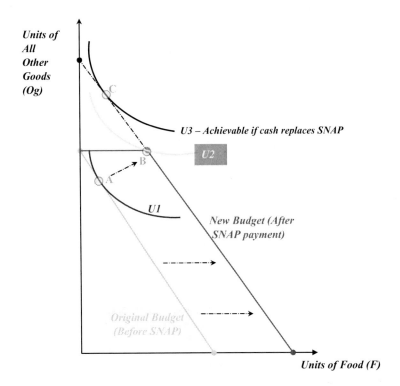

Figure 7.6 Scenario: consumer is better off with cash as compared to in-kind SNAP payment.

In Figure 7.6, the extra SNAP payment does improve the utility position of the Consumer Household (the maximum utility position changes from the U1 to the U2 Indifference Curve, and the optimum moves from Point A to Point B).

However, if SNAP were replaced by an equivalent cash-subsidy program, this type of consumer would be better off. Under a cash payment program, this consumer would attain an even higher level of satisfaction, reaching Optimum Point C on the highest U3 Indifference Curve. The results of this scenario analysis has motivated some economists to suggest replacing SNAP with a cash transfer system.

In Figure 7.7, the extra SNAP payment improves the utility position of the Consumer Household (the maximum utility position changes from the U1 to the U2 Indifference Curve, and the optimum moves from Point A to Point B). This consumer has a different preference schedule than the one shown in the Figure 7.6 scenario.

Figure 7.7 indicates that there is no net loss of satisfaction of transferring funds for SNAP purposes as compared to cash. This outcome offers some assurance that in-kind transfer programs need not reduce economic value. But we really do not have any basis for saying that one type of consumer is more prevalent than another.

Economists examine the results of Figures 7.6 and 7.7, and observe that we cannot use economic theory alone to predict the value of SNAP and related programs. We need to conduct empirical research (gather actual data and analyze it) to arrive at more definitive conclusions.

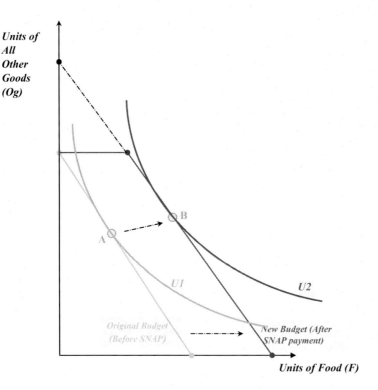

Figure 7.7 Consumer has equal satisfaction with an in-kind SNAP payment, as compared with an equivalent cash subsidy.

The formal consumer optimization analysis of SNAP causes us to address some interesting questions. For example, if SNAP is sometimes a lower-value program than a cash transfer, then why go to the trouble of creating an in-kind transfer program? There are higher administrative costs of figuring out the food needs of low-income households, and some economists suggest that we should just transfer cash, and let households decide what is best for their own welfare.

On the other hand, SNAP and related programs are not sustainable without political support. Whether it is economically efficient or not, taxpayers understand that they ultimately carry the burden for supporting SNAP and similar programs. It is not unrealistic to expect taxpayers to assume a "paternalistic approach" – if funds are to be transferred, taxpayers can demand increased assurance that the funds will support the targeted goals, and not be directed to other competing and undesirable uses (such as alcohol, drugs, etc.).

In simple terms, all government-supported programs share both a political and economic reality. It is advisable to consider "both sides of the coin," when designing and delivering public programs.

The challenges of interpreting the evidence for nutrition program effects on food budgets and security

The microeconomic analysis of in-kind subsidy programs in this chapter's previous section stresses the importance of empirical research to investigate how households actually respond to policy incentives. The theory itself does not offer a definitive single answer.

Thirty years of empirical research in this policy area has yielded surprising results and much "food for thought" (please pardon the pun). Senauer and Young (1986) measured responses of households to additional food stamp funds relative to cash equivalents, and their modeling displayed a *noticeable increase in the food budget with SNAP* in comparison to an equivalent amount of cash transfer.[24]

As noted in Figure 7.7 above (which is known as the "infra-marginal case"), traditional theory predicts *no real difference* in the optimal spending point (when comparing cash to in-kind transfer).

The scenario observed in Figure 7.6 predicts that the SNAP program would have a *smaller* food budget outcome than the equivalent cash transfer. Figure 7.6 is known as the "extra-marginal" case.

Senauer and Young, along with other researchers, engaged in empirical studies, and determined results that *contradicted both* the extra-marginal and the infra-marginal micro-economic theory predictions. The *observed net increase in the food budget* with SNAP (the Food Stamp Program) funding is unexpected.

Senauer and Young offered interesting hypotheses to explain the unanticipated increase in household food-spending budgets associated with SNAP program participation: (1) household recipients may feel *morally obligated* to spend additional "Food Stamp" funds to expand their food budgets; (2) decision making within a household *may pass to another member* who is predisposed to increase the household's food security via a larger food budget, because the legal obligations of SNAP reinforce the preference of that household member; and (3) since SNAP monthly payments occur early, and *if we assume that these households spend all or most of their monthly SNAP allotment when it arrives*, then we can predict that households supplement their food budgets with their own income as they "run out" of food near the end of the month.[25]

To further "stir the pot," between 1995 and 2000, the so-called welfare system (the AFDC and TANF programs) was markedly reformed, and tightened restrictions reduced the "welfare caseload" (i.e. participation rates). Because the offices that handle welfare cases are often the same locations to apply for SNAP benefits, the welfare reforms increased the "transaction cost" of applying for (or renewing) SNAP membership. Consequently, as "welfare rolls" were reduced, so were SNAP participant rates (even in cases where these households were still SNAP eligible). Any modeling of SNAP participation and its consequences must be adjusted for other intervening policy variables that can alter observed results.[26]

What are the policy lessons to be learned? Theory can guide research questions, but it cannot answer them by itself. Empirical analysis is critical, if actual relationships are to be detected and verified.

Parke and Ranney (1996) also emphasized the importance of carefully designing the empirical research to uncover verifiable results.[27] Similar to Senauer and Young, Parke and Ranney determined that consumers do not regard food stamp checks (SNAP payments) to be identical to cash resources; traditional microeconomic theory predictions must be modified to account for the distinct consumer spending responses to alternative funding sources.[28]

The challenges associated with empirical analysis is also a reminder that policies based only on theoretical predictions are likely to be mistaken. Theory is not vacant; but it is not sufficient for complete policy making either. A proper balance between theoretical modeling and pragmatic empirical research yields better insights and more effective policy design.

Nutritional policy paradox: the dual problems of obesity and food insecurity

Our recently completed examination of consumer decision models emphasizes that the field of food and nutrition economics is a fertile source of meaningful research opportunities with real policy consequences. In the twenty-first century, a very high-profile area of study is the unexpected connection between the problems of food insecurity and obesity in the US (and worldwide).

Policymakers are keenly interested in obtaining usable research information on this phenomenon because:

1) They seek to prevent food assistance programs from worsening an already serious set of problems, and
2) They wish to re-design policies in ways that can hopefully begin to sever the food insecurity-obesity connection, and reverse the negative patterns that are associated with each of these challenging problems.

National and international research has focused on how we have arrived at the paradox of household food insecurity being coupled with child and adult obesity. One conclusion that cuts across much of the research is that we are not encountering a cause-and-effect relationship between these two phenomena. Rather, food insecurity and obesity occur simultaneously because they are independently arising from a combination of related factors, including:[29]

- poverty pressures.
- less access to healthy foods.
- marketing and cultural influences.
- cheap energy-dense foods; expensive healthy diets.
- food deprivation and binging cycles.
- barriers to regular physical activity.
- limited access to health care.

The above-listed influences are also discussed by Burns (2004), when she reviewed the literature on the reasons for linkages between food insecurity and obesity. Burns determined that the insecurity-obesity relationship exists in the US, Europe, and Australia.[30]

Drewnowski and Specter (2004) investigated the price incentives for household consumers to purchase energy-dense foods rather than the less dense fruits and vegetables.[31] They document an inverse relationship between food-energy density (MJ/kg) and food-energy cost ($/MJ). Relatively *cheap* processed foods, and relatively *expensive* fruits and vegetables, are a price differential caused by the distinct demand and cost-of-production conditions that exist in these alternative food markets.

Drewnowski and Specter cite an example: the ($/MJ) energy cost of potato chips is about 20 cents (US) /MJ or (1200kcal/$), while the ($/MJ) cost of fresh carrots is 95 cents US/MJ or (250kcal/$). Traditional microeconomics tells us that consumers pay attention to relative prices. They adjust their purchases accordingly as they seek to maximize satisfaction within a budget constraint. For low-income households, where their budget limits are tight, these price differentials really matter.

In addition to the relative price incentive to purchase more energy-dense foods, and to economize on fruits and vegetables, Drewnowski and Specter also observe that processed foods have attractive taste and texture attributes associated with their higher fat and sugar content. Consumer preferences are drawn towards these alluring qualities.

The combined impact of consumer preferences and price differentials presents a powerful economic argument that helps us to better understand the dietary choices of low-income households. Simply put, when poverty afflicts a household, there are strong market incentives to purchase foods that trigger obesity. These results are predicted by the normal and rational economic drive to maximize dietary energy for the least cost.

Examining relationships among SNAP, food insecurity, and obesity

There is a wealth of empirical research on observed relationships between participation in SNAP, household food insecurity, and obesity trends.

The full range of published studies indicates that SNAP has mixed impacts. For example, Gibson (2003, 2006) determined that SNAP participation is positively related to obesity in low-income women; Gibson also observed an increased prevalence of overweight daughters and obese mothers when their SNAP participation is long term.[32,33]

On the other hand, a 2003 study by Jones et al. reported that food-insecure girls who participated in a combination of the SNAP, school breakfast, and school lunch programs were less prone to be overweight than their counterparts in non-program-participating households. In another study, adults participating for 6 months or more in SNAP had a lower body mass index (BMI) than adults with less than 6 months of SNAP experience.[34]

The body of evidence about the obesity impacts of SNAP participation does not reveal many definitive patterns. From a policy standpoint, there is an opportunity to make improvements in the nutritional outcomes of the SNAP program.

The US Department of Agriculture (USDA) and the Department of Health and Human Services (HHS) jointly issued a report known as *The Dietary Guidelines for Americans, 2010*.[35] This joint USDA and HHS document is relevant to the SNAP program because it is built upon three generally applicable principles that can be incorporated into the day-to-day administration of SNAP:

- Encourages and support households to consume *nutrient*-dense foods and beverages.
- Promotes dietary and lifestyle choices that aid each household member to achieve and maintain a healthy weight.
- Includes food safety principles that prevent and avoid foodborne illnesses.

The Food Research and Action Center (FRAC) built upon the USDA-HHS dietary guidelines to identify and recommend strategies to improve SNAP's household nutrition outcomes. Those strategies include:[36]

- Increase SNAP participation.
- Enhance SNAP benefits to assist households to afford adequate diets, including healthier foods.
- Promote fruit and vegetable purchases with SNAP benefits.
- Facilitate SNAP use at farmers' markets, in Community Supported Agriculture (CSA), and other farm-to-consumer settings.

- Augment SNAP Nutrition Education to equip households with accurate dietary and food safety information.
- Boost household access to healthy, affordable, and SNAP-supported foods in under-served communities.

SNAP and the additional sixteen federal nutrition programs have the capacity to reduce US food insecurity. If the USDA-HHS dietary guidelines are properly incorporated into the programs, participating households can improve their diets and health, and lessen the incidence of obese and/or overweight outcomes.

The USDA's Thrifty Food Plan

Our above discussion of the connections between the SNAP program and healthy household diets puts a spotlight on a fundamental question: what primary nutritional goals does the US federal government seek to achieve with the SNAP program, as it is currently designed and administered?

In testimony before the US House of Representatives' Subcommittee on Nutrition and Horticulture, Haskins (2012) offered three main purposes for SNAP:[37]

- Augment the capacity of needy households to afford a low-cost and nutritionally sufficient diet.
- Function as an economic stabilizer for individual household budgets, and for the entire national economy.
- Supplement the low-wages of employed SNAP-participant households.

All three purposes are important, but our focus here is on the first: supplementing the nutritional needs of qualified SNAP recipient households by financially supporting a low-cost balanced diet.

The USDA's Center for Nutrition Policy and Promotion (CNPP) is responsible for using scientific research, current consumption patterns, and actual food costs to formulate a household diet plan that meets national nutritional guidelines at a minimum cost. This USDA effort to define a nutritionally sufficient and most economical diet began in the early 1960s when the Food Stamp Program first became permanent law. Since that time, based on the latest nutritional knowledge, the USDA has periodically updated the mixture of foods and nutrient content included in the low-cost diet. The CNPP's most recent revision of this inexpensive diet occurred in 2006, and it is known as the "Thrifty Food Plan."[38]

Why the Thrifty Food Plan is important

The significance of the Thrifty Food Plan (TFP) arises from both its scientific foundations and its funding effects on the SNAP Program.

From a scientific viewpoint, the TFP is determined using a mathematical optimization process that seeks a minimum budget cost solution, subject to a combination of nutritional goals and constraints. The sophisticated TFP mathematical model incorporates average consumption across 58 food categories for 15 age-gender groups, along with US dietary recommendations and the scientific nutrient profiles of the included food groups.

The role of the TFP in the administration of SNAP program payments is critical. Once the USDA has mathematically determined the TFP formulation for the low-cost diet plan, then *the outcome is used to set the maximum allowable SNAP payment for a household recipient.* In many ways, the TFP methodology is important because it measurably affects the taxpayer cost of the SNAP program. It also directly controls the funding received by qualified households. The size of a SNAP payment has a bearing on the degree to which participating households can improve their food security levels and stabilize their household budgets.

Professional perspectives on the Thrifty Food Plan (TFP)

The CNPP's official TFP publication explains the extensive background, applicable data, and scientific methodology that produced the updated dietary plan. The report emphasizes the careful and detailed effort that was required to create a nutritious diet that households could adopt while on a minimal budget.[39]

Nutrition specialists, food economists, and other observers have independently reviewed the design and implementation of the revised TFP. Their studies of this dietary plan generate some interesting insights and perspectives.

To reach minimum dietary cost, the TFP assumes most ingredients are raw or fresh, and that meals are primarily made "from scratch." Rose (2007) examined the household's estimated meal preparation time associated with the food and recipes included in the TFP. Using TFP recipes, and reasonable assumptions about the time needed to prepare and cook these suggested meals, Rose determined that a household would require an average of 2.3 hours per day for this task, not including the time needed for shopping and cleanup.[40]

The TFP formula implicitly assumes that SNAP participants have a low opportunity cost for the necessary meal preparation time. The problem is that the US Congress expects SNAP participants to seek and secure gainful employment as a condition of SNAP eligibility. The era of accountability has its consequences. In a single-parent household, compliance with SNAP work conditions is contradictory to the TFP premise that there is "plenty of time" to prepare meals from scratch.

Following up on Rose's observations, Davis and You (2010) examined the question of meal preparation from a production function perspective.[41] In this case, basic microeconomics predicts that a rational household will review the input-to-output relationship and pursue the least cost input combination to generate the desired output. Meal preparation, similar to any other production function, taps into the labor resource.[42]

Labor is scarce, and when a household considers the productive options for "meal production," the opportunity cost of the labor resource will be a prominent consideration. Unfortunately, the TFP treats labor time as a plentiful and slack resource. The reality is otherwise.

Rational households, under pressure to earn sufficient income because of normal household maintenance demands, realize that their labor resource is much more valuable than the TFP assumes. Also, recall that US Congressional policy is focused on ensuring that able-bodied SNAP participants are spending time in the workforce, and not at home. In fact, strict adherence to TFP meal-preparation guidelines creates "meal production functions" that simply do not make economic sense to many rational SNAP-participating households.

Drewnowski and Eichelsdoerfer (2010) reviewed the TFP and determined that typical US household food consumption patterns are noticeably dissimilar to the TFP protocols.[43] The TFP presumes that households will seek out and use the suggested low-cost recipes. The TFP model also assumes that households adjust their food intake to replace animal protein with large volumes of legumes and whole-grain pasta. The TFP additionally presumes households will reduce their whole milk and citrus juice consumption to nearly zero. Such scenarios question the applicability of the TFP model to real-world household food preferences and budgets.

Drewnowski and Eichelsdoerfer pose the question of how (or why) households will suddenly change their normal consumption patterns to follow a "government-endorsed" dietary plan. Beyond the socio-psychological challenges of such an extraordinary change in food consumption, these researchers raise practical questions of whether households can realistically adapt to these new foods and recipes.[44]

Given the fact that processed and energy-dense foods often have lower per-unit energy cost, shorter preparation time, increased storage capacity and less spoilage, the TFP recommendations for "from scratch recipes" are often detached from the food consumption incentives that low-income households face daily.[45]

Political considerations associated with the TFP

Our brief review of the TFP uncovers some concerns about its applicability for low-income SNAP-participant households. A variety of suggestions are offered to guide future revisions of the TFP. Some of these recommendations would rearrange the TFP to include different foods and recipes, without measurably affecting the cost of funding the TFP. However, other suggestions would increase the per-household TFP budget in an effort to further improve food security and serve related goals.[46]

When policy makers review recommendations, especially for a large national program such as SNAP, they generally take into account a range of factors such as economic feasibility and political acceptability. In relation to this particular policy situation, certain observations about SNAP and the TFP are worth consideration:

- The USDA's CNPP agency is expected to produce a *minimum-cost* Thrifty Food Plan to determine the *maximum-allowable* SNAP payment to a household. This is no coincidence; it is part of the program design as a control on total government spending for the program.[47]
- The US Congress named SNAP as a "supplemental" program. This perspective emphasizes that Congress intends SNAP to be an "add-on" to a household food budget, rather than a full replacement.[48] While the TFP offers households a diet that could be achieved within the SNAP budget, a more practical viewpoint would recognize that SNAP is to be combined with a household's own resources to address the challenges of food security.

Discussions about the adequacy of the Thrifty Food Plan should probably be expanded to include considerations such as the overall taxpayer cost of the SNAP program and the general pressures to limit federal government spending on all programs. Popular media have few reservations in stating political reasons to reduce or limit spending on SNAP and similar programs.[49]

Before the 2014 Farm Bill was authorized, proposals from both the House and Senate included *spending reductions for SNAP* and related nutrition programs. When the 2014 Farm Bill was approved, Congress had reduced spending on Title IV Nutrition programs by approximately 1 percent as compared with the original baseline. This reduction could have been much larger, as the House was proposing a 5 percent decrease in nutrition program spending.[50]

Why emphasize this political perspective? The answer is pragmatic. Competing pressures often accompany public policy decisions. In the case of SNAP, it is not only important to understand how this nutrition program affects the food security and nutritional status of low-income households, but we must also balance this perspective against concerns that spending on SNAP must be limited, similar to the constraints on all other forms of federal government spending. These forces "play themselves out" in an arena of both politics and economics.

The roles of the low-cost, moderate-cost, and liberal USDA Food Plans

As a complement to the Thrifty Food Plan (TFP; discussed above), the USDA has historically created guidelines for alternative household diet plans that are matched with different income levels. These dietary systems are known as the Low-Cost, Moderate-Cost and Liberal Food Plans. One year after the TFP revision in 2006, USDA (2007) incorporated the latest food consumption patterns along with updated nutritional standards to update the dietary composition of these increasingly *more expensive* plans.[51]

The boundaries for distinguishing the various food plans are population quartiles of food spending, as follows:[52]

Table7.1 US population quartiles of food spending

Quartile Lower Bound	USDA, CNPP Food Plan Category	Quartile Upper Bound
0 percent <	Thrifty Food Plan Quartile	≤ 25th percent
25th percent	< Low-Cost Food Plan Quartile	≤ 50th percent
50th percent	< Moderate-Cost Food Plan Quartile	≤ 75th percent
75th percent	< Liberal Food Plan Quartile	≤ 100th percent

The USDA's Center for Nutrition Policy and Promotion (CNPP) is ultimately responsible for ensuring that each of the four food plans meet current scientifically based nutrition standards and are also relevant to the consumption habits of current consumers. Of course, the CNPP cooperates with many other agencies and experts before it produces a set of recommended food plans for households across the nation.

We have already established that the *Thrifty Food Plan (TFP)* is the primary base for determining the maximum household SNAP payment. The additional three CNPP food plans are not just theoretical derivations; they are also "placed into service."

The *Low-Cost Food Plan* is frequently cited in bankruptcy courts to define the percentage of a bankrupt person's income that constitutes his/her food budget.

Depending upon relevant household income percentiles, divorce courts can match the appropriate USDA food plan to determine a more accurate alimony payment. The *Liberal Food Plan* is used by the US Defense Department to establish the Basic Allowance for Subsistence Rates for all service members.[53]

One reason why the courts and other federal departments use the CNPP's food plan categories as "reference points" for estimating household food values is the objective and consistent estimation methodology that is common to all of the plans. As is the case with the

TFP (described earlier), a mathematical optimization model is used to set the food spending budgets for each population quartile.[54]

Once the dietary requirements and food consumption patterns for each level are entered into the model, the same mathematical calculation system is used each time to arrive at a final budget solution. It would be difficult to prove in court that the estimation procedure was "arbitrary and capricious." In fact, the opposite claim of adhering to consistent methods and scientifically objective criteria in the optimization model has considerable support and evidence.

It is interesting to observe how scientific estimations are applied in different societal circumstances. At first glance, it might not be clear as to the practical value of using a mathematical model to guide household food recommendations and budgets. But as we explore these research efforts, we discover that they have multiple applications that can make a difference, whether it be enhancing the nutritional health of a household or establishing a fair and objective financial judgement for adjudicates in a courtroom.

MyPlate vs. MyPyramid: changing USDA nutritional recommendations to household consumers

Ongoing USDA research to improve the budgeted food plans is evidence of the USDA's commitment to develop and implement nutrition recommendations that can make a difference in the dietary lives of everyday household consumers. SNAP recipients are a primary target of these guidelines, but all Americans can benefit if they follow them. A challenge associated with the four food budget plans is their technical orientation. To reach a wider audience, USDA needed to create an easy-to-understand communication format.

To achieve this marketing goal, the USDA created and published the "stepwise food pyramid" model (between 1992 and 2005) to emphasize that all households should design their daily diet based on the principles of variety, moderation, and sensible proportion.[55]

In 2005, the USDA updated the pyramid model to incorporate the latest science on what should or should not be included in a balanced diet. Then, in 2011, after reviewing consumer confusion of how to convert the food pyramid into everyday life, the USDA changed the visual illustration to "MyPlate."

MyPlate is a plate-shaped display with four colorful "pie-type slices" (representing vegetables, fruits, grains, and protein), and a "glass" (symbolizing dairy products). MyPlate offers general guidelines for a healthy diet by encouraging food consumers to balance their meals across the five food groups. USDA recently introduced a second program with a competitive format – known as MyWins – to encourage consumers to make incremental and relatively easy-to-accomplish improvements in both diet and bodily activity. USDA is promoting MyPlate and MyWins as a joint package in an effort to encourage healthier lifestyles. The joint program is also aimed at combatting the obesity problem in American society.[56]

In comparison to the four budgeted food plans, the MyPlate, MyWins nutritional campaign is much easier for the average household to understand and utilize. All of these nutrition-oriented plans and programs incorporate the science-based system known as the "Dietary Guidelines for Americans." USDA has training and educational materials to allow schools and other organizations to use MyPlate, MyWins as a complete nutrition and lifestyle education program.

USDA's educational and marketing effort is a much-needed component for developing SNAP and related programs into something more than a food safety net. There is a real potential to help households both increase their food security and enhance their quality of life.

Summary and future food policy choices

In this chapter, we have explored a range of important roles for federal nutrition policy:

- Federal nutrition programs serve as a food safety net for needy households.
- Participation in SNAP and other nutrition programs create a counter-cyclical benefit to the national economy, and also produces a local economic stimulus.
- The 2014 Farm Bill and related authorizing legislation created seventeen programs that serve the nutritional needs of alternative demographic groups.
- While the evidence is sometimes mixed, participation in federal nutrition programs generally improves the food security status of needy households.
- More research and improvements in program design are needed to help sever the connection between food insecurity and obesity in children and adults.
- If household participants perceive SNAP payments and cash transfers to be equivalent forms of income, then formal microeconomic consumer analysis predicts these alternative funding sources will create *no difference* between the food budgets of "infra-marginal households."
- Empirical research on household responses to SNAP payments reveal a notable increase in the food budgets of SNAP participants, relative to the same amount of cash transfer. Further survey studies demonstrate that many SNAP households do *not* consider SNAP and cash transfers as identical income sources.
- The USDA's Thrifty Food Plan (TFP) determines a minimum cost budget for household nutrition, and the TFP is the basis for setting the maximum household SNAP payment. The USDA also designs the Low-Cost, Moderate-Cost and Liberal Food plans that are used as reference points in the courts and other government programs.
- USDA's original "food pyramid" model, and now its "MyPlate, MyWins" campaign, are more effective methods to communicate and promote better nutrition and healthier lifestyles to food safety-net households, and more generally to the US public at large.

Past and current nutrition programs have made noticeable economic and societal impacts. Future nutrition policy is likely going to require a sustainable balance between:

1) the goals of improving household food nutrition and food security, and
2) the economic and political pressure to limit government spending on all programs, including food and nutrition programs.

Exploration of food programs and their wide range of impacts helps us to realize that when we consider legislation such as the 2014 Farm Bill, we are actually engaged in a much larger agenda. Farm and food policies are intertwined. As we search for ways to achieve more efficient and effective outcomes, we can search for opportunities to harmonize the various program goals and activities.

In the next chapter, our studies continue to concentrate on the inter-connections between farm, food, and society. Natural resource, energy, and environmental management create quality-of-life impacts that equally affect farm producers and food consumers.

Important questions can be global in nature (e.g. determining if connections exist between farm practices, food consumption patterns, and climate change). Or, the key issues can arise locally or regionally, such as the effect of a buffer strip width on local watershed quality.

As in the case of food and nutrition policy, the issues of environment, energy, and natural resources are not easily simplified, and are sometimes emotionally charged. Our task will be to examine these areas by carefully balancing their normative and positive elements. Let's move onto the next chapter and rise to the challenge.

Notes

1 Vilsack, Thomas. USDA Secretary. "Thrifty Food Plan." Release No. 0073.13. USDA Office of Communications. San Diego, CA. April 18, 2013. Retrieved from: www.fns.usda.gov/tags/thrifty-food-plan

2 Food Research and Action Center. "A Review of Strategies to Bolster SNAP's Role in Improving Nutrition as well as Food Security." Originally published July 2011; last updated January 2013. Retrieved from: www.frac.org/wp-content/uploads/2011/06/SNAPstrategies.pdf

3 Basiotis, P.P., C.S. Kramer-LeBlanc, and E.T. Kennedy. "Maintaining nutrition security and diet quality: the role of the Food Stamp Program and WIC." *Family Economics and Nutrition Review*, 11 (1 and 2), pp. 4–16. 1998. Retrieved from: www.ers.usda.gov/webdocs/publications/fanrr9/32535_fanrr9rf_002.pdf

4 Mabli, J., L. Castner, J. Ohls, M.K. Fox, M.K. Crepinsek, and E. Condon. "Food Expenditures and Diet Quality among Low-Income Households and Individuals." Report to the U.S. Department of Agriculture, Food and Nutrition Service. 2010. Washington, DC: Mathematica Policy Research, Inc. Retrieved from: www.ncbi.nlm.nih.gov/books/NBK206908/

5 Slack, T. "How Did the Great Recession Impact the Geography of Food Stamp Receipt?" *Choices*. Quarter 2, 2014. Retrieved from: www.choicesmagazine.org/choices-magazine/theme-articles/food-and-poverty/how-did-the-great-recession-impact-the-geography-of-food-stamp-receipt

6 Ibid, p. 4.

7 Ibid.

8 A counter-cyclical influence is any variable or activity that acts to soften or moderate the undesired effects of the national business cycle. For example, when the economy is in the recession phase of the business cycle, then Real GDP and consumer spending are decreasing and unemployment is increasing. A counter-cyclical factor, such as increased household food spending with SNAP, tends to reverse the negative trends in Real GDP and household spending, and help generate job creation and lower unemployment. See Gordon, Robert J. *Macroeconomics*. Eleventh Edition. Boston, MA: Pearson Education. Glossary page G-1, 2009.

9 Hanson, Kenneth and Victor Oliveira. "How Economic Conditions Affect Participation in USDA Nutrition Assistance Programs." Economic Information Bulletin No. (EIB-100), p. iii, September 2012. Retrieved from: www.ers.usda.gov/publications/eib-economic-information-bulletin/eib100.aspx

10 An Entitlement Program is one whose expenditures are determined by the number of people who qualify, rather than a preset budget allocation. See Rosen, Harvey S. *Public Finance*. Sixth Edition. Boston, MA: McGraw-Hill Irwin, 2002, p. 531.

11 Aussenberg, Randy Alison and Kirsten J. Colello. "Domestic Food Assistance: Summary of Programs." February 17, 2016 Congressional Research Service 7-5700. Retrived from: www.crs.gov. R42353. Retrieved from: www.fas.org/sgp/crs/misc/R42353.pdf

12 "7 Top Hunger Organizations: The Organizations Fighting Food Insecurity Worldwide." September-October 2013. *Food & Nutrition Magazine*. Retrieved from: www.foodandnutrition.org/September-October-2013/7-Top-Hunger-Organizations/

13 Ellison, Jon. "Hunger in America: A History of Private and Public Responses." Harvard University Scholar Series, 2004. Retrieved from: www.dash.harvard.edu/bitstream/handle/1/8846747/Ellison.pdf?sequence=1

14 USDA, Food and Nutrition Service. "Supplemental Nutrition Assistance Program (SNAP): A short History of SNAP." Last published: November 20, 2014. Retrieved from: www.fns.usda.gov/snap/short-history-snap

15 Aussenberg, Randy Alison and Kirsten J. Colello. "Domestic Food Assistance: Summary of Programs." February 17, 2016 Congressional Research Service 7-5700. Retrieved from: www.crs.gov R42353. Retrieved from: www.fas.org/sgp/crs/misc/R42353.pdf

16 "Supplemental Nutrition Assistance Program (SNAP): A Short History of SNAP." USDA, Food and Nutrition Service. Last published: November 20, 2014. Retrieved from: www.fns.usda.gov/snap/short-history-snap

17 In Appendix A to this textbook, you can examine more detailed descriptions of the goals, recipients, benefits, organization and funding for each of the seventeen federal food programs mentioned here in Chapter 7.

18 Ibid, p. 6.

19 Ibid, p. 7.

20 "Food Insecurity and Hunger in the United States: An Assessment of the Measure." National Research Council. Washington, DC, 2006, pp. 23–51. Retrieved from: www.nap.edu/catalog.php?record_id=11578.

21 Mabli, James, Jim Ohls, Lisa Dragoset, Laura Castner, and Betsy Santos. "Measuring the Effect of Supplemental Nutrition Assistance Program (SNAP) Participation on Food Security." Prepared by Mathematica Policy Research for the U.S. Department of Agriculture, Food and Nutrition Service, August 2013. Retrieved from: www.fns.usda.gov/sites/default/files/Measuring2013.pdf

22 Ibid, p. xxii.

23 This application on consumer choice draws upon the analysis of in-kind transfers that appears in Rosen, Harvey and Ted Gayer, *Public Finance*. Ninth Edition. New York: McGraw Hill/Irwin, 2010, pp. 269–272.

24 Senauer, Ben and Nathan Young. "The Impact of Food Stamps on Food Expenditures: Rejection of the Traditional Model." *American Journal of Agricultural Economics* 68(1), February 1986, pp. 37–42. Retrieved from: www.pdf.usaid.gov/pdf_docs/PNAAV750.pdf

25 Ibid, pp. 41–42.

26 Kaushal, Neeraj and Qin Gao. "Food Stamp Program and Consumption Choices." NBER Working Paper No. 14988. May 2009, pp. 1–35. Retrieved from: www.nber.org/papers/w14988.pdf

27 Wilde, Parke and Christine Ranney. "The Distinct Impact of Food Stamps on Food Spending." *Journal of Agricultural and Resource Economics* 21(1), pp. 174–185, 1996. Retrieved from: www.ageconsearch.umn.edu/bitstream/31002/1/21010174.pdf

28 Ibid, p. 185.

29 Food Research and Action Center. "Why Are Low Income and Food-Insecure People Vulnerable to Obesity?" Washington, DC. 2015. Retrieved from: www.frac.org/initiatives/hunger-and-obesity/why-are-low-income-and-food-insecure-people-vulnerable-to-obesity/

30 Burns, Dr. Cate. "A Review of the Literature Describing the Link between Poverty, Food Insecurity and Obesity with Specific Reference to Australia." Melbourne: Centre for Physical Activity and Nutrition Research. School of Exercise and Nutrition Sciences, Deakin University. 2004. Retrieved from: www.vichealth.vic.gov.au www.secure.secondbite.org/sites/default/files/A_review_of_the_literature_describing_the_link_between_poverty_food_insecurity_and_obesity_w.pdf

31 Drewnowski, A. and S.E. Specter. "Poverty and Obesity: The Role of Energy Density and Energy Costs." *American Journal of Clinical Nutrition* 79, pp. 6–16. 2004. Retrieved from: www.ncbi.nlm.nih.gov/pubmed/14684391

32 Gibson, D. "Food Stamp Program Participation Is Positively Related to Obesity in Low- Income Women." *Journal of Nutrition*, 133(7), pp. 2225–2231. 2004. Retrieved from: www.jn.nutrition.org/content/133/7/2225

33 Gibson, D. "Long-term Food Stamp Program participation is positively related to simultaneous overweight in young daughters and obesity in mothers." *Journal of Nutrition*, 136(4), pp. 1081–1085. 2006. Retrieved from: www.jn.nutrition.org/content/136/4/1081

34 Jones, S.J., L. Jahns, B.A. Laraia, and B. Haughton. "Lower Risk of Overweight in School-Aged Food Insecure Girls Who Participate In Food Assistance: Results From the Panel Study of Income Dynamics Child Development Supplement." *Archives of Pediatric and Adolescent*

Medicine, 157(8), pp. 780–784. 2003. Retrieved from: www.jamanetwork.com/journals/jamapediat rics/fullarticle/481402

35 U.S. Department of Agriculture and U.S. Department of Health and Human Services. Dietary Guidelines for Americans, 2010. Seventh Edition. Washington, DC: U.S. Government Printing Office, December 2010. Retrieved from: www.cnpp.usda.gov/sites/default/files/dietary_guidelines_for_americans/PolicyDoc.pdf

36 Food Research and Action Center. "A Review of Strategies to Bolster SNAP's Role in Improving Nutrition as well as Food Security." January 2013. Retrieved from: www.frac.org/wp-content/uploads/2011/06/SNAPstrategies.pdf

37 Haskins, Ron. "Reflecting on SNAP: Purposes, Spending, and Potential Savings." Brookings Institution: Social Genome Project Research, Number 37 of 51. Testimony May 8, 2012. Retrieved from: www.brookings.edu/research/testimony/2012/05/08-snap-haskins

38 Carlson, A., M. Lino, W-Y. Juan, K. Hanson, and P. Peter Basiotis. "Thrifty Food Plan, 2006." Published 2007. (CNPP-19). U.S. Department of Agriculture, Center for Nutrition Policy and Promotion. Retrieved from: www.cnpp.usda.gov/sites/default/files/usda_food_plans_cost_of_food/TFP2006Report.pdf

39 Ibid, p. 1.

40 Rose, Donald. "Food Stamps, the Thrifty Food Plan, and Meal Preparation: The Importance of the Time Dimension for US Nutrition Policy." *Journal of Nutrition Education and Behavior* 39, pp. 226–232. 2007. Retrieved from: www.prc.tulane.edu/uploads/Food%20StampsThrifty%20Food%20PlanandMeal%20Preparation.pdf

41 Davis, George C. and Wen You. "The Thrifty Food Plan Is Not Thrifty When Labor Cost Is Considered." *Journal of Nutrition*. 2010. The American Institute of Nutrition. Retrieved from: www.jn.nutrition.org/content/140/4/854.full

42 Ibid, p. 2.

43 Drewnowski, Adam and Petra Eichelsdoerfer. "Can Low-Income Americans Afford a Healthy Diet?" *Nutr. Today*. Nov. 44(6): 246–249. 2010. Retrieved from: www.ncbi.nlm.nih.gov/pmc/articles/PMC2847733/

44 Ibid, p. 2.

45 Ibid, p. 3.

46 Food Research and Action Center. "A Review of Strategies to Bolster SNAP's Role in Improving Nutrition as well as Food Security." January 2013. Retrieved from: www.frac.org/wp-content/uploads/2011/06/SNAPstrategies.pdf

47 Carlson, Andrea, Mark Lino, WenYen Juan, Kenneth Hanson, P. Peter Basiotis. "Thrifty Food Plan, 2006." USDA, CNPP-19, April 2007, p. ES-1. Retrieved from: www.cnpp.usda.gov/sites/default/files/usda_food_plans_cost_of_food/TFP2006Report.pdf

48 Sanders, Katie. "Fact-checking Gwyneth Paltrow's $29 Weekly Food Stamps Budget Claim." Punditfact. April 22, 2015. Retrieved from: www.politifact.com/punditfact/statements/2015/apr/22/gwyneth-paltrow/gwyneth-paltrows-29-weekly-food-stamps-budget-flaw/

49 Maass, Harold . "Why Conservatives Hate Food Stamps." *The Week*. September 20, 2013. Retrieved from: www.theweek.com/articles/459770/why-conservatives-hate-food-stamps

50 Aussenberg, Randy Alison. "SNAP and Related Nutrition Provisions of the 2014 Farm Bill (P.L. 113-79)." April 24, 2014. Congressional Research Service 7-5700. www.crs.gov. Report No. R43332. Retrieved from: www.nationalaglawcenter.org/wp-content/uploads/assets/crs/R43332.pdf

51 Carlson, A., M. Lino, and T. Fungwe. "The Low-Cost, Moderate-Cost, and Liberal Food Plans, 2007." (CNPP-20). U.S. Department of Agriculture, Center for Nutrition Policy and Promotion, 2007. Retrieved from: www.cnpp.usda.gov/sites/default/files/usda_food_plans_cost_of_food/FoodPlans2007AdminReport.pdf

52 Ibid, pp. 6–7.

53 Ibid, p. 1.

54 Ibid, p. ES-3.

55 Center for Nutrition Policy and Promotion (CNPP). "A Brief History of USDA Food Guides." USDA, June 2011. Retrieved from: www.choosemyplate.gov/sites/default/files/printablematerials/ABriefHistoryOfUSDAFoodGuides.pdf

56 USDA News Release. "USDA Launches Online MyPlate, MyWins Challenge, Available Throughout National Nutrition Month." Release No. 0063.16. March 16, 2016. Retrieved from: www.usda.gov/wps/portal/usda/usdahome?contentid=2016/03/0063.xml&contentidonly=true

Chapter 8

Economic choices and outcomes for agriculture, natural resources, and the environment

In February 2014, a Buscombe County farmland owner in western North Carolina (NC) agreed to the legal conditions of a "conservation easement" on 52 acres of bottom-land containing large swathes of prime[1] agricultural soils. This prime land of the "Watalula Farm Tract" is leased to the Gaining Ground Farm (GGF) farm operation. GGF raises and markets vegetables and beef for local NC farmers' markets, area restaurants, and USDA's Community Supported Agriculture (CSA) program.[2]

This land preservation outcome was made possible by the farmland owner's foresight, the hard work of the GGF operation, the coordinating effort of the Southern Appalachian Highlands Conservancy (SAHC), and assistance from the USDA's Natural Resources Conservation Service (NRCS) and related agencies. The conservation easement offers considerable legal assurances that the 52-acre land area will remain permanently in agricultural use.[3]

Conservation ethics and economics

Concerted efforts to preserve crucial farmland areas, such as establishing conservation easements in western North Carolina, are evidence that both ethics and economics influence how we use our natural resources.

A landowner's decision to legally and permanently pledge his/her valuable natural asset to a single use (agriculture) is admirable. The economic opportunity cost of this legal easement could be sizable, especially if the bids from alternative land uses are noticeably higher than the agricultural economic value.

The story of farmland preservation in Buscombe County, North Carolina is also one of teamwork and dedication. And it is indicative of a national trend. Across the US, we can find many other examples of US landowners, producers, and volunteer organizations cooperating to achieve conservation goals.[4,5,6] In the Buscombe County case, we can interpret the outcome as an ethical and collective commitment to preserve areas of prime soils for the benefit of current and future generations of farm producers and food consumers.

Preventing an "irreversible change" in land use is another view of this conservation easement. If prime agricultural land is not protected by an easement (or some other use restriction), then industrial, commercial, or residential demanders are often successful in reallocating these prime lands for more intense economic development. It is not too difficult to argue that once prime land has been redirected towards creating an industrial park or a housing complex, then it is highly unlikely that it will ever return to agricultural use.

In this chapter, we investigate the economic phenomena and public policies that influence important interactions among agriculture, natural resources, and our environment. Similar to other topics that we have addressed, this field of study is broad and complex. A full inquiry into this subject necessitates entire collegiate programs of study. Our goal in this chapter is more limited. We survey key areas of interest. We remain focused on how critical aspects of natural resources and the environment relate to the functioning and performance of the US agricultural and food system.

Organization of chapter

We can use a straightforward approach to explore the multiple interfaces that link agriculture, natural resources, and the environment. We begin by introducing a theoretical model to guide our study. The model allows us to explore significant connections among economic and policy variables in a logical format. We can readily apply the model to analyze key scenarios. Equipped with an investigative method that is both consistent and practical, we address important considerations associated with:

- Stock and flow indicators of agricultural, environmental, and natural resources
- Land use and soil conservation indicators
- Agricultural and related influences on the economics of water use
- Agriculture's role in energy and climate change policies

We conclude by examining key trends in US natural resource, energy, and environmental policy.

A model for intertemporal analysis of agricultural, natural resource, and environmental relationships, and economic outcomes

Background and introduction for the analysis

Two American men of letters, Mark Twain and Will Rogers, are both known for this remark: "Buy land, they are not making any more of it."[7] In natural resource economics, their shared comment infers a fixed supply of land. Their observation further emphasizes that our planet has limited physical quantities of exhaustible natural resources. As the world's human population and global economy both grow, they tap into these natural resources. Logic seemingly dictates that ongoing economic growth will eventually deplete a fixed reservoir of natural productive inputs.

Economist John Krutilla, in his 1967 path-breaking article entitled "Conservation Reconsidered," reopened the question of how best to manage non-renewable natural resources to optimize net per-capita economic value for both current and future generations.[8] Krutilla's research and conclusions differ markedly from those of Thomas Malthus in 1798.[9]

Based on the science of his era, Malthus observed an imbalance: human populations were growing exponentially while food production increased arithmetically. Malthus predicted a grim future of global malnutrition, famine, and social unrest as agricultural output failed to keep pace with expanding human demands. But dramatic advances in technology, coupled with higher living standards and reduced population growth rates, changed the anticipated Malthusian calculus. Real market prices for quantities of raw material consistently *trended downward* throughout most of the twentieth century. As a result, Krutilla and most contemporary resource economists concluded that the direst Malthusian predictions were likely to remain unrealized.

However, Krutilla's research indicated that considerable challenges still lie ahead. He focused on ecological natural resource considerations, as well as the demanding economic conditions in less developed countries. Krutilla recognized that natural resources deliver value to the global economy on two levels:[10]

1) the market for naturally supplied quantities of physical productive inputs, and
2) the harder-to-measure benefits and costs of "ecological services" associated with natural and environmental systems.

Roughly speaking, Malthus examined questions on how a growing society manages the "quantity" of its natural resources, while Krutilla draws our attention to "resource quality."

Malthus predicted adverse future welfare effects as exhaustible resources (e.g. iron, copper, crude oil, etc.) were depleted. Thanks to the work of Krutilla and other dedicated professionals, the disciplines of natural resource and environmental economics emphasize that our future welfare also depends on natural quality-of-life conditions derived from the proper functioning of ecological systems (e.g. the benefits of biochemical and hydrologic cycles, genetic diversity, clean air and water, etc.).

Krutilla further noted that modern economies have a tendency to degrade the quality of the earth's ecological services by generating side effects such as environmental pollution. He also observed that the growing global economy could severely damage the sustainable carrying capacity of ecological systems (e.g. by ocean over-fishing, tropical forest deforestation, or generating record-setting and climate-altering carbon concentrations in the earth's atmosphere).

Krutilla applied the "option demand" concept, and extended the meaning of ecological services. He argued for economic mechanisms to properly appraise the worth of unique natural wonders (e.g. the Grand Canyon or Yellowstone Park). Just as there is a real demand to preserve historical sites (e.g. Gettysburg, Manassas), consumers are also "willing and able to pay" to reserve options to protect wildlife habitat, save endangered species, or safeguard prime agricultural land for future generations to experience and enjoy.[11]

Option demand similarly includes the preferences of consumers who seek to *maintain natural attributes in existence*, even if those consumers never personally use them. For example, a consumer may contribute funds to prevent the development of a wilderness area without ever expecting to actually visit the site itself.

Krutilla realized that ecological services often exhibit economic traits associated with *public goods and externalities*. As we learned in Chapter 3, competitive markets can fail to fully estimate values if goods are non-rival or non-excludable, or if they generate external market effects. Krutilla, along with other important contributors to the natural resource and environmental economics literature, recommend a range of private and public incentives to more fully integrate ecosystem-service values into natural resource decision making.

Assumptions and basic framework for the model

Using the above introduction as a foundation, we build an analytical approach to address questions that often arise when we consider the confluence of agriculture, natural resources, and the environment.

Although Krutilla and Malthus differ in their conclusions, they are both focused on common themes:

- How can society best allocate natural resources to meet intergenerational economic goals?
- Is it possible to achieve a sustainable relationship between global economic growth and the planet's scarce natural resources over time?

As we indicated earlier, a comprehensive approach to these global questions would easily occupy an entire course of study. Within the confines of single textbook chapter, we necessarily narrow our focus to core concepts of practical policy significance.

We will use the insightful microeconomic model of intertemporal choice to guide our study. This model is well suited to determining fundamental principles that are at the heart of properly managing natural resources over time. The concepts of resource substitutability, sustainability and environmental externalities are also incorporated into our analysis.

An Economic Model of Intertemporal Production and Consumption. The goal of creating a model of intertemporal choice is to identify the conditions for an optimal balance of present and future consumption and production.[12]

All economic modeling efforts require simplification to achieve a manageable analytical approach. We begin by assuming that individual households must make consumption and production decisions across two time periods: Now (Time 0), and in the Future (Time 1). The household's intertemporal welfare depends on how it balances the output and utility of a single product (V) over time, identified as V_0 and V_1. When the household is acting in its consumer role, it makes saving versus consumption decisions. When the household is engaged in production, the decision to sacrifice current consumption creates an opportunity to invest in and enhance future output.

We assume the household is a rational consumer. The household adjusts its choices between V_0 and V_1 to reach the highest indifference curve that is tangent to its intertemporal budget line. As a result, the rational household achieves optimum utility. The prevailing interest rate determines the budget line's slope, and also defines the trade off between saving and current consumption spending. The wealth position of the household budget line (HBL) is determined by efficient utilization of its intertemporal production function (IPF). See Figure 8.1.

When a household reduces consumption now, then the unconsumed quantity of the current product V_0 can be invested in its IPF as a capital input for generating additional amounts of the future product V_1. This production process is equivalent to a household not consuming a portion of its own soybeans, and planting the held-back beans to later harvest additional new soybeans at end of the growing season. We can use Figure 8.1 to examine the trade offs and the household's intertemporal optimization.

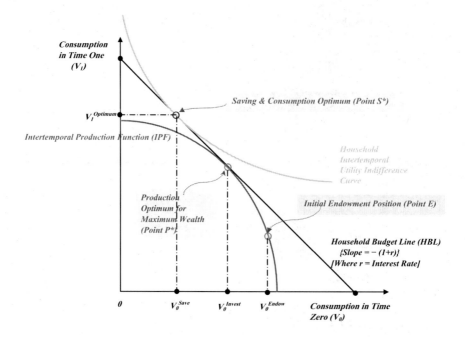

Figure 8.1 Intertemporal model of household consumption and production.

In Figure 8.1, we predict how a household, beginning from an initial endowment position (*Point E*), takes advantage of its own productive opportunities (*along the IPF Curve*) and the lend/borrow market opportunities (*along the HBL*) to achieve optimum wealth and consumer satisfaction outcomes.

Along the horizontal axis in Figure 8.1, the distance ($V_0^{Endow} - V_0^{Save}$) is the total amount that the household saves out its (V_0) initial endowment. Part of the saved (V_0) is invested in the household IPF, and the rest is loaned to the outside market at the going interest rate (r). The distance ($V_0^{Save} - 0$) is the amount of (V_0) that the household consumes now.

The distance ($V_0^{Endow} - V_0^{Invest}$) measures the amount of the household's saving that is invested using the IPF to produce additional quantities of V in Time 1. This investment enables the household to *maximize its wealth*, because as the household "slides along" its IPF (*moving from Point E to Point P**), the household equates its marginal rate of transformation (MRT) with the slope [– (1+r)] of the lend/borrow market (the IPF slope is tangent to the HBL slope). At this tangency (*at Point P**), the household is in the optimal position to participate in the lend/borrow market.

The distance ($V_0^{Invest} - V_0^{Save}$) is the amount of V_0 that the household lends to the market. As a market lender in Time 0, the household reaches a new optimal consumer wealth level (*at Point S**) in Time 1. At Point S*, the household's wealth is superior to what is available along its singular IPF.

We refer to the model displayed in Figure 8.1 to make relevant observations about managing products and natural resources over time. We review the results of intertemporal analysis in Figure 8.1, and note the following:

- To optimize their individual wealth position, rational households equate their IPF's marginal rate of transformation (MRT) to the slope [– (1+r)] of the HBL's lend/borrow market. When we interpret this result, we note that households have a natural and *rational market incentive to* **balance** *current and future consumption* to achieve maximum wealth and optimal consumer satisfaction.

- *The interest rate (r) influences household consumption, saving, and investment decisions in different ways.* For example, as the interest rate (r) increases, two important incentives are at work. *From a consumer perspective,* as (r) rises, future consumption values are discounted more heavily. Immediate consumption is favored.

    From a production standpoint, an increase in (r) motivates capital formation for increased production. This productive response is future oriented.

    What is the lesson? Any policy induced reduction or increase in the discount (interest) rate may not necessarily be the best method to balance the welfare of current and future generations. Interest rate changes "cut both ways."[13]

- *The model in Figure 8.1 assumes* **no** *market distortions exist.* The market interest rate and the household incentives to consume, invest, and save are determined in purely competitive markets.

    What happens when market externalities, public goods, market power, or other factors *drive a wedge between marginal social cost (MSC) and marginal private cost (MPC)?* A revised analysis will yield alternative results.

    Based on the realities of natural resource markets and the likelihood of market distortions mentioned earlier in this chapter, the model introduced in Figure 8.1 must be reexamined to incorporate market conditions that are less than perfect.

Market distortions and intertemporal household decisions

Agricultural production practices are associated with a variety of environmental side effects. For example, bee-keepers and orchard-growers have been managing their mutually beneficial inter-relationship ever since human society transitioned from hunter-gatherer migration to farm-based civilization.

But there are instances where specific agricultural practices create costly side effects. Crop cultivation on marginal lands can erode soils and generate non-point water pollution. Improper application of a pesticide often results in airborne-drift that damages neighboring ecosystems.

Normal competitive markets cannot always fully account for the costs of negative external effects (or the benefits of positive external effects). When farm methods are responsible for these externalities, then the economic consequences should be accurately analyzed.

There is a time dimension to market externalities, especially in the case of natural resource management. The side effects of current production (and/or consumption) activities can have real effects on the future ecosystem productivity. We can apply the model of intertemporal production and consumption to predict expected outcomes when externalities alter productivity over time.

Scenario One: external cost and intertemporal choice

Let's return to the intertemporal choice model in Figure 8.1. The pure market interest rate (r) measures the *market premium* of current versus future value. The current price (P_0) of access to *an extra product-unit now* $\{\Delta(V_0)\}$, can be compared to the consumer's future value

(P_1) of receiving the same marginal product *one time-period later* $\{\Delta(V_1)\}$. In simpler terms, a dollar in hand today is worth more than the same dollar offered to the household in the future. We can display this pure market relationship as:[14]

$$1 + r = (P_0) / (P_1) = -\Delta(V_1) / \Delta(V_0)$$

When a negative externality *in the current production period* causes ecosystem damage that reduces productivity *in the future period* (e.g. current farm practices that cause future watershed damage), then the private market interest rate *does not measure* all of the product's current social cost.

The negative market externality means that the *private market cost in Time Zero* (MPC_0) is less than the *full marginal social cost in Time Zero* (MSC_0). If we represent the extra-market cost with the symbol λ, then the market conditions are displayed in Figure 8.2 below, and as follows:[15]

> $MSC_0 > MPC_0$, *and* $MSC_0 = MPC_0 + \lambda$
>
> **Household Budget Line-Marginal Private Cost:** $1 + r = (P_0) / (P_1) = -\Delta(V_1) / \Delta(V_0)$
>
> **(HBL-MPC has a flatter slope)**
>
> **Household Budget Line-Marginal Social Cost:** $1 + r^* = (P_0 + \lambda) / (P_1) = -\Delta(V_1) / \Delta(V_0 - V_0^{\lambda})$
>
> **(HBL-MSC slope is steeper)**

In Figure 8.2, we predict results when the private market **cannot detect** *the extra production cost caused by a negative externality in Time 0.* Because the market cannot internalize the current external cost, the household encounters a budget line whose slope (interest rate r) is determined by the Marginal Private Cost (MPC) of production. In this scenario, the MPC is less than the Marginal Social Cost (MSC). The household incentive to save and consume is determined by a flatter-sloped HBL-MPC (see Figure 8.2) because the market interest rate cannot detect the external cost in Time 0. From the household viewpoint, the externality means that V_0 appears relatively less scarce than V_1.

Let's analyze movements along the horizontal axis in Figure 8.2. The distance $(V_0^{Endow} - V_0^{Invest})$ is the amount of commodity V_0 that the household invests in its IPF to maximize private wealth when the HBL-MPC budget line dominates. The distance $(V_0^{Endow} - V_0^{MPC})$ is a very modest amount of private saving; in this situation, private saving is less than productive investment. The household taps-into the savings of other persons in the economy to offset its own saving deficiency.

Under the influence of the MPC-generated interest rate, the household reduces its saving, consumes more, and borrows from the rest of society at the "cheaper" interest rate to finance its production. The distance $(V_0^{Invest} - 0)$ is the amount of (V_0) that the household currently consumes, and distance $(V_0^{MPC} - V_0^{Invest})$ is the amount of (V_0) that the household borrows from the general market to invest in its intertemporal production.

Scenario Two: internalized external cost and intertemporal choice

In Scenario 1, production of Commodity V_0 was accompanied by an external cost (e.g. non-point pollution) that the market could not internalize. Nobel Laureate Ronald

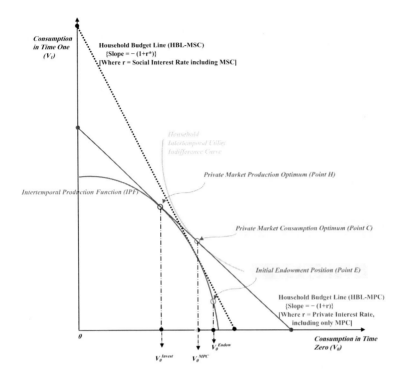

Figure 8.2 Predicted intertemporal choice when an external cost influences household production of V_0.

Coase persuasively argued that externalities are often not internalized because property rights in natural resources (and other resources) are not adequately defined.[16] Following the Coase logic, let's assume a change in institutional structure causes property rights in V_0 to be clarified. A market internalization of external costs occurs. What consequences can we expect?

In Figure 8.3, we predict results when institutional innovation allows for transparency in the assignment of property rights. Under the new arrangement, the private market detects (internalizes) the extra production cost caused by a negative externality in Time 0.

At this juncture, we introduce a simplifying assumption: property rights are assigned equitably in a manner acceptable to all parties. While this assumption is tenuous at best, it allows us to move forward with the scenario analysis.

Compared to the outcome in Figure 8.2, the scenario in Figure 8.3 reveals a different set of final results (i.e. in terms of resource use and production management). An institutional innovation enables the market to internalize the negative externality in Time 0. The market is empowered to take into account the previously-external cost.

With property rights clearly delineated, the household utilizes a budget line whose slope (interest rate r^*) is determined by the Marginal Social Cost (MSC) of production. In this scenario, MPC + λ = MSC. The household incentive to save and consume is determined by

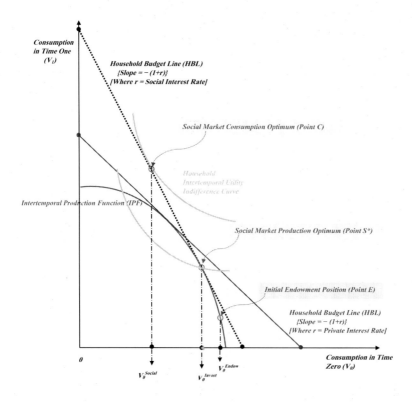

Figure 8.3 Intertemporal choice model of household consumption and production when an external cost is fully internalized in Period 0.

the steeper-sloped HBL-MSC because the market interest rate includes the external cost of producing commodity V in Time 0. From the household viewpoint, the V_0 is now "scarcer" compared to when the MPC determined opportunity cost. The household is encouraged to economize on its volume of V_0 use. See Figure 8.3

Referring to Figure 8.3, we predict results when an institutional innovation internalizes a negative productive externality. *Because the market now bears the full cost of the formerly-external damage, the household encounters the HBL-MSC budget line.* The HBL-MSC has a slope (interest rate r^*) that is determined by the Marginal Social Cost (MSC) of production. The MSC is greater than the Marginal Private Cost (MPC). The household incentive to save and consume is determined by a steeper-sloped HBL-MSC.

Let's analyze movements along the horizontal axis in Figure 8.3. The distance $(V_0^{Endow} - V_0^{Social})$ is the amount of commodity V that the household saves in total. The distance $(V_0^{Invest} - V_0^{Social})$ is the amount of *household private lending*; now, private saving *is more than* household productive investment. The household is satisfying the borrowing needs of other persons (and receiving the higher r^* in return) in the economy to fully utilize its household saving volume. The distance $(V_0^{Social} - 0)$ is the amount of (V_0) that the household currently consumes.

Intertemporal analysis: summary and conclusions

Our model of intertemporal choice logically organizes key variables that influence production and consumption decisions, now and in the future. Let's summarize the economic principles from this analysis:

- Rational, *optimizing decision makers respond to market opportunity cost*, such as the interest rate, as they manage products and resources over multiple time periods.
- *Households participate in intertemporal markets as both producers and consumers.* Price and interest rate changes are expected to not only alter household saving or borrowing behaviors, but the incentive for capital investment.
- *The presence or absence of market distortions matters.* If current external costs cannot be internalized, households will encounter misdirected incentives to save less, invest less, and consume more.
- Intertemporal markets may require *institutional innovations or improved public policies* to remove or mitigate the inefficient outcomes associated with market distortions.

Intertemporal choice and the challenges of sustainable development

Equipped with the microeconomic foundations of intertemporal choice, we can re-examine the scarcity and growth questions that were mentioned earlier in this chapter.

Important new issues arise if we *extend the model of household intertemporal choice to a societal level.* When this inquiry is placed on a global scale, the challenge is to seek the proper intertemporal balance of world economic growth in relation to the earth's ecological capacity to sustain growth.

In 1983, the United Nations (UN) established the World Commission on Environment and Development (WCED) to research the conditions for sustainable global economic growth. Norway's former prime minister, Gro Harlem Brundtland, chaired the WCED. After four years of study, the WCED published a document entitled, "Our Common Future." [17] The WCED's set of recommendations is commonly known today as the "Brundtland Commission Report." Formal definition and investigation of the term "Sustainable Development" is credited to the work of the Brundtland Commission.

Let's review the Brundtland Commission's definition: Sustainable Development is "meeting the needs of the present without compromising the ability of future generations to meet their own needs" (WCED 1987). [18] Our microeconomic intertemporal model is certainly congruent with the view that current and future decisions must be balanced to achieve optimum results.

Other economic models are also compatible with Brundtland's description of sustainable development. Barbier (2003), Krautkraemer (2005), and Bergstrom and Randall (2010), draw parallels between WCED's view of sustainability and the theoretical conditions of balanced per-capita economic growth. [19, 20, 21] From the perspective of economic rationality, the per-person welfare of the next generation should be no worse off than that of the current generation.

While economic growth theory and sustainable development research share commonalities, it is important to understand that controversy is not absent. There are important disagreements about the nature of the growth challenges that lie ahead. The unresolved questions and the differing viewpoints about sustainability trends mean that this subject is wide open for additional study and discussion.

While there are many worthy topics to investigate under the heading of "scarcity and growth," let's examine two opposing viewpoints:[22]

- Weak Sustainability (alternatively identified as strong resource substitutability)
- Strong Sustainability (a.k.a. weak or inelastic resource substitutability)

We encounter two vastly different perspectives on the global economy's future welfare when we discuss the "weak" and "strong" sustainability hypotheses.

Weak sustainability

The term "weak sustainability" actually translates into a relatively *optimistic view* of the global economic future. From an economic theory standpoint, weak sustainability means that a manager can *easily substitute one resource input for another* within a production function. In technical terms, the absolute value of the elasticity of input substitution is greater than one. Further, the weak sustainability premise argues that it is the total sum of all sources of capital that matters for future growth, not the individual scarcity of any one input. Capital is broadly defined to include natural resources, human resources, and physical capital (equipment, facilities, etc.)

To be clear, weak sustainability "weakly depends" on the availability of any one resource. No input, including natural resource capital, is essential to continued growth. Instead, given the correct market signals, producers use more of one resource and less of another to efficiently reach an output goal. Weak sustainability, if it is an accurate explanation of how production works, implies a brighter global future for continued and sustainable economic growth. Exhaustible natural resource deposits can be depleted, but economic growth continues, because producers substitute less scarce alternative resources to replace the scarcer and exhausted natural supplies.

Strong sustainability

If the empirical evidence supports the strong sustainability hypothesis, then we have a more *pessimistic projection* for global economic growth. The fundamental premise of strong sustainability is that resource inputs, particularly natural resources and ecological carrying capacity, are unique and essential to sustainable development. As contrasted with the weak sustainability hypothesis, producers *encounter resource inputs that are complements, not substitutes.* In technical terms, the absolute value of the elasticity of input substitution is less than one. Strong sustainability "strongly depends" on the continued presence and productive quality of each individual resource.

Whenever the strong sustainability hypothesis is the most accurate interpretation of the production process, then sustainable development is not attainable in the traditional sense. Eventually, if current economic growth depletes natural non-renewable inputs, or is responsible for irreversible damage to ecosystem carrying capacity, then future generations will face reduced welfare relative to current consumers and producers.

Alternative perspectives on strong versus weak sustainability

Empirical evidence for weak or strong sustainability is currently mixed. Rather than emphasize sustainability as a dichotomy of weak or strong, Turner (1993) introduces broad criteria to create a four-phase continuum that ranges from very weak to very strong.[23] Christianson and Tyndall (2011) utilize Turner's spectrum to consider how the implementation of innovative and specific agricultural technologies could cause any one of the four sustainability phases to be realized. The particular sustainability outcome would depend on the interaction between the technology and the natural environment.[24]

Neumayer (2004), Pezzey and Toman (2005), and Bergstrom and Randall (2010) emphasize the importance of both *theoretical* and *empirical* sustainability research to establish a broad-minded and objective approach that can address areas of persistent disagreement and controversy.[25, 26, 27]

For example, Pezzey and Toman (2005) propose that we specify and estimate alternative mathematical production functions to test for input substitutability limits under a variety of assumptions about output levels, technologies, ecological capacity constraints, and related conditions.[28] Bergstrom and Randall (2010) recommend approaches to sustainability research that account for intergenerational markets, technological uncertainty, and a reversibility-irreversibility continuum.[29]

Bergstrom and Randall (2010) also propose Cost-Benefit Analysis (CBA) as a more pragmatic means to evaluate the usefulness of policy recommendations when intertemporal decisions are required. The CBA method of determining maximum net present value (*rationally comparing current costs to future benefits*) to make investment decisions offers a practical basis for making intertemporal choices. [30]

Randall and Farmer (1995, 2010) suggest an alternative decision-making method known as the "Safe Minimum Standard" (SMS).[31, 32] In comparison to conventional CBA, the SMS approach provides a decision-making tool that can adjust current resource usage rates to account for uncertainty, very long time horizons and irreversibility. SMS offers guidelines to avoid costly and irreversible changes in ecosystem support capacity while providing a buffer for renewable resources to regenerate their life-supporting potentials.

Overview of the Sustainability Discussion. Intertemporal choice lies at the heart of the sustainability debate. Seeking a proper balance between today's decisions and tomorrow's welfare is an important undertaking.

If there is a neutral position within the weak versus strong sustainability discussion, it centers on continued efforts to perform science-based research in this field of study. There are plenty of meaningful questions to pursue.

We can take a normative stance in this instance. We should continue efforts to build up our knowledge base, and ultimately improve our ability to recommend policies and institutional innovations capable of properly balancing the needs of a growing economy and the capacity of our ecological systems to sustain that growth.

Interpreting empirical trends in US agricultural resource utilization and conservation

Intertemporal choice analysis and sustainable growth theory offer a framework to ask additional questions and organize relevant information. We can now move ahead by assembling and interpreting the empirical evidence.

What conclusions can we reach about the state of our agricultural, natural, and environmental resources, when we examine actual measurements about current and expected future conditions? Is there measurable progress being made as a result of conservation programs and the use of new technologies?

To properly answer these questions, we need an integrated approach to interpret the data. We need to objectively assess the current and future status of our economic and ecological systems.

Fortunately, we do not have to "start from scratch." Solid research has already been done to empirically assess the state of our resources. In 1993, Carlson, Zilberman, and Miranowski edited a comprehensive and integrative text to guide professional empirical research on agricultural and environmental resource economics. Similarly, Simpson, Toman, and Ayres (2005) offered an extensive twenty-first-century update to Barnett and Morse's classic study of scarcity and growth in 1963.

The USDA's Economic Research Service (ERS) and Natural Resources Conservation Service (NRCS) both have done yeoman's work in conducting, organizing, and publishing an impressive record of professional research in the applied areas of agricultural, natural resource, and environmental economics. Another important information source is the National Agricultural Statistics Service (NASS). NASS conducts the US Census of Agriculture, as well as providing wealth of information on production, commodity prices, farm labor and wages, producer demographics, and many other important agriculturally related variables.

Stocks and flows: measuring agricultural resource capacity and environmental quality

As noted in Chapter 2 of this text, the modern consumer has high expectations. Food providers must offer proof of where and how their products are produced. The demand for transparency extends to accurately reporting the natural resource and environmental side effects associated with agricultural production, as well as any externalities originating with the food/feed/fuel marketing supply chain.

One response to this consumer call for "evidence of what the food system actually does" is to regularly compile and publish a series of "resource indicators" that consistently track the resource conditions over time. For more than twenty years, the USDA's ERS and the Organization for Economic Co-operation and Development (OECD) are two agencies who assemble periodic publications to report and interpret *agricultural and environmental indicators*.

The USDA's ERS organizes its "Indicators Bulletin" into farm-related major resource categories, including land use, agricultural productivity, and agricultural production management and conservation policies.

The OECD report is focused on areas such as air and *water quality, biological diversity, forest and fish resources, and municipal waste*. The two reports have some overlap, but taken together, they offer a "status update" on the condition of a fairly wide spectrum of agricultural and environmental resource variables.

We can build a logical connection between the ERS/OECD empirical indicators and the model of intertemporal choice introduced earlier in this chapter. One important aspect of the ERS and OECD reports is the commitment to regularly measure and report changes in the indicator values over time.

Intertemporal choice theory is specifically designed to examine how current choices affect future resource allocations, output amounts, and utility levels. What happens in Time 0 is related to the observable end results in Time 1. As we monitor resource conditions now and in the future, we can differentiate between the "stocks and flows."

A *stock value* is the total value or amount of a resource at one point in time. In contrast, a *flow value* indicates a variable measured per unit time.

To distinguish stocks and flows, let's consider an agricultural scenario. If the results of a recent soil fertility test indicate that a particular field is currently rich in nitrogen and phosphorus, but is short of potassium, then we have a measure of soil's "stock" fertility values.

If, prior to planting a crop, a farm manager crosses the field to apply potassium, and later there is also the normal nutrient uptake to grow the crop, then we have both inflows and outflows to soil fertility occurring during the growing season. To be clear, inflows increase the future soil fertility stock value, while outflows decrease the future stock.

Adapting a visual model developed at the Tufts University's Global Development and Environment (GDAE) Institute, we can organize the agricultural/environmental stocks and flows to display the important intertemporal connections between supply/demand activities now and in the future (see Figure 8.4).

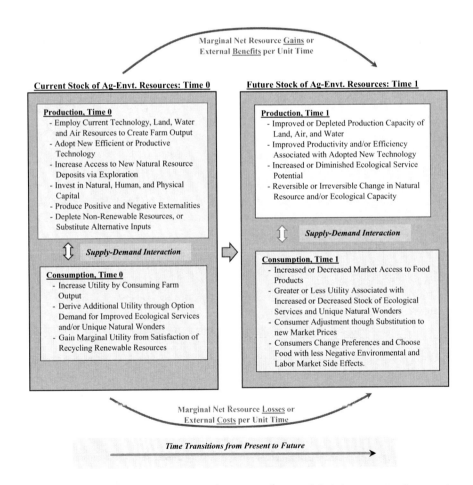

Figure 8.4 Producer and consumer market interactions, and their intertemporal connections to agricultural/environmental stocks and flows, Now (Time 0) and in the Future (Time 1).[33]

In Figure 8.4, *current* production and consumption practices in Time 0 generate flow variables that either augment or diminish the *future* quality or stock value of agricultural, natural resource, and environmental resources in Time 1. We can use Figure 8.4 as a guide for observing and interpreting the trends in resource stocks and flows as reflected in the published ERS/OECD indicators.

Land use and soil conservation indicators

The 2012 ERS Report noted that agricultural-related land uses accounted for about 51 percent of the US's total area of 2.26 billion acres. During 1959 to 2007, US agricultural land use (defined as cropping, grazing (pasture and range), farmsteads, and farm road acreages), *decreased* by approximately 66.56 million acres [M-Acres].[34] This change in farmland use amounts to 6.06 percent acreage decline over 48 years. At the same time, US urban areas *expanded* by about 33.3 M-Acres, or 122.5 percent.[35]

While these acreage numbers seemingly raise a red flag about the future of agricultural production, it is important to recognize that production is a multi-input enterprise. *Farm output is not just a function of how* **extensively** *we utilize the land resource, but it also encompasses* **land use intensity**. Land is obviously an essential agricultural resource. A farm manager generates output by combining each acre with other key inputs, such as labor, physical capital, managerial skill and the adoption of new productivity enhancing technologies.

In its 2012 Agricultural and Environmental Indicators research bulletin, the ERS documents *total US farm output in 2009 as 170 percent greater than in 1948*. Total agricultural input usage increased by only 0.11 percent. The ERS highlights increased farm productivity. These are impressive output gains, averaging a 1.52 percent-per-year increase in Total Factor Productivity [TFP].[36] Technology adoption and increased producer managerial skills play a large role in realizing these productivity advances (i.e. increases in output per unit input).

Another point to remember is that alternative land uses regularly compete for the available acreages. For example, flexibility in switching between crop and pasture allows land uses to fluctuate back and forth. Changing market incentives are often a strong reason for reallocating land uses.

As noted earlier in this chapter, not all changes in land use are reversible. At the urban/rural interface, any farmland converted to intense residential or industrial purposes will rarely return to agricultural use. At this chapter's opening, we noted that it takes moral commitment and real determination to preserve prime agricultural soils from the economic pressures of urban development.

Intensity of land use is also associated with the risk of external effects, such as non-point pollution, excessive nutrient leaching and soil erosion. What evidence do we have about these broader environmental concerns? The data we have indicates that the US is making progress in conserving our stock of natural resources, but there is room for improvement.

The USDA's Natural Resources Conservation Service (NRCS) compiles a *national inventory of soil and water resources*. In April 2010, NRCS reported that between 1982 and 2007, rates of US wind- and water-borne soil erosion were noticeably *lower*. NRCS *cites an* **overall 43 percent reduction in cropland erosion**. Farm owners, operators, conservation officers, and a variety of other participants cooperated to make this result happen, even as farmland production output rose.[37]

In 1982, nearly 169 M-Acres were eroding at above-sustainable rates. By 2007, efforts had *reduced* the number to 99 M-Acres of above-tolerance (T) soil erosive rates. On lands that are classified as highly erodible, erosion rates above the T-level had fallen to 54 M-Acres in 2007, as compared to 84 M-Acres in 1982.[38]

From the standpoint of soil conservation, and of passing along sustainable productive resources to the next generation, the dramatic *drop in the soil erosion rate is a real intertemporal benefit.* On the other hand, close to 100 M-Acres continue to erode at rates that diminish the soil's natural resource stock available for future users. Ongoing efforts to encourage additional conservation gains continue to be a worthwhile endeavor.

Reductions in water- and wind-borne soil erosion not only help retain the land's stock value of farm productivity, they also have beneficial environmental effects. Less erosion mitigates the siltation of watersheds and waterways. *Decreased sheet and rill soil erosion means less turbidity in streams and lakes, and therefore improves ecological capacity, dissolved oxygen and overall quality of freshwater systems.* Less wind erosion reduces the threat of dust storms, and diminishes the adverse impacts of excessive airborne dust particles on the efficiency of machinery, HVAC systems, and facility maintenance.[39]

Participation in soil conservation programs

Taking into account the favorable productivity and environmental effects of proper soil management, the value of USDA soil and water conservation programs is clear. The Natural Resources Conservation Service (NRCS), along with USDA's Farm Service Agency (FSA) administer most of the federal programs that have played a role in the reported and sizable drops in soil erosion rates. Much, but not all, of the funding for NRCS and FSA conservation programs is tied to farm bill authorizations.

Voluntary participation characterizes the design of most federal conservation programs. However, to prevent intensive farm practices from creating excessive erosion on highly erodible or environmentally sensitive lands, farmer eligibility to receive payments from USDA commodity programs is contingent on a farmer adhering to an approved conservation plan. "Cross-compliance" is the name given to the conservation requirement that is connected to receiving financial benefits from other farm programs. In the 2014 Farm Bill, the cross-compliance policy for environmentally sensitive lands was also incorporated into the subsidized Federal Crop Insurance program.[40]

Cross-compliance is noteworthy as a mechanism to directly tie conservation goals to the farm safety net. In comparison, the natural resource impact of USDA's voluntary conservation programs often have greater visible impacts than cross-compliance because the land areas of these elective efforts are measured in many millions of enrolled acres.

Based on the funded conservation programs in the 2014 Farm Bill, we identify four important types of voluntary programs: *land retirement, working lands, easements,* and *regional partnerships.* A more detailed examination of these four areas offers insights into the far-reaching effects of voluntary agricultural conservation policies:

(1) Land retirement programs

In 2016, the FSA-managed and funded Conservation Reserve Program (CRP) allows producers to voluntarily enroll up to 24 M-acres of authorized and qualified farmland. CRP sets up 10- or 15-year contracts to establish native prairie, pollinator-meadow acreages, and/or wildlife habitat on lands that are highly erodible, marginal pasture, or ecologically significant grasslands or wetlands.[41]

There are two CRP sub-programs making measurable and beneficial impacts on environmental quality and future land productivity: the Conservation Reserve and Enhancement Program (CREP) and the Farmable Wetland Program (FWP).[42]

CREP is a team effort of both federal and state conservation programs. CREP is narrower in its scope – the focus is on solving agriculturally related environmental problems. CREP has produced environmental improvement in the Florida's Everglades, Maryland's Chesapeake Bay, and along the Mississippi River Watershed in Southeast Minnesota. Producer sign-ups in CREP are continuous (year-round), and the approved projects are generally awarded larger financial incentives than the CRP provides alone.

Producers join the FWP by enrolling farmable or previously converted wetlands into CRP. Landowners restore wetland hydrology, create vegetative cover and inhibit development. There are specific criteria that must be met if land is to enter the FWP program.

CRP is classified as a *temporary land retirement program*. As a CRP participant, a producer ceases active crop production and introduces an approved conservation system in exchange for receiving an annual government payment. As of February 2016, 23.6 M-acres were already enrolled in the program, and additional CRP demand is anticipated. Based on the trends, it is likely the full 24 M-acres of available CRP will be enrolled.

(2) Working Lands Programs

The Working Lands Programs constitute another large-scale and voluntary approach to encouraging soil and water conservation. Based on Congressional Research Service budget estimates, the 2014 Farm Bill increases the funding of Working Lands Programs while downsizing CRP funding (in comparison with preceding farm bills).

Working Lands Programs offer guidance and financial support for producers to introduce conservation methods while they continue to actively raise crops and/or engage in farm production. The *Environmental Quality Incentives Program (EQIP)* and the *Conservation Stewardship Program (CSP)* are two dominant Working Lands Programs.[43]

EQIP. Producers annually compete for limited EQIP program funds that offer cost sharing to implement conservation projects. EQIP conservation practices are tailored to county-level or regional resource needs. For example, an EQIP project could be used to address the resource concerns of a soil and water conservation district, such as livestock production limitations, damaged plant conditions, water quality degradation, and/or susceptibility to sheet-and-rill water-borne soil erosion.

In an effort to tackle difficult resource challenges and spark advances in conservation technology and cooperation, the 2014 Farm Bill reauthorized the *Conservation Innovation Grants (CIG) program*. CIG was incorporated into EQIP. CIG leverages federal investment to create new initiatives in environmental protection, agricultural production, and forest management.

EQIP is particularly designed to assist producers who seek to initiate a first-time officially recognized conservation system on their farms. EQIP is available throughout the US, and EQIP contracts encompassed 11.2 million acres in Fiscal Year (FY) 2014.[44]

CSP. The Conservation Stewardship Program encourages the *continuation and improvement of* producers' existing conservation systems. A producer must "pre-qualify" to become a CSP participant. Under the 2014 Farm Bill, he/she must have previously tackled at least two resource challenges, and also agree to concentrate on at least one more priority concern during the 5-year span of a CSP contract. Also, CSP is an incentive-based pay-for-performance program. When a CSP producer achieves additional and measurable conservation outcomes, then the CSP payment increases too.

Similar to EQIP, CSP is offered throughout the nation. Initial CSP sign-up began in 2009; by the end of FY2014, producers had enrolled over 67 M-acres. Under the 2014 Farm Bill, there is funding to increase CSP participation up to an additional 10 M-acres per year. [45]

Additional Working Lands Programs. The 2014 Farm Bill also modified the smaller-scale Working Lands Programs. To achieve increased administrative efficiency, the Agricultural Water Enhancement Program (AWEP) and the Wildlife Habitat Incentives Program (WHIP) were rescinded, and their components were folded into other USDA conservation programs. AWEP became part of the Regional Conservation Partnership Program (RCPP), and WHIP is now included within EQIP.

The Agricultural Management Assistance (AMA) program is one additional Working Lands Program that is coordinated with Federal Crop Insurance. AMA is only offered in sixteen states where crop insurance sign-up is deficient. The AMA program is an effort to increase producer incentives to participate in both conservation and multi-peril crop insurance.[46]

(3) Easements

The 2014 Farm Bill created the *Agricultural Conservation Easement Program (ACEP)* largely by renaming and consolidating similar programs from previous farm bills. The former Farmland Protection Program, Grassland Reserve Program, and Wetlands Reserve Program were all repealed and redefined under ACEP. Easement funding for ACEP is now divided into two major areas, identified as:[47]

i   *Agricultural Land Easements (ALE)* – purchase development rights for non-agricultural uses, or

ii   *Wetland Reserve Easements (WRE)* – purchase rights to restore and preserve wetlands.

ALE and WRE both contain largely the same general contract language, including exchange and compliance requirements. ACEP is a national program, and it was used to help preserve about 143,833 acres of farmland, grassland, and wetlands in FY2014.

In contrast to the more temporary nature of CRP, ACEP is a *permanent land retirement program.* A landowner receives a payment that "buys out" development rights. As urban expansion continues relatively unabated, the ACEP program is one mechanism to preserve prime farmland from irreversible conversion to another use.

(4) Regional partnerships

Program consolidation under the 2014 Farm Bill also affected the "Other" category of funded Conservation Programs. The newly created *Regional Conservation Partnership Program (RCPP)* is the result of combining elements from the following repealed programs: Chesapeake Bay Watershed, Cooperative Conservation Partnership Initiative, Great Lakes Basin, and Agricultural Water Enhancement Programs.[48]

Under RCPP, 5-year Regional Conservation Partnership agreements determine the project area and the types of available assistance. Regional partners shoulder a substantial percent of the total project cost, thereby leveraging federal and local financial resources. The NRCS channels the federal RCPP funds through Critical Conservation Areas.

There are federal conservation programs that are **not** *directly authorized via 2014 Farm Bill Funding*. We can briefly summarize these programs:[49]

(1) *Emergency Programs* – Congress periodically approves supplemental appropriations to offer disaster funds to rehabilitate farmlands and watersheds damaged by infrequent catastrophic events (e.g. hurricanes, earthquakes, etc.). The Emergency Conservation Program (ECP), the Emergency Watershed Protection (EWP) program, and the Emergency Forest Restoration Program (EFRP) are examples.
(2) *Technical Assistance Programs* – Often on a fee-for-service basis, USDA can offer producers science-based and technical expertise. Conservation Operations include soil surveys and plant-materials analysis centers.
(3) *Watershed Programs* – NRCS joins with local governments and organizations to rehabilitate watersheds, dams, and related flood structures to achieve goals for soil and water conservation, improved resource utilization, and flood prevention. In these instances, NRCS operates under the authority of Public Law 534 (1944 Flood Control Act) and Public Law 566 (1954 Watershed and Flood Prevention Act).

Summary: land use and soil conservation indicators

Previously in Figure 8.4, we considered the interaction between the "flows and stocks" of our natural resources. In the case of our soil and land resources, we can make some important observations:

- The US is endowed with a stock of *extensive land area* (2.3 billion acres), and just over half is in agricultural use. While agricultural land area decreased over the past 50 years, *land intensity* and agricultural technology increased, resulting in a 170 percent increase in farm output.
- Farm landowners, producers and conservation agencies combined their efforts *to reduce soil erosion rates by 43 percent* over the past quarter century. Soil amendments are a net inflow to the stock value and quality of our soil resources. More improvement is needed as nearly *100 M-acres continue to lose soil above the sustainable T rate.*
- Included in the 2014 Farm Bill, and in other legislation, are a range of *voluntary and cross-compliance conservation programs* offering assistance to reduce erosion, improve soil quality and decrease the negative side effects of soil erosion and non-point pollution. Some agricultural practices reduce the stock value of our natural resources. On the other hand, there are opportunities and funding sources to create inflows, and increase our stock of natural resources.

Related agricultural resource indicators

The ERS Resource Indicators Bulletin (2012), in addition to tracking land use and soil conservation, also examines the status of agricultural research and development, production technology, pesticide use, fertilizer demand, and irrigation efficiency.[50]

- *Agricultural Research and Development (R&D)* – Total US agricultural R&D spending is comprised of both private and public components. Private sector R&D funding accelerated after the year 2000, and continues to do so. Private sector R&D is now larger than US public sector agricultural R&D. The combined total (private + public) shows a net increase over the past 15 years. Public R&D spending has been variable. The 2014 Farm Bill introduced a modest increase in Public R&D funding. Private sector R&D mostly enhances marketable products, while public sector's R&D focus is on basic research. Public R&D primarily aims to generate new knowledge in areas such as health, safety, nutrition, and environmental effects.

- *Production Technology and Pesticide Use* – Advances in bio-technology since 1996 have created genetically engineered (GE) herbicide-tolerant and insect-resistant varieties of corn, cotton, and soybeans. The vast majority of US soybean, corn, and cotton producers have adopted GE varieties because of increased yields, reduced pesticide applications and costs, and improved time management. There has been an increase in herbicide use, and unfortunately, an adverse consequence is a worrisome increase in weed resistance to glyphosate and related herbicides.
- *Fertilizer Demand* – Increased fertilizer prices, coupled with more efficient precision agriculture technologies, contributed to decreased producer fertilizer demand. In addition, the amount of nitrogen fertilizer removed by the crop as a percent of nitrogen applied improved (this is a net gain in nitrogen recovery rates). Nevertheless, nearly 47 percent of corn production is associated with excess nitrogen application. Similar to other US resource-use levels, gains in environmentally beneficial results are occurring, but the results remain a work-in-progress.
- *Irrigation Efficiency* – Enhanced water-use efficiency, combined with changes in regional cropping patterns, produced an impressive result: water applied fell by nearly 100,000 acre-feet as irrigated acres in the western US increased by 2.1 million acres.

OECD environmental indicators

OECD is comprised of 34 member nations, including the US. OECD's reach extends to both advanced and emerging economies throughout the world.[51] The OECD Publication, "Environment at a Glance – 2015," offers a snapshot of natural resource and ecological conditions within the OECD membership, as well as additional global estimates.[52]

Comparing the 2015 indicators to a Year 2000 baseline, the OECD's assessment of changes in the stocks and flows of our environment is similar to the conclusion reached in the USDA-ERS bulletin on agricultural and environmental indicators. Progress is happening, but more effort is still needed.

The reported environment indicators suggest that OECD member nations have *made gains* in reducing atmospheric emissions, increasing fuel efficiency, expanding renewable energy, protecting biodiversity, and improving water-use efficiency.

Simultaneously, the report clearly reveals that while OECD countries have reduced greenhouse gas (GHG) emissions *[a flow value], the OECD countries begin from a current GHG level (9.6 tons/person) [a stock value], that is 2.82 times greater than the GHG level (3.4 tons/person) in the rest of the world.*

The 2015 OECD study emphasizes that *climate change likely represents the most severe threat to the stability of global and local ecosystems.* Irreversible and undesirable changes are predicted. Global GHG emissions are currently expected to change atmospheric concentrations to a level that is nearly three times higher than the CO_2 levels needed to increase the average global temperature by two degrees Centigrade.

With respect to the interactions with agriculture, the OECD study notes that improvements in nutrient uptake and precision applications are associated with a 9 percent drop in phosphate fertilizer use, a 12 percent rise in nitrogenous fertilizer demand, and an increase in total OECD agriculture production by 3 percent between 2000 and 2015. Similarly to the US, OECD *nations experienced a net decrease in agricultural land use, accompanied by an increase in output per acre.* Urban and forestland uses expanded as farmland acres dropped. OECD also noted that organic farming accounts for just 2 percent of total OECD production; organic farming in the European Union is noticeably higher at about 10 percent because of special incentives offered to EU farmers to convert from traditional methods.

Summary and policy considerations

Our purpose in reviewing agricultural and environmental indicators is to use empirical evidence as a basis for assessing the current state of our natural resources. Both the ERS and the OECD arrive at similar conclusions. *The US and other economies are **making progress** in generating beneficial "resource flows" that influence the "stock condition" of our environment. Both agencies also observe that considerably **more gains are needed** to reach stock value levels consistent with long-term sustainability.*

The resource conservation progress achieved thus far is an indication that current successful policies should continue. For example, conservation program funding is included under Title II in the 2014 Farm Bill. When we evaluate the content of Title II funding, our perspective can be compared to the analogy of whether "the cup is half-empty or half-full."

Let's examine the pessimist's viewpoint first. Compared with the 2008 Farm Bill, the *2014 legislation reduced overall budgetary allocations for federal conservation programs.* The maximum total CRP acreage under the 2014 Agricultural Act decreases from 32 M-acres to 24 M-acres. Two primary forces were responsible for this CRP reduction: (1) market forces motivated many producers to non-renew their CRP contracts as crop cultivation became more profitable, and (2) conservation was subjected to "sequestration" and related pressures on Congress to reduce overall federal spending. Budget austerity and streamlining are largely responsible for the 2014 Farm Bill's conservation spending projection to fall by $208 million between 2014 and 2018.

On the other hand, maybe the glass is "half-full." *In the context of the entire 2014 Farm Bill, conservation spending (at 6 percent of the Farm Bill Budget)* is still the third-largest category, after nutrition and crop insurance. The Congressional Budget Office's 5-year forecast that conservation spending will be $28.3 billon means that the 2014–2018 budget will only be ~1 percent below the original 2008 baseline projection. Another observation is that not all conservation programs are expected to diminish. Instead, as CRP acreages drop down to about 24 M-acres, funding is available for producers to add working lands into the EQIP and CSP programs.

To the extent that ongoing conservation programs create agronomic and environmental benefits, continuation of the "farm bill approach" is worthwhile:

- Establish a largely voluntary system, supplemented by cross-compliance requirements
- Offer financial support and incentives to actively engage in conservation practices
- Provide technical expertise when requested

- Engage in educational efforts to facilitate the development and implementation of conservation projects
- Conduct research to advance knowledge, and provide avenues for practical application

One area of caution that remains is the realized and potential irreversible environmental damage associated with the release of GHGs into the earth's atmosphere. Agriculture's impact in this area can either be beneficial or costly. As we look to the future, there are some important policy considerations on what incentives can or should be created within agriculture to help reduce or avoid the most serious ecological consequences connected with climate change. We will address some of these concerns later in this chapter.

Our above discussion has placed considerable emphasis on land-related issues: acreage allocations, erosion, land-use intensity, and externalities. The disciplines of ecology and economics both tell us that all actions in the environment are interrelated. Two key resources definitely tied to land use are water and energy. We next turn our attention to these critical areas.

Agricultural and related influences on the economics of water use

Every natural resource has at least one unique characteristic that strongly shapes its economic value. Land, as we have seen, is a mostly stationary, versatile and highly productive input that exhibits both stock and flow values. In comparison, water is a largely mobile natural resource. Water in a lake might seem stable, but it is simply one part of the constantly changing global hydrologic cycle. Antarctic or arctic ice can immobilize water, but only if temperatures stay below the freezing point.

Earth is a watery planet; seventy-one percent is covered with water.[53] Water is essential to human life, as well as to the survival of nearly all earth's inhabitants. In comparison to other valued natural resources, water use uniquely generates complex interconnections among economic, agricultural, ecological, and physical phenomena. Clearly, water-use decisions often play a key role in determining the welfare of our environment, society, and economy. It is little wonder that we consider water to be a natural resource worthy of special attention.

This textbook is a vehicle to examine resource use from the perspective of agricultural and food policy and its effects on economic participants. The study of water-use economics is quite broad, and extends well beyond the trends in our agri-food system. We necessarily narrow our focus to our targeted goals, while recognizing that this knowledge area is vast and involves many interrelated considerations.

Water use and the agri-food system

Market analysis offers a logical framework to guide a review of the agri-food system's key water-use economic attributes and trends. We organize our effort as follows:

- Elements of water demand in the agri-food system.
- Alternative water supply sources for the agri-food system.
- Market externalities and water quality considerations associated with the agri-system.

- Non-point pollution and the controversy over the "Waters of the United States (WOTUS)" interpretative rule.
- Summary of water policy issues.

Water demand

The agri-food system's water demand derives from water's value as a productive input. In production agriculture, the primary water uses include crop irrigation, livestock watering requirements, and aquaculture. Also, within the supply chain, additional water demands stem from food processing and food safety procedures; these water needs are mostly calculated within the industrial water uses category. Some food-related water demands (restaurants, etc.) access the public water supply. The United States Geological Survey (USGS) periodically collects water use data, catalogues it, and then publishes an all-inclusive inventory. Results of the USGS 2010 comprehensive survey were reported in 2014.[54] In Figure 8.5, the distribution of alternative US water uses based on 2010 USGS data is displayed.

The importance of agriculturally related water uses is illustrated in Figure 8.5. In 2010, overall US freshwater withdrawals were 306.3 billion gallons-per-day (B-gpd), and irrigation demands accounted for just over one-third of that total. While thermoelectric power (38.2 percent) was the single largest water use category, if we add up all three agriculturally related water demands (irrigation + livestock + aquaculture), agriculture is the number-one water user, at 41.3 percent.

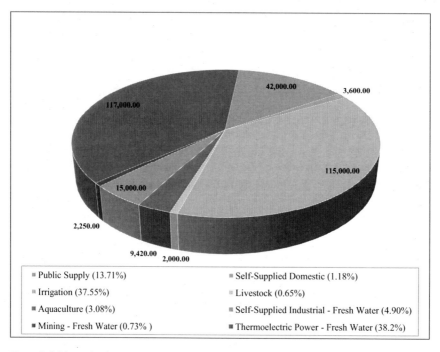

Figure 8.5 Major fresh water uses in the US in 2010 (millions of gallons per day).

Source: USGS (2014).

It is important to note that while the US has increased its population and its real GDP since 1980, *total US water withdrawals (355 B-gpd; fresh plus saline) in 2010 have noticeably declined* below the water demands that prevailed in 1980. Reductions in water withdrawals have dropped in four major use areas: thermoelectric power, irrigation, public supply, and industrial. While aquaculture and mining did see increases in water use, their relatively much smaller base volume could not affect the overall downward trend in US water demand.

What factors are responsible for these declines in US water use? The answer to this question is rooted in investments to upgrade equipment and facilities, the adoption of much-improved water-saving technologies and the application of better water-management practices. Advances in irrigation technology have been particularly significant in making water use more efficient. *Total irrigated acreage in 2010 reached a* **new high of 62 M-acres**, *while* **total irrigated water usage decreased** *from* a 1980 peak of 150 B-gpd to 120 B-gpd in 2010.[55] Irrigation practices have changed considerably since 1985: new and more efficient sprinkler and micro-irrigation methods have noticeably replaced surface flooding and related techniques.

Elsewhere in the US economy, natural-gas-fired thermoelectric plants require much less water for power generation and cooling purposes than the coal-fired power plants that they have supplanted. Similarly, water-saving plumbing devices and household items (efficient toilets, dishwashers, washing machines, etc.) have helped decrease the US per capita demand for water.

Similar to our soil and land resources, researchers again arrive at now familiar conclusions about US water demand:

1) The *gains in water-use efficiency* have facilitated powerful strides in reducing US overall water use.
2) As US population and industrial output continue to expand in the future, the *growth will eventually place a sizable strain on the sustainable capacity* to satisfy increasing demands.

Continued progress in water-use efficiency will be essential to proper water-use management.

Water supply

Earth's oceans constitute 97.2 percent of all water sources, and their saline water composition largely limits their usefulness as a supply directly fit for human use or consumption. And, while global warming will likely have measurable negative impacts on this next statistic, an approximate 2.15 percent of the earth's water is stored as polar ice. *Basic arithmetic says that the remaining 0.65 percent of the planet's water supply is fresh.*[56] Agriculture and all other uses compete with each other for access to the earth's limited fresh water sources.

We sometimes view these water source measurements as static or permanent. In reality, to employ a pun, the situation is quite fluid. The sun powers the earth's hydrologic cycle, and sometimes in very powerful ways. In the US, large amounts of water can be drawn from the Atlantic Ocean and Gulf of Mexico and then deposited on land as fresh water during a hurricane.

Another viewpoint dispels the idea that saline water is not available for direct human use. The nations of Kuwait and Saudi Arabia regularly employ *desalination plants* to convert sea water into potable uses.[57] The issue is expense. Undoubtedly, producing a drinkable glass of fresh water is less expensive along the coast of Lake Michigan in Green Bay,

Wisconsin than it is by drawing saline water from the Red Sea to have a drink of H_2O in Mecca, Saudi Arabia.

Taking nothing away from the science of meteorology, we also can say that *precipitation patterns*, as a fresh water source, are uneven and difficult to predict. The proportional balance between the earth's saline and fresh water may "regress towards mean values," but the variability is considerable. Witness situations of extended drought in one growing season followed by protracted periods of standing water in the next.

Fluctuating water supplies beg the question of what are the founts that supply US agriculture. From the standpoint of irrigated water for US farming and related uses, *57 percent of irrigation taps into surface water supplies, while 43 percent of irrigated water originates with groundwater sources.*[58]

Whether or not ground- or surface-waters are the primary water supply source, the economic perspective emphasizes how a farmer (or any other user) views the marginal cost of employing another gallon of water for a particular purpose. In many circumstances, a farm producer may privately drill a well or build a similar water delivery system. Once the private water-supply investment is complete, there is often a low extra cost of using another water unit from a developed source.

When the marginal cost is low, a rational decision maker continues to use additional water amounts until the law of diminishing marginal utility reduces the extra benefit sufficiently to equal marginal cost. In effect, a minimal marginal cost indicates that water is plentiful (not scarce). Under these circumstances, the demand-side incentive is to use large amounts of water.

If the true social cost of water use is scarcer than what the private marginal cost indicates, then the market communicates an incorrect signal to the water user. Only when the price per unit of water appropriately measures true social marginal cost, will water demanders voluntarily seek to "conserve water."

If inadequate water pricing mechanisms drive a wedge between the social and private costs of water withdrawals, the "Tragedy of the Commons" is a scenario that can arise with groundwater use. In nineteenth-century England, a commons was an open pasture not owned by any one cattle-grazer, but was accessible by all area producers. The tragic aspect, which is also applicable to groundwater use and ocean fisheries, is the absence of any enforceable fees for grazing the commons. Each producer faces a zero private price for extracting a marginal unit of the common's limited resource stock.[59]

The "free" marginal cost falsely implies that extra units of the resource are not scarce. Consequently, each producer reaps a net personal welfare gain by placing an additional animal on the commons, straining its capacity. Since all producers on the commons encounter the same private incentive, the result is a deterioration of the commons' overall productivity. Eventually overgrazing ruins all value in the commons.

Challenges Associated with Groundwater Use and Supplies. Groundwater utilization can be similar to the grazing-land commons described by Hardin. The Ogallala Aquifer is a massive groundwater source that continuously extends northward from west Texas to South Dakota. Until recently, water withdrawal rates for farm irrigation from the Ogallala were a modern-day example of a commons experiencing rapid depletion of a natural resource. Many producers accessed the Ogallala's water reserves for irrigation because the cheap price of withdrawal helped create profitable farm returns. However, similar to the case of the grazing commons scenario, the private marginal cost of drafted water from the Ogallala understated the true social cost of the water extraction.

As with all groundwater sources, we can compare withdrawal to recharge rates. Ogallala groundwater is recharged by rainfall and snowmelt; but the US Great Plains area has an arid climate, so the recharge rate is reduced. Improvements in irrigation technology have noticeably reduced uptake rates, but more improvements are needed, because the entire aquifer is in an overdraft state.

One estimate indicates a nearly 30 percent reduction in the Ogallala's water levels since irrigation for crop production originally became prevalent in the mid-twentieth century. Future declines in the Ogallala's groundwater capacity are expected, but technology and management adjustments have helped slow down withdrawal rates.[60]

Surface Water Supply Challenges. Whenever considerations of sufficient water supply are discussed, projections of future use must be viewed in terms of changing technologies and management choices. While crises in water use can occur, the severity relaxes if new methodologies can more efficiently control water demand while improving water recharge rates. As noted earlier in this chapter, irrigation technology has markedly improved since 1985: precision agriculture, efficient sprinklers, and micro-irrigation techniques have replaced the excessive water-demanding methods such as surface flooding. Today, US agriculture irrigates a historically high number of acres, and does so with less water.

In the US, one additional aspect of the water supply is the wholly *diminished interest* in building "public water projects" that create artificial surface water reservoirs. Large structures assembled during 1930 to 1969, such as the Hoover and Grand Coulee Dams in the western US, were originally praised for their multiple economic benefits (stable water sources, electric power, employment, etc.) However, since the 1970s considerations of adverse environmental consequences and also significant up-front and ongoing maintenance costs now regularly limit the opportunity to engage in additional large-scale future investments in surface water supply projects.[61]

Market externalities and water quality considerations

A sufficient quantity of water supplied is a necessary and obvious farm input. Water quality matters too. Livestock and crops require healthy water sources with low salinity levels, if they are to thrive.

Farm managers understand the importance of water quality within their own operations. Unfortunately, some production practices generate "off-farm and downstream" non-point water pollution.

When fertilizers, herbicides, and pesticides are applied at prescribed rates, the typical results are improved farm productivity and profitability. But when input treatments exceed productive uptake rates, or if the extra nutrients/chemicals are washed away in large storm events, then local watersheds absorb the run-off. The end result is a deterioration in the purity of surface- and ground-waters.[62]

Agriculture is not alone as a source of water-borne externalities. A US Geological Survey (USGS) report (2013) on the ecological health of the nation's streams determined that *urban land uses* had altered the natural state of local aquatic biological systems in 89 percent of studied US watercourses. In the same study, agriculture affected 79 percent of the streams' ecological conditions.[63] Overall, the USGS study concludes that when the side effects of all land uses are combined, an average of 83 percent of 585 US streams experienced impaired ecological health compared to referenced baselines. From a policy perspective, the USGS recommends that better practices are needed in *every land use category* if we are to further improve water quality.[64]

While more work is needed to improve US water quality, it is important to *recognize the progress that has occurred.* The US Congress passed the Water Pollution Control Act (P.L. 92-500) in 1972, and assigned the Environmental Protection Agency (EPA) as the law's primary administrator. This piece of legislation is known as the "Clean Water Act" or CWA. Since the CWA's enactment, the waters of the US are indeed cleaner, with **reduced levels** *of agents that cause biochemical oxygen demand, harmful suspended solids, and dangerous bacteria.* Point sources such as sewage treatment plants and industrial by-products have complied with the CWA's stricter controls, and consequently release significantly less pollutants into the nation's waterways.[65]

The 1972 CWA was a vehicle for progress in water quality because of the initial emphasis on improving *point-source pollution controls.* By the year 2000, the EPA began broadening its approach. EPA stepped up its cooperation with state governments to create programs that could reduce water pollution from non-point sources.

CWA's Section 303 requires *state governments* to establish Total Maximum Daily Load (TMDL) requirements for pollutants that impair US waters. The TMDL targets must be consistent with reaching and sustaining appropriate water quality standards. In cases where *non-point sources* are associated with compromised water quality, the CWA does *not* authorize federal agencies (including the EPA) to administer controls over non-point pollution sources. As a result, EPA does not have direct jurisdiction regulating non-point sources. Implementation of pollution control practices *are state-sponsored programs and regulations* consistent with TMDL water quality standards. State-run programs are typically supplemented with assistance from federal, local, and private sources.[66]

Non-point pollution and the controversy over the "Waters of the United States (WOTUS)" interpretative rule

Agricultural interests are involved in a major dispute over jurisdictional authority associated with CWA's Section 404. Before farm- and other-landowners can dispose of dredge or fill materials into designated wetlands or navigable rivers, CWA Section 404 requires permits administered by the Army Corps of Engineers (ACE). However, language in the CWA empowers the EPA to reject an ACE-approved Section 404 permit, if details of the permit fail to satisfy CWA requirements.[67]

Section 404's permitting process is an encumbrance to those it regulates, particularly the landowners whose properties contain "ephemeral" or "isolated" waters/wetlands (such as drainage ditches) that either flow intermittently or are not physically adjacent to navigable waterways. The sporadic nature of these waterbodies raises the question as to whether transient waters can actually justify federal CWA regulatory action. Considerable litigation has occurred to determine what the limits of CWA's Section 404 implementation are.[68]

The US Supreme Court (USSC) weighed in twice on the jurisdictional issue (USSC cases in 2001 and 2006). Unfortunately, the USSC Justices *did not reach common ground* on specific criteria to differentiate the wetlands/waterways that are (and are not) subject to federal CWA control. Without clear-cut USSC guidance, lower court and administrative decisions on CWA jurisdiction are ascertained case-by-case. Lack of clarity, as well as intense lobbying by both landowners and government agencies, ultimately created the political will to figure out where the CWA's reach began and ended.[69]

In 2011, the EPA and ACE, under the Obama Administration's direction, created a proposal to administratively determine which "Waters of the United States (WOTUS)" are, and are not, covered under the CWA's regulations. The initial proposal was released in March 2014, and the EPA/ACE agencies invited public input through November 2014. After sorting through over a million comments, *the EPA and ACE jointly published a CWA Rule in May 2015.*[70] Subsequent to the final rule's publication, the Farm Bureau volunteer organization initiated an internet campaign known as "Ditch the Rule."[71] The EPA responded with an online program known as "Ditch the Myth." But the EPA's internet campaign was determined to be beyond its range of authority, and the EPA was forced to discontinue its counter-campaign.[72]

While not unexpected, *additional litigation* immediately followed the release of the May 2015 ACE/EPA rule to clarify CWA jurisdiction. With a 2-1 ruling in October 2015, the Federal Sixth Circuit Court of Appeals asserted its authority to address the landowners' and states' petitions. The Sixth Circuit Court *imposed a nationwide stay*, prohibiting implementation of the proposed May 2015 ACE/EPA WOTUS Rule.[73] No timeline has been set for the Sixth Circuit Court to rule on the facts of the case.

As it stands today, with questions about CWA Section 404 federal jurisdiction unresolved until further court action, state governments and their designated agencies will assume leadership roles in non-point water pollution control. For example, in April 2016, Minnesota's (MN's) legislature and governor signed a law to establish vegetation buffers up to 50 feet wide along the state's rivers and streams, and a minimum 16.5-foot buffer strip along public ditches. The goal of these buffers adjacent to MN's waterways is to filter out excess nitrogen, phosphorus, sediment, and other biochemical agents, and prevent these polluting agents from damaging MN's lakes, rivers, and streams.[74]

As with any policy, the heightened role of the states in water quality has its strengths and drawbacks. On the plus side, state and local authorities are often in a position to better understand regional problems. They can more quickly propose and implement solutions than their federal counterparts, and they can perform ongoing monitoring to ensure that improvements are permanent and sustainable. On the down side, rivers and streams follow paths that typically cross state boundaries. Policies acceptable in one state can easily be prohibited in another.

While not impossible, it can be difficult for multiple states to reach agreements with each other on the best methods to achieve cleaner waterways. Aside from political differences that sometimes arise between states, it is just more complicated to coordinate the regulatory efforts of several agencies and authorities. Some states have successfully formed water compacts for this very purpose. To the extent that states can work together, then the chances of achieving progress in water quality are enhanced.

Summary

The central role of water resources in US agricultural and natural resource policy cannot be overstated. As we look to the future, we can expect the following enduring and significant issues to influence how we manage water supply and use:

- *Over 40 percent of US water use is agriculturally related.* Significant efficiencies associated with new technologies and management practices have reduced water demand while the US economy and population has grown.
- On the supply side, *surface waters satisfy 57 percent of agricultural water use, while groundwater supplies the remaining 43 percent.* Large water projects are largely a "policy of the

past," and some groundwater sources are in a state of overdraft. Continuing improvements in water management, technology, and pricing policies will be necessary to balance the growth of water uses against the limits of US water resources.

- *Water quality management, as well as water quantity, is needed to ensure that all users (including agriculture) can access water fit for animals, crops, aquaculture, and human consumption.* Jurisdictional questions regarding the relative roles of local, state, and federal authorities will need to be addressed in ways that facilitate sustained and ongoing quality improvements in US water sources.

Agriculture's role in energy and climate change policies

Agriculture's connection to water and land resources is clear and long-standing. In the twenty-first century, agriculture is also a key factor linked to ongoing developments in US energy and climate change policies. In this chapter section, we first examine agriculture's role in renewable energy, and then review some major climate change considerations.

Agriculture, renewable energy, and the 2014 Farm Bill

Continuing financial support to encourage the development and utilization of renewable energy sources is funded within the 2014 Farm Bill's Title IX, Energy. The sum of both Title IX's mandatory and discretionary budgets for energy projects/programs is estimated as $1.459 billion over 5 years (FY2014–FY2018).[75] The energy program cost share within the 2014 Farm Bill's entire 5-year total is about 0.298 percent (less than one percent of the $489 billion 2014 Farm Bill 5-year budget).[76]

Despite the relatively small budgetary size of energy programs within the 2014 Farm Bill, these funds continue to support important research projects and technological advances that promote renewable energy.

Between 2005 and 2013, numerous renewable programs (e.g. subsidized loans, tax stimuli, grant assistance, and regulatory mandates) funded by a variety of federal agencies (including the Departments of Energy and Transportation, as well as the EPA) expanded renewable energy program budgets far beyond farm-bill incentives. Federal government aid from all sources greatly expanded the nationwide availability of renewable energy, and at one point the sum of federal budget levels exceeded $7 billion annually.[77] A number of state governments also supplemented the federal programs by introducing additional inducements for renewables.

The reasons for the large expenditures and the wide range of federal renewable energy programs in the early- to mid-2000's included the *promotion of US energy independence, generating increased demand for US farm products, and facilitating reduced GHG emissions.*[78]

However, energy markets and energy politics began to change in 2010. The advent of "US fracking technology" began to noticeably increase domestic fossil fuel production, and decrease both energy scarcity and energy prices. The Fall 2010 elections led to a new political climate that emphasized reduced federal spending. The inability of the US executive and congressional branches of government to agree on strategic spending limits ultimately resulted in across-the-board spending cuts known as "budget sequestration." As a result of these combined pressures, *most of the non-farm-bill federal subsidies for renewable energy ended in 2013.* Looking ahead, the primary federal support to promote renewable energy resides within 2014 Farm Bill's Title IX funding.[79]

Renewable energy alternatives are generally cleaner and more climate-friendly when compared to traditional fossil fuels. Many renewable energy options are connected to agricultural and rural land uses. For example, agriculturally related renewable energy sources include:

- Corn-based ethanol or soy-based biodiesel.
- Wind-powered turbines placed on farm sites or in rural locations.
- Harvested-crop and forest biomass utilized as fuel to generate heat for industrial purposes.
- Conversion of animal waste into methane and electric power via anaerobic digesters.

Of the farm-related renewable energy options listed above, corn-based ethanol grew rapidly to become the largest single agricultural renewable energy program. Soy-based biodiesel output also expanded, but at a much slower rate than did corn-starch ethanol production.

In 2001, US ethanol output was 1.8 billion gallons and absorbed about 7 percent of US corn production. By 2015, the US was generating 14.8 billion gallons of corn-based ethanol, and ethanol required 37 percent of 2015's US total corn output.[80] Much of this tremendous rise in ethanol production supplied the US energy market with proportional-blended fuels that power vehicles for transportation and related purposes.

In an effort to identify the impacts that ethanol-based fuels are having on the US economy, the US Department of Energy (DOE) publishes a fact sheet describing the effects of ethanol use and production. The DOE emphasizes that ethanol is a biodegradable fuel. Distiller's Dried Grains with Solubles (DDGS) are a high-protein animal feed and a regular byproduct of ethanol processing. Ethanol generates at least one-third more energy than is used to produce it. Ethanol also decreases GHG emissions by about 20 percent compared to gasoline, and meets tailpipe emission standards when blended with petroleum-based fuels. Finally, ethanol is a high performance and safer octane-booster replacement for the risky MTBE additive.[81]

Increased corn demand associated with the rise of ethanol as a renewable fuel has been a "two-sided coin" from a policy standpoint.

On the one hand, ethanol utilization boosts revenues and profits for corn producers. Because grain markets are competitive and highly interconnected, expanding corn demand tends to enhance the profitability of crop farming in general. There are also economic multiplier effects associated with extra ethanol production as it creates a derived demand for corn as a feedstock, and speeds up the flow of the supply chains for crop inputs and outputs. The rise of ethanol production has additionally stimulated jobs and infrastructure investments in rural America. Ethanol production is a "value-added" industry that offers distributional outlets and markets for corn production.

On the other hand, livestock producers are disadvantaged as heightened ethanol demand boosts corn prices, and consequently increases the animal feeding expenses in agricultural enterprises. Environmental concerns are also voiced because enhanced corn demand, when spurred on by ethanol subsidies, creates economic pressures for farmers to non-renew CRP contracts, and risk increased soil erosion and non-point pollution because higher profits urge producers to convert idle-marginal lands into additional corn-producing acres. Consumer groups complain that rising food prices are associated with the competition between food and fuel demands. Equity issues can arise when subsidized ethanol production is connected with rising food prices that have adverse welfare effects on low-income households.[82]

The disquieting effects of an expanding ethanol sector, including tightened corn markets and related externalities, have motivated a change in focus in federal renewable energy programs towards ethanol feedstocks that have less negative impacts on food markets and the environment.

A review of the grants and incentives for renewable energy research and production in the 2014 Farm Bill reveals the following trends:[83]

- Continued funding for projects initiated under the *Bioenergy Program for Advanced Biofuels (BPAB)*. The BPAB, established under the 2008 Farm Bill, pays producers to further the production of advanced biofuels.
- Extended ongoing support for the *Biomass Crop Assistance Program (BCAP)*. BCAP, which also began with 2008 Farm Bill funding, financially helps farmers to cultivate, collect, harvest, store and transport nontraditional crops as the base feedstocks that can be processed into cellulosic biofuels.
- Retained funding for the *Renewable Energy for America (REAP)*. REAP offers funding for infrastructure projects that encourage efficient rural energy sources, particularly those that promote self-sufficiency and boost biofuels marketing. However, the 2014 Farm Bill specifically excludes REAP funding for retail fuel pumps – the Congressional view is that such investments are now private capital budgeting decisions that retail fuel businesses must make for themselves.

The 2014 Farm Bill's ongoing support for renewable energy research and development is also connected to the even broader issue of reducing agriculture's "carbon footprint" and its GHG emissions. We now turn our attention to the climate change topic.

Rationale for reviewing US agriculture policies in relation to climate change

To understand why US farm and food policies should be reviewed in relation to their effects on climate change, we should briefly describe the nature and scope of the climate problem.

During 2015, the US National Oceanic and Atmospheric Administration (NOAA) reported that the earth's annual-average atmospheric carbon dioxide (CO_2) concentration climbed above 400 parts per million (ppm) for the first time since record-keeping began in 1959. NOAA measures daily atmospheric conditions at the Mauna Loa research facility on Hawaii's Big Island.[84]

Based on ice-core isotope-dating analysis, the earth's CO_2 atmospheric density reached no higher than 280 ppm for thousands of years prior to 1880. From that time forward, the industrial revolution and today's modern economy has relied upon large-scale fossil-fuel combustion activity to power economic growth. The world's market expansion has had the side effect of emitting extra units of CO_2 into the air. The earth's atmospheric CO_2 concentration subsequently climbed ever higher. In April 2016, CO_2 levels attained a monthly average of 407.4 ppm at Mona Loa.[85] In a 2015 *Scientific American* article, David Biello noted that any CO_2 atmospheric concentration above 400 ppm is a level not experienced on the planet since the end of the Oligocene era 23 million years ago (before homo sapiens existed).[86]

Why does the atmosphere's CO_2 level matter? Accepted science tells us that CO_2 soaks up radiated infrared energy, and then re-emits it. As a logical result, when the earth's CO_2 concentration increases, the earth heats up. Earth's average temperature is now 1.4 degrees Fahrenheit (0.8 degrees Celsius) greater than it was in 1880.

While a 1.4-degee change seems trivial, it is not. A massive amount of heat is required to warm the earth's atmosphere, oceans and land by just a marginal amount. The earth entered a 300-year mini-ice-age between 1500 and 1800 when the planet's average temperature dropped by about 2.6 degrees Fahrenheit.[87]

It is also important to understand that some atmospheric CO_2 and related greenhouse gases are essential. If they are absent from our atmosphere, then the planet is a frozen wasteland. But if there is too much CO_2, as there is on Venus (96 percent), then the earth boils over. Similar to the story of Goldilocks, the survival of life as we know it requires just the right amount of CO_2 in the earth's atmosphere. There should not be too much or too little. The current trajectory of increasing CO_2 levels threatens the atmospheric balance.

To the extent that increased CO_2 levels and heightened average planetary temperatures will create economic disruptions (affecting the welfare and profitability of agriculture, food, and many other related industries), policies are needed to mitigate the negative impacts of climatic imbalance.

The US federal government's current adaptation policy

In February 2016, the US Supreme Court issued a stay preventing implementation of an EPA Clean Power Plan aimed at reducing carbon emissions from electric-power generating plants.[88] Similar to the struggles that surround water pollution control, the sticking point is jurisdictional. Where does state government regulatory authority end and federal rule begin? In the meantime, CO_2 emissions continue, and if the science is correct, climate change is inevitable.

While the judiciary branch interprets the limits of regulatory authority, the federal government's other two branches recognize that a changing climate is a risk not to be ignored. The Government Accounting Office (GAO), the US Congress's primary auditing agency, classified climate change as one of federal government's thirty most significant risks. In November 2013, Executive Order 13653 instructed federal agencies in the executive branch to create concrete plans for climate change adaptation.[89]

USDA's adaptation response to climate change

The 2014–2018 USDA Strategic Plan has four primary goals. We can review Strategic Goal #2: "Ensure Our National Forests and Private Working Lands Are Conserved, Restored, and Made More Resilient to Climate Change, While Enhancing Our Water Resources."[90] Within this strategic framework, the USDA aims to assist the US agri-food system to sustainably adapt to a changing climate while also helping to mitigate the damaging effects of climate change.

The USDA is uniquely positioned to work towards achieving its strategic goal. With its nationwide network of FSA and NRCS offices, the USDA has the potential to directly offer research and extension services to the millions of private farmers and ranchers likely to be affected by climate stressors. Some examples of expected agricultural climate challenges include the increased frequency of extreme weather events and the heightened susceptibility to disease vectors and pest infestations.

The USDA can also address climate-change impacts because of its influence on a substantial portion of US public lands. The US Forest Service (FS) falls under USDA jurisdiction. The FS is charged with the supervision of 193 million acres of US national forests and grasslands.[91] Again, basic science tells us that trees and plants have the capacity to absorb CO_2 and accumulate it as sugars, starches, and cellulose while releasing oxygen. Healthy soils also serve as a carbon sink.

These natural cycles and resources represent an opportunity for the USDA to facilitate processes that sequester carbon, improve climate resiliency, and enhance future productivity.

Currently, US agriculture is estimated to produce six percent of all US GHG emissions while also absorbing twelve percent of US greenhouse gases. A USDA strategic objective is to emphasize programs that increase the GHG absorptive capacity while reducing its greenhouse emissions.[92]

USDA has a "suite of programs" matched to the tasks of climate change adaptation and mitigation. Included are voluntary actions, counterbalances, and incentives:[93]

- Encouraging conservation tillage programs and nutrient management practices.
- Supporting the growth of perennial grasses and tree plantings on marginal farmlands, fire impacted landscapes, and built landscapes.
- Helping fund the development of methane digesters to reduce emissions and supply on-site farm power sources.
- Facilitating the application of precision agriculture and related technologies to reduce waste and enhance energy efficiency in agricultural enterprises and rural economies.

The 2014 Farm Bill and climate change policy

Public Law 113-79 (a.k.a. the Farm Bill) lacks a separate climate change title. Nevertheless, at least four identifiable connections exist between farm bill provisions and climate-related policies:[94]

- Instructs the Secretary of Agriculture to revise the Forest Service (FS) strategic plan. In June 2015, the FS complied with this directive, and released a 2015–2020 Strategic Plan that includes: "Strategic Objective A: Foster resilient, adaptive ecosystems to mitigate climate change."
- Extends authority for the FS International Programs Office (FSIPO) through FY2018 to continue its work. FSIPO encourages climate change mitigation and sustainable natural resource management by cooperating with global partners to tackle the planet's vital forestry issues and concerns.
- Includes the "enhancement of carbon sequestration" as an eligible activity with the newly created USDA-NRCS Regional Conservation Partnership Program (RCPP).
- Empowers the Secretary of Agriculture to initiate research on pulse crops to increase nitrogen fixation and reduce agriculture's carbon footprint.

Anticipated climate impacts and adaptations for US agriculture

In November 2015, the USDA's Economic Research Service published a rigorous study of the interactions expected to link climate change, US field-crop response, and water scarcity.[95] The ERS report cited previous studies indicating that US farm and ranch managers will be resilient in adjusting their operations to new climate-changed growing conditions. The study also emphasizes that producers' capacity to adapt will significantly determine how a changing climate influences future productivity, farm income, and food security.

It is likely that geographic comparative advantage for producing alternative crops will shift with long-term climate change, and producers will need to adapt accordingly. To the extent that ERS predictions are reasonably accurate, it makes sense that the USDA strategic plan should emphasize policies with incentives to build up enhanced adaptive capability and figure out practices that can mitigate negative climate outcomes.

Summary

In this chapter, we have explored the interconnections among agriculture, natural resources, and the environment in the US. Our exploration of these important relationships can be summarized as follows:

- Economic models of intertemporal choice provide insights into how current incentives influence the future condition and use of our natural resources. If there are market distortions, the decision makers in the present period will not be offered the correct signals about future resource scarcity. Properly designed policies to internalize externalities can ensure that producers and consumers in the agri-food system are exposed to resource prices and interest rates that equate private and social marginal costs.
- In our examination of land and water resources, we were able to access comprehensive inventories and indicators with key information about the condition of these natural inputs. Using a stock and flow analysis, we arrived at determinations that the US has made progress in creating positive inflows to the stock value of our resources; however, work remains to be done, if true sustainability is to be achieved.
- Investments to increase agriculture's capacity to produce renewable fuels has been significant. The renewable energy sector is evolving towards alternative feed stocks, and the 2014 Farm Bill is encouraging further innovation.
- Agriculture has the potential of making important contributions to mitigating the adverse effects of climate change and reducing the build-up of atmospheric greenhouse gases.

In the next chapter we explore the productivity relationships been agricultural inputs and outputs. Natural resources, energy, and the environment, when combined with technological advances, managerial skill, and, policy incentives, will be key determinants influencing the future trajectory of our output capacity. We now turn our attention to this next important topic.

Notes

1 "The United States Department of Agriculture (USDA) defines prime farmland as the land best suited to food, feed, forage, fiber, and oilseed crops. Prime farmland produces the highest yields with minimal inputs of energy and economic resources, and farming it results in the least damage to the environment." Carver, A.D. and J.E. Yahner. "Defining Prime Agricultural Land and Methods of Protection." Purdue University Cooperative Extension Service. Agronomy Guide. AY-283. Retrieved from: www.agry.purdue.edu/landuse/prime.htm

2 Southern Appalachian Highlands Conservancy (SAHC). "Preserving Farms – And 'A Way of Life.'" www.appalachian.org. February 28, 2014. Retrieved from: https://southernappalachian.word press.com/2014/02/28/preserving-farms-and-a-way-of-life/

3   Ibid.
4   Iowa Department of Natural Resources. "Success Stories from the Solid Waste Management System." March 2014. Retrieved from: file:///C:/Users/User/Downloads/emssuccessstories2014.pdf
5   LandScope America, NatureServe, National Geographic. "A Conservation Success Story - The Tallgrass Prairie Legacy Project, Kansas." 2016. Retrieved from: www.landscope.org/explore/eco systems/disappearing_landscapes/tallgrass_prairie/tallgrass4/
6   Thompson, Jayne. "Colorado Cattlemen's Agricultural Land Trust: Viewing Sage Grouse on Conserved Ranch Inspires Staff." Sage Grouse Initiative. April 20, 2015. Retrieved from: www. sagegrouseinitiative.com/colorado-cattlemens-agricultural-land-trust-viewing-sage-grouse-on-conserved-ranch-inspires-staff/
7   McIntyre, Douglas A. "Memo to Congress: 'Buy Land, They Ain't Making Any More Of It.'" Time: 24/7, Wall St. Wednesday, Jan. 28, 2009. Retrieved from: http://content.time.com/time/business/article/0,8599,1874407,00.html
8   Krutilla, John V. "Conservation Reconsidered." *American Economic Review* 57(4). Sept. 1967, pp. 777–786. Retrieved from: www.rff.org/files/sharepoint/News/Features/Documents/071003%20 Krutilla-ConservationReconsidered.pdf
9   British Broadcasting Company (BBC). "History: Thomas Malthus (1766–1834)." 2014. Retrieved from: www.bbc.co.uk/history/historic_figures/malthus_thomas.shtml
10 Krutilla. "Conservation Reconsidered." pp. 778–779.
11 Ibid, pp. 779–781.
12 Hirshleifer, Jack. *Price Theory and Applications.* Upper Saddle River, NJ: Prentice Hall, 1976, pp. 412–423.
13 Bergstrom, John C. and Alan Randall. *Resource Economics: An Economic Approach to Natural Resource and Environmental Policy.* Third Edition. Cheltenham, UK: Edward Elgar, 2010, pp. 378–379.
14 Hirshleifer, Jack. *Price Theory and Applications,* pp. 415–416.
15 Choi, Kwan. "Ch18. Externalities and the Environment, Part A." 2009. Retrieved from: www2. econ.iastate.edu/classes/econ301/choi/Ch18Ext.pdf
16 Coase, Ronald. "The Problem of Social Cost." *Journal of Law and Economics,* Volume III, October 1960, 1–44. Retrieved from: www.law.uchicago.edu/files/file/coase-problem.pdf
17 Brundtland, Gro Harlem. "Report of the World Commission on Environment and Development: Our Common Future." United Nation WCED: March 1987, pp. 1–300. Retrieved from: www.un-documents.net/our-common-future.pdf
18 Ibid, p. 43.
19 Barbier, Edward B. "The Role of Natural Resources in Economic Development." 2002 Joseph Fisher Lecture. Blackwell Publishing Ltd: University of Adelaide and Flinders University of South Australia. Retrieved from: http://homepage.univie.ac.at/adusei.jumah/natural_resources.pdf
20 Krautkraemer, Jeffrey A. "Economics of Natural Resource Scarcity: The State of the Debate." Washington: Resources for the Future, April 2005. Retrieved from: www.rff.org/files/sharepoint/ WorkImages/Download/RFF-DP-05-14.pdf
21 Bergstrom and Randall. *Resource Economics,* pp. 375–379.
22 Barbier, E. "The Role of Natural Resources in Economic Development," pp. 256–258.
23 Turner, R. Kerry. "Sustainable Development and Climate Change." Norwich, UK: Centre for Social and Economic Research on the Global Environment (CSERGE), Working Paper PA 95-01, ISSN 0967-8875. Dec. 1995. Retrieved from: www.researchgate.net/publication/222492921_ Sustainable_development_and_climate_change
24 Christianson, Laura and John Tyndall. "Seeking a Dialogue: A Targeted Technology for Sustainable Agricultural Systems in the American Corn Belt." *Sustainability: Science, Practice and Policy.* Community Essay: Volume 7, Issue 2, 2011. Retrieved from: http://sspp.proquest.com/archives/ vol7iss2/communityessay.christianson.html
25 Neumayer, Eric. *Weak versus Strong Sustainability: Exploring the Limits of Two Opposing Paradigms.* Cheltenham, UK: Edward, 2004. Retrieved from: https://books.google.com/books/about/Weak_ Versus_Strong_Sustainability.html?id=AzJt-gQUS00C
26 Pezzey, John C.V. and Michael A. Toman. "Sustainability and its Economic Interpretations." *Scarcity and Growth Revisited: Natural Resources and the Environment in a New Millennium.* R. David Simpson, Michael A. Toman and Robert U. Ayres (eds). Washington, DC: Resources for the Future, 2005. Retrieved from: http://people.anu.edu.au/jack.pezzey/PezzeyToman2005.pdf
27 Bergstrom and Randall. *Resource Economics,* pp. 380–383.

28 Pezzey and Toman. "Sustainability and its Economic Interpretations," p. 134.

29 Bergstrom and Randall. *Resource Economics*, pp. 379–397.

30 Ibid, p. 381.

31 Farmer, Michael C. and Alan Randall. "The Rationality of a Safe Minimum Standard." *Land Economics* (1998), 74, pp. 287–302. Retrieved from: http://econpapers.repec.org/article/uwplandec/v_3a74_3ay_3a1998_3ai_3a3_3ap_3a287-302.htm

32 Bergstrom and Randall. *Resource Economics*, pp. 383–385.

33 The graphical model in Figure 8.4 is an adaptation of the General Stock-Flow Diagram developed by the Global Development and Environment Institute (GDAE) at Tufts University. See http://ase.tufts.edu/gdae/. A straightforward description of the GDAE Stock-Flow Diagram is offered in: Ackerman, F., Goodwin, N., Nelson, J., Weisskopf, T., and Institute, G. (2007). Resource maintenance in economies. Retrieved from: www.eoearth.org/view/article/155722

34 Note: these US national numbers include Alaska and Hawaii.

35 Land in Urban Areas, by Region and States, United States, 1945-2007. Retrieved from: www.ers.usda.gov/data-products/major-land-uses/.aspx#25984

36 Osteen, Craig, Jessica Gottlieb, and Utpal Vasavada. *Agricultural Resources and Environmental Indicators, 2012 Edition*. Economic Research Service. EIB Number 98, August 2012. Retrieved from: www.ers.usda.gov/media/874175/eib98.pdf

37 NRCS, USDA. *National Resources Inventory: Soil Erosion on Cropland*. April 2010, pp. 1–2. Retrieved from: www.nrcs.usda.gov/Internet/FSE_DOCUMENTS/nrcs143_012269.pdf

38 Ibid, pp. 2–6.

39 Hill, Peter R. and Jerry V. Mannering. *Conservation Tillage and Water Quality*. Cooperative Extension Service, Purdue University, West Lafayette, IN. WQ-20, 1/95, January 1995. Retrieved from: www.extension.purdue.edu/extmedia/WQ/WQ-20.html

40 Stubbs, Megan. *Agricultural Conservation: A Guide to Programs*. Congressional Research Service, 7-5700 www.crs.gov, R40763, September 30, 2015, p. 2. Retrieved from: http://nationalaglaw center.org/wp-content/uploads/assets/crs/R40763.pdf

41 Politsch, Kent. *USDA Sees Strong Demand for Conservation Reserve Program: Deadline to Submit Offers for Competitive Enrollment is Feb. 26*. USDA News Release. Feb. 11, 2016. Retrieved from: www.usda.gov/wps/portal/usda/usdahome?contentid=2016/02/0039.xml

42 Stubbs, Megan. *Conservation Reserve Program (CRP): Status and Issues*. Congressional Research Service 7-5700, www.crs.gov, R42783, August 29, 2014, p. 15. Retrieved from: http://national aglawcenter.org/wp-content/uploads/assets/crs/R42783.pdf

43 Stubbs, Megan. *Agricultural Conservation: A Guide to Programs*. Congressional Research Service, 7-5700 www.crs.gov, R40763, September 30, 2015, pp. 12, 15–16. Retrieved from: http://national aglawcenter.org/wp-content/uploads/assets/crs/R40763.pdf

44 Ibid, p. 15.

45 Ibid, p. 12.

46 NRCS, USDA. *Agricultural Management Assistance*. Retrieved from: www.nrcs.usda.gov/wps/portal/nrcs/main/national/programs/financial/ama/

47 Stubbs, Megan. *Agricultural Conservation: A Guide to Programs*. Congressional Research Service, 7-5700 www.crs.gov, R40763, September 30, 2015, p. 6. Retrieved from: http://nationalaglaw center.org/wp-content/uploads/assets/crs/R40763.pdf

48 Stubbs, Megan. *Conservation Provisions in the 2014 Farm Bill (P.L. 113-79)*. Congressional Research Service. 7-5700, www.crs.gov, R43504. April 24, 2014, pp. 12–13. Retrieved from: http://national aglawcenter.org/wp-content/uploads/assets/crs/R43504.pdf

49 Stubbs, Megan. *Agricultural Conservation: A Guide to Programs*. Congressional Research Service, 7-5700 www.crs.gov, R40763, September 30, 2015, pp. 8, 23. Retrieved from: http://nationalaglaw center.org/wp-content/uploads/assets/crs/R40763.pdf

50 Osteen, Craig, Jessica Gottlieb, and Utpal Vasavada. *Agricultural Resources and Environmental Indicators, 2012 Edition*. Economic Research Service. EIB Number 98, August 2012, pp. iii–v. Retrieved from: www.ers.usda.gov/media/874175/eib98.pdf

51 OECD – Organization for Economic Co-operation and Development. "Members and Partners." OECD Headquarters, Paris, France. 2016. Retrieved from: www.oecd.org/about/membersand partners/

52 OECD (2015), *Environment at a Glance 2015: OECD Indicators*. Paris: OECD Publishing. Retrieved from: http://dx.doi.org/10.1787/9789264231993-en

53 Lomborg, Bjørn. *The Skeptical Environmentalist: Measuring the Real State of the World*. Cambridge, UK: Cambridge University Press, 2001, p. 149.

54 Maupin, M.A., J.F. Kenny, S.S. Hutson, J.K. Lovelace, N.L. Barber, and K.S. Linsey. "Estimated Use of Water in the United States in 2010: U.S. Geological Survey Circular 1405." 2014. Retrieved from: http://dx.doi.org/10.3133/cir1405

55 Ibid, p. 25.

56 Lomborg, Bjørn. *The Skeptical Environmentalist*, p. 149.

57 Ibid, p. 153.

58 Maupin, M.A. et al. "Estimated Use of Water in the United States in 2010: U.S. Geological Survey Circular 1405," p. 25.

59 Hardin, Garrett. "The Tragedy of the Commons." *Science*, December 13, 1968. Updated March 13, 2005.The Garrett Hardin Society. Retrieved from: www.garretthardinsociety.org/articles/art_tragedy_of_the_commons.html

60 Kromm, David E. "Ogallala Aquifer." *Water Encyclopedia: Science and Issues*. Advameg, Inc. 2016. Retrieved from: www.waterencyclopedia.com/Oc-Po/Ogallala-Aquifer.html

61 Bergstrom and Randall. *Resource Economics*, pp. 361–371.

62 Stubbs, Megan. *Nutrients in Agricultural Production: A Water Quality Overview*. Congressional Research Service 7-5700. www.crs.gov. CRS Report #R43919. February 20, 2015. Retrieved from: http://nationalaglawcenter.org/wp-content/uploads//assets/crs/R43919.pdf

63 Carlisle, Daren M., Michael R. Meador, Terry M. Short, Cathy M. Tate, Martin E. Gurtz, Wade L. Bryant, James A. Falcone, and Michael D. Woodside. "Ecological Health in the Nation's Streams, 1993–2005, National Water-Quality Assessment Program." U.S. Department of the Interior, U.S. Geological Survey, Circular 1391. Published 2013. Retrieved from: http://pubs.usgs.gov/circ/1391/

64 Ibid, p. 5.

65 Copeland, Claudia. "Water Quality Issues for the 114th US Congress: An Overview." Congressional Research Service. 7-5700. www.crs.gov, CRS Report #R43867. February 5, 2016. Retrieved from: http://nationalaglawcenter.org/wp-content/uploads//assets/crs/R43867.pdf

66 Stubbs, Megan. *Nutrients in Agricultural Production*, pp. 21–22.

67 Copeland, Claudia. "Water Quality Issues for the 114th US Congress: An Overview," pp. 3–4.

68 Copeland, Claudia. "EPA and the Army Corps' Rule to Define 'Waters of the United States.'" Congressional Research Service, 7-5700, www.crs.gov. CRS Report #R43455. June 29, 2015, pp. 11–12. Retrieved from: www.fas.org/sgp/crs/misc/R43455.pdf

69 Copeland, Claudia. "Water Quality Issues for the 114th US Congress: An Overview." February 5, 2016, pp. 4–5. Retrieved from: http://nationalaglawcenter.org/wp-content/uploads//assets/crs/R43867.pdf

70 Copeland, Claudia. "EPA and the Army Corps' Rule to Define 'Waters of the United States.'" Congressional Research Service, 7-5700, www.crs.gov. CRS Report #R43455. June 29, 2015, pp. 2–4. Retrieved from: www.fas.org/sgp/crs/misc/R43455.pdf

71 American Farm Bureau Association. "It's Time to Ditch the Rule." 2016. Retrieved from: http://ditchtherule.fb.org/.

72 Snider, Annie. "EPA's water-rule blitz was 'covert propaganda,' GAO says." *Politico*, Dec. 14, 2015. Retrieved from: www.politico.com/story/2015/12/epa-clean-water-rule-propaganda-gao-216750#ixzz3uQNB1GJC

73 United States Court of Appeals for the Sixth Circuit. In Re: Environmental Protection Agency and Department of Defense Final Rule; "Clean Water Rule: Definition of Waters of the United States," 80 FED. REG. 37,054 (June 29, 2015). Decided and Filed: October 9, 2015 before: Keith, McKeague and Griffin, Circuit Judges. Order of Stay. Retrieved from: www.ca6.uscourts.gov/opinions.pdf/15a0246p-06.pdf

74 Minnesota Board of Water and Soil Resources. *Buffer Program: 2016 Buffer Law Amendments*. Buffer Initiative Legislative Summary, Laws of Minnesota 2015, 1st Special Session, Chapter 4, Article 4. March 2016. Retrieved from: www.bwsr.state.mn.us/buffers/assets/buffer-glance.pdf

75 Schnepf, Randy. *Energy Provisions in the 2014 Farm Bill (P.L. 113-79)*. March 12, 2014. Congressional Research Service 7-5700 www.crs.gov. Report #R43416. Page 6. Retrieved from: http://nationalaglawcenter.org/wp-content/uploads//assets/crs/R43416.pdf

76 Economic Research Service, USDA. *Agricultural Act of 2014: Highlights and Implications*. Retrieved from: www.ers.usda.gov/agricultural-act-of-2014-highlights-and-implications.aspx

77 Schnepf, Randy. *Energy Provisions in the 2014 Farm Bill (P.L. 113-79)*. March 12, 2014. Congressional Research Service 7-5700 www.crs.gov. Report #R43416. Page 1. Retrieved from: http://nationalaglawcenter.org/wp-content/uploads//assets/crs/R43416.pdf

78 Ibid.

79 Ibid.

80 Kress, Cathann A. *Ethanol Usage Projections and Corn Balance Sheet (mil. bu.)*. Cooperative Extension Service, USDA. Ames: Iowa State University School of Science and Technology. Retrieved from: www.extension.iastate.edu/agdm/crops/outlook/cornbalancesheet.pdf

81 US Department of Energy. *Biofuels & Greenhouse Gas Emissions: Myths versus Facts*. April 18, 2008. www.eere.energy.gov. Retrieved from: http://energy.gov/sites/prod/files/edg/news/archives/documents/Myths_and_Facts.pdf

82 Malcolm, Scott and Marcel Aillery. *Growing Crops for Biofuels Has Spillover Effects*. Amber Waves. USDA, ERS. March 1, 2009. Retrieved from: http://ers.usda.gov/amber-waves/2009-march/growing-crops-for-biofuels-has-spillover-effects.aspx#.VzPH6vkrK00

83 Schnepf, Randy. *Energy Provisions in the 2014 Farm Bill (P.L. 113-79)*. March 12, 2014. Congressional Research Service 7-5700 www.crs.gov. Report #R43416. Pages 9-21. Retrieved from: http://nationalaglawcenter.org/wp-content/uploads//assets/crs/R43416.pdf

84 NOAA Global Greenhouse Gas Reference Network. *Trends in Atmospheric Carbon Dioxide Recent Monthly Average Mauna Loa CO_2*. Retrieved from: www.esrl.noaa.gov/gmd/ccgg/trends/

85 NOAA Global Greenhouse Gas Reference Network. *Trends in Atmospheric Carbon Dioxide: Up-to-date weekly average CO2 at Mauna Loa*. Retrieved from: www.esrl.noaa.gov/gmd/ccgg/trends/weekly.html

86 Biello, David. "CO2 Levels for February Eclipsed Prehistoric Highs – Global Warming is Headed Back to the Future as the CO_2 Level Reaches a New High." *Scientific American*. March 5, 2015. Retrieved from: www.scientificamerican.com/article/co2-levels-for-february-eclipsed-prehistoric-highs/

87 NASA. Earth Observatory. *The world is getting warmer*. Retrieved from: http://earthobservatory.nasa.gov/Features/WorldOfChange/decadaltemp.php

88 Chappell, Bill. *Supreme Court Puts White House's Carbon Pollution Limits On Hold*. National Public Radio. February 10, 2016. Retrieved from: www.npr.org/sections/thetwo-way/2016/02/10/466258777/supreme-court-puts-white-houses-carbon-pollution-limits-on-hold

89 Leggett, Jane A. *Climate Change Adaptation by Federal Agencies: An Analysis of Plans and Issues for Congress*. February 23, 2015. Congressional Research Service. 7-5700. Pages ii–iii – Summary. www.crs.gov. R43915. Retrieved from: http://nationalaglawcenter.org/wp-content/uploads//assets/crs/R43915.pdf

90 US Department of Agriculture. *Strategic Plan for FY 2014 – 2018*. Page 13. Retrieved from: www.ocfo.usda.gov/usdasp/sp2014/usda-strategic-plan-fy-2014-2018.pdf

91 Leggett, Jane A. *Climate Change Adaptation by Federal Agencies: An Analysis of Plans and Issues for Congress*. February 23, 2015. Congressional Research Service. 7-5700. Pages 34–35. www.crs.gov. R43915. Retrieved from: http://nationalaglawcenter.org/wp-content/uploads//assets/crs/R43915.pdf

92 US Department of Agriculture. *Strategic Plan for FY 2010–2015*. Page 16. Retrieved from: www.ocfo.usda.gov/usdasp/sp2010/sp2010.pdf

93 Ibid.

94 Ramseur, Jonathan L. *Climate Change Legislation in the 113th Congress*. March 12, 2014. Congressional Research Service 7-5700 www.crs.gov. R43230. Page 15. Retrieved from: http://nationalaglawcenter.org/wp-content/uploads/assets/crs/R43230.pdf

95 Marshall, Elizabeth, Marcel Aillery, Scott Malcolm, and Ryan Williams. *Climate Change, Water Scarcity, and Adaptation in the U.S. Fieldcrop Sector*. ERR-201. U.S. Department of Agriculture, Economic Research Service, November 2015. Retrieved from: www.ers.usda.gov/media/1951525/err-201.pdf

Chapter 9

Research, technology, and the growth of sustainable agricultural production

In April 2014, US Secretary of Agriculture Tom Vilsack was invited to join a public conversation sponsored by the Council on Foreign Relations.[1] The Agriculture Secretary commented on a variety of topics associated with the 2014 Farm Bill's enactment. One area of interest during that interview was the trend in US agricultural productivity. Secretary Vilsack was able to articulate the remarkable record of US farm output gains, as follows:[2]

Since 1950, our corn production has increased 300 percent. Now … what this means is we've gone from planting 10,000 seeds per acre of corn to 30,000 seeds per acre.

[In 1950], the average dairy cow was producing 5,500 pounds of milk. Today, that same cow – 22,000 pounds of milk. … You know, extraordinary productivity [is] just based on the science.

[W]orld food needs are going to continue to grow as populations grow. And the challenge for agriculture [is] to meet the needs of 9 billion people … in the next 40 years or so in the world, we have to increase agricultural production by about 70 percent.

So that's why it's important when people look at the Farm Bill – that's why we put a premium on establishing a strong research title [in the bill] because we need to be investing significantly more resources in agricultural research than we've been in the past.

During the same CFR conversation, Secretary Vilsack addressed the related topic of how a changing climate will influence the sustainability of future US agricultural output. A summary of his comments are:

We ignore climate change at our peril … farmers, because they deal with their land every day, they understand the personality of their farm.

And so farmers are very interested in the … technologies that will allow them to … be productive even if they have less water, even if they have a storm that comes through that's extraordinarily intense. So they're very interested in investing in innovation … new seed technology and intellectual property and new machinery and new farming systems that will allow them to mitigate the impact of climate.

[There is] a great interest on the part of the farmers to look at double-cropping or cover crops as a way of dealing with the changes … [a]cover crop would allow the carbon to be sequestered. It would allow moisture that's in the soil to continue to remain. It would re-energize and re-nourish the soil … it could [also] produce the feedstock for a new chemical or a new energy source or a new fuel source.

Now what that does, it creates additional income opportunities for the land owner. It creates new job opportunities … the impact of that is pretty significant.

Organization of chapter

Any discussion of agricultural productivity and its related policies typically draws a sizable audience. Many business interests and government officials have a real stake in agriculture's current and future production capacity.

In recognition of the topic's significance, we begin this chapter by reviewing the main economic forces that influence sustainable US agricultural production. We highlight how research efforts and changing technology have been critical factors in determining US agricultural productivity patterns.

To logically guide our economic analysis, we utilize established production function theory and the latest empirical research. Our goal is to ascertain the factors most closely associated with past, present, and future US agricultural productivity trends.

Next, we explore inter-relationships among productivity, sustainability, and climate change that are expected to shape the US agri-food system's capacity to respond to changing economic and environmental conditions.

Finally, to arrive at additional insights about long-run sustainable US agricultural production, we examine the economic consequences of alternative scenarios, policy options, and outcomes.

Economic forces driving change in agricultural productivity and sustainability

Definitions and terminology

Before engaging in a more in-depth review of changes in sustainable agricultural production, it pays dividends to make an initial investment in clarifying our terms and definitions.

Weighted-value indices of agricultural outputs and inputs. To create an estimate of changes in overall US agricultural productivity over time requires that we use reasonable and accepted methods of aggregating output and input values.

Similar to the index-estimation techniques regularly used in empirical economic research, we determine an agricultural productivity indicator by utilizing a weighted-average aggregate index value for each observation over time in relation to a base-period index value.

For example, if we are interested in the annual percent rates-of-change for agricultural output and/or input data, then the indexed data are calculated relative to base-year index values.

There is a variety of techniques available to calculate indices for time-series data. The USDA's Economic Research Service (ERS) uses the Tornqvist Index-Estimation Methodology.[3]

Differentiating changes in agricultural output and changes in agricultural productivity. US agricultural output, when measured as an aggregated index value, is an estimate of total US agricultural production in a particular time period. In Figure 9.1 (see next page), we use a USDA-ERS production model (2003) to illustrate that US agricultural output levels are a function of both input-usage rates and productivity changes.[4]

As we examine the equation in Figure 9.1, we visualize the multiple sources that generate net changes in US agricultural output. One scenario is where producers are motivated to hire additional inputs to increase their output. We can also observe changes in agricultural output traced to factors such as improved technologies, variable weather patterns, or permanent changes in climate.

Figure 9.1 also suggests that the normal reporting of market-based indices of US agricultural output can be modified by incorporating non-market externalities into the calculation (see the box on the far right in Figure 9.1).

For example, agriculture can produce the positive externality of carbon sequestration or the negative externality of non-point water pollution. At this moment, most indexed measures of US agricultural output are "traditional" – they simply calculate readily available and widely recognized changes in market-based indexes of total output. Adjusting indexed-output values for external effects is a technique receiving increased attention, but more work is needed to arrive at a universally accepted measure of external impacts.[5]

The USDA-ERS has considerable experience in collecting data and developing reliable indices of traditional market-based agricultural input and output values. To capture the important aspects of "Productivity" (see the middle box in Figure 9.1) in determining

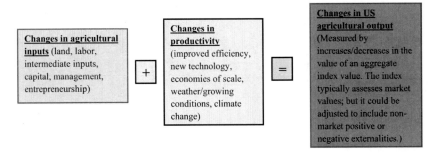

Figure 9.1 US agricultural output changes are determined by changes in inputs and productivity (USDA, ERS 2003).

US agricultural output, the USDA-ERS closely monitors the Ratio of Total Agricultural Output to Total Agricultural Inputs. This ratio is known as *Total Factor Productivity (TFP)*. Whenever the TFP ratio increases over time, it indicates that average agricultural output per unit input is rising. Simply put, overall productivity is growing if the TFP trend is increasing.

TFP growth can be a powerful economic force. Other things being equal, increased TFP means that farm operators and owners have a real opportunity to generate positive profit margins and increased real net income. In addition, as a farm achieves increased TFP, it also operates at a lower average total cost, and is therefore in a stronger competitive position when variable market conditions reduce product prices and thinout profit margins. From a societal standpoint, improved TFP can alleviate the general economic challenge associated with allocating scarce resources.

TFP growth and the technological treadmill

There is also an economic downside to TFP growth. As increased TFP enhances the individual financial condition of each farm enterprise, the *fallacy of composition*[6] takes hold. The fallacy means that a rising TFP has market-wide consequences that differ greatly from the benefits that arise for a single producer.

When applied to agriculture, the fallacy is sometimes better known as the "technological treadmill" (Cochrane, 1958; Levins and Cochrane, 1996).[7,8] The treadmill analogy is appropriate. Farm producers know their fast pace of technology adoption is necessary just to keep up with competitive market demands.

As *all* farm operators reduce cost and increase output through technology adoption, they expand production, increase market supply, and drive down the equilibrium market price. Consequently, the treadmill means that the typical farm operation will struggle to earn a normal profit.

Any farm resisting the technological imperative will "fall off the treadmill" and fail. Surviving farms "run in place as the relentless tech-treadmill turns." The goal of "getting ahead" financially is indeed challenging.

Analyzing TFP changes using production function analysis. The OECD, in a research report on sustainable agricultural productivity growth, used production function analysis to highlight economic sources of TFP growth.[9] The OECD study identifies technical efficiency

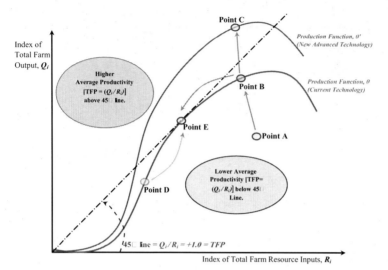

Legend for the Production Functions, $Q_i = \theta(R_i)$ and $Q_i = \theta'(R_i)$, in Figure 9.2:

- Output (Q_i) Changes from **Point A** to **B**: *Improved TFP from Gains in Technical Efficiency*
- Output (Q_i) Changes from **Point B** to **C**: *Technological Advance Increases TFP*
- Output (Q_i) Changes from **Point B** to **E** or Output (Q_i) Changes from **Point D** to **E**: *Improved TFP from Economies of Scale*

Figure 9.2 Production function analysis of the alternative paths to achieving increased total factor productivity (TFP) (OECD 2011).

gains, technological advance, and economies of scale as primary pathways to realize TFP growth, as illustrated in Figure 9.2 below:

We use the graph in Figure 9.2 to emphasize that TFP growth originates from multiple sources. This analytical approach also suggests that we can encourage additional gains in TFP by carefully designing policies that promote gains *in technical efficiency, technological advance,* and *economies of scale.*

Empirical research on changes in US agricultural TFP

In July 2015, the USDA-ERS released an extensive study of US agriculture that examined the trends and sources of changing US farm productivity.[10] When we compare the theoretical concepts in Figure 9.2 to the USDA-ERS empirical research on agricultural output and productivity, we observe the logical connections that we would expect and hope to find.

In particular, the USDA-ERS review of US agricultural productivity identifies "drivers" that have influenced past and current trends, as well as factors that will continue to strongly influence future TFP growth.

The in-depth USDA-ERS productivity study made the following key observations and interpretations:[11]

- The USDA-ERS Study reviewed 63 years of US agricultural productivity data between 1948 and 2011. When the weighted-average index of all farm inputs (land, labor, intermediated goods, and capital) was estimated over this time span, the results were notable for how efficient those resources were utilized. *Aggregate input use* increased at a very modest rate of 0.07 percent per year.

- During the 1948–2011 timespan, the aggregate *agricultural output index* increased at a 1.49 percent annual rate.
- When we combine the results of input use and output generation, we determine that TFP grew at an average rate of 1.42 percent per year. This is an impressive result. Over the entire 1948–2011 observation period, *aggregate output* increased by 156 percent, and the lion's share of that growth is attributable to the gains in TFP.

If we interpret the reported USDA-ERS productivity patterns using our production functions displayed in Figure 9.2, we can reasonably state that the growth in US agricultural output is *primarily attributable to both* **technical efficiency gains** *and* **technological advance** (in the graph, this would be movements between Points A and B, and Points B and C). We make this interpretation because efficiency gains and technological progress require very little or no change in the use of agricultural inputs; and the 1948–2011 record shows that the output growth rate (1.49 percent per year) is approximately 21.3 times larger than aggregate input growth rate (0.07 percent per year).

From years of well-established empirical research, we also know that US agriculture has seen both the *average farm acreage size increase and the number of farms decrease*. It is also true that the total amount of land in agricultural production has *gradually decreased* since 1948.[12]

Consequently, as US farm producers were responsible for tremendous output growth between 1948 and 2011, *they were* **not** *using up more land area to accomplish that feat*. The extensive agricultural land input, measured in acres, lessened.

So, when we measure productivity gains, some changes in TFP can be traced to economies of scale, but variations in scale of operation are also associated with the drive for improved efficiency and technological advance. As a result, the aggregate output trends that are directly traceable to economies of scale are difficult to separate out from the overwhelming incentives for producers to adapt their operations to new efficient methods and technologies.

Recent TFP trends and research opportunities

In May 2016, the USDA-ERS posted an online updated report of US Agricultural TFP entitled, "Findings, Documentation, and Methods."[13] The published results largely confirmed the outcomes identified in their earlier 1948–2011 ERS productivity study.

The 2016 ERS online post took advantage of additional farm TFP data compiled during the 2012–2013 period. Consequently, we can reliably examine US agricultural TFP trends during 1948–2013. The supplementary TFP data enabled the ERS to determine whether current TFP growth is keeping pace with historical trends.

As the increasingly important question of how the agricultural sector will meet growing global food demands is addressed more intently, measures of productivity patterns are receiving greater attention from policy makers and related interest groups.

The 2016 ERS report compares changes in US agricultural productivity in two recent and separate sub-periods: 2000–2007 and 2007–2013. ERS defines a sub-period as the time required for the completion of a peak-to-peak cycle of aggregate economic activity.

The 2000–2007 sub-period was characterized by the surge in US bio-fuel use and production. Over the early 2000s timespan, corn acreage expanded by nearly 15 million acres, corn prices rose, and the rural economy experienced growth in capital investment and job creation. Agricultural input demand was noticeably higher during this cycle of booming bio-fuel markets. The *ag-input* utilization index rose by +0.32 percent per year in the 2000–2007 sub-period, compared to the long-term historical average of +0.07 percent per year.[14]

The rate of *agricultural **output** growth* was roughly the same, increasing an average of +0.9 percent per year, during both the 2000–2007 and the 2007–2013 sub-periods.

The 2007–2013 sub-period was marked by a national macroeconomic recession in 2008–2009, extensive use of precision technologies in US agriculture, and export demand growth for US agricultural and food products. But what differentiated the 2007–2013 economic cycle was the *remarkable decrease in the US agricultural input-use rate*, changing at a pace of −0.54 percent per year. When the negative change in the input index is combined with the +0.9 percent output growth, the *change in TFP jumps to a +1.54 percent annual rate* over the 2007–2013 sub-period, as compared to the +0.6 percent annual rate during the 2000–2007 sub-period.

The US national recession during 2008–2009 was the most severe since the Great Depression, and some of the reduced agricultural input usage during the 2007–2013 sub-period can be attributed to this massive macroeconomic downturn. However, another researchable hypothesis is the influence of precision agricultural technology on farm input usage rates during the 2007–2013 sub-period.[15]

While *precision agriculture methods* require up-front software and hardware investments, the pay-off for producers is the ability to apply extra inputs only in areas that are identified as deficient or would benefit from additional application. The savings, measured in terms of reduced pesticide and fertilizer use, decreased labor time, and related general efficiencies, are significant.

In addition, if we recall the natural resource efficiencies documented during this same sub-period in Chapter 8, we have further reasons to expect producers to achieve smarter use of agricultural inputs (e.g. more efficient water use for irrigation; anaerobic digesters to generate energy and reduce emissions; reductions in soil erosion rates; increased participation in EQIP and CSP conservation programs).

Integrating sustainability and climate change considerations with productivity analysis

As discussed above, the traditional market-based productivity indices show a continuing upward trend. While US agricultural TFP data reflect an impressive record of farm output expansion, researchable questions remain about future sustainable growth because intensive agricultural practices are associated with damaging environmental side effects.

In addition, concerns about sustainability are intertwined with climate-change conditions. At this time there are more questions than there are answers. A growing research agenda is now exploring how environmental degradation and a changing climate will influence the future growth of agricultural productivity.

Linking sustainability to agricultural productivity

In the journal *Nature* (2002), Tilman et al. agreed that global agricultural technologies have significantly boosted the worldwide food supply.[16] However, this research group also notes the unintended but harmful effects of many global farm systems on environmental quality and ecosystem carrying-capacity. In Chapter 8 of our textbook, we discussed how Krutilla[17] and other researchers arrived at similar conclusions.

Today, a growing number of producers are adapting new techniques that increase farm output while preserving future ecosystem services.[18] The expanded focus on "sustainability" (see Chapter 8, p. 13) implies that agriculture should develop and implement environmentally friendly production methods that also meet current global food needs. If we can implement sustainable farming systems now, then future generations can also share the same benefits that we enjoy today: utilizing natural resources and environmental systems to support a successful economy and a desirable quality of life.

Organizations such as the OECD (2014) and the United Nations [UN] (2013) sponsor ongoing research to encourage globally sustainable agricultural growth trends.[19, 20] For example, the OECD's *Green Growth* initiative aims to spur modernization and technological improvements to promote growth patterns that create current prosperity and also conserve the natural resources and environmental conditions needed to safeguard future health and welfare.[21]

Similarly, the UN *Sustainable Development Solutions Network* champions actions such as food-waste reduction, healthy-diet programs, sustainable production technology adoption, and the creation of climate-smart agricultural landscapes.[22] Conservation programs sponsored by the USDA also play a role in identifying specific programs, such as soil-health workshops and cost-shared practices that promote sustainable production.[23]

Climate change and agricultural productivity: challenges and opportunities

Questions about sustainable growth in agricultural production would merit attention even in a climate-stable world. But overwhelming scientific evidence is telling us that the global climate is shifting. In March 2014, the Intergovernmental Panel on Climate Change (IPCC) used the results of extensive and credible research to declare that climate transformation is already in progress, and further variation is expected.[24]

While researchers have worked diligently to construct sophisticated models to simulate and predict interactions between agricultural output trends and climate change, the complexity of the challenge is daunting.

From a biophysical standpoint, it is not just a matter of increased average global temperatures and melting ice caps. The higher concentrations of carbon dioxide (CO_2) and Ozone (O_3) in the earth's atmosphere influence plant transpiration and growth rates. A more energized atmosphere also increases the potential for extreme weather events such as extended droughts or flash floods.[25]

From an economic standpoint, forecasting changes in agricultural productivity go beyond the pure biochemistry and physics of new ecological conditions. Output trends are intertwined with the collective influence of a shifting global climate on the behavioral incentives facing individual farm producers and consumers. Predicted output trends should also reflect how macro- and micro-economic market conditions, as well as government policies, respond to the new circumstances.

Lobell and Gourdji (2012) carefully examined the biophysical effects of projected climate conditions on global crop productivity.[26] Lobell and Gourdji determined that increased CO_2 concentrations would tend to increase crop yields globally, while warming trends would likely offset most of the CO_2 impact by reducing average worldwide yields.

In addition, this biophysical research assesses that climate change will *slow the rate of expected productivity growth* normally connected with new technologies and improved management methods. Lobell and Gourdji (2012) conclude that climate change will not reduce global yields, but will make it more difficult for agricultural productivity to expand as rapidly as would be expected in an alternative climate-stable scenario.

Nelson et al. (2013) undertook the large task of combining biophysical and economic models, and analyzed multiple scenarios to increase our understanding of the range of possible future outcomes.[27] The complexity of their research assignment is made clear when we understand that Nelson et al. utilized the outcomes of seven different biophysical scenarios as inputs into nine separate economic models.

When they consolidated the results from this multi-faceted approach, Nelson et al. (2013) determined that by 2050, climate change will be associated with a 17 percent loss in global yields, but the lost productivity will be nearly offset by an escalating intensity of farm practices and increased farmed-acreages, creating a net 2 percent output loss. Their much more dramatic predictions were economic.

The Nelson et al. model estimated that global consumption will drop by 3 percent and average producer prices will rise by about 20 percent. While Nelson et al. (2013) were not charged with the goal of forecasting the negative welfare impacts of rising global food prices on low-income households, the predicted results of their extensive modeling effort are a reason for considerable concern.

Similar to Nelson et al., Yang, and Shumway (2015) utilized sophisticated modeling techniques to predict how climate change would produce structural economic changes in US agriculture.[28] The differentiating aspect of Yang and Shumway's research is their focus on the predicted adjustment rate for asset utilization as climate change alters market conditions. Yang and Shumway used over 100 years of data to demonstrate that new market situations (created by a stochastic climate or similar dynamic force) cause *quasi-fixed asset modifications* – meaning that the farm assets are not totally fixed, nor are they instantaneously reallocated.

Evidence is strong for quasi-fixity in Yang and Shumway's analysis. While no enterprise adapts immediately, crop adjustments are predicted to occur at twice the rate compared to livestock changes. Yang and Shumway also employ the economic theory of rational expectations to demonstrate that farm production *adjustment rates are much slower and the economic costs are much higher if producers fail to anticipate climate change.*

On other hand, if producers accept that climate change is real, and simply adapt to climate uncertainty, then adjustment costs drop noticeably and the asset reallocation rate for quasi-fixed assets rises. At the start of this chapter, the US Agriculture Secretary warned that we ignore climate change at our peril; his viewpoint is validated by Yang and Shumway's in-depth study of stochastic asset adjustment.

Alternative agricultural productivity scenarios and associated policy options

It is difficult to overstate the importance of ongoing research to determine both the obstacles and the catalysts for continued agricultural productivity growth. Factors such as environmental sustainability and climate change deserve attention if we are to better understand how current conditions influence future trends. The common threads that tie together the entire discussion are the need to both expand our knowledge base and harness the necessary incentives, if sufficient US agricultural productivity growth is to occur in the twenty-first century.

Fortunately, we do not have to create TFP-enhancing strategies "from scratch." There are fundamental principles that guide productivity growth, and we can use them to establish plausible scenarios and policy options. In the 2003 edition of *Agricultural Resources and Environmental Indicators*, the USDA's Economic Research Service (ERS) highlighted the following factors closely associated with productivity growth:[29]

- Research and Development (R&D)
- Extension
- Education
- Infrastructure
- Government policies/programs

Research and development

Innovation in agriculture, as in most industries, is the primary source of TFP growth. Innovation can be small- or large-scale, but its origins are most often the result of systematic investigation, i.e. research and development (R&D). In agriculture, R&D is typically responsible for outcomes such as disease-resistant and higher-yielding crops, improved livestock breeds, enhanced fertilizer and pest-management systems, and superior farm practices.

Twenty-first-century R&D is both privately and publicly funded, and *private sources now generate a majority of agricultural research expenditures*. While there are exceptions, we can distinguish private R&D from public R&D by examining their intended purposes. Private research is most often focused on specific and commercially viable applications, while public funds are primarily channeled towards basic research.

Private firms typically strive to retain intellectual property rights for their innovations via legal mechanisms such as patents, copyrights, and trademarks. The private focus on proprietary rights is essential if the originators of a new process or product are to reap a sufficient return on their R&D costs.

Despite the best legal efforts of private enterprise, newly created knowledge from R&D often generates significant positive externalities. Private firms cannot always capture all of the research benefits that they create. Information about new methods frequently spreads quickly and at low cost to the rest of the economy. As a result, knowledge creation unavoidably creates "public good" outcomes – non-rival and non-excludable benefits (see Chapter 3).

In comparison to commercially oriented R&D, the benefits of basic research are even more clearly in the realm of public goods. Consequently the use of public funds to engage in basic research is economically sensible. Private firms could not earn sufficient returns, and the private market would under-allocate resources towards basic R&D.

R&D often yields benefits that are not purely public or private. In such instances, a rationale for private-public partnerships arises. In fact, without an appropriate institutional apparatus, important and productive research opportunities requiring private-public collaboration would be lost or overlooked.

Recognition of this potential R&D shortcoming led the US Congress to pass the 1980 Technology Innovation Act, and later the 1986 Technology Transfer Act (TTA). The TTA authorized federal departments to establish private-public alliances for joint research.[30] More specifically, the TTA created legal guidelines to arrange private-public contracts known today as *Cooperative Research and Development Agreements (CRADAs)*. The USDA quickly recognized the CRADA as a worthwhile institutional innovation. During 1987–1995 alone, USDA collaborated with private entities to implement over 500 CRADAs.[31]

Joint CRADA projects, along with purely private and purely public R&D, together create the primary sources of agricultural TFP growth. The key role of R&D is the social rate of return on these research-oriented activities. Estimates for core marginal rates of return, reflecting directly measurable and properly discounted benefits and costs, *fall anywhere between a +35 percent and +60 percent internal rate of return*,[32] when all private and public investments in agricultural R&D are included. Such returns are a sizable net gain to society, and highlight the importance of continued support for R&D from all sources.

Extension and education

What time interval is needed for research breakthroughs to affect real output? What factors connect R&D innovations to actual productivity changes? Extension and education efforts are key links in *disseminating, communicating, and implementing* new ideas.

While each system has a separate purpose, extension and education effectively reduce the time required to convert potential research gains into realized returns. If we first focus on the role of agricultural extension agents, we discover a group of professionals dedicated to organizing scientific results into easy-to-use formats. Extension's timely delivery of accessible information means that farmers and ranchers can quickly convert new knowledge into practical technologies that increase their operational efficiency and productivity.

Unfortunately, data on the productivity enhancing effects of extension activities is sparse relative to the evidence of output gains from research. Scant data is one reason why the measured return on investment for extension efforts is variable, ranging between a 20 percent and a 100 percent rate of return.

Extension's purposes are being modified by the twenty-first-century phenomena of the Internet, producer access to self-help technologies, and the rapidly rising influence of private agricultural consulting firms. Federal government funding support for extension has fallen since 1980. State and local governments have found it necessary to reduce the number of agents, and consolidate county-level extension programs into larger regional service areas. *Private consulting and self-service technologies* are partly filling the void created by diminished investments in extension.

Extension programs facilitate the dissemination of specific innovations and technologies to producers. Education, on the other hand, aims to build broad skills in critical thinking and problem solving. Fuglie et al. (2007) estimated that 5.6 percent of US agricultural output growth could be attributed to increased labor quality.[33]

When the farm labor force is better educated, has superior training or gains more experience, then labor quality improves. Additional education facilitates producer technology adoption, as well as teaching consumers the skills they need to properly evaluate new food choices based their actual benefits and risks. Producers surveyed by Joreger et al. (2003) indicated their involvement the Minnesota Farm Business Management Education program was associated with a $5,000 average annual increase in net farm income (Joerger 2003, p. 56).[34]

Infrastructure and government policies/programs

Economic research determined that public infrastructure investments (roads, bridges and highways, water and sewer systems, schools, hospitals, etc.) are linked to gains in productivity.

In agriculture, improved transportation and communication systems increase producer efficiencies for input acquisition and output marketing. Munisamy and Roe (1995) determined that *infrastructure development and R&D were complementary inputs* to agricultural productivity gains.[35]

Short- and long-run agricultural productivity patterns are induced by government policies. Let's first look at temporary government influences. When federal biofuel policies dramatically increased corn production incentives in the early 2000s, producers responded with the rapid hiring of additional inputs (e.g. planting extra corn acres on marginal land) and the TFP growth slowed. By 2012, the federal government reduced or eliminated the majority of biofuel subsidies and corn output expansion leveled off. Input usage dropped, and farmers were also quickly adapting precision agriculture farming techniques. TFP was on the rise again.

Long-term government effects on productivity include macroeconomic policies that encourage technological investments. Government programs that boost agricultural research and innovations also affect long-term TFP. Other broad policies with extended effects include improved mechanisms to protect intellectual property rights and programs similar to CRADA. Legal protections create the correct economic environment for private and public research, because firms will innovate more rapidly if they have confidence in their ability to reap sufficient returns on their investments. We should also recognize the role of international trade policies and agreements that spur US agricultural producers to expand output when they have a global comparative advantage.

Alternative research policies and associated agricultural productivity scenarios

The in-depth 2015 ERS agricultural productivity study referenced earlier in this chapter not only reviewed past farm output developments, but also offered short- and long-term US TFP projections up through the year 2050.[36] ERS developed three TFP scenarios to explore the output growth consequences of different future funding levels for public research.

We can summarize the three alternate ERS assumptions about public agricultural research funding:[37]

- (#1) *The Optimistic Scenario*: U.S. public agricultural research spending rises an average of 1 percent per year percent in real terms, compared to the baseline of the 2005–2009 average level of expenditures.
- (#2) *The Nominally Constant Annual Public Funding Scenario*: Annual US public agricultural research spending through 2050 remains unchanged in nominal dollars at its average 2005–2009 level of $2.5 billion per year.
- (#3) *The Scenario of a One-time 25 percent-Decrease in Federal Public Research Spending*: In this scenario, no subsequent nominal or real funding changes occur if Congress was to significantly reduce public agricultural research in 2014, and then maintains this lower level of public funding indefinitely into the future.

The above three scenarios are distinct federal agricultural research policy choices. Initially, the outcomes of these three funding options do not differ by much. Positive agricultural output growth is projected in all three situations through the year 2020; specifically, US farm production increases by 13 percent, 12 percent, and 12 percent, respectively, in each of the three scenarios during the 2010–2020 stretch of growing seasons. Noticeably different outcomes occur when the entire 2010–2050 projection period is analyzed.

If we review the *optimistic scenario*, the expected TFP growth rate is 1.46 percent per year during 2010–2050, compared with 1.42 percent during 1948–2011. From the standpoint of the future global food supply-demand balance, this is a good outcome.

The *scenario of constant nominal annual public funding* is not as "rosy" as the optimistic one. The annual rate of agricultural TFP growth is 0.86 percent/year between 2010 and 2050; this is 40 percent lower than the 1.42 percent per year historical 1948–2011 growth rate. The predicted result of this policy option is strongly and negatively affected by a 3.73 percent per year increase in expected real research costs projected over the 2010-2050 forecasting interval.

The third scenario, where public agricultural research experiences a 25 percent loss of funding in 2014, and then remains nominally constant per year in future years, US Agricultural TFP growth rate decreases to 0.63 percent per year during 2010–2050. This is a 56 percent reduction in TFP growth, relative to the 1.42 percent per year that the US experienced during 1948–2011.

Why do we care about the alternative growth TFP growth rates in these three scenarios? Heisey et al. (2011) projected that if Scenarios Two or Three become reality, then US agricultural production growth rates likely *will not* match global food demand growth rates.[38] In contrast, Heisey et al. (2011) also forecasted that *if US R&D spending on public agricultural research were to rise by 1 percent per year in real terms subsequent to 2010, then US agricultural TFP will expand at a rate **equal** to the speed of growing domestic and global food demand.*

To meet global food demand, Scenarios #2 and #3 necessitate that US producers accelerate the rates at which they hire additional land, labor, capital, fertilizer, pesticide, and related scarce inputs. The cost of production, and associated food prices, will rise as the marginal cost of hiring additional inputs increases. Increased worldwide food prices create severe burdens on low-income households across the planet.

Without sufficient gains in TFP (Scenarios 2 and 3), more intensive and extensive farmland use is expected. Increased land-use intensity, and increased hiring of extensive marginal lands for crop production, will create environmental challenges. We can expect compromised water quality, increased soil erosion, and reduced wildlife habitat and/or wetlands. The long-run economic and ecological costs of Scenarios Two and Three are significant.

Summary and conclusions: the future of US agricultural productivity possibilities

Undoubtedly, US agricultural productivity trends since 1950 have been remarkable. Can this record continue? Based on established theoretical and empirical evidence, the answer to this question is a largely a matter of policy choice. It is a decision with global consequences.

Is the US prepared to select a path of ongoing investment in agricultural research that will spur future TFP growth sufficient to equal the expanding food demands of an increasing global population? This is a difficult question. Research tells us that the US has the capacity to respond positively. Whether the US will choose to expand its TFP growth rate to meet global food demands is a consideration of political, ethical, and economic significance.

If the US does answer this productivity challenge in a positive way, there are guideposts to guide the needed investments. The growth strategy will involve a coordinated effort to integrate additional investments in research and development (R&D), extension, education, infrastructure, and coordinated government policies/programs.

Research on TFP growth also informs policy design. Short- and long-run productivity trends often diverge. It is necessary to formulate productivity policies that intentionally consider both more immediate and extended outcomes and trends.

In the next chapter we explore the food security question at local and regional levels. Ultimately, US national agricultural productivity influences circumstances at the microeconomic level. It makes sense that we first reviewed broader considerations (in Chapter 9 now) and then narrow them (in Chapter 10) to study what is happening to producers and consumers in individual markets.

Household welfare is the name of the game, in the end. The adaptations required by individual decision makers can only be fully understood when we have properly explained the economic environment that they encounter on a daily basis.

As you turn the page to another chapter, we hope you are sufficiently prepared and motivated to continue this exciting journey of exploring the many facets of US agricultural and food policy.

Notes

1 The Council on Foreign Relations (CFR) is an independent, nonpartisan membership organization, think tank, and publisher.
2 Council on Foreign Relations (CFR), Roger C. Altman, Presider. "Agricultural Technology and Productivity Continue to Make Gains and Ensure U.S. Food Security: A Conversation With Tom Vilsack." CFR Events: Renewing America Series. April 9, 2014. Retrieved from: www.cfr. org/agricultural-policy/agricultural-technology-productivity-continue-make-gains-ensure-us-food-security/p35599
3 The Tornqvist index calculation technique incorporates prices from both the base period and the comparison period to determine the indexed weighted averages. A benefit of the Tornqvist method is that inputs to the production process need not be perfect substitutes. Heimlich, Ralph. *Agricultural Resources and Environmental Indicators*. USDA, ERS Agriculture Handbook AH-722, Chapter 5.1, February 2003. Retrieved from: http://infohouse.p2ric.org/ref/37/36628.htm
4 Heimlich, Ralph. *Agricultural Resources and Environmental Indicators. Chapter 5: Agricultural Productivity and Research*. USDA, ERS. Agricultural Handbook 722. February 2003. http://info house.p2ric.org/ref/37/36628_files/AREI5-1productivity.pdf
5 OECD (2014), Green Growth Indicators 2014. OECD Green Growth Studies, OECD Publishing. Retrieved from: http://dx.doi.org/10.1787/9789264202030-en
6 "Fallacy of Composition: What is true for the individual is not necessarily true for the group." Samuelson, Paul and William Nordhaus. *Economics*. Sixteenth Edition. Boston, MA: Irwin McGraw-Hill, 1998, pp. 6–7.
7 Cochrane, Willard W. 1958. *Farm Prices: Myth and Reality*. Minneapolis, MN: University of Minnesota Press. Retrieved from: http://barrett.dyson.cornell.edu/Papers/IFPRIMay2002.pdf
8 Levins, Richard A. and Willard W. Cochrane. "The Treadmill Revisited." *Land Economics* 72(4) (Nov. 1996), pp. 550–553. Retrieved from: www.jstor.org/stable/3146915?seq=1#page_scan_tab_contents
9 OECD (2011). *Fostering Productivity and Competitiveness in Agriculture*. OECD Publishing. Retrieved from: http://dx.doi.org/10.1787/9789264166820-en, page 25.
10 Wang, Sun Ling, Paul Heisey, David Schimmelpfennig, and Eldon Ball. *Agricultural Productivity Growth in the United States: Measurement, Trends, and Drivers*. ERR-189, U.S. Department of Agriculture, Economic Research Service, July 2015. Retrieved from: www.ers.usda.gov/media/1875389/err189.pdf
11 Ibid, pp. 28–29.
12 Ibid, pp. 17–18.
13 Ball, Eldon, Sun Ling Wang, and Richard Nehring. USDA, ERS. *Agricultural Productivity in the U.S.: Findings, Documentation, and Methods*. Washington: USDA, ERS. Updated: May 9, 2016. Retrieved from: www.ers.usda.gov/data-products/agricultural-productivity-in-the-us/findings,-documentation,-and-methods.aspx#majorfinding
14 Ibid.
15 Schimmelpfennig, David. *Cost Savings from Precision Agriculture Technologies on U.S. Corn Farms*. USDA, ERS Amber Waves. May 2, 2016. Retrieved from: www.ers.usda.gov/amber-waves/2016-may/cost-savings-from-precision-agriculture-technologies-on-us-corn-farms.aspx#.Vz0t_Y-cHIV

16 Tilman, David, Kenneth G. Cassman, Pamela A. Matson, Rosamond Naylor and Stephen Polasky. "Agricultural sustainability and intensive production practices." *Nature* 418, 671–677 (8 August 2002). Retrieved from: www.nature.com/nature/journal/v418/n6898/full/nature01014.html

17 Krutilla, John V. "Conservation Reconsidered." *American Economic Review* 57(4) Sept. 1967, pp. 777–786. Retrieved from: www.rff.org/files/sharepoint/News/Features/Documents/071003%20Krutilla-ConservationReconsidered.pdf

18 Kremen, C., and A. Miles. 2012. "Ecosystem services in biologically diversified versus conventional farming systems: benefits, externalities, and trade-offs." *Ecology and Society* 17(4), p. 40. Retrieved from:http://dx.doi.org/10.5751/ES-05035-170440

19 OECD (2014a). "Green Growth Indicators 2014." OECD Green Growth Studies. Paris: OECD Publishing. DOI: Retrieved from: http://dx.doi.org/10.1787/9789264202030-en

20 Dobermann, Achim and Rebecca Nelson, Chairs of the UN Thematic Group on Sustainable Agriculture and Food Systems of the Sustainable Development Solutions Network. *Solutions for Sustainable Agriculture and Food Systems: Technical Report for the Post-2015 Development Agenda.* 18 September 2013. Retrieved from: http://unsdsn.org/wp-content/uploads/2014/02/130919-TG07-Agriculture-Report-WEB.pdf

21 OECD (2014). "Green Growth Indicators 2014." OECD Green Growth Studies, OECD Publishing. Retrieved from: http://dx.doi.org/10.1787/9789264202030-en

22 Dobermann, Achim and Rebecca Nelson. *Solutions for Sustainable Agriculture and Food Systems: Technical Report for the Post-2015 Development Agenda*, p. 13.

23 USDA, Alternative Farming Systems Information Center (AFSIC). *Sustainability in Agriculture.* National Agricultural Library. May 2016. Retrieved from: https://afsic.nal.usda.gov/sustainability-agriculture-0

24 Sands, Ron. *Economic Responses Offset Potential Climate Change Impacts on Global Agriculture.* USDA, ERS. Amber Waves, October 06, 2014. Retrieved from: www.ers.usda.gov/amber-waves/2014-october/economic-responses-offset-potential-climate-change-impacts-on-global-agriculture.aspx#.V1Xhg5ErK03

25 Lobell, David B. and Sharon M. Gourdji. "The Influence of Climate Change on Global Crop Productivity." *Plant Physiology* 160(4) December 2012, 1686–1697. American Society of Plant Biologists. Retrieved from: http://dx.doi.org/10.1104/pp.112.208298

26 Ibid.

27 Nelson, Gerald C., Hugo Valin, Ronald D. Sands, Petr Havlík, Helal Ahammad, Delphine Deryng, Joshua Elliott, Shinichiro Fujimori, Tomoko Hasegawa, Edwina Heyhoe, Page Kyle, Martin Von Lampe, Hermann Lotze-Campen, Daniel Mason d'Croz, Hans van Meijl, Dominique van der Mensbrugghe, Christoph Müller, Alexander Popp, Richard Robertson, Sherman Robinson, Erwin Schmid, Christoph Schmitz, Andrzej Tabeau, and Dirk Willenbockel. "Climate Change Effects on Agriculture: Economic Responses to Biophysical Shocks." *Proceedings of the National Academy of Sciences*, 111(9), pp. 3274–3279. August 2013. doi: 10.1073/pnas.1222465110. Retrieved from: www.pnas.org/content/111/9/3274.full

28 Yang, Sansi and C. Richard Shumway. Dynamic Adjustment in US Agriculture under Climate Change. *Am. J. Agr. Econ.* (2016) 98(3), pp. 910–924. DOI: 10.1093/ajae/aav042. Retrieved from: http://ajae.oxfordjournals.org/content/98/3/910.full.pdf+html?sid=dfcd0105-f3c7-45a0-9547-9b542184ac7a

29 Heimlich, Ralph. *Agricultural Resources and Environmental Indicators.* USDA, ERS Agriculture Handbook AH-722, Chapter 5.1, *Agricultural Productivity*, pp. 11–15. February 2003. Retrieved from: www.ers.usda.gov/media/873664/agproductivity.pdf

30 Fuglie, Keith, Nicole Ballenger, Kelly Day-Rubenstein, Cassandra Klotz, Michael Ollinger, John Reilly, Utpal Vasavada, and Jet Yee. *Agricultural Research and Development: Public and Private Investments under Alternative Markets and Institutions.* Agricultural Economic Report No. (AER-735) 88 pp, May 1996. Retrieved from: www.ers.usda.gov/publications/aer-agricultural-economic-report/aer735.aspx

31 Fuglie, Keith Keith, Nicole Ballenger, Kelly Day-Rubenstein, Cassandra Klotz, Michael Ollinger, John Reilly, Utpal Vasavada, and Jet Yee. *Public-Private Collaboration in Agricultural Research*, Agricultural Economic Report No. (AER-735), pp. 51–57, May 1996. Retrieved from: www.ers.usda.gov/media/463777/aer735s5_1_.pdf

32 Ibid, pp. 53–56.

33 Fuglie, Keith O., James M. MacDonald, and Eldon Ball. *Productivity Growth in U.S. Agriculture.* USDA, ERS Economic Brief Number 9, September 2007. Retrieved from: www.ers.usda.gov/media/201254/eb9_1_.pdf

34 Joerger, R. M. "Student Perspectives of the Nature, Effectiveness, and Value of the Minnesota Farm Business Management Education Program." *Journal of Agricultural Education* 44(1), pp. 56–69. 2003. Retrieved from Charles R. Holcomb. Producer Attitudes and Farm Management Education. Master's Thesis, University of Minnesota Duluth, 2011. Retrieved from: https://d-commons.d.umn.edu/bitstream/10792/148/1/Holcomb,%20Charles.pdf

35 Munisamy, Gopinath and Terry L. Roe. *Sources of Sectoral Growth in an Economy Wide Context: The Case of U.S. Agriculture.* University of Minnesota Economic Development Center. Department of Economics, Minneapolis Department of Applied Economics, St. Paul. Bulletin Number 95-7, August 1995. Retrieved from: http://ageconsearch.umn.edu/bitstream/7454/1/edc95-07.pdf

36 Wang, Sun Ling, Paul Heisey, David Schimmelpfennig, and Eldon Ball. *Agricultural Productivity Growth in the United States: Measurement, Trends, and Drivers,* ERR-189, U.S. Department of Agriculture, Economic Research Service, July 2015, pp. 53–56. Retrieved from: www.ers.usda.gov/media/1875389/err189.pdf

37 Ibid, p. 54.

38 Heisey, P., S.L. Wang, and K. Fuglie. 2011. *Public Agricultural Research Spending and Future U.S. Agricultural Productivity Growth: Scenarios for 2010–2050.* Economic Brief 17. U.S. Department of Agriculture, Economic Research Service. Retrieved from: www.ers.usda.gov/publications/eb-economic-brief/eb17.aspx

Chapter 10

Exploring the multi-dimensional aspects of food security

Food security is a concern for households worldwide. Achieving a more food-secure status requires a combination of both increased production capacity as well as improved consumption. An example can illustrate. Consider how the parents, teachers, and administrators in the Charlottesville, Virginia school district have teamed up to create a City Schoolyard Garden (CSG).[1]

In 2016, the Charlottesville CSG accepted a USDA Farm-to-School Grant to expand its "Harvest of the Month" Program. On the "production side," high-school teachers used the CSG to build students' entrepreneurial skills to grow and market vegetables, flowers, and spring seedlings. On the "consumption side," school officials literally pushed carts of CSG-harvested products down elementary school hallways; they shared the fresh produce with the youngsters in the classrooms. Teachers used this as a teachable moment for youth to develop their knowledge and appreciation of the essential elements for a healthy diet at an early age.[2]

Let's travel further south, and halfway around the world. We can observe the effort to build a more food-secure world, one household at a time, in West Africa. Many families in Senegal depend on wood energy to cook their meals. Reliance on a single heating source is risky. Changes in weather or socio-political conditions can suddenly and severely hamper the primary means to thoroughly cook foods. Food security is not just ensuring a minimum caloric intake. It includes all of the resources that increase the nutritional value of foods and safeguard their consumption against the threat of pathogens.[3]

Faculty and student-fellows participating in the International Program at the University of Missouri (MU) College of Agriculture, Food and Natural Resources recognized the need for diversified energy sources in West Africa, and decided to act. They proposed a project entitled "Biofuels for Sustainable Rural Livelihoods," and received a USDA Foreign Agricultural Service (FAS) Cochran Fellowship to actively pursue their project goals.

MU staff were able to work with Senegal's National Biogas Program to construct 500 bio-digesters in houses and schools across the Diourbel Region. MU fellows also initiated farmer-training programs in feedstock management and soil conservation. The end result of these efforts is to assist Senegalese households to establish affordable and diversified energy alternatives and improve their food security at the farm level.[4]

The global and local challenges of food insecurity

As we study current conditions and future trends in our twenty-first-century agri-food system, we learn that numerous tests of policymaking effectiveness lie before us. Whether they are located in urban US communities or rural regions of West Africa, poverty and food insecurity are among the most troubling and significant of these challenges.

If our decisions are to produce desired outcomes, then we should concentrate our efforts to overcome the most important socio-economic problems. What can be done to alleviate poverty and help to create a world where households are more food secure?

If we can clearly identify the critical economic impasses, and figure out how to surmount them, then we can improve our potential to make real progress in creating advances in social welfare.

Many key questions require our attention. It is difficult or impossible to address them all. Prioritization is also problematic. Nevertheless, we can and should propose initiatives that can make a difference.

Since the year 2000, organizations such as the United Nations (UN), the G8 and G20 Alliances, the US Agency for International Development (USAID) and the USDA have reached a near-consensus around this single policy theme: [5]

> Coordinating local, regional, and global policies to create a world where every household is food secure.

Such a goal is undoubtedly difficult to achieve, but it also a vision that gathers nearly universal approval and support. This chapter explores the various opportunities currently being pursued to reduce or eliminate food insecurity.

In many ways, food security is a policy agenda that goes beyond solving the immediate problem of hunger. It is nothing less than a concerted effort to address and overcome the root causes of food insecurity. The ultimate goal is to encourage global economic progress, and consequently increase the likelihood that every household can access a nutritional diet.

Ideally, every person should be sufficiently nourished so that they are ready to be productive workers in the labor market or effective learners in school.[6]

Organization of chapter

Food security policy is a wide-ranging topic. The approach that we will take is to first consider how to define food-secure and food-insecure households. Next, we will examine how the United States pursues domestic food security policy. Then we will review the multinational and global efforts to improve nutritional conditions for households worldwide.

Finally, we will make observations about the relationship between household food security (or insecurity) and the operational effectiveness of our agri-food systems. In particular, we can explore the role of "food hubs" in achieving efficient and equitable food distributional outcomes. We will also review the food-security problems associated with geographic areas that are "food deserts." We examine the growing importance of local agri-food systems, regional food networks and public-private partnerships that can help establish sustainable food-secure conditions over the long term.

Defining levels of food security and insecurity

Naylor (2014) offers this basic definition of food security:[7]

> Food Security means having adequate supplies of affordable food throughout the year to ensure a healthy and productive life.

We can measure the presence or absence of food security at a micro, intermediate or macro scale. For example, researchers have conducted studies of food security conditions for households, regions, and entire nations. Studies at different scale levels necessarily emphasize alternative aspects of food security, but there are also common elements. Headey and Ecker (2013)[8] and Naylor (2014)[9] recommend four dimensions to include when assessing whether conditions are food secure or food insecure:

- Availability (employ some physical measure of food supply adequacy).
- Access (economically measure if income is sufficient to purchase food).
- Utilization (gauge whether diets are nutritionally balanced).
- Stability (determine if households, regions, etc. can maintain food availability and sustain food access as markets, politics, and climate fluctuate).

As Naylor (2014) correctly observes, the multi-faceted nature of food security is not easily measured.[10] Producing a stable and long-term food secure condition is also a difficult accomplishment, especially in the developing regions of the world. But even in developed nations such as the US, there are pockets of food insecurity in both rural areas and inner cities.

National and international agencies and governments profess their commitments to help every household achieve a food-secure status. Such goals are praiseworthy, but the obstacles to their accomplishment are considerable. Much work remains to be done if measurable progress is to occur.

It is tough to know if gains in food security are happening without a reliable measurement approach. The USDA developed a classification system to gauge different levels of household food security. The USDA recognizes a "security continuum" that is divided into four ranges. The top two ranges are considered food-secure stages, while the bottom two are deemed as food insecure. The USDA nomenclature is:[11]

- High Food Security
- Marginal Food Security   ↑ *Food Secure Household*

- Low Food Security
- Very Low Food Security   ↓ *Food Insecure Household*

Using the USDA taxonomy, food-secure households either have no problems accessing food (*high food security*), or have periodic problems with food access but no substantial reductions in their food intake (*marginal food security*).

In contrast, *low food-secure households* have reduced economic access to balanced nutritional diets, although household food intake is not substantially less. *Very low food security* causes households to experience real diet disruptions, including decreased frequencies and/ or quantities of food intake. If household members regularly skip meals because of insufficient household income, then we have an instance of very low food security.

The USDA also emphasizes that *food insecurity* and *hunger* are not equivalent concepts. A *food insecure household* is a socio-economic condition that limits or prevents household members' access to healthy nutritional dietary choices. *Hunger* is a physiological sensation associated with personal pain, discomfort, and sometimes illness.[12] Food insecurity can be an important reason why hunger is more prevalent in a household, but it is not the sole reason. Research that explores the consequences of food insecurity has the special challenge of understanding the various cause-and-effect relationships.

When we can pinpoint food insecurity as the primary reason for chronic hunger in children and other household members, we find a nearly universal interest in figuring out how to overcome the root causes of food security problems.

Naylor (2014) and many other researchers conclude that the challenges associated with food insecurity are best understood at the household level.[13] We cannot fully comprehend the true nature of food security conditions by merely comparing the world's population numbers to the total caloric value of global food production. Totals and averages will not offer us any insights into to how we should address the questions of unequal household incomes and food purchasing power.

Economic access, which measures whether a household is both willing and able to pay for a nutritious diet, is arguably the most significant challenge of food security. The United Nations (UN), in an effort to bring about positive change on a global scale in the twenty-first century, identified eight Millennium Development Goals (MDGs). The UN's first MDG is actually no surprise to anyone who studies food security problems:[14]

MDG #1: Eradicate Extreme Poverty and Hunger

The connection between extreme poverty and food insecurity is clear. Naylor (2014) notes that approximately one-third of our global population lives in extreme poverty (households earning less than $1.25 per day). These impoverished households are most susceptible to food insecurity and chronic hunger whenever food prices rise or average incomes fall.[15]

Linking food security definitions to policy directions

Our very brief introduction to the factors influencing food security measurement tells us that we are exploring a complex and multi-dimensional field of study. We also know that few issues are as significant and universal as the food security status of households, both locally and globally.

What contributions can agri-system policies make to improve food security? While we may not be able to arrive at a definitive answer to this question, we can begin to understand the various considerations that must be included if we are to increase the effectiveness of our policy recommendations. In the next section of this chapter, we review efforts in the United States intended to make progress in food security conditions. After we have examined national concerns, we will expand our study to review multinational and global food security initiatives.

Examining US and global responses to food insecurity

Food insecurity in the US

The USDA conducts annual national surveys to estimate US household food security conditions. In 2015, USDA's Economic Research Service (ERS) reported that 83.7 percent of US households were food-secure, and 12.7 percent were food-insecure.[16] Within the broad food-insecure category, 5.0 percent (6.3 million US households) faced the more severe dietary challenges that accompany the "very low food insecurity" classification.

The ERS noted that the proportion of food-insecure US households in 2015 had decreased from a higher level of 14.9 percent (5.6 percent at "very low food security") in 2011. In 2011, the US was still recovering from the negative macroeconomic effects of the 2008–2009 Great Recession.[17]

As noted earlier in this chapter, we expect to observe a connection between socio-economic factors and food-security status. For example, the December 2011 US unemployment rate was 8.5 percent,[18] whereas the unemployment rate had declined to 5.0 percent by the end of 2015.[19] It is not unreasonable to suggest that a decreasing unemployment rate would be associated with a lower frequency of food insecurity. On the surface, these economic linkages appear to be straightforward. But in-depth research reveals that the factors contributing to food insecurity (at least in the US) are more variable than we normally would expect.

Gunderson, Kreider, and Pepper (2011) conducted a thorough review to better understand the economics of US food insecurity.[20] They presented some interesting results. For example, while they reported an anticipated inverse relationship between household income and food insecurity, they also noted that the likelihood of a decline in food insecurity (linked with increased income) was stronger for households who were marginally secure or were low food-insecure, as compared with households who were very low food insecure. Results of this nature suggest that other factors, beyond household income changes, are needed if we are to make progress in reducing the proportion of households who are very low food-insecure.

Gunderson, Kreider, and Pepper [GKP] (2011) also explain that the connection between poverty and food insecurity is surprisingly less apparent, when data are analyzed in detail. GKP's study revealed that 65 percent of households with incomes close to the poverty line were food-secure. Conversely, GKP also determined that nearly 20 percent of households whose incomes are 200 percent above the poverty line were classified as food *insecure*.[21] GKP postulated a number of reasons for these unexpected observations, including:[22]

- Current income may not always be the best predictor of food insecurity. GKP suggest that a 2-year income average might be explored as a more important determinant of food insecurity.
- Asset liquidity and income volatility were also posited as food-insecurity determinants worthy of further study.
- GKP noted that the elasticity of food security was more sensitive to changes in the unemployment rate than to changes in the poverty rate. GKP observe that unemployed households are not necessarily poor; they conclude that other economic factors, in addition to poverty, should be reviewed more thoroughly to uncover their influence on household food-security status.

US food-security policy considerations

Food insecurity and hunger are not identical phenomena, but they are related. Political support and ethical arguments that favor policies to reduce food insecurity typically begin with the belief that it is "the right thing to do" when we offer assistance to hungry children (and adults). Such considerations are powerful factors in establishing a policy.

As we have noted in earlier chapters of this textbook, 75–80 percent of the approximate $95 billion of annual spending on the US Farm Bill is dedicated to creating a "food safety net." Programs such as the Supplemental Nutrition Assistance Program (SNAP) (formerly "food stamps") and the National School Lunch Program (NSLP) are evidence of large-scale policies that directly or indirectly aim to lessen the probability of a household becoming food insecure.

Gunderson, Kreider, and Pepper (GKP) (2011) also indicate, as food security policies are reviewed, that we need to better understand the impacts of related safety-net programs such as WIC, the School Breakfast Program, Medicaid, and housing assistance.[23] Other factors, worthy of study, are the net impacts of privately funded food assistance organizations on food insecurity. More research is needed to determine the food security (or insecurity) status of households who participate in an array of private and public programs. Households will review the totality of their options, and then select alternative budgets that are financially beneficial in relation to their individual food-security status.

If we examine the food security status of US households from the standpoint of cost and benefit, we can gain additional economic insights into the outcomes associated with action in this policy area. GKP (2011) examined correlations between food insecurity and health-related problems. Among the areas of health concern, *food-insecure household members experience higher frequencies of birth defects, anemia, cognitive disabilities, higher levels of depression, and increased instances of chronic disease and long-term physical health problems.* To the extent that we can establish policies that effectively reduce household food insecurity, then society has a better chance of reducing its health care costs.[24]

Other benefits of increasing the frequency of food-secure households occur when citizens are sufficiently nourished to fully contribute to workforce productivity and/or engage in educational pursuits. Using the basic notion of Maslow's Needs Hierarchy, members of a food-secure household are more likely to actively pursue higher-level goals, and consequently they are in a better position to enhance their net positive socioeconomic impacts.

Analyses of SNAP and the NSLP (GKP, 2011) indicate that measurable reductions of household food insecurity are associated with participation in these programs. Such results imply that future attempts to modify or "reform" SNAP and NSLP should consider the effects of new program designs on household participation. Increasing (or, at least, maintaining) participation rates of qualified households in these assistance programs is a path to reducing food insecurity (or preventing food insecurity problems from becoming more severe).[25]

Access to a government-subsidized and robust food safety net is not a common circumstance worldwide. If we transition our discussion of food security to examine conditions on a multinational or global basis, a variety of additional programs and policies become relevant. We now turn our attention to this broader view.

Linkages between US and global food-security initiatives

One method to compare food-security classifications across different nations is to use a common measurement instrument. GKP (2011) cite an 18-question survey to make a food security determination for households with children. That survey instrument is known as the Core Food Security Module (CFSM). GKP suggest that by either using the full 18-question CFSM, or by using a strategic subset of CFSM questions, it will be possible to analyze the differences in food insecurity experiences among classes of households in different countries. This is a wide open area of research, and a policy aimed at supporting basic research on this topic would be very beneficial.[26]

Larger-scale policies aimed at making gains in household food security involve multinational and global commitments that emphasize the principles of humanitarian aid and economic development. For example, the US initiated an endeavor known as "Feed the Future" to specifically offer both financial support and to coordinate the efforts of eleven different US federal agencies to engage in a multinational program to increase household food security worldwide.[27]

One aspect of the US Feed the Future initiative is an intentional effort to synchronize the program with other ongoing programs to prevent needless overlap and improve effectiveness. For example, the US Feed the Future project builds upon a widely recognized set of five guidelines that were proposed and agreed to by multiple nations at a 2009 World Food Summit. By harmonizing the US Feed the Future effort with these five recommendations (globally known as the "Rome Principles"), resources will be more efficiently utilized because unnecessary duplication of effort is prevented. The five principles that provide the foundation for the US Feed the Future initiative can be summarized as:[28]

- Each nation develops a "country-owned plan" to reduce food insecurity that fits the needs of their population, economy, and societal norms. Consultations and partnerships with other nations are built on the premise that if a country believes it has "ownership" of its program, then that program has the best chance of being implemented and the greatest potential to make a real impact.
- Coordinate private, public, and non-government organizational efforts to maximize impact, take advantage of comparative strengths, and prevent programs from overlapping or working at cross-purposes.
- Because progress towards improved food security is multi-dimensional, encourage the development and implementation of plans that are comprehensive in their design.

- Wherever possible, leverage the strengths of multilateral institutions to achieve the necessary size and combination of financial, technological, and human resources to reach desired results.
- Use realizable and substantial benchmarks to set achievable and sustainable food security goals; assess progress and identify areas of needed additional effort; be publicly accountable and transparent about goals and actual outcomes.

The US *Feed the Future* program has its own website (https://feedthefuture.gov/about), and the US contributed $3.5 billion over three years to initiate the process.[29] Nations from the G8 Alliance joined with the US in the financial effort, and consequently an additional $18.5 billion was made available to create a substantial pool of resources to help implement this plan to reduce global food insecurity.

Global Food Security Act of 2016

Investments in food-security initiatives, such as Feed the Future, are commendable. They help households, regions, and entire countries overcome socioeconomic barriers that may have seemed insurmountable. When consumers and entrepreneurs have needed resources, and a new sense of hope that they "have turned a corner," a positive self-reinforcing economic trend can develop.

But in a twenty-first-century world where the rational question of sustainability arises in nearly every endeavor, it is reasonable to ask whether Feed the Future is a just a temporary influence on food security conditions, or is there reason to believe that it can create longer-lasting effects?

Recently there was a boost towards the view that these food policy efforts have real potential to produce both permanent and net beneficial outcomes. Both houses of the US Congress acted in a bipartisan fashion, and they passed Public Law No: 114-195, the Global Food Security Act (GFSA) of 2016. President Obama signed the bill into law.[30]

PL 114-195 creates statutory authority that supports the Feed the Future Program. The law approves nearly $7 billion in additional funding. Under this legislation, Feed the Future is a much more sustainable food security policy.

President Obama noted that this new law would ensure that Feed the Future's record of success would continue. He indicated that Feed the Future had "reached over 9 million farmers across the globe, reducing hunger, boosting yields, and increasing incomes . . . poverty has been cut by up to a quarter. Stunting is down by as much as a third. Nearly 18 million more children are getting better nutrition."[31]

The US Agency for International Development can operate Feed the Future under PL 114-195 to promote food security programs worldwide. GFSA does not replace the US traditional Food for Peace program; it complements it.

GFSA is intended to create long-term effects. This bill will help developing nations increase their agricultural production and distribution capacity. Progress towards self-sufficiency for both households and entire countries is the envisioned result.

The GFSA also financially supports the Emergency Food Security Program (EFSP). EFSP is an electronic voucher program that allows for locally purchased commodities to help people in troubled food-insecure areas. Support for EFSP means that financial assistance can take advantage of local food sources, rather than exclusively depend on US food shipments.[32]

Finally, the potential for the GFSA to deliver real gains in global food security stems from its demands for accountability and transparency. PL 114-195 requires the President to coordinate agencies, establish monitoring and evaluation systems, and create platforms for consultation with stakeholders and Congressional committees. The President was required to submit the GFSA's overall organizational and reporting strategy to the Congress by October 1, 2016.[33]

What is the world's food insecurity condition?

Congressional requirements for maintaining transparency, as the GFSA is implemented, puts a spotlight on the measured outcomes of efforts to reduce food insecurity on our planet. Using available data, what do we know about the trends in global food insecurity?

There are three worldwide organizations seeking to make global progress towards improved food security: The United Nation's Food and Agriculture Organization (FAO), the International Fund for Agricultural Development (IFAD) and the World Food Programme (WFP). The FAO, IFAD, and WEP jointly publish an annual report known as *The State of Food Insecurity in the World*.[34]

In 2015, this report tells a story of genuine advancement. The proportion of food-insecure households in 2015 was 12.9 percent of the world's population, as compared with 23.3 percent in 1990–1992. The 2015 publication declared that 72 of 129 monitored countries (56 percent) had achieved the Millennium Development Goal (MDG) of reducing the rate of malnutrition by half.[35]

While the accomplishments in global food security are important and impressive, more work needs to be done. Nearly 795 million households worldwide remain food insecure. Reaching out to nearly another 1 billion people is a huge task, but it is no longer seen as impossible. There are now projections that global food insecurity could be eradicated in the future, if the various policies and programs continue to make headway.

The condition of food insecurity is not being ignored. There are sizable ongoing efforts being conducted by the FAO, IFAD, and WFP, along with the US Feed the Future and Food for Peace programs. It is also necessary to recognize the impacts of private efforts, such as programs sponsored by the Global Alliance for the Future of Food and other similar groups.[36]

What is the International Food Security Assessment (IFSA)?

The global eradication of hunger and malnutrition is an appealing goal from many perspectives. A world where no child must go to bed hungry is ethically, socially, and even politically desirable. Is this future vision economically possible?

Since the late 1970s, the USDA's Economic Research Service (ERS) has performed economic modeling to analyze, assess, and make future projections of food availability in developing countries. In 2016, this research has become known as the International Food Security Assessment (IFSA).[37] The IFSA is an economic modeling technique used to make 10-year projections about future trends in food security conditions worldwide.

The span of the IFSA assessments increased over time. In the 1970s, the forecasts focused on whether particular countries were likely to encounter food deficits or surpluses. ERS analysts incrementally modified and improved their economic models over time to analyze the broader view of food security as a multi-faceted phenomenon.

In the *International Food Security Assessment (IFSA), 2016–2026*, the ERS economic model projects that 10-year market growth patterns will produce a combination of lower food prices and rising household incomes. As a result of this encouraging forecast, the IFSA predicts that the share of food-insecure households in 76 developing nations will decrease from 17 percent in 2016 to 6 percent in 2026.[38] While the IFSA primarily makes projections on households reaching a targeted threshold of 2,100 calories per day, as compared to broader food security measurements, the trend towards additional progress in reducing food insecurity increases our confidence that global aspirations for making a real difference in future conditions are achievable.

Exploring relationships between food security and food systems

Projections of future global food security conditions are one way to understand the economic factors that influence household nutritional status. We also know that food security is a multi-faceted concept. We should apply a wide-ranging set of analytical techniques to more fully comprehend the causes and consequences of food security (and insecurity).

In the final section of this chapter, we consider the question of food insecurity from the broad perspective of household access to foods that are both nutritious and reasonably priced. It seems counterintuitive to discuss the US problems of obesity and diet-related diseases as topics related to household food insecurity. But there are economic factors that logically link these concerns together.

A food-secure household does more than consume at a prescribed level of caloric food intake. Food security implies access to a well-rounded diet.[39] Consequently, households who lead healthier lifestyles because they consume balanced and nutritional diets fit a description of food security that is more consistent with a holistic perspective.

Food-insecure households in the US may lack the food choices necessary for nutritionally healthy diets. Instead, food insecurity can be interpreted to include the household consumption of more readily accessible foods that lack nutritional balance and increase the likelihood of obesity and related dietary problems.[40]

Households in diverse US geographic areas, varying from rural locales to inner-city neighborhoods, may have greater accessibility to convenience stores and fast-food outlets than they do to supermarkets. There are serious concerns about the association between poor diets and the absence of nutritious food options. In a broad sense, this is a food security issue.

This question of limited geographic access to nutritional food choices is addressed in the 2008 Farm Bill, where the term "food desert" is formally defined:[41]

> A food desert is an area in the United States with limited access to affordable and nutritious food, particularly such an area composed of predominantly lower income neighborhoods and communities. (Title VI, Sec. 7527)

Food-secure US households may "take for granted" the capacity of our food system to provide a wide range of nutritious food options to meet their dietary needs. The situation facing households located in food deserts can be quite different.

A 2001 household survey indicated that about 6 percent of US households experienced deficiencies of needed or desired foods because access was limited or absent. An ERS study of food deserts noted that about half of these households located in food deserts also did not have sufficient income to purchase all of the needed foods. A question of causality must be addressed in this instance, because we do not have the data or evidence to determine whether income or geographic access is the most significant limitation.[42]

What policies can be pursued to help reduce the nutritional challenges associated with food deserts? The ERS recommends that we need more research to determine the root causes of the limited access. For example, suppose we have substantial evidence that supermarkets are discouraged by locational diseconomies to place outlets closer to food-limited areas. Perhaps zoning restrictions can be relaxed or tax-reduction enticements can be introduced to encourage supermarkets to set up outlets in locations that better serve households and "make the desert bloom."

Suppose SNAP participants do not travel to, and patronize, farmers' markets because of the absence of technologies to utilize their EBT cards? Policies to subsidize or otherwise encourage technological investments needed to allow EBT payments at farmers' markets could increase access to fresh fruits and vegetables to households who perceive their access to nutritious options as limited.

Policies may also be needed to spark change on the "demand side." If households lack all the information they need to make improved nutritional food choices, then a public educational campaign to raise awareness of healthy options may be needed. If the question is the absence of transportation to reach the supermarket, perhaps local and regional governmental agencies and private donors can offer financial support to help create the necessary transit linkages to increase access to nutritional food options.[43]

The capacity of local food system innovation to improve household food security in the US

In addition to policies directly aimed at alleviating food security problems posed by food deserts in the US, we can also consider the beneficial effects on household welfare associated with market system innovations. In 2015, at the request of the House Agriculture Committee, the ERS published an extensive report on the changes taking place in regional and local food systems.[44]

US food markets experienced considerable growth in US consumer interest and demand for locally and regionally produced foods between 2006 and 2014. Evidence of this expansion of "local food systems" is observed in at least three different food marketing channels:[45]

- During 2006–2014, the number of farmers' markets grew by 180 percent, reaching a total of 8,268 markets in 2014.
- A cooperative system of aggregating locally produced foods, known as "regional food hubs," emerged as a way to distribute foods to wholesale, retail, institutional, and individual buyers. The number of food hubs increased 288 percent during 2006–2014.
- Locally sourced farm-to-school food programs serve both educational and nutritional goals for school districts and their farm suppliers. The USDA Farm-to-School Census indicated that 4,322 school districts were operating with these programs in 2014, a 430 percent increase since 2006.

The rise in the value and frequency of local food systems creates new opportunities to make impacts on US household food security. Government agencies and private volunteer organizations have a range of new supply options to increase access to nutritional foods. The rapid pace of change in local food systems means that we do not yet know what all the options or possibilities are. But there is certainly room for research and experimentation. Evidence of efforts to tap into these new alternatives is beginning to build.

In 2013, Schmit, Jablonski and Kay investigated the economic impacts of a food hub in New York State.[46] While indicating that the applicability of their study may be limited, they determined that a food hub can expand the availability of locally produced farm products in a region. They also observed that the food hub encouraged farm business expansion. Local farmers also benefitted from the food hub's capacity to access local consumer markets and offer storage options for product delivery.

Households located in food deserts could potentially be linked to a food hub distribution network. Consequently, a range of new and potentially healthier food options could affordably be made available to food-deficient households.

O'Hara (2015) directly links the potential of urban food hubs to help solve the problems of urban food deserts.[47] Recognizing the multi-dimensional aspects of food security, O'Hara analyzes a locally sourced "urban food hub" as a system comprised of four interrelated components:

- Introducing intensive food production methods, such as aquaponics and hydroponics.
- Using professional food preparation practices, cooperating with commercial kitchens.
- Achieving food distribution goals (e.g. increasing household food access in food deserts) through farmers' markets, grocery stores, and related retail outlets.
- Achieving full food-system sustainability, by implementing effective waste reduction and waste re-using methods (for example, composting and water management techniques).

O'Hara also urges that university-level research is needed to establish food system protocols. It is important to identify key operational relationships that are observable in smaller-scale experimental urban food-hub systems.

For example, O'Hara highlights the importance of conducting feasibility studies, such as those sponsored as part of the "Urban Food Hub System Concept" project by the University of the District of Columbia's (UDC's) College of Agriculture, Urban Sustainability and Environmental Sciences (CAUSES). The approach taken by CAUSES aims to not only improve food security, but also to enhance job creation and promote urban sustainability by using the food hub system to strengthen socio-economic, cultural, and environmental conditions.[48]

Private–public partnerships, local leadership, and the future of sustainable food-secure solutions

"Resilience" is a voluntary program that supports efforts such as the Urban Food Hub System (O'Hara, 2015) to increase US household food security. *Resilience* is sponsored by the Post-Carbon Institute, a non-profit organization.[49] Private-sector initiatives are increasingly significant contributors to economic progress in the US. When these volunteer exertions are properly coordinated with public policies, the results can be politically influential and economically powerful.

In the United States, successful policies often have to strike a balance between individual initiative and social welfare. For example, if we are considering policy actions that aim to make measurable gains in US household food security, it is very important that the households themselves engage in the improvement process. Members of US households generally have strongly held beliefs that they should have "ownership" in what is being accomplished. In many instances, the involvement and influence of volunteer private-sector organizations can help shape and implement policies in a manner that is perceived as non-threatening and cooperative, and is appealing to independent-minded households.

For example, AGree is a private sector initiative that receives input from forty-four different agri-businesses, farmers, non-profit organizations, volunteer groups, university professors, and charitable foundations.[50] AGree's stated goal is to spark beneficial change in the food and agriculture system by encouraging leaders to take action and highlight the national priorities associated with food and agriculture in the United States. The Meridian Institute is the organizational home of the AGree Initiative.

In the area of improving US household food security, the AGree Initiative has assisted in promoting programs such as:[51]

- *The Wholesome Wave Fruit and Vegetable Prescription (FVRx) Program.* FVRx creates a partnership among healthcare providers, farmers markets, and families with diet-related diseases. FVRx offers assistance to overweight and obese children through access to parental nutrition counseling. In addition, there is a $1 per day voucher redeemable at farmers' markets.
- *The Arcadia Center for Sustainable Food and Agriculture's Mobile Market* is a non-profit organization that helps organize a farmstand-on-wheels. The mobile unit distributes locally produced food to food-insecure communities in the Washington, DC Area.
- *The Double-Up Food Bucks (Double-Up) Program,* sponsored by the Fair Food Network, provides SNAP beneficiaries with a financial dollar-for-dollar match to increase their purchases of locally grown fruits and vegetables.

Private-sector involvement by organizations such as AGree and Resilience can directly affect household economic welfare. As we look to the future, partnerships between private organizations and public agencies provide a range of opportunities that would be difficult to offer by public policy on its own. US society generally benefits when local leaders, business professionals, and other experts decide to "give back to society" and take voluntary action to make a difference.

Summary, conclusions, and a look forward

Food Security is one of the few policy goals that has the potential to gain the immediate attention and nearly the universal support of policy makers, interest groups, and everyday citizens. Perhaps it is the fact that human beings easily recognize that we all must eat to survive.

Each of us may have experienced a hunger-pang at some point in our lives. Empathy for food security is a natural human response.

What is happening in the food security arena? While the problem of food insecurity is far from solved, considerable progress has occurred on a global level to reduce the most severe instances of food insecurity. Agencies such as the FAO and the USAID offer evidence that efforts to improve household food security are making real gains. Let's hope that the trend towards alleviating food insecurity continues.

One of the influences that can achieve beneficial results in creating food-secure homes is rural economic development. If the economic vitality of rural areas can be stimulated and sustained, the overall economic growth of a region can have a powerful effect on the ability of households to find gainful employment and be in a position to be more fully food secure. We certainly should have an interest in the potential contributions of rural development. We take on that task in the next chapter of this textbook.

Notes

1 Hagy, Tegan. "Grants, Gardens and Green Beans: Charlottesville's Growing Farm to School Program." USDA Blog. USDA Food and Nutrition Service. Nov. 29, 2016. Retrieved from: http://blogs.usda.gov/2016/11/29/grants-gardens-and-green-beans-charlottesvilles-growing-farm-to-school-program/

2 Ibid.

3 Thomas, Desiree. "Research in Energy Security Helps Lead to Food Security in West Africa." USDA Blog. USDA Foreign Agricultural Service. Nov. 28, 2016. Retrieved from: http://blogs.usda.gov/2016/11/28/research-in-energy-security-helps-lead-to-food-security-in-west-africa/#more-67578

4 Ibid.

5 G8 L'Aquila Summit. "L'Aquila Joint Statement on Food Security – L'Aquila Food Security Initiative." L'Aquila, Italy: July 10, 2009. Retrieved from: https://feedthefuture.gov/sites/default/files/resource/files/afsi_jointstatement_2009.pdf

6 The White House – The US Government's Global Hunger and Food Security Initiative. "About: Feed the Future." Washington, DC: Beth Dunford and Nancy Stetson, Deputy Coordinators of the Feed the Future Initiative, 2016. Retrieved from: https://feedthefuture.gov/about#Rome%20Principles

7 Naylor, Rosamond L. "The Many Faces of Food Security," in *The Evolving Sphere of Food Security*. Naylor, Rosamond L. (ed). Oxford, UK: Oxford University Press, 2014, pp. 3–27.

8 Heady, D.D. and O. Ecker. "Rethinking the Measurement of Food Security: From First Principles to Best Practice." *Food Security* 5(3), pp. 327–343, 2013.

9 Naylor, Rosamond L. "The Many Faces of Food Security," p. 7.

10 Ibid.

11 Coleman-Jensen, Alisha, Matthew P. Rabbitt, Christian A. Gregory, and Anita Singh. "Household Food Security in the United States in 2015, ERR-215." U.S. Department of Agriculture, Economic Research Service, pp. 3–4, September 2016. Retrieved from: www.ers.usda.gov/webdocs/publications/err215/err-215.pdf

12 Ibid, note 7, p. 4.

13 Naylor, Rosamond L. "The Many Faces of Food Security," p. 8.

14 United Nations. "We Can End Poverty – Millennium Goals and Beyond 2015: Fact Sheet." New York: UN Department of Public Information. September 2013. Page 1. Retrieved from: www.un.org/millenniumgoals/pdf/Goal_1_fs.pdf

15 Naylor, Rosamond L. "The Many Faces of Food Security," p. 8.

16 Coleman-Jensen, Alisha, Matthew P. Rabbitt, Christian A. Gregory, and Anita Singh. "Household Food Security in the United States in 2015, ERR-215." U.S. Department of Agriculture, Economic Research Service, p. 6, September 2016. Retrieved from: www.ers.usda.gov/webdocs/publications/err215/err-215.pdf

17 Ibid.

18 Bureau of Labor Statistics, US Dept. of Labor. "Unemployment Rate falls to 8.5% in December 2011." Washington, DC. January 9, 2012. Retrieved from: www.bls.gov/opub/ted/2012/ted_20120109.htm

19 Bureau of Labor Statistics, US Dept. of Labor. "News Release: The Employment Situation – December 2015." Washington, DC. January 8, 2016. Retrieved from: www.bls.gov/news.release/archives/empsit_01082016.pdf

20 Gundersen, Craig, Brent Kreider, and John Pepper. "The Economics of Food Insecurity in the United States." *Applied Economic Perspectives and Policy* 33(3), pp. 281–303, 2011. Retrieved from: http://aepp.oxfordjournals.org/content/33/3/281.full.pdf+html

21 Ibid, pp. 295–299.

22 Ibid, pp. 285–288.

23 Ibid, p. 298.

24 Ibid, p. 289.

25 Ibid, pp. 291–295.

26 Ibid, pp. 283–285.

27 The White House – The US Government's Global Hunger and Food Security Initiative. "About: Feed the Future." Washington, DC: Beth Dunford and Nancy Stetson, Deputy Coordinators of the Feed the Future Initiative, 2016. Retrieved from: https://feedthefuture.gov/about#Rome%20Principles

28 Food and Agriculture Organization, United Nations. "World Summit on Food Security." Rome, Nov. 16–18, 2009. Declaration of the World Summit on Food Security. November 2009. Retrieved from: www.fao.org/fileadmin/templates/wsfs/Summit/Docs/Final_Declaration/WSFS09_Declaration.pdf

29 The White House – The US Government's Global Hunger and Food Security Initiative. "About: Feed the Future." Washington, DC: Beth Dunford and Nancy Stetson, Deputy Coordinators of the Feed the Future Initiative, 2016. Retrieved from: https://feedthefuture.gov/about#Rome%20Principles

30 Davies, Stephen. "Obama Signs Global Food Security Act." Agri-Pulse Communications. July 20, 2016. Retrieved from: www.agri-pulse.com/Obama-signs-Global-Food-Security-Act-07202016.asp

31 Ibid.

32 Ibid.

33 Library of Congress. "S.1252 – Global Food Security Act of 2016. Summary: S.1252 – 114th Congress." (2015–2016). Retrieved from: www.congress.gov/bill/114th-congress/senate-bill/1252

34 FAO, IFAD and WFP. 2015. "The State of Food Insecurity in the World 2015. Meeting the 2015 international hunger targets: taking stock of uneven progress." Rome, FAO. Retrieved from: http://reliefweb.int/sites/reliefweb.int/files/resources/a-i4646e.pdf

35 Ibid, pp. 4–5.

36 Global Alliance for the Future of Food. "Who We Are." 2016. Retrieved from: http://futureoffood.org/about-us/who-we-are/

37 Rosen, Stacey, Karen Thome, and Birgit Meade. International Food Security Assessment, 2016-2026, GFA-27, U.S. Department of Agriculture, Economic Research Service, June 2016. Retrieved from: www.ers.usda.gov/media/2109786/gfa27.pdf

38 Ibid, Report Summary.

39 Naylor, Rosamond L. "The Many Faces of Food Security." p. 8.

40 ERS Report to Congress. Economic Research Service (ERS), Food and Nutrition Service (FNS), and the Cooperative State Research, Education, and Extension Service (CSREES), USDA. Michele Ver Ploeg, Report Director. "Access to Affordable and Nutritious Food: Measuring and Understanding Food Deserts and Their Consequences." ERS, USDA. June 2009. Retrieved from: www.ers.usda.gov/webdocs/publications/ap036/12716_ap036_1_.pdf

41 Ibid, p. 1.

42 Ibid, p. iv.

43 Ibid, pp. 103–114.

44 Low, Sarah A., Aaron Adalja, Elizabeth Beaulieu, Nigel Key, Steve Martinez, Alex Melton, Agnes Perez, Katherine Ralston, Hayden Stewart, Shellye Suttles, Stephen Vogel, and Becca B.R. Jablonski. "Trends in U.S. Local and Regional Food Systems, AP-068." U.S. Department of Agriculture, Economic Research Service, January 2015. Retrieved from: www.ers.usda.gov/media/1763057/ap068.pdf

45 Ibid, pp. 2–3.

46 Schmit, T.M., B.B.R. Jablonski, and D. Kay. "Assessing the Economic Impacts of Regional Food Hubs: the Case of Regional Access." Cornell University. September 2013. Retrieved from: http://dx.doi.org/10.9752/MS145.09-2013

47 O'Hara, Sabine. "Food Security: The Urban Food Hubs Solution." The Solutions Journal 6(1), pp. 42–53, January 2015. Retrieved from: www.thesolutionsjournal.com/article/food-security-the-urban-food-hubs-solution/

48 Ibid.

49 Post Carbon Institute, Resilience. "Food Security: The Urban Food Hubs Solution." Santa Rosa, CA. 2016. Retrieved from: www.resilience.org/stories/2015-04-22/food-security-the-urban-food-hubs-solution

50 AGree, Transforming Ag and Food Policy. "Local Food: Revitalizing Community-based Food Systems." Washington, DC: Meridian Institute, AGree Initiative. 2015. Retrieved from: www.foodandagpolicy.org/sites/default/files/AGree_LFI_2015_0.pdf

51 Ibid, p. 5.

Chapter 11

Twenty-first-century perspectives on rural development

An opening viewpoint: business succession and rural development

How is farm ownership transferred efficiently from one generation to the next? This question is not only relevant for individual farm operations, but also for the economic stability of all rural areas. In addition, achieving successful business succession is a challenge to the local economy that extends beyond farm and agribusiness entities. It is a general business concern.

The economic vitality of rural communities depends on a combination of dedicated citizens, viable businesses, and innovative thinking. The smooth intergenerational transfer of business ownership may not be the most exciting aspect of regional development, but it is essential.

In many rural communities, the responsiveness of small businesses to local customers is at the heart of their ongoing economic success. Ownership succession plans, when properly executed, can provide reassurances to clientele that their expectations of a business's trustworthiness and customer service will continue to be fulfilled. If government policies and programs can facilitate farm business ownership transitions, then the rural economy's ongoing vitality will benefit.

An example of such institutional innovation is USDA's Business and Industry (B&I) Guaranteed Loan Program. The B&I Program provides options that reduce the transactions costs of business ownership transfer in two different areas:[1]

- First, if the business ownership changeover is *within a family*, then the B&I program offers new financing alternatives in cases where the exiting business owner needs sales revenue to finance his/her own retirement.
- Second, in cases where the business owner's *children have no interest* in owning and managing the business, then the normal 100 percent transfer of ownership requirement can be delayed. An "outside group" can be offered a financing alternative.

The B&I Guaranteed Loan Program's flexibility helps preserve the integrity of small business ownership. The USDA B&I Program also fosters the financial stability and viability of farm and non-farm rural businesses. Rural development can move forward when businesses in transition can maintain quality service, provide steady local employment opportunities, and be a reliable contributor to a local community's economic base.[2]

Introduction

Researchers and policy makers know there are real and measurable benefits of engaging in rural development. We can cite specific instances where economic projects have made a positive difference in the lives of rural households and businesses.[3] Nevertheless, it is often difficult to exactly define the scope and mission of rural development efforts. There are challenges in determining how extensive a "rural area" is, and what features of "development" are the most appropriate and efficient.[4]

In the twenty-first century, we realize that efforts to promote the ongoing success of the rural economy depends on implementing broad-based and integrated policy approaches. True and effective rural development is no longer viewed as a simple extension of agricultural policy.

Advances in the agriculture sector can still make notable economic contributions. But rural vitality in the modern age requires that we institute multi-sector models to effectively combine public infrastructure investments with innovative private markets. Rural development must trigger mechanisms that efficiently connect diverse productive factors. In this view, rural development involves managing many of the same influences that are economically important in urban areas.

Today, rural regions generate Real GDP growth by orchestrating comprehensive approaches that utilize technological capacity, build transportation-communication networks, access financial assets, and institute infrastructural services. Rural development policy must be carefully considered, properly planned, and correctly implemented to realize quantifiable and valuable results.

One additional challenge is that no single economic model exists to guide rural development policy. Strong empirical research and robust assessment methods are needed to determine the best approaches in particular circumstances. We compensate for the absence of a primary rural development theory by seeking out guidelines that help us to formulate the right questions to ask.

Fortunately, professional researchers who study rural development have done yeoman's work in helping to discern key patterns and considerations as we consider policy directions in this field. A key objective for this chapter is to utilize the current body of knowledge to increase our understanding of the considerations that should be guiding rural development policy.

Organization of chapter

Our exploration of the rural development landscape begins by examining agriculture's changing role within the rural economy over time. The evolution of agricultural production and marketing trends, in relation to overall local and regional economic trends, means that we should understand how current conditions set the pattern for future change. For example, industrial and technological influences on US agriculture have motivated the substitution of capital for labor, reduced the need for on-farm employment, and triggered the drive towards using off-farm income as an important means of diversifying farm operations.

Considering the changing character of agriculture in rural development, we organize the remainder of this chapter to consider the following perspectives on rural policy:

- Evolving role of agriculture in rural development
- The need for comprehensive approaches to rural development
- Proposals to modernize rural development policies
- Analyzing US and global rural development patterns
- Anticipating future challenges and opportunities in rural development policy

As in many other areas of public policy, there are both promising opportunities and serious challenges when we address rural development issues. It is a broad and interesting field of study. As we move forward into this chapter, we encounter a wide spectrum of researchable questions that require critical thinking and analytical proficiency to discern workable policy solutions.

Evolving role of agriculture in rural development

Hodge and Midmore (2008) reviewed the design and implementation of rural development models in Europe and the US after World War II.[5] Immediately following the war, rural and agricultural policies were closely linked. In that era, agriculture often constituted a significant proportion of the rural GDP. Policies to expand commodity production and marketing offered substantial and measureable gains to the rural economy.[6]

Times change. Modernization affected all phases of agriculture. Reduced farm labor demand stimulated a rural to urban exodus. To adjust to the new reality, rural economies diversified; they actively sought to attract non-farm businesses and industry. As a result of these changing conditions, rural development efforts based largely on the agricultural "multiplier effect" lost much of their clout. It was soon apparent that new approaches were needed to stimulate rural growth.

Policies that spur advances in multiple economic sectors, coordinate development across geographic regions, or encourage local communities to innovate are among the diverse strategies now covered under the "umbrella" of rural development. A visit to the USDA Rural Development website illustrates this broad perspective. The USDA highlights the importance of rural development initiatives that promote safe and affordable housing, general business support and infrastructure investment.[7]

The need for comprehensive approaches to rural development

Ideally, development efforts should be adaptable to the diverse needs of different rural economic regions. Fully effective development efforts introduce policy designs that take advantage of the specific resource potentials of a particular rural area.

Ward and Hite (1998) addressed the diverse nature of rural development as they summarized four professionally refereed papers focused on applications of rural economic models.[8] Ward and Hite noted that this field of study does not lend itself to reliance on a single theory formalized in one rigorous stand-alone model. But they did identify essential recurring themes that offer useful guidelines for international rural development policy. In particular, Ward and Hite (1998) emphasize that development strategies consider:[9]

- Private market liberalization coupled with public-sector structural adjustment.
- Progressive global integration – from inception to completion.
- Physical infrastructure investments – e.g. establish/enhance transportation and communication networks.
- Social and institutional investments – e.g. institute/maintain the rule of law, a functioning democracy, and ongoing and reliable investments in human capital (education, training).

Ward and Hite (1998), as they review rural development with reference to these four guidelines, stress that we must be ready to redefine terms such as "rural" and "remote" in light of changing technologies. And, the evolution of our concepts means that our policies must also progress, if they are to stay current with relevant economic factors. Policy designs and outcomes must be regularly reviewed. When policies are informed by proper assessment mechanisms, then they can be modified and updated in light of new economic realities.[10]

Case study: palm oil production and its connection to Nigerian rural development

We can apply Ward and Hite's (1998) guidelines to examine the opportunities and challenges for rural development in Southeastern Nigeria. In this case study, we briefly examine how economic activities associated with palm oil production affect rural Nigeria's average standard of living.

In 2002, the United Nations (UN) Food and Agriculture Organization (FAO) published an agricultural services bulletin describing the economic significance of palm oil. This edible oil is a highly marketable product that can potentially improve economic growth in rural Nigeria.[11]

The oil palm tree originated in Africa's tropical rainforests. Africans have been processing oil palm fruit into edible oil for over 1,000 years. Other parts of the oil palm tree are also useful – for example, palm fronds are essential in creating thatched roofs, can serve as a ruminant feed source, or can promote soil conservation and nutrient recycling when placed between rows in palm-tree plantations. The economic importance of processed palm oil has a long history and its value continues in the twenty-first century. It is a sought-after ingredient that both local and international consumers consider a necessity when preparing their cuisines.[12]

It is normal to have a curiosity about the nature of any agricultural production enterprise. The biochemistry of palm oil reveals a carotenoid product. When the fruit is processed it has a highly pigmented red color. Palm oil is also a saturated fatty acid. Its combined characteristics create a viscous semi-solid texture.

Palm oil production and marketing represent a rural economic development opportunity that has yet to be fully realized in rural Southeast Nigeria. A review of past and current Nigerian market conditions reveals why the potentials for economic renaissance associated with creating a palm oil farm-to-consumer supply chain have yet to emerge.

Ward and Hite (1998) emphasize that successful rural development depends on regions who invest in the necessary physical infrastructure as well as foster a societal system that enforces the rule of law. Nigerian transportation and communication systems offer some market support, but Southeastern Nigeria would definitely benefit from additional infrastructure investment. Other challenges arise from inadequate access to electric power and potable water.

The BBC recently reported on problems originating from the absence of a transparent Nigerian legal system. The country does have modern technologies to help process the palm oil, but local producers choose not to access them because police officers demand bribes as the product is transported to modern processing machinery. Traditional production methods prevail because institutional protections are not adequate to shield farmers from corruption. As a result, customary palm oil production technologies continue to prevail in rural Nigeria.[13]

Palm oil cultivation and production practices have sometimes been criticized as a source of negative environmental externalities. While there are side effects from palm oil output that require attention, they are not more serious than the side effects of many other types of agricultural enterprises. A recent editorial in the *New York Times* emphasized that the economic development benefits of palm oil production more than offset the hazards.[14] The negative externalities of palm oil output are far less of an environmental concern than the external costs associated with Nigeria's petroleum industry.

Global decreases in the price and profit of the global petroleum industry have recently convinced Nigerian government authorities to seek ways to diversify and strengthen their national economy. Agrimoney.com, an international online media source, recently (2016) reported that the Nigerian government is now rethinking its investment strategies, and is pursuing economic reforms to support and rejuvenate the economic potentials of palm oil production, processing, and marketing.[15]

Hopefully, Nigerian officials will take note of the rural development advice and experience offered by Ward and Hite (1998) and other analysts. The goal should be to optimize the net gains by jointly establishing a prosperous palm-oil farm economy and a systematic rural development effort.

As we have been learning in this chapter, rural regions are better off when there are comprehensive efforts to stimulate the economy. In this case, a key aspect will be the ability to utilize Nigeria's comparative advantage in building up its palm-oil market potentials. Increases in palm-oil production, as well as its supply-chain capacity, could generate real benefits for its farm producers, domestic consumers, and for export. This investment would be an exciting chance to make a real difference in a region that could greatly benefit from its rural development potentials.

Proposals to modernize rural development policies

The Organization for Economic Cooperation and Development (OECD) is an international forum where "governments can work together to share experiences and seek solutions to common problems."[16] In October 2006, the OECD released a study entitled, "Reinventing Rural Policy."[17] Similar to Ward and Hite (1998), the OECD underscores the need to revise our thinking about rural economic conditions.[18]

The OECD report notes that access to the Internet and advanced communications networks mean that rural people can participate in the global economy equally as well as their urban counterparts. Transportation systems have also improved and become more affordable, so the notion of what we call "remote" needs redefinition. Finally, rural areas can experience a net inflow of resources and economic activity, if the amenities and social character of rural life are marketed as a reason for businesses and consumers to relocate to rural areas from more urban settings.

In light of the changing socio-economic circumstances, the OECD has advanced a "New Rural Paradigm."[19] The OECD summarizes the major components of the new paradigm as follows:

- Instead of aiming to equalize farm and non-farm incomes, rural policy should capitalize on the competitive advantages of rural areas, and encourage innovations that tap into rural areas' under-utilized resources.
- Rather than exclusively focusing on agricultural sector growth, also engage in policies that enhance the value of alternative rural economic engines, including eco- and agro-tourism, rural quality of life, and industries suited to rural workforce skills and availability. Rural development can also promote strategic technology-based infrastructure investments in communications systems and Internet access to allow rural regions to effectively compete with urban centers for industries that can "operate anywhere."
- Stress the use of rural private-public partnerships that rely on investment criteria to attract business and industry, as compared with the model of government subsidies to encourage the growth of targeted industries.
- Invite and involve cooperative or collaborative organizations/associations of private businesses, non-government organizations (NGO's), local and state government agencies as well as national (federal) government support to coordinate and organize rural development projects and programs. This joint approach differs from initial rural development efforts that often were guided solely by national government agencies and policies.

Honadle (2001) reviewed the status of US rural development strategy.[20] In her analysis, Honadle cited the economic need for many of the reforms recommended by the subsequent OECD report. Honadle's contribution to the rural policy discussion suggests that the changes will encounter political resistance by agricultural and related groups.[21]

The predicted conflicts are understandable. Interest groups accustomed to receiving benefits from status quo rural development projects are likely to oppose changes that redistribute program resources to a broader constituency. This viewpoint, which emphasizes the powerful effect of politically relevant influences, indicates that changes in rural development policy will be gradual. Policy makers must balance the competing needs of their constituencies. These decision makers must seek compromise in creating polices that align the goals of alternative interest groups.

Regardless of the barriers, there are interests who continue to seek rural policy reform. Honadle (2001) highlights a trend that the OECD (2006) also considers to be critical to sparking real change in rural development approaches. [22, 23] In particular, Honadle explores the influence exercised by State Rural Development Councils (SRDCs) as part of a coordinated National Rural Development Partnership (NRDP). These associations fit into the OECD paradigm where local, state, and regional groups can help national rural development efforts to be more targeted and effective in rural communities and economies.

Analyzing US and global rural development patterns

In the US, the methods and priorities for rural development are clearly exhibited in the 2014 Farm Bill. As the USDA implements the farm bill's congressionally prescribed rural development goals, we can observe an agenda that extends considerably beyond a simple extension of agricultural policy:

- A direct quote from a USDA document is:[24]

  The Agricultural Act of 2014 reaches far beyond our farms — it touches the lives of every American. The Act authorizes and directs key rural programs that help promote local economic development — from connecting rural communities to broadband Internet to providing much needed, and often unavailable, financing for rural small businesses, communities, and individuals.

- USDA's implementation of the 2014 Farm Bill's intent for rural development includes:[25]

  o   Initiating grant programs for small and emerging businesses (non-farm and farm) to increase the overall employment rate in rural areas.
  o   Creating housing programs to help all rural people access safe and affordable housing.
  o   Advancing alliances among community groups to promote sustainable and broad-based economic development.
  o   Investing in local public infrastructure.

The above is not an exhaustive list of all rural development project areas targeted by the 2014 Farm Bill. But the character and content of these initiatives is telling. While other aspects of the 2014 Farm Bill still direct considerable federal support to farm-related activity, we can observe that the economic backing for rural development is more comprehensive in nature. US rural development policy is evolving.

If we take a second look at the 2006 OECD report on rural policy, we can detect that other nations around the globe also recognize the need to redesign rural development to address a much broader agenda. The OECD report examines notable changes in rural development policy taking place in the United Kingdom, the Netherlands, Canada, Finland, Germany, and Mexico.[26]

To summarize aspects of the new rural paradigm being implemented in these six countries, the OECD identifies the following patterns:

- Enhancements to rural "amenities," including the importance of supporting activities that conserve natural resources and improve environmental quality. Globally, many nations understand that improved rural quality of life serves as an economic advantage that can help attract business and generate employment opportunities.
- Continuing reforms of general agricultural policies can help nations and regions develop trade relationships based on true economic comparative advantage.
- Decentralization of rural development projects to increase the role of encouraging regions to build up their competitiveness, as compared to receiving government subsidies that target only one industry.

Anticipating future challenges and opportunities in rural development policy

Funding priorities in the 2014 Farm Bill and the OECD development guidelines provide us with strong indications about the future direction of rural policy. And, as we look ahead, it is reasonable to seek out and identify economic policies with the best promise of achieving beneficial and measurable results.

Policy makers searching for guidance can profit from the insights of specialists in rural development research. These analysts help us to understand important lessons learned from past development efforts. They can also share their perceptions into key considerations regarding the current state of affairs.

Microeconomic perspective on rural development

Blank (2005, 2008) investigates the microeconomic consequences of rural development from an agricultural household and business perspective.[27,28] Blank's research helps us to address a very fundamental question: what are the economic results that we should expect from a successful rural development policy?

Microeconomic theory would direct us to consider how development activities influence opportunities for profit maximization (and long-term wealth maximization) in farm and non-farm rural businesses. Blank (2008) also reminds us that rural area markets are a two-way street; not just comprised of businesses, but also utility maximizing households.[29]

Blank asks us to consider that an agricultural producer's goal of long-term wealth maximization is simply one component contributing to the farm household's overall utility maximization. When we start from this premise, then we can begin to understand that rural development policy should touch upon more than just production and profit.

Changes in household utility are naturally sensitive to new levels of wealth and income, but utility also responds to changes in a range of other factors (e.g. amenities, quality of life, and overall well-being). Blank's analysis strongly reinforces the perspective that successful rural development policy, looking to the future, must be comprehensive in both its design and delivery.

Addressing diverse conditions in rural development

As we have indicated earlier in this chapter, Hodge and Midmore's (2008) research is part of a larger professional literature documenting the diverse nature of rural areas.[30] They argue that successful rural development policy requires an approach that can include the agriculture sector, but must also address other sectors and be more comprehensive in nature.

Hodge and Midmore emphasize that we should evaluate the economic consequences of any rural policy choice in a comprehensive manner. We can begin by employing traditional microeconomic measures of efficiency, equity, and policy effectiveness. From this viewpoint, the efficiency of rural development policy can be gauged in terms of changes in Real GDP, changes in product quality, and gains in institutional efficiency. Assessing equity impacts can involve determinations of whether development programs increase rural community viability, create a more even income distribution, upgrade labor conditions, and/or enhance access to vital resources and services that contribute to a better quality of life.

Hodge and Midmore also raise the question of "causality" as an important methodological issue. How do we know whether observed changes in rural economic conditions are actually traceable to rural development efforts? Are there plausible and competing explanations of what is actually driving change in rural areas? We need methods that help us to validate what effects are truly linked to enacted rural policies.

Establishing legitimate responses to questions of causality, efficiency, and equity are undoubtedly important. They are output indicators. But rural development challenges also involve whether plans are properly executed, and whether they focus on the issues most pertinent to rural areas relative to urban zones. As a result, we need "process indicators": ways to assess the accuracy and adequacy of rural policy implementation.

For example, an appropriate indicator of rural progress may be improvements in the availability constituent access to social services. In comparison, the typical urban concern about whether policies can help alleviate overcrowded housing has much less relevance in rural settings.

Similarly, data collection and measurements in rural and urban areas may not always be comparable. For example, an urban Census enumeration district might be effective for studying differences in urban household income distribution; but attempts to use the same data-gathering approach in a rural area might not allow income distribution research to move forward because rural data are more aggregated.[31] When it comes to development planning and evaluation, "one size does not fit all."

Strengths and shortcomings of past rural development strategies

Naylor (2014) offers an international perspective on successes and failures in rural development. The World Bank, a global organization dedicated to alleviating poverty and assisting less developed nations to make progress, utilized the "integrated rural development model" (IRPM) to sponsor projects worldwide in the 1970s and 1980s.[32]

The principles that underlie IRPM are theoretically appealing: within a defined geographic region, rural development projects would coordinate all government and NGO agencies at the local level by means of a regional planning authority. Planning authorities could tap into the comparative advantages of the different ministries by collaborating on improving health care, roads, irrigation, agricultural credit, and technology adoption. Ideally, with IRPM, the whole would be greater than the sum of its parts.

Implementation barriers proved to be a major stumbling block for IRPM, and its promises of revolutionizing rural development were never fully realized. Naylor (2014) clearly explains that regional planning authorities were not able to convince the various agencies included with IRPM projects to work together.[33] Lines of communication across agencies never really formed because the decision makers within agencies had powerful economic incentives to maintain spheres of influence within their own areas of authority and expertise. These agencies had no tradition of coordinating their efforts, and the existence of an IRPM project was insufficient motivation to break through pre-existing barriers.

The achievement of rural development goals via regional coordination was a reasonable hypothesis, but this approach was unfortunately not feasible in practice. In 1988, the World Bank abandoned IRPM as a development model in the late 1980s and early 1990s.

An alternative to IRPM is a more centralized rural development method. The Centralized Model (CM) empowers national agencies/ministries to administer policies aimed at stimulating targeted rural development activities closely associated with each agency's own mission. Using this approach, development might proceed more narrowly and sequentially, as opposed to the multi-pronged tactics that IRPM had promoted.

Compared to IRPM projects, the CM strategy institutes a set of nationwide policy incentives. Markets and/or individual producers rationally and voluntarily respond to the CM strategy through new investments, technology adoption, infrastructure improvements, etc. The CM model suggests that individual decision makers willingly engage in development activity, given the correct incentive environment. Naylor (2104) proposes that the CM approach is consistent with the producer-based development recommendations that Nobel laureate Theodore W. Schultz articulated in *Transforming Traditional Agriculture* (1964).[34]

The CM strategy also has its drawbacks. While individual agencies or ministries are much better equipped to engage in economic activities that fall within their particular jurisdictions, there are rural development problems that would be best solved by a coordinated effort. There also may be questions of whether sufficient resources can be brought to bear to fully fund the intended policies.

Looking towards the future of rural development, lessons learned from the trials associated with the IRPM and CM strategies are instructive. It may be possible to create new paradigms for making real impacts by incorporating the best parts of previous attempts, while preventing the repetition of past mistakes.

Seeking principles to guide future rural development

A question that often arises when considering the future of rural development is the appropriate role of agriculture. Blank (2008) investigated regional agricultural patterns in the western US, and identifies some important factors that deserve further study.[35] For example, the rising popularity of "localized agriculture" has implications for rural development policy.

Blank (2008) probes the localization movement from the perspective of its long-term viability in relation to the counter-influence of globalization. Further, Blank encourages us to examine alternative approaches to rural development models, in light of their capacity to account for phenomena such as small-scale farm economics, efficient geographic clusters, and locational amenities. Blank's contribution to our understanding of rural development are the powerful insights to be learned when we carefully apply microeconomic theory.

Ashley and Maxwell (2001) reviewed historical, institutional and theoretical influences on rural development, and concluded that rural development strategies need real reform.[36] Ashley and Maxwell offer guidelines to direct these reforms, and they begin with a central premise: successful rural development policies should lessen rural poverty.

If we accept poverty reduction as a common thread that ties together efforts to engage in rural development, then we can establish a coherent set of organizing principles.

Ashley and Maxwell (2001) are diligent in examining the relevant rural development policy factors that can affect the causes and consequences of poverty. They derive five principles to guide rural development policy in ways that can alleviate poverty and improve the quality of life in rural areas:[37]

- Recognize rural diversity.
- Respond to past, present, and future changes in rural socio-economic conditions.
- Establish development policies logically consistent with other poverty reduction efforts.
- Engage in rural development strategies that support democratic decentralization.
- Assist rural areas to advance the comparative advantages of their productive sectors in a manner that reduces poverty and encourages real GDP growth.

Earlier in this chapter we reviewed OECD guidelines for rural development. Careful inspection of the principles offered by Ashley and Maxwell (2001) shows a convergence of ideas.[38] It appears that the research on rural development is identifying the path that leads us forward. What remains is the implementation, and an assessment of outcomes. The work ahead is challenging, but also worthwhile.

Conclusions, and what's next?

Our inquiry into rural development has been a good opportunity to explore fundamental issues. What is rural? What should be the purposes of rural development strategies? With the diverse nature of rural areas in the US, and around the world, how do we develop a set of principles to guide rural development? These are key questions deserving of careful research and well-managed policy making.

The linkages between rural development in this chapter, and the special topics covered in the upcoming Chapter 12, are strong and readily observed. A healthy and growing rural economy in the twenty-first century is very dependent on factors such as new entrants into agriculture, the local foods movement, organic agriculture, and societal agricultural literacy. We still have plenty of work to do as we continue our intellectual journey towards a better understanding of food and agricultural policy.

Notes

1 Rikkers, Sam. "Taking Charge: How Rural Residents Are Switching from Employees to Business Owners." USDA Rural Business Service. December 12, 2016. Retrieved from: http://blogs.usda. gov/2016/12/12/taking-charge-how-rural-residents-are-switching-from-employees-to-business-owners/#more-67752

2 Ibid.

3 McConville, Megan. USDA, Rural Development (RD) Agency. "Working Together to Develop Local Strategies for Strong Rural Communities." Washington, DC. Sept. 29, 2016. Retrieved from: http://blogs.usda.gov/2016/09/29/working-together-to-develop-local-strategies-for-strong-rural-communities/. Alton, Missouri, with a population of 870, participated in a USDA rural development grant program, Smart Growth America, to improve the local economy. Alton, with the support of a USDA RD grant, implemented a comprehensive plan, capitalized on cultural heritage, enhance regional food access, and increased eco-tourism, etc.

4 Ward, William A. and James C. Hite. "Theory in Rural Development: An Introduction and Overview." *Growth and Change* 29, pp. 245–258. Summer 1998. Retrieved from: www.researchgate. net/publication/229779918_Theory_in_Rural_Development_An_Introduction_and_Overview

5 Hodge, Ian, and Peter Midmore. "Models of Rural Development and Approaches to Analysis Evaluation and Decision-Making." *Économie Rurale* 307, pp. 23–38. Retrieved from: www. researchgate.net/publication/38452142_Models_of_Rural_Development_and_Approaches_To_ Analysis_Evaluation_And_Decision-Making

6 Ibid, p. 25.

7 USDA, Rural Development (RD) Agency, Site Map. "Rural and Community Development." Washington, DC. Last Date Modified: March 18, 2015. Retrieved from: www.usda.gov/wps/portal/ usda/usdahome?navid=rural-development

8 Ward and Hite, p. 246. Retrieved from: www.researchgate.net/publication/229779918_Theory_ in_Rural_Development_An_Introduction_and_Overview

9 Ibid, p. 249.

10 Ibid, p. 256.

11 Poku, Kwasi. *Small-scale Palm Oil Processing in Africa.* FAO Agricultural Services Bulletin #148. United Nations. 2002, pp. 3–8. Retrieved from: ftp://ftp.fao.org/docrep/fao/005/y4355E/y4355E00. pdf

12 Ibid, pp. 3–6.

13 BBC News. "In Pictures: Nigerian Palm Oil." 2016. http://news.bbc.co.uk/2/shared/spl/hi/picture_ gallery/08/africa_nigerian_palm_oil/html/8.stm

14 Ayodele, Thompson. "The World Bank's Palm Oil Mistake." *New York Times.* The Opinion Pages – Op-Ed Contributor. Oct. 15, 2010. Retrieved from: www.nytimes.com/2010/10/16/ opinion/16ayodele.html?_r=1&src=sch&pagewanted=all

15 Ashreena, Tanya. "Nigeria Makes Progress in Releasing 'Untapped Potential' in Palm Oil." Wednesday, 5 Oct 2016. Agrimoney.Com. Retrieved from: www.agrimoney.com/feature/nigeria-makes-progress-in-releasing-untapped-potential-in-palm-oil—466.html

16 Organization for Economic Cooperation and Development (OECD): Better Policies for Better Lives. "About the OECD." Paris, France. 2016. www.oecd.org/about/

17 OECD, Public Affairs Division. "Reinventing Rural Policy." Nicola Crosta, nicola.crosta@oecd. org. 2006. Retrieved from: www.oecd.org/gov/regional-policy/37556607.pdf

18 Ward and Hite, p. 247.

19 OECD, Public Affairs Division. 2006. P. 4. Retrieved from: www.oecd.org/gov/regional-policy/ 37556607.pdf

20 Honadle, Beth Walter. "Rural Development Policy in the United States: Beyond the Cargo Cult Mentality." *Journal of Regional Analysis and Policy* 31(2), 2001. Retrieved from: http://ageconsearch. umn.edu/bitstream/132202/2/2001-2-7.pdf

21 Ibid, p. 100. Retrieved from: http://ageconsearch.umn.edu/bitstream/132202/2/2001-2-7.pdf

22 Ibid, pp. 100–102. Retrieved from: http://ageconsearch.umn.edu/bitstream/132202/2/2001-2-7.pdf

23 OECD, Public Affairs Division. 2006. Pp. 4–6. Retrieved from www.oecd.org/gov/regional-policy/ 37556607.pdf

24 USDA, Rural Development Agency. "USDA Rural Development: Highlights of the Agriculture Act of 2014." April 2014. Retrieved from: www.rd.usda.gov/files/RDFarmBillHighlights.pdf

25 Ibid, pp. 1–4.

26 OECD, Public Affairs Division. 2006, p. 5. Retrieved from: www.oecd.org/gov/regional-policy/ 37556607.pdf

27 Blank, S., K. Erickson, and C. Moss. "The Business of an Agricultural Way of Life." *Choices* (20)2, pp. 161–166, 2005.

28 Blank, Stephen C. *The Economics of American Agriculture: Evolution and Global Development.* Armonk, NY: M.E. Sharpe Publishers, 2008, pp. 349–377.

29 Ibid, p. 351.

30 Hodge, Ian and Peter Midmore. "Models of Rural Development and Approaches to Analysis Evaluation and Decision-Making." *Économie Rurale* 307, p. 25. Retrieved from: www. researchgate.net/publication/38452142_Models_of_Rural_Development_and_Approaches_To_ Analysis_Evaluation_And_Decision-Making

31 Ibid, p. 31.

32 Falcon, Walter P. "Food Security for the Poorest Billion." In Naylor, Rosamond L. (ed). *The Evolving Sphere of Food Security.* Oxford, UK: Oxford University Press, 2014, pp. 43–45.

33 Ibid, p. 44.

34 Schultz, Theodore W. *Transforming Traditional Agriculture*. New Haven, CT: Yale University Press, 1964.
35 Blank, Stephen C. *The Economics of American Agriculture*, pp. 359–377.
36 Ashley, Caroline and Simon Maxwell. "Rethinking Rural Development." *Development Policy Review* 19(4), pp. 395–425, 2001. Retrieved from: http://s3.amazonaws.com/academia.edu. documents/6626749/rethinking_rural_development.pdf?AWSAccessKeyId=AKIAJ56TQJRTWSM TNPEA&Expires=1475177415&Signature=ngbEh0B%2FsuGfoiwRBkWoBctFpfs%3D&response-content-disposition=inline%3B%20filename%3DRethinking_rural_development.pdf
37 Ibid, p. 418.
38 Ibid, pp. 419–420.

Chapter 12

Current developments and new dynamics influencing agricultural and food policy

Twenty-first-century US agriculture is witnessing important changes in demographics and typical career paths. By 2050, we can expect a "new normal" in the US domestic farm economy. Women, veterans, and socially disadvantaged groups are entering US Agriculture because discerning food consumers, new technologies, and supportive government policies are creating fresh market growth opportunities. It is instructive to examine some real-world examples to highlight the new and exciting trends in US agriculture. Let's take a look.

In Spokane, Washington, Beth Robinette exemplifies the dynamic influence of women in US agriculture. Beth is an owner-operator of a *grass-fed beef operation and the co-founder of a farmer- and worker-owned cooperative food hub*.[1] A sample of Ms. Robinette's management outlook is informative:

> My favorite part of I think we should delete the period here. [the cooperative food hub] is growing the business. Every dollar we bring into the business represents a dollar reinvested in our local economy ... My favorite part of ranching is just being on the land ... I am constantly learning ... [it] might mean improving my stockmanship, or learning ... how the land responds to different grazing pressures at different times, or figuring out how to adapt ... to changing climatic conditions.[2]

Michelle Dudley manages the Crossroads Farmers Market ("The Crossroads") in Takoma Park, Maryland. Just north of Washington, DC, this open market allows immigrant vendors to offer 131 different fruits and vegetables to over 1,000 visitors per week. The Crossroads helps US immigrants from El Salvador, Guatemala and other Central American countries create a vibrant market economy where farmer-vendors and low-income consumers engage in mutually beneficial trade for traditional vegetables and plants.[3]

A US combat veteran from Operation Desert Storm and Operation Iraqi Freedom II, Eric Grandon of West Virginia (WV), was encouraged to farm through the WV Veterans and Warriors Agriculture program. Mr. Grandon discovered that farming had tremendous therapeutic value in managing his PTSD. Bee-keeping proved to be among the best ways to achieve personal peace and healing. Veterans like Eric Grandon bravely served their country, and the WV farm program helps these heroes productively assimilate back into the civilian economy.[4]

Similar to the WV program, the USDA's Agricultural Research Service (ARS) cooperates with the University of Arkansas in Fayetteville and the National Center for Appropriate Technology (NCAT), to offer an "Armed to Farm" boot camp that teaches veterans agricultural fundamentals and practices via workshops, online courses, and internships at various sites throughout Arkansas.[5]

A Rwandan refugee, and now a naturalized American citizen, Janine Ndagijimana and her family immigrated to Burlington, Vermont. Janine works diligently with the University of Vermont Extension Service as part of the New American Farmer Program. Janine rents acres to grow and market eggplants locally; she also exports them to nearby Canada. Janine enlisted the help of USDA's Natural Resources Conservation Service (NRCS) to properly manage cover crops and improve her farm's soil health, as well as to participate in the Environmental Quality Incentives Program (EQIP). Through EQIP, Janine is offered technical support and financial assistance to employ high tunnels and extend the brief VT growing season for sensitive crops such as vegetables, herbs, and berries.[6]

Organization of chapter

Important and exciting socio-economic transformations are taking place within US agriculture. Reflecting the demographic changes occurring within the entire US population, the age, ethnic, and attitudinal characteristics of the agri-food system are trending in new directions.

Among the many societal forces modifying the future of US agriculture, we focus on a few critical factors in this chapter. Our approach to this dynamic area of study is to initially review broader considerations and then concentrate on topics of special interest. Consequently, this chapter sequentially examines the following topics and trends affecting the US agri-food system:

- Theoretical and empirical factors influencing the economic potentials of new entrants (including women, socially disadvantaged groups, and veterans) and smaller-scale operations.
- Socioeconomic forces and policies associated with the agri-food system's roles for women, socially disadvantaged groups, and veterans.
- The socioeconomic effects of changing consumer attitudes and the local foods movement.
- The increasing role of organic farming and marketing.
- The vital functions of agricultural and food education in the twenty-first century.

The face of US agriculture is changing "as we speak." It is important to carefully consider the meaning of these major trends and new circumstances.

We can certainly be grateful for the accomplishments of the market participants, past and present, who created the highly productive and reliable US agri-food system that we have today. But we must also look to the future to see who will be next to "carry the baton" and excel in the race to successfully and sustainably satisfy growing global food demands.

As we move forward with the topics in this chapter, we have a chance to consider what the future holds. While there will be challenges, there is also a sense of promise and possibilities in the capacity of the US agri-food system to transform itself and meet those challenges.

Analyzing the economic potentials of women, socially disadvantaged groups, and veterans as new market entrants and small-scale operators

Small-scale versus large-scale farm operations

In Chapter 2 of this textbook, and throughout the agricultural economics literature, we emphasize the economic and technological forces that drive US agriculture towards a market structure of *decreasing farm numbers* and *increasing farm size*. That aspect of market concentration is well documented.[7]

But the increasing entry of new and beginning farmers in recent years, especially led by women in American agriculture, and also by socially disadvantaged groups and veterans, is a novel source of vitality in the farm and food sectors. Changing demographics introduce a new market dynamic.

Large-scale agriculture in the US is not disappearing; in many ways, it is as strong as ever. But at the other end of the market spectrum, when we examine small family farm trends, key changes are influencing both the image and the fundamental character of who will be guiding the US agri-food system in the years ahead.

For anyone with an interest in the future of the agricultural and food sector in our economy, the new market patterns are significant, exciting, and worthy of study. To understand the nature of the upcoming changes, we first "set the stage" by describing the current market structure of US agriculture.

The total number of US farms in 2014 was 2,084,000, based on USDA Agricultural Resource Management Survey (ARMS) data. Total farm acres were 913 million, which means an average of 438.1 acres per farm.[8]

Small family farms, with an annual average Gross Cash Farm Income (GCFI) of less than $350,000, constituted 90 percent of the *total number* of US farms; these smaller operations also generated 21.9 percent of the *total value* of US agricultural production and controlled 46 percent of *total US farmland.*[9]

Approximately 68 *percent of the **total value*** *of US farm production* occurs on 9 *percent of the **total number*** *of US farms* classified as either *mid-size or large-scale* family farms. The GCFI is $350,000 to $999,999 for mid-size farms, and over $1,000,000 for large-scale farms. Together, medium and larger farms also utilized 51 percent of total US farmland.[10]

If we just examine the distribution of GCFI, we might conclude that the largest farms are the most economically viable. The driving forces of technology adoption, specialization, and government policies have certainly created powerful incentives for the average farm size to increase.

But the economic forces influencing change in the US agricultural market structure are more complex. A USDA-ERS study (2013) reported that the *number of small crop farms has been increasing* since the year 2000, reversing a downward trend that had prevailed during the last half of the twentieth century.[11] What factors revived the growth of smaller farms? There are a number of variables that help explain this market rejuvenation.

Strengths and limitations of small-scale farm operations

Owner-operators of small farm operations can be *entrepreneurial*, and quickly adjust their "product mix" to take advantage of new market trends. Using a maritime analogy, it is easier to change course with a small speedboat than a large ocean cruiser. The growth of women, socially disadvantaged groups, and veterans as new entrants into agri-food markets is a dynamic component of the entrepreneurial resurgence in small-scale agriculture.

Where large farms normally benefit from specialization, small farms more readily engage in *diversification*. Small farms can supplement their income and control their risk by broadening their economic base and creatively employing their resources in alternative enterprises.

Another avenue open to smaller-scale producers is to "contract" their production. A contract provides farmers or ranchers with an assured market for their output. Small producers agree to deliver their products to customers seeking commodities with particular qualities on a prescribed timeline.[12]

It is also important to understand the drawbacks to small-scale farm enterprises. Smaller farms may not fully benefit from new technologies designed to be cost efficient when investment costs are spread across more acres and/or increased output. Compared to large-scale operators, producers on smaller farms may have more difficulty demonstrating credit-worthiness or their capacity to absorb downside financial risk. Also, government policies such as tax advantages and commodity program benefits, may favor larger-sized operations relative to smaller ones.

Why are the trends and economic viability of small-scale farms important? The answer to this question is multifaceted:

- "New and beginning farms" typically enter the industry as small-scale operations.
- From a demographic standpoint, growth in the number of small farms is an opportunity to revitalize US agriculture with a younger and more diverse group of owner-operators. The average age of principal US farm operators was 58.3 years in 2012, compared to an average of 50.5 years in 1982.
- Opportunities for women, socially disadvantaged groups and veterans to enter into farming as new participants are likely to be in the category of small-scale start-up businesses.

Socioeconomic considerations and the market entry of small-scale farm operators

While it is desirable that small farms are themselves economically viable operational units, their worth extends further. Numerical growth in small farms yields positive impacts for the vitality of rural and regional economies. Small farm operators typically earn significant off-farm income. A USDA-sponsored farm bill forum noted that *off-farm income* accounts for 85–95 percent of farm household income.[13] If we recall the power of the macroeconomic multiplier effect, rural businesses and communities benefit when numerous small-farm households spend their combined farm- and nonfarm-income to purchase goods and services in the local economy.

Small farm operators can also make sizable economic contributions if they engage in direct marketing. Examples include farmers' markets and cooperative food hubs. Direct marketing is a chance to increase a farm's profit margin, particularly when a small producer can serve niche markets where consumers willingly pay extra for qualities such as product freshness and personal service.

In these instances, small-scale producers help consumers satisfy their desire to properly balance price and choice within their food budgets. Basic microeconomics tells us that the market entry of new firms into an industry creates a livelier competitive market. When small farm operators join the market, then consumers have increased opportunity to judge real product value, because enhanced competition inevitably sets solid benchmarks for price and quality.

Earlier research on the benefits of participating small farm operations (and their associated households) for enhancing the strength and vigor of rural communities still has relevance today.[14] Small or part-time farmers tend to support activities conducive to community growth, development, and vitality.

Characteristics and contributions of women farm operators in US agriculture

The 2012 Census of US Agriculture tells us that *13.7 percent of all principal US farm operators are women.* If the participation of women as second- or third-farm operators is also included, then 30.5 percent of all US farm operators are female (969,672 in number), according to the 2012 Ag Census.[15] When women are the principal farm operators, most *(91 percent) of their farms earn between $0 and $49,999 in total annual sales.* In our above discussion, we identified the economic benefits when new, smaller farms enter today's markets. Women farm owners and managers are definitely making real contributions to farm market vitality as they establish and run these smaller start-up operations.

In 1982, women were the principal farm operators on just 5.4 percent of farms, and were also 12.2 percent of all operators (1st, 2nd, or 3rd). Times have changed. *The role of women in production agriculture has increased by 150 percent over a 30-year period (1982–2012).*[16]

If we look deeper into the US Ag Census, we observe that the total number of female US farm operators increased continuously between 1982 and 2007, and then slightly decreased between the 2007 and 2012 Ag Census.

It remains to be seen whether the recent dip (during 2007–2012) in women farm-operator numbers is an anomaly or a new trend. But it is interesting to note the breakdown of the changes that took place in that 5-year span.

For instance, in the category between $0 and $9,999 in annual farm sales, we find a noticeable decrease in the number of female principal operators (a net decrease of 21,122 during 2007–2012). All other sales categories of greater than $10,000 in annual farm sales experienced **greater** numbers of women as principal operators (a net increase of 17,945).[17]

There are a variety of considerations worth mentioning about the events that occurred between the 2007 and 2012 Census of US Agriculture. In 2008–2009, the US experienced its worst national recession since the 1930s. In addition, there were substantial agricultural economic pressures deriving from bio-energy demands to non-renew CRP contracts and place land back into crop production. Another key observation is the *3.1 percent decline in the total number of all farm operators (1st, 2nd or 3rd; male or female) during the 2007–2012 time period.* In comparison, the total number of women operators declined by only 1.6 percent. After all of the changes, women as a percent of all US farm operators *slightly increased* during 2007–2012.

As we carefully examine the 2007 and 2012 Census of Agriculture, an interesting picture of women in twenty-first-century US Agriculture begins to emerge. For example, we can hypothesize farm expansion as one reason why the number of women declined in the lowest annual sales category ($0 to $9,999), while all other larger sales categories rose in number. *Some of those smaller operations managed by women simply evolved upwards to into larger enterprises.*

It is also possible that some women operators who managed the land while receiving CRP payments, let their CRP contracts expire, and then took advantage of the chance to earn larger returns because bio-energy market growth markedly increased the profitability of crop production. In such instances where land was placed back into production, a farm operation could easily generate sales greater than $10,000/year.

Smaller operations often produce specialty items that are direct-marketed to urban centers. During the 2008–2009 recession, considerable economic turmoil likely reduced or upset many urban food markets, and smaller farm operations struggled to succeed under these stressful circumstances.

Finally, relative to men, women owner-operators *are equally influenced* by the technological imperative transforming agriculture to an industry with smaller numbers of larger farms. The disappearance of small women-operated farms during 2007–2012 may be partly caused by the pressures of long-term structural changes that affect all farm markets.

In many ways, volatility in agricultural market is not necessarily a new development. The decline in overall farm numbers during 2007–2012 indicates that farm economic forces have broad impacts. When the demographic changes are viewed in their totality, it is safe to conclude that the trend of an expanding role for women in US agriculture will continue.

Commodities marketed by US principal women farm operators in 2012

When women are the principal farm operators, what products are their farms producing? We can examine the 2012 Census of Agriculture to help answer this question. One way to measure their impact is to examine a measurement known as the annual *$Value of Sales by Commodity Group* ($VSCG). When $VSCG is summed across all commodities sold by principle women operators in 2012, we find a total of $12.897 billion (about 3.3 percent of $VSCG on all farms).[18]

The Census categories of *Poultry and Eggs, Cattle and Calves, and the combined grouping of Grains, Oilseeds, Dry Beans, and Dry Peas* accounted for the *highest-valued* $VSCG for these women farmers; *together these commodity sales were **56.9 percent** of the women principal operator $VSCG total.*

If we examine the commodities *associated with the **greatest number*** of principal women farm operators, the 2012 Ag Census tells us that *Cattle and Calves, Poultry and Eggs, and Other Crops and Hay* constitute the most "popular" commodities among women principal operators, *accounting for **50.1 percent of the number of female primary producers** in 2012.*

Another way to understand this data on women as principal operators is to examine the *average $VSCG per farm operator*. A "drill down" into the Census data reveals the set of commodities where principal women operators earn an average $VSCG of $100,000/ year or more. These higher-grossing areas include: *Milk from Cows, Cotton and Cottonseed, Aquaculture, Poultry and Eggs,* the grouped category of *Grains, Oilseeds, Dry Beans and Dry Peas,* and also the additional category of *Nursery, Greenhouse, Floriculture, and Sod.* These larger operations are economically important – while they account for just 23.5 percent of all principal women operators, *they generate 60.9 percent of the total $VSCG for this group of producers.*[19]

Characteristics and contributions of underserved minority operators in US agriculture

The increased participation of women in agriculture is partly a reflection of changing societal attitudes towards increased gender equity in our twenty-first-century US economy. Ethnic and racial minorities have also been seeking greater economic equality in America.

While the pursuit of social justice is an ongoing work-in-progress, there are additional population dynamics at work in the US economy. The twenty-first-century US population is considerably more ethnically diverse than it was in the twentieth century. All parts of the US economy, including the food and agricultural sectors, now reflect the reality of increased diversity.

The rise in US agriculture's ethnic diversity is reflected in census data. A review of Table 12.1 reveals that the number of minority farm operators increased across the board between 2007 and 2012. The largest percent changes occurred within the Asian and Hispanic categories.

The growth rates noted in Table 12.1 are gradually changing the complexion of US agriculture. The 2012 Census of Agriculture reports that 8 percent of all principle operators were minorities, compared to about 7 percent in the 2007 Ag Census.

While these statistics seemingly indicate that socially disadvantaged groups have yet to make significant inroads in US agricultural markets, we should carefully observe both the proportional and numerical changes taking place over time. A +15 percent annual rate of

Table 12.1 Number of minority principal operators and percent change, based on the 2007 and 2012 Census of US agriculture

	2007 Ag Census	2012 Ag Census	Percent Change
Asian	11,214	13,699	+22.2 percent
Black	30,599	33,372	+9.1 percent
American Indian	34,706	37,857	+9.1 percent
Hispanic*	55,570	67,014	+20.6 percent
Total	132,089	151,942	+15.0 percent

Source: USDA NASS, 2012 Census of Agriculture, Preliminary Report.[20]

increased influence in agriculture is actually very substantial. If this +15 percent rate of increase is sustained, and if we use the "rule of 72" to figure out how long it will take for the role of minority principle operators to double, only about 5 years are needed for their impact to increase twofold.[21]

How does this increasing role of underserved groups participating in agriculture compare to the national economic trends for all minorities in America? They are comparable. Wilkins (2014) uses US Census data to determine that both the Asian and Hispanic/Latino segments of the US population had increased by 50 percent or more between the years 2000 and 2012. All other minority groups also saw double-digit growth over the same time period.[22]

Given the demographic trends influencing the overall American population, the increasing role of minorities as a productive force within our agricultural economy is very predictable. If these demographic changes are properly recognized and supported, the role of ethnic diversity can create new niches and sources of comparative advantage that can enhance the future competitiveness of US agriculture.

Using the 2012 US Agricultural Census information in Table 12.2, we can interpret economic characteristics and trends for US farm-businesses supervised by women and minorities. A brief scan of Table 12.2 reveals that women and socially disadvantaged groups are predominantly managing smaller-scale farms as principle operators. Over time, given the technological forces at work in American agriculture, it is reasonable to expect that many of these smaller-sized operations will gradually advance into larger-scale farms. Of particular

Table 12.2 Share of farms by economic class for selected groups, identified by principal annual operator sales, using data from the 2012 Census of US agriculture

	Operator Sales < $50,000/Year	Operator Sales ≥ $50,000/Year
All Farms	75 percent	25 percent
Female	91 percent	9 percent
Hispanic	85 percent	15 percent
American Indian	92 percent	8 percent
Black	94 percent	6 percent
Asian	65 percent	35 percent

Source: USDA NASS, 2012 Census of Agriculture, Preliminary Report.[23]

interest, when anticipating the potential economic evolution of minority-operated farms, is the significant proportion (35 percent) of Asian-operated farms that are already earning more than $50,000/year.

While the recent net gains of minorities becoming farmers and ranchers (see Table 12.1) are important, it will take time for the full potential of ethnic diversity to be realized in US agriculture. From a demographic standpoint, minorities collectively represented nearly *37 percent of the entire US population in 2012, while 8 percent of principal farm operators are from these ethnically diverse groups.*[24,25] The capacity exists for a greater influx of minorities into agriculture.

In addition, as we examine Table 12.2, we notice that minority groups (other than the Asian category) are more highly concentrated in managing small farm operations than is the case for all farms. That imbalance will likely adjust itself over time as producers of all backgrounds adapt to the technological imperative towards larger-sized farms.

There are many reasons for the current ethnic disparities. Limitations originated because disadvantaged groups and veterans were either not aware of the opportunities or falsely believed that they lacked eligibility. But active efforts are underway to create more opportunities and easier access to the tools that minorities are seeking to become even more active participants in the US farm economy. We next review how federal programs and policies are attempting to open additional doors for minorities in American agriculture.

Opportunities and incentives for socially disadvantaged groups to participate in US Farm Bill programs

The USDA's Natural Resources and Conservation Service (NRCS) offers programs specifically aimed to provide support and technical services for socially disadvantaged farmers and/or ranchers. Because it is important that the intended groups targeted for assistance actually receive the help, the NRCS (and all USDA agencies) relies on a formal definition of who qualifies, as follows:

> A *Socially Disadvantaged Farmer/Rancher* (SDF/R) is any farmer or rancher who has been subjected to racial or ethnic prejudices because of their identity as a member of a group without regard to their individual qualities. The included SDF/R groups are African Americans, American Indians or Alaskan natives, Hispanics, and Asians or Pacific Islanders.[26]

A USDA program expressly designed to enhance farming opportunities for socially disadvantaged groups was initiated in the 1990 Farm Bill. Identified as the Outreach and Assistance to Socially Disadvantaged Farmers and Ranchers (OASDFR) program, it was authorized under the 1990 Farm Bill's Section 2501. OASDFR has been reauthorized in succeeding farm bills, and is often referred to as simply the "the 2501 program."[27]

The 2501 Program requires the USDA to actively engage in outreach activities and technical assistance that facilitates the entry of these disadvantaged groups into farm markets as viable businesses. The program is implemented via grants managed by land grant universities, tribal governments, Latino-serving institutions, veterans groups, state-controlled institutions, community-based organizations, and nonprofits.

In the 2008 Farm Bill, Congress authorized the creation of an Office of Outreach and Advocacy (OOA) to administer and coordinate the OASDFR program. *The 2014 Farm*

Bill extended the OASDFR coverage to include veterans.[28] The OOA's responsibilities include efforts to help socially disadvantaged groups and veterans become aware and ultimately access specially designed benefits from a range of USDA agencies, including NRCS conservation programs, Farm Service Agency (FSA) financial assistance programs, Sustainable Agriculture and Research and Education (SARE) programs, and programs offered through state government departments of agriculture.

The OOA has helped more than 300 local partners to offer socially disadvantaged and veteran farmers and ranchers access to approximately $74 million in USDA assistance since 2010.[29] To ensure continuing positive impacts, the 2014 Farm Bill approved $10 million per year in mandatory OASDFR funding over the FY2014–FY2018 time horizon.[30]

The growth and diversity of the US agricultural economy are facilitated by government policies (such as the 2014 Farm Bill) that promote the entry of new and beginning farmers, socially disadvantaged groups, veterans, and women as entrepreneurs, and skilled laborers into farm and food markets. Injecting additional scarce and valuable human-based resources into the production process is an established means of increasing the agri-food system's real output potential.

Successful progress for any economy requires expanding outlets that can *demand and utilize the growth* in productive capacity. In the next section of this chapter, we explore the mounting consumer interest in local food systems.

While the local food movement is still in its early development stages, it is a growth sector in the US agricultural economy. As new and beginning farmers strengthen their presence in the agri-food system, the increasingly diverse gender and ethnic backgrounds of these new producers represent a real opportunity to harmonize wide-ranging productive potentials with the varied demands of local food markets.

The expanding role of local food markets in the US agri-food system

The twenty-first century has witnessed a rising trend towards linking US consumers with locally produced foods. Some traditional direct marketing options, such as farmers' markets and "you pick" enterprises have increased in frequency and popularity. Newer types of market arrangements have also broadened and extended the trend. For example, Jenny Bostick is both a farmer and a coordinator for the Family Connections Regional Partnership located in rural Georgia's Mitchell County. As a female farm operator, Jenny sought to expand her enterprise to supply locally grown produce to area school districts.[31]

Jenny's goals to increase the reach of her farm operation benefitted from two USDA programs: (1) the Farm-to-School local foods program, and (2) the 2501 socially disadvantaged farmer and rancher (SDFR) program. Training and technical assistance were necessary to assure the success of this local foods initiative. Workshops coordinated by Southwest Georgia Project for Community Education and the USDA helped Jenny learn and apply practices that met school district food requirements and business supply protocols. The investments of time and effort paid off, and Jenny became a local produce supplier for two school districts.[32]

Based on USDA estimates, total annual local food sales in the US were $4.8 billion in 2008, and $6.1 billion in 2012. This sales expansion is a 6.2 percent annual growth rate. *Approximately 164,000 farmers **(8 percent of all US farms) marketed local foods** to account for 1.5 percent of total US agricultural sales in 2012.*[33]

Difficulties in definition

How do we define a local food system? Unfortunately, there is no widely accepted definition of what constitutes "local." It is even difficult to specify a common set of criteria to fully classify a local market.

Section 6015 of the 2008 Farm Bill offers the following definition of "local": "products transported less than 400 miles or within the state in which they are produced."[34] This farm bill description of a local food market is necessary because it partially determines a producer's *eligibility to participate in USDA's Business and Industry loan program*. While this Section 6015 definition has its limitations, it does emphasize the geographical aspect of what describes a local food system.

For the purposes of this textbook, we can consider that "local" includes particular social and/or supply chain features in both production and geography. Production characteristics for "local food" are generally associated with, but not limited to, smaller family farms, urban gardens, and sustainable/organic operations.

Geographical distance between producer and consumer also matters if the classification of "local food" is to have meaning. As mentioned already, one criterion is whether the food is grown and marketed within state lines. In surveys, many consumers tend to think of local as within a 100-mile radius, or simply as food grown on nearby small farms.[35]

A variety of farm operations and/or market connections can be classified within the realm of a local food system:[36]

- Community and school gardens.
- Farm-to-school programs.
- Community-Supported Agriculture (CSA)* and related direct-to-consumer marketing arrangements.
- Farmers' markets, roadside farm stands, pick-your-own operations.
- Food hubs, market aggregators, community kitchens.
- Food cooperatives and buying clubs.
- On-farm sales/stores and Agri-tourism.

*In Community-Supported Agriculture (CSA), groups of local residents agree to be shareholders or subscribers who financially support the production costs of a farm or community garden in exchange for receiving shares of the farm's output during the growing season.[37]

Federal farm policy effects on local food system development

Government support for local food systems and markets falls into two broad categories:

- Programs specifically aimed to help establish and/or maintain local food systems.
- Programs available for all farm systems, and which also benefit local food systems.

Specific federal policies facilitating local food system development

The 2014 Farm Bill re-authorizes a range of pre-existing and new programs that can be accessed by communities and organizations to initiate and/or provide ongoing support targeted for local food systems. The legislative initiatives in the farm bill can be summarized as follows:[38]

- USDA competitive grants that are open for local food system proposals in two related areas:
  i) The *Farmers' Market Promotion Program* (FMPP) has expanded opportunities and increased funding for direct farm-to-consumer projects, and
  ii) The *Local Food Marketing Promotion Program* (LFPP) opens up USDA support for intermediary supply-chain enterprises who coordinate a distribution network to deliver local or regional foods.

- USDA efforts to establish crop valuation methods and reliable crop price histories for locally produced foods increases the access to business loans and/or credit for regional food producers.
- Increased SNAP-recipient purchasing power helps qualified households adjust their budgets to incorporate increased fruit and vegetable consumption by including preferences for projects that involve local food and direct-to-consumer sales venues.
- The 2014 Farm Bill simply reauthorizes a number of programs that have already been supporting the development of markets for locally and regionally produced foods.
- The Obama Administration implemented the USDA "Know Your Farmer, Know Your Food" initiative to coordinate existing USDA programs that facilitate the formation of local food systems.

General federal policies accessible to support local food systems

The 2014 Farm Bill, and all of its predecessors, are not intended to provide a farm safety net exclusively to assist any particular set of US farms. Rather, the goal is to ensure that broad economic stabilizers are in place to assist an entire agricultural industry confronted by both natural and market factors that generate market instability.

Federal farm programs are envisioned as *equally accessible* to decision makers within markets of any geographic dimension: local, regional, national, or international. Consequently, farm bill programs provide support to *local food systems* simply because US agricultural markets in general can access the farm bill's risk-reducing and/or cost-sharing options. Broadly applicable USDA programs also utilized by local food markets include:[39]

- marketing and promotion.
- business assistance and agricultural research.
- rural and community development.
- nutrition and education.
- farmland conservation.

Examples of broad-based programs available to facilitate the development and/or maintenance of local food systems include conservation cost-sharing options, research and cooperative extension programs, rural cooperative grant and loan programs, child nutrition programs, USDA-administered farm support and grant programs, and related direct and indirect benefits available to local producers from other federal agencies.

Reviewing the economic effects of organic, sustainable, and related certifications on US local, regional, and national food markets

As discussed above, changing consumer demands, shifting producer demographics, and favorable government policies have combined to foster the ongoing development of local food systems. The goals and popularity of USDA's "Know your farmer, know your food" program indicate a rapidly growing interest among consumers to personally review the productive origins and nutritional content of the foods they eat.[40] Beyond just dietary and health demands, today's consumers often want to know how their food purchases affect natural resource conservation, environmental quality, the local economy, and the overall quality of life in their communities.

If we fully understand this twenty-first-century context, where consumer expectations have both broadened and escalated, we can anticipate that markets will emerge to fill these expanding needs. In particular, it is important that we review how today's consumers have driven the robust growth of organic and related "alternative" options within the US agri-food economy.

A connection between organic production and local food systems

A 2012 Utah State Extension report, documenting the growing strength of the local food movement, indicates that US agricultural direct-to-consumer sales rose $399 million (49 percent) between 2002 and 2007.[41] In a related study, the USDA Economic Research Service (ERS) used data from the 2007 Agricultural Resource Management Survey (ARMS) to note that of 21,669 surveyed *organic farms*, 45.7 percent (9,896) were engaged in direct marketing of their products to consumers.[42]

From the standpoint of economics and profitability, the decision of organic producers to engage in direct marketing has been rewarding. The 2007 Census of Agriculture indicates that organic-farm direct marketers earned 75 percent more than the annual average of all direct-sales farms. Further evidence of organic farm financial performance is impressive. Of the 20,474 farms with organic sales in the 2007 Agricultural Census, 41 percent sold $131 million of organic farm output directly to consumers.[43]

While direct marketing theoretically reaches national or even international markets, an additional ERS study (Kremen et al. 2004) observed that consumers who frequent farmers' markets have a significant demand for organic products.[44] ERS researchers are confident that organic producers have utilized direct marketing to play a major role in the expansion of local and regional food markets.

Dynamic changes in organic production and marketing

As indicated above, organic production and marketing have grown rapidly in economic importance. It is clear that organics are a key component driving the advance of both the US local food movement and the direct-to-consumer food markets. However, if we are to have a more complete picture of how organic farm operations and organic food markets are changing the US agricultural economy, we must consider an even wider spectrum of data and evidence.

Dmitri and Oberholtzer (2009) conducted an in-depth USDA study of the dynamic changes occurring in organic food markets.[45] Undoubtedly, increased consumer sophistication and willingness to pay have both been very powerful forces behind the expanding market opportunities for organics. Policy changes have been important too.

When it endorsed the Organic Foods Production Act of 1990, Congress directed the USDA to establish a set of both prohibited and permitted substances associated with organic production and handling operations. This task was a massive undertaking. One decade later, the USDA-approved regulations that comprised the National Organic Program (NOP) were published in 2000, and then implemented in 2002.[46]

The advent of the NOP means that a verifiable national system for organic certification is a reality. This is a milestone in the ongoing development of organic food markets because the certification process is recognized as credible. The certified "organic label" has real meaning. Consumer trust improves dramatically, and the stage is set for significant market growth.

Between 2002 and 2011, organic crop acres markedly expanded (1.3 million to nearly 3.1 million acres). Simultaneously, US organic farm numbers grew from 5,021 to 8,493. Certified organic farm size, on average, swelled from 268 to 477 acres during 1997–2005. Extraordinary growth in certified pastureland acres was largely responsible for augmenting the average farm size of these organic operations.[47]

Increases in organic corn acres and production have been spurred by substantial growth in the organic dairy sector. Certified organic milk cow numbers grew from 67,000 to 255,000 in the 2002–2011 timeframe.[48]

Retailing of organic products also progressed. In 1997, direct-to-consumer markets and natural foods stores were typical organic outlets. By 2008, *nearly **half** of all organic foods were distributed by traditional retail market intermediaries* (supermarkets, big-box stores, etc.). Fresh produce is the most popular sales item among organics, but the growth of organic dairy products, beverages, breads, and grains has also been strong.

Consumer sovereignty is one of the hallmarks of any market economy. New trends in consumer preferences transform markets. What is the appeal of organic food to consumers? What is sparking the growth? As we already stated in this textbook, twenty-first-century consumers may still enjoy the staples (e.g. "meat and potatoes"), but their food purchase decisions often incorporate many other variables such as ethical values, environmental awareness, local economic vitality, and global concerns.

Many of today's consumers seek out organic foods for a variety of reasons. First, there is the perception that organic foods are a healthier option than processed foods. Also, socially conscious consumers may view organics as an environmentally responsible purchase. Organic production can help conserve natural resources because organic agricultural production methods involve crop rotations, natural pest controls, recycled manure and crop residues, and less pollution of waterways. And, if organics are known to be locally produced, the consumer may view their purchase as a boost to the regional economy where he or she lives and works.

Organic production and certification procedures in relation to other alternative farm systems and practices

Certified organic production methods are challenging to implement because they are often more labor-intensive in comparison to conventional farming. In addition, the hiring of approved organic inputs can be difficult because they are scarce or difficult to locate. Organic certification is meaningful because its standards are rigorous and regularly enforced.

As the local food movement and organic markets achieved considerable momentum, the US agri-food system has attracted a variety of additional and related certifications, endorsements, and claims. For example, in meat and poultry markets, consumers may encounter products that are labeled variously as:

- free-range
- antibiotic free
- cage-free
- hormone free
- grass-fed
- natural

The above list of promoted food characteristics is not comprehensive. If you do the research, you will discover an even longer list of claimed food traits (e.g. *certified humane, vegetarian fed*, etc.) that aim to inform consumers about the nature of their food options, and also serve as a form of promotion to encourage consumer purchases.

None of these other labels are equivalent to the formal USDA organic certification. In some ways, the Latin warning of "*Caveat emptor* (Let the buyer beware)" is relevant in this instance. Some of these food labels are voluntary certifications that may or may not have guidelines and verification systems to ensure that the claims are accurate. Consumers are wise to investigate which claims are substantial, and which ones have less evidence to support them.

"Sustainable" is a term that has recently increased in its prevalence, especially in its applications to the US agri-food system. While the terms "sustainable" and "organic" may sound similar, it is important to understand that there currently is *no* commonly accepted set of verifiable standards to precisely determine which food production methods are "sustainable." In comparison, USDA organic production and food certification systems are thoroughly vetted.

What is the meaning and purpose of "sustainability" in the US agri-food system?

Sackett, Shupp, and Tonsor (2016) recently investigated the range of consumer responses to claims of the "sustainable," "organic" or "local" labels placed on their foods.[49] Their research revealed that consumers struggle to identify the precise differences that distinguish the claims made by the various "eco-labels" that they encounter. The research also notes that if consumers feel confident that the claims are properly supported, then they are willing to pay a premium to purchase and consume these alternatively produced foods, as compared with conventional offerings.

"Sustainability" is a claim that has grown in popularity and importance in recent years. As noted by Sackett, Shupp, and Tonsor (2016), if the appropriate documentation is supplied, the USDA will review food labeling proposals such as "sustainably produced." But, unlike the rigorous organic application process, the producer who makes the sustainability assertion is not physically inspected before the labeling decision label is made.

The process of establishing applicable protocols that substantiate claims about food quality or production methods is an arduous task. The NOP for organics required over 10 years to be fully developed and implemented. If consumer demand for "sustainability" remains strong, it is possible that we can develop more exacting guidelines to determine when food items are properly labeled as "sustainably produced." But extra time and effort will be required.

The foundations for instituting sustainability guidelines exist. In the 1990 Farm Bill, Congress defined sustainability in the context of the US agri-food system, and that definition remains in statute today (U.S. Code Title 7, Section 3103):[50]

> *Sustainable agriculture* is an integrated system of plant and animal production practices having a site-specific application that will over the long-term:
>
> - satisfy human food and fiber needs;
> - enhance environmental quality and the natural resource base upon which the agriculture economy depends;
> - make the most efficient use of nonrenewable resources and on-farm resources and integrate, where appropriate, natural biological cycles and controls;
> - sustain the economic viability of farm operations; and
> - enhance the quality of life for farmers and society as a whole.

The above Congressional definition is often condensed into three simple objectives for sustainable agriculture: economic profitability, environmental health, and social and economic equity. For many farm producers, these are simply "the three legs of the sustainability stool."

To implement the Congressional goals for sustainable agriculture, USDA's National Institute of Food and Agriculture (NIFA) oversees funding for the Sustainable Agriculture Research and Education (SARE) program. SARE's charge is to jointly improve producer profitability, environmental conditions, and social justice through grants, research, and education. SARE is administratively guided by volunteer administrative councils in each of four US Regions (Western, Southern, North Central, and North East). Each region can determine priorities for grant programs that are best suited to its own agricultural sustainability needs.[51]

The mounting importance of agricultural literacy

As we explored questions about "sustainable" and "organic" agriculture in this chapter, Sackett, Shupp, and Tonsor (2016) made a noteworthy comment: US consumers must endeavor mightily, if they are to understand the distinctions between various agricultural terms and their true meanings. Unfortunately this set of circumstances, where the typical US consumer is either confused, mystified, or misinformed about the agri-food system, is not unusual. In fact, it is often the norm.

In a 2012 article published by the Council of State Governments, Nebraska Senator Kate Sullivan noted that agriculture is her state's largest industry, but it is one of the least understood. Sullivan is concerned that ignorance about agriculture and its importance in our everyday life leads to mistakes in public policies that can adversely affect agriculture.[52]

An example of where agricultural science and political priorities recently collided occurred when a group of more than 100 Nobel Laureate scientists signed a public letter and released it to the media. The letter issued a message demonstrating how these scientists differed with the Greenpeace Organization on the safety and advisability of using genetic modification to develop new strains of foods to address world hunger problems.[53]

Because the disagreement between the scientists and the Greenpeace organization took place in a highly charged and emotional public setting, it is questionable as to whether the dispute between the two groups helped to advance the general public's agricultural literacy. What is really needed are proper forums where all considerations are carefully reviewed, and people are given the opportunity to review the evidence in a calm and objective manner.

There is much to be gained if the agricultural literacy of the average consumer can be improved. Many professionals in agricultural and food markets understand the scope and significance of this "disconnect" between the twenty-first-century American consumer and the agricultural economy that provides them with one of life's essentials. Efforts are underway that aim to close this educational gap.

To be fair, the modern average US consumer does not often interact directly with the farm economy. Less than 2 percent of the US population is involved with production agriculture. For many consumers, a visit to a supermarket or a big-box store is their point of contact with their food supply.

Agencies such as USDA's NIFA provide a valuable service when they help sponsor communication plans and informational programs to educate consumers about the consequences of their food choices. One promising effort is to intentionally introduce agriculture-based curricula into US primary and secondary school systems. It is known as the Agriculture in the Classroom (AITC) program.[54] State-government agencies, who receive NIFA support, are working to promote the use of AITC curriculum in K-12 school systems across the country.

AITC has rigorous academic foundations. AITC defines Agricultural Literacy as "having the ability to understand and communicate the source and value of agriculture as it affects our quality of life."

A publication known as "National Agricultural Literacy Outcomes" (NALOs) is having an impact. NALOs determine benchmarks for progress in agricultural literacy in each of the following K-12 educational levels:[55]

- Early Elementary [K-Grade 2]
- Upper Elementary [Grades 3–5]
- Middle School [Grades 6–8]
- High School [Grades 9–12]

In addition, the NALOs are broken down into major areas of academic achievement:

- Agriculture and the Environment Outcomes
- Plants and Animals for Food, Fiber, and Energy
- Food, Health, and Lifestyle
- Science, Technology, Engineering, and Math (STEM)
- Culture, Society, Economy, and Geography

The depth of the NALO educational curriculum is also reinforced by a "Logic Model" that offers a national guide on the steps needed to achieve increased Agricultural Literacy. The logic model is a stepwise process that utilizes educational inputs and programmatic outputs to produce targeted outcomes of improved agricultural literacy. The steps of the logic model can be portrayed as follows:[56]

AITC goals are ambitious. The need for coordinating curricula and active participation is clear. Many professionals have "gone the extra mile" to develop high-quality and usable approaches that are dedicated to boosting agricultural literacy nationwide.

Table 12.3 AITC Logic Model for Agricultural Literacy Programming

Educational Inputs	Programmatic Outputs	Agricultural Literacy Outcomes
Financial Resources	**Activities & Participants**	Knowledge
Human Resources	PK-20 Educators Training	Attitudes
Program Resources	Student/Youth Activities	Skills
Collaboration	Policymaker Information	Behaviors
Partnerships	Consumer-based Information	Practices

In addition to federal and state government involvement, a number of volunteer organizations are also making sizable contributions to the effort, including the National Association of Agricultural Educators (NAAE), as well as all of the NAAE's state-level affiliates. And it would be a major oversight if the contributions of the Future Farmers of America (FFA) and 4-H programs were not included in the discussion. Despite the excellent and collective exertions of these organizations and government agencies, much remains to be done to make additional headway in increasing US agricultural literacy.

Conclusions

The absence of agricultural literacy in modern society is a cause for concern. An uninformed public will have difficulty understanding current conditions in farm markets and systems. The fast pace of change in agriculture makes the educational task even more of a challenge. It is encouraging that concerted efforts are being made to address the literacy problem though an academically and logically sound approach.

Even if they are hard to completely grasp, the new trends in American agriculture are an exciting development. Women, veterans, and socially disadvantaged groups are untapped resources that have much to offer an agri-food system that faces aging demographics and related issues. Local foods, organics, and questions of sustainability are now real elements creating an interesting future as the twenty-first century continues to unfold.

Our modern agri-food system is not easily understood. A lack of knowledge can sometimes lead to undesirable combinations of policy decisions. In the next chapter, we examine circumstances where conflicting policies arise, and we consider options that can help to mitigate the adverse consequences of these sometimes contradictory choices.

Notes

1 McCarron, Jessica. "In Conversation with #WomeninAg: Beth Robinette." USDA Deputy Press Secretary. Welcome to the USDA Blog. April 29, 2016. Retrieved from: http://blogs.usda.gov/2016/04/29/in-conversation-with-womeninag-beth-robinette/#more-64533

2 Ibid.

3 Neal, Arthur. "Mapping out Farmers Market Success." USDA AMS Deputy Administrator. Welcome to the USDA Blog. May 18, 2016. Retrieved from: http://blogs.usda.gov/2016/05/18/mapping-out-farmers-market-success/#more-64873

4 Rikkers, Sam. "Agriculture Saved a Veteran's Life." USDA Rural Business Service. Welcome to the USDA Blog. April 29, 2016. Retrieved from: http://blogs.usda.gov/category/new-and-begin ning-farmers/

5 O'Brien, Dennis. "ARS Helps Veterans Weigh a Career in Agriculture." USDA Public Affairs Specialist. Welcome to the USDA Blog. April 12, 2016. Retrieved from: http://blogs.usda.gov/category/new-and-beginning-farmers/

6 Overstreet, Amy. "Refugee Farmers Set Down Roots, Honor Traditions in Vermont." USDA Public Affairs Specialist. Welcome to the USDA Blog. April 18, 2016. Retrieved from: http://blogs.usda.gov/2016/04/18/refugee-farmers-set-down-roots-honor-traditions-in-vermont/#more-64294

7 Carolyn Dimitri, Anne Effland, and Neilson Conklin. *The 20th Century Transformation of U.S. Agriculture and Farm Policy.* USDA, Economic Research Service. EIB-3, 2005, p. 5. Retrieved from www.ers.usda.gov/media/259572/eib3_1_.pdf

8 USDA, National Agricultural Statistics Service (NASS). *2015 Agricultural Statistics Annual, Chapter IX: Farm Resources, Income, and Expenses.* Last Modified: 6-24-2016. Retrieved from: www.nass.usda.gov/Publications/Ag_Statistics/2015/index.php

9 Hoppe, Robert and James M. MacDonald. *Understanding America's Diverse Family Farms.* Amber Waves, USDA, ERS: January–February 2016. Retrieved from: www.ers.usda.gov/amber-waves/2016-januaryfebruary/understanding-america%E2%80%99s-diverse-family-farms.aspx#.V3lrzrgrK00

10 Ibid.

11 MacDonald, James M. Penni Korb, and Robert A. Hoppe. *Farm Size and the Organization of U.S. Crop Farming.* USDA, ERS Research Report, Number 152, August 2013. Retrieved from: www.ers.usda.gov/media/1156726/err152.pdf

12 Hoppe, Robert A. *Structure and Finances of U.S. Farms: Family Farm Report, 2014 Edition.* USDA Economic Research Service. Economic Information Bulletin Number 132, December 2014, p. 17. Retrieved from: www.ers.usda.gov/media/1728096/eib-132.pdf

13 USDA Farm Bill Forum Comment, Summary and Background. *Farm Family Income.* 2004. Retrieved from: www.usda.gov/documents/FARM_FAMILY_INCOME.doc

14 Brown, Adell Jr., Ralph D. Christy, and Tesfa G. Gebremedhin. "Structural Changes in U.S. Agriculture: Implications for African American Farmers." *The Review of Black Political Economy* 22(4), pp. 51–71, June 1994. Retrieved from: http://mj7kn4np9m.scholar.serialssolutions.com/?s id=google&auinit=A&aulast=Brown&atitle=Structural+changes+in+US+agriculture:+Implicatio ns+for+African+American+farmers&id=doi:10.1007/BF02689979&title=The+Review+of+Black +political+economy&volume=22&issue=4&date=1994&spage=51&issn=0034-6446

15 USDA, NASS. *United States Farms with Women Principal Operators Compared with All Farms.* 2012 Census of Agriculture. Retrieved from: www.agcensus.usda.gov/Publications/2012/Online_Resources/Race,_Ethnicity_and_Gender_Profiles/cpd99000.pdf

16 Hoppe, Robert and Penni Korb. *Characteristics of Women Farm Operators and Their Farms.* USDA, ERS. Economic Information Bulletin No.111, pp. iv–v, April 2013. www.ers.usda.gov/media/1093194/eib111.pdf

17 USDA, NASS. *United States Farms with Women Principal Operators Compared with All Farms.* 2012 Census of Agriculture. Retrieved from: www.agcensus.usda.gov/Publications/2012/Online_Resources/Race,_Ethnicity_and_Gender_Profiles/cpd99000.pdf

18 Ibid.

19 Ibid.

20 USDA, NASS. *Preliminary Report Highlights U.S. Farms and Farmers, Issued February 2014.* 2012 Census of Agriculture. Retrieved from: www.agcensus.usda.gov/Publications/2012/Preliminary_Report/Highlights.pdf

21 The "Rule of 72" estimates the number of years required to double a value, if the annual growth rate is known. The rule states to take 72, and divide it by the growth rate, expressed as a percentage. For example, if the annual growth rate is 9 percent, then the rule estimates that $72 \div 9 = 8$ years (approximately) is required for the value to double. Note the value of 9 is in the denominator, not 0.09. Retrieved from: www.investopedia.com/terms/r/ruleof72.asp

22 Wilkins, Kate. *Why Diversity Matters: The Importance of Racial and Ethnic Equality in Conservation.* Natural Resource Ecology Laboratory, Colorado State University: Eco-Press. May 12, 2014. https://nrelscience.org/2014/05/12/why-diversity-matters-the-importance-of-racial-and-ethnic-equality-in-conservation/

23 USDA, NASS. *Preliminary Report Highlights U.S. Farms and Farmers, Issued February 2014.* 2012 Census of Agriculture. Retrieved from: www.agcensus.usda.gov/Publications/2012/Preliminary_Report/Highlights.pdf

24 Wilkins, Kate. *Why Diversity Matters: The Importance of Racial and Ethnic Equality in Conservation.* Natural Resource Ecology Laboratory, Colorado State University: Eco-Press. May 12, 2014. Retrieved from https://nrelscience.org/2014/05/12/why-diversity-matters-the-importance-of-racial-and-ethnic-equality-in-conservation/

25 National Agricultural Statistics Service (NASS), USDA. *Preliminary Report Highlights: US Farms and Farmers: 2012 Census of Agriculture-February 2014*. Page 3. Retrieved from: www.agcensus. usda.gov/Publications/2012/Preliminary_Report/Highlights.pdf

26 USDA, NRCS. Limited Resource Farmer and Rancher – (LRF/R) Socially Disadvantaged Farmer Definition. Updated 11/01/2010. Retrieved from: http://lrftool.sc.egov.usda.gov/SDFP_Definition.aspx

27 Johnson, Renée and Tadlock Cowan. *Local Food Systems: Selected Farm Bill and Other Federal Programs*. Congressional Research Service 7-5700, www.crs.gov, R43950, p. 13, February 5, 2016. Retrieved from: www.fas.org/sgp/crs/misc/R43950.pdf

28 National Sustainable Agriculture Coalition (NSAC). *Outreach and Assistance For Socially Disadvantaged and Veteran Farmers and Ranchers (Section 2501)*. NSAC Publications, October 2014. Retrieved from: http://sustainableagriculture.net/publications/grassrootsguide/farming-opportuni ties/socially-disadvantaged-farmers-program/#history

29 Farm Futures. *$8.4 million available to reach out to socially disadvantaged, tribal and veteran farmers*. July 1, 2016. News Stories. http://farmfutures.com/story-84-million-available-reach-socially-disadvantaged-tribal-veteran-farmers-0-143481

30 Johnson, Renée and Tadlock Cowan. *Local Food Systems: Selected Farm Bill and Other Federal Programs*. Congressional Research Service 7-5700, www.crs.gov, R43950, p. 13, February 5, 2016. Retrieved from www.fas.org/sgp/crs/misc/R43950.pdf

31 USDA, Office of Advocacy and Outreach. "Partner Success Stories: Farm-to-School Produce. W *Staying Connected* 2(1): 3, January–March 2014. Retrieved from: www.outreach.usda.gov/docs/ January%20-%20March%202014%20w-Carolyn%20Christian%20final1.pdf

32 Ibid, p. 3.

33 Johnson, Renée and Tadlock Cowan. "Local Food Systems: Selected Farm Bill and Other Federal Programs." Congressional Research Service 7-5700. www.crs.gov. Report # R43950. March 12, 2013, p. 1. Retrieved from: www.fas.org/sgp/crs/misc/R42155.pdf

34 Martinez, Steve, et al. "Local Food Systems: Concepts, Impacts, and Issues." ERR 97, U.S. Department of Agriculture, Economic Research Service, May 2010. Page iii. Retrieved from: http://ers.usda.gov/media/122868/err97_1_.pdf

35 Rushing, James. "Buying into the Local Food Movement." ATKearney, Industries: Consumer Product and Retail. January 2013. Retrieved from www.atkearney.com/consumer-products-retail/ ideas-insights/featured-article/-/asset_publisher/KQNW4F0xInID/content/buying-into-the-local-food-movement/10192

36 Ibid, pp. 4–5.

37 Ibid, pp.7–9.

38 Johnson, Renée and Tadlock Cowan. "Local Food Systems: Selected Farm Bill and Other Federal Programs." Congressional Research Service 7-5700, www.crs.gov, R43950, pp. 2–4, February 5, 2016. Retrieved from www.fas.org/sgp/crs/misc/R43950.pdf

39 Ibid. p. 4.

40 Ibid. p. 25.

41 Brain, R. (2012, September). "The Local Food Movement: Definitions, Benefits, and Resources." USU Extension Publication: Sustainability/ 2012/09pr. Available at: https://extension.usu.edu/ files/publications/publication/Sustainability_2012-09pr.pdf

42 Bagi, Faqir Singh and Richard Reeder. "Farm Activities Associated With Rural Development Initiatives." ERR-134, U.S. Department of Agriculture, Economic Research Service, May 2012, pp. 7–9. Retrieved from: www.ers.usda.gov/media/601606/err134_1_.pdf

43 Martinez, Steve, et al. "Local Food Systems: Concepts, Impacts, and Issues." ERR 97, U.S. Department of Agriculture, Economic Research Service, May 2010. Page 22. Retrieved from http://ers.usda.gov/media/122868/err97_1_.pdf

44 Kremen, A., C. Greene, and J. Hanson. "Organic Produce, Price Premiums, and Eco-Labeling in U.S. Farmers' Markets." VGS-301-01, U.S. Department of Agriculture, Economic Research Service, 2004, Retrieved from: www.ers.usda.gov/Publications/VGS/Apr04/VGS30101/

45 Dimitri, Carolyn, and Lydia Oberholtzer. *Marketing U.S. Organic Foods: Recent Trends From Farms to Consumers*. Economic Information Bulletin No. 58. U.S. Dept. of Agriculture, Economic Research Service. September 2009. Retrieved from www.ers.usda.gov/media/185272/eib58_1_.pdf

46 Gold, Mary V. *Organic Production/Organic Food: Information Access Tools*. Alternative Farming Systems Information Center, USDA National Agricultural Library. June 2007, Reviewed April 2016. Retrieved from www.nal.usda.gov/afsic/organic-productionorganic-food-information-access-tools

47 Dimitri, Carolyn, and Lydia Oberholtzer. *Marketing U.S. Organic Foods: Recent Trends From Farms to Consumers*. Economic Information Bulletin No. 58. U.S. Dept. of Agriculture, Economic Research Service. September 2009. Page 10. Retrieved from www.ers.usda.gov/media/185272/eib58_1_.pdf

48 McBride, William D., Catherine Greene, Linda Foreman, and Mir Ali. "The Profit Potential of Certified Organic Field Crop Production." ERR-188, U.S. Department of Agriculture, Economic Research Service, July 2015. Page 2. Retrieved from www.ers.usda.gov/media/1875181/err188.pdf

49 Sackett, Hillary, Robert Shupp, and Glynn Tonsor. "Differentiating 'Sustainable' from 'Organic' and 'Local' Food Choices: Does Information about Certification Criteria Help Consumers?" *International Journal of Food and Agricultural Economics* 4(3), pp. 17–31, 2016. Retrieved from: www.foodandagriculturejournal.com/vol4.no3.pp17.pdf

50 Cornell University Law School, Legal Information Institute. *7 U.S. Code § 3103 – Definitions*. Section (19). Retrieved from: www.law.cornell.edu/uscode/text/7/3103

51 NIFA, USDA, Sustainable Agriculture Research and Education (SARE). "SARE Vision and Mission." University of Maryland, SARE, 2012. Retrieved from: www.sare.org/About-SARE/Vision-and-Mission

52 Orr, Carolyn. "Concerns about the Lack of 'Agricultural Literacy.'" Council of State Governments Knowledge Center – Stateline Midwest. July 2012. Retrieved from: http://knowledgecenter.csg.org/kc/content/concerns-about-lack-agricultural-literacy

53 James, Brooke. "GMO not Dangerous, over 100 Nobel Laureates State." Science World Report. July 1, 2016. Retrieved from: www.scienceworldreport.com/articles/43030/20160701/gmos-dangerous-over-100-nobel-laureates-state.htm

54 NIFA, USDA. *About Agriculture in the Classroom (AITC)*. Retrieved from www.agclassroom.org/get/about.htm

55 Spielmaker, D. M. (2013). *National Agricultural Literacy Outcomes*. Logan, UT: Utah State University, School of Applied Sciences and Technology. Retrieved from: http:// agclassroom.org/teacher/matrix.htm

56 Spielmaker, D. M., Monica Pastor, and Denise Stewardson. "Logic Model for Agriculture Literacy Programming." NIFA, USDA Conference on an Agricultural Literacy – Logic Model Development Committee. Retrieved from: www.agclassroom.org/affiliates/doc/logic_model.pdf

Chapter 13

When policies work at cross-purposes
Addressing challenges and pursuing opportunities

In his ground-breaking work, *The Logic of Collective Action*, Mancur Olson persuasively argued that groups whose members share common interests *do not always* act in unison to consistently achieve their collective purposes. Olson published this advice more than a half a century ago.[1] But his ideas continue to have relevance today. Olson makes his point in eloquent fashion:

> [I]f the members of some group have a common interest or objective, and if they would all be better off if that objective were achieved, it has been thought to follow logically that the individuals in that group would, if they were rational and self-interested, act to achieve that objective.
>
> But it is *not in fact true* that the idea that groups will act in their self-interest follows logically from the premise of rational and self-interested behavior.[2]

How do Mancur Olson's observations apply to the development and implementation of US agricultural and food policies? From a broad societal perspective, all participants in the

US agri-food system benefit from a policy environment where the wide variety of program goals and market incentives are well coordinated and harmonized.

On the other hand, when special interests influence policy proposals, there is a rational tendency for these narrower groups to promote programs that serve their private needs. There is typically little regard for creating comprehensively beneficial economic impacts in these instances.

Olson recognized the importance of these different group motivations. He emphasized that not all groups who have a stake in establishing economic policies are created equal. Smaller-sized groups ("privileged groups," in Olson's nomenclature) readily assess that their lobbying efforts can return handsome rents (above-normal returns) for themselves, and they will work relentlessly to secure those gains.

Conversely, larger groups (Olson's "latent groups") are often comprised of consumers and taxpayers who find it costly and difficult to organize themselves to jointly lobby for their common interests. Also, when we examine the dynamics of large-numbered groups, we observe that the rational calculus for individual participation is not promising.[3]

The benefit of an improved policy design for a single person (as a member of a large group) is likely to be small and dispersed. When compared to the cost of lobbying for a socially efficient policy design, the individual benefit is not sufficient to trigger action. An extra challenge that generally arises in a large group is the temptation to be a "free rider" – an individual refrains from taking an active role, and seeks to reap benefits that may emerge as a result of the efforts of a few dedicated volunteers.

In summary, the policy-making environment may not readily lend itself to creating coordinated and efficient results. Olson's counsel is that collective action is often characterized by goals and objectives that serve the narrow and concentrated interests of privileged groups. The "public good" benefits sought by large-numbered latent groups are not realized. These dispersed groups cannot easily organize themselves to act on behalf of their common good.

While collective action by a larger group is difficult, Olson argues that it is not impossible. He suggests that if common interests are to be successfully pursued, then groups must strongly organize, compel participation, and impose compulsory membership requirements.[4]

Recent research on the topic of collective action has also raised some interesting questions. We live in an Internet age, and the cost of organizing dispersed groups has changed dramatically. In 1965, when Mancur Olson was contemplating the challenges of group action, he could not have foreseen or imagined the instantaneous communication patterns that we now commonly accept as "twenty-first-century standard operating procedures."[5]

Organization of chapter

As we have been working our way through the varied topics in this textbook, we have considered an extensive array of US agricultural and food policies. If we are mindful of Mancur Olson's admonitions, we can anticipate situations where individual programs and policies are not all well coordinated with each other.

Inefficient outcomes are a likely end result when the agendas for our food and agricultural systems themselves lack synchronicity, or in circumstances where agri-food policy purposes are at odds with broader national or international interests. What can be done to resolve or avoid these conflicts?

In this chapter, we examine the origins and consequences of discordant policies, and investigate the challenges associated with overcoming the differences. We also explore options that could either harmonize future policy designs or mitigate their conflicting purposes.

This is a wide-ranging research topic. The constraints of a textbook chapter means that we narrow our focus. We address the following areas where agriculture and food policy goals can exhibit divergent interests and agendas:

- Trade policies
- Environment, natural resource, and climate policies
- Nutrition policies

The above is not a comprehensive list. Other areas of policy conflict exist. But there is much that we can learn by studying these areas where policies have worked at cross purposes.

The remainder of the chapter examines efforts to intentionally align policy goals, including conservation cross-compliance, and proposals to better synchronize global food and agricultural policies.

Challenges of agricultural and food policy coordination

A brief review of Farm Bill decision making and outcomes

In Chapter 2 of this textbook, we examined the multifaceted legislative process required to design and approve the 2014 Farm Bill. Subsequent research and analysis of this massive 12-title piece of legislation (again, see Chapter Two) indicate noticeable shortcomings in terms of harmonized policy goals and designs.[6] The content and outcomes of the 2014 Farm Bill are largely disconnected from overarching goals such as resource efficiency or income equity.[7] Mancur Olson, using his collective action theory, would not be surprised by this result.

Some titles within the farm bill (e.g. resource conservation and scientific research support) have a consistent policy design and content. But the majority of the 2014 Farm Bill is a loosely connected assortment of farm and food legislative initiatives.

Similar to situations encountered during the passage of previous farm bills, the 2014 version emerged from a sometimes emotional, and not always predictable, political-economic environment. Intense special-interest lobbying, legislative logrolling, strategic voting, and related political phenomena were necessary to produce a viable 2014 Farm Bill.

The niceties of a theoretically coherent legislative initiative take a back seat to the realities of crafting a proposal that can gather sufficient political support. In almost any circumstance, it is difficult to create an omnibus bill that can successfully pass through both Houses of Congress and receive the President's signature.

Congressman Frank Lucas (R – Oklahoma), member of the House Agriculture Committee, and a key player in negotiating successful passage of the 2014 Farm Bill, plainly identified the object of the legislation:

> [T]he ultimate goal remains the same – to provide a strong safety net so we can continue to be the preeminent source of food and fiber for the world.[8]

Lucas also noted that the twin goals of establishing a safety net and ensuring a stable food supply are not new. These purposes have an 80-year history dating back to the original farm bill in 1938. The challenge, as we look to the future, is whether these traditional aims are appropriate for the economic and social conditions that will be important in the twenty-first century.

The interest in agri-food system policy innovation

Private organizations, academic institutions, and related interests who carefully study the relationships among food needs, agricultural output potential, and sustainable environmental capacities are calling for major changes in policy. Farm bill programs, while they have some permanency and typically include a title on international trade, are primarily relevant during their approximate 5-year legislative intervals and are largely designed to address domestic US safety net and supply concerns.

At Stanford University, Rosamond Naylor (2014) collaborated with a professional research team to establish a Center on Food Security and the Environment (FSE).[9] Stanford's FSE Center is dedicated to generating new knowledge and policy solutions through integrated research on improving agri-food systems, mitigating hunger, enhancing the environment, and encouraging interdisciplinary inquiry.[10]

Naylor and her colleagues conclude that policies should evolve towards a well-reasoned approach that fosters long-run global food security. In the preface to Naylor's edited volume, Kofi Anan, former Secretary-General of the United Nations, summarizes the need for cohesive worldwide agri-food policies, as follows:

> Improving food and nutrition security is a matter of good governance, rigorous science, soil and water management, innovation, health, vision, courage, leadership and human compassion. It also depends on us putting into place the right policies to reduce poverty and inequality, promote gender equality, strengthen land rights, and accelerate wider economic and social development.[11]

Similar to Naylor's goals and efforts at the FSE Center, research sponsored by the Meridian Institute's AGree Initiative (see www.foodandagpolicy.org) identified "four challenges" that should be the focus of agri-food system policy innovations. Listed below, these four challenge areas clearly reflect Kofi Anan's vision:[12]

- Meeting future demand for food.
- Conserving and enhancing water, soil, and habitat.
- Improving nutrition and public health.
- Strengthening farms, workers, and communities.

The AGree Initiative promotes a broad-based and systematic effort that can meet the four challenges (cited above) in a transformative manner. AGree seeks to spur real action and produce "positive change" in the agri-food system.

What is AGree? It is a private association of advisors and partners whose membership includes farmers and ranchers (both conventional and organic), input suppliers, retailers, environmental groups, international rural development practitioners, nutrition experts, and health professionals. AGree receives funding from an impressive group of food, agriculture, and international development foundations.[13]

One further example of diverse interests coalescing to improve agri-food system outcomes is the Global Panel on Agriculture and Food Systems for Nutrition (a.k.a. the Global Panel). The Global Panel begins from a fundamental premise: the overarching goal of agri-food policies is to systematically and holistically improve the nutrition of children and adults worldwide.[14]

The Global Panel emphasizes that policy interventions must be chosen judiciously because their impacts can produce either beneficial or harmful effects on human nutrition. The Global Panel advises governments to carefully design and implement science-based policies in a manner that intentionally enhances both food quality and quantity for favorable nutritional outcomes.

When we compare the methodology of the Global Panel to the FSE Center or the AGree Initiative, we see a familiar pattern. The Global Panel argues for an organized approach among "four domains" of food systems that need to be properly managed for their nutritional impacts:[15]

- Agricultural production.
- Markets and trade systems.
- Consumer purchasing power.
- Food transformation and consumer demand.

The Global Panel suggests that it is possible to organize efficient "pathways" among the four agri-food system domains to advance the "nutrition sensitivity" of policy design and implementation. The Global Panel recommends that we pay attention to consumer dietary patterns, market supply-chains, and socio-economic interactions to select policies that have the best opportunity to improve the diversity, adequacy, and safety of nutrients available to and/or accessed by consumers.[16]

One simple observation that we can make, when we jointly examine the research work of the FSE Center, the AGree Initiative and the Global Panel, is a consistent call for policy coordination within our agri-food system. Such pleas to harmonize rules, programs, and agendas are an indication that agri-food policy contradictions are a real challenge. Dynamic reforms are needed if we are to make progress in policy synchronization. In the next section of this chapter we examine specific examples of mismatched policies, and the future prospects for achieving better organization and results.

Reviewing 2014 Farm Bill program goals in relation to US WTO trade commitments

When the 2014 Farm Bill was signed into law in early 2014, a number of legislators hailed the measure as a "win for common sense" because the Direct Payment Program (DPP) was eliminated with its passage. Many Congressional leaders viewed the DPP as politically untenable because DPP-eligible producers received DPP payments regardless of farm market and income conditions.

Especially during the intervening period between the 2008 and the 2014 Farm Bills, US farm producers had experienced an unusual cycle of high commodity prices and strong income at the very same moment that the general US economy was going through the worst recession in 80-plus years. The notion that agricultural producers were reaping high private-sector earnings while continuing to receive DPP payments was a scenario that politicians could not properly explain or defend to their constituents.

What was the policy role of the DPP prior to its discontinuation? In 2013, Purdue University extension economist Roman Keeney produced a well-written newsletter to explain DPP's origins, and also described the expected economic after-effects of its elimination.[17] DPP was included in the 1996 Farm Bill to establish one simple farm subsidy payment as a substitute for a whole set of above-market-priced commodity programs.

Congressional leaders in 1996 viewed DPP as a temporary program to help producers transition away from receiving farm subsidies. Politicians at the time envisioned that US farm producers were about to become solely dependent on private-market revenues. Viewed through the lens of the generous commodity market conditions in the mid-1990's, legislators anticipated that producers' needs for the DPP would diminish and disappear by 2002.[18]

Unfortunately, not all forecasts are accurate. When the 2002 Farm Bill was being assembled, commodity prices and farm incomes were on the downside of the cycle, and suddenly the DPP was no longer being viewed as just a transition subsidy. Producers needed immediate financial assistance in 2002, and the DPP was a ready-to-go program – legislators did not have to "reinvent the wheel". So, the DPP became a more permanent fixture in US farm policy between 2002 and 2014.

Times change, and in 2014 views towards the DPP soured. One lesson we can learn by exploring the DPP's history is to realize that almost any farm bill program is a "creature with a temporary lifespan." While farm bill programs certainly are longer-lived than many other government projects that depend on annual legislative approval, the 5-year span of any farm bill actually goes by fairly quickly. In policy, we should perhaps be more skeptical when we hear that some program has "permanent funding." Journalists in today's world often engage in fact-checking, and in the case of farm programs, the practice of fact-checking is likely to be a very rational behavior.

The domestic backstory on the DPP is important, but as Roman Keeney points out, there is an international DPP perspective that also must be explored. Keeney reminds us that before the 1996 Farm Bill was enacted, the US (in 1995) had joined the World Trade Organization (WTO).[19]

During the 47 years prior to its WTO membership, the US was a prominent player in the WTO's predecessor association, known as the General Agreement on Tariffs and Trade (GATT). The GATT promoted the economic benefits of free trade. GATT negotiations to reduce trade barriers among participating nations began shortly after the end of World War II in 1945. Unrestricted international trade was seen as a means of rebuilding the world's economies after a worldwide recession and two world wars. The year 1947 saw a successful first round of GATT negotiations in Geneva. Additional GATT rounds followed and laid the foundation for establishing the WTO on January 1, 1995.

What is the connection between DPP farm subsidies and US's WTO membership? If we closely examine the DPP program's structure, we observe that DPP producer subsidies are not "triggered" by any event in the private commodity markets. Prices or production worldwide could fluctuate up or down in a particular marketing year, and DPP producer payments remain unchanged according to defined support levels written into the farm bill.

Why is it important for farm program subsidies to be unrelated to market incentives? Well, basic economics and WTO policies tell us that markets are most efficient in resource allocation when price and income incentives are "pure" – unadulterated by temporary government policies. In the parlance of WTO protocols, it is desirable for farm and food policies to be "decoupled" from the private market mechanism. In this way, producers and consumers regulate their rational behaviors in relation to prices that reflect actual resource scarcities in the world's economy, instead of reacting to artificial incentives created by some short-term government program.

When the DPP program was operational, the US could justly claim that this farm subsidy was "decoupled" from the market system. As a result, the US could demonstrate its commitment to creating a free-trade environment as a WTO member. Here is a case where the purposes of US trade policy and the impacts of a US farm policy (the DPP) *were not in conflict*.

The DPP is now history. How did the Congress alter its farm subsidy system after eliminating the DPP? Beyond the removal of the DPP, the 2014 Farm Bill also eliminated the Counter-Cyclical Payment (CCP) program and the Average Crop Revenue Election (ACRE) program that existed under the 2008 Farm Bill. Then Congress established the Price Loss Coverage (PLC) program and the Agriculture Risk Coverage (ARC) Program. From the standpoint of international trade and the US commitments to the WTO, what is the net influence of the PLC and ARC subsidy programs?

The short answer is that PLC and ARC are *not* entirely decoupled from market incentives. See Chapter 4 of this textbook for more complete explanations of how the PLC and ARC programs operate.

Suffice it to say, both PLC and ARC elicit increased subsidy payments to producers when market prices or farm revenues drop below designated farm-bill levels. PLC and ARC generate payments that *are connected* ("coupled") to private market incentives.

Patrick Westhoff, Scott Gerlt, and Joseph Glauber (2015) studied the actual pattern of commodity program payouts to American farm producers via the 2014 Farm Bill.[20] Westhoff et al. note that the US participated in GATT agricultural trade negotiations during the 1986–1994 Uruguay Round Agreement on Agriculture (URAA). Today, the WTO fully supports the URAA's outcomes.

As a URAA signatory, the US consented to a trade system that aims to ultimately eliminate market-distorting farm subsidies. The URAA designates market-distortion severity using a colored-box classification method. Green box policies create minimal distortion. Blue box policies are tolerated because farm subsidies are accompanied by production restrictions. Amber box policies create clear market distortions.

The DPP was widely recognized as a URAA Green Box farm subsidy policy. Both the PLC and ARC programs are considered Amber Box policies.

Congressional design of commodity programs in the 2014 Farm Bill largely ignored WTO implications. A decoupled DPP program was replaced with two farm subsidy methods linked to private market signals. Unfortunately, trade and farm policies are working at cross purposes in this instance.

Differences not only exist between farm and trade policy goals. Other areas are also subjects of concern. Let's examine them.

Agri-food policies and their interactions with natural resources, the environment, and climate change

In his textbook on the *Economics of American Agriculture*, Dr. Steven C. Blank suggests that the future growth of government support for US farm subsidies will strongly depend on the actions of agricultural producers who convincingly demonstrate that they are true "land stewards".[21]

Blank's analysis references a market environment where sophisticated consumers and informed taxpayers actively seek assurance that their private purchases and their government tax payments make a difference. These knowledgeable decision makers have both the will and the capacity to support suppliers/markets that clearly adhere to sustainable production methods and generate desirable food quality/quantity outcomes. These same consumers can withdraw their support for farm programs if their preferences are ignored or left unfulfilled.

In this viewpoint, the impact of "sustainability" as a social movement exceeds any scientific definition or the intent of any government policy or program. Sustainability is not just an agenda item promoted by some narrow and inconsequential interest group. It is a *market imperative* that affects market prices and producer incomes.

What are the sustainability concerns of these consumers and taxpayers? The conversation is wide-ranging, and there are real tensions that exist between agriculture and the environmental interests which participate in the discussion.

It is no wonder that conflicting purposes arise when we address agro-environmental policies. The issues are complex. A variety of academic professionals, non-government organizations (NGOs), political lobbyists, private citizens, and many others join in the discussion.

If a reasoned policy is to emerge from this cacophony of voices, it is necessary to carefully consider the evidence that lies behind such diverse views, and hopefully develop balanced proposals that properly weigh the various facts and perspectives.

The Public Library of Science (PLOS)-Biology is an online refereed journal where members of the biological-scientific community have made contributions to the discussion. A team of UK scientists at Cambridge University (Tanentzap, Lamb, Walker, and Farmer, 2015) recently reviewed the inherent competitive interactions that characterize agricultural and environmental land uses.[22]

Tanentzap et al. (2015) argue that agriculture generates unsustainable environmental costs. In their study, Tanentzap et al. use published research to estimate that 80 percent of global deforestation and 53 percent of the threatened extinction of earth's terrestrial species are associated with the global expansion of agricultural land uses. Tanentzap et al. also link accelerated eutrophication of the earth's waters to the release of human-synthesized nitrogen fertilizers into the environment. Tanentzap et al. also criticize farm management practices that degrade and exhaust soils; as natural soil resources are depleted, ongoing food demand growth requires additional land conversion to compensate for diminished natural resource capacity.[23]

ERS economists Claassen and Ribaudo (2016) note that some agricultural production practices discharge greenhouse gasses into the atmosphere, and consequently augment planetary climate change. Large areas of monoculture tend to crowd out wildlife habitat and negatively affect biodiversity.[24]

On the other hand, Claassen and Ribaudo cite the environmental progress associated with farm operations that have adopted conservation and related sustainable methods that enhance natural resource capacity and control undesirable emissions.[25]

However, Claassen and Ribaudo remind us there are also concerns about negative interactions between climate change events and farm systems. For example, there are significant environmental consequences when off-season extreme storm events rapidly drop substantial rainfall amounts on exposed soils. Amplified phosphorus loads in Lake Erie are associated with the heightened incidence of very strong rain storms in late winter and early spring. To adjust to these severe climate-generated episodes, it may be necessary to construct sediment basins or terraces.[26]

Government conservation programs offer subsidies and cost-share arrangements to encourage producers to implement environmentally friendly practices and land uses. Eric Lichtenberg (2014) observes that while these efforts often create measurable gains in natural resource sustainability, there are extra undesirable effects.[27]

For example, conservation subsidies supplement producer incomes, increase farm wealth and create the financial capacity for converting natural habitat to farm enterprises. Therefore, as conservation programs increase ecologically sound uses, there is often an escalation of agricultural operations. This unintended growth of farm production is known as program "slippage." Lichtenberg cited evidence of program slippage in three econometric analyses where 100-acre increases in CRP are accompanied by an average increase of 20 acres of non-cropland altered to initiate crop use.[28]

Lichtenberg also raises concerns about "additionality" when producers qualify for and participate in government-funded conservation programs. The question posed by "additionality" is to estimate how much extra conservation happens when producers participate in the program, as compared to the amount of conservation effort that would have happened anyway, with no program in place. Lichtenberg's additionality inquiry is important, but it is difficult to properly measure. Nevertheless, taxpayer support for subsidized conservation programs is likely to grow or wane, depending on the answer to the additionality question.[29]

As the Congress considered the appropriate direction for conservation policy during the debates that culminated in the 2014 Farm Bill's passage, two additional matters created conflicts with the goal of achieving increased alignment of agricultural practices and environmental sustainability:

- National political pressure to reduce the federal budget deficit through government spending reductions.
- Market pressures during 2008–2014, in the form of unusually high commodity price profit levels, creating incentives for additional crop production through land conversion and more intensive crop management methods.

Lubben and Pease (2014) compared the funding and structure of conservation-related programs in the 2008 and 2014 farm bills. Citing Congressional Budget Office projections, Lubben and Pease report a 10-year 6.56 percent reduction (relative to the 2008 budget) of conservation spending during 2014–2023.[30]

The 2014 Farm Bill also consolidated and streamlined conservation programs. However, what is likely the more important change in government-sponsored conservation programs is a resource reallocation: increased funding for the EQIP and CSP working-lands programs, and reduced spending on the Conservation Reserve Program (CRP). Lubben and Pease indicate that the growing role of working land program and a diminished CRP function has been a trend since the 1996 Farm Bill.[31]

We can predict some noteworthy economic impacts to be associated with changing conservation subsidy configurations. Reduced CRP funding, along with more limited program acreages, open the door to further cropland expansion as CRP contracts expire. Janssen et al.'s study (2007) of South Dakota CRP contracts infers that 61 percent of expiring CRP agreements re-enter farm operations as crop enterprises, and another 30 percent are expected to produce grass hay or support livestock production.[32]

CRP cessation and crop expansion may impose measurable environmental and economic *opportunity costs*. Lubben and Pease cite an analysis (Wu and Weber 2012) documenting the CRP's net economic contributions associated with reduced soil erosion, increased wildlife habitat, improved recreation opportunities, and increased land values.[33] The net impact on environmental conditions will partly depend on the success of the EQIP and CSP programs that encourage conservation practices while land is actively cropped and harvested.

Closely connected with the growing role of the EQIP and CSP working-lands conservation programs is the question of additionality. How much extra conservation takes place when a producer participates in EQIP and CSP, as compared to the producer's typical and unsubsidized farm practices? The absence of data on additionality means that ongoing monitoring of practices and results will be necessary over the next few years. Taxpayers and related interest groups will want to know how much extra "land stewardship" is occurring, if their support for conservation programs (restructured or not) is to continue.

CSP, EQIP, and CRP are subsidized voluntary conservation programs. As the full impact of budget cut backs and program restructuring in the 2014 Farm Bill is realized, tracking the outcomes will certainly be important. Lubben and Pease also remind us that there is still another influence on the competing agricultural and environmental interests: required compliance with conservation goals built into the Farm Bill.[34]

The 2014 Farm Bill not only reauthorized conservation compliance requirements as conditions for producer participation in PLC and ARC Commodity Programs, it also included the same proviso on subsidized federal crop insurance. The combined impacts of these so-called "Sodbuster and Swampbuster" requirements could be substantial. We will be looking at this question more closely near the end of this chapter.

Identifying linkages and disconnects between US agricultural and nutrition policies

In Chapter 7 of this textbook, we cited a Congressional Research Service report indicating that nearly 70 federal programs had connections to food and nutrition policy. We also noted that 79 percent of the annual spending in the 2014 Farm Bill is dedicated to SNAP, WIC, school breakfast and lunch programs, and related initiatives.[35]

At first glance, we might assume that program coordination would naturally arise as agriculture and food policies are simultaneously being formulated and multi-billion dollar budgets are proposed and implemented. Unfortunately, despite efforts to align these related policies, the relationship between agricultural policy and nutritional health is unclear. The evidence is mixed. Because there is a lack of definite proof, differential viewpoints on the connection or disconnection of these policies exist. Various ideas become published, and they compete for the public's perception of what the relationship is.

In some quarters, the link between agricultural and nutritional health policies is severely criticized. Other researchers arrive at alternative conclusions. We will use this section of the chapter to explore some of the concerns, and also examine some suggested means to better coordinate future policies.

In April 2011, Dr. Neal Barnard (M.D.) published a commentary examining the connection between agricultural subsidies and nutritional health. Dr. Barnard's arguments received national media attention.[36] A summary of his research appeared in the *Huffington Post* (2011)[37] and are also accessible on the Physicians Committee for Responsible Medicine website.[38]

Barnard observes that US commodity policy and subsidies tend to distort the normal market price mechanism. He argues that agricultural subsidies are partly responsible for some foods to be more plentiful and lower-priced, such as animal products, refined fats, and corn-based sweeteners. In contrast, Barnard notes that other crops, such as fruits and vegetables, remain relatively unsubsidized. In Barnard's analysis, consumers notice the relatively greater scarcity and higher prices of the foods that lack government program support. Barnard predicts that consumers reduce their purchases of the scarce items and increase their use of the plentiful products.

Barnard is also concerned about producer response to government subsidies. He argues that the rational response of farmers is to plant more of the crops that have the strongest government support, and reduce the output of crops where there are no government protections against downside financial risk.[39]

Barnard suggests that the consumer response to these food price differentials is predictable. He also notes that the subsidized food consumption patterns differ considerably from the recommended food consumption models that appear in the 2010 USDA publication, *Dietary Guidelines for Americans*.[40] The USDA pamphlet urges consumers to reorganize their diets by increasing their fruit and vegetable consumption, while reducing their intake of saturated fats, cholesterol, processed grains, and sugars.

Barnard notices that the current structure of US agricultural policies and subsidy levels primarily reduces the cost of foods with fats, cholesterol, etc., while the prices of fruits, vegetables, and related "healthier" foods are more expensive in comparison. In his commentary, Barnard urges reform of US agricultural policy to change or eliminate the farm subsidy system, such that the average consumer household will receive new price signals about what actually constitutes a healthy diet.

Rikard, Okrent, and Alston (2012) investigated agricultural subsidy impacts by conducting a multi-market food-and-caloric-intake modelling simulation.[41] Their approach differed from Barnard's broader policy analysis. They estimated economic impacts on American consumption patterns in the absence of agricultural subsidies. Rikard, Okrent, and Alston gathered data on nine food categories and ten agricultural commodities; they calculated three different consumer subsidy/support measures in 1992, 1997, and 2002 to predict US food consumption and caloric intake effects. Rikard, Okrent, and Alston (2012) determined that the absence of the subsidies had only a minimal effect in reducing household caloric intake.[42]

Whether or not agricultural policy has a major or a minimal influence on the effectiveness of nutrition health policies, there is still the question of public opinion relative to these connections. Sociological principles tell us that when people perceive a situation as real, then their response is conditioned by that viewpoint. In other words, perceptions matter.

Will Masters, a Nutrition Science and Policy specialist at Tufts University, argues that we need to actively work to align agricultural and nutrition policy goals, if we are to achieve better US nutritional outcomes. Masters recommends: (1) tailoring programs to efficiently utilize agricultural-nutrition linkages to attain measurable outcomes for specific consumer groups with real dietary needs; and (2) diversifying diets, markets, programs, and products in the agricultural-nutrition supply chain to anticipate nutritional requirements, and achieve nutritionally healthy outcomes.[43]

In Chapter 12 of this text, we examined some of the local food market initiatives, such as Community Supported Agriculture (CSA) associations that are generating a more diverse set of consumer food options. USDA's Know Your Farmer, Know Your Food program is similarly an effort to increase the variety of food choices open to consumers. While these efforts have only recently started to gain momentum, they do appear to be addressing the need to better coordinate agricultural production and food distribution systems.

Intended and actual effects of conservation cross-compliance

The above discussion examines a variety of questions that encompass the proper coordination of agricultural and nutritional health policies. When solutions to problems of policy harmonization are offered, many proposals seek *incentive programs* that motivate decision makers to *voluntarily* alter their choices.

However, some approaches to synchronizing sets of policies go beyond offering attractive subsidies or rewarding inducements for voluntary action. There are instances where so-called "tougher" methods are introduced. For example, since 1985 agricultural producers who qualify for and collect commodity program payments and related benefits *are required to comply with* certain conservation requirements as an eligibility condition for the receipt of farm-bill benefits. That sterner approach to program coordination still exists, and has an expanded role in the 2014 Farm Bill.[44]

In these cases, if a producer desires to remain as a qualified recipient of taxpayer-funded farm subsidies, the producer *is required to* meet specified conservation standards. This method of tying the goals of two programs together using legally enforceable obligations is known as "cross-compliance."

The support for, or the opposition to, cross-compliance policy, often depends on which interest group is surveyed. Independent-minded entrepreneurs (including farm owner-operators), who prefer making choices rather than adhering to government-imposed rules, are less likely to favor a policy based on compulsory requirements. On the other hand, environmentalists, conservationists and some taxpayers may consider cross-compliance policy as a reasonable trade-off: producers are offered a taxpayer-supported safety net in exchange for obeying a requirement to either protect highly erodible lands and/or preserve natural wetlands.

The 2014 Farm Bill has been criticized in some quarters for its reduced emphasis on the voluntary CRP program. Also, interest groups who vigorously support sustainability and related natural resource conservation efforts were not happy about across-the-board budget reductions that affected conservation funding. However, one important change inserted into the 2014 Farm Bill could have broad and positive conservation impacts: cross-compliance policy was extended to encompass subsidized federal crop insurance.[45]

The potential impact of this additional conservation requirement is substantial because the 2014 Farm Bill increased funding for crop insurance subsidies while eliminating both the Direct Payment Program (DPP) and Average Crop Revenue Election (ACRE) program. The funds saved from commodity program elimination were re-routed to provide subsidies to reduce premiums and spur additional producer participation in federal crop insurance.

Because the federal government premium subsidies are substantial (as high as 65 percent of the true cost), it is expected that additional producers will join the federal crop insurance program. The 2014 Farm bill explicitly conditions eligibility for the subsidies on compliance with conservation requirements.

In 2014, federally subsidized crop insurance provided coverage for 294 million acres of crops in production. To provide a perspective, the Congressional Research Service (CRS) reports that 83 percent of US crop acreage was insured in 2014.[46] The sheer size, in total insured acreage, is sufficiently large to consider that the connection between cross-compliance and federal crop insurance is not a trivial policy. Its impacts are potentially national in scope.

Any taxpayer who likes to see policy coordination within government may take solace in a cross-compliance rule that connects a subsidy recipient to a conservation requirement. Unfortunately, in some cases, the reality of cross-compliance can fall short of the promised harmonization.

A CRS report (referenced above) notes that conservation compliance follows the normal rule of law.[47] Alleged violators of conservation requirements are presumed innocent until proven otherwise. The USDA agencies (FSA and NRS) expected to enforce required cross-compliance are not accustomed to imposing regulatory restrictions. These agencies are much better equipped to offer assistance associated with voluntary USDA programs. For example, FSA and NRCS often develop consultative relationships with producers who voluntarily decide to install conservation practices that involve joint cost-sharing. But, in the case of cross-compliance, these agencies have to switch roles and act as "police" to ensure adherence to required conservation practices.[48]

The federal Government Accountability Office (GAO) and USDA's Office of the Inspector General (OIG) both reviewed the FSA's and NRCS's record of conservation-compliance enforcement. As might be expected, the GAO discovered that not all cross-compliance conservation constraints were being enforced. Reasons for the breakdown in these agencies include resource constraints, the absence of training, and the prioritization of other agency responsibilities above compliance enforcement. The GAO report raised concerns about the lack of evidence to fully support NRCS assertions that 98 percent of the reviewed areas are in full compliance.[49]

The GAO also questioned the FSA practice of granting compliance waivers without producers supplying all appropriate documentation. FSA County Review Committees are generally comprised of farmers and are elected by in situations of compliance enforcement.

The GAO noted that the FSA waived nearly 61 percent of cases where farmers were cited for conservation violations. Since the GAO Report was published, both the FSA and NRCS have made strides to tighten controls and ensure that conservation compliance is occurring. Nevertheless, the GAO and OIG oversight reports highlight the difficulties associated with a policy based on the enforcement of compulsory participation.[50]

The prospects for agri-food policy innovation

Throughout this chapter we have examined situations where the purposes and/or outcomes of important agri-food policies either lack harmonization or are inconsistent. Thoughtful and dedicated organizations, such as AGree, the FSE Center, and the Global Panel have called for renewed efforts to re-invent agri-food policies in ways that can synchronize policies to achieve considerable gains in economic efficiency and equity.

Mancur Olson's arguments, which emphasize the difficulties of realizing the benefits of logical collective action, tell us that the task of policy coordination is characterized by a troublesome combination of both high individual costs coupled with low individual benefits. If individuals were somehow able to overcome personal disincentives, there would be high collective payoffs. It is not impossible to make progress in this arena, but it is also not easy.

As we confront the challenges arising from conflicting policies, we should be seeking out opportunities for creating approaches that are mutually beneficial and reinforcing. The pathways to improved policy outcomes are not really new. They include better education, real leadership, lower cost technologies, and a renewed motivational ideology.

Real progress may involve participants setting aside the normal rational calculus of individual gratification, and intentionally seeking to pursue the common good. It is a tall order. But with today's social media and related technologies, the costs have never been lower for coordinating many individuals into an organization that can exercise some "clout".

Undoubtedly, traditional focused interest groups will also act to protect the gains associated with maintaining a status quo policy. On the other hand, the so-called "Internet of Things" means it is entirely plausible that large and more dispersed interests have a potential to coalesce and bring about policy coordination by the processes of negotiation and compromise.

In the next and final chapter of this textbook, we review where we have been with policy formation and implementation, and use it as a basis for probing the future. In many ways, everyone in the world has a stake in the performance of our agri-food system. We all need a nutritional diet if we are to survive.

What is exciting about the future of food and agriculture is the opportunity to do more than aim for survival only. We have the knowledge and tools that can promote prosperity and improve people's daily lives.

Such a dynamic future will not happen by itself. It will depend on our choices. Let's move onto the next chapter to see what lies ahead.

Notes

1 Olson, Mancur. *The Logic of Collective Action: Public Goods and the Theory of Groups*. Cambridge, MA: Harvard University Press. Harvard Economic Studies, Volume CXXIV. 1971. Pages 1–3.
2 Ibid, p. 1.
3 Ibid, pp. 49–50.
4 Ibid, pp. 48.
5 Bollier, David. "The Logic of Collective Action: The Fall of an Iconic Theory?" News and Perspectives on the Commons. March 7, 2013. Retrieved from http://bollier.org/blog/logic-collec tive-action-fall-iconic-theory
6 Goodwin, B.K. and V.H. Smith. 2014. "Theme Overview: The 2014 Farm Bill, An Economic Welfare Disaster or Triumph?" *Choices Magazine*. Quarter 3. Retrieved from: http://choicesmagazine. org/choices-magazine/theme-articles/3rd-quarter-2014/theme-overview-the-2014-farm-billan-economic-welfare-disaster-or-triumph. See more at: www.choicesmagazine.org/choices-magazine/ theme-articles/3rd-quarter-2014/theme-overview-the-2014-farm-billan-economic-welfare-disas ter-or-triumph#sthash.7DijFkIm.dpuf
7 Babcock, B. 2014. "Welfare Effects of PLC, ARC, and SCO." *Choices Magazine*. Quarter 3. Retrieved from: http://choicesmagazine.org/choices-magazine/theme-articles/3rd-quarter-2014/ welfare-effects-of-plc-arc-and-sco. See more at: www.choicesmagazine.org/choices-magazine/ theme-articles/3rd-quarter-2014/welfare-effects-of-plc-arc-and-sco#sthash.FbVSgy69.dpuf
8 Lucas, Rep. Frank. "Farm Bill Provides Safety Net for Producers and Consumers." Feb. 6, 2014. "Frankly Speaking – Issues: Agriculture, Economy and Jobs, Lower Taxes and Government Spending." Retrieved from: https://lucas.house.gov/frankly-speaking/farm-bill-provides-safety-net-producers-and-consumers
9 Naylor, Rosamond (ed). *The Evolving Sphere of Food Security*. New York: Oxford University Press, 2014.
10 Stanford University. Center on Food Security and the Environment. Freeman – Spogli Institute at Stanford. http://fse.fsi.stanford.edu/
11 Naylor (ed). *The Evolving Sphere of Food Security*. New York: Oxford University Press, 2014, pp. ix–x.
12 AGree Initiative. "Facing the Future: Critical Challenges to Food and Agriculture." Washington, DC: Meridian Institute. May 2012. Retrieved from: http://foodandagpolicy.org/sites/default/files/ Facing_the_Future.pdf
13 AGree – Transforming Food and Ag Policy. "AGree's Mission, Vision and Who We Are." Retrieved from: www.foodandagpolicy.org/about-us
14 Global Panel on Agriculture and Food Systems for Nutrition. 2014. "How can Agriculture and Food System Policies Improve Nutrition?" Technical Brief. London, UK: Global Panel on Agriculture and Food Systems for Nutrition. Retrieved from: www.glopan.org/sites/default/files/ Global%20Panel%20Technical%20Brief%20Final.pdf
15 Ibid, p. 8.
16 Ibid, p. 9.
17 Keeney, Roman. "The End of the Direct Payment Era in U.S. Farm Policy." Purdue Extension: APEX—Ag Policy Explained. EC-774-W. Dec. 2013, Retrieved from www.extension.purdue.edu/ extmedia/ec/ec-774-w.pdf

18 Ibid, pp. 1–2.
19 Ibid, p. 1.
20 Westhoff, Patrick, Scott Gerlt, and Joseph Glauber. "Farm Program Elections, Budget Costs, and the WTO." *Choices Magazine.* 3rd Quarter 2015, 30(3). Retrieved from: www.choicesmagazine.org/UserFiles/file/cmsarticle_458.pdf
21 Blank, Steven. *The Economics of American Agriculture: Evolution and Global Development.* London, UK: Routledge, pp. 443–449, 2008.
22 Tanentzap, Andrew J., Anthony Lamb, Susan Walker, and Andrew Farmer. "Resolving Conflicts Between Agriculture and the Natural Environment." Public Library of Science (PLOS)-Biology: Sept. 9, 2015. Retrieved from: http://dx.doi.org/10.1371/journal.pbio.1002242
23 Ibid, retrieved from: http://dx.doi.org/10.1371/journal.pbio.1002242
24 Claassen, R. and M. Ribaudo. 2016. "Cost-Effective Conservation Programs for Sustaining Environmental Quality." *Choices Magazine.* Quarter 3. Retrieved from: www.choicesmagazine.org/choices-magazine/theme-articles/theme-overview-water-scarcity-food-production-and-environmental-sustainabilitycan-policy-make-sense/cost-effective-conservation-programs-for-sustaining-environmental-quality
25 Ibid.
26 Ibid.
27 Lichtenberg, E. 2014. "Conservation, the Farm Bill, and U.S. Agri-Environmental Policy". Choices. Quarter 3. Retrieved from: http://choicesmagazine.org/choices-magazine/theme-articles/3rd-quarter-2014/conservation-the-farm-bill-and-us-agri-environmental-policy
28 Ibid.
29 Ibid.
30 Lubben, B., and J. Pease. 2014. "Conservation and the Agricultural Act of 2014". *Choices Magazine.* Quarter 2. Retrieved from: http://choicesmagazine.org/choices-magazine/theme-articles/deciphering-key-provisions-of-the-agricultural-act-of-2014/conservation-and-the-agricultural-act-of-2014
31 Ibid.
32 Janssen, L., N. Klein, G. Taylor, E. Opoku, and N. Holbeck. "Conservation Reserve Program in South Dakota: Major Findings from 2007 Survey of South Dakota CRP Respondents." Economics Research Report 2008–1. Department of Economics, South Dakota State University. Retrieved from: http://ageconsearch.umn.edu/bitstream/37936/2/CRP2008.pdf.
33 Wu, J. and B. Weber. "Implications of a Reduced Conservation Reserve Program." The Conservation Crossroads in Agriculture: Insight from Leading Economists. Council on Food, Agricultural, and Resource Economics, 2012. Retrieved from: http://issuu.com/c-fare/docs/implicationssofareducedconservationreserveprogram.
34 Lubben, B., and J. Pease. "Conservation and the Agricultural Act of 2014". *Choices Magazine.* Quarter 2, 2014. Retrieved from: http://choicesmagazine.org/choices-magazine/theme-articles/deciphering-key-provisions-of-the-agricultural-act-of-2014/conservation-and-the-agricultural-act-of-2014
35 Randy Alison Aussenberg and Kirsten J. Colello. "Domestic Food Assistance: Summary of Programs". February 17, 2016 Congressional Research Service 7-5700. Retrieved from: www.crs.gov. R42353. www.fas.org/sgp/crs/misc/R42353.pdf
36 Barnard, Neal. "Farm Subsidies Tax Our Health." *Newsday,* OpEd – Opinion. April 14, 2011. www.newsday.com/opinion/oped/farm-subsidies-tax-our-health-1.2818804
37 Kucinich, Elizabeth. "How Agricultural Policies Are Making Us Sick." *Huffington Post:* The Blog. April 21, 2011. Retrieved from: www.huffingtonpost.com/elizabeth-kucinich/agriculture-subsidies-are-making-u_b_851468.html
38 Barnard, Dr. Neal. "Agricultural and Health Policies in Conflict: How Food Subsidies Tax Our Health." Physicians Committee for Responsible Medicine. April 11, 2011. www.pcrm.org/health/reports/agriculture-and-health-policies-ag-versus-health
39 Ibid.
40 U.S. Department of Agriculture and U.S. Department of Health and Human Services. Dietary Guidelines for Americans. Seventh Edition, Washington, DC: U.S. Government Printing Office, December 2010. Retrieved from: www.cnpp.usda.gov/sites/default/files/dietary_guidelines_for_americans/PolicyDoc.pdf

41 Rickard, B.J., A.M. Okrent, J.M. Alston. "How have agricultural policies influenced caloric consumption in the United States?" *Health Econ* 22(3), pp. 316–339, March 2013. Retrieved from: www.ncbi.nlm.nih.gov/pubmed/22331635

42 Ibid.

43 Masters, Will. "Aligning Agriculture and Nutrition: Can Understanding our Differences help us Meet Common Goals?" Tufts University – Grand Challenges Annual Meeting: Agriculture-Nutrition Track, October 6–7, 2014. Retrieved from: http://worldfoodcenter.ucdavis.edu/docs/gates_pres/masters_gates.pdf

44 Lubben, B., and J. Pease. 2014. "Conservation and the Agricultural Act of 2014". *Choices Magazine*. Quarter 2. Retrieved from: http://choicesmagazine.org/choices-magazine/theme-articles/deciphering-key-provisions-of-the-agricultural-act-of-2014/conservation-and-the-agricultural-act-of-2014

45 Shields, Dennis A. "Federal Crop Insurance: Background." Congressional Research Service 7-5700, www.crs.gov, Report # R40532. August 13, 2015, pp. 22–23. Retrieved from: www.fas.org/sgp/crs/misc/R40532.pdf

46 Ibid. p. ii.

47 Ibid, p. 22.

48 Stubbs, Megan. "Conservation Compliance and U.S. Farm Policy Analyst in Agricultural Conservation and Natural Resources Policy." April 2, 2012. Congressional Research Service 7-5700, www.crs.gov, Report # R42459. Retrieved from: www.fas.org/sgp/crs/misc/R42459.pdf

49 Ibid, pp. 10–11.

50 Ibid, p. 11.

Chapter 14

Anticipating future trends in agricultural and food policy

The Global Food Security Act of 2016

On July 20, 2016, a consortium of diplomats, entrepreneurs, bankers, physicians, US Agriculture Secretary Tom Vilsack, US National Security Advisor Susan Rice, and other international leaders participated in a US White House Summit on Global Development.[1] The summit panelists actively discussed strategies that could assist the world's developing nations improve their own economies. Important themes for this conference included the identification and implementation of policies that could improve farm productivity, combat hunger, promote better nutrition, fight poverty, and stimulate economic growth on a global scale.[2]

Just prior to convening the Summit, President Obama signed a related Congressional bill into law. Known as the Global Food Security Act of 2016 (GFSA), this legislative initiative originated at the "ground level." It received strong bipartisan Congressional support in both Houses.[3] The cooperative attitude that prevailed in Congress while crafting this law was a refreshing change to the contentiousness that can sometimes characterize legislative action on agricultural and food policies.

An impressive coalition of private and public entities rallied to support the GFSA's passage.[4] The enactment of the Global Food Security Act of 2016 is an example of how the common good can be actively pursued when ethical, political, and economic goals are aligned. This scenario, where decision-makers work together to unite policies and achieve desired outcomes, clearly contrasts with instances where programs and objectives are in conflict (see Chapter 13).

The GFSA is founded on a set of goals, actions, and principles that have garnered broad-based support:[5]

- GFSA requires that the US President plan and execute a transparent strategy that promotes global food security, resilience, and nutrition, and is consistent with prior national food security investment plans.
- GFSA specifies that it is in the US national security interest to:
  - Engage in comprehensive and agriculturally led growth strategies that reduce global poverty, hunger, and malnutrition.
  - Improve the efficiency and incomes of small-scale farm producers worldwide.
  - Create socio-economic resilience to food market shocks, and therefore decrease excessive dependence on emergency food assistance.
  - Enhance women's and children's nutrition, and health.
  - Harmonize US agricultural, scientific, trade, technological and nutrition strategies, and investments to gain a higher return, in the form of significant global food security progress.

- GFSA includes requirements to demonstrate that its programs are efficient and achieve measureable outcomes:
  - GFSA expects federal government agencies to coordinate efforts to achieve coherence in program monitoring and evaluation.
  - GFSA demands the establishment of effective platforms to spur collaboration with key stakeholders and consultation with relevant congressional committees.
  - GFSA emphasizes that its programs have reliable reporting mechanisms to demonstrate effective use of taxpayer dollars.

The legislated conditions outlined above indicate that the GFSA has strong ethical foundations: transparency, accountability, enhanced public health, and open government. Divergent political factions can find common ground and support GFSA and similar proposals when they are based on universal principles such as honesty, integrity, and fair dealing.

Our textbook is focused on agricultural and food policy. The GFSA is important and relevant to our studies because this law emphasizes that the agricultural and food environment is global in scope, and plays an essential role in the success of developing nations' growth agendas.

The GFSA, and all related initiatives, aim to break the harmful cycle of poverty and malnutrition that prevents households from achieving upward economic mobility. Proper alignment of agricultural and food policies can promote the right combination of investment and development conditions to produce a more food secure and sustainable global economy.

The promise of the GFSA in generating beneficial outcomes is considerable, if its potentials are fully realized. A central question is whether the GFSA can be implemented in a fashion that completely taps into its capacity to yield desired results.

As we move forward in the final chapter of this textbook, we consider the future of the GFSA within a larger context: *what will be the general direction of US farm and food policy?* The answer to this question is difficult to decipher. We argue that the effort to answer it is rational. On net, we are better off if we carefully explore our options and anticipate the possible outcomes.

Organization of chapter

Throughout the previous chapters in this textbook, we have explored a variety of current farm and food policy decisions and reviewed their economic effects. Because policies from the past often have relevance today, we have also addressed programs from an historical perspective. However, our main objective in this text has been to offer a "forward-looking" approach.

In this concluding chapter, we believe it is valuable to maintain our "think ahead" strategy. To accomplish this aim, we address two related questions, one positive in nature, and the other more normative in its focus:

- What are the likely future trends in US agricultural and food policy?
- What should be the future of US agricultural and food policy?

As we address these two questions, we strive to offer plausible predictions and reasonable recommendations. But errors in our expectations are inevitable. We do not claim to propound a definitive depiction of what lies ahead. Rather, as in all efforts to anticipate upcoming changes, we focus on trends and outcomes where the current evidence points towards their continuing relevance and importance.

If we can increase our awareness of probable events, then we can prepare accordingly. We can strategically consider which policies are robust enough to be useful within a realistic range of circumstances.

To take a "look ahead," we sequentially structure this final chapter as follows:

- We interpret the significant positive and normative influences that are currently driving changes in US agricultural and food policy.
- We examine the choices and consequences associated with two contrasting methods of policy change: broad-based major transformation, or gradual marginal adjustment.[6]
- We analyze three connected but different areas of policy change: food, environmental, and agricultural policy.

- We summarize why it is essential to continue to review and interpret US farm and food policies.
- We utilize Albert Hirschman's *Exit, Voice, and Loyalty* paradigm to suggest strategies that can influence the future development and implementation of effective agricultural and food policies.
- We summarize the general goals of this textbook, and suggest a future pathway.

The outline of topics above offers a roadmap to guide our understanding of how the future of agricultural and food policy may unfold. As we navigate through the various policy pathways in this chapter, we can begin to predict how current choices create alternative economic consequences.

Positive and normative influences on the future of agricultural and food policy

During the annual Aspen Ideas Festival in 2014, the Senior Editor for *The Atlantic Magazine* (Korby Kummer) interviewed two US Secretaries of Agriculture (Dan Glickman and Tom Vilsack) about the future direction of US food policy. In the course of this engaging three-person discussion, Secretary Glickman made a very telling observation (note: this quotation is paraphrased):[7]

> In the past, the philosophy that drove US agriculture was characterized by this statement: 'If we grow it, they will buy it.' But in today's world, it is more accurate to say the philosophy has changed to, 'If they buy it, then we will grow it.' There has been a role reversal, and the food system is increasingly a consumer-driven process.

Secretary Glickman's insight is an effective introduction to the question at hand: what are the powerful forces currently influencing the US agriculture and food system, and what policy adjustments will be necessary to adapt to the new realities?

If we research professional publications and the general literature, there is a remarkable consensus about the major factors influencing the agri-food system's future.[8] The catalysts spurring policy change include:

- Evolving US Consumer Demand – Shifts in consumer preferences and purchases are sparking farm producers and food providers to change their overall market strategies and product offerings. Today's knowledgeable consumers expect the agri-food system to:
  - Provide accurate information on food origin, content, and nutritional value.
  - Meet high expectations and offer verifiable evidence for:
    - Scientifically determined food safety standards.
    - Determining how the food production process affects environmental quality, sustainability and climate change.
    - Food quality, taste, and economic value.
    - The impact of food purchases on the well-being of the local economy.
- Advances in Technology – Public and private research stimulates technological change that improves the agri-food system's productivity, risk management, food quality, food safety, and market efficiency. Examples include:

o Promoting and managing new agricultural knowledge in areas such as bio-genetics, precision agriculture, integrated pest management, and related advanced production techniques.

o Developing advanced methods to prevent food contamination events, and improve the sensitivity for detecting disease vectors before they create damaging outbreaks.

o Research technologies that improve both productivity and sustainability.

- Climate Change – Our warming planet is already affecting the productivity, reliability, and sustainability of the agri-food system. New policy approaches are needed to:

  o Encourage technological and management adjustments that can compensate for higher frequencies of extreme weather events and changes in the prevalence of disease vectors.

  o Develop agri-food technologies and practices that reduce the greenhouse gas emissions and adapt to the new environmental conditions that are emerging because of climate change.

- International Trade and Development – US government policy decisions to participate in, or exit, multilateral trade agreements will have large economic effects on the US agri-food system.

  In addition, the trade and development relationships between advanced economies (such as the US and the EU) and the developing nations will significantly influence long-term global economic growth. Opportunities to provide reliable information about trade and development impacts will depend on:

  o Supplying evidence-based and scientifically sound research on the economic consequences of rejecting or accepting membership in the WTO and related large-scale multilateral trade agreements (such as the TPP or the T-TIP) that reduce trade barriers.

  o Creating and implementing policies such as the GFSA to encourage cooperative efforts to reduce global poverty, alleviate malnutrition and mitigate adverse health conditions.

  o Restructuring the agri-food system to target the long-term goal of sustainable and healthy global nutrition rather than simply produce marketable commodities.

- Changing Demographics – The agri-food system's ethnic composition and age distribution, as well as overall US societal demographics, are changing considerably, and will continue to shift for the foreseeable future. Agri-system policies should be modified to account for, and benefit from:

  o The increasing role of women and diverse ethnic groups in the production, distribution and consumption of farm and food products.

  o Management practices that incorporate the increasing need for smooth farm succession transitions. In the twenty-first century, a major challenge is the intergenerational transfer of farm ownership and control.

- Logic of Collective Action – The multi-year farm bill, and related legislative initiatives, are regularly influenced by a political-economic environment where special interests in the agri-food system have the power to rationally manipulate public policy to benefit their individual social welfare.[9]

Larger and dispersed societal groups generally lack sufficient incentives to restructure policies to realize results that would improve their welfare and also serve the greater public interest.

Achieving outcomes with more efficient and/or equitable outcomes typically requires new policy approaches. Singular interests often have the political leverage to maintain the status quo. In situations where private motives can counter public welfare outcomes, it is unclear whether collective action to achieve the "greater good" is possible. Changes in public policy, under these circumstances, will likely require:

○ Coalition-building and activism among members of the broad and widely dispersed interest groups.

○ Use of social media and related technologies to reduce the costs of collective action; if the costs of combined action are sufficiently reduced, then the economic calculus can change, and cooperative efforts to transform policies become rational activities.

○ Coordinated efforts by private foundations, journalists, and individual citizens to educate citizenry about the welfare gains and losses of policy change in the agri-food system.

○ Risk-taking by politicians and other key decision-makers to recognize the need for policy change, and to champion that cause.

The above list of policy-influencing factors is not comprehensive. Additional considerations, such as **environmental sustainability** or **food safety**, might also be separately highlighted as reasons why current farm and food policy will change. Our intent is not to underestimate their influence. Rather, we are also interested in the economic and political mechanisms that may bring to bear these interests and concerns.

In a pure market system, we often emphasize the power of consumer sovereignty. As Secretary Glickman observes, we are in an era where informed consumers are using both their voices and purses to send a message to the agri-food supply system. Times are changing, and *when consumers demand food safety and environmental sustainability as essential components of the "products" they seek*, it is advisable for producers to listen, adjust and satisfy those demands.

We have clear evidence that the supply chain is paying attention to food consumers. Major "big-box store" retailers such as Walmart have already made major modifications in the food products they agree to market. They are also making new guarantees about food safety and quality.

Are agricultural and food policies keeping pace with the changes being initiated by our farmers, agribusinesses, distributors, and their consumers? This is an open question, and a variety of responses and opinions arise when it is posed.

If policy adjustments are lagging behind market trends, we perhaps should not be too quick to judge or criticize. As we have mentioned briefly in this chapter, and in more depth in Chapter 13, collective action is rationally constrained. Needed policy changes are not impossible to achieve and implement, but the democratic (small "d") political system is not exactly designed to be as responsive as are efficient markets.

Humorous insights sometimes compensate for the frustration associated with the sluggish nature of true policy change. At a recent agricultural conference, a panelist[10] recalled an observation about the US political process: "US policy makers will choose the correct approach, but only after having exhausted all other options."[11]

In the next section of this chapter, we continue to focus on the future of agricultural and food policy. We contrast the idea of a large-scale policy transformation with change occurring as smaller incremental steps in a longer-term process.

Structural transformation versus marginal adjustment: how will US agri-food policy change?

Is there general satisfaction with the current set of policies influencing the US agri-food system? The status quo is likely acceptable to some special interests. But, if "no" is the response to the question, then the need for reform rationally follows.

What should be the nature of US agri-food system policy reform? Our options include, but are not limited to:[12]

a)   a complete changeover, or;
b)   a series of modest incremental improvements, or;
c)   a set of transitions that are not transformational, but are sufficiently different from the status quo to constitute more than an ordinary change.

Of the three above-mentioned scenarios, which alternative is the most likely to prevail? Which option has the best chance of creating societal welfare results that are both reasonable and desirable? Is one of the options rationally superior, either from an individual and/ or a societal standpoint? Unfortunately, we cannot honestly answer these questions in a definitive manner.

From a purely objective and scientific perspective, we should comment on the strengths and weaknesses of each of the three policy-change scenarios. For readers who seek a more decisive retort to these questions, perhaps a dose of humor is the correct prescription. Former US President Harry Truman opined that what he really needed was a one-armed economic advisor; in this way, it would not be possible for the consultant to appeal to arguments "on the other hand."[13]

Transformational policy change

Should a "systematic overhaul" of the US agri-food system occur? Can it?

Ardent supporters of the 1996 Farm Bill believed that US farm policy had transformed from an era of heavily subsidized crop production to a new epoch as a "market-driven farm sector." There is little doubt that the 1996 Farm Bill authors believed that they had drastically altered the nature of US farm policy. Unfortunately, when the 2002 Farm Bill was being crafted, commodity market prices and profits had significantly plummeted from higher 1996 levels. Political pressures to use subsidies to "save the farm" were very strong in 2002, and they eventually prevailed.[14]

What can be learned from this economic history? A simple lesson is the difficulty in transforming farm policy towards an unsubsidized and pure-market approach. The events surrounding the 2002 Farm Bill's enactment suggests that Congress creates a "farm safety net" in cases where the normal cycle of "boom and bust" in commodity markets creates financial stress in the agricultural economy.

If past history is an indicator of future policy decisions and performance, then it is *not* likely that the current system of farm subsidies supplementing farm producer incomes will be completely and sustainably replaced by sole reliance on market prices and profits to determine farm incomes.

In the past, various non-farm interest groups have lobbied for agricultural markets to be released from farm income subsidies. These interests argue that federal farm subsidies rarely assist low-income producers. Rather, the largest and most dominant farms receive the bulk of the Farm Bill payments that offer farm income support.[15]

Can the traditional system of farm income subsidies be quickly and completely overturned? Of course, we must acknowledge that any political outcome is possible. But the financial pressures that prevailed in determining policy in past farm bills still exist today.

The political power of interest groups and lobbyists who developed the current set of farm income subsidy policies is as strong as ever. Any change in farm subsidy policy will first need the support of these special interests. These lobbying groups are fully rational and informed, and will not consent to wholesale policy reform unless it is compatible with their private interests.

Incremental policy improvements

If economic principles are applied to policy reform, then we predict changes to occur incrementally ("at the margin") instead of happening on a large scale.

The marginalist approach recommends that we evaluate whether a policy choice is rational based on its extra benefit relative to its extra cost. Ideally, as long as the extra gain to society exceeds the marginal cost, then the next policy change should occur. Rationally, the policy modifications continue while net gains are achieved, and cease when the marginal benefit of the last policy change just equals its marginal cost. To implement any further change, where the net return would be negative, is not rational and therefore avoided.

There are drawbacks to a marginalist philosophy. If the long-term goal is to amend the system on a larger scale by gradually making a series of smaller changes, the proper sequencing of the incremental modifications may be difficult or costly to orchestrate. In such cases, implementing a number of marginal changes may not build towards achieving a greater overarching objective, but simply become a set of unconnected adjustments that lack organization or sustainability.

Eubanks (2013) offered a thoughtful analysis of farm policy change, and contrasted the opportunities for large-scale fundamental change to the prospects for making incremental advances.[16] Eubanks concluded that while the more dramatic results of a wholesale transformation would be very satisfying for the interests seeking such an outcome, the modest effects of marginal change are more realistic and achievable. Eubanks also argued that the incremental method often has a better chance of achieving a targeted goal that is both measurable and meaningful.

While marginalism has its limitations, there are techniques that can overcome or mitigate the shortcomings of the incremental approach. The industrial concepts of "quality assurance" and "continuous improvement" can be integrated into marginal decision-making methods. By instituting standard benchmarks, emphasizing regular and transparent communications that inform stakeholders of both challenges and progress, and creating measurement and documentation systems that stimulate honest assessments, the marginal approach has a much better chance of producing meaningful long-term change. The recommended changes become intentional and systems-oriented, rather than random and disjointed.[17]

Transitional policy change

If we apply the principles of organizational change associated with management theory, we can classify transitional policy change to include:[18]

a)   Planned change
b)   Remedial change
c)   Developmental change

From a management standpoint, *planned change* is an outcome of an organized effort that recognizes a problem to solve or goal to achieve, and then generates a strategic planning process to deliberately accomplish an identified objective.

Title Twelve in the 2014 Farm Bill offers an example of *planned change*. An important US societal problem currently involves the reintegration of war veterans (e.g. from the Iraqi and Afghan conflicts) into the civilian economy. Title XII creates a Military Veterans Agricultural Liaison (MVAL) position to assist veterans to access agricultural program opportunities and facilitate the utilization of veterans' education benefits to initiate a farm or ranching career.[19] The goal of this program is easily understood by most observers. If it works, the results will be measurable, and its effects will receive universal support from most taxpayers and interest groups. This is a simple illustration of *planned change*.

Remedial change can be considered as a sub-component of a strategic plan. In this scenario, there is a recognized shortcoming, and an effort is mounted to remedy the situation to solve the problem and create a better outcome. An illustration of *remedial change* is the overall effort to reduce the frequency of infectious and disease outbreaks in the food system by instituting a "prevention philosophy" as the Food Safety Modernization Act (FSMA) is implemented.[20]

Developmental change is an effort to build on current success, and seek to make even further progress. Strategic planning typically incorporates aspects of developmental change. An example of developmental change is occurring as Title VI (Rural Development) in the 2014 Farm Bill improves the effectiveness and access for rural development program participants by streamlining the application process, improving coordination of rural college investments and measuring progress for assessment and accountability purposes.[21]

The *Transitional* and *Incremental* approaches to policy change are not mutually exclusive. Planned, remedial and developmental change include principles and practices that can be integrated to further strengthen the Incremental Policy Approach. The various reforms can be systematically combined to improve the chances of achieving meaningful policy change over time.

What are the prospects for agri-food policy reform?

A rhetorical question is whether "the cup is half-full or half-empty?" As we carefully examine both the possibilities and the limits of achieving beneficial agri-food policy reform, we can adopt a normative position. We can downplay philosophies of excessive optimism or pessimism, and instead consider pragmatic realism as a recommended approach to make predictions about future decisions and trends.

For example, the history of policymaking in successive farm bills indicates incremental change is the most likely outcome. Critics of current policy often cite the numerous shortcomings and inconsistencies of our current policy environment, and logically argue that the solution is systemic change.

In reality, as noted by welfare economists, almost any overhaul of current policies is *not* "Pareto-optimal." It is nearly impossible to discover and implement a new policy option that assists some interest groups to be better off, while not somehow making others worse off.

The more common case is that major policy proposals provide measurable benefits to some economic participants while disenfranchising others. In such instances of non-Pareto-optimal change, *science cannot be applied to determine a "best outcome."* Instead, we are left with situations where policymakers must resort to their personal ethics and logrolling politics to arrive at an outcome that balances competing interests. They must weigh the gains against the losses, and make difficult decisions about "whose ox will be gored."

Having cited the above challenges, and they are considerable, we do not necessarily extinguish all hope of making progress. Systemic policy change, especially in the short term, is highly unlikely. But possibilities for moving forward remain.

Eubanks (2013) observes that today's agri-food policy mix includes support for progressive, albeit small-scale, programs. He argues that the need for real policy change is slowly being recognized.[22] If we agree with his position, then we can be encouraged that we have programs rewarding producers to engage in ecologically sound practices and to market products that offer genuine nutritious options for food consumers. And, from a management perspective, opportunities to engage in planned change are another reason why progress is possible, even if it falls short of being systemic.

Reconciling divergent agendas: food policy, environmental policy, and agricultural policy

Challenges associated with the agri-food system's diverse economic interests

There are important instances where agri-food system policy objectives fail to align (see Chapter 13). While common economic interests do exist, divergent policy objectives arise among innovative farm producers, high-tech agribusinesses, environmental activists, and food nutrition advocates.

In an ideal market environment, Adam Smith's vision of a competitive market system could harness the power of divergent private incentives to generate beneficial societal market outcomes and efficiently allocate scarce resources. Smith's paradigm, where market economies yield efficient results, continues to be influential in twenty-first-century policy making.

But the promise of Smith's capitalism has limits. Real world markets cannot measure up to perfectly competitive standards. Market efficiency requires free entry and free exit, the absence of market power, internalized externalities, and costless access to market-relevant information (such as enterprise profitability and production technology).

The reality of the agri-food economic system is a series of exceptions to the rules of perfectly competitive markets:

- *Entry and exit* from agricultural and food markets encounters considerable barriers; the reality is far removed from the assumption that both free entry and free exit generate fluid market expansions and contractions.
- *Market power* prevails among the agri-system's economic decision makers. Instead of numerous and powerless price-taking entrepreneurs, farm input markets (e.g. fertilizers, pesticides, seed companies, etc.), as well as value-added agribusinesses (international grain marketers, food aggregators and processors, etc.), exhibit oligopolistic and/or

monopolistically competitive behaviors that adversely influence the economic efficiency of input markets and product prices.

- Instead of pure markets where equilibrium prices reflect true resource costs, farm producers, agribusiness and related entities often generate *market externalities* (these are both/either costly and/or beneficial side-effects) that cannot be properly measured by market-determined prices and costs in the agri-food market system.
- Agriculture is characterized by *asset fixity*, instead of the profit-motivated free flow of capital among industries, as envisioned by Adam Smith and his advocates.
- Production technologies in the real world are not public information to be shared. Instead, they are controlled as proprietary information to be protected by patents and *legal constraints that prevent copying of technologies* without a consent agreement and a rental rate amenable to the inventor/owner of the technology.

Market imperfections are common in the agri-food system, even if agricultural commodity markets themselves are quite competitive.

What are some key effects of the market imperfections? One result is that the agri-food system does not include all of the features that generally guarantee efficient results. If we fully understand the agri-food economic system's shortcomings, we are less surprised to discover that sectoral markets and policies fail to operate in concert with one another.

What can we learn from these observations of conflicting policy goals? One lesson is the need for intentional effort. We cannot rely solely on Smith's invisible hand to deliver improved economic results. The reality is that we do not have perfect markets. But the need for better policy results is also real. We will not achieve a better future by letting the system run on autopilot. Deliberate action is required.

Challenges originating from divergent research agendas

Just as the various economic interests in the agri-food systems have their disagreements about appropriate policy objectives, we can also observe conflicting views originating from various branches of the professional academic literature on agricultural, environmental, and food-nutrition related topics.

Every scientific discipline has a set of intellectual foundations that guides the research agenda. Different disciplines rely on diverse premises. The key sectors and decision makers in the agri-food system are linked together by many important logical connections. However, the nature of disciplinary research is to create new knowledge within a particular sphere of the agri-food system, abstracted from the other related elements.

The narrower focus of disciplinary research can overlook or de-emphasize systematic connections. As a consequence, differing interpretations of policy can emerge as disciplinary investigations independently study methods to improve agricultural production, enhance environmental sustainability, or stimulate healthy nutritional food consumption patterns.

Each discipline has its own distinct advantages, so there are many cases where it is healthy and valuable to examine problems from alternative scientific perspectives. Separate themes and policy insights can emerge from analysts with specialties in agricultural policy, environmental policy, and food policy. All of these research efforts have value.

But there is also value in seeking meaningful and rational policy alignment. To achieve this objective, researchers must engage in substantive cross-disciplinary conversations. We can be intentional about coordinating research agendas to achieve a systems viewpoint on how to solve problems.

If real-world policy makers are to produce coherent policies, then the "experts" they rely upon for technical advice should figure out techniques to properly merge their research agendas for solving the interdisciplinary problems that exist within the agri-food system.

What is being suggested here is more difficult than it sounds. In many research institutions, the production of disciplinary scholarly work is highly rewarded (with tenure and salary perks). While some changes in the reward system are taking place, there are challenges associated with creating sufficient incentives for interdisciplinary research efforts.

In the long term, we not only need policy reforms in agri-food markets, we also require systems of professional recognition for interdisciplinary research. Some institutions are already moving in this direction, and we are now seeing more investigations where the disciplines are working in concert to tackle the complex problems with a systems approach.

There is no doubt that interdisciplinary research is challenging and requires a comprehensive effort. But the payoffs are considerable. Coordinated research on the agricultural, environmental, and nutritional aspects of the agri-food system are worthwhile academic pursuits.

What is the future of farm and food policy and why should we care about it?

In May 2016, the Bipartisan Policy Center (BPC) published an important report on the future of farm and food policy authored by the CEO Council on Sustainability and Innovation (a.k.a., the CEO Council). The composition of the CEO Council includes top executives from five major agricultural- and food-related US corporations: Kellogg, DuPont, Hormel, Elanco, and Land O'Lakes.[23]

The CEO Council's recommendations about the future are convergent with other professional and volunteer organizations that have been addressing the same types of questions. A consensus is beginning to emerge on what should be the direction of the US agri-food system's operations and policies. This is a reassuring and promising outcome.

The CEO Council's report is an in-depth and serious document. The report highlights three action areas:[24]

- Sustainable Productivity – Improve livelihoods, productivity, and resiliency through more sustainable practices.
- Transparency – Engage customers and consumers through transparent communications around food and agriculture.
- Collaborative Decision Making – Increase collaborative decision making across the food and agriculture supply chain.

There is an international aspect of the CEO Council's policy approach. They welcome and support the United Nations (UN) 2030 Agenda for Sustainable Development, including the UN's seventeen Sustainable Development Goals (SDGs). Successful SDG results will largely depend on making real progress in reaching global goals for food and agriculture.

Earlier in this chapter, we mentioned the need for purposeful efforts if needed reforms in agri-food policies are to become more than just a plan with good intentions. There are positive signs that real policy change is possible. If there is follow-through on the Global Food Security Act of 2016 (see opening of Chapter 14) and CEO Council's report, there could be some exciting changes taking place in farm and food policy.

Why do we care about the future of these policies? Ultimately, there is the expectation and the hope that they make a difference. As we have explored a wide range of interests and concerns in this textbook, we have learned that real challenges lie ahead. Taking into consideration factors such as the nutritional needs of a growing global population, the rising stress on our natural resources and environment, the known and unknown threats of climate change, and the lingering questions about the limits of international cooperation to solve these problems, we know that much is at stake.

When we really think hard about all of these factors, we conclude that it is probably time to "take stock" about where we are now, and what we want our future direction to be. Optimistically, our research tells us that we are beginning to understand the scope of the problems we face, and what will be required to help solve them. If there is any doubt or pessimism, it probably lies in whether we, as decision makers, will properly act on the knowledge that we have. It may be necessary to figure out ways of overcoming the rational limitations associated with collective action.

It might seem unlikely that a comic strip can offer us wisdom, but one of the more famous quotations from the character Pogo is perhaps appropriate: "We have met the enemy, and he is us."[25] We do know how to prevail against the enemy. It is a matter of the will to do so.

Ideas to consider: what can be done to learn, influence, and improve agri-food system policy?

Albert Hirschman published *Exit, Voice, and Loyalty* (1970) to explore how consumers/citizens respond to situations where organizations/states are offering products/services that do not meet their expectations.[26]

Hirschman observed that when individuals face circumstances of inferior products being offered in perfectly competitive markets it is quite common and rational for those consumers to exercise the "exit option": they withdraw from the organization and its products, and take their business elsewhere.

Hirschman also perceived a different behavior that is sometimes exhibited when individuals are dissatisfied. They exercise the "voice option." Instead of immediately departing from the organization, they may file a complaint, ask "to see the manager," or even publicize their displeasure. Exercising voice can be a more costly alternative than quietly exiting the organization to seek better treatment from an alternate source.

Under what circumstances does voice become a rationally superior option? Hirschman argued that if a consumer has developed an emotional and/or intellectual loyalty to the supplier, then there can be the powerful perception of a true loss associated with departure. If organizational loyalty is a strong enough influence, the consumer can judge the voice option to be a rational choice.

How can we apply Hirschman's insights to the prospects for reforming policies in the agri-food system? The answer to the question is not immediately obvious, but it revolves around how an individual develops a sense of loyalty to an organization or a cause.

If individuals believe they are "members" responsible for maintaining the organization's vitality, or if they share an ideology associated with the organization's history and/or current values, or if they are sufficiently "emotionally invested" to overlook the rational response to sunk costs, then the loyalty "quotient" can be powerful enough for individuals to use their voice in attempts to affect change, as compared with simply leaving the organization.

Hirschman's hypothesis of the key connection between voice and loyalty can be further interpreted when we link to Mancur Olson's logical limits to collective action. Collective action can become rational if loyalty motivates individuals to perceive that when they join voices with others, then the chances of affecting change increase. Instead of "exit or non-action" being seen as the most rational behaviors, the notion of activism becomes meaningful.

Creating an atmosphere where individuals have a sense of loyalty and believe that their voice matters requires leadership. In the agri-food system, leaders are emerging to announce their commitment to create a better future. It can be very inspiring when organizations such as AGree, the Bipartisan Policy Council, the CEO Council, and the UN Agenda for Sustainable Development are largely "speaking with one voice" to argue for real reform.

Throughout this textbook, we have noted how everyday citizens are participating members in small volunteer groups, as well as in larger organizations, because they believe that they can make a difference in their own lives, and the lives of others. Loyalty to the principles that these organizations espouse can be a potent force for people to exercise the "voice option" and press for needed change.

A summary of the lessons and perspectives offered in this agri-food policy textbook

In this concluding textbook chapter, it is appropriate to review our educational goals, evaluate the usefulness of our endeavors, and suggest possible future applications of what we have learned.

Throughout this examination of US agricultural and food policy, we have been striving to develop a balanced and forward-looking perspective. The emphasis has been to use the tools of economic analysis to better understand alternative policy choices and their outcomes.

A roadmap analogy illustrates this textbook's instrumental educational value. We began this journey by familiarizing ourselves with the "agricultural and food policy landscape." The first two chapters of this text increase our understanding of how key past trends continue to affect the future of farm and food markets. We additionally explore the critical influence of new policy initiatives in food safety, the farm bill and international trade on outcomes such as economic efficiency, market stability, and long-term sustainability.

Roadmaps guide us to a preferred destination. Similarly, decision makers institute policies to achieve desired ends. We examine a variety of policies and programs in this textbook. Farm commodity and crop insurance programs (Chapter 4) aim to create a financial farm safety net, while nutrition programs (Chapter 7) offer a food safety net for low-income households. The Food Safety Modernization Act (FSMA) (see Chapter 5) seeks to prevent the spread of harmful food-borne illnesses.

We use roadmaps to identify an efficient itinerary. We utilize economic tools such as Cost-Benefit Analysis (CBA) (Chapter 5) to help determine whether we are effectively achieving the FSMA's disease-prevention goals. In addition, we engage in consumer and producer surplus analysis to predict who will shoulder the costs and who will be the primary beneficiaries of the policy.

A trained cartographer employs appropriate navigation tools – e.g. interpreting the map legend and orienteering via a compass. In Chapter 3 of our textbook, we introduce a "toolbox" of economic analysis techniques to build skills in identifying the efficiency gains and losses associated with agri-food system policies. We apply an intertemporal analysis model

(Chapter 8) to predict how we can sustainably manage our natural resources. In Chapter 6, we utilize an iterative logical model to predict how globalization patterns influence trade policy choices. A feedback loop further integrates the effects of globalization on the agricultural and food economy.

Technologies change. GPS and precision agriculture replace maps and compasses. In Chapter 9, we investigate the dramatic impacts of changing technology on agricultural productivity. We also study the prospects for an expanding production capacity to maintain pace with growing global food demand as agricultural technologies interact with climate change.

Investment and development modify landscapes, and maps are redrawn. In Chapter 10, we study how new policies aim to make real progress in improving the food security status of needy households locally and throughout the world. One transformation under consideration is to better utilize food hubs to remedy the problems of food deserts. In Chapter 11, we probe how policies must systematically influence both the agricultural sector and the broader-based non-farm rural economy to advance rural development and improve the average rural household's standard of living.

Demographics affect geography. Correspondingly, in Chapter 12, we explore how women, socially disadvantaged groups, and veterans are taking advantage of progressive policies to make important contributions as participants in the dynamic US agri-food system. Related to this discussion is the growing prominence of local food markets, organic agriculture and agricultural literacy trends.

Maps can lead us to either desirable or unwanted end points. In Chapter 13, we probe the reasons for initiating policies that generate contradictory outcomes. Conflicting policy purposes can be intended or unintended. Regardless of their original aims, the resulting inefficiencies are detrimental. In Chapter 13 we seek pathways to remove obstacles and seek mutually beneficial results. The route to policy improvement has familiar guideposts: they include an appeal to enhanced education, real leadership, superior technologies, and a renewed commitment to coordinating efforts to achieve a common purpose.

This concluding chapter represents an opportunity to assess where we have been, and where we want to go next. If there is one lesson we can learn, it is the realization that effective policy is not something that happens naturally. Intentional and informed participation are required. A goal of this textbook is to raise awareness of the challenges that lie ahead and the importance of making informed choices to meet those challenges. Ideally, careful readers of this textbook will not view the concluding chapter as the end of their agricultural and food policy education, but rather as the start of an endeavor to remain knowledgeable and actively participate in creating a more sustainable and food-secure world.

Notes

1 Crescente, Fernanda. "Obama Signs Global Food Security Act to End Hunger." USA Today. July 21, 2016. Retrieved from: www.usatoday.com/story/news/politics/2016/07/20/obama-signs-global-food-security-act-to-end-hunger-invest-in-agriculture/87358640/

2 US Agency for International Development (USAID). "White House Summit on Global Development: Real Lives, Real Outcomes." Washington, DC, July 20, 2016. Retrieved from: www.usaid.gov/sites/default/files/documents/1869/White_House_Summit_On_Global_Development_Program_072016.pdf

3 US House of Representatives, 114th Congress (2015-2016). H.R.1567 – Global Food Security Act of 2016. www.congress.gov/bill/114th-congress/house-bill/1567

4   AGree Initiative. *Letter Endorsing Global Food Security Act.* Washington, DC: Meridian Institute. March 2016. Retrieved from: http://foodandagpolicy.org/sites/default/files/2016%20Global%20 Food%20Security%20Act%20Letter_Paul%20Ryan.pdf

5   US House of Representatives, 114th Congress (2015-2016). *H.R.1567 – Global Food Security Act of 2016.* www.congress.gov/bill/114th-congress/house-bill/1567

6   Eubanks, William S., II. "The Future of Federal Farm Policy: Steps for Achieving a More Sustainable Food System." *Vermont Law Review,* 37, 957 (2013). Sept. 28, 2012. Retrieved from: http://papers. ssrn.com/sol3/papers.cfm?abstract_id=2182032

7   Aspen Ideas Festival 2014. Kummer, Korby, Moderator. "US Food and Farm Policy: Past and Present – Where Does the Future Lie?" Retrieved from: www.aspenideas.org/session/us-food-policy-past-and-present-where-does-future-lie#HuHG-fCj0Jk

8   United Nations Department of Economic and Social Affairs. Division for Sustainable Development. "Food and Agriculture: The Future of Sustainability." Sustainable Development in the 21st Century (SD21). Retrieved from: https://sustainabledevelopment.un.org/content/documents/1443sd21brief.pdf

9   Olson, Mancur. *The Logic of Collective Action: Public Goods and the Theory of Groups.* Cambridge, MA: Harvard University Press. Harvard Economic Studies, Volume CXXIV. 1971. Pages 1–3.

10 Hardin, John Jr. Panelist for "Not your Grandparents' Farm Bill (or Does the US Farm Bill Still Matter." AAEA 2016 Annual Meeting, Boston, MA. August 1, 2016. John Hardin, Jr. is the Board Vice-Chair for the American Farmland Trust. Retrieved from: www.farmland.org/our-story/senior-leadership

11 Eban, Abba, Israeli politician and diplomat. June 1967. Eban is credited with this comment: "he (Eban) was hopeful a new system of interstate relationships might come to pass. His optimism was expressed as: 'Nations do behave wisely once they have exhausted all other alternatives.'" Retrieved from: http://quoteinvestigator.com/2012/11/11/exhaust-alternatives/

12 Daszko, Marcia and Sheila Sheinberg. "Survival Is Optional: Only Leaders with New Knowledge Can Lead the Transformation." Theory of Transformation: Final to Short Article. April 2005. Retrieved from: www.mdaszko.com/theoryoftransformation_final_to_short_article_apr05.pdf

13 Buttonwood. "One-armed Economists." *The Economist,* Buttonwood's notebook, Financial Markets. June 7, 2010. Retrieved from: www.economist.com/blogs/buttonwood/2010/06/inflation_deflation_and_asset_allocation

14 Blank, Steven. *The Economics of American Agriculture: Evolution and Global Development.* London, UK: Routledge, pp. 446–447, 2008.

15 Ibid, p. 436–437.

16 Eubanks, William S., II. "The Future of Federal Farm Policy: Steps for Achieving a More Sustainable Food System," pp. 957–986; article last revised 10 August 2013. Sept. 28, 2012. http://papers.ssrn. com/sol3/papers.cfm?abstract_id=2182032

17 Saylor Academy. *The Sustainable Business Casebook: 4.1 Sustainability Reporting.* Retrieved from: https://saylordotorg.github.io/text_the-sustainable-business-case-book/s08-01-sustainability-reporting.html

18 Authenticity Consulting, LLC. "Major Types of Organizational Change." Field Guide to Consulting and Organizational Development. Retrieved from: http://managementhelp.org/misc/types-of-orgl-change.pdf

19 USDA, ERS. "Military Veterans Agricultural Liaison (Title XII)." Agricultural Act of 2014: Highlights and Implications: Socially Disadvantaged and Veteran Farmers and Ranchers. Retrieved from: www.ers.usda.gov/agricultural-act-of-2014-highlights-and-implications/socially-disadvantaged-and-veteran-farmers-and-ranchers.aspx

20 US Department of Health and Human Services, Food and Drug Administration. "Food Safety Modernization Act." Guidance and Regulation. Updated September 2, 2016. Retrieved from: www.fda.gov/Food/GuidanceRegulation/FSMA/

21 USDA, ERS. "Accessibility, Accountability, and Effectiveness of Existing Programs." Agricultural Act of 2014: Highlights and Implications: Rural Development. Retrieved from: www.ers.usda.gov/agricultural-act-of-2014-highlights-and-implications/rural-development.aspx

22 Eubanks, William S., II. "The Future of Federal Farm Policy: Steps for Achieving a More Sustainable Food System," pp. 957–986; article last revised 10 August 2013. Sept. 28, 2012. http://papers.ssrn. com/sol3/papers.cfm?abstract_id=2182032

23 Bryant, John A., James C. Collins, Jr., Jeffrey M. Ettinger, Chris Policinski, and Jeff Simmons, CEO Council on Sustainability and Innovation. "Food for Thought: A Call to Action on the Future of Sustainable Agriculture." Bipartisan Policy Center. Washington, DC. May 2016. Retrieved from: http://cdn.bipartisanpolicy.org/wp-content/uploads/2016/05/BPC-CEO-Council-Sustainability-Innovation.pdf

24 Ibid, pp. 5–6.

25 Kelly, Walt. "We have met the enemy, and he is us." This Day in Quotes. April 22, 2015. Retrieved from: www.thisdayinquotes.com/2011/04/we-have-met-enemy-and-he-is-us.html

26 Hirschman, Albert O. *Exit, Voice and Loyalty: Responses to Decline in Firms, Organizations, and States.* Cambridge, MA: Harvard University Press, pp. 1–20, 1970.

Index